Incidental Model

Social Competence in Developmental Perspective

NATO ASI Series

Advanced Science Institutes Series

A Series presenting the results of activities sponsored by the NATO Science Committee, which aims at the dissemination of advanced scientific and technological knowledge, with a view to strengthening links between scientific communities.

The Series is published by an international board of publishers in conjunction with the NATO Scientific Affairs Division

A Life Sciences	Plenum Publishing Corporation
B Physics	London and New York
C Mathematical	Kluwer Academic Publishers
and Physical Sciences	Dordrecht, Boston and London
D Behavioural and Social Sciences	
E Applied Sciences	
F Computer and Systems Sciences	Springer-Verlag
G Ecological Sciences	Berlin, Heidelberg, New York, London,
H Cell Biology	Paris and Tokyo

Social Competence in Developmental Perspective

edited by

Barry H. Schneider

School of Psychology,
University of Ottawa,
Ottawa, Canada

Grazia Attili

Istituto di Psicologia,
Consiglio Nationale Delle Ricerche,
Rome, Italy

Jacqueline Nadel

Laboratoire de Psychobiologie de l'Enfant,
Conseil National de Recherche Scientifique,
Paris, France

and

Roger P. Weissberg

Department of Psychology, Yale University,
New Haven, Connecticut, U.S.A.

Kluwer Academic Publishers

Dordrecht / Boston / London

Published in cooperation with NATO Scientific Affairs Division

Proceedings of the NATO Advanced Study Institute on
Social Competence in Developmental Perspective
Les Arcs, France
July 8–18, 1988

Library of Congress Cataloging in Publication Data

```
Social competence in developmental perspective / edited by Barry H.
  Schneider ... [et al.].
       p.   cm. -- (NATO ASI series. Series D, Behavioural and social
  sciences ; vol. 51)
    Includes bibliographical references.
    ISBN 0-7923-0400-4
    1. Social skills in children.  2. Socialization.   I. Schneider,
  Barry H.  II. Series: NATO ASI series.  Series D, Behavioural and
  social sciences ; no. 51.
  BF723.S62S63   1989
  305.23'1--dc20                                            89-15557
```

ISBN 0–7923–0400–4

Published by Kluwer Academic Publishers,
P.O. Box 17, 3300 AA Dordrecht, The Netherlands.

Kluwer Academic Publishers incorporates the publishing programmes of
D. Reidel, Martinus Nijhoff, Dr W. Junk and MTP Press.

Sold and distributed in the U.S.A. and Canada
by Kluwer Academic Publishers,
101 Philip Drive, Norwell, MA 02061, U.S.A.

In all other countries, sold and distributed
by Kluwer Academic Publishers Group,
P.O. Box 322, 3300 AH Dordrecht, The Netherlands.

Printed on acid free paper

Contents

Preface

What determines the focus of a researcher's interest, the sources of inspiration for a study, or the variables scrutinized? If we were to examine the antecedents of these decisions, they would surely emerge as accidents of circumstance--the personal experiences of the researcher, the inspiration of early mentors, the influence of contemporary colleagues--all tempered by the intellectual currents that nurture the researcher's hypotheses. Among the accidents that mold the careers of researchers is geographic location. The culture in which a research program emerges helps determine both its very subject and its method.

The primary purpose of this book is to assist those interested in the scientific study of children's social competence in transcending the boundaries imposed both by geography and by selective exposure to the highly diverse schools of thought that have led to interest in this field. Most of these ideas were presented and exchanged at an Advanced Study Institute entitled "Social Competence in Developmental Perspective" held in Savoie, France, in July 1988. This Institute was attended by scholars from France, England, Northern Ireland, Germany, Italy, Norway, Spain, Portugal, Netherlands, Canada, the United States and Brazil. Those who participated will recognize that the metamorphosis from lecture to chapter has necessitated many changes. In order to accommodate the reader who may be unfamiliar with the field, more attention has been paid here to identifying the theoretical contexts of the research described. The presentation of empirical data in the chapters that follow is more selective, guided by the need to support recurring arguments and illustrate frequent themes. The intent here is to equip the reader to better appreciate the contents of professional journals in this area, not to usurp the function of an empirical journal. Finally, many of the positions argued herein have been refined as a result of contact with each other at the Institute.

Both newcomers to the field and veterans will be struck by the heterogeneity of the contributions that follow. One must reflect upon the many pathways that have led to interest in social relations in order to understand adequately this heterogeneity. The following enumeration of the roots of the work presented throughout the book is by no means exhaustive.

Personality theory. Early opponents of Freudian personality theory attributed much of human behavior to peer experience. "Social interest" is a primary motivating force in Adler's system, while feelings of inferiority are seen as underlying much psychopathology. Though Adler did not dispute Freud's view that the core of an individual's personality is determined in early childhood, his open parent/child guidance sessions may have helped to demystify the process of applying psychological principles in promoting mental health in communities; subsequent efforts in this regard have focused on enhancing peer relations (Ansbacher & Ansbacher, 1956). Moreno's (1934) sociometric technique emphasized the diversity of roles played by individuals within various social systems. It influenced both research and psychotherapy.

Erikson (1950) achieved an integration of psychoanalytic theory with the influences of peers and society at large. Harry Stack Sullivan (1953) is perhaps most responsible for the inclusion of peer influence in personality theory. He emphasized the individual's need for friendships and more intimate relationships. In the process, he underscored the developmental perspective far more than any predecessor. Within his system, the crucial personal tasks faced by an individual differ fundamentally according to age and stage of development.

Child development. Personality theorists such as Sullivan adopted a developmental model as part of the process of tracing adult personality features back through child and adolescent experience. In contrast, scholars in the area of developmental psychology have increasingly adopted a life-span perspective and, in doing so, seek to identify which behaviors are specific to a particular stage and which are more enduring. This life-span perspective was not unknown to pioneers in the field. Systematic longitudinal investigations designed to elucidate continuities between child and adult behavior (e.g., Northway, 1944) were launched in the years between the two world wars. Children's social interaction was studied by means of direct observation and peer assessment in child development laboratories established on the campuses of North American universities (Hartup, 1985; Jack, 1934). These techniques have survived to this day as mainstays of research methodology. Piaget's many insights into the development of children's thinking had a profound impact on the peer relations field. He demonstrated important developmental differences in the ways children think about others and about the rules constraining interpersonal behavior. Theory-building in the field of children's development was further revolutionized by the views of the Soviet theorists Vygotsky and Lurie, who explored the complex cognitive and linguistic mechanisms that mediate children's interactions with their environments.

Human ethology. Inspired by evolutionary theory, ethologists have employed observational methods to study the group behavior of various species. Such processes as affiliation, aggression, and dominance have figured prominently in their work. The extension of this type of inquiry to the peer relations of children was a logical one. Furthermore, much recent ethological research with non-human primates has focused on individual differences in patterns of interaction between young primates and their peers, as well as the link between these interactions and aspects of the offsprings' interaction with their parents.

Social psychology. Interperonal attraction, leadership and attitudes towards others have been key variables in the social psychology literature since its beginning. More recent thinking in social psychology has also considered more intimate friendships and close relationships. Argyle and colleagues (Argyle, 1967) conducted detailed studies of the rules that govern human relationships and applied this research in helping individuals seeking to establish and enhance friendships. However, social psychological theory has not been traditionally widely applied in the study of children's behavior.

Preventive mental health. While the fields of medicine and clinical psychology have traditionally restricted their role to the treatment of disorders once they arise, attention has increasingly been paid to the need for preventing disorder and to the factors associated with successful adaptation in the face of adversity (Garmezy & Rutter, 1983). Because unsuccessful peer relations are often a forerunner of psychological maladjustment, and because satisfying interpersonal relationships may assist individuals in overcoming the stresses of an otherwise pathogenic situation, children's social competence relations have attracted the keen interest of the preventive mental health movement.

Systems theory. Awareness of the reciprocal influences of children, families, schools, subcultures and societies has increased within several of the disciplines already described, especially child development, social psychology, and preventive mental health. Bronfenbrenner (1977) criticized developmental psychology's failure to consider the context in which child development occurs. Albee (1986) emphasized the impact of adverse socioeconomic conditions on an individual's psychological well-being.

Self-concept theory. Scholars in psychology and education, as well as laypersons, have been profoundly aware of children's images of themselves and the impact of self-concept on behavior. Some have considered self-concept the core of human personality (Lecky, 1945). Theorists are nearly unanimous in emphasizing the social origin of self-concept (see, e.g. Cooley 1902; Harter, 1983) and have thus spurred the study of children's peer relations.

Behavior therapy. Procedures derived from learning theory have been used extensively to assist youngsters with maladaptive peer relations. Behavior analysts have also contributed greatly to the refinement of observational methods in studying children's peer interaction, because stringent observational data are generally used to document the effectiveness of this type of intervention. Because the basic principles of classic S-R (Stimulus-Response) theory do not vary according to age or stage, a developmental perspective has not characterized this field in the past. However, greater awareness of developmental factors will surely emerge as the field of behavior therapy continues its current flirtation with the study of the cognitive and affective influences on behavior.

Thus, scholars whose interests have converged on children's peer relations hail from diverse intellectual heritages. One would imagine that these different schools of thought might operate as warring camps vigorously debating the validity of each other's work. This is hardly the case. The varying approaches reflect differences in background and interest, their idiosyncratic characteristics nurtured in part by isolation. Lack of contact, but not lack of respect, should be inferred from the heterogeneity described above. Though these highly varied theoretical backgrounds do not distribute strictly according to nationality, there are striking differences in the relative influence of each as one crosses international boundaries. The principles of behavior therapy, for instance, are predominant in the basic training of psychologists in North America, but not in Continental Europe. In contrast, European researchers are much more familiar with ethological approaches than most of their American counterparts. International exchange has facilitated the growth of the field to a certain extent. For example, the psychologies of Adler and Moreno, introduced above, originated in Europe, and were transported to America as part of the great upheaval that accompanied the two world wars. Peacetime exchanges among colleagues have of course occurred, albeit they are often hampered by insufficient familiarity with the basic vocabulary, methodology, and biases of psychological research in other countries. It is hoped that the exchanges of ideas documented in this volume will help remedy this state of affairs.

The purpose of this book is to facilitate communication among these approaches, not to attempt a contrived synthesis of highly disparate interests and methods. The reader is invited to appreciate the individuality and internal logic of each approach as well as its contribution to the study of children's social behavior. Nevertheless, there are a number of recurring issues and common problems. Many of the contributors decry--and some attempt to resolve--the enduring obstacle imposed by the lack of consensus on the definition of social competence and skill. The need for a systems perspective, already introduced, is evident in chapters devoted to conceptual issues, descriptive research and applied intervention alike. Similarly, there is considerable attention throughout to the difficulties in accurately measuring children's social competence and the problems this poses in interpreting research findings of all types. However, the central theme is the need for greater awareness of developmental issues in social development research. The importance of a developmental perspective sounds obvious, almost proverbial. The most pressing need in this regard is not to lament the deficiencies of previous research but to determine how, where, and when to incorporate considerations of age, stage, and gender differences, among others, in building theories and designing research. Ideas along these lines are contained in several of the chapters that follow.

This book is divided into five sections, each of which begins with an editorial introduction. In Section I, entitled *Social Competence in Developmental Perspective: Conceptual Issues*, the importance of social competence is discussed and reaffirmed. Several important theoretical problems are addressed, including the definition of social competence and its relation to general adaptive ability. Important methodological dimensions, especially with respect to longitudinal investigations, are introduced. Section II is devoted to the *Emergence of Social Competence in Early Childhood*. It contains deliberations as to the nature of the child's first social contacts and descriptions of the rapidly evolving forms of social exchange during the preschool years. Section III is a selective examination of *Ongoing Social Development in Middle Childhood and Adolescence*. Special consideration is given to the impact of actual and pretend aggression on relations among peers. *Setting Factors in Children's Social Development: The Influences of Families and Schools* are considered in Section IV. Separate chapters within that section present evidence for the effects of families and schools on the social interaction of both preschoolers and school-age children. The final section of the book, *Translating Theory Into Practice: Social Competence Promotion Programs*, focuses on applied interventions based on social development research. In addition to the full-length chapters, several brief conversation summaries, based on discussions by participants at the Institute, have been included in order to clarify selected crucial issues. The appendices contain abstracts of individual studies conducted by participants at the Institute.

The Organizing Committee is grateful to the NATO Scientific Affairs Division for its funding of the Institute and to the University of Ottawa which provided supplementary support. Special thanks are extended to the student assistants and secretaries for their devoted attention to the many organizational matters inherent in bringing together scientists from many countries and in helping prepare the manuscript: Biran Mertan, Ann McKendry, Irene Sullivan, Carolina Rott, Paula McCann, Philip Fleurian Chateau, Patricia Van Buren, Zoltan Dienes, and Nadia Kurylyzn. Susan J. Cohan, our dedicated copy editor, made many useful suggestions, and helped overcome the obstacles imposed by differences between countries in usage and format. Dr. Alastair Younger of the University of Ottawa collaborated extensively with the Organizing Committee in many aspects of the organization of the Institute and of this book.

We hope that this book facilitates international collaboration among scientists in the peer relations field, and that the fruits of these collaborative endeavors enhance the peer relations of colleagues in many countries and the children with whom they work.

References

Albee, G. (1986). Toward a just society: Lessons from observations on the primary prevention of psychopathology. *American Psychologist, 41*, 891-898.

Ansbacher, H. L. & Ansbacher, R. R. (Eds.) (1956). *The individual psychology of Alfred Adler.* New York: Harper & Row.

Argyle, M. (1967). The psychology of interpersonal behavior. Harmondsworth, United Kingdom: Penguin Books.

Bronfenbrenner, U. (1977). Toward an experimental ecology of human development. *American Psychologist, 32,* 513-531.

Cooley, C. (1902). *Human nature and the social order.* New York: Scribners.

Erikson, E. H. (1950). *Childhood and society.* New York: Norton.

Garmezy, N. & Rutter, M. (Eds.). (1983). *Stress, coping and development in childre.* New York: McGraw-Hill.

Harter, S. (1983). Developmental perspectives on the self-system. In P. Mussen (Ed.), *Handbook of child psychology,* Vol. 4, (pp. 275-386). New York: Wiley.

Preface

Hartup, W. W. (1985). Forward. In B. H. Schneider, K. H. Rubin, and J. E. Ledingham (Eds.), *Children's peer relations: Issues in assessment and intervention* (pp. vii-xi). New York: Springer-Verlag.

Jack, L. (1934). An experimental study of ascendant behavior in preschool children. *University of Iowa Studies in Child Welfare* (Vol.12, No.3).

Lecky, P. (1945). *Self-consistency: A theory of personality.* New York: Island.

Moreno, J. L. (1934). *Who shall survive?* Washington, DC: Nervous and Mental Disease Publishing Company.

Northway, M. (1944). Outsiders: A study of personality patterns of children least acceptable to their agemates. *Sociometry, 7,* 10-25.

Sullivan, H. S. (1953). *The interpersonal theory of psychiatry.* New York: Norton.

Barry H. Schneider
Grazia Attili
Jacqueline Nadel
Roger P. Weissberg

Aix-les-Bains, France
July, 1988

List of Contributors

Michel Alain, Ecole de Psychologie, Pavillon Felix Antoine Savard, Université Laval, Québec, Ste Foy, Québec, Canada G1K 7P4

Monique Alles-Jardel, 28, rue Paul Langevin, Résidence Plein Sud II, 38130 Echirolles, France

Françoise D. Alsaker, Department of Personality Psychology, Oysteinsgt. 3, N-5007-Bergen, Norway

Jens Asendorpf, Max Planck Institute for Psychological Research, Leopoldstrasse 24, D-8000 Munchen 40, West Germany

Steven Asher, University of Illinois, Bureau of Educational Research, 1310 S. Sixth Street, Champaign, IL 61821, U.S.A.

Grazia Attili, Istituto di Psicologia, Consiglio Nazionale delle Richerche (CNR), Viale Marx 15, 00137 Roma, Italy

Pierre-Marie Baudonnière, Laboratoire de Psychobiologie de l'enfant, 41, rue Gay-Lussac, 75005 Paris, France

Michel Boivin, Ecole de Psychologie, Pavillon Felix Antoine Savard, Université Laval, Québec, Canada   G1K 7P4

Denis Boucher, Département de Psychologie, Université de Moncton, Moncton, N.B., Canada   E1A 3E9

Paul E. Bourque, Département de Psychologie, Université de Moncton, Moncton, N.B., Canada   E1A 3E9

Maria Campart, Istituto di Filosofia, Scienza dell'educazione e Laboratorio sperimentale di Psicologia, Universita' di Genova, Genova, Italy

Marlene Caplan, Psychology Department, Yale University, Box 11A, Yale Station, New Haven, CT 06520-7447, U.S.A.

Pierre Charlebois, Ecole de Psycho-éducation, 750, boul. Gouin est, C.P. 6128, succursale A, Montréal, Québec, Canada   H3C 3J7

Christina Christopoulos, Psychology Department, Duke University, Durham, North Carolina 27705, U.S.A.

Toon Cillessen, Department of Psychology, Catholic University of Nijmegen, P.O. Box 9104, 6500 HE Nijmegen, Netherlands

List of Contributors

John Coie, Psychology Department, Duke University, Durham, North Carolina 27705, U.S.A.

Jennifer Connolly, Department of Psychology, York University, 4700 Keele Street, North York, Canada   M3J 1P3

Angela Costabile, Dipartimento di Scienze dell'Educazione, Universita' della Calabria, Italy

Nicki Crick, Box 512, Peabody, Department of Psychology and Human Development, Vanderbilt University, Nashville, TN 37203, U.S.A.

Orlanda Cruz, Faculdade de Psicologia e Ciencias da Eduçaco, University of Porto, Rua das Taipas 76, 4000 Porto, Portugal

Phyllis Daen, 4700 Langdrum Lane, Chevy Chase, MD 20815, U.S.A.

Tina Daniels-Beirness, Psychology Department, Carleton University, Ottawa, Ontario, Canada   K1S 5B6

Zilma de Moraes Ramos de Oliveira, Faculdade de Eduçaco da U.S.P.E.D.M., Avenida da Universidade 308, Cidade Universitaria, CEP 05508 - Sao Paulo, Brazil

Guilhem de Roquefeuil, INSERM Unite 70, 388, Rue de Mas Prunet, F-34070 Montpellier, France

Michel Djakovic, INSERM Unite 70, 388, Rue de Mas Prunet, F-34070 Montpellier, France

Kenneth A. Dodge, Department of Psychology and Human Development, George Peabody College, Vanderbilt University, Nashville, Tennessee, 37203, U.S.A.

Steve Duck, 151-CSB, Communication Studies, University of Iowa, Iowa City, IA 52242, U.S.A.

Tamara Ferguson, Department of Psychology, Utah State University, Logan, Utah, U.S.A.

James A. Fitzsimmons, 4700 Langdrum Lane, Chevy Chase, MD 20815, U.S.A.

Anne Marie Fontaine, Laboratoire de Psychobiologie de l'enfant, 41, rue Gay-Lussac, 75005 Paris, France

Sharon Foster, Department of Psychology, Box 6040, West Virginia University, Morgantown, WV 26506-6040, U.S.A.

Wyndol Furman, Department of Psychology, University of Denver, Denver, Colorado 80208, U.S.A.

List of Contributors

Claude Gagnon, Ecole de Psycho-éducation, 750, boul. Gouin est, C.P. 6128, succursale A, Montréal, Québec, Canada   H3C 3J7

Norman Garmezy, Department of Psychology, University of Minnesota, Elliott Hall, 75 East River Road, Minneapolis, Minnesota 55455, U.S.A.

Pierre Garrigues, INSERM Unite 70, 388, Rue de Mas Prunet, F-34070 Montpellier, France

Leslie A. Gavin, Department of Psychology, University of Denver, Denver, Colorado 80208, U.S.A.

Evelyne Genest, Université de Provence, Aix-Marseille, France

Maria-Luisa Genta, Dipartimento di Scienze dell'Educazione, Universita' della Calabria, Italy

Ronita Giberson, Department of Psychology, University of Denver, Denver, Colorado U.S.A.

Carollee Howes, Graduate School of Education, University of California, Los Angeles, CA 90024-1521, U.S.A.

Gary W. Ladd, 216 CDFS, Purdue University, West Lafayette, IN 47906, U.S.A.

Serge Larivée, Ecole de Psycho-éducation, 750, boul. Gouin est, C.P. 6128, succursale A, Montréal, Québec, Canada   H3C 3J7

Jane Ledingham, Child Study Centre, University of Ottawa, Ottawa, Ontario, Canada K1N 6N5

Alain Legendre, Laboratoire de Psychobiologie de l'Enfant, 41, rue Gay-Lussac, 75005 Paris, France

Jacqueline Liégeois, Laboratoire de Psychobiologie de l'Enfant du CNRS, 41, rue Gay Lussac, 75005, Paris, France

John E. Lochman, Division of Medical Psychology, Duke University Medical Center, Box 2906, Durham, N.C. 27710, U.S.A.

Mara Manetti, Istituto di Filosofia, Scienza dell'educazione e Laboratorio sperimentale di Psicologia, Universita' di Genova, Vico S. Antonio 5/7, Genova, Italy

Ersilia Menesini, Dipartimento di Psicologia, Via della Pergola, 48, 50122 Firenze, Italy

Biran Mertan, 14, Rue Michelet, 3700 Tours, France

Juliette Michel, Laboratoire de Psychobiologie de l'Enfant du CNRS, 41, rue Gay Lussac, 75005, Paris, France

List of Contributors

Rosemary S.L. Mills, Department of Psychology, Psychology Building, University of Waterloo, Waterloo, Ontario, Canada N2L 3G1

Laurent Mottron, 6, rue de la Grange des Dimes Vallière Fondette, 37230 Luynes, France

Jacqueline Nadel, Laboratoire de Psychobiologie de l'Enfant du CNRS, 41, rue Gay Lussac, 75005, Paris, France

Louis Oppenheimer, Vakgroep Ontwikkelingspsychologie, Weesperlein 8, 1018 XA Amsterdam, Netherlands

Jeffrey Parker, University of Illinois, Department of Psychology, Champaign, IL 61821, U.S.A.

Linda Rose-Krasnor, Psychology Department, Brock University, St. Catherines, Ontario, Canada L2S 3A1

Maria Clotilde Rossetti Ferreira, Faculdade de Educaco da U.S.P.E.D.M., Avenida da Universidade 308, Cidade Universitaria, CEP 05508 - Sao Paulo, Brazil

Kenneth Rubin, Department of Psychology, Psychology Building, University of Waterloo, Waterloo, Ontario, Canada N2L 3G1

Barry H. Schneider, School of Psychology, University of Ottawa, 120 University, Ottawa, Ontario, Canada K1N 6N5

Peter Smith, Department of Psychology, The University, Sheffield, England S10 2TN,

Fred Strayer, Laboratoire d'Ethologie Humaine, Département de Psychologie, Université du Québec à Montréal, C.P. 8888, Montréal, Québec, Canada H3C 3P8

Robert Terry, Psychology Department, Duke University, Durham, North Carolina 27705, U.S.A.

Line Thomassin, Ecole de Psycho-éducation, 750, boul. Gouin est, C.P. 6128, succursale A, Montréal, Québec, Canada H3C 3J7

Richard E. Tremblay, Ecole de Psycho-éducation, 750, boul. Gouin est, C.P. 6128, succursale A, Montréal, Québec, Canada H3C 3J7

Giovanna Tomada, Department of Psychology, University of Florence, Italy

Nel Warnars-Kleverlaan, Vakgroep Ontwikkelingspsychologie, Weesperlein 8, 1018 XA Amsterdam, Netherlands

Roger P. Weissberg, Department of Psychology, Box 11A, Yale Station, New Haven, CT 06520-7447, U.S.A.

List of Contributors

Marie-José Garcia-Werebe, Laboratoire de Psychobiologie de l'Enfant du CNRS, 41, rue Gay Lussac, 75005, Paris, France

Elizabeth A. Wehner, Department of Psychology, University of Denver, Denver, Colorado 80208, U.S.A.

Allison S. White, Department of Psychology, University of Denver, Denver, Colorado 80208, U.S.A.

Section I

Social Competence in Developmental Perspective: Conceptual Issues

Introduction to Section I

Barry H. Schneider

This first section of the book is largely devoted to reaffirmation of the importance of social competence, deliberation about its nature, and reflection on the implications of a developmental perspective.

In Chapter 1, Steven R. Asher and Jeffrey G. Parker discuss theoretical models and research findings pertaining to the development of peer relationships. While these researchers have traditionally focused on the child's social status in larger peer contexts such as classroom groups, they devote considerable attention in this chapter to the processes involved in forming and maintaining more intimate friendships with a select group of individuals. In doing so, they make reference to a number of related affective dimensions, especially the child's feelings of loneliness. Their chapter closes with a comprehensive and critical review of longitudinal data that illustrate the link between childhood social competence and subsequent psychological adjustment.

This interest in childhood social competence as it relates to general well-being is shared by Norman Garmezy (Chapter 2). While Asher and Parker specifically target social competence in their research, Garmezy's model is broader and includes both social and nonsocial aspects of general competence. In a seminal research program that has had marked impact on the fields of children's social development, child psychopathology, and child clinical psychology, Garmezy and his colleagues have studied social and general competence as factors that assist children in overcoming the harmful effects of unfavorable early environments. Chapter 2 contains a summary of their theoretical position and findings.

The thorny issue of how social competence should be defined is tackled by Louis Oppenheimer in Chapter 3. It has been noted that defining competence "is like trying to climb a greased pole" (Phillips, 1984, p. 24). Theorists' failure to reach consensus on uniform usage of the terms *social competence* and *social skill* is highly frustrating and has been quite detrimental to the field (Zigler & Trickett, 1978). However, this lack of agreement concerning basic definitional issues should come as no great surprise given the diversity of reasons for interest in this field, discussed in the Preface. As one might expect, scholars from different backgrounds have included in their models and definitions of social competence elements that reflect their own needs and interests. Oppenheimer reviews and evaluates a number of previous approaches to the definition of social competence but devotes most of his chapter to the explication of his own systemic model, which is intended to encompass more of the basic factors that impinge on social development than existing conceptualizations of social competence.

In Chapter 4, Jens Asendorpf introduces a number of conceptual issues related to longitudinal studies of children's social competence. Longitudinal investigations have been highly valued within the field for over 60 years despite their high cost. They are arguably the most accurate means of studying developmental change. The results of many previous studies featuring the longitudinal perspective are reviewed by Asher and Parker in Chapter 1. Many of the conceptual problems addressed by Asendorpf evolve from the difficulty

B. H. Schneider et al. (eds.), Social Competence in Developmental Perspective, 3–4.
© 1989 by Kluwer Academic Publishers.

inherent in defining stability with respect to an individual's social behavior over the course of development because that individual's behavior, as well as the behavior of the peers, will change markedly with maturity. Asendorpf illustrates his views using data from a longitudinal study of children's shyness.

In a brief summary of a conversation hour at the NATO Advanced Study Institute on Social Competence in Developmental Perspective, Jane Ledingham continues the discussion of problems in longitudinal research. Her views are based on experience accrued in designing and implementing a large-scale longitudinal study of aggressive, withdrawn, and aggressive-withdrawn children in Montreal. The main topic of discussion was the conceptual difficulties of designing longitudinal studies because the initial measures collected when children are young become outdated or inapplicable as the subjects grow older.

In Chapter 5, Steve Duck presents a series of conceptual issues related to the essential nature of social competence. Traditional models of social competence are as much under siege as they were in Oppenheimer's chapter, but here, the attack emanates from different directions. This chapter is of particular interest because it introduces many of the theoretical issues that pervade the adult social competence literature, many of which turn out to be no less relevant to children. Duck's views are aimed at moving the field of social competence to an interpersonal communications perspective, with heightened emphasis on behaviors occurring within close interpersonal relationships. The analysis of conversations is promulgated as a promising research tool.

Section One closes with a consideration of whether existing models and measures of social competence apply equally to individuals of both sexes. Tina Daniels-Beirness notes a number of fundamental differences in the properties of boys' and girls' groups, as well as in the course of boys' and girls' social development, in Chapter 6. Her examples, and her suggestions for improvement, pertain to sociometric instruments, which will be discussed in greater detail in Section Three.

Many of the conceptual and methodological issues debated in Section One will receive continued but diminished attention in the other four sections. Because there are many models and definitions of social competence, with important differences among them, it is incumbent on everyone working in the field to clearly enunciate their concepts of social competence in describing their research.

References

Phillips, G. M. (1984). A competent view of "competence." *Communication Education, 32,* 25-36.
Zigler, E. & Trickett, P. L. (1978). IQ, social competence and the evaluation of early childhood intervention programs. *American Psychologist, 33,* 789-798.

1

Significance of Peer Relationship Problems in Childhood

Steven R. Asher and Jeffrey G. Parker

University of Illinois at Urbana-Champaign

In his 1917 sixteen-volume series *Practical Child Training*, educator R. C. Beery offered advice to mothers whose children have few friends and are reticent to approach others. Beery urged mothers to facilitate get-togethers with peers, such as backyard picnics that include the child's schoolmates, and to help the children "have a royal good time" (p. 1325). Beery also suggested what to do when a child is fearful about approaching other children: "If your child ever comes to you to bury his head in your skirts, you should not scold or make any scene, but simply appear to pay no attention to him" (p. 741).

Whatever the specific merits of his suggestions, Beery was responding to a sentiment expressed by parents and educators alike--namely, concern for children who have difficulty establishing ties with peers. In recent years, many psychologists and educational researchers have translated this concern into systematic programs of research. As a result, there now exists an extensive body of research on the origins, maintenance, and modification of low acceptance in the peer group (see Asher & Coie, in press, for a comprehensive treatment of this topic). From this research, it is clear that large individual differences can be found in children's degree of acceptance and friendship among their peers. Indeed, a distressingly large number of children are not liked by most of their classmates and have few, if any, friends (e.g., Coie & Dodge, 1983; Gronlund, 1959; Hymel & Asher, 1977). These individual differences in group acceptance and friendship tend to be relatively stable, even over extended periods of time (e.g., Coie & Dodge, 1983; Newcomb & Bukowski, 1984). Moreover, there is accumulating evidence that individual differences in peer acceptance are the consequence of variability in children's behavioral and social-cognitive competence (for recent reviews, see Coie, Dodge, & Kupersmidt, in press; Dodge & Feldman, in press; Putallaz & Wasserman, in press).

Although wide variability in peer acceptance and social competence is not in doubt, the significance of such variability is less well understood. Reliable individual differences do not in and of themselves establish the importance of a phenomenon. The critical question is whether serious peer relationship difficulties have important negative implications for children's development and well-being. In this chapter, we will argue that concern for poorly accepted children is well placed because peer rejection has important

5

B. H. Schneider et al. (eds.), Social Competence in Developmental Perspective, 5–23.
© *1989 by Kluwer Academic Publishers.*

implications for children's short- and long-term social and emotional adjustment. In advancing this argument, we will draw upon three somewhat distinct literatures. First, we will make the conceptual argument that children having peer relationship problems miss out on important functions that friendships serve in children's lives. Second, we will draw upon an emerging body of empirical work indicating that poorly accepted children are lonelier and feel less satisfied not only with their peer relationships in general, but with the friendships that they do have. Finally, we will summarize another body of empirical work indicating that low-accepted children are at risk for serious later life problems, including dropping out of school, delinquency and criminality, and mental health disturbances.

The Functions of Friendships

In this section, we will highlight several of the myriad benefits that children derive from continuing, successful integration into the peer group. By focusing on how children benefit from their friendships, we hope to make clear the important experiences that are missed by children who are poorly accepted and lack friends. Over the years, a number of authors have suggested that children benefit in important ways from their friendships. One of the earliest of these authors was Harry Stack Sullivan (1953), who focused on the friendships of preadolescents. Sullivan proposed that friendship in the preadolescent period marks a watershed in children's developing capacity to participate in collaborative, intimate personal relationships. According to Sullivan, preadolescent friendships serve several related functions in children's lives: They offer children consensual validation of their interests, hopes, and fears; bolster children's feelings of self-worth; and provide affection and opportunities for intimate self-disclosure. In addition, Sullivan felt that friendships promote the growth of interpersonal sensitivity and serve as early models for later romantic, marital, and parental relationships.

In the three decades since Sullivan's formulation there have been several additional attempts to catalog the benefits of friendships (Asher, 1978; Duck, 1983; Furman & Robbins, 1985; Hartup & Sancilio, 1986; La Gaipa, 1981; Solano, 1986; Wright, 1978). On the whole, seven friendship functions appear with some regularity across various formulations: a) fostering the growth of social competence, b) serving as sources of ego support and self-validation, c) providing emotional security in novel or potentially threatening situations, d) serving as sources of intimacy and affection, e) providing guidance and assistance, f) providing a sense of reliable alliance, and g) providing companionship and stimulation. We turn next to a discussion of each.

Friendship and the Socialization of Social Skills

Developmental theories have long recognized that children's friendships may foster the development of specific competencies that may eventually be generalized to other interpersonal contexts, both current and future. Piaget is usually credited with drawing early attention to this, but Sullivan (1953) was perhaps the earliest theorist to write extensively about this possibility. In Sullivan's view, individuals progress through a series of developmental periods, which he called "epochs," each marked by the emergence of a specific social need that motivates them to prefer certain forms of social interaction and to seek out certain key social relationships (see Buhrmester & Furman, 1986, for an excellent summary of Sullivan's theory). According to Sullivan (1953), intimacy needs arise in preadolescence and promote the formation of close, same-sex friendships. This relationship represents for the child "a perfectly novel relationship.... Nothing remotely like this has

6

ever happened before" (p. 245). In particular, through intimate self-disclosure with a friend, preadolescents for the first time gain an appreciation of the "personhood" of the participants in a relationship. This appreciation manifests itself as a newfound sensitivity to and genuine concern for the welfare of another, which, in turn, promotes the development of particular social competencies and values, including empathy, compassion, loyalty, and altruism. Several key elements of Sullivan's theory receive continuing attention by Youniss (1980), who emphasizes that it is the reciprocal, symmetrical aspect of friendship that makes advances in interpersonal sensitivity and understanding possible.

Other authors have also written about the role of friendship in the socialization of social competence. Fine (1980, 1981), for example, discusses friendship as a context for the emergence and elaboration of self-presentation and impression-management skills--skills for positioning oneself effectively and adaptively in social situations. Drawing upon symbolic interactionist theories (e.g., Cooley, Mead, Goffman) and his own observation research, Fine (1981) points out that friendships can serve as staging areas in which children explore the boundaries of allowable behavior and gain social poise under stress. His view is that the friendship bond:

> creates a setting in which impression-management skills are mastered and in which inadequate displays will typically be ignored or corrected without severe loss of face. Outside of friendship bonds, preadolescents have a critical eye for children's behaviors that are managed inadequately. (p. 41)

Further, Fine (1981) believes that friendship acts as a social institution whose purpose includes the transmission of information relevant to the problems of growing up:

> There are several topic areas in which children are interested but that they cannot learn about from adults: the practice of sex, informal rules of institutions (how *really* to succeed in school), the art of making negative evaluations (insults), and how to have excitement and adventure (pranks, mischief, and illegal behavior). (p. 44)

Similarly, Gottman and Parker (Gottman & Parker, 1986; Parker & Gottman, 1989) have suggested that friendships may play a role in the development of skills for managing emotions in interactions and interpreting internal emotional experiences. For example, they suggest that friendship interaction in early childhood has the implicit goal of maximizing the level of enjoyment that children experience in play. For this to occur, friends must be successful in coordinating their behavior to a high degree, and this, in turn, necessitates that the children learn skills for inhibiting action and maintaining organized behavior and attention in the face of arousal, excitement, and frustration.

Self-Validation and Ego Support

An additional function of friendship is that of self-validation and ego support. Friendships help children develop and maintain an image of themselves as competent, attractive, and worthwhile (e.g., Duck, 1983; Furman & Buhrmester, 1985; Furman & Robbins, 1985; Hartup & Sancilio, 1986; Reisman, 1985; Sullivan, 1953; Weiss, 1974; Wright, 1978). This function has been hypothesized to be especially important when children are going through periods of stress and transition, but it is undoubtedly important at other times as well.

Embodied in this notion is the expectation that friends are more overtly validating and supportive than nonfriends; that is, that friends are more likely to compliment one another, to express care and concern about one another's problems, and to boast to peers about a friend's accomplishments in the friend's presence. But the notion of self-validation and ego support is not limited to overt expressions of praise or concern; it is meant to apply equally well to the other, less direct ways in which friends influence one another's self-esteem and self-image. For example, Duck (1983) suggests that by attending to one another's actions, by listening, and by asking for advice, friends communicate that they value one another's opinions and hold one another in high regard. It also has been suggested that the child who befriends a more attractive child may do so in part because of the sense of pride and self-acceptance that arises from being associated with a highly desirable partner (Elkind, 1980).

In addition, a number of authors have pointed to the important opportunities that friendships provide for self-discovery and social comparison (e.g., Asher, 1978; Duck, 1983; Fine, 1981; Parker & Gottman, 1989; Rubenstein, 1984; Sullivan, 1953; Wright, 1978). These authors emphasize that a continuing and close relationship with a best friend affords children a relaxed, nonthreatening context in which to compare their own interests, attitudes, and anxieties to those of someone they like and admire. In this way, friendships can serve as anchor points for children to evaluate their own opinions, beliefs, and emotional reactions. By discovering that their own attitudes and beliefs are shared by friends, children come to view their beliefs as valid and, in the process, come to know and accept themselves--a process that Sullivan (1953) refers to as consensual validation.

The self-validating, ego-enhancing quality of friendship apparently is not lost on children: From early childhood onward, children's conceptions of friendship indicate in various ways that they expect friends to support, accept, nurture, and understand one another (Bigelow, 1977; Bigelow & La Gaipa, 1975; Douvan & Adelson, 1966; Gamer, 1977; Hunter & Youniss, 1982; Kon, 1981; La Gaipa, 1981; Reisman & Shorr, 1978; Smoller & Youniss, 1982). Moreover, children's and adolescents' descriptions of their actual friendships indicate that they see these relationships as supportive, tolerant, and understanding (Berndt, 1986a; Crockett, Losoff, & Peterson, 1984; Furman & Buhrmester, 1985; Richey & Richey, 1980; Sharabany, Gershoni, & Hofman, 1981).

Emotional Security

Another valuable function of friendship, one that has often been overlooked, is to provide children with a sense of emotional security in novel or threatening situations. By emotional security we are referring to the kind of reassurance, or even enhanced confidence, that children seem to gain from even the simple presence of a best friend. Friends help children explore new environments, try new behaviors, and take the kind of small and large risks often associated with growth.

The emotional security function of friendship has not been well studied. It appears, though, that even in the earliest of childhood friendships, the comforting value of a peer's presence is evident. For example, Ispa (1981), in a study conducted in the Soviet Union, observed children between 1 1/2 and 3 years of age when they were in a strange room. The children were placed either with a familiar peer from their nursery school group, with an unfamiliar peer from another nursery school group, or without another peer present. Children in this study exhibited the most comfort with a familiar peer present, the least comfort when they were alone, and an intermediate level of comfort when they were with an unfamiliar peer. Ispa also compared the level of comfort that children exhibited when they were with a peer compared to when they were with a familiar adult caretaker. Interestingly, the children were actually less comfortable with an adult than when in the presence of a familiar peer. This finding suggests that in some situations a peer can actually provide a level of security that an adult does not. This finding is especially remarkable given the age of the children involved.

An earlier study by Schwarz (1972) also examined the kind of emotional security that peers can provide in unfamiliar circumstances. Schwarz sent 4-year-old children into a strange room by themselves, with an unfamiliar peer, or with a friend. The room contained various novel but potentially interesting toys, and the children were observed in this room to see whether they explored the environment or exhibited anxiety and remained relatively immobilized. Children were found to exhibit the most comfort and to explore the room the most when they were with a friend as opposed to when they were with an unfamiliar peer or were alone.

Except for this work on very young children, little else is known about the emotional security function of friendship. It is likely that friends' role in helping children deal with novel and potentially threatening circumstances surfaces in varied forms throughout childhood and on into adolescence. It is interesting to note, for example, that the majority of both boys and girls of dating age prefer double-dating with friends or dating in groups as opposed to single-dating (Broderick, 1966). Presumably, part of what prompts adolescents to double date is the security that they derive from their same-sex friend's presence as they explore the awkward world of early cross-sex relations.

Intimacy and Affection

The role of friendship in providing opportunities for intimate self-disclosure continues to receive widespread prominence in scholarly literature on friendship (e.g., Duck, 1983; Furman & Buhrmester, 1985; Hartup & Sancilio, 1986; Sullivan, 1953) as well as in self-help books (e.g., Brenton, 1974) and popular North American films (e.g., *Stand By Me, The Breakfast Club*). Indeed, psychologists generally view the amount of reciprocal intimate self-disclosure in a particular relationship as a measure of the closeness of that relationship-- of the affection and trust that prevail between two individuals, child or adult. Conversely, they are reluctant to label a particular relationship a close friendship in the absence of a demonstrated willingness to share personal or private thoughts and feelings with each other (Mannarino, 1976; Oden, Herzberger, Mangione, & Wheeler, 1984; Serafica, 1982; Sullivan, 1953).

Children come to share this view as well. As they get older, children increasingly emphasize intimacy, self-disclosure, openness, and affection as components of friendship, both in their general beliefs about friendships (Bigelow, 1977; Bigelow & La Gaipa, 1975; Douvan & Adelson, 1966; Furman & Bierman, 1984; Hunter & Youniss, 1982; Reisman & Shorr, 1978; Selman, 1981; Smoller & Youniss, 1982) and in their descriptions of their actual friendships (e.g., Berndt, 1986a; Berndt & Perry, 1986; Crockett et al., 1984; Sharabany et al., 1981). Older children of both sexes also possess more intimate knowledge of their friends (Diaz & Berndt, 1982), describe their friends in a more differentiated and integrated manner (Peevers & Secord, 1973), and see their friendships as more exclusive and individualized (Sharabany et al., 1981; Smoller & Youniss, 1982). Girls, in particular, are thought to grow increasingly conscious of the intimate aspects of friendship, although the empirical evidence concerning sex differences is actually rather equivocal (cf. Berndt, 1986a; Berndt & Perry, 1986; Bigelow & La Gaipa, 1975; Bukowski & Newcomb, 1985; Crockett et al., 1984; Douvan & Adelson, 1966; Furman & Bierman, 1984; Furman & Buhrmester, 1985; Gamer, 1977; Hunter & Youniss, 1982; Sharabany et al., 1981). Not surprisingly, children of all ages report more intimacy in same-sex as opposed to cross-sex friendships, although this difference may disappear in late adolescence among girls (Sharabany et al., 1981).

It should be noted, however, that developmental trends in intimacy between friends do not imply that young children's friendships are devoid of affection and intimate self-disclosure. Reisman and Shorr (1978), for example, found that talking about a problem with a friend was reported by more than half of all 7- to 8-year-old children. Pursuing a related avenue of research, Ladd and Emerson (1984) found that as early as first grade (approximately 6 to 7 years of age), close friends know more about each other and are more aware of the important ways in which they are similar to and different from their partners than is the case with pairs of children who have a less close relationship. Apparently, then, young children do disclose information to one another, even though they do not spontaneously highlight this aspect of friendship in interviews and questionnaire assessments (La Gaipa, 1981).

One question that has sometimes surfaced with regard to friendship intimacy is how it relates to the intimacy that children experience in their family relations. Some authors (e.g., Dickens & Perlman, 1981; Wright & Keple, 1981) suggest that as the individual matures, the primary source of interpersonal intimacy shifts from family to friends. This was the position of Sullivan (1953), who is generally credited with first calling attention to the intimate, affectionate quality of friendship during preadolescence (see Buhrmester & Furman, 1986). Other authors point out that intimacy in friendship can be independent of intimacy in family relationships (Furman & Buhrmester, 1985; Rubenstein, 1984), or that there are important links between family relations and friendship relations in this regard (e.g., Cooper & Ayers-Lopez, 1985; Hunter & Youniss, 1982). The best empirical evidence suggests that the growth of intimacy in adolescent friendships does not come at the expense of intimacy between children and their parents (Crockett et al., 1984; Furman & Buhrmester, 1985).

Guidance and Assistance

Like most adults, children appreciate their friends partly because friends are willing to use their own time, energy, and material resources to help the individual meet his or her needs or obligations (Duck, 1983; Furman & Buhrmester, 1985; Weiss, 1974; Wright, 1984). In addition to tangible aid, friends also provide constructive criticism, counsel, and information. Of special importance is the spirit of helping and sharing in friendship. Clark (1984) likened children's friendships to a communal relationship, such as that which exists among kin or romantic partners. In a communal relationship, members feel a special obligation to be responsive to one another's instrumental needs. This is in contrast to an exchange relationship, such as that which exists between business partners, in which members are responsible for benefiting one another in direct proportion to benefits received, without any special sense of obligation to fulfill unmet needs.

Children of all ages almost always mention sharing and helping in their references to friendship obligations and in their descriptions of their actual friendships (Berndt, 1986a; Reisman & Shorr, 1978; Sharabany et al., 1981; Smoller & Youniss, 1982;). Moreover, friends emphasize equity in the distribution of rewards and obligations to a greater extent than nonfriends (Newcomb, Brady, & Hartup, 1979), and children who spontaneously share with a friend often mention friendship as the basis for their actions (Carlton-Jones, 1985). Sex differences favoring girls have sometimes been found with regard to children's references to instrumental aid, helping, and sharing in friendships (e.g., Berndt, Hawkins,

& Hoyle, 1986; Bukowski & Newcomb, 1985; Sharabany et al., 1981), but other studies find no differences in this regard (e.g., Berndt, 1986a; Furman & Buhrmester, 1985).

Research on friends' actual behavior, however, indicates that sharing and helping among friends are more contextually dependent than children's verbal reports would suggest. Berndt's (1986b) review of this issue indicates that in situations structured so as to allow children to work toward equality of outcomes (i.e., noncompetitive situations), friends share and help each other more often than nonfriends and that this pattern grows stronger across the middle childhood years. However, when sharing and helping are assessed in competitive situations, friends may be less likely to share or help than nonfriends. Berndt (1986b) proposes that friends share less than nonfriends in competitive situations because friends are more cognizant of social comparison in these situations, and more motivated to avoid losing.

The emphasis that friends place on advice, sharing, helping and other forms of instrumental aid relative to other functions of the relationship is generally thought to peak sometime in middle childhood, when it is thought to give way to an emphasis on intimacy and understanding (Bigelow & La Gaipa, 1975; Furman & Bierman, 1984). However, Richey and Richey (1980), in a questionnaire survey of 17- to 25-year-olds, remarked:

> Best friends apparently expect an astonishing (to us) amount of material and psychological support from their friends. Of 32 kinds of assistance listed--from staying with the subject at the time of a death in the family, to lending him/her two weeks' income, to remaining his/her friend even if the subject did something unethical --at least 51% of subjects believed that their friends would do 26 of the things listed. (p. 537)

It seems, then, that the expectancy of guidance and assistance from friends continues into adulthood.

Reliable Alliance

Weiss (1974) introduced the phrase "reliable alliance" to refer to the sense of security and reduction in perceived vulnerability that derives from knowledge that one can count on another's continuing loyalty and availability. He suggested that an individual's sense of reliable alliance in a relationship was somewhat independent of the actual level of other provisions of the relationship, and of the relationship's intimacy. Weiss (1974) felt that reliable alliance was primarily a function of kin relationships. However, Furman and Robbins (1985) point out that children's friendships can also serve as important sources of reliable alliance, and the available data support this view (Furman & Buhrmester, 1985).

Perceptions of loyalty and faithfulness in friendship, important components of reliable alliance, have been studied in some detail. Three conclusions seem warranted. First, children expect loyalty and faithfulness in their friendships; friends should not pick fights, talk behind one's back, lie and cheat, or get one in trouble (Austin & Thompson, 1948; Berndt, 1986a; Douvan & Adelson, 1966; La Gaipa, 1981). The closer the friendship, the greater the expectations for loyalty.

Second, the emphasis placed on loyalty and faithfulness in friendship expectations and in descriptions of actual friendships rises to a peak in middle or late childhood (Berndt, 1986a; Bigelow & La Gaipa, 1975; Douvan & Adelson, 1966; Gamer, 1977; Reisman & Shorr, 1978), after which point, it may stabilize (Reisman & Shorr, 1978) or even decline (Smoller & Youniss, 1982).

Finally, girls appear to stress loyalty to a greater extent in their general friendship expectations than boys do (e.g., Berndt, 1986a; Douvan & Adelson, 1966), but the evidence

11

for sex differences when children are asked to describe their actual friends is more mixed (cf. Berndt, 1986a; Berndt & Perry, 1986; Sharabany et al., 1981).

Companionship and Stimulation

Several years ago, La Gaipa (1981) noted:

> I suspect that fuller observations of the behavior of friendships in their natural setting would quickly reveal the "lighter" side of friendship. There is more to friendship than manifestations of prosocial behavior. . . . We would conjecture that it is difficult to maintain a friendship that is devoid of fun and laughter. (pp. 182-183)

The "lighter side" of friendship is companionship and stimulation, and as La Gaipa points out, this aspect of friendship should not get ignored by researchers as they focus on other functions such as emotional and physical support. With a friend, children gain access to a familiar, willing partner and playmate, someone who likes to spend time with them and who gladly joins them in collaborative activities--mundane or otherwise. The difference that a friend can make in terms of the quality of children's social lives is illustrated in the observational data of Roopnarine and Field (1984): In a playroom full of preschool children (3 to 5 years of age), those without friends had fewer children to talk to and to engage in fantasy play with. Instead, they were more likely to spend their time watching other children and their friends or to fight with other friendless children.

Friends spend a great deal of time in one another's company, particularly as they get older. One recent survey of early adolescents (Crockett et al., 1984) found that most report interacting with their best friend on a daily basis. The most common site of friendship interaction was at school. But friends also typically had as much as 3 hours of contact with their best friend outside of school, much of it spent conversing over the telephone. Similarly, Fine (1980) reports on the daily friendship contacts of a group of preadolescent boys:

> These respondents spent an average of 4.2 hours with friends of their same age, as compared with 3.5 hours with their parents and 1.7 hours alone. Time with friends included such activities as bicycle riding, sports (soccer, football, basketball, bowling), playing games, "hanging around," and watching television. (p. 314)

Measures of the sheer quantity of time that friends spend together do not reveal the content of friendship interaction, however. What children do when they are on their own with friends is not well documented (Hartup, 1984). Available data indicate that children report being happy while in the company of their friends (Csikszentmihalyi, Larson, & Prescott, 1977) and that in contrast to time spent alone, time with friends involves physically active or robust play and activities (Medrich, Roizen, Rubin, & Buckley, 1982). Further, play with friends is more coordinated, successful, extended, and nonstereotyped than play with nonfriends (Gottman & Parkhurst, 1980; Labinger & Holmberg, 1983; Roopnarine & Field, 1984; Rotherham & Phinney, 1981). Friends also create a more pleasing affective climate in their interaction than nonfriends do (Foot, Chapman, & Smith, 1980; Newcomb et al., 1979). Moreover, some activities that children enjoy--such as harmless Halloween pranks--almost never occur without the co-conspiring participation of a friend (Fine, 1980). It is apparent that friendship has much to offer children by way of excitement, amusement, and satisfaction.

Children certainly appreciate the extent to which companionship and stimulation are an important component of friendship. At all ages, children emphasize these qualities in their descriptions of actual friendships (Austin & Thompson, 1948; Berndt, 1986a; Berndt & Perry, 1986; Furman & Buhrmester, 1985; Hayes, Gershman, & Bolin, 1980) and in their beliefs about friendship in general (Bigelow, 1977; Bigelow & La Gaipa, 1975; Douvan & Adelson, 1966; Furman & Bierman, 1984; La Gaipa, 1981; Reisman & Shorr, 1978; Smoller & Youniss, 1982).

Summary

This discussion of the functions of friendship points to a rich and rewarding world that is potentially available to children who have friends. It is doubtful that deliberate planned efforts by adults to enrich the lives of children could ever duplicate the complex learning environment that occurs spontaneously in children's day-to-day lives with their friends. Friends serve as valued companions, confidants, and helpers; as reliable allies; and as sources of emotional support. Children also gain social knowledge and social skills from their friendship relations. All in all, these vital functions make us aware that to be rejected by peers, to lack friends in the peer group, is to miss out on important contexts in which social and emotional growth occur.

Loneliness and Relationship Dissatisfaction

Several of the functions of friendship discussed in the previous section suggest that children who lack friends would experience a variety of negative emotional consequences. Functions such as self-validation and ego support, emotional security, intimacy and affection, guidance and assistance should have beneficial consequences for children's feelings of self-worth, feelings of being included, and feelings of competence and confidence. Conversely, children who lack these friendship functions in their lives would likely experience lower self-esteem, greater loneliness, and greater social anxiety.

Indeed, in recent years, researchers have begun to examine the links between peer relationship problems and various forms of emotional maladjustment. Work has emerged on social anxiety (Hymel & Franke, 1985), perceived social competence (Wheeler & Ladd, 1982), and social self-esteem (Harter, 1982). In this section we are going to focus on recent research concerned with children's feeling of loneliness and dissatisfaction with their social relationships.

It might seem obvious to expect that children whose acceptance by peers is low would feel lonely. On the other hand, it could be argued that not everyone can be popular and that children who have few friends might nonetheless be quite content with their social world. Poorly accepted children might be content either because they place relatively little value on social relationships and really do not mind being poorly in-tegrated into the peer group, or because they enjoy one or two very satisfying friendships from which they derive considerable pleasure, even though they are not well accepted by the majority of their peers.

Loneliness and Peer Rejection

Despite long-standing interest in children who lack friends, researchers have only recently begun to study the feelings of children who are poorly integrated into the peer group. Within recent years, measures of loneliness have been developed by investigators in Canada (Heinlein & Spinner, 1985), Belgium (Marcoen & Brumagne, 1985), and the United States (Asher, Hymel, & Renshaw, 1984). It is clear that loneliness in children can be reliably measured (e.g., Asher et al., 1984), that children have well-developed conceptions of loneliness (Cassidy & Asher, 1988a; Hayden, Turulli, & Hymel, 1988), and that children's feelings of loneliness are fairly stable, even over a one-year period (Hymel, Franke, & Freigang, 1985).

The measure developed by Asher et al. (1984) has been used to study the links between integration into the peer group and feelings of loneliness. This measure contains 16 primary items centering on feelings of loneliness and social dissatisfaction and 8 filler items asking about hobbies, interests, and school subject preferences. The 16 primary items include direct statements of loneliness (e.g., "I'm lonely"), assessments of one's current peer relationships (e.g., "I don't have any friends"), indicators of recognition that key social provisions of relationships are not being met (e.g., "There's no other kids I can go to when I need help in school"), and statements related to perceived social competence (e.g., "I'm good at working with other children"). In subsequent research (Asher & Wheeler, 1985), the wording of some of the items was modified slightly to ensure that all 16 of the primary items had an explicit focus on the school peer group (e.g., "I'm lonely at school"; or "I don't have any friends in class"). Children responded to each item on a five-point scale, indicating the degree to which each statement is a true description of themselves (i.e., "that's always true about me; that's true about me most of the time; that's sometimes true about me; that's hardly ever true about me; that's not true at all about me").

This questionnaire has now been used in several studies (Asher & Wheeler, 1985; Asher & Williams, 1987; Crick & Ladd, 1988) with third- through sixth-grade children (approximately 8 to 11 years of age), in one study (Parkhurst & Asher, 1989) with seventh- and eighth-grade students (approximately 12 to 13 years of age), and in one study (Cassidy & Asher, 1988b) with kindergarten and first-grade children (approximately 5 and 6 years of age). In each study, factor analyses of questionnaire responses have revealed a principal factor with all 16 of the primary items loading on that factor. The items with the highest loadings are those specifically concerned with loneliness (e.g., "I'm lonely at school"; "I feel alone at school"). Furthermore, the internal reliability of the measure has been found to be quite satisfactory. The Cronbach *alpha* is .90 or .91 in the studies with children 8 years of age and older, and the coefficient is .79 for 5-and 6-year-old children.

Asher, Parkhurst, Hymel, and Williams (in press) have recently reviewed research on the link between acceptance by the peer group and feelings of loneliness and dissatisfaction with one's peer relationships. As they note, two different types of analyses have typically been performed. First, children's scores on the loneliness questionnaire have been correlated with sociometric ratings of how well children are liked by classmates. This correlation was -.31 in one study (Asher et al., 1984) and -.33 in another (Hymel, 1983).

The link between loneliness and sociometric status has also been studied by examining loneliness scores as a function of children's status group classification. In these analyses, children were classified, following Coie and Dodge's (1983) use of sociometric nomination data, as popular, rejected, neglected, controversial, or average in status. Popular children receive many positive nominations from their classmates and few negative nominations. Rejected children receive few positive nominations, but many negative nominations. Neglected children receive few positive or negative nominations. Controversial children receive many positive and many negative nominations, and average status children receive an average number of positive and negative nominations.

Asher et al. (in press) summarize the results of five studies with relatively large samples in which status group differences in loneliness were examined. In all five studies, rejected children were significantly more lonely than other status groups. Interestingly, neglected children in these studies did not show the same high levels of loneliness that rejected children reported. Indeed, neglected children were no more lonely than average status children. Apparently, it is not simply lacking friends in a class that leads to strong feelings of social isolation or alienation, but rather, it is being actively disliked by many of one's peers.

Together, then, the results of correlational analyses and the results of status group comparisons refute the argument that poorly accepted children are somehow content with their social world and do not mind being poorly integrated into the peer group. On the contrary, the evidence suggests that many of these children experience subjective distress about their general social circumstances. As we will see in the next subsection, low-accepted children's dissatisfaction even extends to their feelings about their best friends.

Low-Accepted Children's Views of Their Friendships

It is increasingly recognized that overall acceptance by the peer group and having a best friend are distinct phenomena (Asher & Hymel, 1981; Berndt, 1984; Bukowski & Hoza, 1989; Furman & Robbins, 1985; Mannarino, 1976; McGuire & Weisz, 1982; Parker, 1986). Children who are well liked or accepted by everyone in their class may nonetheless have no best friends in that group. Likewise, children who are poorly accepted or disliked by most of their classmates could still have mutual friendships with certain classmates. Indeed, it has been suggested that low-accepted children may form their own distinct classroom "subculture" (Gottman, 1986). Researchers' and educators' concerns about the emotional well-being of low-accepted children might be attenuated if it could be established that many such children have satisfying one-to-one friendships. Thus, it is of interest to learn how many low-accepted children have friendships and how satisfying those friendships are to the children involved.

We recently conducted a study to address this issue (Parker & Asher, 1988). We identified low-accepted children who had at least one mutual best friend and compared the quality of their friendships to the quality of average- and high-accepted children's friendships. Two hundred and seventy-eight children in grades three to six participated in the study. To identify children with best friends, children were asked to indicate their three best friends from a roster of all classmates. Children who nominated each other were considered best friends. By this criterion, 75% of all children had at least one best friend, and 45% had more than one best friend. As would be expected, fewer low-accepted children (54%) had best friends than average-accepted (79%) or high-accepted (91%) children. Low-accepted children also had fewer friends (mean .82) than average-accepted (mean 1.41) and high-accepted (mean 1.90) children. Nonetheless, it is significant that over half of all low-accepted children had at least one friend.

To assess relationship quality, we modified and factor analyzed a self-report measure developed by Bukowski, Hoza, and Newcomb (1987). The measure assesses children's perceptions of distinct features of their friendship, such as levels of companionship, trust, conflict, conflict resolution, and support. Children indicated on a 5-point scale how true each of 40 items was of their relationship with their mutual friend. The friend's name was embedded in every item. For example, to assess children's perceptions of their friend's loyalty, children indicated their agreement with statements such as "Becky would stick up for me if another kid was causing me trouble."

Findings from this measure indicated that low-accepted children with friends reported as much companionship and conflict in their friendships as did other children. They also seemed as likely as other children to consider their friend to be a special individual in their lives. But importantly, they viewed their friendships as less supportive and as having less

15

trust and loyalty. Low-accepted children also reported more difficulty resolving conflicts with friends than did better-accepted children. Thus, although a significant number of low-accepted children had mutual best friendships, they did not seem as satisfied with their friends as did other children. Again, like the data on loneliness, these data indicate that low-accepted children are less satisfied with their social world.

Long-Term Implications of Poor Peer Relationships

In this section, we turn from an emphasis on the concurrent implications of poor peer relationships--such as the opportunities missed by poorly accepted children or the sense of social dissatisfaction that they experience--to consider the issue of whether poor peer relationships in childhood place children at long-term risk for serious adjustment problems in later life.

Developmental and clinical psychologists have historically been quite receptive to the idea that poor peer relationships in childhood might portend adjustment problems in adolescence and adulthood (see Parker & Asher, 1987). Much of this receptivity follows from what we have presented so far: If one is convinced that friendships serve several important socialization and supportive functions in children's lives, and if one attaches significance to the fact that rejected children are lonely and unhappy about their peer relations, then it seems plausible that children with long-standing peer relationship difficulties should experience later adjustment difficulties. Such children, by definition, are growing up in an atypical and disadvantaged social context. We would expect these children to become more extreme and more idiosyncratic over time in their modes of thought and behavior. Furthermore, without the support of friends, these children can also be expected to be inordinately vulnerable to both normative stressors such as school transitions and nonnormative stressors such as the death of a parent. And because academic pursuits take place in a social context, poor peer relationships early in life might undermine subsequent academic progress as well. Elsewhere (Parker & Asher, 1987), we have referred to this line of reasoning as a "causal" model of peer relations and later adjustment.

There is, however, an alternative view of the possible link between early adjustment to peers and later personal adjustment, one that makes no assumption that peer relationship problems cause later maladjustment. This model--which we have referred to as an "incidental" model (Parker & Asher, 1987)--assumes that early forms of disorder that will emerge fully in adulthood have a negative influence on interpersonal relationships in childhood. In this view, it is the early forms of disorder that are responsible for both the early disturbances in peer adjustment and the ultimate maladaptive outcomes. Peer relationship disturbances may be potentially useful for screening purposes, but they would not be expected to make any independent contribution to later maladjustment and there is no reason to expect that children who are rejected by peers for reasons other than underlying disorder will have later maladjusted outcomes, according to this model.

Whether one subscribes to a causal model or an incidental model, or whether one believes that both models pertain, at least one empirical expectation is shared: It ought to be possible to demonstrate that poorly accepted children stand a greater chance than others of developing later life difficulties. We turn to this issue next.

1. Peer Relationship Problems

Methodological and Conceptual Issues

The literature on the long-term risk of children with peer relationship problems is widely scattered across disparate disciplines and research traditions. Perhaps as a result, claims of risk are often made without adequate attention to variations in studies' designs or the way peer difficulty is conceptualized and measured (see Parker & Asher, 1987). To avoid repeating this error, it is necessary to take three basic methodological and conceptual distinctions into account.

First, it is essential to resist treating findings from sociometric measures as interchangeable with findings from measures of status-relevant behavior, such as aggressiveness and shyness or withdrawal. We characterize this as a distinction between asking "Is the child liked?" and asking "What is the child like?" Measures of peer acceptance (e.g., sociometric measures) are indexes of the collective attraction of a group of children toward one another. They address the question "Is the child liked?" By contrast, reports about children's behavioral style address the question "What is the child like?" Since any particular behavioral dimension is only imperfectly correlated with acceptance by peers, whether a child is liked cannot be confidently inferred from knowledge of what the child is like.

Second, risk studies generally fall into one of two types of research designs, follow-up and follow-back, with one markedly more informative than the other. Follow-back designs begin by selecting a sample of adults or young adults who are deviant on some adjustment outcomes and selecting a second sample of adults who are adjusted, and then examining available childhood school or clinic records to determine the aspects of childhood functioning that are associated with adult problems. Such studies ask, for example, whether a disproportionately greater number of high school dropouts than high school graduates were rejected by peers in childhood. By contrast, follow-up designs begin by selecting groups of children who differ in acceptance and comparing their subsequent adjustment. In such studies, for example, the numbers of accepted and rejected children who eventually drop out are compared. Although follow-back studies are much easier to conduct, they can be quite misleading if used to address issues of predictive risk. For example, it is quite possible to find that most dropouts were low-accepted children in elementary school without it necessarily being the case that most low-accepted children will drop out. The latter, probabilistic type of prediction can only come from follow-up designs, which document the incidence of a particular disorder in target and comparison samples.

Finally, distinctions need to be made among types of samples. The two most common types of samples in the risk literature are samples of schoolchildren and samples of children who have been referred to clinics for evaluation or therapy. In addition, a few studies involve samples of so-called high-risk children who are the offspring of psychiatrically disturbed parents, such as schizophrenics. All other things being equal, the sample with the potential for the clearest interpretation and the widest generalizability of findings is the school sample.

With these issues in mind, we recently reviewed the available empirical evidence concerning the premise that children with poor peer relations are "at risk" (Parker & Asher, 1987). We concentrated on three important outcomes: dropping out of school, juvenile and adult criminality, and adult psychopathology. In all, we located almost 40 studies that addressed in some way the relationship between earlier peer adjustment and these later outcomes. Many of these studies contained multiple predictors, multiple outcomes, and more than one sample. Our approach was to take each outcome separately and examine the issue of risk as a function of: (a) the type of peer relations measure (acceptance, behavioral style), (b) the type of longitudinal design (follow-back or follow-up), and (c) the nature of the sample (school, clinic, or high-risk). We also made a distinction between judgments of peer adjustment derived from teachers and judgments derived from the peers themselves. For a detailed presentation of our findings, the reader is referred to our original, larger review. Here, we will summarize several important conclusions that we reached in that review.

Are Children With Poor Peer Relations at Risk?

The question of whether low-accepted children are at risk cannot be answered apart from consideration of the type of peer relations measure and the particular outcome of interest. Regardless of the outcome considered, low acceptance and aggressiveness are more consistent predictors of later negative outcomes than shyness/withdrawal. In fact, we found very little evidence to link shyness/withdrawal to later negative outcomes, at least in the follow-up sense. It should be mentioned, however, that shyness/withdrawal has been studied most often through teacher rather than peer report, most often in connection with psychopathology rather than dropping out or criminality, and most often in clinic rather than school samples. Thus, we should be cautious in drawing conclusions about shyness/withdrawal, since the existing findings are confounded by the source of judgment, type of outcome, and type of sample. It is perhaps fairest to say that the ideal study of shyness/withdrawal has yet to be done.

In addition, the power of particular predictors varies as a function of the outcome under consideration. Specifically, measures of acceptance and measures of aggressiveness show somewhat different relationships to later dropping out or criminality in terms of consistency of prediction. Low acceptance was most consistently predictive of later dropping out. In study after study, children identified as low in peer acceptance dropped out at rates 2, 3, and even 8 times as high as other children. In percentage terms, on average, about 25% of low-accepted elementary school children dropped out later compared to about 8% of other children. By contrast, aggressiveness was most consistently predictive of later criminality. Studies with measures of aggressiveness indicated that aggressive boys and girls were, on average, nearly 5 times more likely than other boys and girls to be involved in later crime, and in some studies these rates rose to 8 or 10 times more likely. In percentage terms, on average, 33% of all aggressive children were later involved in juvenile or adult crimes, compared to about 10% of nonaggressive children.

Finally, the risk premise appears to be on surer ground with regard to dropping out and criminality than it is for adult psychopathology. It should be noted that the literature regarding psychopathology was on the whole the least sophisticated methodologically and the most skewed toward nonschool samples. Also, what seems to be needed is a better-articulated conception of the kinds of mental health outcomes that might be expected to be associated with different sorts of peer problems. Most of the research on early peer relations and later psychopathology either has focused on schizophrenia or has obtained some general indicator of an individual's mental health status, such as receipt of mental health services. Perhaps childhood peer relationship problems would better predict specific outcomes such as extreme loneliness, anxiety, depression, or feelings of alienation.

Another important issue that we have discussed (Parker & Asher, 1987) concerns the sensitivity and specificity of prediction. Sensitivity refers to the extent to which predictions based on peer adjustment result in few, if any, false-negative predictions (i.e., few children destined for disorder escape detection). Specificity, on the other hand, refers to the extent to which predictions based on peer adjustment result in few, if any, false-positive predictions (i.e., children who are not at risk are not labeled as being at risk).

Consideration of the specificity and sensitivity of prediction indicates that peer relations measures of all types tend to show the same pattern of error of prediction: They tend to be relatively sensitive to those children who will ultimately show problematic outcomes but at the same time overselect many children who are not actually at risk. As a practical matter, both the direction and the degree of prediction error that is acceptable depend on why children are being selected. If children are being selected for intervention, and if one's concern is to avoid intervening with children not actually in need of treatment, then the tendency to overselect children is a concern. On the other hand, if all children would benefit from the intervention and no stigma is attached to program participation, then overselection need not be problematic.

Conclusion

The various lines of inquiry reviewed in this chapter provide strong support for the view that children who are poorly accepted by the peer group should be the focus of our concern. Not only do these children miss out on valuable friendship functions, they report greater loneliness and dissatisfaction with their social relationships, and they appear to be more at risk for later life adjustment difficulties, especially early withdrawal from school. Together, these lines of inquiry suggest that children with peer relationship problems should be viewed as a group "at risk" and that further efforts should be made to understand the origins of peer rejection in childhood and to intervene effectively with children who lack friends in school.

In concluding this chapter, we wish to stress that the goal of researchers has not been to help rejected children become the most popular children in their classrooms, but rather to help them gain acceptance and the ability to form and maintain friendships. There is no evidence that children need to achieve a high degree of popularity in order to benefit from their social lives at school. Indeed, research indicates few differences between average-accepted and popular children in either their social competence or their feelings of well-being (e.g., Asher et al., in press; Coie et al., in press). Rather than transforming poorly accepted children into social "stars," researchers have set their sights on the more fundamental goal of helping such children acquire skills for gaining group acceptance and friendship. In the past two decades, considerable progress has been made toward this goal (see, for example, Ladd & Asher, 1985). Certainly, the material reviewed in this chapter indicates that achieving this goal can make an important difference in children's lives.

Acknowledgment: The research reported in this chapter was supported by National Institute of Child Health and Human Development Research Grant HD05951 and by National Institute of Child Health and Human Development Training Grant HD07205.

References

Asher, S. R. (1978). Children's peer relations. In M. E. Lamb (Ed.), *Social and personality development* (pp. 91-113). New York: Holt, Rinehart and Winston.
Asher, S. R., & Coie, J. D. (in press). *Peer rejection in childhood.* New York: Cambridge University Press.
Asher, S. R., & Hymel, S. (1981). Children's social competence in peer relations: Sociometric and behavioral assessment. In J. D. Wine & M. D Smye (Eds.), *Social competence* (pp. 125-157). New York: Guilford Press.
Asher, S. R., Hymel, S., & Renshaw, P. D. (1984). Loneliness in children. *Child Development, 55,* 1456-1464.

Asher, S. R., Parkhurst, J. T., Hymel, S., & Williams, G. A. (in press). Peer rejection and loneliness in childhood. In S. R. Asher & J. D. Coie (Eds.), *Peer rejection in childhood*. New York: Cambridge University Press.

Asher, S. R., & Wheeler, V. A. (1985). Children's loneliness: A comparison of rejected and neglected peer status. *Journal of Counseling and Clinical Psychology, 53*, 500-505.

Asher, S. R., & Williams, G. A. (1987, April). New approaches to identifying rejected children at school. In G. W. Ladd (Chair), *Identification and treatment of socially rejected children in school settings*. Symposium conducted at the annual meeting of the American Educational Research Association, Washington, DC.

Austin, M. C., & Thompson, G. G. (1948). Children's friendships: A study of the bases on which children select and reject their best friends. *Journal of Educational Psychology, 39*, 101-116.

Beery, R. C. (1917). *Practical child training*. New York: Parents Association.

Berndt, T. J. (1984). Sociometric, social-cognitive, and behavioral measures for the study of friendship and popularity. In T. Field, J. L. Roopnarine, & M. Segal (Eds.), *Friendships in normal and handicapped children* (pp. 31-52). Norwood, NJ: Ablex.

Berndt, T. J. (1986a). Children's comments about their friendships. In M. Perlmutter (Ed.), *Minnesota symposia on child psychology: Vol. 18. Cognitive perspectives on children's social and behavioral development* (pp. 189-212). Hillsdale, NJ: Erlbaum.

Berndt, T. J. (1986b). Sharing between friends: Contexts and consequences. In E. C. Mueller & C. R. Cooper (Eds.), *Process and outcome in peer relationships* (pp. 105-127). New York: Academic Press.

Berndt, T. J., Hawkins, J. A., & Hoyle, S. G. (1986). Changes in friendship during a school year: Effects on children's and adolescents' impression of friendship and sharing with friends. *Child Development, 57*, 1284-1297.

Berndt, T. J., & Perry, T. B. (1986). Children's perceptions of friendships as supportive relationships. *Developmental Psychology, 22*, 640-648.

Bigelow, B. J. (1977). Children's friendship expectation: A cognitive developmental study. *Child Development, 48*, 246-253.

Bigelow, B. J., & La Gaipa, J. J. (1975). Children's written descriptions of friendships: A multidimensional study. *Developmental Psychology, 11*, 857-858.

Brenton, M. (1974). *Friendship*. New York: Stein & Day.

Broderick, C. B. (1966). Socio-sexual development in a suburban community. *Journal of Sex Research, 2*, 1-24.

Buhrmester, D., & Furman, W. (1986). The changing functions of friends in childhood: A neo-Sullivan perspective. In V. J. Derlega & B. A. Winstead (Eds.), *Friendship and social interaction* (pp. 41-62). New York: Springer-Verlag.

Bukowski, W. M., & Hoza, B. (1989). Popularity and friendship: Issues in theory, measurement, and outcome. In T. J. Berndt & G. W. Ladd (Eds.), *Peer relationships in child development* (pp. 15-45). New York: Wiley.

Bukowski, W. M., Hoza, B., & Newcomb, A. F. (1987). *Friendship, popularity, and the "self" during adolescence*. Unpublished manuscript, University of Maine, Orono.

Bukowski, W. M., & Newcomb, A. F. (1985). *Friendship conceptions among early adolescents: A longitudinal study of stability and change*. Unpublished manuscript, University of Maine, Orono.

Carlton-Jones, D. (1985). Persuasive appeals and responses to appeals among friends and acquaintances. *Child Development, 56*, 757-763.

Cassidy, J., & Asher, S. R. (1988a). *Loneliness in young children*. Manuscript in preparation, University of Illinois, Urbana-Champaign.

Cassidy, J., & Asher, S. R. (1988b). *Young children's conceptions of loneliness*. Manuscript in preparation, University of Illinois, Urbana-Champaign.

Clark, M. S. (1984). A distinction between two types of relationships and its implications for development. In J. C. Masters & K. Yarkin-Levin (Eds.), *Boundary areas in social and developmental psychology*. (pp. 241-270). New York: Academic Press.

Coie, J. D., & Dodge, K. A. (1983). Continuities and changes in children's social status: A five-year longitudinal study. *Merrill-Palmer Quarterly, 29*, 261-281.

Coie, J. D., Dodge, K. A., & Kupersmidt, J. (in press). Peer group behavior and social status. In S. R. Asher & J. D. Coie (Eds.), *Peer rejection in childhood*. New York: Cambridge University Press.

Cooper, C. R., & Ayers-Lopez, S. (1985). Family and peer systems in early adolescence: New models of the role of relationships in development. *Journal of Early Adolescence, 5*, 9-21.

Crick, N. R., & Ladd, G. W. (1988). *Rejected and neglected children's perceptions of their peer experiences: Loneliness, social anxiety, and social avoidance*. Paper presented at the meeting of the Southeastern Conference on Human Development, Charleston, SC.

Crockett, L., Losoff, M., & Peterson, A. C. (1984). Perceptions of the peer group and friendship in early adolescence. *Journal of Early Adolescence, 4*, 155-181.

Csikszentmihalyi, M., Larson, R., & Prescott, S. (1977). The ecology of adolescent activity and experience. *Journal of Youth and Adolescence, 6,* 281-294.

Diaz, R. M., & Berndt, T. J. (1982). Children's knowledge of a best friend: Fact or fancy? *Developmental Psychology, 18,* 787-794.

Dickens, W. J., & Perlman, D. (1981). Friendship over the life cycle. In S. Duck & R. Gilmore (Eds.), *Personal relationships: Vol. 2. Developing relationships* (pp. 91-122). New York: Academic Press.

Dodge, K. A., & Feldman, E. (in press). Issues in social cognition and sociometric status. In S. R. Asher & J. D. Coie (Eds.), *Peer rejection in childhood.* New York: Cambridge University Press.

Douvan, E., & Adelson, J. (1966). *The adolescent experience.* New York: Wiley.

Duck, S. (1983). *Friends, for life: The psychology of close relationships.* New York: St. Martin's Press.

Elkind, D. E. (1980). Strategic interactions in early adolescence. In J. Adelson (Ed.), *Handbook of adolescent psychology* (pp. 432-444). New York: Wiley.

Fine, G. A. (1980). The natural history of preadolescent male friendship groups. In H. C. Foot, A. J. Chapman, & J. R. Smith (Eds.), *Friendship and social relations in children* (pp. 293-320). New York: Wiley.

Fine, G. A. (1981). Friends, impression management, and preadolescent behavior. In S. R. Asher & J. M. Gottman (Eds.), *The development of children's friendships* (pp. 29-52). New York: Cambridge University Press.

Foot, H. C., Chapman, A. J., & Smith, J. R. (1980). Patterns of interaction in children's friendships. In H. C. Foot, A. J. Chapman, & J. R. Smith (Eds.), *Friendship and social relations in children* (pp. 267-287). New York: Wiley.

Furman, W., & Bierman, K. L. (1984). Children's conceptions of friendship: A multimethod study of developmental changes. *Developmental Psychology, 20,* 925-931.

Furman, W., & Buhrmester, D. (1985). Children's perceptions of the personal relationships in their social networks. *Developmental Psychology, 21,* 1016-1024.

Furman, W., & Robbins, P. (1985). What's the point?: Selection of treatment objectives. In B. Schneider, K. H. Rubin, & J. E. Ledingham (Eds.), *Children's peer relations: Issues in assessment and intervention* (pp. 41-54). New York: Springer-Verlag.

Gamer, E. (1977, May). *Children's reports of friendship criteria.* Paper presented at the annual meeting of the Massachusetts Psychological Association, Boston.

Gottman J. M. (1986). The world of coordinated play: Same- and cross-sex friendship in young children. In J. M. Gottman & J. G. Parker (Eds.), *Conversations of friends: Speculations on affective development* (pp. 139-191). New York: Cambridge University Press.

Gottman, J. M., & Parker, J. G. (Eds.) (1986). *Conversations of friends: Speculations on affective development.* New York: Cambridge University Press.

Gottman, J. M., & Parkhurst, J. T. (1980). A developmental theory of friendship and acquaintanceship processes. In W. A. Collins (Ed.), *Minnesota symposia on child psychology: Vol. 13. Development of cognition, affect, and social relations* (pp. 197-253). Hillsdale, NJ: Erlbaum.

Gronlund, N. E. (1959). *Sociometry in the classroom.* New York: Harper and Brothers.

Harter, S. (1982). The perceived competence scale for children. *Child Development, 53,* 87-97.

Hartup, W. W. (1984). The peer context in middle childhood. In W. A. Collins (Ed.), *Development during middle childhood: The years from six to twelve* (pp. 240-282). Washington, DC: National Academy Press.

Hartup, W. W., & Sancilio, M. F. (1986). Children's friendships. In E. Schopler & G. B. Mesibov (Eds.), *Social behavior in autism* (pp. 61-80). New York: Plenum.

Hayden, L., Turulli, D., & Hymel, S. (1988, May). *Children talk about loneliness.* Paper presented at the biennial meeting of the University of Waterloo Conference on Child Development, Waterloo, Ontario, Canada.

Hayes, D. S., Gershman, E., & Bolin, L. J. (1980). Friends and enemies: Cognitive bases for preschool children's unilateral and reciprocal relationships. *Child Development, 51,* 1276-1279.

Heinlein, L., & Spinner, B. (1985, April). *Measuring emotional loneliness in children.* Paper presented at the biennial meeting of the Society for Research in Child Development, Toronto, Ontario, Canada.

Hunter, F. T., & Youniss, J. (1982). Changes in functions of three relations during adolescence. *Developmental Psychology, 18,* 806-811.

Hymel, S. (1983, April). *Social isolation and rejection in children: The child's perspective.* Paper presented at the biennial meeting of the Society for Research in Child Development, Detroit.

Hymel, S., & Asher, S. R. (1977, April). *Assessment and training of isolated children's social skills.* Paper presented at the biennial meeting of the Society for Research in Child Development, New Orleans.

Hymel, S., & Franke, S. (1985). Children's peer relations: Assessing self-perceptions. In B. H. Schneider, K. H. Rubin, & J. E. Ledingham (Eds.), *Children's peer relations: Issues in assessment and intervention* (pp 75-92). New York: Springer-Verlag.

Hymel, S., Franke, S., & Freigang, R. (1985). Peer relationships and their disfunction: Considering the child's perspective. *Journal of Social and Clinical Psychology, 3*, 405-415.

Ispa, J. (1981). Peer support among Soviet day care toddlers. *International Journal of Behavioral Development, 4*, 255-269.

Kon, I. S. (1981). Adolescent friendship: Some unanswered questions for future research. In S. Duck & R. Gilmore (Eds.), *Personal relationships: (Vol. 2): Developing personal relationships* (pp. 187-204). New York: Academic Press.

Labinger, M. R., & Holmberg, M. C. (1983, April). *Dimensions of sharing and helping in preschool children with friends and acquaintances.* Paper presented at the biennial meeting of the Society for Research in Child Development, Detroit.

Ladd, G. W., & Asher, S. R. (1985). Social skill training and children's peer relations. In L. L'Abaté & M. Milan (Eds.), *Handbook of social skills training and research* (pp. 219-244). New York: Wiley.

Ladd, G. W., & Emerson, E. S. (1984). Shared knowledge in children's friendships. *Developmental Psychology, 20*, 932-940.

La Gaipa, J. J. (1981). Children's friendships. In S. Duck & R. Gilmore (Eds.), *Personal relationships: Vol. 3. Developing personal relationships* (pp. 161-185). New York: Academic Press.

Mannarino, A. P. (1976). Friendship patterns and altruistic behavior in preadolescent males. *Developmental Psychology, 12*, 555-556.

Marcoen, A., & Brumagne, M. (1985). Loneliness among children and young adolescents. *Developmental Psychology, 21*, 1025-1031.

McGuire, K. D., & Weisz, J. R. (1982). Social cognition and behavioral correlates of preadolescent chumship. *Child Development, 53*, 1478-1484.

Medrich, E. A., Roizen, J., Rubin, V., & Buckley, S. (1982). *The serious business of growing up: A study of children's lives outside of school.* Berkeley: University of California Press.

Newcomb, A. F., Brady, J. E., & Hartup, W. W. (1979). Friendship and incentive condition as determinants of children's task-oriented social behavior. *Child Development, 50*, 878-888.

Newcomb, A. F., & Bukowski, W. M. (1984). A longitudinal study of the utility of social preference and social impact sociometric classification schemes. *Child Development, 55*, 1434-1447.

Oden, S., Herzberger, S. E., Mangione, P. L., & Wheeler, V. A. (1984). Children's peer relationships: An examination of social processes. In J. C. Masters & K. Yarkin-Levin (Eds.), *Boundary areas in social and developmental psychology* (pp. 131-160). New York: Academic Press.

Parker, J. G. (1986). Becoming friends: Conversational skills for friendship formation in young children. In J. M. Gottman & J. G. Parker (Eds.), *Conversations of friends: Speculations on affective development* (pp. 103-138). New York: Cambridge University Press.

Parker, J. G., & Asher, S. R. (1987). Peer relations and later personal adjustment: Are low-accepted children at risk? *Psychological Bulletin, 102*, 357-389.

Parker, J. G., & Asher, S. R. (1988, July). *Peer group acceptance and the quality of children's best friendships.* Paper presented at NATO Advanced Study Institute, "Social competence in developmental perspective," Savoy, France.

Parker, J. G., & Gottman, J. M. (1989). Social and emotional development in a relational context: Friendship interaction from early childhood to adolescence. In T. J. Berndt & G. W. Ladd (Eds.), *Peer relationships in child development* (pp. 95-131). New York: Wiley.

Parkhurst, J. T., & Asher, S. R. (1989). *Social life in middle school: Peer rejection, behavioral style, and loneliness.* Unpublished manuscript, University of Illinois at Urbana-Champaign.

Peevers, B. H., & Secord, P. F. (1973). Developmental changes in attribution of descriptive concepts to persons. *Journal of Personality and Social Psychology, 27*, 120-128.

Putallaz, M. F., & Wasserman, A. (in press). Children's entry behavior. In S. R. Asher & J. D. Coie (Eds.), *Peer rejection in childhood.* New York: Cambridge University Press.

Reisman, J. M. (1985). Friendship and its implications for mental health or social competence. *Journal of Early Adolescence, 5*, 383-391.

Reisman, J. M., & Shorr, S. E. (1978). Friendship claims and expectations among children and adults. *Child Development, 49*, 913-916.

Richey, M. H., & Richey, H. W. (1980). The significance of best-friend relationships in adolescence. *Psychology in the Schools, 17*, 535-540.

Roopnarine, J. L., & Field, T. M. (1984). Play interactions of friends and acquaintances in nursery school. In T. Field, J. L. Roopnarine, & M. Segal (Eds.), *Friendships in normal and handicapped children* (pp. 89-98). Norwood, NJ: Ablex.

Rotherham, M. J., & Phinney, J. S. (1981, April). *Patterns of social overtures among preschool friends and non-friends.* Paper presented at the biennial meeting of the Society for Research in Child Development, Detroit.

Rubenstein, J. (1984). Friendship development in normal children: A commentary. In T. Field, J. L. Roopnarine, & M. Segal (Eds.), *Friendships in normal and handicapped children* (pp. 125-135). Norwood, NJ: Ablex.

Schwarz, J. C. (1972). Effects of peer familiarity on the behavior of preschoolers in a novel situation. *Journal of Personality and Social Psychology, 24,* 276-284.

Selman, R. L. (1981). *The growth of interpersonal understanding: Developmental and clinical analysis.* New York: Academic Press.

Serafica, F. C. (1982). Conceptions of friendship and interaction between friends: An organismic-developmental perspective. In F. Serafica (Ed.), *Social-cognitive development in context* (pp. 100-132). New York: Guilford Press.

Sharabany, R., Gershoni, R., & Hofman, J. (1981). Girlfriend, boyfriend: Age and sex differences in intimate friendship. *Developmental Psychology, 17,* 800-808.

Smoller, J., & Youniss, J. (1982). Social development through friendship. In K. H. Rubin & H. S. Ross (Eds.), *Peer relationships and social skills in childhood* (pp. 277-298). New York: Springer-Verlag.

Solano, C. H. (1986). People without friends: Loneliness and its alternatives. In V. J. Derlega & B. A. Winstead (Eds.), *Friendship and social interaction* (pp. 227-246). New York: Springer-Verlag.

Sullivan, H. S. (1953). *The interpersonal theory of psychiatry.* New York: Norton.

Weiss, R. S. (1974). The provisions of social relationships. In Z. Rubin (Ed.), *Doing unto others.* Englewood Cliffs, NJ: Prentice Hall.

Wheeler, V. A., & Ladd, G. W. (1982). Assessment of children's self-efficacy for social interactions with peers. *Developmental Psychology, 18,* 795-805.

Wright, P. H. (1978). Toward a theory of friendship based on a conception of self. *Human Communication Research, 4,* 196-207.

Wright, P. H. (1984). Self-referent motivation and the intrinsic quality of friendship. *Journal of Social and Personal Relationships, 1,* 115-130.

Wright, P. H., & Keple, T. W. (1981). Friends and parents of a sample of high school juniors: An exploratory study of relationship intensity and interpersonal rewards. *Journal of Marriage and Family, 43,* 559-570.

Youniss, J. (1980). *Parents and peers in social development: A Sullivan-Piaget perspective.* Chicago: University of Chicago Press.

2

The Role of Competence in the Study of Children and Adolescents Under Stress

Norman Garmezy

University of Minnesota

"Stress" and "coping" have virtually become paired associates in numerous titles of books, chapters, and journal articles (e.g., Antonovsky, 1979; Compas, 1987; Compas, Malcarne, & Fondacaro, 1988; Field, McCabe, & Schneiderman, 1985; Garmezy & Rutter, 1983; Holroyd & Lazarus, 1982; Lazarus & Folkman, 1984; Milgram, 1986; Roth & Cohen, 1986). By comparison, the linkage of "stress" and "competence" is a less common pairing. The term "competence" refers to those skills, capacities, and knowledge that enhance cognitive, social, and emotional adaptation (see White, 1979; Garmezy, Masten, Nordstrom, & Ferrarese, 1979). It is the central theme of this chapter that it is more productive to integrate the competence construct in studying adaptation to stress than to employ the more elusive and unstable formulations of coping. Three sections of this chapter seek to justify this somewhat atypical viewpoint.

The first section focuses on a heterogeneous literature linking competence to adaptive functioning in children and adults confronted with chronic and acute stressful life events. That linkage can be seen both in the idiography of case studies and in the nomothetics of group observations. Numerous studies now available suggest that there is a continuity of competence that bodes well for individuals caught up in disadvantaged circumstances, and supports the possibility of escape from high stress environments. Such continuity, for which one can find some degree of support even in longitudinal studies of severely disordered persons, can be demonstrated in research conducted in different geographic settings, using different subjects sampled in terms of variations in age, nationality, and ethnicity, under different stressor conditions, employing different outcome measures.

While no single study can clearly establish the power inherent in the stress-competence-adaptation sequence, the relevant studies, looked upon as a collective, do attest to the power of competence indices in the domains of work, social, and cognitive functioning for predicting adaptation under stress.

This relationship can be illustrated and shown to hold true   for a wide range of stressful experiences, including poverty, foster home placement, delinquent subcultures,

B. H. Schneider et al. (eds.), Social Competence in Developmental Perspective, 25–39.

traumatic separation and loss, child abuse, divorce, parental psychopathology, war and its vicissitudes, the Holocaust, and others (Garmezy, 1985).

The second section of the chapter will be devoted to a comparison of the power of the "coping" versus the "competence" construct. In my view, the various instruments used to measure "coping" have serious limitations. These, including their psychometric properties, create uncertainty about the transsituational generalizations that can be made based upon so-called "coping" measures.

In the third section of the chapter, I provide a brief overview of the power of the competence construct in the context of adaptation to stress as revealed by an ongoing Minnesota longitudinal study of stress resistance in children. This research program, aptly titled *Project Competence*, originally focused on a central city cohort of some 200 families and the offspring then enrolled in elementary school grades 3-6 (8-11 year olds). These children, now late adolescents and young adults, are currently being followed in an effort to study over time continuities and discontinuities in competence and in resilience under stress. The initial studies (Time 1) emphasized the measurement of the children's competence qualities and the collection of correlated familial data, much of it derived from 6 hours of interviews with the mothers. A description of the multimethods used to evaluate competence and its correlates will be presented in the context of Time 1 findings.

The transition from childhood to adolescence and adulthood (Time 2) is fraught with increasing demands--societal, familial, biological, and personal--on the young people who are our focus of interest. The questions to be answered are of considerable importance in identifying resilient children. For example: Is efficacy in meeting these later demands in part a function of past as well as present indicators of social, cognitive, and motivational competence? To what extent do continuities of competence exist for the period from middle childhood to late adolescence? Do specific aspects of competence in adolescence parallel similar competencies exhibited in childhood? When continuity is present, what are the adolescent outcomes in competence as exhibited in school and work settings, peer relations, and involvement in the community? What role do social, cognitive and motivation competence play in the maintenance of positive functioning under stress?

Where discontinuities exist over time (competent --> incompetent; incompetent --> competent), can generalized explanations prevail? Or must such explanations be essentially idiographic, necessitating extensive case histories to provide specific explanatory hypotheses for the changes? These questions will serve as a basis for discussion of the viewpoints expressed in the chapter. The data that may answer some of these questions will begin to be reported in publications due to appear over the next several years.

Studies of Stress-Resistant Children

It is something of an anomaly that the phenomenon of resilience in children and adults under stress, which is so commonplace and so well-known to the lay public that people can often readily recite personally known individual cases, should be neglected in the literature of stress and stress-responsivity. Lois Murphy (1962) early posed the evident neglect of the positive adaptations made by most individuals under stress in this way:

> It is something of a paradox that a nation which has exulted in its rapid expansion and its scientific-technological achievement, should have developed in its studies of childhood so vast a "problem" literature, a literature often expressing adjustment difficulties, social failures, blocked potentialities, and defeat...In applying clinical ways of thinking formulated out of experience with broken adults, we were slow to see how the language of adequacy to meet life's challenges could become the subject of

psychological science. Thus there are thousands of studies of maladjustment for each one that deals directly with the ways of managing life's problems with personal strength and adequacy. (p. 3)

When 20 years later (Garmezy, 1985) I sought to collate that small body of literature on "personal strength and adequacy" so neglected in 1962, I found that the situation had not markedly improved. The article reviewed a very diverse (and partial) literature that had to be extracted from a varied array of journals and books. I titled the manuscript "Stress-Resistant Children: The Search for Protective Factors". The word "search" was well-chosen for the paper was truly the product of an effort to locate instances of the phenomenon of protective factors--a term Michael Rutter (1979) had used earlier in his review.

"Risk" factors have long been the central focus of epidemiologists. These are factors statistically associated with higher incidence rates of a disease or disorder. Risk factors can be state or trait factors, exogenous precipitants of disorder such as stressful life events, or long term stable and often chronic factors that are associated with disorder. The requisites of risk factors include such qualities as measurability, stability, modifiability, relevance, sensitivity, and specificity (Regier & Allen, 1981). The latter two concepts, when applied to risk factors, refer to the validity of a diagnostic indicator with respect to true positive and true negative rates. Thus, sensitivity refers to the proportion of individuals identified as being at risk by virtue of a given risk factor who later develop the disease or disorder; specificity refers to the proportion of individuals identified as not having the risk factor who later do *not* develop the disorder.

The relationship between risk and stress is obvious. Stressors, too, can be risk factors in that they can enhance the probability of disorder. An acute stressor can potentiate a disturbed state; a chronic stress can induce vulnerabilities that can be precursor to or a predisposing element in disorder (Masten & Garmezy, 1985). Interactive effects are often evidenced between and among stressors.

One of the best illustrations of the additive and interactive effects of stressors has been provided by Rutter and his colleagues (Rutter, Cox, Trepling, Berger, & Yule, 1975). In examining and comparing 10-year-old children on the Isle of Wight and an inner city London borough, Rutter and his colleagues determined that six family variables were often significantly associated with child psychiatric disorder: 1) severe marital discord; 2) low socio-economic status; 3) overcrowding or large family size; 4) paternal criminality; 5) maternal psychiatric disorder; and 6) foster home placement of the child. The presence of these multiple factors when cumulated, increased the offspring's risk. Thus, the presence of a single risk element, despite chronic family distress, did not increase the rate of children's psychiatric disorder relative to children whose families exhibited no risk factors; any two risk factors heightened the probability of psychiatric disorder four-fold, while 4 or more factors resulted in a tenfold increase in that rate.

Unlike the substantial literature on risk, the concept of a protective factor requires introduction. Such a factor is one that often in coexistence with the presence of risk factors is accompanied by a reduction in the probability that the disorder will be actualized. Rutter and his colleagues asked this critical question: Is it possible that a good parent-child relationship can protect against the effects of deprivation and stress? In a subsequent study, the sample consisted of children living in families marked by two risk elements: 1) at least one parent had been under psychiatric care; 2) discord, disharmony, and unhappiness characterized the family atmosphere.

From within the sample the investigators chose children whose relationship with one parent, despite family discord, was characterized by "high warmth and the absence of severe criticism". These children were compared with other children who lacked a good relationship with both parents. In evaluating conduct disorder in these offspring it was observed that 75% of those in the latter group showed psychiatric disorder. However, in the group of children with a loving parent the prevalence of conduct disorder, despite the presence of the two risk factors, reduced the prevalence rate to 25%.

Apparently, a warm loving attachment to a parent even amidst risk factors provides some protective armor for a child. In a related study Rutter (1971) compared children born into families with mentally ill parents who were placed in harmonious, happy homes versus those raised amid parental discord in their biological families. Again conduct disorder (i.e., psychiatric risk) was more strikingly evident (2 1/2 times greater) in the children reared by their biological parents.

Rutter has pioneered the study and identification of protective factors as did Lois Murphy in an earlier era (1962). Until recent years, risk remained the predominant concern of stress researchers. Currently, there is a growing interest in pursuing the study of the attributes and developmental careers of children who are manifestly adaptive despite the presence of stress and disadvantage. Studies of resilient children have begun to appear in the literature of developmental and clinical psychology and psychiatry,and the range and findings of these studies warrant review. In this area recognition of the long-term research contributions of Block and Block (1980) to the construct of "ego resilience" deserves mention. As the Blocks define, the construct "ego resilience" describes a broad dimension of ego functioning, defined at one end by "resourceful adaptation to changing circumstances", and the ability to use a flexible set of problem-solving strategies. At the other extreme there are manifestations of inadequate adaptation, difficulty in responding to new situations, tendencies to perseveration or disorganization under stress, and difficulty in recouping from traumatic experiences (p. 48).

In initiating an area of study, single case instances often serve to energize the investigator's interest. It is important for behavioral and psychiatric scientists not to desert this important method of study for it can serve as a gateway to large scale group research (Garmezy, 1982; Kazdin & Tuma, 1982; Runyan, 1982).

If single case instances constitute a starting point, what often follows is the collation of such cases in order to derive more general principles. For example, the trials and tribulations of great figures who achieved eminence in adult life have been catalogued in three books appropriately titled *Lessons from Childhood* (Illingworth & Illingworth, 1966), *Cradles of Eminence* (Goertzel & Goertzel, 1962), and *300 Eminent Personalities* (Goertzel, Goertzel & Goertzel, 1978). These books describe the adverse early years of individuals who later became famous for their achievements. While they make fascinating reading, such reviews of eminent lives remove the study of "stress resistance" from the realm of the commonplace to a low base-rate context of the extraordinary. The traumatic familial, physical, or social circumstances of childhood of such greats as Beethoven, Thomas Edison, Kepler, Helen Keller, Eleanor Roosevelt, Albert Einstein, Louis B. Armstrong, G.B. Shaw, Dylan Thomas, Franz Kafka, T.E. Lawrence and others, scarcely seem the foundation stones on which to build a research program of resilience under stress observed in ordinary children. Many of the individuals cited in these volumes came to greatness with rather extraordinary predispositional qualities and potential talents. A focus on eminence, whether viewed from the cradle or the rocking chair, can cause us to lose sight of the many children and adults who lead ordinary lives, but whose very "ordinariness" can be seen as heroic when considered   against the highly traumatizing backgrounds from which they have come.

Nevertheless, there could be a linkage between those of genius and those of more ordinary achievements. It may lie in the nature of the stressors endured, the presence of specific temperaments which foster resistance, and although somewhat lower in a continuum of competencies, the presence of competence qualities that can be marshalled to meet the challenges posed by comparable stressful life events.

More about that in the following section. For now one considers evidence for the presence of protective factors that accompany resilience under stress, viewed not from idiographic case histories, but rather from nomothetic investigations that can be found in the literature of stress.

Reviews of some of the findings of different research efforts illustrating potential protective factors have been reported elsewhere (Garmezy, 1983, 1985; Garmezy & Rutter, 1985). In these reviews a diverse set of studies have been evaluated. These include epidemiological research on the Isle of Wight and an inner London borough as previously cited; a significant longitudinal study of some 30 years' duration by Werner & Smith (1982) of an infant cohort born on the Hawaiian island of Kauai in which earlier vulnerabilities were suggested by exposure of the babies to perinatal stress and later to poverty, family instability, limited parental education, and in some cases serious mental health problems of the parents; a longitudinal study of the Berkeley cohort of children ranging from their pre-school years to late adolescence (Block & Block, 1980); a review of competent black children of the inner city first conducted in 1970 and now in the process of being updated 18 years later (Nuechterlein, 1970; Loraas, 1988); a study of divorce and its aftermath conducted by Wallerstein and Kelly (1980); a 20 year longitudinal study conducted by Professor Manfred Bleuler (1978) with a cohort of schizophrenic patients who were followed clinically and whose cases were also reviewed in terms of their family life and the adaptation of their offspring; studies of Israeli and Irish children caught up in the maelstrom of war (Spielberger, Sarason, & Milgram, 1982; Harbison, 1983); a study of children of the Holocaust grown to adulthood (Moskovitz, 1983), a follow-up study in adulthood of persons who had been sexually abused as children (Zimrin, 1986), a followup report of the lives of successful men from criminogenic backgrounds (Farrington, Gallagher, Morley, St. Ledger & West, 1988); a comparative analysis of the family life and school achievement of poor black children who succeed in school versus others who fail (Clark, 1983); an evaluation of the adult adaptation of black children reared to adulthood in foster homes (Festinger, 1983); and Rutter & Quinton's (1984) follow-up into adulthood of the outcomes of institutionally reared girls whose continuous placement in that setting had begun in infancy or childhood.

These citations are a varied lot, indeed, but their very heterogeneity provides an advantage. For if one can find a concurrence of correlated factors that accompany successful adaptation under stress, it would greatly enhance the reliability of such protective factors.

In general, I see no reason to depart from the original coherence that I perceived to exist in my earlier 1985 review. At that time, I suggested that a triad of factors seemed to be reflected in the data of many of the studies. First, there were dispositional attributes of resilient children that could be viewed as positive temperament variables. These may include a reasonably good level of intelligence, a capacity for inhibition of response, persistence, the activation of control mechanisms, an adaptability to new situations, vigor of output, etc. Second there is the presence of a supportive family milieu and a positive relationship with parents. Third, there is the strength afforded by an external support system, that encourages and reinforces a child's adaptive efforts, and strengthens these through the inculcation of a consistent set of positive values.

Consistent with this triad is an underlying substrate of what is best termed "competence", as evidenced in a range of behaviors descriptive of cognitive, social, and emotional maturity. The cognitive component is reflected in the ability to problem-solve and to remain evaluative in stressful situations; a companion attribute is an achievement orientation. Social maturity is best evidenced in good peer relationships, the ability to form close friendships, and to interact meaningfully with adults. Emotional maturity is reflected in emotional regulation and the ability to constrain excessive and distorted emotional outbursts, as well as the capability not to allow emotionality to overwhelm and inhibit effective cognitive functioning.

As an illustration of this last point, I cite the recent publication of Asarnow, Carlson, & Guthrie (1987) indicating that suicidal children spontaneously generated fewer cognitive coping strategies to deal with stressful life events, than did a comparison group of nonsuicidal children. It is also interesting to note that suicidal children perceive their family environments as non-supportive, conflictful, and lacking in cohesiveness.

In offering these extensions, I have moved to an interpretation of the reported behaviors of children who seemingly are adaptive under stress. Far more research is needed in all three protective domains. Most of the observations made in the aforementioned studies, have not been oriented to the systematic exploration of these and other potential protective factors. But it is evident that multiform competencies differentiate those who effectively meet adversity and cope constructively with it, as opposed to others who have proved incapable of dealing with varied types of stressors.

There are other types of societal protective factors as well, ones that appear to provide gains for disadvantaged children. Rutter, Maughan, Mortimore & Ouston (1979) in the volume *Fifteen Thousand Hours* have reported the results of a research program designed to test whether the ethos of a secondary school can play an important role in fostering the competencies and adaptation of its students.

The study began as part of a large scale epidemiological investigation of children aged 10-11 living within an inner city London borough. The children were then in their final primary grade. At that point they were given a series of evaluations that included measures of non-verbal intelligence, reading comprehension, and teachers' assessments of their behavior. Family data were also collected. The children were then followed through their secondary school years, with systematic measurements at ages 14 and 16 of their behavior, attendance, and academic attainments. Police records were checked for delinquent acts, and the study provided for one year of post-school information to gather and evaluate employment patterns.

The London schools, located in disadvantaged areas, showed marked differences in their rates of delinquency, behavioral disturbances, attendance patterns, and academic attainments. These differences remained even when statistical controls were used to compensate for differences in the children's backgrounds, personal characteristics, and the types of primary schools they had attended.

What seemed to account, in part, for the latter differences, were some common school features that were present in the high attainment schools. In effect, certain attributes of the schools seemed to serve as protective factors despite adverse family conditions. What were these characteristics? They were factors that made up the "ethos" of the school: its academic emphasis; teachers' action in the classroom, including their preparation and planning; a high level of structure in the classroom; the giving of homework and exams; the use of incentives and rewards; the availability of after-school extracurricular activities; the presence and use of library facilities; faculty concern with academic and work-oriented goals; a willingness on the part of school officials to allow pupils to take responsibility for their actions and activities in the school; a prosocial atmosphere; an expressed appreciation to students for good work; and the presence of a substantial nucleus of children of at least average intellectual ability. With regard to this last factor there is apparently a "tilt point" that can influence group school performance. If a substantial portion of the children attending a specific school are of below average intellectual ability, then even the more able students will suffer the consequences of such an ill-formed distribution.

Factors that did *not* enhance the social and cognitive competence of the children or reduce behavioral disturbance in the classroom, included the age and size of the school, the availability of space, the age of the school, and grade placement in terms of pupil talent.

Now a new and confirmatory study (Mortimer, Sammons, Stoll, Lewis & Ecob, 1988) of the primary school milieu has appeared, that reaffirms the power of the ethos of the school, for strengthening children's competence and thus prepare them for many of life's vicissitudes that lie ahead.

In the United States too, the success of various school programs, including Head Start, appear to confirm the power of certain schools to provide experiences conducive to more healthful outcomes for disadvantaged children (The Consortium for Longitudinal Studies, 1983).

Competence Versus Coping in Reaction to Stressful Situations

These studies of school influence bring me to the second major topic of this chapter. I assert it as a proposition: The perceived importance of competence indicators can serve as protective factors that often transcend the effects of age variables, social status variables, stressor elements, and a potential for disordered behavior. The previous studies I have cited, when considered together, attest to the power of manifest competence in the domains of work, social and interpersonal functioning, and intellective challenge as being powerful predictors of adaptation to a diverse set of markedly stressful experiences. I find in the concept of competence a construct of such power, that it can even predict, if rated premorbidly, recovery from the most severe mental illnesses (Garmezy, 1985; Kantor and Herron, 1966). If competence can counteract the overpowering effects of mental disorder, then surely it has the power to play a definitive role in response to lesser or equally powerful stressors.

The notion that competence is the bearer of protection against traumatic events has a somewhat prosaic, molar character. It carries little of the drama of the *coping* construct, which is far more popular and suggests a molecular relationship with how persons will behave under stress. Effective coping suggests an ongoing behavioral process designed to mitigate the effects of stress or trauma. The process underlying such efficacy tends to be neglected and we are left with the specifics of behavioral responses, that typically take the form of post-event categorizations. An example: a recent article on the coping responses of crime victims (Wirtz & Harrell, 1987) presents as coping responses, such highly specific behaviors as "changed phone", "stayed home more", "don't go out alone", "bolt locks more", "carry or purchased weapon", "more cautious", etc.

By contrast, Moos and Schaefer (1986) provide a category set of more generalized, presumably transsituational responses: appraisal-focused coping; problem-focused coping; and emotion-focused coping. If we select problem-focused coping and examine its three components, namely "seeking information and support", "taking problem-solving actions", and "identifying alternative rewards", we can recognize clearly that such category subsets can best be generated in a context of manifest competence. Appraisal-focused coping too provides components that also reflect intellective competence (e.g., "logical analysis and mental preparation", "cognitive redefinition", "cognitive avoidance or denial").

A similar position has been espoused by Murphy and Moriarty (1976), who defined coping, in part, as "active ways of solving problems", pointing out that children have differential reactions to stress:

> Each child struggles to find solutions and out of these struggles and these solutions develops an implicit or explicit view of life as well as self. And so the personality is not just a pattern of predetermined (genetic) givens, but an achievement or outcome of coping with the challenges and opportunities life has offered...When, as with most of this group (of vulnerable infants) a child has been able to muddle through--by some combination of selection, escape, protest, or reconstruction of the situation--tolerance, strength, creativity, or triumph, or all of these, may be the outcome. (p. 13)

I take these wise words very seriously, for they pose a formidable challenge to those who would attempt to give definite content and form to the coping construct, expressing it in terms of a set of behavioral categories, to be applied to real or imaginary traumas, as an indication of the *generalized* coping qualities of the individuals being studied.

In an extensive review, Moos (1974) has described the wide variety of psychological techniques that are available to assess adaptive behavior and the manner in which people handle major life crises and everyday life stressors. In describing these various methods, Moos has posed three critical questions:

(1). How complex and how true to life is the stimulus situation confronting the subject?

(2). What type of response must the subject make; how complex and "real" is it?

(3). How complex and difficult is the analysis of the data required by the investigator? (p.337)

These questions are not dissimilar to the relationship of laboratory analogues to real world situations. Laboratory analogues can take the form of subject analogues, stimulus analogues, and response analogues. If subjects, stimuli, and responses appear to be veridical with real life situations to which generalizations are to be made, then the laboratory task approximates reality and the researcher can use data so obtained, as a near real world representation that sustains generalization. If all three are essentially distant and artificial analogues, then any generalization from obtained data must be very cautiously appraised. Thus hypothetical situations (a stimulus analogue) accompanied by multiple choice categories of response (a response analogue) with individuals recreating presumed stressors (a subject analogue), represent three futile strikes and in American baseball parlance, the researcher is retired.

Similarly, dichotomous "coping" responses made to situations and described as problem-focused versus emotion-focused, or social support categorized as "emotional", "tangible", or "informational", lends itself to response analyses that may assume more precision than is warranted.

Issues surrounding denial behavior under stress provide an interesting illustration of how complexity can be supplanted by simplicity. Lazarus and Folkman (1984) have written of the virtue of denial in response to severe stress. This is in contrast to the hapless response accorded denial in psychoanalytic thinking, based on its status as a rather rudimentary defense mechanism utilized by the young and in later life, by those of lower SES status (Haan, 1977). For Lazarus and Folkman (1984; see also Breznitz, 1983) denial following marked stress, initiates inactivity or depressed activity, as a means of restoring psychological equilibrium and mobilizing anew one's energy before confronting the stressful situation. Conversely, there are other contexts in which denial is handicapping, as in the postponement of a physical examination, when early symptoms suggest the possibility of a life-threatening illness. These simple examples are offered merely to illustrate that categorical responses require a knowledge of the context, before the researcher can decide upon either its adequacy or its predictive power for revealing adaptability or maladaptation under stress.

The issue does not rest on the declaration of a simple plus or minus, as with an evaluative grade. Rather, it involves the need to consider behavior on a continuum, that ranges from adaptability to maladaptability. The placement of an individual somewhere on such a continuum will require knowledge of both the processes activated by numerous stressors and the adequacy of the assessment method that is intended to reflect such processes.

Additional problems are posed by current methods for measuring coping, among which is the issue of continuity and discontinuity in an individual's response to a stressor. Discontinuities can be a function of many variables: age changes, patterns of growth and development, developmental transition points, cumulative stressors, shifts in economic status, family dissolution, extensive social change, and the imposition of environmental constraints. All these factors and others can not only alter the behavioral responses of individuals under stress, but they can also affect the reliability of systems presumed to categorize coping styles or coping methods.

An additional shortcoming of the coping construct, as reflected in the literature, is that coping as measured is typically an after-the-event measure. Research on the power of coping indicators in one stressful situation to predict responses in other stress situations, is in remarkably short supply. By contrast, this is not true of the integrative construct of competence/incompetence, which serves as a more powerful substrate for predicting efficacy or nonefficacy, in "coping" with stressful events, even prior to their occurrence. The view of our research group is that the nature of competence behavior, as reflected in such domains as intellective performance (including social cognition), work efficiency, social exchange, and achievement motivation enables one to measure continuities or discontinuities over time and consistency or inconsistency of adaptive behavior under stress. Coping is evanescent; competence is stable. The former invites discontinuity by its unreliability and its lack of transsituational generality; the latter ensures a reasonable likelihood of successfully measuring continuities or discontinuities in adaptation over time.

Perhaps the image of disagreement between coping and competence is more apparent than real. When Lazarus and Folkman (1984) describe coping resources such as health and energy, positive self regard, problem solving skills, social skills, social support, and material resources, they are referring specifically to competence indices or competence derivatives. In these examples, problem-solving skills and social skills can be classified as competence indices; social support and available material resources are often regarded as competence derivatives.

When Antonovsky (1979) writes of "generalized resistance resources" (GRR), he refers initially to a) adaptability on the physiological, biochemical, psychological, cultural, and social levels; b) profound ties to concrete, immediate others; and c) commitment of the individual to institutional ties between the self and the total community. While one can make a case for competence as an embracing construct, the fit is at best a partial one. However, Antonovsky's early volume on *Health, Stress, and Coping*, these GRR's, as he identified them, appeared to be markedly similar to the competence construct, as my research colleagues and I have used it: a) a preventive health orientation (i.e., the wisdom to avoid dangerous situations that can be debilitating); b) the availability of material resources that accompanies higher social status (often as an antecedent to or a consequent of manifest competence); c) good interpersonal relations including power, status and the utilization of available services; d) knowledge-intelligence; e) ego identity. Knowledge-intelligence", writes Antonovsky, "is the decisive GRR in coping with stressors." Ego identity, for Antonovsky, is comparable to the Eriksonian composite of good mental health: constitutional quality, manifest capabilities, consistent roles, effective defenses, significant identifications--a composite of those very elements that constitute the basis of efficacy and self-esteem.

When Antonovsky evaluates good coping strategies, the tie to competence as the underlying substrate becomes evident. Rationality, flexibility, and farsightedness become the definitive attributes, each of which reflects aspects of cognitive competence: rationality which implies accurate and objective assessments; flexibility, the ability to generate alternative solutions; farsightedness; the anticipation of consequences; planful behavior on a longer-term basis. Such defining attributes bring us full circle to the integrating construct of competence.

In our Minnesota research on stress-resistant children, we define "resiliency" as the maintenance of competence under stress. The roots of that definition are many. My early research career was spent studying the relationship of premorbid competence to outcome in schizophrenic .disorder. Process and reactive schizophrenia was for a long period a recognized dichotomy in schizophrenia (Garmezy, 1970). It is interesting to note that the developmental histories of these two classes of schizophrenics differed in terms of premorbid history, and in the potentiators that preceded the disorder. Reactive schizophrenics showed a premorbid history marked by social, sexual, and work competence and comparative familial stability; an identifiable stressor was associated with the onset of the disorder; symptoms were affectively stormy; and recovery and return to the community, even in the absence of the pharmacological interventions of today, tended to be the life history pattern. The process schizophrenic typically was marked by premorbid incompetence, the absence of a specific stressful potentiator, regressive negative symptoms, non-responsiveness to the earlier forms of treatment, and a long-term failure to recover from the psychosis. (More recent pharmacotherapeutics, fortunately, have achieved greater success in generating remissions within the chronic schizophrenic group).

The tie between premorbid competence, stressor, and recovery in clear and evident cases of a major psychosis, served as the prototype for our later studies of children of schizophrenic mothers, and subsequently of children resilient under marked familial stress. It strengthened the basis of our belief that competence indicators, and not coping strategies, were the proper focus for research on stress-resistance. This emphasis provided an antidote to risk factors and a way station for studying those protective factors that inhibit the expression of disordered behavior.

To return to one of the studies previously cited, Werner and Smith's *Vulnerable But Invincible* (1982), we can clearly see the protective role played by competence.

In the third volume of the Kauai studies, the authors chose sub-cohorts of "resilient" adults, and compared them with peers from the original cohort who were coping inadequately. The resilient adults, as children, and their parents bore the early and later hallmarks of competence. "Resilients" had better relationships with parents, who were less frequently absent from the home. The competence of the parents was indexed in terms of the support they provided to their children, the family stability and closeness, rule setting, discipline, and the parents' respect for the individuality of their children.

In turn, the children's competence qualities were evidenced by better health histories, more rapid recuperation from illness, an "active" childhood and adolescence, evidence of social responsibility, autonomy, and a positive social orientation. Other signs of maturity in the group of resilient girls (despite early disadvantage) were a lowered prevalence of fewer teen-age marriages and teen pregnancies, and fewer accidents. Further, these children were skillful in selecting and identifying with resilient models and cognizant of the availability of sources of support such as peers, older friends, ministers, and teachers to whom they could turn when necessary.

Patterns such as these parallel Antonovsky's categories of generalized resistance resources, which in turn, reflect powerful and attractive competence qualities in the resilient children.

The University of Minnesota's Project Competence

I can only touch briefly on Minnesota's Project Competence led by a three co-principal investigatorship team that includes Professors Ann Masten, Auke Tellegen, and the author. Since these studies have been described in considerable detail in journal articles and book chapters, I will not provide an extensive accounting here (Garmezy, Masten, & Tellegen, 1984; Garmezy & Tellegen, 1984; Masten & Garmezy, 1985; Masten, Garmezy, Tellegen, Pellegrini, Larkin, & Larson, 1988). However, I note briefly that we are engaged in a follow-up study that was launched some 8-9 years ago when we selected a community cohort of 200 families residing in the central city of Minneapolis. This diverse and somewhat heterogeneous sample includes middle class families, working blue collar class families, and single mothers on welfare who agreed to join our research program focused on stress-resistance in children.

Our basic plan was to study competence in the children of these families which varied in their exposure to stressful circumstances and life events. Among the data we gathered were 6 hours of interviews with mothers and 2 hours of additional interviews with the index children.

The children were also given an individual achievement test, an abbreviated intelligence test, and a variety of laboratory procedures designed to measure social cognition, problem-solving, divergent thinking, humor comprehension, humor appreciation, humor generation, delay of gratification, and impulsivity and reflectiveness. The collated competence indices included cumulative school records which were analyzed and rated; sociometric data were obtained from classmates with their cooperation; and teachers rated all the children in their classes on aspects of their motivation and citizenship irrespective of their ability level.

Analyses of these data focused on correlational and factor analytic explorations of the internal structure of specific domains. In this way we replaced a large number of single indicators with a smaller number of composite measures representing the domains of *competence, social cognition, reflectiveness-impulsiveness*, and *stress* (measured by both life events schedules and the interviewer's ratings following 6 hours of interviews with the mother, her SES status, etc.). In the first wave of (Time 1) studies we were able to factor analyze peer and teacher ratings of the competence qualities of the participating children. We identified two factors reflecting a portion of the competence domain: *engaged-disengaged* and *classroom disruptiveness*.

Four potential modifying factors of the stress-competence relationships were analyzed:

    a)   sex (girls vs. boys)
    b)   IQ (high vs. low)
    c)   Socio-economic status (SES) (high vs. how)
    d)   parental competence qualities (family stability and cohesion vs. the lack of these attributes)

Children with greater assets (higher IQ, SES, and positive family attributes) were found to be more competent. Of greater significance these children were more socially engaged with their peers and more active in their classroom. By contrast, children with fewer assets under stress tended to be more disruptive. Children with greater assets, under high stress tended to disengage from activities but did not become disruptive. Disruptive children heightened their disruptiveness under stress. We infer that positive family attributes appear to serve a protective function against children's disruptive-aggressive responses to stress. These attributes appear to reflect the quality of the parent-child relationship, the adequacy of family communication, the degree of the parents' perceptiveness about the child, and the overall competence of the parents.

Another aspect of competence proved to be the child's social comprehension as reflected in interpersonal understanding, problem-solving ability (Pellegrini, 1985) humor comprehension, appreciation, and production (Masten, 1986).

Included in the family-related modifiers of competence and stress were indices of family stability and organization (e.g., positive family mores, marital stability, a work history, evidence of mother's concern for the physical upkeep of the home, and family cohesion (frequency of family activities, level of manifest affection, presence of rules regarding offspring's behavior, adequacy of communication in the family, etc.).

Children with these more advantageous family characteristics were more intelligent, more competent, and less likely to be disruptive under high levels of stress.

By contrast, children in families marked by lower SES, and fewer positive familial qualities of stability, organization, and cohesion were more likely to be exposed to stressful life events and were also, less competent and less intellectually able. Under high stress, these children were manifestly more disruptive. Thus, there appears to be a cumulative quality to levels of stress and multiple risk factors which contribute to reducing engagement in competent children, and to increased disruptiveness in less competent children.

In conclusion three points are worthy of mention:

1. Follow-up data obtained recently when the children are now in late adolescence or early adulthood suggest a continuity in the competence of their mothers. The continuity of competence in the offspring must await further analyses of our data as reflected in going lengthy interviews and laboratory tests.

We hypothesize correlated transgenerational continuities in competent functioning over Time 1 and Time 2. Along with current evaluations of exposure to ongoing stress are efforts to study the interactions in the stress-competence relationships for mothers and their offspring.

2. We do have first gleanings that IQ and "Parenting Quality" as measured in childhood contribute significantly to the prediction of adaptation in adolescence even after earlier measures of childhood competence are taken into account.

It appears that both competence and the internal and external resources that accompany competence are reasonably stable and predictive of various aspects of later adjustment. Academic achievement, and externalizing behavior problems in childhood are particularly stable and broadly predictive of different patterns of adaptation in late adolescence. IQ and parenting quality seemingly function as broad markers of adaptive abilities and environments that are probably inseparably related to competence (Masten et al, 1988).

3. The stability and level of competence achieved are likely modifiers of the range of alternatives open to an individual under stress. The power of social cognition has been affirmed in our Project Competence studies as one partial index of competence. This suggests that the utilization of cognitive alternatives in stressful situations likely reflects a more generalized level of competence. In this sense competence can serve both as a

precursor as well as a basic substrate for the manifestation of differing types of adaptive strategies that are so popular in contemporary stress research. Faced then with a choice between coping and competence indicators, the latter would appear to be the more powerful and predictive measures of choice.

Acknowledgments: Preparation of this chapter was facilitated by grants from the William T. Grant Foundation, and the National Institute of Mental Health and a Research Career Award (NIMH) to the author. Appreciation is expressed to Drs. Ann Masten and Auke Tellegen, coprincipal investigators of Project Competence at the University of Minnesota.

References

Antonovsky, A. (1979). *Health, stress, and coping.* San Francisco: Jossey-Bass.

Asarnow, J. R., Carlson, G. A., & Guthrie, D. (1987). Coping strategies, self-perceptions, hopelessness, and perceived family environments in depressed and suicidal children. *Journal of Consulting and Clinical Psychology, 55,* 361-366.

Bleuler, M. (1978). *The schizophrenic disorders: Long-term patient and family studies.* New Haven, CT: Yale University Press.

Block, J. H., & Block, J. (1980). The role of ego-control and ego-resiliency in the organization of behavior. In W.A. Collins (Ed.), *Development of cognition, affect, and social relations: The Minnesota Symposia on Child Psychology* (Vol. 13, pp. 39-101). Hillsdale, NJ: Lawrence Erlbaum.

Breznitz, S. (Ed.) (1983). *The denial of stress.* New York, NY: International Universities Press.

Clark, R. M. (1983). *Family life and school achievement: Why poor black children succeed and fail.* Chicago: University of Chicago Press.

Compas, B. E. (1987). Coping with stress during childhood and adolescence. *Psychological Bulletin, 101,* 393-403.

Compas, B. E., Malcarne, V. L., & Fondacaro, K. M. (1988). Coping with stressful events in older children and young adolescents. *Journal of Consulting and Clinical Psychology, 56,* 405-411.

The Consortium for Longitudinal Studies (1983). *As the twig is bent: Lasting effects of preschool programs.* Hillsdale, NJ: Erlbaum.

Farrington, D. P., Gallagher, B., Morley, L., St. Ledger, R. J., & West, D. J. (1988). Are there any successful men from criminogenic backgrounds? Psychiatry, 51, 116-130.

Festinger, T. (1983). *No one ever asked us: A postscript to foster care.* New York: Columbia University Press.

Field, T. M., McCabe, P. M., & Schneiderman, N. (Eds.) (1985). *Stress and coping.* Hillsdale, NJ: Erlbaum.

Garmezy, N. (1970). Process and reactive schizophrenia: Some conceptions and issues. *Schizophrenia Bulletin* (2), 30-74.

Garmezy, N. (1982). The case for the single case in research. In A. E. Kazdin & A. H. Tuma (Eds.), *Single case research designs* (pp. 5-17). San Francisco: Jossey-Bass.

Garmezy, N. (1983). Stressors of childhood. In N. Garmezy & M. Rutter (Eds.), *Stress, coping, and development in children* (pp. 43-84). New York: McGraw-Hill.

Garmezy, N. (1985). Stress-resistant children: The search for protective factors. In J. E. Stevenson (Ed.), *Recent research in developmental psychopathology* (pp. 213-233). Elmsford, NY: Pergamon Press.

Garmezy, N., Masten, A., Nordstrom, L., & Ferrarese, M. (1979). The nature of competence in normal and deviant children. In M. W. Kent & J. E. Rolf (Eds.), *Primary prevention of psychopathology:* Vol. III. *Social competence in children* (pp.23-43). Hanover, NH: University Press of New England.

Garmezy, N., Masten, A. S. & Tellegen, A. (1984). The study of stress and competence: A building block for developmental psychology. *Child Development, 55,* 97-111.

Garmezy, N., & Rutter, M. (Eds.) (1983). *Stress, coping, and development in children.* New York: McGraw-Hill.

Garmezy, N. & Rutter, M. (1985). Acute reactions to stress. In M. Rutter & L. Hersov (Eds.), *Child and adolescent psychiatry: Modern approaches* (2nd ed., pp. 152-176). Oxford, England: Blackwell.

Garmezy, N. & Tellegen, A. (1984). Studies of stress-resistant children: Methods, variables, and preliminary findings. In F. Morrison, C. Lord, & D. Keating (Eds.), *Advances in applied developmental psychology* (Vol. I, pp. 231-287). New York, NY: Academic Press.

Goertzel, M. G., Goertzel, V., & Goertzel, T. G. (1978) *Three hundred eminent personalities.* San Francisco, CA: Jossey-Bass.

Goertzel, V., & Goertzel, M. G. (1962). *Cradles of eminence.* Boston, MA: Little, Brown.

Haan, N. (1977). *Coping and defending.* New York, NY: Academic Press. Harbison, J. (1983). *Children of the troubles.* Belfast, Northern Ireland: Stranmillis College.

Holroyd, K. A., Lazarus, R. S. (1982). Stress, coping and somatic adaptation. In L. Goldberger & S. Breznitz (Eds.), *Handbook of Stress* (pp. 21-35). New York, NY: Free Press.

Illingworth, R. S., & Illingworth, C. M. (1966). *Lessons from childhood.* Edinburgh, Scotland: Livingstone.

Kantor, R. E., & Herron, W. G. (1966). *Reactive and process schizophrenia.* Palo Alto, CA: Science and Behavior Books.

Kazdin, A. E., & Tuma, A. H. (Eds.). (1982). *Single-case research designs.* San Francisco, CA: Jossey-Bass.

Lazarus, R. S., & Folkman, S. (1984). *Stress, appraisal and coping.* New York, NY: Springer.

Loraas, J. A. (1988). *Competent, disadvantaged black children: An update.* Unpublished undergraduate honors thesis. University of Minnesota, Minneapolis.

Masten, A. S. (1986). Humor and competence in school-aged children. *Child Development, 57,* 461-473.

Masten, A. S. & Garmezy, N. (1985). Risk, vulnerability and protective factors in developmental psychopathology. In B. B. Lahey & A. E. Kazdin (Eds.), Advances in clinical child psychology (Vol. 8, pp. 1-52). New York, NY: Plenum.

Masten, A. S., Garmezy, N., Tellegen, A., Pellegrini, D. S., Larkin, K., & Larsen, A. (1988). Competence and stress in school children: The moderating effects of individual and family qualities. *Journal of Child Psychology and Psychiatry, 29*(6), 745-764.

Milgram, N. A. (Ed.). (1986). *Stress and coping in time of war.* New York, NY: Brunner/Mazel.

Moos, R. H. (1974). Psychological techniques in the assessment of adaptive behavior. In G. V. Coehlo, D. A. Hamburg, & J. E. Adams (Eds.), *Coping and adaptation* (pp. 334-399). New York, NY: Basic Books.

Moos, R. H., & Schaefer, J. A. (1986). Life transitions and crises: A conceptual overview. In R. H. Moos (Ed.), *Coping with life crises* (pp. 3-28). New York, NY: Plenum.

Mortimore, P., Sammons, P., Stoll, L., Lewis, D., & Ecob, R. (1988). *School matters: The junior years.* Somerset, England: Open Books.

Moskovitz, S. (1983). *Love despite hate: Child survivors of the Holocaust and their adult lives.* New York, NY: Schocken Books.

Murphy, L. B. (1962). *The widening world of children: Paths toward mastery.* New York, NY: Basic Books.

Murphy, L. B., & Moriarty, A. E. (1976). *Vulnerability, coping, and growth from infancy to adolescence.* New Haven, CT: Yale University Press.

Nuechterlein, K. (1970). *Competent disadvantaged children: A review of research.* Unpublished undergraduate honors thesis. University of Minnesota, Minneapolis.

Pellegrini, D. S. (1985). Social cognition and competence in middle childhood. *Child Development, 56,* 253-264.

Regier, D. A., & Allen G (Eds.). (1981). Editor's Summary. In *Risk factor research in the major mental disorders* (pp. 193-203), DHHS Publication No. ADM 81-1068. Rockville, MD: National Institute of Mental Health.

Roth, S., & Cohen, L. J. (1986). Approach, avoidance, and coping with stress. *American Psychologist, 41,* 813-819.

Runyan, W. M. (1982). *Life histories and psychobiography.* New York, NY: Oxford University Press.

Rutter, M. (1971). Parent-child separation: Psychological effects on the children. *Journal of Child Psychology and Psychiatry, 12,* 233-260.

Rutter, M. (1979). Protective factors in children's responses to stress and disadvantage. In M. W. Kent & J. E. Rolf (Eds.), *Primary prevention of psychopathology: Vol III. Social competence in children* (pp. 49-74). Hanover, NH: University Press of New England.

Rutter, M., Cox, A., Trepling, C., Berger, M., & Yule, W. (1975). Attainment and adjustment in two geographical areas: I. The prevalence of psychiatric disorder. *British Journal of Psychiatry, 126,* 493-509.

Rutter, M., Maughan, B., Mortimore, P., & Ouston, J. (1979). *Fifteen thousand hours.* Cambridge, MA: Harvard University Press.

Rutter, M., & Quinton, D. (1984). Long-term follow-up of women institutionalized in childhood: Factors promoting good functioning in adult life. *British Journal of Developmental Psychology, 18,* 225-234.

Rutter, M., Yule, B., Quinton, D., Rowlands, O., Yule, W., & Berger, M. (1975). Attainment and adjustment in two geographical areas: III. Some factors accounting for area differences. *British Journal of Psychiatry, 126,* 520-533.

Spielberger, C. D., Sarason, I. G., & Milgram, N. A. (Eds.). (1982). *Stress and anxiety* (Vol. 8). Washington, DC: Hemisphere Publishing.

Wallerstein, J. S., & Kelly, J. B. (1980). *Surviving the breakup: How children and parents cope with divorce.* New York, NY: Basic Books.

Werner, E. E., Smith, R. S. (1982). *Vulnerable but invincible: A study of resilient children.* New York, NY: McGraw-Hill.

White, R. W. (1979). Competence as an aspect of personal growth. In M. W. Kent & J. E. Rolf (Eds.), *Primary prevention of psychopathology: Vol. III. Social competence in children* (pp. 5-22).

Wirtz, P. W., & Harrell, A. V. (1987). Victim and crime characteristics, coping responses, and short- and long-term recovery from victimization. *Journal of Consulting and Clinical Psychology, 55,* 866-871.

Zimrin, H. (1986). A profile of survival. *Child Abuse and Neglect, 10,* 339-349.

3

The Nature of Social Action: Social Competence Versus Social Conformism

Louis Oppenheimer

Universiteit van Amsterdam

Abstract

The purpose of this chapter is to provide a critical evaluation of the concept of social competence. On the basis of a discussion of literature dealing with theory, models, and assessment of social competence as well as empirical research with regard to social competence, it is argued that the terminology used and the interpretation of the empirical findings do not characterize the development of children but rather the environment in which they must function socially. Hence, many of the abilities that have been assessed and that are thought to involve "social skills" merely reflect children's abilities to conform to the demands and expectations of the social environment. Consequently, the development of socially desirable behavior has been studied, not the development of social competence. To understand the latter development, a dynamic interactional model of development (i.e., an activity-levels model of development) will be presented. The interaction between the needs of the organism, the expectations and demands of the developing child and those of the social environment are presented. On the basis of this model, empirical data will be discussed and reinterpreted.

The Nature of Social Action: Social Competence Versus Social Conformism

In his attempt to study children, or "your pupils, because you certainly do not know them" (p. vi), Rousseau (1762) adopted a sociological, or more general societal, perspective in describing our ultimate goals in educating children--that is, adaptation to adult society with its institutions and to adulthood with its characteristics. Such a perspective is almost completely absent in contemporary developmental psychology. Development is described in terms of end-states relating to adulthood and adult society, which in no way reflect the qualities of adult social functioning and adults' affective, cognitive, and behavioral successes. The need to include such a reflection in our thinking about social development becomes paramount if we realize, for instance, that the role of peer relations in children's development is affected by the constraints of the cultural context (Hartup, 1983). Consequently, the study of both the contribution of peer relations to social competence and social competence itself could easily become a narrowly focused study of national and societal values and norms instead of a broadly based study of cross-cultural developmental

B. H. Schneider et al. (eds.), Social Competence in Developmental Perspective, 41–69.

phenomena. When social competence is described in detail below, this problem will become even more evident.

The purpose of this chapter is to critically evaluate the construct of "social competence." It will be argued that many of the social skills thought to characterize social competence in fact reflect children's abilities to comply or cope with the demands and expectations of social environments (i.e., they involve conformism). White (1979) defines this problem even more sharply by stating that "much of what has been written in recent years about the problems of youth points to social enslavement and alienation from self" (p. 20). Social competence "represents an evaluative term based on judgments (given certain criteria) that a person has performed a task adequately" (Gresham, 1986, p. 146). That is, the classification of social behaviors or outcomes as socially "competent" or "incompetent" is based on the standards, norms, and values prevalent in a particular society. Consequently, there is no place within the construct of social competence for *the subjective evaluation of the acting individuals themselves* with respect to their behavior. The construct of social competence, however, should also encompass behaviors that though judged *incompetent* by the social environment, are considered totally competent from the point of view of the child in question. Societal values, then, should be included as mere parameters in such a construct. Although these parameters may, for instance, restrict the range of social, proper behaviors or goals to be pursued, they may also result in adverse or pathological courses of action.

Social Competence

A major determinant of social behavior and adjustment is the "way in which one reasons about other people and about social situations" (Pelligrini, 1985, p. 253). Inadequate social skills, such as deficits in communication skills (Ladd, 1981), prevent the attainment of peer acceptance (Bierman & Furman, 1984); hence, peer-related social "incompetence" is the result of deficits in "peer-related social interactions and the absence of specific individual social behaviors" (Guralnick & Groom, 1985, p. 140). Social competence defined by social effectiveness is again related to cognitive competences such as problem solving and social-cognitive competences such as affective and cognitive role taking (Wright, 1980). Insufficient social competences, then, will often result in children's experiencing social difficulties; these children are labeled socially incompetent, and their behaviors are seen as maladjusted (Dodge, McClaskey, & Feldman, 1985).

This short summary of statements from a representative sampling of research articles offers a picture of the confused use of such terms as *social competence, social behaviors, social skills, social outcomes,* and *socially inadequate* and *maladjusted behaviors* of children on the one hand and *cognitive, social-cognitive,* and *social competence* on the other. Gresham (1986) is one of the few who explicitly distinguishes between social competence and social skills. According to him, social competence is an "evaluative term based on judgments that a person has performed adequately," while social skills are "specific behaviors that an individual exhibits to perform competently on a task" (pp. 145-146). Nevertheless, Dodge (1985) aptly notes that "the number of definitions of social competence in the developmental literature today approaches the number of investigators in the field" (p. 3). According to Greenspan (1981a), social competence is a "slippery construct" (p. 3). Although, he continues, "some progress toward understanding [social competence] has undoubtedly been made, there is a pervasive feeling that a consensual definition of social competence is still far outside our grasp" (p. 3).

This is problematic because also in the field of mental retardation social competence rather than intellectual ability is now used as the ultimate criterion in classifying an individual as mentally retarded (Greenspan, 1981b; Gresham, 1986; Oppenheimer & Rempt, 1986; Zigler & Trickett, 1978). Despite the conviction of a 1973 panel of experts that social competence is not identical to general intelligence and that the difference between the two must be defined in order to permit the stimulation and evaluation of children's social development (Anderson & Messick, 1974), neither a comprehensible measure nor a clear explication of the construct of social competence is presently available.

Social competence represents a "catch-all" concept that encompasses a large variety of often very different variables that play a role in social interactions. There is little consensus about what social competence actually is or about how the various variables are related to each other (see, for instance, Rubin & Ross, 1982; Schneider, Rubin, & Ledingham, 1985, for an impression of the present state of affairs).

Two Comprehensive Models of Social Competence

To date, few attempts have been made to order the various variables in a comprehensive way. Dodge (1985) proposes "a scheme or model of the various components of social interaction, which could lead to hypotheses concerning the manner in which various aspects of social interaction are related to each other" (p. 3). Similarly, a comprehensive model of social competence could be developed "which could serve as a basis for both research and clinical work with children and youth with problems" (Greenspan, 1981a, p. 24). Greenspan (1981a) and Dodge (1985) are among the few who have attempted to order contemporary ideas about social competence and the variables involved in social interaction. In the following subsections, both of their models will be discussed in greater detail.

Greenspan's Proposed Model of Social Competence

The prevailing lack of consensus about the exact meaning of social competence is, according to Greenspan (1981a), the result of the different approaches to social competence taken by different investigators. Three general approaches can be distinguished: an outcome-oriented, a content-oriented, and a skill-oriented approach.

The outcome-oriented approach concerns the individual's ability to attain desired social objectives. Within this approach, a distinction is made between various related abilities, such as the ability to deal with a changing world (Foote & Cottrell, 1955), to interact effectively with the environment (White, 1959), to adequately respond to the complexity of living in a society (Phillips, 1968), to learn alternative behavioral responses or courses of action to attain a given goal (Gladwin, 1967), and to accomplish the desired effects through one's actions (Edmonson, 1974). The various abilities will result in particular interpersonal outcomes, such as popularity, success or failure in various social roles (e.g., as friend, lover, or parent), performance in school, and success or failure in dating and marriage. The outcome-oriented approach therefore is a practical approach that serves as an indicator of the individual's social status. This approach functions as an excellent indicator, or index, of social, interpersonal problems. It does not, however, offer any insight into the causes of those problems.

In the content-oriented approach, attempts are made to identify behavioral traits that may contribute to socially successful outcomes. Greenspan (1981a) distinguishes two different strategies to identify such traits. In the first--the "bag of virtues strategy" (p. 7)--all possible behaviors are enumerated, preventing any distinction between social competence per se and other forms of competence, such as physical and emotional variables. In short, this strategy involves four global trait categories or competences: (a) physical health and growth, (b) cognitive ability (e.g., IQ), (c) educational achievements, and (d) motivational and emotional variables (cf. Anderson & Messick, 1974; Zigler & Trickett, 1978). In the second strategy--the "factorial strategy" (p. 9)--a limited number of behavioral dimensions are identified based on confining behavioral traits more strictly to interpersonal behavior. Examples of this strategy are the two-category taxonomy consisting of the niceness-nastiness and social activity-passivity dimensions (Kohn, 1977; Kohn & Rosman, 1972), Schaefer's (in Greenspan, 1981b) reflection-impulsivity dimension, and Guilford's (1977) "calmness-emotionality" dimension. While Guilford (1977) considered it more adequate to order these four dimensions into an "emotional health factor" (i.e., niceness-nastiness and calmness-emotionality) and a "stylistic factor" (i.e., activity-passivity and reflection-impulsivity), Greenspan (1981a) proposes to label these factors a "character factor" and a "temperament factor" (p. 12) respectively.

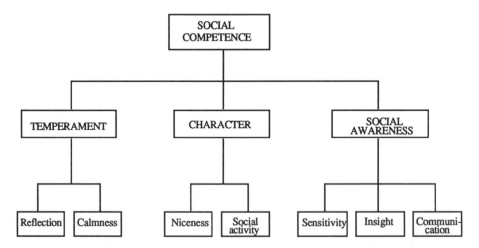

Note: From "Defining Childhood Social Competence: A Proposed Working Model" by S. Greenspan, 1981, in *Advances in Special Education* (Vol. 3, p. 26), edited by B.K. Keogh, Greenwich, CT: JAI Press. By permission.

Figure 3.1

Greenspan's proposed model of social competence, consisting of social awareness, character, and temperament.

Finally, the skill-oriented approach to social competence within Greenspan's model refers to the individual's social awareness. Social awareness is defined by the individual's skills, abilities, and processes to gain his or her social objectives, for instance, and to master the social environment; it is the ability to engage effectively in complex interpersonal interactions and to use and understand people effectively--that is, social cognition (Chandler, 1977; Flavell, 1985; Selman, 1976; Shantz, 1983). Greenspan (1981a) distinguishes three different aspects of social awareness: social sensitivity (i.e., role taking and social inference), social insight (i.e., social comprehension, psychological insight, and moral judgment), and social communication (i.e., referential communication and social problem solving) (See Figure 3.1.)

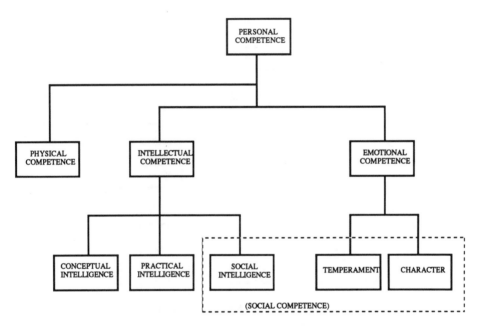

Note: From "Defining Childhood Social Competence: A Proposed Working Model" by S. Greenspan, 1981, in *Advances in Special Education* (Vol. 3, p. 29), edited by B.K. Keogh, Greenwich, CT: JAI Press. By permission.

Figure 3.2

Greenspan's proposed model of personal competence.

Social competence can now be defined in terms of the above aspects. According to Greenspan (1981a) social competence is "that portion of an individual's perceived effectiveness in interpersonal situations and social roles which is attributable to qualities of temperament, character, and social awareness" (p. 24) (See Figure 3.2.). To give an idea of how social competence is related to general "personal competence," a schematic representation of the relationships is shown in Figure 3.3.

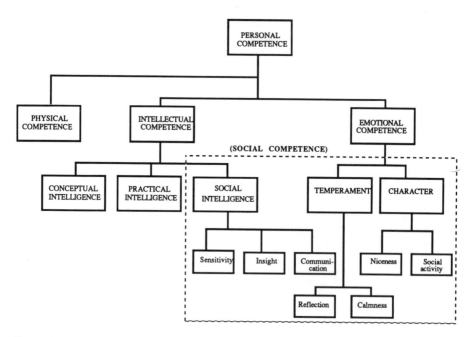

Note: Adapted from "Defining Childhood Social Competence: A Proposed Working Model" by S. Greenspan, 1981, in *Advances in Special Education* (Vol. 3), edited by B.K. Keogh, Greenwich, CT: JAI Press.   By permission.

Figure 3.3

The relationships between social and personal competence.

Dodge's Scheme of the Conceptualization of Social Interactions

According to Dodge (1985), the numerous definitions of social competence have two general features in common. The first concerns the child's responsiveness to environmental stimuli, and the second concerns the emphasis on social effectiveness in almost all definitions. Besides these commonalties, one or more different facets or aspects of social interaction are often emphasized in the different definitions, such as assertion (Bornstein, Bellack, & Hersen, 1977) and frequency of interaction (Furman, Rahe, & Hartup, 1979), as examples of behavioral facets, and the child's self-concept (Harter, 1982) and cognitive skills (Gottman, Gonso, & Rasmussen, 1975).   Each facet represents a component of social interaction and is relevant for an understanding of social competence.

In Dodge's (1985) scheme social behavior is placed in a social context. The social context may present the individual or child with a specific task: "Social behavior can [then] be conceptualized as occurring in response to specific tasks" (i.e., stimuli, settings, situations, contexts, and domains; p. 4). These tasks represent coherent amounts of information and may be very complex. The child is thought to approach such a task "with a set of prior experiences which help the child cope with its complexity" (p. 4). This set constitutes a filter that enables the child to selectively process information about the situation and, among other components, consists of particular perceptual strategies, social goals, and the self-concept. This filter, or set of prior experiences, is termed *unconscious influences* (Dodge, 1985). The *processing* of the perceived or selected information passes through six sequential steps, including encoding, interpretation, response search, response evaluation, enactment, and self-monitoring. The last step refers to the implementation of the selected response--that is, the actual behavioral response (i.e., *behaviors displayed*). The behavioral response is then evaluated by other social agents who are either participating in or observing the specific task. These judgments (i.e., *evaluations by others*) constitute the final aspect of social interaction (See Figure 3.4.).

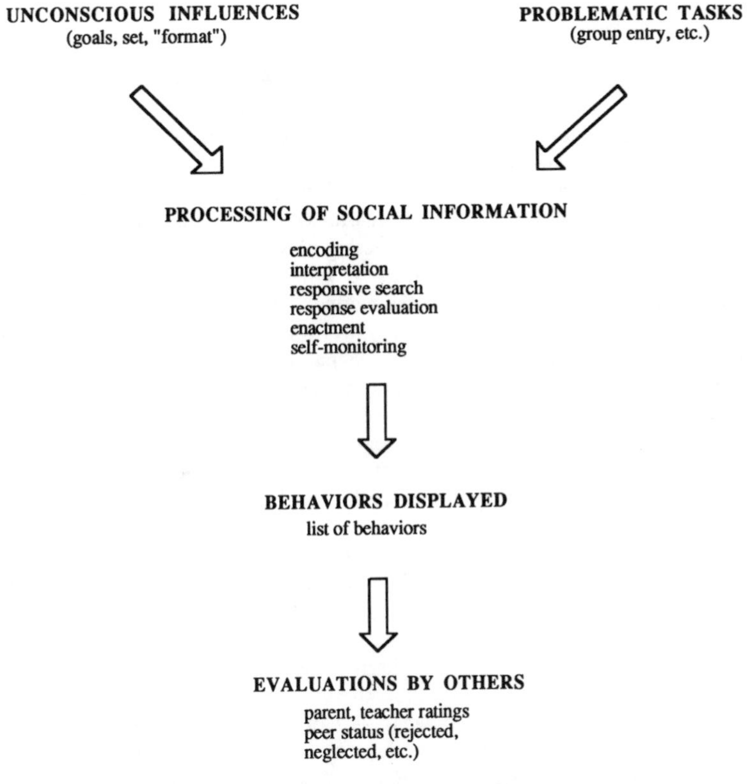

UNCONSCIOUS INFLUENCES   PROBLEMATIC TASKS
(goals, set, "format")   (group entry, etc.)

PROCESSING OF SOCIAL INFORMATION

encoding
interpretation
responsive search
response evaluation
enactment
self-monitoring

BEHAVIORS DISPLAYED
list of behaviors

EVALUATIONS BY OTHERS
parent, teacher ratings
peer status (rejected,
neglected, etc.)

Note: From "Facts of Social Interaction and the Assessment of Social Competence in Children" by K.A. Dodge, 1985, in *Children's Peer Relations: Issues in Assessment and Intervention* (p.4), edited by B.H. Schneider, K.H. Rubin, and J.E. Ledingham, New York: Springer-Verlag. By permission.

Figure 3.4

Dodge's model for "assessing social competence."

Both the Greenspan and Dodge models can be characterized as correlational models. They group a number of variables in such a way that empirically verifiable hypotheses can be formulated with regard to relationships among these variables and components. Without doubt, both models will contribute substantially to more structured approaches to the concept of social competence and its role in social interaction. Of interest is the difference between the two models. While Greenspan's (1981a) model represents a classic correlational model, Dodge's (1985) model tends more toward an information-processing model that suggests conditional, causal relationships (i.e., quasi-causal or implied causal relationships between its components). Hence, while Greenspan (1981a) invites the investigator to formulate hypotheses with respect to conditional or prerequisite relationships between the components in the model, Dodge (1985) attempts to specify a number of such relationships. The latter type of model (i.e., the information-processing model) within the area of social competence is also employed by Argyle (1985) and Krasnor (1985).

Two Additional Models of Social Competence

Argyle (1969; 1985) suggests the existence of similarities between the performance of social and motor skills. Motor skills, such as driving a car, can be represented by a simple information-processing model (see Figure 3.5), which closely parallels Miller, Galanter, and Pribram's (1960) "Test Operate Test Exit (TOTE)" model. Argyle's information-processing model involves a "goal" or "motivation," the perception of the situation, its translation, and the selection of a motor response. The similarities between this model and the third component in Dodge's (1985) model--the "processing of social information"--is evident. The motor response results in effects on the outside world; these effects (i.e., changes) are evaluated by the *individual* with respect to their effectiveness, and other, or new responses are given. Krasnor's (1985) model presents a typical routine for an information-processing model. This model, based on social problem solving (Rubin & Krasnor, 1986), considers the relation between a social goal and the appropriate strategy to attain this goal. Again, the model contains the components of task assessment, generation of strategies, selection of a strategy, and implementation of the strategy, as well as assessment of the outcome.

Although these models represent serious attempts to order a multitude of variables now thought to play a role in social competence, each model describes only a selected part of the total construct of social competence. Given this state of affairs, it is again and again surprising to note the considerable number of intervention studies that focus on isolated parts of the social competence structure, while none of the interveners has any certainty about how central or marginal the particular part might be with respect to social competence. As Gresham (1986) notes, "it seems premature to develop rather elaborate treatment strategies for behavioral deficits without knowing at a conceptual level the deficits we are trying to remediate or how to assess these deficits reliably or validly" (p. 143). Furthermore, very little is known about what part of the social competence structure is directly related to social interactional processes or socially (in)competent behaviors or outcomes. For instance, no unequivocal data are available concerning what variables underlie a child's popularity or make a child nice or well liked. It may sound like a mere semantic argument, but it can easily be demonstrated that the terms *popular, nice* and *well liked* mean rather different things for children of the same age as well as for children of different ages. As Hartup (1985) aptly notes, students in the field of social competence "are no longer content to assume that frequency of social contacts or general sociometric indices provide sufficiently differentiated diagnostic measures" (p. ix). As long as the deficiency of peer relations is dependent on the context in which those relations are assessed and the particular social skills thought to be involved, doubts can be raised about the assumption that children with "poor relations, in fact, lack social skills" (Hartup, 1985, p. ix). To increase this uncertainty (or confusion), the area of social competence is elaborated with new constructs or variables such as the "self-system" and self-esteem (Harter, 1983), locus of control (King & Galejs, 1985), and causal attribution (Sobol & Earn, 1985).

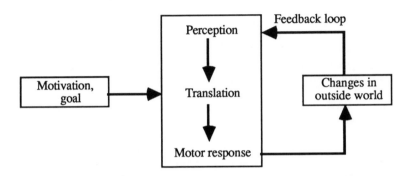

Note: From "Social Behavior Problems and Social Skills Training in Adolescence" by M. Argyle, 1985, in *Children's Peer Relations: Issues in Assessment and Intervention* (p. 214), edited by B.H. Schneider, K.H. Rubin, and J.E. Ledingham, New York: Springer-Verlag. By permission.

Figure 3.5

The "motor skill model" proposed by Argyle.

Hartup (1985) considers these new doubts, criticisms, and elaborations within the field of social competence to be indicators of a progressive discipline: "old wine in new bottles--with the flavor much improved. New vintages are also well represented in the collection. And, finally, there is some indication that next year's harvest will be a good one" (p. x).

An Alternative Approach to Social Competence

There is, however, reason to doubt Hartup's optimism. To "decant" knowledge from old bottles into new bottles will not necessarily lead to qualitatively more (let alone much) improved knowledge. Furthermore, new "knowledge vintages" will only contribute to our knowledge of the construct of social competence and its development if they can be "added" to our existing knowledge. However, wines are often characterized by their incompatibility. Let me illustrate this phenomenon with Aebli's (1984) lecture to the Sixth Congress of German Developmental Psychology (Regensburg, West Germany, 1983).

Aebli reported on a very elegant study that sheds light on Hartup's (1985) idea of "old wine in new bottles." Children who are not yet able to grasp the concept of the conservation of liquid believe that a given amount of water in a tall, thin glass is *greater* than the same amount of water in a short, wide glass simply because the water level in the tall, thin glass is higher than the water level in the short, wide glass. Based on this knowledge--that is, that nonconserving children equate "more" with a higher liquid level--Aebli (1984) developed the following research procedure. Nonconserving children were confronted with a doll who was seriously ill. Because of this illness, the doll had to drink a lot of water. In front of the child were placed two identical glasses filled with water. In front of the doll were placed two empty glasses, one tall and thin and one short and wide. After discussing the doll's illness with the child, the experimenter poured one of the child's glasses into the doll's short, wide glass. This resulted in a considerably lower water level in the doll's short, wide glass as compared to the water level in the child's remaining glass. The experimenter commented on this situation with the statement that the doll actually had less water than the child. After the child concluded for herself or himself that the doll indeed had less water, indeed, she or he was asked to show the experimenter how the doll could get "more" water. To everyone's surprise the children did not pour their remaining glass of water into the tall, thin glass but instead added their remaining water to the water in the short, wide glass. According to Aebli (1984) the children explained their actions by the argument that 'pouring the same quantity of water in a glass of another form would not mean that you get more; more means that you should add water.'

Similarly, to profit from increasingly detailed information about the development of social functioning, we need a meaningful structure for this knowledge. Although nonconserving children are aware that "new bottles" will not suffice to attain "more," within the field of social competence, new bottles are still produced.

The reasons for this phenomenon may be twofold. Even with the appearance of Piagetian theory within contemporary developmental psychology (cf. Cairns, 1983; Bruner, 1960; Flavell, 1963; Hunt, 1961), the child is still predominantly regarded as a "preprogrammed feedback system, whose inputs, outputs and inner workings can be given many interpretations" (Hollis, 1977, p. 5). The major advantage of such a passive conception of the developing human being is the single mode of explanation and well-worked-out causal models that can be employed. In the opposite conception of the child, the child is seen as possessing "some species of substantial self within" (Hollis, 1977, p. 5). That this conception is less popular is caused by the difficulty of making this type of child a topic of research. There is no "explanatory account of autonomy, the active self is the . . . we-know-not-what" (Hollis, 1977, p. 15). In the developmental model corresponding to the autonomous conception of the child,

> development and its potential plasticity both contribute to and result from embeddedness in the context. Reciprocal interactions between individual and context involve functions of the active individual--for example, of his or hercognitions...and repertoire of specific behaviors and skills--influencing the very context that influences him or her. (Lerner, 1986, p. 181)

Consequently, the study of the developmental courses by which children structure and come to understand their (social) environments (i.e., contexts), the way in which they perceive and understand themselves and their roles within contexts (Markus & Wurf, 1987; Oppenheimer & Oosterwegel, in press), and their ability to interact with others are of great importance in understanding children's the social functioning.

The second reason may stem from the absence of a global theoretical framework that would encompass the many and varied pragmatic theoretical models available. As a consequence, it is entirely unclear whether identical phenomena are explained by different models or whether the models are essentially identical and the phenomena essentially different. There has also been no attempt to determine in what way the different models may relate to each other. Theoretical models are characterized by an inner stubbornness that does not allow for any easy integration.

The Reciprocal, Interactional (or Activity-Levels) Approach

The reciprocal, interactional approach to developmental processes has resulted in a number of theoretical frameworks that emphasize the presence of interrelated systems (e.g., the ecological approach: Bronfenbrenner, 1977, 1979; the dialectical theory: Riegel, 1975; the life-span approach: Baltes, Reese, & Nesselroade, 1977; contextualism: Lerner, Hultsch, & Dixon, 1983). The purpose of these theoretical frameworks is to detail the complex interactions between the developing organism and the environment. The systems approach evident in these theoretical frameworks can also be found in a recent approach in developmental psychology--the psychobiological approach. According to Cairns (1979), development can only be understood by understanding the processes by which biological, interactional, and social components are fused during the individual's development. In other words, "behavior, whether social or nonsocial, is appropriately viewed in terms of an organized system and its explanation requires a holistic approach" (Levine, 1982, p. 30). The developing organism, then, can be defined in terms of a system consisting of numerous interacting and mutually impacting systems (henceforth referred to as activity levels) that develops within a context consisting of increasingly complex societal systems (i.e., activity levels).

On a slightly different plane, the holistic approach to the study of human development can be observed in the theory of Heinz Werner (1948). In his opinion, the development of perception and cognition cannot be dissociated from actions, feelings, and sensations. This holistic and "organismic" approach to development is characterized by *microgenesis*, which refers to the developmental, "self-renewing" process, that occurs each time we are confronted with new tasks or problems. According to Werner (1948), development is multilinear--that is, three qualitatively different types of thinking can be distinguished that developmentally succeed each other and that will remain simultaneously present. These types of thinking are to sensory-motor and affective thinking, perceptual and physiognomic thinking, and conceptual thinking. The similarity to the stage-mixture model (Turiel, 1974) within Piaget's epistemological theory is obvious. What we actually are dealing with are activity levels within activity levels, in which "earlier stages provide the basis (foundations, rudiments, seeds) for a later stage;...the earlier stage is incorporated into a later stage as a part, but it is qualitatively changed. It is present there but in a different guise, having taken on new emergent properties" (Kitchener, 1986).

According to Piaget, the different stages of cognitive or operational development reflect levels of equilibration between the subject and his or her environment. The earlier operational stages consist of less well equilibrated activity levels that are replaced or encompassed by more adequate operational activity levels. In the course of this substitution process, the earlier (preceding) levels continue to exist but do not remain the same activity levels the moment they become part of and are included in a larger system. Piaget (1976) assumes that development has a direction and is rational: "Though gradual progress towards equilibrium involves a direction, it never involves finality, much as, in thermodynamics, the increase in entropy, though admittedly directed, is not finalized" (p. 226). This description of equilibrium contains no normative definition. That is, the final end-state of optimal adaptation and the ultimate degree of equilibrium are unknown to the agent (and fortunately also to the theorist). Do lower levels of equilibration imply inadequate levels of adaptation to the demands and expectations of the environment, or do they merely imply *other* forms of adaptation--forms of adaptation that may not be sufficiently sophisticated to solve the experienced conflict between the "needs" of the organism and the opportunities offered by the environment to fulfil those needs (Piaget, 1981) or that may have completely different purposes? The successive stages of operational thinking, then, represent different levels of activity or systems of operational thought, which form part of an increasingly larger cognitive system.

Adaptation is regarded as a problem-solving activity, the resolution of mismatches between systems varying in size from atoms to clusters of galaxies. Problem-solving activities as attempts to achieve optimal adaptation will lead to genotypical and/or phenotypical reconstructions or accommodations. Reconstructions or accommodations of activity functions are not only evident on the epistemological level--that is, the development of knowledge--but will occur, depending on the type of adaptational problem and the species confronting it, on all organismic levels of activity. The purpose of these accommodations is to solve a problem, to achieve a renewed balance between the "malfunctioning" activity and the demands made by the external, as well as the internal, environment. The teleological goal-directedness characterizing the phylogenetic levels (Popper, 1972; Schneirla, 1957) can therefore also be applied to the intra-organismic activity levels and the stages of ontogenetic development. For each activity level, conflicts can be assumed to occur between its functioning and the real outcomes, or the adaptive value, or the efficiency of this functioning. Each activity level, then, is subject to disequilibria between its real adaptational value and the desired adaptational end-state. On the basis of these arguments, it can be assumed that disequilibria constitute the origins of any adaptational activity and that all these activities are goal-directed and serve the purpose of attaining optimal adaptation--that is, an "end-state" unknown to the agent. Disequilibria reflect the needs of an activity level or organism to improve its functionality. *Needs are manifest disequilibria* (Piaget, 1981).

The activity-levels-within-activity-levels postulate is not new within developmental psychology and was already noted in Urie Bronfenbrenner's (1977) ecological approach to human development. Bronfenbrenner argues that four interrelated systems are involved in the developmental process. They can be characterized by an increasing complexity of organization. These systems, which are interdependent, are (a) the individual-psychological microsystem, which is composed of "the complex of relations between the developing person and environment in an immediate setting containing the person" (Bronfenbrenner, 1977, p. 515); (b) the mesosystems which "comprise the interrelations among major settings containing the developing person at a particular point in his or her life" (p. 515); (c) the exosystems, which are defined as "one or more settings that do not involve the developing person as an active participant, but in which events occur that affect, or are affected by, what happens in the settings containing the developing person" (Bronfenbrenner, 1979, p. 25); and (d) the macrosystem, which is composed of historical events, as well as cultural values and beliefs that may affect the other ecological systems. In a similar way, Riegel's (1977) dialectical theory and the life-span developmental approach presented by, among others, Baltes et al. (1977) reflect this postulate in varying degrees of explicitness and levels of organization.

The range of solutions to manifest disequilibria that may be applied by the developing individual is co-determined by the different organismic and societal systems. Consequently, the range of preferences or interests that developing individuals are allowed to pursue, although regarded as optimal by the individuals themselves, will be restricted. Preferences or interests (also referred to as goals), involve the relationship between needs (i.e., the manifest disequilibria) and objects, people, or events thought to be capable of satisfying those needs (i.e., the attainment of equilibria; Piaget, 1981).

However, because disequilibria will occur on different activity levels within the organism, it can be argued that a considerable part of human preferences is not conscious (James, 1929). Children's apparently inherent curiosity, which results in the need to explore and to manipulate the environment to acquire schemes of knowledge, may be an example of such a preference originating as a disequilibrium on an unconscious activity level.

If, indeed, all our actions are dictated by interests and goals, as Piaget (1981) assumes, this will pose a number of interesting problems for the understanding of human action and its development. We have to realize that the initiation of actions may be co-determined by disequilibria on different and often unconscious activity levels, such as that of the genetic code. The interaction, synchronization, or dialectics between these different activity levels results in the concrete actions that we observe.

The claim that children's abilities to pursue preferences or interests (i.e., their social skills or planning abilities) are age-related can be defended easily and empirically (cf. Friedman, Scholnick, & Cocking, 1987; Pea, 1982). These abilities reflect progressive--in some instances, stage like--changes. It is much more difficult, however, to defend the same claim for the preferences or interests themselves. Although, as children grow older these preferences or interests may and will change in terms of their contents (i.e., the objects, people, or events to which the manifest disequilibria become directed; Oppenheimer & Van der Wilk, 1984), the claim that the nature of the disequilibria on the various intra-organismic activity levels will also change is much less tenable.

The changes in the *contents* of preferences or interests are the result of socialization processes. This process is one of conceptualization: Because the passage from unconsciousness to consciousness requires reconstructions, the "cognizance (or the act of becoming conscious) of an action scheme transforms it into a concept and therefore that cognizance consists basically in a conceptualization" (Piaget, 1976, p. 332). Reported changes in preferences or interests (Oppenheimer & Van der Wilk, 1984) are not characterized by a succession of different types of interests, but rather by an increase in the variety of different types of interests. That is, the directly pleasure-related preferences that characterize young children are still present when vocational interests emerge at the onset of adolescence. The later, more intellectualized vocational interests may also be (social) rationalizations of the pleasure-related interests evident during the first 4 to 7 years of life. This may be the result of the restricted range of possible (vocational) interests that children are allowed to pursue at different ages. With respect to vocational interests, we can even observe differences in this range of possible courses of action (i.e., vocational expectations in the macro-, exo-, and mesosystems) between girls and boys (Van der Wilk & Oppenheimer, 1987).

An Activity-Levels Model of Development: Organism-Environment Interaction

The theoretical perspective presented here refers to the child as a developing system consisting of many interacting activity levels. Each of the organismic activity levels (e.g., the genetic and information-processing activity levels or structures), as well as the nonorganismic activity levels (e.g., the affective, cognitive, and behavioral [knowledge] structures) or the activity levels based on interactions among these activity levels (e.g., the self-system), is characterized by functional or adaptational "needs," or disequilibria. The restoration of these disequilibria to equilibria, or the satisfaction of these needs, requires the presence of states, objects, people, or events thought capable of satisfying the needs.

53

Consequently, each activity level is acting, either consciously or unconsciously, with a purpose--that is, toward equilibration. In a number of instances, equilibration will result in progressive reconstructions of the structure underlying the activity level, as is the case with the cognitive (Piaget, 1976) or the genetic structures (i.e., by way of phenocopying; Baldwin, 1902; Piaget, 1978). In other instances, equilibration will be a goal in itself without direct consequences for the structural characteristics of the equilibrating activity level, as can be illustrated by the digestive activity level. Nevertheless, in this theoretical perspective, each *disequilibrium* on whatever activity level will affect the functioning of other activity levels because reciprocal interactions between activity levels are postulated. For instance, when somebody is hungry, his or her performance or achievement will decrease, and emotional problems will prevent optimal social behavioral functioning. Maslow's (1943) needs, in his theory of motivation, could easily be incorporated into the present theoretical framework, though not necessarily in a hierarchical order. Consequently, the prevention of equilibration inside or outside the organism will result in functional changes within the organic activity levels and subsequently in the relationship between the organism and the contexts in which it functions. To illustrate the theoretical perspective involved (Oppenheimer, 1988), the organism (Figure 3.6), the environment (Figure 3.7) and their interaction (i.e., the child; Figure 3.8) are schematically represented.

In Figure 3.6, the organism is depicted as a set of interacting activity levels corresponding to Riegel's (1977) *individual-psychological* system or Schneirla's (1957) *genotype*. As was argued before, the organism is a system consisting of many interacting activity levels, such as the *genetic, affective, cognitive* and *behavioral* activity levels. For instance, the *self-system* is defined as consisting of elements from at least the cognitive, behavioral, and affective activity levels (Harter, 1983). Serving and subject to these activity levels is the *inner-biological* system (Riegel, 1977), which, among others, includes the information-processing capacities of the individual-psychological system. If the model is placed along a time dimension, reference will be made to *maturation* (Schneirla, 1957). An illustration of such a maturational timetable is "the myelination of the very long neurons of the pyramidal tracts which control the motor neurons [and] predict quite nicely the dramatic gains in neuromuscular function during the first years of life" (Korner, 1979, p. 104).

The schematic model shown in Figure 3.6 also negates Greenspan's (1981a) proposal to differentiate between physical, intellectual and emotional competence on a higher level and conceptual, practical, and social intelligence on a lower level in the study of social competence. Whether or not equivalent activity levels could be discerned in the organism (i.e., such as the self-system), they are always constituted by, or consist of, competence-specific and competence-general elements of other reciprocally interacting activity levels.

In Figure 3.7 the environment is presented as three separate but interacting activity levels. The names of these activity levels--the meso-, exo-, and macrosystems--are derived from Bronfenbrenner's (1977, 1979) ecological theory. The definitions for these systems have been slightly changed. The *macrosystem* represents the culture or subculture, consisting of belief systems or ideology, and encompasses the exo- and mesosystems. The *exosystem* includes those settings "that do not involve the developing person as an active participant, but in which events occur that affect, or are affected by, what happens in the settings containing the developing person" (Bronfenbrenner, 1977, p. 25). These latter settings involving the developing person constitute the *mesosystem*: the different social contexts in which a child actively participates. As an illustration, the *family, peer*, and

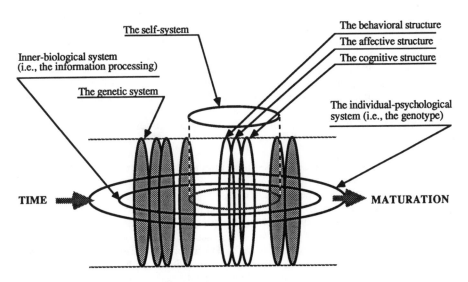

Figure 3.6

The organism presented as a system consisting of of interacting activity levels.

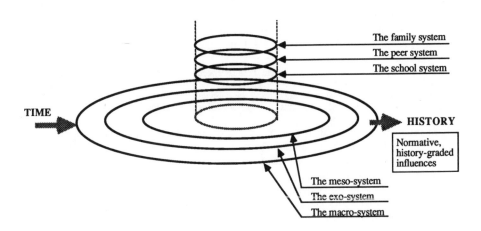

Figure 3.7

The environment presented as three separate, interacting activity levels or systems.

school systems have been distinguished within the mesosystem. If placed along a time dimension, reference is made to Baltes et al.'s (1977) *normative, history graded influences* on development (i.e., changes that take place within societal structures or institutions, values, and standards over time and history).

The link between the organism and the environment is the *microsystem*, or Schneirla's (1957) third source of development--the child himself or herself (i.e., the phenotype). The child is the final system (see Figure 3.8) representing the interaction or dialectics between the two major systems (i.e., the organism and the environment) and refers to *the product of this dialectic*. It is characterized by development of *normative age-graded influences* as the result of changing interaction patterns and changes in the nature of the dialectic over time (i.e., maturation and history-graded influences). Parallel with these three time dimensions, there exists a fourth dimension, which involves to Baltes et al.'s (1977) *nonnormative life events*, which can take forms ranging from traumatic experiences such as incest, rape, an accident, or the death of a spouse to an earthquake, nuclear catastrophe, or war.

The schematic representation of the three interacting systems in Figure 3.8 (i.e., the organism, the environment, and the child herself or himself) indicates the complex interactions between "multi-activity-level systems." Behavior or actions in contexts, then, are the result of these interactions. This is not a new approach (see also Laosa, 1979). Similar ideas can be found in Weber (1966) and Parsons (in Parsons & Shils, 1959), among others. For instance, Parsons & Shils (1959) note that actions do not occur in a void but in "constellations which we call systems" (p. 54). He distinguishes between three forms of activity or "modes of organization of elements of action" (p. 54). These modes of organization are called the social systems, the personality systems, and the cultural systems. Social systems and personality systems involve modes of organization for *motivated* action. In social systems, motivated action is
organized with respect to the reciprocal relations of actions, whereas in personality systems, motivated action is organized in reference to the living organism. Cultural systems, however, consist of organizations of symbolic patterns, which are transmitted among social systems by diffusion and among personalities by learning. The systems within the personality and social systems are conceived to be actors. Their actions are thought to be oriented toward goals and the gratification of situation-related need-dispositions. Most important, in Parsons & Shils (1959) view, is the conclusion that

> the analysis of the cultural system is essential...because systems of value standards...and other patterns of culture, when *institutionalized* in social systems and *internalized* in personality systems, guide the actor with respect to both the *orientation to ends* and the *normative regulations* of means and of expressive activities, whenever the need-dispositions of the actor allow choices in these matters. (pp. 54-57)

It is of interest to note that in recent reviews of, and books on, social competence and interaction (cf. Hartup, 1983; Rubin & Ross, 1982; Schneider, Rubin, & Ledingham, 1985), no reference to Parsons & Shils (1959) can be found, especially since concepts such as "institutionalization", "internalization", "orientation to ends", and "normative regulation" appear many times in the various works on social competence, although expressed in different terminologies and not embedded in a more encompassing theoretical framework that defines the meaning of these concepts.

Interests are the link between "needs" (i.e., Parsons' "need-dispositions"), or "manifest disequilibria," and the objects, events, and so forth thought to be capable of satisfying those needs. Therefore, an individual's goals reflect objectivized interests. Consequently, goals and their underlying "internalized value standards," or "duties" (Von Wright, 1976), "manifest disequilibria," "need-dispositions," or "wants" (Hollis, 1977) are of great importance in explaining an individual's behavior. They put the individual's behavior "into context, [so that] the appropriateness and effectiveness of social actions can be judged" (Krasnor, 1985, p. 59). It should be noted, however, that the manifest disequilibria and their resulting objectivations derived from the direct organismic "consumenatory and riddance" value system (Pepper, 1966, p. 552; i.e., affective values), the "appetitive and aversive purpose structure" (p. 552; i.e., conative achievement values) and the "natural selection" value system (p. 552; i.e., survival values) are different from those derived from the social value systems (Pepper, 1966). The values from the latter systems--such as the "personal situation," the "personality structure," and the "social situation" value systems--lack any "intrinsic dynamics" (Pepper, 1966, p. 552), and hence, the resulting disquilibria are not intrinsically, but extrinsically, given or motivated. Consequently, in the present theoretical framework, an individual's goals, though only attainable in social contexts, are not of necessity "relevant social goals" (Krasnor, 1985, p. 58). It is also not possible to study social behavior (i.e., its competence and effectiveness) without relating it to other competences (Greenspan, 1981a) nor to regard children's goals as mere "vague consequences of prior experiences" (Dodge, 1985, p. 15)--that is, the perception of the individual as a sophisticated, preprogrammed feedback system.

Social Competence Reconsidered

Although it will not be denied here that the human being is a social animal, "relevant social goals" do not exist for the individual; they exist only for society. These are the demands and expectations of the macro-, exo-, and mesosystems, the institutionalized cultural patterns (Parsons & Shils, 1959) that have to be internalized by the child. The child must accomplish his internalization despite the possibility that these patterns may run counter to the his or her interests based on needs or need-dispositions originating on conscious and unconscious organismic activity levels (cf. James, 1929). To what extent, then, do present conceptions of social competence reflect anything more than the child's ability to conform to these cultural patterns? To what extent does the social pressure to conform result in the prevention of equilibrations, which, as should by now be obvious, may lead to disequilibria for one or more interacting organismic activity levels such that social dysfunctioning or "incompetent social behavior" will be the consequence? Again, this is not a new argument. Similar ideas can be found in Freud (1923) and Janet (in Schwartz, 1955). For instance, according to Janet, psychopathology may result from the failure to attain the goal of action, because this goal is "to transform the external world by the removal of obstacles and the advancement of the profitable" (p. 45). To understand children's social behaviors or actions, it is necessary to understand their interests and their relations with the demands and expectations of the environment. Social competence, then, should involve the individual's ability to cope with the resulting discrepancies between socially relevant and individually relevant goals within social contexts. If this is true, then individuals in social contexts (i.e., parents, peers, and teachers) can only be the worst judges of social competent behaviors, though they might be the best judges of socially desirable behaviors.

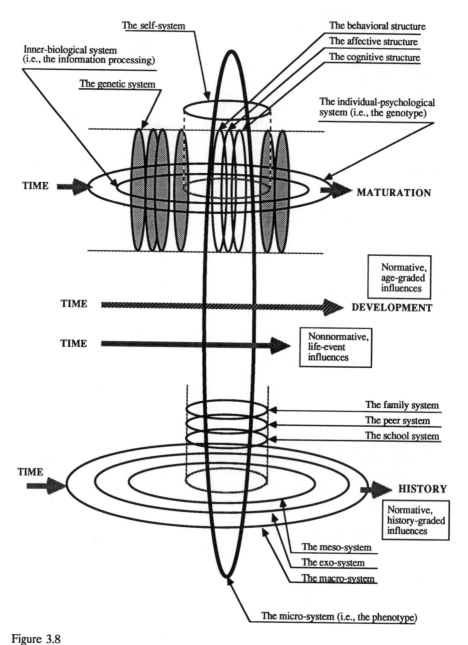

Figure 3.8

The interaction between the organism and the environment--that is, the developing child.

Social Competence and Individually Relevant Goals

The presentation of the activity-levels-within-activity-levels model of the origins of social behavior and the discussion of its consequences for social competence has offered a theoretical basis for the assumption that relevant social goals will often not be identical to relevant individual goals. The extent to which society (i.e., the contexts) determines what goals should be socially relevant is illustrated by the findings of Adams (1983) and King and Galejs (1985), who report that parents and teachers "perceive boys and girls differently when the relationship between children's locus of control perceptions and competence measures are considered" (King & Galejs, 1985, p. 15). The latter authors suggest that these differences, although most salient among older children, are the result of different cultural expectations for girls and boys. Hence, the mesosystems in which the children actively participate determine what is "socially relevant." Individuals in these contexts subsequently judge the appropriateness of children's behavior in relation to the standards (i.e., cultural patterns) prevalent in each particular context.

However, socially competent behavior, as defined by social contexts, need not necessarily have any relation to competent behavior as defined by the individual. The latter behavior is geared toward relevant individual goals, the former toward relevant social (i.e., societal) goals. The importance of this conclusion is further highlighted when one takes into account that it is questionable whether children with "poor relations... lack social skills" (Hartup, 1985, p. ix) and that only "low moderate correlations [exist] between social competence measures [and] peer friendship and likeability" (Beck, Collins, Overholser, & Terry, 1985, p. 43).

According to Asher (1983), the poor correlation between observed behavior and children's social status may be explained by the assumption that actual behavior is irrelevant as long as the actor is thought "to be well-intentioned" (p. 1432). That is, people focus on others' goals rather than on their behavior. Although this type of explanation is "rarely acknowledged in the literature" (Asher, 1983, p. 1432) on social competence, in the theoretical perspective presented in this chapter, Asher's (1983) explanation is postulated as fundamental for an understanding of social competence. People behave or act to attain their goals or interests (Piaget, 1981) motivated by the need to equilibrate. Good personal relationships (e.g., peer relations) as a consequence of these behaviors will only be a derivative, while the acceptability of the individual's goals--that is, their being well intentioned--will determine the attitudes that others in the social contexts have toward the acting individual.

Such a hypothesis requires a shift in perspective when it comes to theorizing about social competence and the definition and operationalization of socially competent behaviors, social effectiveness, and social skills--that is, the end-states of socialization defined by the prevailing societal standards (i.e., cultural patterns). If such an attitude is adopted, then the data from empirical studies dealing with children's social competence, behavior, and well-being have to be reinterpreted.

A Reinterpretation of Empirical Data

The social acceptability of a child's interests or goals can be regarded as a function of the correspondence between activity levels. Each organismic or environmental system is characterized by its own disequilibria (or demands) and abilities (or opportunities). Interactions between system-related activity levels serve a function: the maintenance or restoration of an equilibrium. Consequently, to determine the particular equilibrium involved in an interaction, both the interests of the organism and those of the social contexts should be considered (i.e., the relevant individual and social goals, respectively).

From a developmental point of view, it is clear that the contexts in which the child will actively participate (i.e., the mesosystems) or the systems that will affect the mesosystems (e.g., the exosystems) will increase in number (i.e., differentiate) and be hierarchically organized. From birth (actually, from conception), the child will experience the outcomes of the match between two major systems (i.e., the organism-caretaker interaction). At this stage will be developed the basis for the child's abilities to pursue "the elementary interests...linked to fundamental organic needs" (Piaget, 1981, p. 34) and the child's trust in the social context to *respect* those needs or interests and to *enable* the child to objectivize them (cf. Erikson, 1963).

Although this hypothesis is derived from the activity levels perspective that is the focus of the present chapter, it agrees with similar ideas in the theories of Claparède (1909), Janet (1935), and Kurt Lewin (1935).

The role of early interactions between the organism and the "primary" mesosystem (i.e., the caretaker[s] or parent[s]) is also emphasized within the field of research on friendship (cf. Sroufe, 1983). According to Sroufe (1983), the early child-caregiver relationship is essential for the child's ability to regulate affect in child-child relationships. More specifically Sroufe notes that the quality of attachment predicts the expression and control of affections during the preschool period (ages 0-4 years). An additional search of the literature (cf. Mueller & Vandell, 1979; Vandell & Wilson, 1982) reveals a complex interaction between the infant and the caregiver. Despite the finding that the infant-caretaker relationship is important for the development of peer relations, this relationship should not be thought of as a one-way or unidimensional transmission of information or affection from the caregiver to the child. On the contrary, both systems (i.e., the organism and the caregiver) mutually affect each other: They interact (Leferink, 1986).

To study the role of the mesosystem (i.e., the child-caregiver interaction) in determining children's social status, Leferink (1986) developed a questionnaire designed to elicit children's ideas about their relationships with their caregivers (i.e., parents). This questionnaire consisted of 10 questions dealing with (a) need gratification, (b) independence and, (c) authority. Need gratification refers to the opportunities that the parents give the child to do what he or she likes to do (e.g., "Are you always allowed to do what you want or like?" and "Are there things you very much want, but which you are not allowed to do?", Leferink, 1986, p. 35). Independence is assessed by questions such as "Do you yourself come up with the things you want to do or are the things you do thought of by your parents?" and "Are there things you have to do which you think you cannot do at all?" (p. 35). Finally, authority refers to the child's role with respect to decisions concerning himself or herself (i.e., "Do you deliberate at home about what should happen?" or "Would you sometimes like your parents to be the boss?", p. 35).

The questionnaire was presented to 81 children divided into three age groups (i.e., 7-, 9-, and 11-year-olds). These 81 children were selected from a larger population on the basis of an elaborate sociometric scale (Koenigs & Oppenheimer, 1985) as popular ($n = 27$), unpopular ($n = 27$), and in-between children ($n = 27$).

A factor analysis of the questionnaire items revealed 10 independent factors, which suggests that each question assesses or deals with a different aspect of the caregiver-child relationship. A stepwise regression analysis revealed that while popularity and children's ideas about their relationship with their parents are related ($F(9,71) = 8.40, p < .001$), the first item on the questionnaire alone (i.e., "Are you always allowed to do what you want or like?") explained 43% of the variance in popularity ($F(1,78) = 63.22, p < .001$). None of the remaining questionnaire items showed a significant contribution to popularity. This finding does not imply that "being allowed to do what one wants" (i.e., direct need gratification) is essential for popularity. On the contrary, an examination of the responses of the popular and unpopular children revealed that the popular children are *not* allowed to do everything they like. For instance, they are not allowed to go alone to the amusement park in the evening or outside when it is raining. Based on the children's reasons for these restrictions, it was concluded that "these wants were not in the interest of the child" (Leferink, 1986, p. 43). The responses of the unpopular children suggest considerably different restrictions. For instance, they were not allowed to "make a mess of their rooms, or at home" (p. 43) or were not allowed to eat candy or sweets. Often, they could not give the reason for these restrictions.

The findings from this study suggest a number of interesting insights. The assumption that the "primary" systems interaction (i.e., between the organism and the caregiver) during infancy is fundamental for the development of children's abilities to satisfy their organic need-related interests is not limited only to infancy. While these "elementary interests...later will be intellectualized and become scales of values" (Piaget, 1981, p. 34), the way in which the family system (i.e., the interaction between the child and the caregivers) deals with these intellectualized interests during childhood affects the child's popularity. The differences between the way parents of popular and unpopular children deal with their children's interests may be related to the degree to which the children's individually relevant goals are respected and preferred to socially relevant goals (e.g., being allowed to make a mess of one's room or being prohibited doing so). Given that popular children are also restricted in the degree to which they are allowed to pursue their own interests, the restrictions on popular children suggest an educational or socialization strategy that has as its purpose making children aware of what objects, people, or events are worthwhile to objectivize for the gratification of their need-dispositions. This is done without any direct attempts to change those need-dispositions. These children may be socialized to select well-intentioned goals (Asher, 1983) within particular contexts, without any pressure to renounce their needs (i.e., manifest disequilibria). Within the present theoretical framework, the proficiency in equilibrating will result in higher levels of well-being and "happiness" and, consequently, in individuals with whom one readily wants to interact (see, for instance, the ability to regulate affect in interpersonal relationships; Sroufe, 1983). If social competence refers to children's or adults' abilities to select goals that are considered well intentioned, then, indeed, social behaviors may be subordinate to these goals.

In a second study (Oppenheimer & Thijssen, 1983), we explored the relationship between children's thinking about friendship, their perspective-taking competences, and their popularity. To assess children's thinking about friendship, a questionnaire was employed that consisted of 17 items dealing with concepts about friendship per se ($a = .89$), 5 items dealing with processes leading to friendships, and 6 items dealing with general information about the actual state of affairs with regard to friends. The different measures were presented to 48 children representing four age groups (i.e., 6-, 8-, 10-, and 12-year-olds). By means of a sociometric measure, half the children in each age group were assessed as popular, the other half as unpopular. In agreement with previous findings (cf. Selman, 1976), the children progressively decentered in their conceptualizations about friendship. This conceptual development--that is, from more concrete, materially related to more abstract and covert psychologically related conceptions of friendship--was closely related to the development of perspective taking (Selman, 1976) and differentially related to popularity. Contrary to, the theoretical assumptions about perspective-taking competences being prerequisites for social behavior (Hartup, 1983), no relation whatsoever was evident between popularity and social perspective-taking skills (a similar finding is reported by Rubin, 1972).

Although the development of concepts about friendship plays a differential role in the degree of popularity at various ages, this relationship is certainly not the rule. Unpopular children evidenced high conceptual and social-cognitive developmental levels. A principal component analysis with Varimax rotation of all the variables employed in this study (with the exception of the process items) resulted in five general factors with eigenvalues larger than 1. These factors were interpreted as (a) a social-cognitive developmental dimension, (b) a dimension of formation and maintenance of friendship relationships or a dimension of isolation versus social involvement, (c) a dimension of popularity, (d) a personality dimension or a dimension of "affinity towards others" (p. 75; see also Rubin, 1972), and (e) a dimension of gender. After a multiple-group method analysis (Nunnally, 1967), the interrelationships among these factors also suggest that children's popularity as an index of social behavioral consequences depends upon their conceptions about friendship and need for social involvement as well as their gender and personality features (see also Rubin, 1972).

These findings agree with those of many other studies. Nevertheless, it is important to note that popularity, as an index of socially competent behavior (cf. Greenspan, 1981a), is the result of a multitude of variables that comprise elements of various organic and nonorganic systems. It is a function of the need-dispositions of the organism and the characteristics of the child herself or himself. The level of social-cognitive development and the development of concepts about friendship can be accepted neither separately nor in combination as accurate indicators of popularity. High social-cognitive developmental levels may be negated by the child's personality or by the absence of any need for social involvement. The reverse is also true. Low social-cognitive developmental levels may be offset by the child's personality or by a high need for social involvement.

The personality dimension consisted of questions dealing with whether the child would like to play with others or be alone, whether the child should share everything with a friend, whether the gender of the other child would affect the friendship, and what is considered to be a good friend. It may be that the clustering of these particular items is the result of children's concern about the available "elbow room" for maintaining their own interests. It is here hypothesized, however, that this dimension of affinity toward others shows the children's need for assurance that particular behaviors serving "well-intentioned" goals will be tolerated. Certainty about the acceptability of such behaviors will make a child nice to interact with and allows an optimal regulation of affect.

From a different perspective, we (Oppenheimer, Stet, & Versteeg, 1986) studied the relationships among conceptions of control, autonomy, and other personality variables. For the present discussion, the conceptions of control (i.e., locus of control or LOC) and the personality variables are relevant. The latter variables were assessed by two diagnostic instruments--the Amsterdam Biographical Questionnaire for Children (i.e., the ABVK) and the Achievement Motivation Test for Children (i.e., the PMTK). The ABVK consisted of four dimensions. The first two deal with neurotic lability, manifested either by psychoneurotic or by functional/physical complaints (i.e., the N and NS items, respectively). The third dimension refers to the personality characteristic of extraversion-introversion (E items). Finally, the fourth dimension assesses the children's test attitude (T items). Test attitude involves the children's reactions to their performance on tests, which can be either self-defensive or self-critical.

3. Social Action

The PMTK also consists of four dimensions. The first dimension assesses children's achievement (i.e., the P items), here defined as the amount of energy that the children are prepared to invest in order to perform well. The second and third dimensions concern debilitatory and facilitatory anxiety (the DA and FA items, respectively). Debilitatory anxiety is manifested in relatively unstructured situations and causes children to dysfunction. Facilitatory anxiety is manifested in structured and unstructered situations and enhances the children's functioning. The fourth dimension of the PMTK deals with the children's perception of their role in social contexts--that is, whether their own behavior is perceived as socially desirable (SD items).

Locus of control (i.e., the perceived competence of the self as a sufficient cause) was assessed by a questionnaire consisting of 32 items ($KR.20 = .79$). The use of open-ended questions in this instrument permitted a more shaded scoring of the responses. The first two types of responses represent the distinction between externally (score = 0) and internally (score = 1) oriented perceptions of control. Two additional higher-order perceptions or conceptions of control were included. These were responses demonstrating the presence of internal and external causes of control (i.e., additive; score = 2) and of reciprocal and integrated components of internal *and* external causes of control (score = 3).

Table 3.1

The Pearson product-moment correlation coefficients between conceptions of control (CCQ) and the dimensions of the PMTK and ABVK

	PMTK N = 64					ABVK N =131		
	N	NS	E	T	P	DA	FA	SD
CCQ	.17*	.19*	.08	-.28**	-.22	.34**	-.25*	-.18

Note. From "Relationships Among Conceptions of Control and Autonomy and Other Personality Variables: A Developmental Approach" by L. Oppenheimer, A. Stet, and E. Versteeg, 1986, *European Journal of Psychology of Education, 3,* p. 98.

 * $p < .05$; ** $p < .001$. N = neurotism expressed by psychoneurotic complaints; NS = neurotism expressed by functional/physical complaints; E = extraversion-introversion; T = test attitude; P = achievement motivation; DA = debilitating anxiety; FA = facilitating anxiety; SD = social desirability (i.e., conformism).

The results--that is, the correlations between LOC and the variables assessed by the ABVK and the PMTK--are presented in Table 3.1.

In addition to the finding that children's understanding of the causes that affect the outcomes of their behavior demonstrated a shift from external, through internal, to integrated internal and external causes, the correlations between the assessed variables are surprising. Children who realize that the outcomes of their behavior are affected by internal and external control variables are neither extraverted, nor introverted. They show a self-critical attitude toward their test performance (i.e., they see themselves rather than others as being responsible for their failure), and they demonstrate neither a high nor a low

63

achievement motivation. They do, however,evidence relatively strong debilitating anxiety and little facilitating anxiety and are clearly nonconformists--that is, they show little socially desirable (i.e., conforming) behavior. This nonconformism may present a potential source of conflicts between the child and the social environment. These conflicts and the high level of debilitating anxiety may be the causes for the higher proneness to neurotic lability shown by these children. The converse is also true. Children showing more external perceptions of control are characterized by low debilitating anxiety but a high facilitating anxiety, they are self-defensive when they fail tests (i.e., they regard failure as not being their own fault), and they show socially desirable behavior. The latter, more conformist behavior, then, will result in approval rather than disapproval from, or conflicts with, the social environment, which may cause the lower proneness to neurotic lability (Oppenheimer et al., 1986, pp. 99-100).

The results of this study suggest that socially desirable behavior--that is, behavior positively evaluated by the environment--is related to a more external perception of control. It is argued here that socially desirable behavior can be characterized as a form of conformism to social regulation. At least, it results in a minimum of conflicts between the demands and expectations of the environment and the behavior of the child. As noted previously, these conflicts result in an increase in the child's proneness to neurotic lability and debilitating anxiety. These consequences of behavior cannot be assumed to be "important social outcomes for individuals." Hence, if "behavior can be considered socially competent if it predicts important social outcomes for individuals" (Gresham, 1986, p. 146), then "nonconformism", or socially "undesirable" behavior, should be classified as "socially incompetent" behavior. Because external LOC is related to a large variety of deficient social and academic competences (cf. Lefcourt, 1976), children with external perceptions of control are considered a risk group both in the literature dealing with personality development and in educational and academic settings. As a consequence, most interventions that aim to promote the development of LOC are directed toward promoting the development of *internal* perceptions of control. Internal perceptions of control, however, will result in children's showing less socially desirable behavior, and subsequently, it will result in children who are less socially competent as judged by the environment.

Conclusion

Contradictions like these in the practical outcomes or consequences of empirical data from two distinct fields of study within developmental psychology again highlight the need for a more encompassing theory. The discussion of empirical data in the previous section, of course, is completely speculative. None of the studies presented there had as its purpose to verify a hypothesis derived from the earlier-presented activity-levels model of development in general and social competence in particular. The reinterpretation of empirical data, however, does emphasize the complexity of human behavior and its origins. Reference is again made to the crucial question in psychology: "Why do people act the way they do?" After more than a century of experimental psychology, it can be concluded that we have not yet come close to answering this question (cf. Sophie Haroutunian, 1983).

It would appear that developmental psychological research--the enormous quantity of information we possess about the maturing organism and the developing child, in terms of the child's physiological, neurological, behavioral, cognitive, and affective functioning--has no explanatory basis. Without any coherence, this information, spread over a multitude of journals or stored in numerous computers, does not enable us to formulate a satisfactory account of behavior. Furthermore, much of this information makes sense only as long as it can be related to the observable characteristics of the maturing organism and the developing child--that is, within the conceptual context used to structure the world. Hence, the conceptual understanding of the developing child is regarded as being akin to our "rational understanding" of the surrounding environment. However, it does not necessarily follow that this rational understanding corresponds with the real nature of the developing child. Based on the previous discussion with respect to social competence, it can be argued that to be able to develop the "right" explanatory principles for human behavior and its development, we must step beyond the observable (Oppenheimer, 1987a). If we express the problem in terms of Piaget's equilibration theory, the apparent disequilibrium between the available empirical, psychological data on the development of behavior and real behavior may be the result of accumulative assimilation processes without the necessary accompanying accommodation processes. New accommodatory schemes will have to be developed to enable the ordered or hierarchical organization of almost irreconcilable differentiated information about development.

Within the field of social competence, this accomodation process is very much needed. The present presentation of an activity-levels model of development is not considered to be a satisfactory response to this manifest disequilibrium. It should be regarded instead as a first attempt to reformulate existing ideas about social competence, its definition, function, and development. It is an attempt to remedy the one-sided emphasis on the unidimensional, adult-societal approach to social behavior, which requires that the developing child conforms to adults' or society's demands and expectations. In the latter approach, the needs of the maturing organism as well as the demands and expectations of the developing child have primarily been neglected. The activities or behavior of individuals is thought to be best understood as interest-guided actions (Oppenheimer, in press; Oppenheimer & Heller, 1984). Individuals or children purposefully link their own constructions of events to desired goals or end-states. From the activity-levels model of development presented here, an encompassing research program could be derived through which "social competence" could be very clearly defined. In this program, children's growing appreciation of and participation in the framework of interest- guided actions could be studied. For example, when and how, in the course of their development do children begin to articulate and understand their own actions as prompted by identifiable interests, aimed at the achievement of particular goals? Similarly, the course by which they come to identify such goals in others should be explored (Oppenheimer & Veerman, 1980). Irrespective of their level of understanding, the interests and goals of particular children will not always coincide, and means for resolving such perceived conflicts must be developed (Oppenheimer, 1987b). This perception of the need to resolve such conflicts and the ability to do so present critical developmental tasks for children that are at present poorly understood and largely unconsidered in developmental psychological research. Finding answers to these distinct but conceptually interdependent developmental questions will permit us to study "social competence" as the child's ability to cope with the discrepancies between socially relevant and individually relevant goals within social contexts.

Finally, during the preparation of this chapter, one of Rabindranath Tagore's little poems suddenly took on new meaning.

> Every child arrives with the message
> that God is not yet discouraged
> about men
> (from *Zwervende vogels*, 1963, p. 27)

References

Adams, G. R. (1983). Social competence during adolescence: Social sensitivity, locus of control, empathy, and peer popularity. *Journal of Youth and Adolescence, 3*, 203-211.

Aebli, H. (1984). Kognitive Entwicklung: Was entwickelt sich, und bei welchen Anälssen? [Cognitive development: What develops, and under which conditions?]. In K. E. Grossmann and P. Ltkenhaus (Eds.), *Bericht über die 6. Tagung Entwicklungspsychologie* [Proceedings of the 6th Confenerence on Developmental Psychology] (pp. 50-61). Regensburg, W. Germany: Druckerei der Universität Regensburg.

Anderson, S., & Messick, S. (1974). Social competency in young children. *Developmental Psychology, 2*, 282-293.

Argyle, M. (1969). *Social interaction.* London: Methuen.

Argyle, M. (1985). Social behavior problems and social skills training in adolescence. In B. H. Schneider, K. H. Rubin, & J. E. Ledingham (Eds.), *Children's peer relations: Issues in assessment and intervention* (pp. 207-224). New York: Springer-Verlag.

Asher, S. R. (1983). Social competence and peer status: Recent advances and future directions. *Child Development, 54*, 1427-1434.

Baldwin, J. M. (1902). *Development and evolution.* London: Macmillan.

Baltes, P. B., Reese, H. W., & Nesselroade, J. R. (1977). *Life-span developmental psychology: Introduction to research methods.* Monterey, CA: Brooks/Cole.

Beck, S., Collins, L., Overholser, J., & Terry, K. (1985). A cross-sectional assessment of the relationship of social competence measures to peer friendship and likeability in elementary-age children. *Psychological Monographs, 111*, 41-63.

Bierman, K. L., & Furman, W. (1984). The effects of social skills training and peer involvement on social adjustment of preadolescents. *Child Development, 55*, 151-162.

Bornstein, M., Bellack, A. S., & Hersen, M. (1977). Social skills training for unassertive children: A multiple-baseline analysis. *Journal of Applied Behavior Analysis, 10*, 183-195.

Bronfenbrenner, U. (1977). Toward an experimental ecology of human development. *American Psychologist, 32*, 513-531.

Bronfenbrenner, U. (1979). *The ecology of human development.* Cambridge, MA: Harvard University Press.

Bruner, J. S. (1960). *The process of education.* Cambridge, MA: Harvard University Press.

Cairns, R. B. (1979). *Social development: The origins and plasticity of interchanges.* San Francisco: Freeman.

Cairns, R. B. (1983). The emergence of developmental psychology. In P. H. Mussen (Ed.), *Handbook of child psychology: Vol. 1. History, theory and methods* (pp. 41-102). New York: Wiley.

Chandler, M. J. (1977). Social cognition: A selective review of current research. In W. F. Overton & J. M. Gallagher (Eds.), *Knowledge and development.* (Vol. 1, pp. 93-147). New York: Plenum.

Claparède, E. (1909). *Psychologie de l'enfant et pdagogie exprimentale* [Child psychology and experimental educational psychology] (2nd ed.). Genève, Switzerland: Libraire Kündig.

Dodge, K. A. (1985). Facets of social interaction and the assessment of social competence in children. In B. H. Schneider, K. H. Rubin, & J. E. Ledingham (Eds.), *Children's peer relations: Issues in assessment and intervention* (pp. 3-22). New York: Springer-Verlag.

Dodge, K. A., McClaskey, C. L., & Feldman, E. (1985). Situational approach to the assessment of social competence in children. *Journal of Consulting and Clinical Psychology, 53*, 344-353.

Edmonson, B. (1974). Arguing for a concept of competence. *Mental Retardation, 12*, 14-15.

Erikson, E. H. (1963). *Childhood and society.* New York: Norton.

Flavell, J. H. (1963). *The developmental psychology of Jean Piaget.* Princeton, NJ: Van Nostrand Reinhold.

Flavell, J. H. (1985). *Cognitive development.* Englewood Cliffs, NJ: Prentice Hall.

Foote, N. N., & Cottrell, L. S. (1955). *Identity and interpersonal competence.* Chicago: University of Chicago Press.

Freud, S. (1923). *The ego and the id.* London: Hogarth.

Friedman, S. F., Scholnick, E. K., & Cocking, R. R. (Eds.). (1987). *Blueprints for thinking: The role of planning in cognitive development.* New York: Cambridge University Press.

Furman, W., Rahe, D. F., & Hartup, W. W. (1979). Rehabilitation of socially withdrawn preschool children. *Child Development, 50*, 915-922.

Gladwin, T. (1967). Social competence and clinical practice. *Psychiatry, 30*, 30-34.

Gottman, J. M., Gonso, J., & Rasmussen, B. (1975). Social interaction, social competence, and friendship in children. *Child Development, 46*, 709-718.

Greenspan, S. (1981a). Defining childhood social competence: A proposed working model. In B. K. Keogh (Ed.), *Advances in special education* (Vol. 3, pp. 1-39). Greenwich, CT: JAI Press.

Greenspan, S. (1981b). Social competence and handicapped individuals: Practical implications of a proposed model. In B. K. Keogh (Ed.), *Advances in special education* (Vol. 3, pp. 41-82). Greenwich, CT: JAI Press.

3. Social Action

Gresham, F. M. (1986). Conceptual issues in the assessment of social competence in children. In P. S. Strain, M. J. Guralnick, & H. M. Walker (Eds.), *Children's social behavior: Development, assessment, and modification* (pp.143-179). New York: Academic Press.

Guilford, J. P. (1977). Will the real factor of extraversion-introversion please stand up? A reply to Eysenck. *Psychological Bulletin, 84,* 412-416.

Guralnick, M. J., & Groom, J. M. (1985). Correlates of peer-related social competence of developmentally delayed preschool children. *American Journal of Mental Deficiency, 90,* 140-150.

Haroutunian, S. (1983). *Equilibrium in the balance: A study of psychological explanation.* New York: Springer-Verlag.

Harter, S. (1982). The perceived competence scale for children. *Child Development, 53,* 87-97.

Harter, S. (1983). Developmental perspectives on the self-system. In P. H. Mussen (Ed.), *Handbook of child psychology: Vol. 4. Socialization, personality, and social development* (pp. 275-385). New York: Wiley.

Hartup, W.W. (1983). Peer relations. In P. H. Mussen (Ed.), *Handbook of child psychology: Vol. 4. Socialization, personality, and social development* (pp. 103-196). New York: Wiley.

Hartup, W. W. (1985). Foreword. In B. H. Schneider, K. H. Rubin, & J. E. Ledingham (Eds.), *Children's peer relations: Issues in assessment and intervention* (pp. vii-xi). New York: Springer-Verlag.

Hollis, M. (1977). *Models of man--philosophical thoughts on social action.* Cambridge, England: Cambridge University Press.

Hunt, J. McV. (1961). *Intelligence and experience.* New York: Ronald Press.

James, W. (1929). *The varieties of religious experience: A study in human nature.* New York: Modern Library.

Janet, P. (1935). *L'intelligence avant le langage* [Intelligence prior to language]. Paris: Flammarion.

King, A., & Galejs, I. (1985). *The relationship of locus of control and its components with preschool children's social competence and popularity* (Journal Report No. 332). Ames: Home Economics Research Institute, Iowa State University.

Kitchener, R. F. (1986). *Piaget's theory of knowledge: Genetic epistemology and scientific reason.* New Haven, CT: Yale University Press.

Koenigs, A. M., & Oppenheimer, L. (1985). Development and training of role-taking abilities with emotionally disturbed preschoolers: A pilot study. *Journal of Applied Developmental Psychology, 6,* 313-320.

Kohn, K., & Rosman, B. L. (1972). Social competence scale and symptom checklist for the preschool child: Factor dimensions, their cross-instrumental generality, and longitudinal persistence. *Developmental Psychology, 6,* 430-444.

Kohn, M. (1977). *Social competence, symptoms, and underachievement in childhood: A longitudinal perspective.* Washington, DC: Winston.

Korner, P. I. (1979). Central nervous control of autonomic cardiovascular function. In K. M. Spyer (Ed.), *Handbook of physiology* (Vol. 1, Sect. 2). Bethesda, MD: American Physiological Society.

Krasnor, L. R. (1985). Observational assessment of social problem solving. In B. H. Schneider, K. H. Rubin, & J. E. Ledingham (Eds.), *Children's peer relations: Issues in assessment and intervention* (pp. 57-74). New York: Springer Verlag.

Ladd, G. W. (1981). Effectiveness of a social learning method for enhancing children's social interaction and peer acceptance. *Child Development, 52,* 171-178.

Laosa, L. M. (1979). Social competence in childhood: Toward a developmental, socioculturally relativistic paradigm. In M. W. Kent and J. E. Rolf (Eds.), *Primary prevention of psychopathology, Vol. 3. Social competence in children* (pp. 253-279). Hanover, NH: University Press of New England.

Lefcourt, H. M. (1976). *Locus of control: Current trends in theory and research.* Hillsdale, NJ: Erlbaum.

Leferink, H. (1986). *Vriendschap: De relatie tussen populariteit en conception over de ouder-kind relatie* [Friendship: The relationship between popularity and concepts about parent-child relations]. Unpublished master's thesis. Amsterdam, Netherlands: Universiteit van Amsterdam.

Lerner, R. M. (1986). *Concepts and theories of human development.* New York: Random House.

Lerner, R. M., Hultsch, D. F., & Dixon, R. A. (1983). Contextualism and the character of developmental psychology in the 1970s. *Annals of the New York Academy of Sciences, 412,* 101-128.

Levine, S. (1982). Comparative and psychobiological perspectives on development. In W.A. Collins (Ed.), *The concept of development.* Hillsdale, NJ: Erlbaum.

Lewin, K. (1935). *Principles of topological psychology.* London: McGraw-Hill.

Markus, H., & Wurf, E. (1987). The dynamic self-concept: A social psychological perspective. *Annual Review of Psychology, 38,* 299-337.

Maslow, A. (1943). A dynamic theory of human motivation. *Psychological Review, 50,* 370-396.

Miller, G. A., Galanter, E., & Pribram, K. H. (1960). *Plans and the structure of behavior.* New York: Holt, Rinehart and Winston.

Mueller, E., & Vandell, D. (1979). Infant-infant interaction. In J. D. Osofsky (Ed.), *Handbook of infant development* (pp. 519-549). New York: Wiley.

Nunnally, J. C. (1967). *Psychometric theory.* New York: McGraw-Hill.

Oppenheimer, L. (1987a, October). *The concept of development: Beyond the observable.* Invited lecture presented at the Max Planck Institute, Berlin.

Oppenheimer, L. (1987b). Cognitive and social variables in the plan of action. In S. F. Friedman, E. K. Scholnick, & R. R. Cocking (Eds.), *Blueprints for thinking: The role of planning in cognitive development* (pp. 356-392). New York: Cambridge University Press.

Oppenheimer, L. (1988). Culture and history, but what about theory?: Valsiner's cultural-historical theory of development. *Comenius, 32,* 413-426.

Oppenheimer, L. (in press). The concept of action: A historical perspective. In L. Oppenheimer & J. Valsiner (Eds.), *The origins of action: Interdisciplinary and international perspectives.* New York: Springer-Verlag.

Oppenheimer, L., & Heller, J. (1984). Development of cooperation and help-seeking activities: An action theoretical approach. In E. Staub, D. Bar-Tal, J. Karylowski, & J. Reykowski (Eds.), *Development and maintenance of prosocial behavior* (pp. 177-200). New York: Plenum.

Oppenheimer, L. & Oosterwegel, A. (in press). Identiteit: Op zoek naar een konkretisering [Identity: A search for a concretization]. In A. Koenigs (Ed.), *Identiteit en eenzaamheid over de levensloop* [Identity and loneliness over the life-span]. Lisse, Netherlands: Swets & Zeitlinger.

Oppenheimer, L., & Rempt, E. (1986). Social cognitive development with moderately and severely retarded children. *Journal of Applied Developmental Psychology, 7,* 237-249.

Oppenheimer, L., Stet, A., & Versteeg, E. (1986). Relationships among conceptions of control and autonomy and other personality variables: A developmental approach. *European Journal of Psychology of Education, 3,* 68-78.

Oppenheimer, L., & Thijssen, F. (1983). Children's thinking about friendships and its relation to popularity. *The Journal of Psychology, 114,* 69-78.

Oppenheimer, L., & Van der Wilk, F. (1984). Interests and goals and how to achieve them: Development and gender-differences. *De Psycholoog, 19,* 642.

Oppenheimer, L., & Veerman, H. (1980). The plan of action: Explorations of several of its components. *Newsletter Soziale Kognition, 3,* 53-71.

Parsons, T., & Shils, E. A. (Eds.) (1959). *Toward a general theory of action.* Cambridge, MA: Harvard University Press.

Pea, R. D. (1982). What is planning development the development of? In D. L. Forbes and M. T. Greenberg (Eds.), *Children's planning strategies* (pp. 5-27). San Francisco: Jossey-Bass.

Pelligrini, D. S. (1985). Social cognition and competence in middle childhood. *Child Development, 56,* 253-264.

Pepper, S. C. (1966). *Concept and quality.* LaSalle, IL: Open Court.

Phillips, L. (1968). *Human adaptation and its failures.* New York: Academic Press.

Piaget, J. (1976). *The grasp of consciousness: Action and concept in the young child.* Cambridge, MA: Harvard University Press.

Piaget, J. (1978). *Behavior and Evolution.* New York: Pantheon.

Piaget,J. (1981). *Intelligence and affectivity.* Palo Alto, CA: Annual Reviews.

Popper, K. R. (1972). *Objective knowledge.* London: Oxford University Press.

Riegel, K. F. (1975). Toward a dialectical theory of development. *Human Development, 18,* 50-64.

Riegel, K. F. (1977). The dialectics of time. In N. Datan & H. W. Reese (Eds.), *Life-span developmental psychology: Dialectical perspectives on experimental research* (pp. 4-46). New York: Academic Press.

Rousseau, J. J. (1762). *Emile ou de l'Education* [Emile or education]. LeHaye, France: J. Néaulme.

Rubin, K. H. (1972). Relationship between egocentric communication and popularity among peers. *Developmental Psychology, 7,* 364.

Rubin, K. H., & Krasnor, L. (1986). Social cognitive and social behavioral perspectives in problem solving. In M. Perlmutter (Ed.), *The Minnesota Symposium on Child Psychology* (pp. 1-68). Hillsdale, NJ: Erlbaum.

Rubin, K. H. & Ross, H. S. (Eds.). (1982). *Peer relationships and social skills in childhood.* New York: Springer-Verlag.

Schneider, B. H., Rubin, K. H., & Ledingham, J. E. (Eds.). (1985). *Children's peer relations: Issues in assessment and intervention.* New York: Springer-Verlag.

Schneirla, T. C. (1957). The concept of development in comparative psychology. In D. B. Harris (Ed.), *The concept of development* (pp. 78-108). Minneapolis: University of Minnesota Press.

Schwartz, L. (1955). *Les névroses et la psychologie dynamique de Pierre Janet.* [The neuroses and the dynamic psychology of Pierre Janet]. Paris: Presses Universitaires de France.

Selman, R. L. (1976). Toward a structural analysis of developing interpersonal relations concepts: Research with normal and disturbed preadolescent boys. In A. Pick (Ed.), *X Annual Minnesota Symposium on Child Psychology* (pp. 156-200). Minneapolis: University of Minnesota Press.

Shantz, C. U. (1983). Social cognition. In P. H. Mussen (Ed.), *Handbook of child psychology: Vol. 3. Cognitive development* (pp. 495-555). New York: Wiley.

Sobol, M. P., & Earn, B. M. (1985). What causes mean: An analysis of children's interpretations of the causes of social experience. *Journal of Social and Personal Relationships, 2,* 137-149.

Sroufe, L. A. (1983). Infant-caregiver attachment and patterns of adaptation in preschool: Roots of maladaption and competence. In M. Perlmutter (Ed.), *Minnesota Symposium on Child Psychology* (Vol. 16, pp 41-83). Hillsdale, N.J.: Erlbaum.

Tagore, R. (1963). *Zwervende vogels* [Stray birds]. Amsterdam, Netherlands: Wereldbibliotheek.

Turiel, E. (1974). Conflict and transition in adolescent moral development. *Child Development, 45,* 14-29.

Van der Wilk, R., & Oppenheimer, L. (1987, April). *Academic choices: Difficult for some, not for others. A motivational study.* Paper presented at the Second European Conference for Research on Learning and Instruction, Tübingen, W. Germany.

Vandell, D. L., & Wilson, K. S. (1982). Social interaction in the first year: Infants' social skills with peers versus mother. In K. H. Rubin & H. S. Ross (Eds.), *Peer relationships and social skills in childhood* (pp. 187-208). New York: Springer-Verlag.

Von Wright, G. H. (1976). Determinism and study of man. In J. Manninen & R. Tuomela (Eds.), *Essays on explanation and understanding* (pp. 415-435). Dordrecht: Reidel.

Weber, M. (1966). *The theory of social and economic organization.* New York: The Free Press.

Werner, H. (1948). *Comparative psychology of mental development.* New York: International Universities Press.

White, R. W. (1959). Motivation reconsidered: The concept of competence. *Psychological Review, 66,* 297-333.

White, R. W. (1979). Competence as an aspect of personal growth. In M. W. Kent & J. E. Rolf (Eds.), *Primary prevention of psychopathology, Vol. 3. Social competence in children* (pp. 5-22). Hanover, NH: University Press of New England.

Wright, M. J. (1980). Measuring the social competence of preschool children. *Canadian Journal of Behavioral Science, 12,* 17-32.

Zigler, E., & Trickett, P. K. (1978). IQ, social competence, and evaluation of early childhood intervention programs. *American Psychologist, 33,* 789-798.

4

Individual, Differential, and Aggregate Stability of Social Competence

Jens Asendorpf

Max Planck Institute for Psychological Research
Munich, Federal Republic of Germany

The quest for the stability of individual differences despite universal developmental change has attracted many personality psychologists as well as developmental psychologists. With respect to social competence from a developmental perspective, the question becomes: How stable are interindividual differences in social competence over time despite age-related changes in social competence? Will a very competent preschooler become a very competent first grader? If individual differences in social competence are predictable to some extent from one developmental stage to another, are all children equally predictable, or are some children better predictable than others? And if so, which children are the more readily predictable ones? Can we predict children's differential stability in social competence based on their other characteristics?

The purpose of this chapter is to take a fresh approach to these long-standing questions. Since present discussions of stability and change in development are often plagued by inconsistent conceptualization and terminology, the chapter starts by drawing some important distinctions between different types of stability that are sometimes confused in the literature. Then, the chapter describes a new method of assessing differential stability and presents first results obtained by using this approach in a longitudinal study of children's emerging social competence during the preschool and kindergarten years.

Three Developmental Views

Within the developmental perspective on social competence, three different views of development can be distinguished (cf., e.g., Wohlwill, 1973). The *individual view* is concerned with just one person: How does this person's social competence change over time? Does it grow, does it decline, or is it constant? This is what most laypersons are interested in when they ask developmental questions. Psychological research rarely takes this single-case view. However, in addition to being professional psychologists, we are also lay psychologists, and the individual view often sneaks into our *interpretations* of data even when these data are assessed and analyzed from one of the other two developmental views. This will become obvious later in the chapter.

B. H. Schneider et al. (eds.), Social Competence in Developmental Perspective, 71–86.

The *general view* is concerned with developmental changes that are shared by all, or nearly all, individuals: Do certain aspects of social competence increase, for instance, between the ages of 3 and 5? Within this general view, all people are treated alike; the (mostly implicit) assumption is that individual differences with respect to development are minor ones, not of theoretical or practical significance, and can be attributed to error. This view, in turn, has fostered the habit of studying general developmental change by analyzing the change in population *means*. If all, or nearly all, individuals developed in the same way, this methodological approach would be perfectly valid because the changes observed at the level of the population at large would apply to each individual as well.

However, the truth is far different when it comes to human development. The *differential view* acknowledges the diversity in developmental change by focusing on differences among the individual changes. Methodologically, individual or subgroup changes are contrasted with changes in other individuals or subpopulations or with changes in the population mean. In both cases, propositions become *relativistic*: This child's social competence has increased between the ages of 3 and 5 years *relative* to that child's competence. This proposition is compatible with the observation that from the individual view, the competence of both children has decreased during the 2-year interval.

In order to clearly distinguish between these three views of development, I will use the terms *individual, general,* and *differential development*. Individual development refers to age-related changes in a person's score with respect to some variable. General development refers to age-related changes in the mean of a population. And differential development refers to age-related changes in individual deviations from the population mean.

Constancy/Change Versus Stability/Instability

Distinguishing between these three views of development is commonplace in psychology, but the next step takes us onto slippery terminological ground. A key concept in the differential view of development is *stability*. Stability refers to the constancy of *differential* development: A psychological entity is said to be stable if the interindividual differences in that entity do not change with age - that is, if the individual deviations from the population mean are constant over time.

Stability is a key concept for psychology for two reasons. First, stability is the prerequisite for inferring individual development from general development. If the stability of aggressiveness is high between the ages of 4 and 6 years in a particular sample, and if mean aggressiveness clearly increases during this age period, we can safely infer that most of the children in the sample became more aggressive. However, if aggressiveness is not stable, the increase in mean aggressiveness does not even imply that the majority of the children in the sample became more aggressive. As Figure 4.1 illustrates, the increase in mean aggressiveness may be due to a minority of children - perhaps a certain subgroup of boys - who strongly influenced the sample mean by their extraordinary increase in aggressiveness.

The second reason why stability is a key concept for psychology is that high stability implies high predictability of interindividual differences despite general developmental change. If aggressiveness were stable over time, we could easily predict adults' aggressiveness from preschool children's aggressiveness, although mean aggressiveness may change considerably during these years.

BEHAVIOR

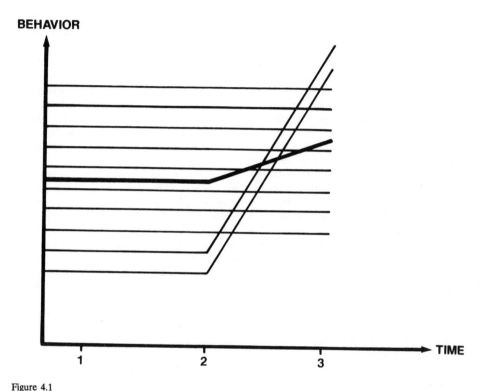

TIME

1   2   3

Figure 4.1

Illustration of how mean change can be due to a minority of subjects if stability is low.

The first point of confusion about stability is that stability is sometimes mixed up with constancy. In principle, the stability of interindividual differences and the constancy of population means are completely independent - as independent as general and differential development. The fact that periods of strong change in general development, such as the end of the 2nd year or adolescence, are also periods of high instability points to an empirical relation between instability and change but does not imply any logical relation between the two (cf. also Moss & Susman, 1980, and Rutter, 1984, for the difference between constancy and stability).

Three Types of Stability

A second point of confusion about stability pervades most of the literature on differential development. Stability is a concept that is commonly applied to a population or a sample of individuals - that is, to an *aggregate* of persons. Consequently, stability is measured by the

73

correlation between two assessments of the same variable or a conceptually equivalent variable at two different ages. Other statistical coefficients such as the mean or the variance share this property of the correlation as a measure of stability: They all apply to the aggregate level, not to the level of the individual. Hence, they cannot be applied to the individual members of the aggregate to which they refer.

Whereas this problem has been recognized for a long time with respect to the mean of change scores (Bakan, 1954; Lewin, 1931), psychologists seem to be less aware of the fact that this problem also applies to correlations in general (but see Valsiner, 1986) and to correlations as measures of stability in particular. Stability at the aggregate level, henceforth called *aggregate stability*, does not necessarily apply to the persons who constitute the aggregate. A correlation of .50 between aggressiveness at age 4 and aggressiveness at age 6 does *not* imply that many, or even most, of the individual children observed will show "medium stability" with respect to their aggressiveness. It is not that most of the children themselves necessarily have the property of being moderately stable but rather that this sample of children as a whole has the property of being moderately stable in terms of the interindividual differences within the sample.

Valsiner (1986) showed that undergraduates in psychology, doctors of psychology, and the authors of *Child Development* have a strong tendency to interpret correlational findings as if these findings told us something about relations at the individual level - for example, individual change. In the case of aggregate stability, the error in interpretation essentially lies in confusing aggregate stability with its individual counterpart (the constancy of individual deviations from the population mean) or even worse, confusing aggregate stability with constancy within the individual view of development.

Figure 4.1 also illustrates this point. Between Time Points 1 and 2, all persons are completely constant in their behavior, both from the individual and from the differential view of development; also, there is perfect constancy at the aggregate level. Between Time Points 2 and 3, there is an increase in the mean, a constancy of 80% of the subjects in terms of their individual development, and a change on the part of *all* the subjects in terms of their differential development: Not a single person continues to have the same deviation from the mean. In order to clearly distinguish the constancy of raw scores from the constancy of deviation scores, I will call the latter the *individual stability*. Thus, what Valsiner (1986) criticized is the widespread confusion of aggregate stability with individual stability.

Now I will advance via a leap of logic. There are interindividual differences in individual stabilities - in the same way as there are interindividual differences in the constancy of raw scores. To be straightforward, let us call the deviation of a person's individual stability from the aggregate stability (i.e., from the correlation) the *differential stability of the person* and the variance between the individual stabilities in a population the *differential stability in the population*.

What we have now done is similar to what Stern (1911) did when he created differential psychology by differentiating general psychology: We have, in turn, differentiated differential psychology. It is this recursivity in the logical reasoning, I suppose, that has so long prevented psychologists from performing a more sophisticated analysis of the stability of interindividual differences.

As far as I know, little attempt has been made in the literature to clearly distinguish between individual, differential, and aggregate stability and to develop coefficients for measuring individual and differential stability. There appears to be only one exception. Ghiselli proposed to regard the absolute value of each individual's *residual score in the regression equation* as a measure of each person's "individual predictability" and to predict these scores by external variables ("prediction of predictability"; Ghiselli, 1960, 1963). However, this approach proved not to be very successful, mainly because the predictors found were quite specific to the criterion variables and could not be cross-validated. For this reason, Ghiselli's approach was not pursued further, although some authorities still regard it as an interesting one (cf. Paunonen & Jackson, 1985, footnote 7; and Wiggins, 1973, chapter 2).

Besides its apparent failure to yield stable results in empirical applications, Ghiselli's approach seems to have a fundamental flaw. Ghiselli chose each person's deviation from the regression line as a measure of differential stability. Thus, he compared each person's change with the change that would be expected in terms of the "regression-to-the-mean effect." It is a widespread belief among psychologists that the regression to the mean is some kind of "natural law" governing psychological data sets. As Rogosa, Brandt, and Zimowski (1982) and others have pointed out, this belief is a myth. A regression-to-the-mean effect may or may not occur depending on the variable observed; certainly, it could be expected only if all instability at the aggregate level (and, hence, all differential stability) were just random. If there are psychologically meaningful differences among the individual stabilities, differential stability is not random, and correcting for a falsely expected regression to the mean will throw off the interpretation of the differential stability that remains. It is primarily for this reason that I find Ghiselli's approach invalid.

A Coefficient of Individual Stability

Given this apparent gap in methodology, I developed a method for measuring differential stability based on a coefficient of individual stability. Since I have presented the rationale for the proposed coefficient of individual stability as well as its mathematical and statistical properties elsewhere (Asendorpf, in press a), a short description of the ideas underlying this approach will suffice here.

An appropriate coefficient of individual stability should have the following properties. First, it should be zero if, and only if, children's *z* scores are *identical* between the two measurement points. This requirement reflects the differential view that underlies the definition of individual stability and does not assume a regression-to-the-mean effect. Second, the coefficient should monotonically decrease with an increasing *absolute z*-score difference between the two assessments: The more children's *z*-scores change (increase or decrease), the less stable they should be - an obvious requirement. Third, the coefficient should be consistent with the correlation as a measure of aggregate stability in the sense that its population mean should be *identical* with the correlation. This is a strong assumption, which could be replaced by the weaker requirement that the correlation be a strictly monotonic function of the mean of the coefficients.

Simple computation shows that the variable

$$i_{XY} = 1 - \frac{(z_X - z_Y)^2}{2}$$

where z_X and z_Y are the z transformations of two variables X and Y, assigns to each person j a coefficient $^iXY(j)$ that satisfies all of the above three conditions; in particular, it is

$$r_{XY} = \frac{1}{n} \cdot \sum_{j=1}^{n} i_{XY}(j)$$

for the correlation ^rXY between the variables X and Y.

It can be shown (cf. Asendorpf, in press a) that this coefficient of individual stability has an undesirable property: Its distribution tends to be strongly skewed to the left. For example, if X and Y are bivariate normally distributed, the coefficient of individual stability is as skewed as the chi^2 distribution. This poses a problem if we want to *explain* the differential stability in a sample by correlating the individual stabilities with some external variable because variables with highly skewed distributions affect the possible range of correlations between them and other variables.

I have shown with Monte Carlo studies for approximately bivariate normally distributed variables (Asendorpf, in press a) that the strictly monotonic transformation

$$Ti_{XY} = \begin{cases} \dfrac{1}{2} \cdot \ln \dfrac{1.001 + i_{XY}}{1.001 - i_{XY}} & \text{for } 0 \le i_{XY} \le 1 \\[2em] \ln \dfrac{1}{1 - i_{XY}} & \text{for } i_{XY} < 0 \end{cases}$$

is very effective in normalizing the skewed distribution of the individual stabilities. This transformation is a modification of the well-known Z transformation of correlations introduced by Fisher. In various applications to real data sets - including Q-sort data, rating data, and behavioral observations - I found that in nearly all instances, the above transformation successfully normalized the individual stabilities. Thus, the coefficient $^{Ti}XY(j)$ appears to be an appropriate measure of individual stability. Figure 4.2 demonstrates the normalizing property of the proposed transformation for various levels of correlation obtained for approximately bivariate normal distributions.

An Illustrative Example

I will now begin to illustrate the rationale of my approach with data reflecting the stability of a certain aspect of children's social competence. These data as well as the other data reported below stem from the Munich Longitudinal Study on the Genesis of Individual Competencies - LOGIC (Weinert & Schneider, 1986; cf. also Asendorpf, in press b, for first results related to social competence). In my part of the study, I follow a sample of 126

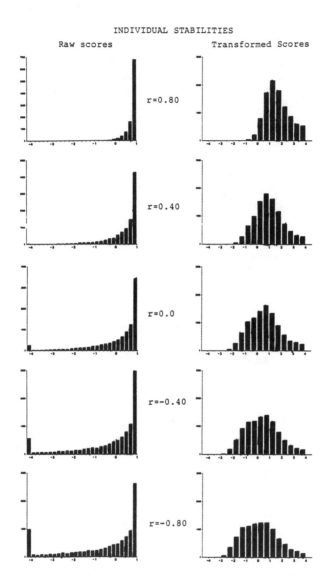

Figure 4.2

Distribution of the raw and the transformed individual stabilities for approximately bivariate normal distributions with correlations of varying size.

children from the beginning of preschool (age 3-4) through elementary school; the major focus of this part of LOGIC is the emergence and stabilization of interindividual differences in competence with respect to initiating contact with peers and adults.

Figure 4.3 shows the scatterplot of the one-year stability of the observed rate of shy contact initiations among all initiations directed to peers and teachers during free play in preschool. A shy initiation was coded whenever a child approached a peer or a teacher, then stopped, and looked for at least 3 seconds at the other person without speaking; this behavior was called "wait-and-hover" by Gottman (1977) and Dodge, Schlundt, Schocken, and Delugach (1983). In the first year of assessment, the rate of shy contact initiations, which was based on a 2-hour sampling of each child's behavior each year, correlated .38 with a parental scale assessing shyness toward peers and .39 with a teacher Q-sort index of shyness.

The scatterplot indicates that children's rate of shy behavior showed a substantial differential stability. This can easily be seen by comparing their scores with the *stability line* $y = (s_Y/s_X)(x - m_X) + m_Y$, where s_X and s_Y are the standard deviations of X and Y, and m_X and m_Y are the means of X and Y. The stability line is identical with the regression line for
$r_{XY} = 1$.

As Figure 4.3 shows, Child 1 and Child 5 were very unstable in their rate of shy behavior; for instance, Child 5 was observed to be shy in over 60% of the observed contact initiations during the first measurement period at age 4; one year later, no shy behavior at all was observed. If the 2 unstable children are excluded from the sample, the correlation rises to $r = .47$
($n = 66, p < .0001$).

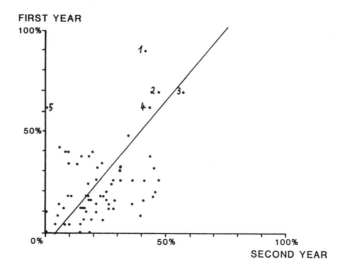

Figure 4.3

Scatterplot of the bivariate distribution of children's shy contact initiations in 2 years of assessment.

This one-year stability, which is rather high for observed behavior in field settings, rests to a great extent upon the scores of Child 2, Child 3, and Child 4 (4.5% of the remaining sample). If these 3 children are also excluded, the correlation drops to $r = .26$ ($n = 63$, $p < .04$). Thus, minimal changes in the sample may lead to major changes in the sample's mean stability.

In the present case, this strong effect of an extreme minority of the sample on the sample mean is due to the fact that the 5 children considered had extreme scores for both measurement points. More generally, correlations are very much influenced by extreme scores in the bivariate distribution; a few stable extreme z scores will cause a substantial aggregate stability (i.e., correlation), and a few extreme but unstable scores can obscure a substantial aggregate stability in the rest of the sample.

Table 4.1 contains some descriptive scores for the 5 children whose rate of shy behavior is marked in Figure 4.3.

Table 4.1 indicates that Child 5 is extremely unstable in the observed rate of shy behavior. An inspection of this child's data in the first 3 years of observation revealed highly stable and extremely high scores in rated shyness/inhibition based on parental and teacher ratings and on all other behavioral observations; it is not clear from the data why the one observational period during the 2nd year of assessment, when the rate of shy contact initiation behavior was found to be zero, deviated so much from this general pattern.

Table 4.1

Descriptive Scores for the 5 Children Whose Rate of Shy Behavior is Marked in Figure 4.3

Score	Child				
	1	2	3	4	5
z score of 1st assessment (z_1)	3.92	2.80	2.78	2.32	2.32
z score of 2nd assessment (z_2)	1.30	1.72	2.50	1.44	-1.77
$\|z_1 - z_2\|$	2.62	1.08	0.28	0.88	4.09
Individual stability	-2.48	0.41	0.96	0.61	-7.49
Transformed individual stability	-1.25	0.44	1.95	0.71	-2.14

The other 4 children have a rate of shy behavior more than one standard deviation above the sample mean for both measurement points. Their individual stabilities still vary considerably, from the virtually perfect stability of Child 3 to the considerable instability of Child 1. Thus, the coefficients of individual stability (particularly the untransformed scores) are very sensitive to differences within extreme scores.

The dependence of the individual stabilities upon the scores of the two assessments being compared was analyzed by correlating the transformed individual stabilities with these

scores (the untransformed stabilities should not be used for these analyses because of their highly skewed distribution). A correlation of
$r = -.41$ ($p < .001$) was found for the first assessment, and one of $r = -.12$ (*ns*) was found for the second assessment. Thus, the higher children's rates of shy behavior during the first observation period, the less stable their rates of shy behavior over the one-year period.

For a closer analysis, the scatterplot of the correlation of $r = -.41$ was investigated (cf. Figure 4.4). The scatterplot indicates that the negative correlation between the scores of the first assessment and the individual stabilities strongly depended upon the 2 children whose scores were the least stable (Child 1 and Child 5 from Figures 3 and 4). If these 2 children are excluded, the correlation decreases to $r = -.28$ ($n = 66$,
$p < .03$). On the other hand, the negative relation between the initial scores and the individual stabilities is not just an artifact. When the individual stabilities were correlated with nearly 100 different measures of the children's social behavior and cognitive functioning obtained during the 1st and the 2nd years of assessment, a clear picture emerged. Only variables assessing children's shyness correlated at least $r = |.30|$ with the individual stabilities for shy contact initiation behavior, and all of these correlations were negative. Besides observed shy contact initiations, the parental rating of children's shyness toward other children in the 1st year of assessment ($r = -.39$) as well as in the 2nd year ($r = -.36$), a teacher Q-sort score of "shy in the preschool group" in the 1st year ($r = -.30$), and the mean length of silences in children's conversations with an adult stranger ($r = -.42$) showed substantial negative correlations with the individual stabilities (in each case, $p < .02$).

This correlational pattern supports the notion that the shyer children were at the beginning of preschool, the less stable this behavior was over time within this setting. This result agrees with the data from the Harvard longitudinal study on the genesis of behavioral inhibition (Reznick, Kagan, Snidman, Gersten, Baak & Rosenberg, 1986). Some of the children who participated in this extreme group study changed from high shyness, as measured in the 3rd year of life, to low shyness 2 years later, whereas no single instance of a change from low shyness to high shyness was observed during this 2-year period.

In the remainder of this chapter, I will present some analyses of the LOGIC data that attempt to answer three basic questions about the differential stability of social competence among children of preschool and kindergarten age: (a) How great is the differential stability of various aspects of social competence, and is it systematically related to the method of assessing social behavior? (b) Are children's individual stabilities consistent across different measures that assess the same construct? (c) Can we identify which children will be more stable than others with respect to a given social characteristic?

The Degree of Differential Stability

Table 4.2 contains data about the 2-year differential stability of various variables obtained in LOGIC: four measures of the children's shyness, three measures of their aggressiveness, a measure of the social desirability of their overall personality, and - for comparison - the children's nonverbal IQ. Social desirability scores were obtained for each child by correlating the child's Q-sort profile in a German 54-item teacher form (Göttert & Asendorpf, in

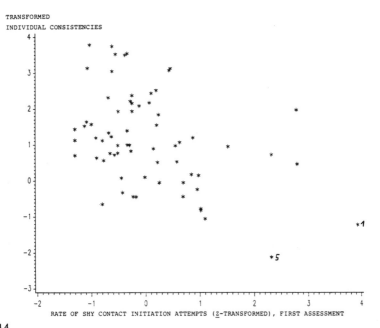

TRANSFORMED
INDIVIDUAL CONSISTENCIES

RATE OF SHY CONTACT INITIATION ATTEMPTS (Z-TRANSFORMED), FIRST ASSESSMENT

Figure 4.4

Scatterplot of the bivariate distribution of children's individual stabilities in shy contact initiations and their initial scores in this variable.

press) of the California Child Q-Set (Block & Block, 1980) with the profile of a "desirable child" that was obtained from four German kindergarten teachers (their agreement was *alpha* = .96, and this profile correlated .87 with the profile of a "socially desirable child" defined by U.S. psychologists; cf. Waters, Noyes, Vaughn, & Ricks, 1985).

Table 4.2 shows that the standard deviations of the individual stabilities were substantial in all cases. Also, the distribution of the individual stabilities did not significantly deviate from normality for any variables except observed aggressiveness. These findings indicate a considerable degree of differential stability in this sample of children. The mean of the transformed individual stabilities did not closely covary with the correlation (the usual measure of aggregate stability); this discordance is due to the fact that the transformed individual stabilities are less sensitive to extreme changes of the z scores than the raw individual stabilities upon which the correlation is based; thus, the mean of the transformed individual stabilities is a more robust measure of aggregate stability than the correlation.

Table 4.2 indicates that the 2-year stabilities vary considerably among children for many aspects of their competence but do not seem to be systematically related to the method of assessment. Is a child's individual stability a characteristic that is simply attributable to measurement error, or is it specific to a particular social setting?

Table 4.2

Degree of Differential Stability Over a 2-Year Period

Measure	N	Aggregate stability[d] Corre-lation	Individual stabilities[e] Mean	SD	Min.	Max.
Parental shyness scale	79	.69	1.47	1.05	-1.03	3.68
Teacher shyness score[a]	151	.50	1.22	1.22	-1.84	3.78
Observed shy contact initiation[b]	68	.30	1.15	1.42	-1.53	3.78
Latency of first spontaneous verbal utterance toward adult stranger	71	.57	1.37	1.20	-1.22	3.80
Parental aggressiveness scale	79	.50	1.28	1.22	-1.32	3.79
Teacher aggressiveness score[a]	151	.62	1.37	1.16	-1.21	3.79
Observed aggressive attacks[b]	68	.36	1.51	1.25	-1.26	3.61
Nonverbal intelligence[c]	168	.56	1.24	1.06	-1.83	3.79
Social desirability of personality[a]	151	.50	1.18	1.17	-1.43	3.76

[a]Correlation between 54-item Q-sort and prototypic Q-sort for "shy child", "aggressive child" respectively "socially desirable child."
[b]Rate of wait-and-hover respectively aggressive attacks among all contact initiations during free play in school.
[c]Columbia Mental Maturity Scale (Burgemeister, Blum, & Lorge, 1972).
[d]Correlation between assessment at ages 3-4 and at ages 5-6.
[e]Transformed individual stabilities.

The Consistency of Individual Stabilities Across Measures and Settings

One way of trying to answer the question posed at the end of the preceding section is to analyze the consistency of the individual stabilities across measures obtained from the same setting and from different settings. If the differential stability observed is systematically related to characteristics of the children within a setting, the individual stabilities of measures that assess these characteristics should show significant intercorrelations within this setting. Furthermore, the cross-setting consistency of the individual stabilities relating to the same construct can be assessed.

In order to test the consistency of children's individual stabilities within the same setting, I chose the construct of social initiative (the amount of various kinds of initiations directed toward peers during play). Children at the age of 5 years played with a familiar same-sex peer for 15 minutes and then cooperated in a construction task for about another 10 minutes; the same procedure was repeated one year later with a different peer. Children's social initiations directed toward the peer were coded in each situation with two coding systems: frequency of manager, teacher, or learner initiations ("role initiations"), coded according to the coding system developed by Stoneman, Brody, and MacKinnon (1984), and frequency of verbal and nonverbal requests, coded according to the coding system developed by Rubin and Emptage (1985); compare with Asendorpf (1986, 1987) for the German adaptations of these systems and reliability data.

by Rubin and Emptage (1985); compare with Asendorpf (1986, 1987) for the German adaptations of these systems and reliability data.

The frequency of role initiations aggregated over both situations and the frequencies of requests in each situation correlated between .52 and .82 in both years of assessment and constituted an internally consistent measure (*alpha* = .89, 1st year; *alpha* = .87, 2nd year) of children's social initiative; the 1-year aggregate stability was .51 for 79 children. The individual stabilities of the three measures of social initiative correlated between .25 (*p* < .03) and .38 (*p* < .001) and reflected moderate internal consistency (*alpha* = .57) as a measure of children's differential stability between the 2 years of assessment. Thus, children's individual stabilities were moderately consistent across the three measures of social initiative obtained from the same setting.

In order to test for the consistency of the individual stabilities across settings, I chose the construct of shyness, because measures of shyness were obtained in quite different settings and using quite different methods of assessment (cf. Table 4.2). The first four variables on Table 4.2 are all related to shyness. The teacher score and the preschool observational measure assessed shyness in preschool, and the parental scale and the latency measure related to shyness toward adult strangers. Their intercorrelations varied between .28 and .53 in the 1st year of assessment; all correlations were highly significant, and the internal consistency of the aggregate of the four measures was *alpha* = .71. In the 2nd and the 3rd year of assessment, the internal consistency dropped to .51 due to insignificant correlations between observed shyness in school and the laboratory and parental measures (although the correlation between observed shyness in school and the teacher judgments remained significant). These data point to a considerable setting specificity for shyness, although some cross-setting consistency was also observed.

The individual 2-year stabilities of the four measures of shyness were not consistent. Only the teacher judgments and the behavioral observations in preschool, and the parental judgments and the latency measure tended to be consistent (in both cases, *r* > .31, *p* < .05). This did not appear to be due to insufficient aggregation because the stability of each of the four measures did not even marginally correlate with the mean of the stabilities of the remaining three measures. An analysis of the three measures of aggressiveness (cf. Table 4.2) yielded a similar result. Thus, the differential stabilities could not be generalized across different settings. On the other hand, all measures as well as their aggregates showed a substantial aggregate stability (the 2-year stabilities were both .62 for the aggregated measures of shyness and aggressiveness).

The following is a possible explanation for this finding: Social initiative, shyness, and aggressiveness relate to temperamental dispositions of children that are stable over time and consistent across different settings. These "basic dispositions" are moderated, however, by children's setting-specific dispositions, which reflect their learning experiences in the particular settings. These setting-specific dispositions may also be moderately stable over time within settings but unstable across settings. Therefore, the differential stability of these constructs may relate to the stability of setting-specific dispositions.

The Explanation of Differential Stability

Table 4.3 presents data showing the dependency of the individual stabilities on the initial and final raw scores as well as on their absolute values; the latter dependency reflects the "regression-to-the-mean effect" discussed above.

by a *unipolar* dependency (cf., e.g., observed shyness or aggressiveness). It would have been misleading to correct statistically for the regression to the mean in these cases because the strong unipolar dependency would have been falsely corrected, too.

The dependency on the raw scores can be explained to some extent. Note that aggressiveness and shyness often showed a negative dependency, and the desirability of personality a positive dependency, on children's initial raw scores. Since aggressiveness and shyness are socially undesirable characteristics of children, this pattern of results suggests an intriguing hypothesis: The more desirable a child's position on some dimension of personality, the more stable the child is on that dimension.

Table 4.3

Dependency of Individual Stabilities on Initial and Final Scores

Measure[a]	Dependency		"Regression to mean"	
	Initial[b]	Final[b]	Initial[c]	Final[c]
Parental shyness	-.21	.02	-.08	-.03
Teacher shyness	-.01	-.08	-.11	-.23**
Observed shyness	-.32**	-.36**	-.43***	-.48***
Latency of first utterance	.20	.18	-.21	.11
Parental aggressiveness	.04	-.05	-.34**	-.28*
Teacher aggressiveness	-.33***	-.15	-.02	.08
Observed aggressiveness	-.63***	-.49***	-.58***	-.23*
Nonverbal intelligence	.13	.08	-.18*	-.14
Desirable personality	.29***	.08	-.14	.01

[a]For more details about the measures, compare with Table 4.2.
[b]Correlation between the transformed individual 2-year stabilities and the initial (1st-year) respectively final raw scores (3rd year).
[c]Correlation between the transformed individual 2-year stabilities and the initial respectively final absolute scores.
*p < .05. **p < .01. ***p < .001.

In order to test this hypothesis, I correlated each variable shown on Table 4.3 as well as various other variables with children's desirability scores for the first year of assessment; in this way, I obtained social desirability scores for a total of 16 variables, which did not correlate above .60 with each other. I then correlated these social desirability scores with the dependency of the individual stabilities on the initial raw scores (since this was a correlation of correlations, the correlations were Fisher-Z-transformed). A correlation of .69 was found between social desirability and dependency. Correlations of a comparable size were also found for the two one-year stabilities in these variables. Thus, the more desirable a high score on some dimension of personality is, the more stable are the scores of children who score high on that dimension.

If desirable characteristics of children are more stable than undesirable ones, this should also apply to the whole personality profile: The more desirable a child's profile is, the more stable the profile should be (in terms of a correlation between two assessments of the profile separated in time). In fact, the correlation between the social desirability of children's Q-sort at the age of 3-4 years and the 2-year stabilities of their personality profiles was .59 (*n* = 151).

children's Q-sort at the age of 3-4 years and the 2-year stabilities of their personality profiles was .59 ($n = 151$).

These surprisingly high correlations between social desirability and individual stability can be explained by an effect of socialization: Undesirable characteristics are "trained away" and therefore become unstable. An alternative explanation is genetic canalization: Children are genetically prepared for certain universal developmental outcomes; hence, deviations from paths leading to these outcomes are less stable and are regarded as undesirable in most cultures. These two hypotheses are not incompatible; both may be true.

Conclusion

The data on the stability of young children's social competence presented here reveal a considerable differential stability: For various aspects of social competence, children differ greatly in the extent to which they remain stable or change relative to their peers. The consistency of the individual stabilities across different measures of the same construct within the same setting shows that differential stability cannot be attributed solely to measurement error. Since the individual stabilities were not found to be consistent across different settings even if they were related to the same construct, the findings seemed to reflect changes in setting-specific dispositions.

Despite this setting specificity of children's stability in social competence, the analyses revealed one major factor that seems to influence the amount of individual stability: The more socially desirable a child's position was on various dimensions of social competence, the more stable the child remained on that dimension. The same was found to be true for children's overall patterns of social competence comprising many different variables.

All in all, these explorations into second-order differential phenomena of development (interindividual differences in the changes in deviation scores over time) suggest that we should go beyond correlations if we are interested in the differential development of social competence.

References

Asendorpf, J. (1986). *Manual zur Kodierung des Rollenverhaltens von Kindern (Manual for coding children's role relationships*; Research Rep., Paper 18/1986). München: Max-Planck-Institut für psychologische Forschung.

Asendorpf, J. (1987). *Manual zur Kodierung des sozialen Problemlöseverhaltens von Kindern (Manual for coding children's social problem solving behavior*; Research Rep., Paper 7/1987). München: Max-Planck-Institut für psychologische Forschung.

Asendorpf, J. (in press a). The measurement of individual consistency. *Methodika*.

Asendorpf, J. (in press b). Shyness, unsociability, and peer avoidance. *Human Development*.

Bakan, D. (1954). A generalization of Sidman's results on group and individual functions, and a criterion. *Psychological Bulletin, 51*, 63-64.

Block, J. H., & Block, J. (1980). The role of ego-control and ego-resiliency in the organization of behavior. In W. A. Collins (Ed.), *Minnesota Symposium on Child Psychology* (Vol. 13, pp. 39-101). Hillsdale, NJ: Erlbaum.

Burgemeister, B., Blum, L., & Lorge, J. (1972). *Columbia Mental Maturity Scale*. New York: Harcourt Brace Jovanovich.

Dodge, K. A., Schlundt, D. C., Schocken, I., & Delugach, I. D. (1983). Social competence and children's sociometric status: The role of peer group entry strategies. *Merrill-Palmer Quarterly, 29*, 309-336.

Ghiselli, E. E. (1960). The prediction of predictability. *Educational and Psychological Measurement, 20*, 3-8.

Ghiselli, E. E. (1963). Moderating effects and differential reliability and validity. *Journal of Applied Psychology, 47*, 81-86.

Göttert, R., & Asendorpf, J. (in press). Eine deutsche Version des California-Child-Q-Set, Kurzform. (A German short form of the California Child Q-Set). *Zeitschrift fur Entwicklungspsychologie und Padagogische Psychologie*.

Gottman, J. M. (1977). Toward a definition of social isolation in children. *Child Development, 48*, 513-517.

Lewin, K. (1931). The conflict between Aristotelian and Galileian modes of thought in contemporary psychology. *Journal of General Psychology, 5*, 141-177.

Moss, H. A., & Susman, E. J. (1980). Longitudinal study of personality development. In O. G. Brim, Jr., & J. Kagan (Eds.), *Constancy and change in human development* (pp. 530-595). Cambridge, MA: Harvard University Press.

Paunonen, S. V., & Jackson, D. N. (1985). Idiographic measurement strategies for personality and prediction: Some unredeemed promissory notes. *Psychological Review, 92*, 486-511.

Reznick, J. S., Kagan, J., Snidman, N., Gersten, M., Baak, K., & Rosenberg, A. (1986). Inhibited and uninhibited children: A follow-up study. *Child Development, 57*, 660-680.

Rogosa, D., Brandt, D., & Zimowski, M. (1982). A growth curve approach to the measurement of change. *Psychological Bulletin, 92*, 726-748.

Rubin, K. H., & Emptage, A. (1985). *A manual for coding communicative and social competence in children.* Unpublished manual, Department of Psychology, University of Waterloo, Canada.

Rutter, M. (1984). Continuities and discontinuities in socioemotional development. In R. N. Emde & R. J. Harmon (Eds.), *Continuities and discontinuities in development* (pp. 41-68). New York: Plenum.

Stern, W. (1911). *Die differentielle Psychologie in ihren methodischen Grundlagen (Methodological foundations of differential psychology).* Leipzig: Barth.

Stoneman, Z., Brody, G. H., & MacKinnon, C. (1984). Naturalistic observations of children's activities and roles while playing with their siblings and friends. *Child Development, 55*, 617-627.

Valsiner, J. (1986). Between groups and individuals: Psychologists' and laypersons' interpretations of correlational findings. In J. Valsiner (Ed.), *The individual subject and scientific psychology* (pp. 113-151). New York: Plenum.

Waters, E., Noyes, D. M., Vaughn, B. E., & Ricks, M. (1985). Q-sort definitions of social competence and self-esteem: Discriminant validity of related constructs in theory and data. *Developmental Psychology, 21*, 508-522.

Weinert, F. E., & Schneider, W. (Eds.) (1986). *First report on the Munich Longitudinal Study on the Genesis of Individual Competencies (LOGIC)* (Research Rep.). München: Max-Planck-Institut für psychologische Forschung.

Wiggins, S. J. (1973). *Personality and prediction: Principles of personality assessment.* Reading, MA: Addison-Wesley.

Wohlwill, J. F. (1973). *The study of behavioral development.* New York: Academic Press.

What to Do while the Kids are Growing Up: Changing Instrumentation in Longitudinal Research

Jane E. Ledingham

University of Ottawa

Longitudinal research designs have the capacity to provide us with some of the most interesting data on how social competence emerges and changes over time. However, the challenges of selecting appropriate measures of social development at different ages in longitudinal research are great. They demand that thought be given to both theoretical and methodological issues relevant to developmental change. More than any other approach to the problem, longitudinal research demands that one consider social competence not as a static condition but rather as a dynamic process that includes both the continuity and the discontinuity inherent in the child's social development. Compounding the difficulties is the fact that, as the children grow older, the investigator is likely to be confronted with an age group that is outside of his or her primary area of expertise.

This discussion is geared towards identifying relevant issues rather than towards providing clear answers about how to proceed. There are at least four questions that must be addressed in order to choose sensitive and meaningful measures at all stages of the research.

1. What ages should be investigated to provide information most relevant to the questions of interest?

Answering this question requires knowledge about when transition points occur in development, and on how large the windows are on the steady states of development. The main guides to important transition point come from the theoretical contributions of writers such as Piaget (1926), and more recently Sroufe (1979), who has suggested what the primary tasks of the preschool period are. Adding to such descriptions are empirical studies that describe the course of development across landmark events such as the emergence of language (Nadel, this volume), the move from the play world to the educational world (Rubin, Daniels-Beirness, & Bream, 1984), from middle school to high school, and from the prepubertal to the postpubertal state (Jones, 1965; Jones & Mussen, 1958; Mussen & Jones, 1957).

B. H. Schneider et al. (eds.), Social Competence in Developmental Perspective, 87–90.
© *1989 by Kluwer Academic Publishers.*

2. What are the principal characteristics of social skill at each age and what are the changes that occur in social competence between two ages?

It is evident that using an identical measure at widely disparate ages will not provide us with an effective measure of the child's emerging capabilities. Assessing social competence at ages three, eight, and thirteen will demand that quite different measures be employed at each age. However, there is very little information in the literature to help us understand how these transformations in social skill come about. For example, how is the preschooler's capacity for fantasy play related to the elementary school aged child's group entry skills and to the adolescent's cross-sex intimate relationships? Kagan (1969) has elegantly described the problem: the continuity of external behavior (the phenotype) does not guarantee that the basic psychological process (or genotype) underlying the external behavior has also remained constant, and in fact many of the most interesting forms of continuity involve constancy of the genotype but not of the phenotype. The most well established demonstrations of genotypic continuity in social behavior include the relation of attachment status to later interactions with peers (Waters, Wippman, & Sroufe, 1979) and the transformation of physical and instrumental to verbal and hostile aggression in the preschool years (Goodenough, 1931; Hartup, 1974; Jersild & Markey, 1935). However, deciding what measure should be used with tenth graders that reflects the same underlying process as the undifferentiated like best - like least sociometric used with kindergarten students is a difficult proposition. Because behavior and perceptions of behavior seem to become more differentiated as age of the child increases (Ledingham 1981; Younger, Schwartzman, & Ledingham, 1985), it is probable that for older children a composite measure that includes several quite different measures (Such as a measure of overall peer acceptance in addition to measures of same-sex and cross-sex friendships) will provide a more comparable equivalent to the simple sociometric used with preschoolers as a measure of genotypically constant social competence.

One of the most dramatic examples of the problem of how to assess continuity comes from studies designed to shed light on the nature of schizophrenia by studying young children at high risk for the disorder. Investigators in this area have attempted to identify measures that will predict to later symptomatology of schizophrenia such as hallucinations and delusions that do not occur until adulthood in this disorder. Researchers have chosen one of two strategies in their attempts to identify the precursors of such behaviors. The first is to measure variables reflecting general competence, while the second is to try and identify the specific downward extensions of deviant behaviors seen only in adulthood (Weintraub & Neale, 1984). Waters & Sroufe (1983) argue that, in the absence of clear evidence about how continuity is preserved, more general measures of behavior will be most likely to add to our information about how competence develops over time.

3. Who is the most appropriate informant at each age?

In part, this question concerns who knows most about the phenomenon of interest, but also involves the issue of whether there are specific sorts of response bias associated with certain observers, and of what the degree of overlap is between different observers. Decisions made about who should report on the behaviors of interest will depend on the behavior to be assessed and on the age of the child. Achenbach, McConaughy, & Howell (1987), in a report of a meta-analysis of correlations between different types of informants, concluded that externalizing problems were rated with more agreement than were internalizing problems, and that younger children were given more consistent assessments by different informants than were older children. Agreement was also lower when the context reported on or the role of the respondents was different. These authors suggest that, whenever possible, multiple informants should be used. However, different reporters have different types of interactions with the target individual (Ledingham & Younger, 1985). Thus, for assessing a specific aspect of behavior, the greater exposure of one type of observer to situations containing that behavior may make that observer the preferred choice.

When peers are selected to report on behavior, sex of rater may also be an important factor to consider. (see Daniels-Beirness, this volume). Hayden-Thomson, Rubin, & Hymel (1987) have found that ratings of opposite sex children were consistently lower when children in kindergarten through sixth grade were asked to rate each classmate's likeability on a three-point scale. Girls' ratings of boys were significantly lower than boys' ratings of girls. However, same-sex and both-sex ratings were highly correlated, and differences were greater at younger ages. In contrast to ratings or nominations of likeability, nominations for items descriptive of more behaviorally-specific items may be less affected by sex of the nominator. In addition, as the child approaches adolescence, the perceptions of opposite-sex peers may provide a more complete picture of social competence, regardless of their agreement with same-sex assessments.

4. Is the feature of central interest global peer popularity, intimate interactions with friends, or typical behavior in natural groups?

Recent research has demonstrated that focussing on each of these measures will yield quite a different picture of development. For example, while the number of nominations received for the "best friend" sociometric is highly correlated with number of reciprocal friendships, the number of reciprocal friendships is only weakly related or unrelated to nominations received on a general likeability factor (Feltham, Doyle, Schwartzman, Serbin, & Ledingham, 1985). Interactions with friends differ qualitatively from those with other peers: reciprocal friends' interactions are more socially responsive and mutual (Nelson & Aboud, 1985; Newcomb & Brady, 1982), and friendship status was found to be related to levels of altruism and affective perspective-taking, while popularity was not (McGuire & Weisz, 1982). Naturalistic observations of social play will provide a good representation of typical situations in which the child is involved, but may not indicate which of a multitude of experiences is most highly related to highest levels of functioning.

References

Achenbach, T.M., McConaughy, S.H., & Howell, C.T. (1987). Child/adolescent behavioral and emotional problems: Implications for situational specificity. *Psychological Bulletin, 101*, 213-232.

Feltham, R.M., Doyle, A.B., Schwartzman, A.E., Serbin, L.A., & Ledingham, J.E. (1985). Friendship in normal and socially deviant children. *Journal of Early Adolescence, 5*, 371-382.

Goodenough, F.L. (1931). *Anger in young children*. Minneapolis: University of Minnesota Press.

Hartup, W.W. (1974). Aggression in childhood: Developmental perspectives. *American Psychologist, 29*, 336-341.

Hayden-Thomson, L., Rubin, K.H., & Hymel, S. (1987). Sex preferences in sociometric choices. *Developmental Psychology, 23*, 558-562.

Jersild, A.T. & Markey, F.U. (1935). Conflicts between preschool children. *Child Development Monographs*, no. 21.

Jones, M.C. (1965). Psychological correlates of somatic development. *Child Development, 36*, 899-911.

Jones, M.C., & Mussen, P.H. (1958). Self-conceptions, motivations, and interpersonal attitudes of early and late maturing girls. *Child Development, 29*, 491-501.

Kagan, J. (1969). The three faces of continuity in human development. In P.A. Goslin, (Ed.), *Handbook of socialization theory and research* (pp. 983-1002). Chicago: Rand-McNally.

Ledingham, J.E. (1981). Developmental patterns of aggressive and withdrawn behavior in childhood: A possible method for identifying preschizophrenics. *Journal of Abnormal Child Psychology, 9*, 1-22.

Ledingham, J.E., & Younger, A.J. (1985). The influence of the evaluator on assessments of children's social skills. In B.H. Schneider, K.H. Rubin, & J.E. Ledingham (Eds.), *Children's peer relations: Issues in assessment and intervention* (pp. 110-121). New York: Springer-Verlag.

McGuire, K.D. & Weisz, J.R. (1982). Social cognition and behavioral correlates of preadolescent chumship. *Child Development, 53*, 1485-1491.

Mussen, P.H. & Jones, M.C. (1957). Self-conceptions, motivations, and interpersonal attitudes of early and late maturing boys. *Child Development, 28*, 243-256.

Nelson, J. & Aboud, F.E. (1985). The resolution of social conflicts between friends. *Child Development, 56*, 1009-1017.

Newcomb, A.F. & Brady, J.E. (1982). Mutuality in boys' friendship relations. *Child Development, 53*, 392-395.

Piaget, J. (1926). *The language and thought of the child.* London: Routledge & Kegan Paul.

Rubin, K.H., Daniels-Beirness, T., & Bream, L., (1984). Social isolation and social problem solving: A longitudinal study. *Journal of Consulting and Clinical Psychology, 52*, 17-25.

Sroufe, L.A. (1979). The Coherence of Individual Development: Early Care, Attachment, and Subsequent Developmental Issues. *American Psychologist, 34*, 834-841.

Waters, E. & Sroufe, L.A. (1983). Social competence as a developmental construct. *Developmental Review, 3*, 79-97.

Waters, E., Wippman, J., & Sroufe, L.A. (1979). Attachment, positive affect, and competence in the peer group: Two studies in construct validation. *Child Development, 50*, 821-829.

Weintraub, S. & Neale, J.M. (1984). The Stony Brook high risk project. In N.F. Watt, E.J. Anthony, L.C. Wynne, & J.E. Rolf (Eds.), *Children at risk for schizophrenia: A Longitudinal Perspective* (pp. 243-263). Cambridge University Press, Cambridge.

Younger, A.J., Schwartzman, A.E., & Ledingham, J.E. (1985). Age related changes in children's perceptions of aggression and withdrawal in their peers. *Developmental Psychology, 21*, 70-75.

5

Socially Competent Communication and Relationship Development

Steve Duck

University of Iowa

Various workers from a number of different disciplinary shadings have been intrigued by the notion that social behavior is a skill demanding competent performance by the actor. There is nothing new about the idea, which probably goes back at least as far as the ancient Greeks, but the focus of attention and the elements of performance examined by each investigator show considerable variety. In most of its forms, however, the notion boils down to a kind of *communication* competence, although it is often treated in some other context, such as a psychological, developmental, or environmental one.

In a recent analysis, Spitzberg and Cupach (1985) teased apart some of the subtleties here, but while my analysis is closely based on theirs, I intend to use it to tie together some of the threads that I have already laid out elsewhere (Duck, Miell, & Gaebler, 1980). In brief, that earlier work showed that there is a distinct parallelism between the cues to which adults attend in getting acquainted and the cues to which children attend as they develop their ways of forming friends from early childhood to late adolescence. Based on this, it is my contention that there are significant parallels between certain types of competence, the stages of a relationship's development, and the nature of the development of children's understandings of the basis of friendship. I also contend that deficiencies in different types of skills lead to different consequences for relationships and I therefore hope to offer an organization for the literature that, in this context, relates to social competence across the life cycle. I argue for a developmental view of competence in relationships in two senses: a) across the life of the person and b) across the life of the relationship. Into this framework I increasingly weave the concept of language as we proceed. I then briefly introduce a new methodology for studying memory for language in social encounters and finally raise eight questions for future research on children's social competence.

Although my review of "the children's literature" is minimal in this chapter, part of my point is to show the value that work on adult relationships has for research on children's relationships. Theoretical issues that are presently "hot" in the adult field--such as "To whose perspective do we accord the most status in describing relational phenomena?"--seem to me to have very important direct relevance to a literature on children's unpopularity that presently uses teachers' and peers' ratings of rejection interchangeably and does not often ask the "incompetent" child about the goals that the child intended to achieve but that, as rated by outsiders, failed to achieve. While my analysis is thus working steadfastly toward an argument that allows me to propose eight questions about children's competence that could usefully be researched, the questions themselves are based on a parallel reading of the literature on children's friendships and other chapters in this volume that I do not detail

B. H. Schneider et al. (eds.), Social Competence in Developmental Perspective, 91–106.
© 1989 by Kluwer Academic Publishers.

here. At this point I will offer a preview of these eight questions (which will be discussed in some detail in the last section of the chapter) in order that readers may keep these questions in mind as I pursue the argument that leads to their being asked:

1. Does competence differ as a function of perspective?
2. What is the role of (different) observers' beliefs about friendship in rating a child's social competence?
3. Why do we focus on the ways in which competence grows with the child and do so little work on the development of competence across the life of a child's relationships?
4. Do we too often act as if a child were merely reactive in his or her friendship formation rather than an active social being?
5. Are different competencies required in order to relate to peers, to parents and to teachers?
6. Do we pay enough attention to network factors?
7. Do we too often assume that all children know all peers equally well?
8. Does the personal importance of a rejection depend on who is doing the rejecting?

Types of Social Competence

Even a casual examination of the range of research into social competence across the life cycle shows that the terms "skill" and "competence" have not been consistently used in the scholarly literature. Some speak of social skills at the nonverbal level, some of relationship initiation skills, some of deficiencies in partner attention skills, others of conversational involvement, yet others of linguistic competence, and others of relational skills.

In most recent work on competence, a fundamental level of ability is assumed in the form of cognitive capacities or mentalistic elements that allow competent performance, which is viewed as the ability to achieve desired outcomes and show adaptability across contexts. The emphasis falls on the developmental processes that facilitate or hinder acquisition of adaptability--elements of performance and skill that are assumed rather than elaborated upon by such researchers. Furthermore, McFall's (1982) distinction between trait and molecular approaches to competence is accepted, and social competence models tend to be trait models that search for personality or cognitive factors that predict competent performance, with empathy and role taking singled out as likely suspects. Given the purposes of this chapter, my first question is: At what stages of relating will these factors be most influential? My second thought is: How does language fit in here? To develop an attack on these questions, I will select four levels from those elaborated on by Spitzberg and Cupach (1985) and relate these, in the rest of the chapter, to the notion that even children's relationships can develop in intimacy over time:

1. Social skills. These skills are usually studied by examining the specific behaviors related to the *perception* of competence (such as those leading to impressions of anxiety, attractiveness, etc.). Research here tends to be "molecular", in the terminology introduced above (McFall, 1982), and to look for particular, situation-specific behaviors that are, may, or may not be related to personality characteristics of the particular persons involved. The assumption is that, to a significant extent, social behavior is based on motor activity that can be taught and learned, and that particular impressions follow from particular patterns of motor activity. At least in early models, the impressions seemed to be treated as very largely context-independent. In normal relationships, competence in such motor activity is usually presupposed, yet in some rejected children competence may be deficient and this shortcoming may prevent their entry into any relationships at all.

2. Interpersonal competence. Assessing interpersonal competence generally involves the study of effectiveness or the achievement of interpersonal objectives. It is seen in terms of the ability to accomplish tasks successfully, particularly *interpersonal* goals, framed within a context of interdependence. The context of performance is important here: The criterion for skill is context-specific and resides externally. Thus, a person's rewardingness and the amount of self disclosure that he or she uses are not inherent in the notion of competence but are strategic elements that may, but may not, be relevant to a judgment of competence in a given case (Parks, 1977). If we are looking for *developing* competence based on an increased understanding of fine points, then this is an important notion.

3. Communication competence. This area of study focuses on interactive behaviors appropriate to a given context. Even if Person X knows what is appropriate to the context, however, he or she still often has a range of behaviors available to achieve the goal and must select competently between them. It is here that the concept of skilled performance is frequently intermixed with the notion of mere competence. Skillful strategic choice between available modes of action often goes beyond simple mechanical competence and the notion of skill normally implies mastery of a wider range of possible behaviors and knowledge of how to act in a wider range of circumstances rather than just a polished mechanical performance of specific behaviors. Such communicative skill seems to presuppose a knowledge of rules of self-presentation and a degree of understanding of such concepts as hierarchies and roles within society as well as an ability to differentiate situations and people. Such abilities may be deficient in children of certain ages (or degrees of social development) or in children who lack experience in social relationships because of deficits in the categories listed above.

4. Relational competence. In examining relational competence, we must keep in mind that this type of competence sometimes depends on the nature of the relationship in question (e.g., emotional expressiveness is more necessary in marriage than in a relationship at work). Thus, the mere ability to perform specific behaviors is not to be regarded as "skilled" performance here and this higher-order level of social competence presupposes a sophisticated understanding of differences between types of relationships and between possible relationship partners. One question, for example, is whether anyone could achieve mastery of this skill very decisively before adolescence, and it seems more likely that many do not, even in adulthood.

The four-level hierarchy presented above is a useful one, in that it deals with competency issues at several different levels and can be viewed as a relationally developmental hierarchy in which each skill presumes and builds on the skills at the previous level(s). The implications for relationships are different in each case, pointing to a need to supplement this hierarchy with a developmental model of relationships. A second need is for work on social competence to attend to the recent dramatic developments that have taken place in the research on adult relationships (Duck, 1988) since these bear on one's interpretation of the meaning of social rejection in particular children. In a nutshell (one that is worth opening elsewhere), these developments propose that relationships are processes and not states (Duck & Sants, 1983) and that they therefore change and develop in ways that require skilled reactions from relaters in the area of adaptation to processual change--skills that rejected or neglected children may lack; that different viewers of the same relationship have legitimately different perspectives on the relationship, whose legitimacy is not really a problem for researchers but certainly does require further study; that even in children's relationships, the interactants are not interchangeable strangers but have important psychological and historical connectors that are ignored at the risk of nonsensical interpretations of behavior; and that the routine business of everyday life plays a more important role in sustaining relationships than has previously been acknowledged (see Duck, 1988, for an elaboration and review of these points).

Let us now explore three of these skills (actually a fusion of the above four into three, as will become clear) in greater depth and tie them more closely to the concept of the development of relationships in children.

Social Skill as Fundamental Nonverbal Competence

In social psychology, a vast amount of work has been done relating social skill to competence in nonverbal behavior (Argyle, 1983). Such work, which is devoted to the microanalysis of social behavior, examines the sequencing of nonverbal activity, especially in relation to speech content, and nonverbal communication as an indicator of attitudes toward an interaction partner (see, for example, Argyle, 1983; Trower, Bryant, & Argyle, 1978). Thus we discover that eye contact not only conveys attitudes about oneself (such as self esteem) but also indicates attitudes toward one's partner (such as liking or disliking) and signals attitudes toward an encounter (such as ease or unease). All of these nonverbal messages are indirectly relevant to the long- term formation and conduct of personal relationships and are directly relevant to competent performance in the interactions that make up relationships. Without such abilities, social encounters are inconceivable, even in children. These skills are essential in order for an individual to initiate relationships and induce others to view him or her as worthy of relational attention.

Another important element in nonverbal communication in relation to competence, however, is its role in the "mechanical" conduct of conversations. A minimally acceptable relationship between speech content and nonverbal sequencing is generally a prerequisite for the satisfactory and effective conduct of social interactions. Work in this tradition has had the primary objective of establishing the correct rules for social behavior and helping to identify appropriate ways of training those who show deficiencies of performance. Thus, Trower et al. (1978) indicate that those with social and mental problems typically have abnormal patterns of eye movements and poor correspondence between nonverbal communication and verbal utterances. For instance, schizophrenics avoid eye contact, and the socially withdrawn tend to do the same. Such skills constitute an important assumed basis for relationship formation, and indeed, in studies of lonely persons, Shaver, Furman, and Buhrmester (1985) have argued that the lonely who show such deficiencies actually lack relationship initiation skills.

Such evidence is usually interpreted in the context of adult relational problems but can apply equally well to children. It suggests that persons whose deviant nonverbal communication are not only difficult but also unrewarding, over and above their failures to display minimally acceptable mechanical competence. As a consequence, observers' judgments indicate that these individuals are likely to be disregarded as potential associates (Rodin, 1982), partly because they are so unrewarding or boring, but mostly because the disrupted nonverbal communication leads to negative *perceptions* of the person and of the person's personality by outside viewers, adopting their own perspectives. The implications for social relationships that derive from this source prefigure any direct incompetence in friendship roles and instead lead to observers choosing to neglect or disregard (Rodin, 1982) rather than to their expressing dislike or unpopularity directly. In the case of an individual who is incompetent at this level, others presumably do not even get as far as judging his or her personal acceptability or personal rewardingness. Judgments of disregard here stem from perceptions of the incompetent or inappropriate performance of relatively mechanical skills rather than the performance or misperformance of roles. In other words, the impact of nonverbal ineptness is likely to be felt at the point of initiation of a relationship with a stranger rather more than at other points, and rejection for this reason is relatively impersonal--at least it is not based on any deep personal knowledge. In brief, if one child views another as "strange" on the basis of such disregard cues, then the first child is likely to ignore, reject, or ridicule the second child.

Such a point is vital because of the intrinsic importance of the outsider's perspective with respect to the other person, over and above the "true meaning" of the behavior. Communication researchers have subsequently confirmed in sophisticated studies of interaction that shy persons' nonverbal communication, for example, is typically interpreted as indicating *hostility*. Burgoon and Koper (1984) showed that shy persons' behavior toward a stranger was rated as hostile by other strangers who viewed the encounter on videotape. On the other hand, friends of the same shy persons viewing exactly the same tape are perfectly able to judge the behavior as shy rather than hostile and so to perceive their shy friend as more nearly normal and friendly than strangers see them as being. This suggests that "shy or incompetent nonverbal communication" leads to initial judgments of disregard but that these judgments are correctable or surmountable when the interaction is continued, despite its unpromising beginnings. In other words, the "meaning" of the behavior (in terms of social competence) is rooted not only in the behavior as "objectively" rated but also in the observer's knowledge base concerning the person who is being observed and rated. We should bear this point in mind here as we consider the different notions of competence and their possibly different influences both during the development of a relationship and during the development of a person.

For instance, let us consider the view that nonverbal communication patterns are not merely incidental but critical to long-term relationships. Cappella (1988) has pointed out that research on specific interactions and on the development, maintenance, and deterioration of relationships has for too long been regarded as separate from research on nonverbal behavior, and as dealing with issues that are distinct from those dealt with by research on nonverbal behavior. Furthermore, it is now clear that although researchers often focus on the skills and knowledge required to initiate or develop relationships, there are also certain types of skills and knowledge that are required just to maintain them (Duck, 1988) and that the issues of relationship maintenance are themselves ones that require skill and strategic competence on the part of the relational partners (Dindia & Baxter, 1987). Initiation of relationships, while it calls for one form of skill, does not exhaust the types of nonverbal patterning skills that are required in a competent relater of any age. Cappella (1988) also sees links between patterns of interaction and relationship "states" that have not been sufficiently investigated and have not been fully and clearly explained in *the context of the societal and cultural values in which relationships exist*. In a given culture--say, the culture of a children's playground--certain interaction patterns are presumed to be relevant to the continuance of relationships. For present purposes, these important observations have three implications. First, they encourage us to see the connection between nonverbal communication and relationships in more complex terms rather than regarding it as merely involving the mechanical performance of small behaviors; second, they emphasize both the context surrounding relationships and the important relativities of relational behavior; third, they emphasize that the meaning of the mechanical performance of social skills will change as context changes and as requirements at the different stages of a relationship change. What is tolerated at the beginning of a relationship may not be appropriate later, although the reverse seems, paradoxically, more likely (Burgoon & Koper, 1984).

Now that I have considered the nonverbal aspects of social skill, I will turn to the role of language.

Social Competence as Conversational Involvement

The important direct and mediating influences between interaction patterns and relationships, one of which is clearly language, obviously need more study in this context, since these are the aspects of interaction to which nonverbal communication theorists often tie their work, but only indirectly or by implication. We can develop this point by looking at work that treats "social skill" and competence as being related to the ability to hold the interest of a conversational partner. Jones, Hansson, and Cutrona (1984) and Jones, Hobbs, and Hockenbury (1982) for example, refer to social skill in the context of research on loneliness and argue that lonely persons (both the young and the elderly lonely) often lack the basic "interestingness" that holds conversational partner's attention. They are poor at asking questions or at showing interest in the other person's conversation; they engage in egocentric monologues, omit rewarding responses to another's remarks, tend to be unwilling or unable to signal involvement in another's talk, and do not ask follow-up questions that indicate interest in what the other has said. Jones *et al.* (1984) report a number of programs and techniques designed to train people who are incompetent in this sense and at this level. It appears that such higher order techniques serve to improve competence in conversational involvement quite satisfactorily.

We should note that incompetence in this sense produces essentially the same effect as nonverbal incompetence but by a subtly different route. In the case of nonverbal communication, the incompetent performer is judged to be strange or hostile at the outset and is therefore disregarded and not "engaged" as a possible relational partner; in the case of lack of conversational skills, the person is disregarded *at a later point* in acquaintance, because of essential unrewardingness, and is avoided or actively rejected not because the person is judged to be initially hostile but because he or she lacks the ability to hold and engage interest.

In both cases, the serious consequence for the incompetent performer is a negative assessment, by other social beings, of his or her general suitability for relationships. For us researchers, however, the consequences point to different avenues of concern. In the case of conversational incompetence, it is likely that a child experiences some social relationships but finds them unsatisfactory, whereas in the case of nonverbal incompetence, it is possible that the child may be entirely isolated socially. A child with the latter type of problem probably complains about having no relationships at all, whereas the child with the former type of problem probably complains about a lack of depth to the relationships that he or she does have--different issues, needful of different solutions. Again, talk enters the picture even more forcefully the more we study the later stages of developing relationships and focus on broader issues of linguistic ability.

Communication Competence as Linguistic Ability and Persuasiveness

Let us first look at the notion of linguistic competence and how that notion has developed in scope. The ancient Greeks, for example, would probably have been intrigued and gratified by the development of interest in social competence. Their main interest was at a different level, which some would argue has primary importance (Spitzberg & Cupach, 1985). Their concern over proper social performance began with language. In particular, they were concerned with communication competence as achieved by the study of rhetoric and persuasion, originally so that citizens could argue competently in courts to settle property disputes. The work of the rhetoricians and Sophists was primarily intended at first to help citizens argue for their rights. After several centuries of development, the art of rhetoric was extended by Cicero to the art of speaking "with fullness and variety" on any subject, a definition extended still further by Quintillian to the "art of speaking well".

An essential element in such conceptualizations, which is still implicit in our thoughts about social competence, is the ability to speak with tact, later extended by Renaissance thinkers to aestheticism, decorum, and other-orientation, which, as they used the concept, roughly translates to "ingratiation". Even later, the notion became more recognizable as the modern "good conversation" and extended beyond the textual message itself to behaviors such as voice modulation, gestures and the speaker's appearance, and to concerns over the ability to engage one's audience and move their emotions, make them feel good, or enlighten them (Spitzberg & Cupach, 1985). We might expect that these different forms of communicative ability would develop, moderate, and change with age, just as other abilities do. These issues, again, are important in their own right but assume added significance for dealing with children's competence in light of recent work that points to the connection between language and the symbolic forms inherent in relationships.

The Role of Rhetoric in Competent Relating

Even children can be seen to use rhetorical persuasion in their dealings with other people. This section of the chapter analyses some modern views of rhetoric as a way to incorporate linguistic competence and show the role of rhetorical persuasion in children's friendships. I begin by examining some of the work of Kenneth Burke, a modern rhetorical theorist who has had a major influence on conceptualizations of rhetoric. His work is based in sociological interpretations of society and emphasizes language and talk as a means of cutting through estrangement, anomie, and divisiveness in society. Burke (1945, 1950) recognizes humankind as *essentially* a symbol-using people seeking "consubstantiality" with others (i.e., union of thinking, support for outlooks). For Burke, rhetoric involves sharing symbolic meanings and being able to grasp and address what is in the other person's mind.

In research on everyday social relationships, a large body of venerable reports similarly tells us that attraction into relationships involves comprehension, expression, and matching of attitudes and opinions (e.g. Byrne, 1971). More recently, I have argued (Duck ,1986, 1988) that such matching normally works through everyday communication rather than through *special* communicative acts and that it is important that researchers in this growing field come to understand the ways in which relaters communicate similarity or dissimilarity everyday through such symbolic means. This type of approach argues that we should attend to the everyday functions of discourse in children and try to develop methods that will capture it.

In recent social psychological work, it has always been assumed--but in a literature relatively unconnected with the literature on social relationships--that the mechanism for such communion is conscious self disclosure, but Duck and Pond (in press) recently issued a challenge to, and extension of, the usual form of this idea. The bulky work on the role of self disclosure in the development of relationships usually presumes that satisfactory self disclosure is a prerequisite for satisfactory relationship development (see, e.g., Miell & Duck, 1986). Too little is known, nonetheless, about self disclosure across the life cycle in general and in children's friendships in particular. Also unexplored is the hidden assumption that subjects have the linguistic and communicative competence to effectuate their self-disclosure needs and goals, although at least some evidence suggests that this assumption may be unwarranted (Spitzberg & Canary, 1985). More worthy of future study, argue Duck and Pond (in press), is the more general point that individuals communicate and maintain, develop, or diminish their relationships by the symbolic uses that they make of language and the general *forms* of communicative structure that they employ, through metaphor or style, as Burke proposed in other contexts. (As an impertinent example [Duck, 1987a], consider how researchers' focus on trajectories of relationship development encourages us to think in terms of routes through relationships, turning points, and directions of movement, whereas an insectival or biological metaphor would encourage us to think in terms of metamorphosis or transformation and hence to pose different research questions.)

However it actually works, self disclosure and other forms of relational communication require specific communicative abilities and knowledge. Although unheralded until recently (Duck & Pond, in press), there are substantial and important overlaps between Burke's conceptualization of rhetoric, the nature of symbolic action, the notion of communicative competence, and the satisfactory conduct or development of social and personal relationships, both in terms of development across the life cycle and in terms of development from initial acquaintance through intimacy. While these topics have been studied in connection with direct and obvious communication strategies (such as self disclosing or affinity seeking), they also relate to the various ways in which individuals make sense of their relationships, in the past, in the present, and for the future. To develop this point as something relevant to the long-term view of social competence, it is valuable to look at competence in relationships and try to determine the extent to which it depends on linguistic understanding and a grasp of social symbolic forms. For instance, Sants (1984) found that in 6-year-old children, levels of friendship conception correlated with verbal IQ and that while concepts of friendship probably depend on vocabulary to some degree, vocabulary is actually used in daily life and is not a mere abstraction. All too often, we researchers overlook the fact that an enormous amount of the day--whether in childhood, adolescence or adulthood--is spent talking with others and that relational talk is an important part of that chunk of time. One thesis of this chapter is that apparently trivial everyday relational talk is fundamental to relational competence and as such requires more urgent attention than it presently receives. At the younger end of the life cycle, it is also clear that any such ability to manipulate symbols develops with age as does the ability to forage for symbols in other people's heads (La Gaipa, 1981). Thus, we can expect children's everyday talk to function as a means of creating, sustaining and managing relationships just as much as we can in adults.

Relational competence and rhetoric

Such a point leads us to the proposal that language has a direct influence on relationships and to a comparison of various techniques that adults use to develop and sustain amity. I contend that children need some form of these techniques too. The previous forms of competence are, as it were, *presumed* to lead toward satisfactory accomplishment of relationships. Yet in addition to these basic components, there is a strategic sort of relationship competence that necessarily organizes and develops the other competencies, namely, relational competence. It is essential here to have a full grasp of certain higher-order principles of appropriateness, social roles, and the rules; to know the other person, and to understand relationships, language, and strategies to effect relational goals. Thus, research on relationship rules shows that when nonverbal communication is not at issue, people in different cultures recognize both universal elements to relationships and some shadings that apply specifically in their own culture. Argyle and Henderson (1984) showed, for example, that all cultures endorse rules of exchange and obligation, but some do not endorse rules of verbal or physical intimacy. Perhaps such research suggests, too, that subcultures also exist with respect to the forms in which a relationship is expressed and that, in children's relationships, the modes of expressing friendship are especially subject to development and change (Sants, 1984).

Expression of friendship is guided by social forms and rules that a given individual--adult or child--must learn. Adult relationships do not progress merely through a person's self disclosing at every opportunity, but through the person's doing so in appropriate contexts and on appropriate occasions. As Montgomery (1984) has shown, open communication depends on appropriateness, not merely on the amount of disclosure. As Cappella (1988) also noted, nonverbal communication patterns have an appropriateness factor, too, that is to some extent dictated by social and cultural values of which a given interactant needs to be aware.

Strategic issues also arise in relationships, and a child's ability to cope with them is a further measure of relational competence. Relationships do not just begin on their own but have to be consciously steered, at least at some point. Bell and Daly (1984) show that adults typically attempt to develop opportunities for affinity seeking, such that they adopt particular styles of communicating as strategies that will enhance their attractiveness. Douglas (1987) further demonstrated that subjects typically test out their partner's willingness for a relationship by various direct and indirect means in the course of testing affinity. For example, people will withdraw from the conversation in order to see whether their partner is really interested enough to try to bring them back into it. Another problem of relationship development that requires both sensitivity and skillful management is the privacy-intimacy dialectic. Baxter and Wilmot (1985) have illustrated the existence of taboo topics, the antithesis of self-disclosure, such that a partner needs to know not only which topics to talk about but which to avoid. Knowledge of all of these factors is a prerequisite for competent relationship development, even if the initiation of the relationship has proceeded adequately. Perhaps the childish equivalent of such strategies is also necessary in a child's world of friendship. The manipulation of such influences on satisfactory relationship conduct depends more and more on communicative skills as a person matures to adulthood, but there are instructive parallels between these kinds of skills and two other factors: the development of relationships themselves and development of children's understanding of relationships (Duck *et al.*, 1980). Basic skill involves getting noticed in the right, promising ways; conversational involvement skills require comprehension of a basic need to be rewarding to other people; communication competence requires the ability to deal with self-disclosure and to present different sorts of rewardingness; relational skills require management abilities that depend on an understanding of another person's needs and likely responses, as interdependence increases. In a parallel finding, Duck *et al.* (1980) reported some consensus by different researchers that children's friendship concepts develop from egocentric through reciprocal cooperation to mutual understanding based on knowledge of internal/psychological factors. A third parallel is provided by work on friendship development in adults, indicating the influence of superficial cues to start with, followed by an increasing influence of deeper cues based on personality factors (Duck & Craig, 1978).

These parallels are intriguing, and a fully developed model of social competence across the life cycle would need to apply the "right" competency criteria to the right stage or aspect of relational development, maintenance, or decline in light of the right expectations about the subjects' knowledge levels. As an individual matures, these skills, relational needs, and relational knowledge will increasingly depend on language as used in everyday life.

Apart from pointing out such parallels between different conceptions of competence, the development of children's concepts of relationships, and relationship development in adults, the present chapter claims that rhetoric and the comprehension of rhetorical symbol usage play a major role in relating. Not only in adults but in children as well, relationships are based on subtle linguistic forms. As relationships develop, so the language and personal idioms used to conduct them changes also (Hopper, Knapp, & Scott, 1981). Thus individuals develop private languages and uses of language that act as barriers to outsiders and make the relationship special for the participants. More than this, language serves as a fundamental index of relational progress, with changes in language style and content being a major vehicle for relational development: The form and style of the language change as much as do the topics selected for discussion (Norton, 1983). Language is also *instrumental* in relational development, with many studies showing that changes in topic and content are used to make relationships progress, the studies on self-disclosure being a major part of such work (Miell & Duck, 1986). Duck and Pond (in press) have pushed the point further and argued that uses of language are *essential* in relationships--that is, they *are* at some level what the relationship is. I have argued (Duck, 1986, 1987b, 1988) that over and above changes in topic and style, *patterns* of communication will change as a function of relationship change; namely, people will talk to different others about different topics as a function of and an index of relationship change. In children, these changes occur as contexts change (such as a move from home to school) and force them to awareness of and adaptation to different social and linguistic perspectives.

In the context of competence, especially given the above remarks, it becomes important to recognize that the ways in which subjects represent or are capable of representing their relationships in language function as an index of their psychological attitudes toward the relationship and the partner. Thus, changes in language abilities as a child develops will serve to modify the child's potential for relationships; so also will changes in levels of competency results (La Gaipa, 1981).

Developing the ICR (Iowa Communication Record)

So far in this chapter I have proposed a developmental model of relationships based on a developmental hierarchy of social competence. In reaching this point in the argument, I will now present a method for analysing some of these issues.

Duck and Pond (in press) have argued that the recall of relational "events" indicates the subjects' metaphorical styles as well as the means by which they recall and present their relationships to others and that these patterns of recall reflect inherent and implicit *future* forms for the relationship. A person who says that he or she is stuck on a partner is saying more than a person who uses the magnetic metaphor and claims to be attracted to the other person's qualities and presumably has different expectations about the relationship. In this regard, Duck and Pond (in press) proposed that the forms of language used and recalled by competent and incompetent relaters would differ. In order to investigate these ideas, a new method is being developed to help in studying the role of talk and memory for talk in relating. If we accept that children's social competence is influenced by, and occurs in the context of, talk with other children, parents, teachers, and siblings, then such a method could be modified to be useful in dealing with some of the issues raised here.

Ever since the establishment and development of the Rochester Interaction Record, usually known as the RIR (Wheeler & Nezlek, 1977), there has been much interest in developing records of relational behavior based on diary reports. Although such work has increased our knowledge of relational activity in very important ways it does not address the mediating mechanisms of the communication through which social interaction is sustained nor the memories for communication that embody and ratify those interactions and conversations (Duck & Pond, in press). Such extensions of the method are necessary to make it particularly relevant to the important work that must be done to apply it to communicative exchanges.

The RIR is primarily used to investigate the characteristics of disengaging, stable, and growing relationships, but without directly measuring any conversational reports--again, therefore, recording "facts" and processes of relationships without any indication of the communicative vehicles by which they are accomplished. Nevertheless, parallel development in the area of research on, say, courtship progress (e.g., Surra, Arizzi, & Asmussen, 1988) now point to the central importance of understanding negotiative processes in mate selection and calls for process-oriented research on relationships (Duck & Sants, 1983) are now much more frequently taken up and applied to a wider range of issues, such as gender influences in relating (Hendrick, 1988). In developing such work, we can clarify the routines of daily communication, the negotiative and mediational influences on children's long-term relationships and the ways in which outsiders are brought into a child's creation of a relationship's mental and social representation.

The role of communication extends to some deep-structure theoretical issues having to do with social memory and the social construction of relational history (or future) in parallel with the diachronic development of relationships in "real" terms. Since relationship development--even in children--does not just involve the psychological processes of increasing intimacy but also entails discussion with particular partners and networks (e.g., Milardo, 1982), we must tie conversation to interaction and not allow one to be studied without the other's influence being considered simultaneously, especially in the context of competence, where these processes have to be handled effectively. We researchers still do not know much about the subject matter of interactions, the kinds of topics that the subjects remember discussing, and the ways in which these interactions promote the increases in intimacy that are presumed to occur in real life.

While this type of descriptive base has been called for by many prominent ethological theorists, beginning with Hinde (1979), there are other theoretical reasons for expecting such a technique to be valuable at several different and complementary levels simultaneously:

1. A method that records a subject's memories of conversation could indicate whether the person's communication patterns vary as a function of competence and/or whether those patterns change as a function of relational changes; for example, we could learn whether a child's interpretation of communications (and hence, possibly, of rejections) is influenced as a function of his or her memory style for conversations;

2. Such a method could help us see the extent to which, in real-life interactions, various psychological variables--such as competence, loneliness, and communicative strategies--influence the nature of topics selected for conversation, satisfaction with the outcomes of conversation, and memory patterns for conversation, giving us a means to check out differences in conversational recall in children who have different levels of social ability;

3. Such a method could indicate the differences in recall between subjects with particular characteristics, such as an unusual appearance, lack of popularity, or a handicap--by recording the different perspectives of two parties to the same interaction and

thereby give us some insights into the systematic differences or changes that occur as relationships develop across age and in intimacy;

4. The method could illustrate the ways in which conversations are responsible for the growth or decline in intimacy that has long been assumed to take place in the course of relationship change but that we often do not investigate in children--as if their relationships were "all or nothing" throughout childhood. The method could also clarify the role of reflection and consideration about interaction (Duck, 1988) as well as the different tracks that may be taken in competent and incompetent relationships.

The Iowa Communication Record (ICR), developed in response to the aforementioned needs, is a self-report form on which respondents record their recollection of conversations. It assesses some facts about an interaction (when, where, with whom) and also provides subjective reports of the nature, flow, and quality of the conversation and the ways in which it was perceived to influence the relationship with the other participants. While the ICR reports retrospective data, part of its purpose is to permit a systematic study of the changes that occur over time in recall of conversation as a function of personality variables, the observer's perspective, or relational events.

A series of studies has already been conducted to obtain data from subjects in a variety of contexts (such as reporting on the two most significant interactions each day for two weeks or reporting on five interactions in one day). To date, we have not conducted studies on children or in the context of social competence before adulthood, but work with adults suggests that there are tantalizing differences of perspective between the competent and the incompetent relater. For example, when we asked lonely and non-lonely subjects to recall "a successful date" and "an unsuccessful date" (using their own definition of these terms), it turns out that the lonely subjects' memories of both the successful and the unsuccessful dates are rather indistinct (Duck, Hoy, & Strejc, 1988). They report low satisfaction not only with the unsuccessful dates but with the successful ones as well! However, as compared to nonlonely subjects, they do not perceive differences in levels of conflict or the frequency of communicative breakdowns. They just enjoy all the dates less without having particularly identifiable reasons.

The results also show that bad dates are seen as being controlled by one party or the other rather than as being mutually controlled. It might have been expected that a perception of control by the other person would lead to ratings of a negative sort, whether from boredom or a sense of being powerless (Rogers & Millar, 1988), but in cases where subjects see themselves as controlling the conversation, it suggests that subjects are bored by the need to put so much energy into steering the conversation --a suggestion that merits further study in view of the fact that persons who actually control a conversation more are rarely aware of the fact, or, if they are aware of it, often do not regard such control in a negative light (Leary, 1983). Clearly, the issue of control over the conversation and how it arises is also rather important here since competence training frequently involves teaching subjects to take control of conversations (Jones et al., 1984), even though the above results suggest that this approach may not work.

These and other findings available from the author suggest that social competence and incompetence are characterized at least in part by perceptions of experiences rather than by the experiences themselves, a possibility that is being explored further in ongoing work. The ways in which relational events are remembered are obviously a critical factor in the competent development of relationships, their maintenance, and perhaps their breakdown or disruption--in children as well as in adults. Based on these findings, researchers can test a range of possibilities concerning such theoretical issues as the competent and incompetent management of communication in children's relationships, together with hypotheses concerning the patterning of communication in the social network and the memories or origins of communicative deficiencies in unpopular children.

By combining a variety of techniques ranging from self-report to behavioral observations, the intention is to fortify the data base against criticisms that are particularly intriguing in the context of social competence in children. For instance, there is the apparently methodological point that retrospective data such as these are inherently flawed and uninformative. In fact, such a criticism is a deep theoretical point and embodies a view of reality that in itself needs to be checked. It credits outside public observers of private relational phenomena with a status that I presently see as prejudicial and premature, and also fails to emphasize the fact that in the realities of the exchanges and conversations in everyday life, subjects are often searching for a description of what is real and often amend their beliefs about relational reality on the basis of conversations with other people. With regard to children's friendship and competence, this issue surfaces as the question of whether children themselves or their teachers or their peers or their parents are the "best" judges of children's achievement of friendship goals, and of course, the issue reverts to the question of "best for what purpose?".

By focusing on the language forms that subjects use to recall conversation as well as the language that they use to describe relationships, this chapter also calls on those who study language acquisition to apply their skills to the ways in which children report and represent their relationships in discourse with others. By noting the parallels between relationship growth, the development of relationship concepts, and types of social competence, the chapter also indicates some ways of extending notions of social competence by ensuring that we ask some of the right questions at some of the right times. The development of relationships requires different skills at different times, just as we see different skills developing in children as they mature. Skills for managing progress require high-order adaptability. Extended use of the ICR will help us to see whether people have the types of skills that we have believed they did.

Eight Questions for Future Research

The foregoing discussion leads me to raise the following eight questions that future research could profitably address in the area of children's social competence:

1. Does "competence" differ as a function of perspective? Unless we know a person's goals, we can hardly assess whether these goals have been achieved, and the goals that we attribute to a child may not be those that the child actually has. If we merely guess at what a child's social goals may be and then use such guesses as the basis for assessing competent achievement of the presumed goals, we should at least acknowledge the risks that we run in so doing. An interesting question related to this is whether a child whose relationship skills are rated directly (rather than inferred from popularity ratings) and who is rated very differently by different observers is a special sort of child distinct from one about whom all raters are in relatively good agreement.

2. What is the role of (different) observers' beliefs about friendship in rating a child's social competence? Teachers or parents whose knowledge of and beliefs about children's friendship styles and development is sophisticated are likely to judge a child's competence (and to foster or comment upon it) in ways that are different from teachers or parents whose relevant knowledge and beliefs are not sophisticated. Such knowledge and beliefs are researchable in their own right, but in any case, we investigators should not assume that all parents or teachers are equally useful commentators or raters or judges when it comes to assessing social competence, and we should, therefore, report information about our raters in studies of social competence.

3. Why do we focus on the ways in which competence grows with the child and do so little work on the development of competence across the life of a child's relationships? It seems to me that we researchers often pay close attention to developmental differences between children of different ages and are aware of the differences between the relationships of children who are located at different points in the life cycle, but we are paying virtually no attention to the ways in which children's relationships develop in intimacy from first meeting to best friendship. In contrast, those studying adult relationships pay attention to very little else, and we have much to learn by bringing the principles of the two separate literatures together.

4. Do we too often act as if a child were merely reactive in his or her friendship formation rather than an active social being? Children do not become friends merely by being present in one another's company; as is the case with adults, they must make other children like them, interact with them and choose them as friends. Children also need to maintain their relationships, just as adults do, and may need higher-order levels of accomplishment than merely the ability to be popular. For example, a child may need to learn the skills of coping with frustration or thwarting by another child and probably has to learn to be a good persuader--persuading others into relationships, persuading partners to stay as partners and various other social graces that depend on some level of rhetorical ability.

5. Are different competencies required in order to relate to peers, to parents, and to teachers? While we often treat "a competent child" as being *universally* competent, there is no certainty in my mind that such a generality will actually prove to be true in all cases. Peers, parents, teachers, siblings, and older or younger children on the playground each represent different sorts of relational challenge. Researchers would be well advised, I believe, to attend to the literature on adult friendship types and to the different rules and skills that apply to them (e.g. Argyle & Henderson, 1984).

6. Do we pay enough attention to network factors? Children's social choices and relationships occur in the context of other relationships within the peer group. Not only does it take two to tango, but it takes many to make a classroom or a social network. A child who loses a friend in the middle of the school year may be faced with problems that are different from those faced by a child who loses a friend earlier in the school year before the relational networks in the class have become established. In adolescence, individual relational disasters often have rippling effects that spread widely throughout the network and are not merely individual or dyadic in their consequences. We err as researchers if we treat children as individual pool balls on the relational pool table. Individuals do not roam about until they haphazardly bump into friends; they are part of (or are excluded from) interacting, lively networks and systems of existing relationships.

7. Do we too often assume that all children know all peers equally well? Some children's reports of rejection or admiration of other children may reflect deep personal knowledge of the other children, while some may be based on prejudice, fashion or ignorance. In assessing whether a child is unpopular, we must take this into account. "Rejection" and "choice" do not always have the same basis in fact.

8. Does the personal importance of a rejection depend on the person who is doing the rejecting? All rejections are not created equally hurtful, just as all peers are not created equally important to a given child. We need to pay attention to the psychological importance of specific rejections in assessing the pains of rejection.

5. Socially Competent Communication

Researchers in the field of social competence are very fortunate. Not only are there significant social and practical reasons for doing this sort of research, but the area holds out continuing challenges, intellectual stimulation and important questions for us to address. As Editor of the *Journal of Social and Personal Relationships*, I frequently see variations on the phrase "More research needs to be done". In the present case, I can myself use that phrase with a mixture of confidence and excitement.

Author Notes: Requests for a full copy of the ICR should be directed to Steve Duck, 151-CSB, Communication Studies Building, University of Iowa, Iowa City, IA 52242, USA.

References

Argyle, M. (1983). *The psychology of interpersonal behavior*, (4th ed.). Harmondsworth, United Kingdom: Penguin.

Argyle, M., & Henderson, M. (1984). The rules of friendship. *Journal of Social and Personal Relationships*, *1*, 211-237.

Baxter, L. A., & Wilmot, W. (1985). Taboo topics in close relationships. *Journal of Social and Personal Relationships, 2*, 253-269.

Bell, R. A., & Daly, J. A. (1984). The affinity-seeking function of communication. *Communication Monographs, 51*, 91-115.

Burgoon, J. K., & Koper, R. J. (1984). Nonverbal and relational communication associated with reticence. *Human Communication Research, 10*, 601-626.

Burke, K. (1945). *A grammar of motives*. New York: Prentice Hall.

Burke, K. (1950). *A rhetoric of motives*. New York: Prentice Hall.

Byrne, D. (1971). *The attraction paradigm*. New York: Academic Press.

Cappella, J. N. (1988) Personal relationships, social relationships and patterns of interaction. In S. W. Duck (Ed) *Handbook of Personal Relationships* (pp. 325-342). Chichester, United Kingdom: Wiley.

Dindia, K., & Baxter, L. A. (1987). Maintenance and repair strategies in marital relationships. *Journal of Social and Personal Relationships, 4*, 143-158.

Douglas, W. (1987). Affinity-testing in initial interaction. *Journal of Social and Personal Relationships, 4*, 3-16.

Duck, S. W. (1986). *Human Relationships: An introduction to social psychology*. London: Sage Ltd.

Duck, S. W. (1987a). Adding apples and oranges: Investigators' implicit theories about personal relationships. In R. Burnett, P. McGhee, & D. Clarke (Eds.), *Accounting for relationships* (pp. 215-224). London: Methuen.

Duck, S. W. (1987b). How to lose friends without influencing people. In M. E. Roloff & G. R. Miller (Eds.), *Interpersonal processes: New directions in communication research*. (pp. 279-298). Beverly Hills, CA: SAGE, Inc.

Duck, S. W. (1988) *Relating to others* Chicago: Brooks/Cole/Dorsey and London: OpenUp Press.

Duck, S. W., & Craig, G. (1978). Personality similarity and the development of friendship: A longitudinal study. *British Journal of Social and Clinical Psychology, 17*, 237-242.

Duck, S. W., Hoy, M., & Strejc, H. (1988, November) *Developing the Iowa Communication Record (ICR): First dates*. Paper presented to the annual convention of the Speech Communication Association, New Orleans.

Duck, S. W., Miell, D. K. & Gaebler, H. C. (1980). Attraction and communication in children's interactions. In H. C. Foot, A. J. Chapman, & J. R. Smith (Eds) *Friendship and social relations in children* (pp. 89-115) Chichester, United Kingdom: Wiley.

Duck, S. W. & Pond, K. (in press) Friends, Romans, Countrymen, lend me your retrospections: Rhetoric and reality in personal relationships. In C. Hendrick (ed) *Review of Social Behavior and Personality, 10: Close Relationships* Newbury Park, CA: SAGE, Inc.

Duck, S. W., & Sants, H. K. A. (1983). On the origin of the specious: Are personal relationships really interpersonal states? *Journal of Social and Clinical Psychology, 1*, 27-41.

Hendrick, C. (1988). Roles and gender in relationships. In S. W. Duck (Ed.), *Handbook of personal relationships*. (pp. 429-448) Chichester, United Kingdom: Wiley.

Hinde, R. A. (1979). *Towards understanding relationships*. London: Academic Press.

Hopper, R., Knapp, M. L., & Scott, L. (1981). Couples' personal idioms: Exploring intimate talk. *Journal of Communication, 31*, 23-33.

Jones, W. H., Hansson, R. O., & Cutrona, C. (1984). Helping the lonely: Issues of intervention with young and older adults. In S. W. Duck (Ed.), *Personal relationships 5: Repairing personal relationships.* (pp. 143-161). London & New York: Academic Press.

Jones, W. H., Hobbs, S., & Hockenbury, D. (1982) Loneliness and social skill deficits. *Journal of Personality and Social Psychology, 42,* 682-689.

La Gaipa, J. J. (1981) Children's friendships. In S.W. Duck & R. Gilmour (eds) *Personal Relationships 2: Developing Personal Relationships* (pp. 161-187). London: Academic Press.

Leary, M. R. (1983). *Understanding social anxiety: Social, personality and clinical perspectives.* Beverly Hills, CA: Sage.

McFall, R. M. (1982) A review and reformulation of the concept of social skills. *Behavioral Assessment, 4,* 1-33.

Miell, D. E. & Duck, S. W. (1986) Strategies in developing friendship. In V. J. Derlega & B. A. Winstead (eds) *Friendship and social interaction* (pp. 129-144). New York: Springer Verlag.

Milardo, R. M. (1982). Friendship networks in developing relationships: Converging and diverging social environments. *Social Psychology Quarterly, 45,* 162-172.

Montgomery, B. M. (1984). Behavioral characteristics predicting self and peer perceptions of open communication. *Communication Quarterly, 30,* 233-240.

Norton, R. (1983). *Communicator style: Theory, applications, and measures.* Beverly Hills, CA: SAGE, Inc.

Parks, M. R. (1977) Issues in the explication of communication competence. Paper presented to the Western Speech Communication Association, Phoenix, AZ.

Rodin, M. J. (1982). Non-engagement, failure to engage, and disengagement. In S. W. Duck (Ed.), *Personal relationships 4: Dissolving personal relationships.* (pp. 31-50). New York: Academic Press.

Rogers, L. E. & Millar, F. (1988) Relational communication. In S. W. Duck (Ed.) *Handbook of Personal Relationships* (pp. 289- 305). Chichester, United Kingdom: Wiley.

Sants, H. K. A. (1984). Conceptions of friendship, social behavior and school achievements in six-year-old children. *Journal of Social and Personal Relationships, 1,* 293-309.

Shaver, P. R., Furman, W., & Buhrmester, D. (1985) Aspects of a life transition: Network changes, social skills and loneliness. In S. W. Duck & D. Perlman (Eds.), *Understanding personal relationships* (pp. 193-219). London: Sage Ltd.

Spitzberg, B. H., & Canary, D. (1985). Loneliness and communicationally competent communication. *Journal of Social and Personal Relationships, 2,* 387-402.

Spitzberg, B. H. & Cupach, W. R. (1985). *Interpersonal Communication Competence* Beverly Hills: SAGE, Inc.

Surra, C. A., Arizzi, P., & Asmussen, L. (1988). The association between reasons for commitment and the development and outcome of marital relationships. *Journal of Social and Personal Relationships, 5,* 47-63.

Trower, P., Bryant, B., & Argyle, M. (1978). *Social skills and mental health.* London: Methuen.

Wheeler, L. & Nezlek, J. (1977). Sex differences in social participation. *Journal of Personality and Social Psychology, 35,* 742-754.

6

Measuring Peer Status in Boys and Girls: A Problem of Apples and Oranges?

Tina Daniels-Beirness

Carleton University

Peer acceptance or popularity refers to the degree to which a child's peers wish to have some form of associative contact with him or her. Peer acceptance is commonly assessed using sociometric techniques. These procedures require children to evaluate other children in terms of their likability or general competence. Research has shown that children identified by these procedures as having poor relationships are at risk for both concurrent and subsequent adjustment problems. Since the identification of these children has very important consequences in terms of their future it is imperative that we be able to identify these children accurately. It has been argued that peers are the best source for identifying these children because they have frequent opportunities to observe their peers and they operate from a child's frame of reference. However, little is known about the frame of reference that children utilize when making judgments about the social status of their peers. Although sociometric procedures are highly favored and frequently used to study children's social relationships, little consideration has been given to the variables that influence children's sociometric choices. This chapter examines the influence of gender on the frame of reference children use in making sociometric decisions.

The following is a conversation that I had with Brian on the first day of kindergarten (age 5):

B: "Get her away from me."
T: "That's not a her; that's a him."
B: "No it's not. Get her away from me. I don't want to play with her.

This conversation was in reference to a small, slight boy with longish hair. Clearly, Brian has a frame of reference that he is working from. The boy wanting to play with Brian looked like a girl, and boys don't play with girls. This example highlights the salience of gender and the role that it plays in social relationships from a very early age. Not only does gender restrict social relationships, but experience within this restricted social group has an impact on children's modes of interacting and the way in which they structure their peer group (Maccoby and Jacklin, in press). This chapter argues that researchers in the area of sociometric assessment must be sensitive to the impact of gender on the frame of reference that children use to evaluate peer behavior. Differences in the organization of boys' and girls' peer groups may be reflected in the criteria that they employ when asked to nominate friends or to rate peers in terms of their likability. The major aim of this

B. H. Schneider et al. (eds.), Social Competence in Developmental Perspective, 107–120.

chapter is to examine the organizational and normative context in which boys' and girls' sociometric assessments occur.

Sex Segregation in Boys' and Girls' Peer Groups

Preference for same-sex friendships from preschool (ages 3-5) throughout childhood and into adolescence has been noted by a number of researchers conducting observational studies of children's social relationships. For example, Lockheed and Klein (1985) reviewed 16 studies that document sex segregation in school settings among children ranging in age from preschool to fifth and sixth grade (ages 10-11). These studies consistently demonstrated that children begin to prefer same-sex playmates sometime during the third year of life but that girls may develop this preference somewhat earlier than boys. LaFreniere, Strayer, and Gauthier (1984) reported that by 27 months of age, girls attending day care were directing two-thirds of their affiliative behaviors -- such as smiles, approaches, affectionate touching, and social vocalizing -- toward other girls. This rate of same-sex interaction was found to remain constant for girls until 66 months. In comparison, boys at 28 months were not found to demonstrate same-sex preference; however, same-sex preference was increasingly evident at 36 and 48 months. By 66 months, boys directed 75% of their affiliative activity toward same-sex peers. Girls showed an initial spurt in their attraction to same-sex peers that did not increase in the later preschool years, whereas boys showed a later interest that continued to increase as a linear function of age.

The degree of gender segregation seems to be quite large even at young ages. Serbin, Tonick, and Sternglanz (1977) found that when preschool children were engaged in parallel play, the partner was twice as likely to be a same-sex as an opposite-sex child. For cooperative interaction, the disparity was even greater -- 4 to 1. Similarly, Luria and Herzog (1985) found that in nursery school (ages 3-5), two-thirds of the play was in the same-sex groups. In addition, they observed a higher degree of segregation (80% same-sex) on the school playground as opposed to in the classroom setting. Maccoby and Jacklin (in press) also found that nursery school children showed a substantial gender bias in their choice of playmates. Although, at this age, a good deal of time -- at least a third -- was spent in mixed-sex groups, it was still considerably more common to find a child playing with one or more same-sex children than with one or more opposite-sex children. Two years later, the gender bias was much more obvious. At this age, children were spending only about 6% of their social playtime in a pair or group having only opposite-sex others, and the occurrence of play in mixed groups had also declined.

In our own research (Daniels-Beirness & LeShano, 1988), we have found a high degree of sex segregation in eight-year-old children's social interactions outside of school. Over a one-week period during summer vacation, 100% of boys' friendship contacts were found to be with other boys; 82% of girls' contacts were with other girls.

Our findings contrast somewhat with those of Maccoby and Jacklin (in press), who found that the degree of same-sex bias was similar for preschool boys and girls. Our research suggests that girls in elementary school (age 8) may have more cross-sex relationships than boys do. It is unclear at the present time whether these differences reflect an age effect and/or a difference in setting.

Age effects have been reported by other researchers. For example, LaFreniere et al. (1984) found a similar degree of same-sex segregation for both boys and girls at 3 and 4 years of age. However, by 5½ years of age, they found that boys engaged in a significantly greater degree of same-sex segregation than did girls. Thus, Maccoby and Jacklin's (in press) finding that 4-year-old boys and girls did not differ in the degree of their preference for same-sex playmates and our finding that 8 year-old boys and girls do differ in the degree of their preference for same-sex playmates may both be valid if gender-based social preferences develop to differing degrees and at different ages in boys and girls. Further research of a longitudinal nature is needed to determine whether this is in fact the case.

The discrepancy in findings may also be a function of the setting in which children were observed. Gottman (1986) has made a strong argument for the role that setting may play in cross-sex friendships. He reports that cross-sex friendships are more common outside of school than within. He suggests that when children enter school, close cross-sex friendships are broken off or are maintained only at home. The effect of setting on sex segregation has also been reported by other researchers. Same-sex preference has been found to be more extreme on the school playground than in the classroom and to be more extreme in the absence of adults (Lockheed & Klein, 1985). In addition, gender segregation has been found to be greater in traditional school settings than in open-concept settings (Bianchi & Bakeman (1978). Because our study examined children's social relationships within their home environment and Maccoby and Jacklin (in press) observed peer interactions within a classroom setting, the differences noted may reflect, at least in part, setting differences. Girls, if more inclined to play with cross-sex peers, may find the home environment most conducive to, or least punitive of, such relationships. Further research on children's peer interaction in a variety of social environments is needed to address this issue.

Although Maccoby and Jacklin (in press) found no difference in the overall degree of sex bias shown by young boys and girls, they did find more variability among girls' same- and cross-sex preferences than among boys'. At 4 years of age, girls showed more intragroup differences in their preferences for same- versus cross-sex playmates than did boys.

In summary, preference for same-sex playmates manifests itself very early in children's lives, at least by age 3. The degree of this preference seems to increase with age. However, the degree of segregation does vary as a function of setting, with cross-sex friendships more common at home than at school. In addition, there is some evidence to suggest that the well-documented "same-sex peer preference" shown by boys and girls may not be equally endorsed by both sexes. It appears that girls may engage in more cross-sex interactions than do boys (although the large majority of their interactions are with same-sex peers) and that this difference may become evident by about 5 years of age. These findings suggest that social development and peer socialization should be examined separately, from the point of view of each sex. Further research of a longitudinal nature is needed to document the magnitude of same- versus cross-sex playmate preferences among boys and girls at various ages in order to address this issue adequately.

The Role of Sex Segregation in Sociometric Choice

An obvious question that one might ask at this point is, "How is sex segregation in children's social interactions reflected in their sociometric choices?" Indeed, same-sex biases in sociometric assessments have been noted by a number of researchers (Criswell, 1939; Hymel & Asher, 1977; Singleton & Asher, 1977, 1979). In general, the percentage of cross-sex friendship nominations made by children is small. In a cross-sectional sample of fourth through sixth graders (ages 10-12), Hallinan (1979) found that only 5% of children's best-friend nominations were cross-sex. In addition, Hallinan (1980) found no cross-sex members of boys' or girls' cliques at this age (clique membership was determined on the basis of unlimited best-friend nominations; each member of a clique chose and was chosen as a best

109

friend by two-thirds of the other members of the group). While some cross-sex friendship nominations were made at all grade levels, in no case were these dyadic friendships a part of the larger friendship network of the clique.

Not only do children select same-sex classmates when asked to complete sociometric measures, but this preference for same-sex peers has been found to increase with age. Gottman and Benson (1975, cited in Gottman, 1986) found that when unlimited best-friend nominations were solicited, 67% of kindergartners' (age 5), 68% of first graders' (age 6), 76% of third graders' (age 9) and 84% of fourth graders' (age 10) selections were same-sex. Hallinan (1979) found this preference for same-sex peers to continue and to become stronger at older ages. She found that 86% of fourth graders, 88% of fifth graders (age 11) and 94% of sixth graders (age 12) nominated same-sex peers on an unlimited-choice best-friend sociometric measure. Gottman and Benson (1975, cited in Gottman, 1986) also found that the number of reciprocal cross-sex best-friend choices dropped dramatically with age. Not only is there a tendency for children to report few cross-sex friendships, but there is also a tendency to nominate opposite-sex peers as negative choices. Asher and Hymel (1981) found that third- through fifth-grade children received, on average, 1.95 negative nominations from opposite-sex peers compared to 0.93 negative nominations from same-sex peers. These findings suggest that children's preferences for same-sex playmates, observed behaviorally both in school and at home, are reflected in their sociometric choices of friends.

Sociometric ratings of likability have also been found to be influenced by children's preference for same-sex peers. Asher and Hymel (1981) found that third- through fifth-grade children received much lower ratings of likability from cross-sex peers ($X=1.93$) than from same-sex peers ($X=3.58$). Similarly, Singleton and Asher (1977) reported cross-sex ratings ($X=2.09$) to be lower than same-sex ratings ($X=3.81$) for third-grade children, as did Singleton and Asher (1979) for third and sixth grade children (same-sex ratings: $X=3.91$ and 3.73 for third and sixth grade, respectively; cross-sex ratings: $X=2.11$ and 1.94 for third and sixth grade, respectively). Reese (1966) also reported cross-sex ratings at or below the neutral point on a five-point sociometric rating scale of likability for fifth- through eighth-grade (ages 11-14) children ($X=2.38, 2.97, 3.1,$ and 3.15 respectively for grades 5, 6, 7 and 8 [ages 11, 12, 13 and 14]). Although these ratings are higher (i.e., more positive) than those reported by Asher and his colleagues, it is difficult to determine whether these differences reflect an increase in cross-sex likability with age or are a function of the methodology and the sample employed. The number of same-sex nominations for Reese's sample was not reported, making it difficult to determine whether ratings of likability for this sample are inflated generally across same- and cross-sex peers or whether these higher likability scores represent an increase in cross-sex likability at older ages. Longitudinal research examining changes in the same- and cross-sex likability ratings of boys and girls over several years is needed to address this issue. In conclusion, there is clear evidence that same-sex playmate preferences are reflected in children's friendship sociometric choices and in their ratings of likability from kindergarten through eighth grade.

Given that girls may engage in more cross-sex peer interaction than boys do, the next question to ask is, "Do sociometric selections reflect more of a gender bias among boys than among girls?" On a sociometric rating scale of likability, Reese (1962, 1966) found that fifth-grade boys accepted girls significantly less than girls accepted boys ($X=2.08$ and 2.67 for boys and girls, respectively) but that in sixth and seventh grade, boys were more accepting of girls than girls were of boys ($X=3.05$ and 2.89 for sixth-grade boys and girls, respectively; $X=3.22$ and 2.98 for seventh-grade boys and girls, respectively). In grade 8, no difference between boys' and girls' cross-sex ratings was observed (X=3.15 and 3.14 for boys and girls, respectively). Singleton and Asher (1979) found that boys' cross-sex ratings were slightly higher than girls cross-sex ratings in third grade (X=2.21 and 2.01 for boys and girls, respectively) but that the differences were minimal in sixth grade (X=1.92 and 1.96 for boys and girls, respectively). Despite the statistical significance of Reese's findings, the magnitude of the differences is small and the differences cluster about the neutral point on the rating scale. Significance tests are not reported by Singleton and Asher; however, the differences are small enough that it is unlikely that they are statistically significant. It would appear, from an examination of these differences, that boys and girls have similar feelings toward opposite sex peers. They do not actively dislike each other; rather, they feel neutral toward opposite-sex peers or they do not have enough experience with them to make a judgment in terms of likability. Thus, cross-sex peer ratings cluster close to the middle or neutral point on the scale. It would also appear that the degree of cross-sex liking or disliking is similar for both sexes. Although there is some suggestion in the literature that boys show a stronger preference for same-sex playmates than girls do, this preference does not seem to be reflected in ratings of likability for cross-sex peers.

Given the strong evidence that children interact primarily with children of their own sex from kindergarten until early adolescence, and because this preference is reflected both in children's nominations of friends and in their ratings of likability, it has become the norm in sociometric research to use only same-sex peer nominations (Hymel & Asher, 1977; Oden & Asher, 1977). This procedure approach solves the problem of children's having little or no experience with cross-sex peers in that they are asked to make judgments only about children with whom they frequently interact. Asher and Hymel (1981) compared this procedure, which restricts choices to same-sex nominations and ratings, with the procedure that includes both same- and cross-sex nominations. They found that the majority of positive nominations came from same-sex peers (X=2.63 & 0.37 for same- and cross-sex peers respectively) and that the majority of negative nominations came from cross-sex peers (X=0.93 and 1.95 for same- and cross-sex peers, respectively). Children also received much lower ratings from cross-sex peers (X=1.93) than from same-sex peers (X=3.58). In addition to there being differences in the mean number of nominations received and in the mean ratings of likability, there also appeared to be differences in the distribution of scores depending upon whether same- or cross-sex peers are doing the nominating. The correlations between same- and cross-sex peer nominations and same- and cross-sex ratings are only moderate in magnitude (r=0.41 for positive nominations; r=0.54 for negative nominations; r=0.48 for play ratings). As the authors note, the small magnitude of these correlations suggests that boys and girls are using different standards or norms in their nominations and ratings of classmates.

In summary, gender segregation is reflected in children's sociometric choices. Children's preference for same-sex playmates is reflected in their choice of same-sex peers for friendship nominations. Cross-sex peers are more likely to be selected as those individuals with whom children would least like to spend time, play or work (negative nominations). Preference for same-sex playmates is also reflected in children's sociometric ratings of likability. Both boys and girls give likability ratings close to the middle or neutral point on the scale for cross-sex peers. Finally, there appears to be only a moderate relationship between same-sex and cross-sex sociometric nominations and ratings. This suggests that boys and girls are relying on different criteria when making their nominations and ratings. These findings argue for restricting sociometric nominations and ratings to same-sex peers. Evidence that both boys and girls use the middle point on the rating scale for cross-sex peers and give few positive or negative nominations to cross-sex peers suggests that cross-sex peers are, in general, a group that children have minimal experience with and little knowledge of. Finally, the fact that boys and girls may rely on different criteria in nominating peers as friends or giving likability ratings suggests that using scores based on input from both sexes may be ill advised.

The Internal Structure of Boys' and Girls' Peer Groups

It is now well established that somewhat different "cultures" develop in all-boy and all-girl peer groups (see Maccoby, 1986 for a review). Research suggests that all-female groups differ in terms of their internal structure from all-male groups. These studies indicate that boys and girls differ in the kinds of social experiences that they have rather than in the number or importance of their social interactions. There appear to be fundamental sex differences in the organization of boys' and girls' informal peer groups.

Intensivity of Boys' and Girls' Peer Groups

One of the most consistently documented differences between boys' and girls' peer groups is the size of the group. Research has consistently shown that by the time that children enter school, girls are interacting in groups of two or three, whereas boys are playing in large groups. For example, Laosa and Brophy (1972) found that girls 5 to 7 years of age played in pairs significantly more than boys, whereas boys played more frequently in groups of three or more. Based on similar findings in 7½-year-olds Waldrop and Halverson (1975) coined the phrases *intensive* and *extensive* to characterize these differences in girls' and boys' peer groups. Girls' almost exclusive contact with one or two best friends was characterized as intensive; boys' play in large groups was characterized as extensive. Waldrop and Halverson's use of this terminology has frequently led researchers to conclude that the friendships of girls and boys differ in intimacy and/or closeness. However, an examination of the findings indicates that this is not the case (see Gottman, 1986, for a discussion of this issue). Rather, the findings suggest that boys who are above average in extensiveness (as measured by ratings based on children's comments regarding such activities as playing ball or being on a playground and/or spending time outside with a group of children) are more socially at ease, spend more hours with peers, and are judged to find peers more important to them than boys who are below average in extensiveness. Girls who are above average in intensiveness (as measured by ratings based on frequent mentioning of a best friend, the mother speaking of the importance of this friend, and frequent interaction with this friend) are more socially at ease, spend more hours with peers, and are judged to find peers more important to them than girls who are below average in intensiveness. These findings do not suggest that girls' peer relationships are more intimate but rather that girls who are peer-oriented and highly social prefer frequent interactions with a single best friend. In comparison, boys who are peer-oriented and highly social prefer frequent interactions with groups of boys.

Similar findings have also been reported for older children. Omark, Omark, and Edglman (1975) found that boys 5 to 9 years of age tended to move about the school-yard in large swarms, whereas girls in that age range were found to play in groups of 2 or 3. Lever (1976, 1978) found that 11 year-old-boys and girls, although spending approximately the same amount of time alone (20%), differed in the size of their peer group when they were involved in social play. Observations during recess showed boys playing in much larger groups than girls. Boys were typically involved in team sports that required 10 to 25 or more participants. Girls were rarely observed playing in groups as large as 10. Girls more often engaged in activities that could be played with 2 or 3 participants. Girls reported being most comfortable in pairs, less so in triads, and least comfortable in groups of 4 or more. In addition, observations made on the school playground showed boys playing in much larger groups than girls to a far greater extent than they did at home (as measured by self-report in diaries). Whether this reflects an actual difference in play-group size as a function of setting or whether it reflects differences in the methods of data collection across the two settings is an empirical question still to be addressed.

Exclusivity of Boys' and Girls' Peer Groups

Not only do boys and girls differ in the size of their peer groups, but there is also evidence to suggest that boys' and girls' social relationships differ in terms of their exclusivity (Eder & Hallinan, 1978). That is, girls' dyadic friendships are more exclusive than boys dyadic friendships. Eder and Hallinan based this conclusion on information collected from 9- to 12-year-olds' unlimited best-friend sociometric choices collected at six-week intervals throughout the school year. The proportion of triads containing mutual best-friend dyads at a given point in time suggested that girls had more exclusive dyadic friendships than boys did. For example, in two of the classes observed, the average frequency of dyadic friendship was more than twice as great for girls as for boys. These differences in dyadic friendship were not found to be a function of the number of friendship choices made by boys and girls. There was no evidence of a tendency for one sex to make more friendship choices than the other. Instead, it is the structural organization of boys' and girls' friendship networks that differs, not the quantity of their peer contact.

Girls were also found to seek out dyadic friendships more frequently than boys did. When triadic friendships were not initially exclusive, there was a high probability that girls would establish a more exclusive dyadic friendship as the school year progressed (Eder & Hallinan, 1978). Boys' dyadic friendships were found to expand to include others over time. After contact with a third person, girls were more likely than boys to return to a mutual dyad. This was found to occur whether the newcomer initiated the contact or a member of the exclusive dyad initiated the contact. Boys more frequently than girls responded positively to a friendship offer from a third person. Feshbach and Sones (1971) reported similar findings for adolescents. In a study of seventh- and eighth-grade children, the reaction of established pairs of same-sex close friends (as determined by teachers and verified by the children) to a newcomer was examined. They found that girls judged newcomers less favorably than did boys, were less welcoming, and were more likely than boys to ignore the newcomer's bids to join the group. These findings suggest that girls do not form dense friendship triads over time but rather return to exclusive mutual dyads after contact with a third person. Boys' social networks on the other hand, become denser as they expand their dyadic friendships to include others. This finding is further supported by Berndt and Hoyle (1981, cited in Berndt, 1983), who found that girls who had many friends at the beginning of the school year tended to make fewer friends during the year than did other girls. The opposite was found to be true for boys.

Because of the exclusivity of girls' relationships, shifting alliances are more common among girls' groups than among boys' groups (Maccoby, 1986). Douvan and Adelson (1966) found that groups among girls were infrequent and that the ties that girls had to these larger groupings were not strong, frequently undergoing breaking and rejoining cycles. Savin-Williams (1980) found that in adolescence, girls were less likely than boys to form stable and consistent groups. Shapiro (1967, cited in Savin-Williams, 1980) found that

113

among 232 children 8-15 years old in a summer camp, girls' friendships were more prone to dissolution than boys' friendships. Girls tend to be most comfortable when they are with a single best friend, and because of their concern with the exclusivity of that relationship, jealousy may be more likely to arise than in boys' groups (Rubin, 1980), resulting in more disruption to social relationships. Rubin presents the following example of the emphasis that girls place on exclusive dyadic social relationships. Eleven-year-old Sarah reports: "Joan's now trying to hang around the older kids so as to be admitted into their gang so she has no time to be with Liz who therefore tries to be friends with Christine which doesn't please Sally" (p. 108). Here, we clearly see the emphasis that girls place on dyadic friendships. We see that Liz, who has lost her exclusive relationship with Joan, tries to establish a new relationship with Christine. This, however, presents a whole new problem for the peer group. Sally is threatened in her exclusive relationship with Christine because of Liz's bids for Christine's friendship. The most obvious solution -- for all three to be friends --is not considered. In this example, as is the case in general for girls, "Two's company, and three's a crowd."

Stability of Boys' and Girls' Peer Groups

Research suggests that in general, peer preferences remain stable over time (Hartup, 1970). Such stability characterizes both same-sex friendship choices (the particular peers that a child nominates as his or her friends) and same-sex peer acceptance (the status accorded the child by the group as a whole). Research suggests, however, that cross-sex friendships, when they do occur, are quite unstable. Gronlund (1955) conducted two sociometric surveys 4 months apart. Only 20% of the cross-sex friendship choices made on the first survey were also made on the second survey. In contrast, children's same-sex choices were about three times as stable (i.e., were more likely to be intact 4 months later).

Research examining between-group differences in the stability of boys' and girls' sociometric nominations has been reported infrequently and, when reported, almost always focuses on the stability of peer acceptance over time. Much less attention has been paid to the stability of boys' and girls' specific friendship choices over time. Three studies do provide some suggestion that stability of friendship choices may differ for boys and girls. Horrocks and Thompson (1946) and Thompson and Horrocks (1947) found no reliable sex differences in the friendship fluctuations of 905 rural and 969 urban children (ages 10-18) when they considered children's three best-friend nominations over a 2-week period. They did, however, find a greater tendency for girls than for boys to select the same person as their first-choice best friend across the 2-week interval. Speroff (1955), in a small study of kindergarten children, reported similar findings. Using most-like-to-play-with nominations, Speroff sociometrically tested a group of 11 kindergarten children (4 boys and 7 girls) every 2 weeks for a period of 10 weeks to determine the nature and extent of the stability of their nominations. Girls were found to be less variable (i.e., more stable) in their sociometric choices than were boys.

Although based on a small sample, these findings do raise questions as to the underlying basis of boys' and girls' selections on sociometric measures. Do these differences in the stability on sociometric measures reflect differences in stability of boys' and girls' friendships, or are they an artifact of the methodology? Because girls are more likely to conform, to engage in socially desirable behaviors, and to comply with adults (Block, 1976), are they more reluctant than boys to make changes in their sociometric choices? This question requires further research before it can be answered.

In summary, despite the lack of stability found in girls' groups, their best-friend relationships seem to be more stable than those of boys. Our own work (Daniels-Beirness & LeShano, 1988) provides some behavioral data to support this contention. We found that 8-year-old girls had known their best friends 1½ years longer than had boys.

Reciprocity of Boys' and Girls' Friendships

Reciprocity seems to be more important in girls' relationships than in boys' relationships. Girls have been found to make more reciprocal friendship nominations than boys, and their reciprocated friendships were found to be more stable (Epstein, 1983; Hansell, 1981; Karweit, 1976, cited in Karweit & Hansell, 1983). Peer groups in which all members are connected by reciprocal choices have also been found for girls but not for boys (Coleman, 1961). Cohen (1977), in a reanalysis of the sociometric data collected by Coleman (1961), found that cliques (defined as groups of four or more persons, each of whom is involved in a mutual-choice relationship with at least two other persons in the group) were three times as frequent for girls as for boys. Finally, girls with exclusive reciprocated friendships do not accept friendship bids from others, whereas boys do (Berndt, 1983).

The Role of Internal Group Structure in Sociometric Choice

In summary, there are clear differences in the size of boys' and girls' groups, in the exclusiveness of their friendships, in the stability of their friendships, and in the importance of reciprocity in their friendships. Girls' friendships are dyadic, intense, reciprocal, and exclusive. Their groups are less stable than are boys' groups but their best friendships are more stable. In comparison, boys have dense, inclusive friendship networks and are more likely to incorporate newcomers into the group rather than to shift alliances.

One of the major implications of these findings is that once these friendship patterns are formed, they promote further differential interaction patterns, leading, in turn, to the development of different kinds of social skills in boys and girls. In addition, the characteristics of the groups in which children participate will have implications for their sociometric choices by shaping the criteria that they rely on in making sociometric choices. For girls, the boundary between friends and nonfriends seems to be sharper than for boys (Berndt, 1983). Such a finding argues for unlimited sociometric choices rather than for the frequently used "3-best-friends" nomination sociometric. Limited-choice sociometrics presume that boys and girls use the same criteria and experiences as a basis for selecting their 3 best friends or the 3 people with whom they most like to work or play. Findings regarding the structure of boys' and girls' peer groups suggest that girls may have difficulty generating three best friends, because they prefer and spend the majority of their time in an exclusive dyadic relationship. In contrast, boys may have difficulty limiting their friendship choices to 3 because they have denser social networks, and this may become an increasing problem as the school year progresses. If forced to select 3 friends, girls may be selecting 1 best friend and 2 other girls with whom they play on occasion. In contrast, boys, if limited to 3 friendship choices, may be required to make arbitrary decisions in selecting three pals from a group of 4 to 10 with whom they frequently play.

Status Hierarchies in Boys' and Girls' Peer Groups

Status represents the linkage between an individual and larger social and organizational groups. Hartup (1970) has identified status as being essential to the development of groups. He suggests that: "It is not truly a group until leaders and followers have emerged or until labour has been divided in some way" (p. 370). Savin-Williams (1980) has suggested that the result of group formation is usually a hierarchical structure with status differentiations among group members. However, the nature of both boys' and girls' peer group organization must be considered in order to determine whether one or both groups conform to this notion of hierarchical structure.

Research suggests that social interaction among boys tends to be oriented around issues of dominance and the formation of a pecking order (Maccoby & Jacklin, in press). Boys' groups are more likely to have a specific leader, and leadership is more likely to take the form of issuing commands. For girls, leadership tends to involve making suggestions and initiating or organizing the group's activities, and all group members participate more in the decision process than in boys' groups. There is also some suggestion in the literature that girls are aware of whom the leaders are but have no such awareness of a series of ordered positions beyond the first (Dunphy, 1969; Gordon, 1957; Jennings, 1950; Sherif, Kelly, Rodgers, Sarup, & Tittler, 1973). While relatively little can be stated with certainty concerning the total structure of girls' peer networks, it seems that girls may have little awareness of status hierarchies beyond the broad categories of leaders and followers (Savin-Williams, 1980).

These differences in the organization of boys' and girls' peer groups are reflected in the type of play in which they engage. Boys play competitive games more often than girls do. Lever (1976) found that 65% of the play activities of fifth-grade boys were formal games (i.e., competitive interactions governed by a set of rules and aimed at achieving an explicit, known goal), as compared to 35% of girls' activities. Girls were more likely to play turn-taking games in which there was little role differentiation (e.g., jumping rope) and minimal competition.

Additional evidence to support the hypothesis that status is more salient to the formation of male relationships than it is to the formation of female relationships is found in the work of Karweit and Hansell (1983). A sample of 20,345 high school students (ages 14-18) was asked to make same-sex nominations in answer to the question "Of the boys/girls in this school who do you go around with most?" Four lines were provided for students to name their friends, but no limit was put on the number of friends to be named. Status criteria such as college plans, curricular track, father's education, father's occupation, and a school status index consisting of 16 items that gauged the student's position in the school's informal social system were then determined for each student. It was hypothesized that if status were more salient to the formation of male relationships than female relationships, then males would exceed females in the number of unreciprocated choices made from lower- to higher-status peers. The results of this study confirmed a fundamental sex difference in the organization of informal friendship networks. Males more frequently chose as unreciprocated friends individuals of higher status, while girls more frequently chose unreciprocated friends of similar status.

This tendency for boys to select higher-status peers as those with whom they would like to be friends provides some evidence that the importance of status differs for boys and girls. Males may use friendships for status acquisition and maintenance more than do females. Karweit and Hansell (1983) speculate that male networks are more elaborated in the vertical status dimension, whereas female networks are developed in the horizontal dimension. Further research is needed to clarify whether there are indeed differences in the way boys and girls structure their social networks.

6. Measuring Peer Status

The Role of Status Hierarchies in Sociometric Choices

Maccoby and Jacklin (in press) raise several issues related to differences in the way boys and girls structure their social networks. They question whether members of all-boy and all-girl play groups make finer distinctions among themselves than they do with respect to the gender out-group. Research has shown that within each sex, there is fairly good agreement as to the dominance hierarchy, although agreement is greater within boys' groups (Omark, Omark, & Edelman, 1975). These authors also question whether boys have a clearer picture of male hierarchy than do girls -- whether girls, in effect, homogenize boys and ignore distinctions among them that are salient to the boys themselves. This is a very likely hypothesis if one considers the differences in the ways in which boys and girls are believed to organize their own peer groups. Since girls do not appear to structure their peer groups on the basis of status, while boys do, it seems likely that asking girls about boys' peer groups would result in girls examining or evaluating boys' peer groups from a horizontally structured orientation. In scoring sociometric choices, the assumption is made that social relationships (both boys' and girls') are rank-ordered from the highest to the lowest position. If this is not the case for both sexes, then boys and girls may be relying on very different criteria in completing this task. Evidence to support such a hypothesis comes from the work of Asher and Hymel (1981). They have demonstrated that the correlations between sociometric scores of same-sex and cross-sex ratees are only moderate (r=0.41, 0.54 and 0.48 for positive nominations, negative nominations, and play ratings, respectively). The lack of a strong correlation between same-and cross-sex ratees' determination of the peer groups' status hierarchy indicates that girls and boys do indeed see their social world differently, and this finding has serious implications for the administration and use of sociometric measures.

A common practice, in the use of sociometric assessments, is to collect same-sex nominations or ratings, calculate each child's sociometric scores, and then rank-order all the children (boys and girls together) from the highest to the lowest on the basis of these scores. Criterion cut off scores are then imposed (often one standard deviation from the mean is used) to identify those who are at the extremes in terms of the number of positive and negative nominations that they received. This procedure makes the assumption that although boys and girls may not be aware of the status hierarchies of their cross-sex peers (hence, the need for same-sex nominations or ratings), they are utilizing the same criteria in nominating or rating their peers. On the basis of this assumption, girls and boys are lumped together, and the same criterion is imposed for both in identifying extreme groups.

The findings reviewed above would argue against making such an assumption. The horizontal nature of girls' peer groups, in comparison to the hierarchical nature of boys' groups, suggests that the concept of "status" is not the same for these two groups. If this is the case, peer status should be determined separately for boys and girls. In addition, separate criteria may need to be employed for the identification of extreme groups. Support for such an argument comes from the findings of Coie, Dodge, and Coppotelli (1982) as well as others (e.g., Rutter, 1976) who find that boys are more likely to be identified in the extreme groups (i.e., rejected) than are girls using a one-standard-deviation cut off score.

Although this procedure may, in part, solve the problem, there is an underlying theoretical issue that must still be addressed. If girls' groups are not structured hierarchically, does it make any sense conceptually to rank-order girls in terms of the number of positive and negative nominations that they receive and to identify girls at the extremes of the continuum? These girls may not differ dramatically from girls identified as falling in the middle of the continuum. Consistent with this argument is the finding that boys are more frequently found in extreme groups than are girls using the criterion cut off presently employed. Is this a function of forcing girls' sociometric nominations to fit a model that does not reflect the structure of their peer group? Are we indeed trying to add apples and oranges?

Moving to differential criterion cut off scores may be useful. However, the whole idea of extreme groups in girls' must be examined empirically. Much research has been devoted to studying girls' best friends, but little is known about girls' relationships at the lower end of the continuum. Some studies suggest that although girls do not perceive their peer group to be ordered hierarchically, they are able to identify girls at the extremes of the continuum (Savin-Williams, 1980). If this is the case, then the use of sociometric procedures as they are presently employed may be appropriate for girls if externally valid criterion cut off scores can be established for this population. However, until girls' social relationships are more clearly understood within a normative context, many questions about the use of sociometric procedures remain unanswered.

Conclusions

In this chapter, I have reviewed some of the varied and diverse findings with regard to the organization and structure of boys' and girls' peer groups. Throughout the literature, there is clear evidence that boys' and girls' peer relationships are sex-segregated from a very early age and that the structure of these all-boy and all-girl groups differs in terms of intensivity, exclusivity, stability, reciprocity, and hierarchical organization. Boys play in large, hierarchically structured groups; they have dense friendship networks; and they are open to the development of new friendships. Girls, on the other hand, play predominately in dyads; they have one-to-one, closed, reciprocal relationships. Their social networks are structured horizontally and based on equality. These differences in social structure suggest that the criteria on which boys and girls rely in making sociometric assessments may differ considerably.

The present chapter suggests that the use of same-sex nominations and the use of unlimited nominations may help to reduce these differences across male and female raters. In addition, peer status should be determined separately for boys and girls, and separate criteria for the identification of extreme groups should be employed in order to address the fundamental differences found in girls' and boys' peer groups.

The points discussed in this chapter highlight the fact that sociometric assessments are just heuristic devices for studying social adaptation (Asher & Dodge, in press). The groups defined by sociometric criteria are not discrete entities. Rather, they reflect arbitrary decisions and have been artificially imposed upon the children being studied. As such, we as researchers must carefully examine what we are asking children to do and we must carefully consider whether children are in fact doing what we believe they are doing.

References

Asher, S.R., & Dodge, K.A. (in press). Identifying children who are rejected by their peers. *Developmental Psychology.*

Asher, S.R., & Hymel, S. (1981). Children's social competence in peer relations: Sociometric and behavioral assessment (pp. 125-157). In J.D. Wine & M.D. Smye (Eds.), *Social competence.* New York: Guilford Press.

Berndt, T.J. (1983). Social cognition, social behavior, and children's friendships. In E.T. Higgins, D.N. Ruble, & W.W. Hartup (Eds.), *Social cognition and social development: A sociocultural perspective.* Cambridge, United Kingdom: Cambridge University Press.

6. Measuring Peer Status

Bianchi, B., & Bakeman, R. (1978). Sex-typed affiliation preferences observed in preschoolers; Traditional and open school differences. *Child Development, 49*, 910-912.

Block, J.H. (1976). Issues, problems and pitfalls in assessing sex differences: A critical review of "The Psychology of Sex Differences" *Merrill-Palmer Quarterly, 22*, 285-308.

Cohen, J.M. (1977). Sources of peer group homogeneity. *Sociology of Education, 50*, 227-241.

Coie, J.D., Dodge, K.A., & Coppotelli, H. (1982). Dimensions and types of social status: A cross-age perspective. *Developmental Psychology, 18*, 557-570.

Coleman, J.S. (1961). *The adolescent society.* New York; Free Press.

Criswell, J.H. (1939). A sociometric study of race cleavage in the classroom. *Archives of Psychology*, 1-82.

Daniels-Beirness, T.M., & LeShano, S. (1988, July). Children's social relationships outside of school. Paper presented at the NATO Advanced Study Institute: Social Competence in Developmental Perspective, Savoy, France.

Douvan, E., & Adelson, J. (1966). *The adolescent experience.* New York: Wiley.

Dunphy, D.C. (1969). *Cliques, crowds and gangs.* Melbourne, Australia: Cheshire.

Eder, D., & Hallinan, M.T. (1978). Sex differences in children's friendships. *American Sociological Review, 13*, 237-250.

Epstein, J. (1983). Friends among students in schools: Environmental and developmental factors. In J. Epstein and N. Karweit (Eds.), *Friends in school: Patterns in selection and influence in secondary schools* (pp. 3-18). New York: Academic Press.

Feschbach, N., & Sones, G. (1971). Sex differences in adolescent reactions toward newcomers. *Developmental Psychology, 4*, 381-386.

Gordon, W. (1957). *The social system of the high school.* Glencoe, II: Free Press.

Gottman, J.M. (1986). The world of coordinated play: Same- and cross-sex friendship in young children. In J.M. Gottman & J.G. Parker (Eds.), *Conversations of friends. Speculations on affective development* (pp. 139-191). Cambridge, United Kingdom: Cambridge University Press.

Gronlund, N.E. (1955). The relative stability of classroom social status with unweighted and weighted sociometric choices. *Journal of Educational Psychology, 46*, 345-354.

Hallinan, M.T. (1979). Structural effects on children's friendships and cliques. *Social Psychology Quarterly, 42*, 43-54.

Hallinan, M.T. (1980). Patterns of cliquing among youth. In H.C. Foot, A.J. Chapman & J.R. Smith (Eds.), *Friendship and social relations in children* (pp. 321-343). New York: Wiley.

Hansell, S. (1981). Ego development and adolescent social networks. *Sociology of Education, 54*, 51-63.

Hartup, W.W. (1970). Peer interaction and social organization. In P.H. Mussen (Ed.), *Carmichael's manual of child psychology* (Vol. 2, pp. 361-456) New York: Wiley.

Horrocks, J.E., & Thomson, G.G. (1946). A study of the friendship fluctuations of rural boys and girls. *Journal of Genetic Psychology, 69*, 189-198.

Hymel, S., & Asher, S.R. (1977). Assessment and training of isolated children's social skills. Paper presented at the biennial meeting of the Society for Research in Child Development, New Orleans.

Jennings, H.H. (1950). *Leadership and isolation* (2nd ed.). New York: Longmans, Green.

Karweit, N. & Hansell, S. (1983). Sex differences in adolescent relationships: Friendship and status. In J. Epsetein & N. Karweit (Eds.), *Friends in school: Patterns in selection and influence in secondary schools* (pp. 115-130) New York: Academic Press.

LaFreniere, P., Strayer, F.F., & Gauthier, R. (1984). The emergence of same-sex affiliative preferences among preschool peers: A developmental/ethological perspective. *Child Development, 55*, 1958-1965.

Laosa, L.M., & Brophy, J.E. (1972). Effects of sex and birth order on sex-role development and intelligence among kindergarten children. *Developmental Psychology, 6*, 409-415.

Lever, J. (1976). Sex differences in the games children play. *Social Problems, 23*, 478-487.

Lever, J. (1978). Sex differences in the complexity of children's play. *American Sociological Review, 43*, 471-483.

Lockheed, M., & Klein, S. (1985). Sex equality in classroom organization and climate. In S. Klein (Ed.), *Handbook for achieving sex equality through education* (pp. 263-284). Baltimore: Johns Hopkins University Press.

Luria, Z., & Herzog, E. (1985). Gender segregation across and within settings. Paper presented at the biennial meeting of the Society for Research in Child Development, Toronto, Ontario, Canada.

Maccoby, E.E. (1986). Social groupings in childhood: Their relationship to prosocial and antisocial behavior in boys and girls. In D. Olweus, J. Block, & M. Radke-Yarrow (Eds.), *Development of antisocial and prosocial behavior: Research, theories, and issues* (pp. 263-284). San Diego: Academic Press.

Maccoby, E.E., & Jacklin, C.N. (in press). Gender segregation in childhood. In H. Reese (Ed.), *Advances in child behavior and development.*

Oden, S., & Asher, S.R. (1977). Coaching children in social skills for friendship making. *Child Development, 48,* 495-506.

Omark, D.R., Omark, M., & Edelman, M.S. (1975). Formation of dominance hierarchies in young children: Action and perception. In T. Williams (Ed.), *Psychological anthropology* (pp. 289-315). The Hague: Mouton.

Reese, H.W. (1962). Sociometric choices of the same and opposite sex children in late childhood. *Merrill-Palmer Quarterly, 8,* 173-174.

Reese, H.W. (1966). Attitudes toward the opposite sex in late childhood. *Merrill-Palmer Quarterly, 12,* 157-163.

Rubin, Z. (1980). *Children's friendships.* Cambridge, MA: Harvard University Press.

Rutter, M. (1976). *Helping troubled children.* London: Plenum Press.

Savin-Williams, R.C. (1980). Social interactions of adolescent females in natural groups. In H.C. Foot, A.J. Chapman, & J.R. Smith (Eds.), *Friendship and social relations in children* (pp. 343-363). New York: Wiley.

Serbin, L.A., Tonick, I.J., & Sternglanz, S.H. (1977). Shaping cooperative cross-sex play. *Child Development, 48,* 924-929.

Sherif, C.W., Kelly, M., Rodgers, H.L., Jr., Sarup, G., & Tittler, B.I. (1973). Personal involvement, social judgement and action. *Journal of Personality and Social Psychology, 27,* 311-328.

Singleton, L.C., & Asher, S.R. (1977). Peer preferences and social interaction among third-grade children in an integrated school district. *Journal of Educational Psychology, 69,* 330-336.

Singleton, L.C., & Asher, S.R. (1979). Racial integration and children's peer preferences: An investigation of developmental and cohort differences. *Child Development, 50,* 936-941.

Speroff, B.J. (1955). The stability of sociometric choice among kindergarten children. *Sociometry, 18,* 129-131.

Thompson, G.G., & Horrocks, J.E. (1947). A study of the friendship fluctuations of urban boys and girls. *The Journal of Genetic Psychology, 70,* 53-63.

Waldrop, M.F., & Halverson, C.F. (1975). Intensive and extensive peer behavior: Longitudinal and cross-sectional analyses. *Child Development, 46,* 19-26.

Section II

The Emergence of Social Competence In Early Childhood

Introduction to Section II

Jacqueline Nadel

Many basic issues regarding the emergence of social competence in early childhood remain wide open to debate, especially the selection of relevant models and methods. Indeed, the origin of social competencies is one of the most controversial in the field of early development. Are social relations the prime mover of cognitive development? Or, conversely, are social relations a mere secondary manifestation of cognitive prerequisities? Is the interpresonal environment the teacher that that engenders the progressive appearance of social competencies? Or are these competencies subject to the child's initiative, implying that children are endowed with the means to select the sources of stimulation that will facilitate their evolution? Or should we postulate a subtle balance among forces not fully understood, with whatever the environment elicits and stimulates in the young organism's social functioning, whatever social stimuli the environment provides for the youngster to process, placed on one side of the scale? On the other side is whatever is elicited by the child acting on the environment and the social stimuli generated by the child for the environment to process.

F. F. Strayer expounds a psychobiological model of social development, inspired by the heuristic distinction between experience-dependent and experience-expectant development, which was introduced by Greenough, Block and Wallace (1987). In his model, Strayer seeks to account for the regularities in development across the species as well as phenotypic variations in development. Within this framework, he focuses on the impact of early experiences on the emergence of individual differences in social adaptation. He traces the continuities and discontinuities in the behaviors and social status of young children over a two-year period within a stable peer group. Therby, he brings a substantial data base to his hypothesis, which he recognizes as provocative, that the ontogenesis of cognitive and affective functions is dependent upon initiative deployed by the organism to maximize interaction with social partners. This interaction paves the way for optimal use of behavioral resources available at that point in time.

My own contribution (Chapter 7) is related to Strayer's in basic purpose and scope. It includes not only an examination of behavioral features that represent steady forward progression in development, but also some attention to behaviors which have a particular function at a given period that is temporary and disappears afterwards. "Experience-expectant" development must be at least partially governed by these transitory adaptive mechanisms. This point of view is underscored by hypothesizing that social factors may be primary but transitory. Imitation processes should play a temporary but decisive role in determining subsequent cognitive development, because they constitute an elementary means for the young child to actively control his/her physical human environment and to engage in learning based on the synchronization of activities. A comparative approach involving language-endowed and autistic children in undertaken within this framework.

B. H. Schneider et al. (eds.), Social Competence in Developmental Perspective, 123–125.
© *1989 by Kluwer Academic Publishers.*

Methodological issues

The choice of research methods, the search for the best descriptors of social development, is the second area of heated debate within the field. None of the five contributions to Section Two is concerned with asymmetric social interactions, such as those between adults and infants. While there was no intent to exclude contexts other than peer systems, one might point out that exchanges between partners of the same functional level surely permit a sharper distinction between experience-dependent and experience-expectant development. This is because asymmetric social situations promote response to stimulation much more than active searching for stimulation. To be less sketchy, I would point out that the focus on early child-child interaction remains constant throughout Section Two, which facilitates the comparison of findings across diverse experimental settings and and divergent operational criteria. Strayer's chapter is devoted to the beginnings of social competence as observed in relatively large collective group settings, whereas in two other chapters (Baudonnière et al., Nadel & Fontaine), the conclusions are supported by data obtained in quasi-experimental situations involving dyads paired by the experimenters. Carollee Howes' methods fall somewhere between these two extremes, since they combine such indirect measures of social behavior, such as sociometrics, with behavioral measures useful in directly distinguishing dyads of friends from other types of dyad.

Pierre-Marie Baudonnière points out several shortcomings of children's everyday large-group environments as suitable seetings for the exploration of social competence. He reminds us that each setting is a micro-culture which bears the imprint of many exogenous influences whose effects are not easily delineated when one appreciates the marked differences from one setting to the next. Therefore, the ecological validity of the findings obtained may turn out to be no greater than in an experiment where at least some impinging variables can be controlled. His own methodological decision has been to use experimental procedures in which the choice of dyadic composition, as well as the location and conditions of the dyadic encounter, are varied. Three degrees of familiarity between children are systematically compared in his studies: unknown partner, previous acquaintance and friend. Under similar coniditions of encounter, and at comparable age levels, Baudonnière demonstrates the importance of such parameters as orientation of gaze, physical proximity, imitation--as measured by common use of identical objects--and verbalizations in discriminating the interpersonal communication that typifies exchanges between partners of each degree of familiarity. He then draws implications for social competence.

Carollee Howes shares Baudonnière's interest in friendship as a measure of early social competence. Her observations herein are based on a three-year longitudinal study using large cross-sectional samples of children, initially aged 16 through 33 months, who belong to stable peer groups. Diverse methods were used, but a remarkable concordance among them emerged in the end. These included such indirect sources of information as teachers and peers and direct behavioral observation, as discussed above. Among these measures was, physical proximity to friends in a dyadic situation, also used by Baudonnière. It is encouraging to note the convergence between findings relevant to the same indicator obtained in situ and in an experimental situation. I am also heartened by Strayer's findings with regard to the importance of imitation processes for group cohesion at the same ages at which imitation seems to play an important role in peer communication according to our own results. Thus, there are some promising signs of consensus.

An ecologically-valid knowledge base in child development can be constructed from components which reflect diverse heuristic and methodological options. We must remind ourselves of McCall's (1977) challenge, still highly pertinent though it is ten years old: Even if experimental procedures allow us to answer the "can questions" (i. e. "Can Factor X under certain circumstances produce or affect Behavior Y?"), we cannot extend the findings to "does questions" ("Does Factor X, under typical life circumstances produce or affect Behavior Y?"). To overcome these limitations, we have developed, in our own work with Pierre-Marie Baudonnière, open-ended controlled procedures which permit us to observe, by invisible camera, the types of information children seek from, and provide to, their social and physical environment, as well as how they elicit stimulation and respond to it. We study these phenomena on the basis of the children's own behavioral choices, uninfluenced by daily routines, the presence of adults, or instructions to the child. By these methods, we hope to come closer to the "does questions". Nevertheless, we must square our findings with those obtained naturalistically in various micro-cultures (family, school-- see Section IV of this volume) that give direction to behaviour and contribute to its cause, if we hope to avoid the emergence of two separate types of validity devoid of mutual contact. As McCall claims: If a laboratory study demonstrates that under certain conditions X can lead to Y, if there is a relationship between X and Y in naturalistic settings, if X can be imposed in a naturalistic or quasi-naturalistic environment and it leads to Y, then several observations coalesce on the tentative proposition that X does cause Y in naturalistic circumstances. Each approach is inadequate by itself, but each makes a vital contribution to the conclusion (p. 336)". Surely, this is the goal envisaged by all contributions which collectively help to elucidate the developmental perspective on social competence.

References

Greenough, W., Black, J., & Wallace, C. (1987). Experience and brain development. *Child Development, 58,* 539-559.

McCall, R. (1977). Challenges to a science of developmental psychology. *Child Development, 48,* 333-344.

Friendships in Very Young Children: Definition and Functions

Carollee Howes

University of California at Los Angeles

The problem and setting

Increasing numbers of infants and toddlers have daily and intimate contact with a stable peer group. These experiences occur in child care centers, family day care homes and in informal play groups. I see these groups as an excellent opportunity to study early affiliative relationships within the peer as opposed to the adult-child social system. The purpose of this conversational hour was first to discuss how to define and identify early friendships and then to explore the functions of early friendships.

Definitions of friendship

In my work I now define friendships using two criteria: reciprocity and affect (Howes, in press). The reciprocal nature of friendships helps distinguish them from measures of popularity. Each child must select the other as a friend. The affective criteria for friendship means that children like adult friends enjoy each other's company. Friendships are a context for the display of affect, both positive and negative.

Developmental issues

In my work I have assumed that the definition of friendship across developmental periods is constant. For infants, toddlers, children, and adults a friendship consists of a reciprocated affective bond. I also assume that an infant has the necessary cognitive and emotional prerequites for forming such a bond if they can form attachments with adults. Thus I expect, all else being equal, that friendships between children should emerge at approximately one year. All else is not always equal, young friendships appear only to be possible under some very specific social and cultural conditions. These include regular and consistent contact with at least one other child of approximately the same age. I suspect that the social and cultural conditions also include a both sufficiently secure relationship with the adult caregiver to permit exploration of peer relations and sufficient time away from adults and from adult attention to engage freely with peers.

I also assume that there are developmental changes in friendships. For example toddlers rarely engage in harmonious and complex play with nonfriends while preschoolers

B. H. Schneider et al. (eds.), Social Competence in Developmental Perspective, 127–129.

regularly play rather skillfully with children who are not friends. I have developed a model of developmental changes in friendships between infancy and preschool. This model has been validated with a cross-sectional sample but not yet with a longitudinal (Howes, 1983). In infancy children may have preferred partners but not yet friendships. In the early toddler period (13-24 months) the child may have one to two friendships which remain stable across time. The stability of these friendships is tied to the toddler's reliance on ritualistic action based social interaction. In the late toddler period (25-36 months) children have greater abilities to communicate and thus more flexibility in friendships. The number of friends increases and the child has both short and long term friends. By preschool (3-5 years) children differentiate friends from playmates so that friends become the way that children construct the social fabric of the group. Children base entry to play groups on friendship status, gossip about friends, and reliably complete sociometric assessments.

Functions of friendship

Children's friendships can fill several functions including companionship, access to play groups, self-comparison and fun. I have focused on the function of friendships for providing children with emotional security. To investigate this function I have examined friendship maintenance and separation from friends.

Sample. To explore these issues I have been working with a sample of over 300 children between the ages of 13 months and 6 years. All of these children were enrolled full time in center based child care of varying quality. The sample is ethnically mixed and included children of working and professional class parents. Forty-one of the children were seen for three years, as early toddlers, late toddlers, and preschoolers and 223 children distributed across all three periods were seen for two years.

Measures and procedures. The children were observed in their child care centers, and were assessed by their teachers, and as preschoolers by sociometric interviews (Howes, in press). Friendships were identified behaviorally (children had to be within three feet of each other at least 30% of the observation period and had to express shared positive affect while playing together), by teacher nominations, and by reciprocated sociometric nomination. There was high agreememt between these three methods.

Keeping friends. Children tended to maintain friendships. Two thousand five hundred and seventy-six dyads remained in stable peer groups over either two or three years. The friendships status of the dyad (reciprocal, unilateral, or nonfriend) tended to remain stable over the two year period but not over three years.

Separation from friends. Most children lost a friend over the course of the study primarily because the child's parents changed child care centers or because the friend was moved to a different room within the center. Most children also kept a friend and ended a friendship even though the friend remained in the peer group. For each child who remained in a stable peer group I computed the proportion of friendships kept, ended, or lost. I then correlated these proportions with measures of the child's social skill, sociometric and teacher ratings in subsequent years. Children who kept a higher proportion of friendships were observed to be more socially skilled, and had higher positive sociometric and teacher ratings. Children who ended a higher proportion of friendships had lower sociometric ratings and higher teacher ratings of difficulty with peers. Children who lost a higher proportion of their friends were rated by teachers as more hesitant with peers and were observed to engage in less social pretend play.

These data while not conclusive do suggest that one function of early friendships is emotional security. The friend may provide the child with the security to explore and develop positive social skills and relationships.

References

Howes, C. (1989). Peer interaction of young children. Monographs of the *Society for Research in Child Development*, #217, Vol. 53, no. 1.
Howes, C. (1983) Patterns of friendship. *Child Development, 54*, 1041-1053.

7

Communicating by Imitation: A Developmental and Comparative Approach to Transitory Social Competence

Jacqueline Nadel and Anne-Marie Fontaine

Laboratoire de Psychobiologie de l'Enfant, Paris

The primary research activities of our team at the Laboratoire de Psychobiologie de l'Enfant in Paris involve the development of social communication during the first 3 to 4 years of life. We have focused on what might be called the hidden face of early social competence. More precisely, we have been involved in the functional analysis of transitory adaptation -- the examination of behavior that either declines or disappears during the early stages of development.

These decreasing or disappearing behaviors serve as the means by which adaptive functions such as social adjustment or communication can be elicited and maintained before more mature expressions develop. These transitory means, however, should not be regarded as precursors. To some extent, they are the opposite of precursors because they do not imply structural continuity. They permit a function to be actualized or to play its adaptive role. They are markers of current internal capacities that are adjusted to the external conditions for their actualization.

We believe that some things about ontogenetic processes can only be learned by studying these specific transitory adaptations, insofar as such studies take into account two principal aspects of the basic controversy concerning continuity versus discontinuity in development. The first aspect is that different behavioral outputs may be functionally equivalent but may nonetheless be indicative of different underlying processes and different developmental stages. The second aspect is that similar behavioral outputs may serve entirely different functions depending on a child's age.

The field of social adaptation is highly relevant to this perspective. It requires 3 full years before children master basic verbal communication skills and the elementary conventional rules of social relationships. Nevertheless, at a far earlier age, they display some capacity to initiate or maintain interaction with others, which can be considered an early form of social competence. Furthermore, they express wants and needs; this can be considered a manifestation of the adaptive function of communication.

B. H. Schneider et al. (eds.), Social Competence in Developmental Perspective, 131–144.
© 1989 by Kluwer Academic Publishers.

According to our theoretical model, before speech is mastered, successive transitory systems of socially sustained exchanges play a predominant role in communication between peers. The emotional system emerges first, followed by the imitative system, and finally the cooperative system. We postulate that these transitory prelinguistic communication systems have two main properties in common. First, they depend on the physical and social features of the immediate environment for "here and now" mediators. Therefore, it is very important to identify the features that are determining factors in peer communication at various ages. Second, the successive transitory systems display the imprint of emotional exchange because emotion is the only available source of information in prelinguistic sustained interactions.

Continuing developments in communication would foster progressive autonomy with respect to the physical, social, and emotional context. On the one hand, the development of social competence permits progressive contextual independence and, in particular, autonomy from attachment figures; an ability to deal with unfamiliarity; and a capacity to interact with multiple partners. On the other hand, the development of competence is due to cognitive changes that enable symbolic behaviors to be mastered, permitting autonomy from "here and now" mediators.

We will discuss this theoretical model within the framework of two specific studies. The first is a developmental investigation involving the manipulation of different environmental conditions that promote or weaken peer-peer social exchanges during the 3rd and 4th years of life. The other project involves a comparative approach to the study of autistic children as an illustration of a psychobiological model of social incompetence.

An ecological approach that stresses the influence of spatial and sociospatial conditions on the occurrence of peer interactions in group settings and utilizes the same framework is presented by Alain Legendre (elsewhere in this book). In proposing conceptual links between physical or social conditions and transitory systems of communication, our methodological choice is to manipulate the external conditions in order to ascertain which manipulations will strengthen or weaken the operating communicative system.

Transitory Social Adaptation from a Developmental Perspective

A consequence of the widespread tendency to focus exclusively on emerging behaviors is that behaviors have been selected for study because of their supposed developmental significance rather than because of their functional role in present levels of adaptation. As a result, part of the behavioral repertoire has been overlooked by developmental psychologists. Synchronized imitation is one of the behaviors that research has neglected. Our view, influenced by the French Darwinian developmental psychologist Henri Wallon (1934), is that imitation is one of the cornerstones of ontogenesis, especially with respect to the development of communication (Nadel, 1980, 1986a, 1987).

This proposal is linked to the following theoretical framework. The genesis of social competence does not consist of a progression from lack of interest in social objects and social events to increasing cognitive capacities to take others' points of view into account. The genesis of social competence is more aptly described in terms of qualitative transformations rather than in terms of quantitative increases in social outcomes. This view agrees with current trends documented by Brazelton and colleagues (see, for instance, Brazelton, Koslowski, & Main, 1974) and particularly by Trevarthen and Hubley (1978).

According to Wallon (1934), these changes are linked to stages of individuation of the self. Wallon's theory describes three fundamental stages in the differentiation of the self and in the associated modes of interaction. The stage of *affective mimicry*, beginning at

6 months, is characterized by immediate coping with emotional expression, which permits the sharing of common feeling states. Therefore, mutual imitation (referred to as "mimetism") between mothers and infants during the 1st year functions primarily to establish a symbiotic affective bond. The developmental objective of this emotional matching is not acquisitive but instead involves the incorporation of, or complete identification with, the model. While serving the purpose of incorporation, repetition also facilitates the process of active distinction. By 15 months of age, toddlers become capable of *minimal distancing*, in the sense of attributing their own personal motives to the other's behavior. This is concomitant with the appearance of *sympathy* which is expressed by selective emotional imitation of the partner and must be differentiated from an incorporation of the partner's state. At the beginning of the 3rd year, *true co-construction emerges*. Children of this age are aware of the differentiation between their own and others' motives and emotional states. This resolves the paradox of dualism and emotional "sharing" in synchronous instrumental imitation. As we understand it, noninduced synchronous imitation is a central social behavior whose evolving function as a mediator of interpersonal exchange is intermeshed with progressive individuation of the self. (We are indebted to E. Moss and F. Strayer [1988], Laboratory of Human Ethology, UQAM, Montreal, for a comprehensive summary of our view in *Contemporary Psychology*).

In order to take this evolving function into account, it is necessary to distinguish immediate imitation from delayed imitation, to distinguish induced imitation from selective imitation (Yando, Seitz, & Zigler, 1978), and to replace the traditional expert-novice dyad with a symmetric pairing. Within this framework, reciprocal immediate imitation should convey a sense of shared identity and constitute a medium through which the young child actively differentiates the self from others. Our hypothesis is that synchronous imitation should allow the child to play an active role in the passage from symbiotic relational modes to the attainment of complete individuation.

At the beginning of our work with Baudonniere in 1979, this role of immediate imitation in the development of prelinguistic peer relations had not been studied, although Maratos (1973) and Pawlby (1977) had documented its social function in infant-mother dyads. Since 1979, Uzgiris (1981; Uzgiris & Kruper, in press) has pointed out the communicative function of imitation in infant-mother dyads, and Grusec and Abramovitch (1982) reported its positive social consequences in group settings; Eckerman, Davis, and Didow (in press) are currently studying its positive effects in dyadic play.

Our personal view was that in going from mimetic emotional exchanges to the differentiation of initiations and answers in cooperative play and verbal exchanges, one necessary step is to imitate the peer/partner as a way of creating shared experiences. This objective behavioral identification causes a positive emotional "shock." Synchronous imitation may then be understood as a mode of calling or inviting the other to interact by issuing the message "I am interested in you"; the subsequent counterimitation used by the initial model to answer the original message is "I am interested in you, too."

In previous work with Baudonniere (Nadel & Baudonniere, 1980, 1982) and with Fontaine (Nadel, Baudonniere, & Fontaine, 1983), we demonstrated that synchronized imitation is the predominant means of exchange in the 3rd year of life. These findings were obtained with triads of familiar peers meeting in an adult-free experimental setting that contained 10 objects in triplicate. Thus, a child could choose an object either for its intrinsic attractiveness or because the partner chose it. In mean percentage per child, 70% of the session's duration involved the children's holding one or several identical objects, thus indicating that holding identical objects was given preference over holding different objects. Furthermore, simultaneously holding identical objects led to similar (postural, motor, or symbolic) use of the identical objects (Nadel et al., 1983). The prevalence of synchronous imitations on the part of the partners was assessed. Furthermore, these imitations were reciprocal. The partners did not consistently play the role of model or imitator but alternated in these roles, supporting the hypothesis that reciprocal imitation is used by toddlers as a means of communication (Nadel & Baudonniere, 1982).

Several questions arise concerning validity. Does the absence of an adult lead to stress, causing the toddlers to behave identically as a way of comforting themselves? Is the presence of identical objects as a paradigmatic condition an artifactual that provokes imitative social behaviors? These two questions were addressed in several studies. The first question, concerning the effect of adult presence, was considered by Mertan (1988). The study compared the social behaviors of 3-year-old familiar peers who met for 12 minutes in the presence of a familiar adult programmed with a neutral protocol, and were left alone during the second part of the session. Although an adult was not present, significant improvements in verbal and positive emotional interactions appeared, while no differences were observed with respect to imitative behaviors.

The second question, concerning the effect of the presence of identical objects on the manifestation of imitative behaviors, led to an experiment comparing the same 3-year-old dyads in two experimental settings. The first setting contained 20 single objects, while the second setting contained 10 pairs of identical objects. Results showed that in the single-objects setting, toddlers expressed equal interest in the objects and the partner. The same children were more interested in the partner in the double-objects setting. This was not due to an increase in familiarity with the partner by the time of the second meeting, because a comparison with Baudonniere's study in which the dyads first met in the double-objects setting shows similar results and even more social encounters (Baudonniere, 1986). These findings indicate that the paradigmatic design involving identical objects is not an artifactual basis for imitation but rather a condition that enables synchronized imitation to take place when it is the most powerful means of exchange. It appears to be a feature of the physical context that facilitates social exchanges (Nadel, 1986b).

Following these findings, our hypothesis was that if physical gestures of the environment are "here and now" mediators that support momentary means of communication, facilitating features will evolve according to communicative means. In other words, while identical objects were demonstrated to be the most powerful mediators of peer communication in the 3rd year, single objects should become as powerful mediators as identical objects, and perhaps even more suitable mediators, at age 4, when self/others differentiation has been mastered, because single objects permit greater differentiation of social roles. To address this issue, a comparison was made between 10 dyads of three-year-old children (2 1/2 to 3 years old) and 10 dyads of 4-year-old children (3 1/2 to 4 years old) who met first in the single-objects setting (Condition 1) and then in the double-objects setting (Condition 2).

The dependent measures were: (a) orientation of interest: object-oriented or socially oriented, as measured by looking while acting (cf. Mueller & Lucas, 1975) (note that social orientation can occur with or without object mediation); (b) type of social orientation: (SOS) short social orientation (i.e., an utterance that is not answered or a one-turn interaction) or (LSO) long social orientation (i.e., an interaction that lasts for more than one turn) (cf. Jacobson, 1981; Mueller & Brenner, 1977); (c) structure of long social orientation: repetition of the same role (i.e., imitative play) or differentiation of roles (i.e., cooperative play).

The level of attraction to the experimental conditions in the two settings (a single set of 20 objects or two sets of 10 objects) and for the two ages (3 and 4) was assessed by measuring the time spent handling objects. No differences were found between ages and between settings (mean duration of handling: 88% to 94% of total session time, in percentage per child). Yet the results show striking differences between the two age groups with respect to the effects of the two settings on communication.

These differences can be summarized in three sets of findings. First, at age 3, the effect of the setting on social versus object orientation was highly significant. With single objects (Condition 1), toddlers were equally oriented toward objects in solitary play (OO, object-oriented) and toward the partner (SO, subject-oriented), whereas with double objects (Condition 2), social orientation was predominant. At age 4, the setting was found to have no effect. Social orientation was always predominant and stronger than at age 3, regardless of the setting (see Figure 7.1). An important cross-factor effect accounts for these results - - $F(1, 38) = 16.53, p<.001$.

Orientation of interest according to

age and object condition

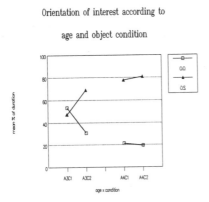

Figure 7.1

Orientation of interest according to age and object condition

Second, the effect of the setting on the duration of social orientation was similar for the two ages. Social orientation was stronger in condition 2. However, the effect involved short exchanges at age 3 and long exchanges at age 4, suggesting a developmental impact on the duration of social orientation (see figure 7.2).

Finally, in Condition 2, we found a strong age effect on the structure of long exchanges. At age 3, long exchanges having an imitative structure were largely predominant, whereas at age 4, cooperative structures involving differentiated social roles were as frequent as imitative structures. Consistent with this result, the setting appeared to have no effect at age 4 with respect to cooperative structures. A significant cross-factor effect accounts for these findings -- $F(1, 38) = 9.65, p<.01$ -- and is shown in Figure 7.3.

Further analyses were performed on every social event that occurred during the session with identical sets of objects in four dyads of 3-year-olds and four dyads of 4-year-olds. Analyzing event-by-event occurrences and co-occurrences (time-sample unit = 1 second) of social behaviors led to the following findings: (a) At age 3, initiations of contact were more frequently successful (i.e., answered) when they took place during imitative sequences

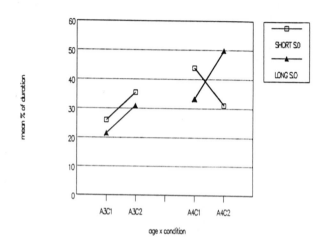

Figure 7.2

Type of social orientation according to age and object condition

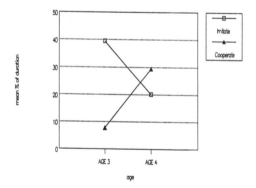

Figure 7.3

Structures of long social orientation according to age for each condition

136

($t = 6.8$, $p<.01$) than at other times, although this was not the case for the age 4 dyads; (b) at age 3, social signals such as smiles, vocal or verbal utterances, and nonverbal social behaviors occurred more frequently during the imitative sequences ($t = 5.5$, $p<.01$). This indicates both the functional role of imitation in early toddler-peer communication and its transitory effect, because imitative sequences did not support more social signals than other exchange structures at age 4 (Veuriot & Nadel, 1988).

These findings offer an example of the context dependency of early communication between peers. The context effect points to physical mediators of exchanges and their links to a transitory interactive structure. Alain Legendre (elsewhere in this book) documents the influence of sociospatial conditions on the occurrence of peer-toddler exchanges in group settings and provides further support for these links. Social-context effects are also evident. Baudonniere's results (presented elsewhere in this book) account for how social dependency changes according to the transitory means of exchange used. These findings suggest that our basic interest in transitory means of social adaptation can lead to an integrative developmental view of the apparently chaotic interaction between biological and environmental conditions in early communication. Furthermore, these results indicate the need for further comparative investigation of transitory social competence.

Transitory Adaptation from a Developmental and Comparative Perspective

An emphasis on transitory adaptations can also provide a basis for studying social incompetence, such as withdrawal or isolation, from a developmental and comparative perspective. If it is accepted that a behavior can assume a transitory role and then disappear or change in function, it can likewise be accepted that behaviors described as symptoms in pathologic ontogeny may also be considered in terms of their current, and perhaps transitory, adaptive efficacy.

As an outgrowth of the ontogenetic value of immediate imitation in the early development of social competence, we offer the hypothesis that synchronized echoing of gestures, as well as some kinds of echolalia, might supply a means of communication even in the case of atypical development, and particularly in autism. This idea is not new. Kanner (1943), followed by Schuler (1979), Prizant (1983), Prizant and Duchan (1981), and McCaleb and Prizant (1985) have pointed out the functional role of immediate echolalia in autistic children ("yes answer"). In addition, several authors (Bartak, Rutter, & Cox, 1975; Curcio, 1978; Dawson, 1986; De Myer, Aipern, Barton, De Myer, Churchill, Hintgen, Bryson, Pontius & Kimberlin, 1972) have suggested a link between gestural-imitative level and autistic aloofness. However, the process of communicating by imitation in atypical social development has yet to be investigated systematically.

Within the range of developmental disorders, autism, defined by Kanner (1943) as a "set of autistic abnormalities in affective contact," is an interesting model for testing sequences in the early growth of communicative skills and, in particular, the ontogenetic value of imitation. Recently, Fein, Pennington, Markowitz, Braverman, and Waterhouse (1986), investigating the overlap of sets of criteria used by researchers and clinicians, found that "aloofness from people is the only criterion which finds its way into every set" (p. 199). According to the authors, this social unrelatedness is inferred from clinical observations of a variety of specific behaviors that may differ between and within autistic children. They range from gaze aversion (Rutter, 1978; Wing, 1976), to little or no interest in human speech (Ornitz, Guthrie, & Farley, 1978) and emotional expressions (Hobson, 1986), to no development (or extremely delayed development) of imitation (Cohen, Paul, & Volkmar,

1987; De Myer, Hintgen, & Jackson, 1981; Rutter & Garmezy, 1983; Wing & Gould, 1979). More often cited is "Rutter's tetrad" of social isolation, communication disturbances, sameness, and early appearance (Rutter, 1978), with associated signs (cf. American Psychiatric Association, 1987) including disturbed responses to sensorial stimuli, motor abnormalities (stereotypies, self-mutilation), global deficits, and inappropriate affect. Imitative disabilities are also frequently reported and are regarded as crucial deficits. Prior (1979) reports that autistic children are particularly deficient in the ability to imitate and rarely do so spontaneously" (p. 363).

There is an increasing tendency to hypothesize a neurological etiology of autism, contrary to earlier psychogenetic theories. Thus, social deficits have come to be considered secondary consequences of primary cognitive impairment. This means that the question of whether the etiology of autism is neurological or psychological has not been separated from the question of whether social impairments are primary or secondary. Yet, as Fein et al. (1986) claim, "a neurological etiology does not necessarily imply that the social deficits are secondary; it could be the case that autism is a neurological disorder which primarily disrupts social or affective development" (p. 198). From this perspective, a comparative developmental approach would be interesting. The behavior of autistic children provides considerable information about the prerequisites of social competence.

Wing and Gould (1979), Rutter (1983), and Fein et al. (1986) offer new perspectives in the controversy over primary factors in autism. Wing (1982) suggests, based on the findings of her previous epidemiological study (Wing & Gould, 1979), that the problems of the children in the socially impaired group are of a different order than those in the sociable severely retarded group. The socially impaired children lacked "a whole complex pattern of actions and responses that makes human beings recognizable" (Wing, 1982, p. 309), while the sociable severely retarded group remains both understandable to others and predictable. Rutter (1983) is close to this conclusion when he attributes a cognitive causality to social and affective abnormalities in autism, except that he describes this cognitive deficit as involving stimuli carrying emotional or social "meaning."

Fein et al. (1986), although clearly indicating that they are not advocating a strict dichotomy between social and cognitive or perceptual development, proposed a convincing set of arguments supporting a neuropsychological model of infantile autism in which social, not cognitive, deficits would be primary. In particular, they pointed out that current findings show modest or complex links between cognitive and social impairments (Bartak & Rutter, 1976; Fein et al. 1986; Wing & Gould, 1979), that cognitive deficits cannot be regarded as the root of social impairments that appeared at an earlier age, and that more precise examination of the cognitive functions linked with social deficits (Sigman & Ungerer, 1984) shows that these cognitive functions (language and symbolic play) depend on social relatedness. It is therefore difficult to decide on a causal determinant. Fein et al. (1986) conclude that "both the rarity of social isolation, even in severely damaged babies, and its resistance to treatment in autism, reinforce the notion of the primacy of the social deficit in autism" (p. 209).

In fact, the most striking point in this controversy over primary factors in autism is the lack of precision about what can be called primary social factors. It is informative to clearly distinguish two levels of social factors. The first would be primary, species-specific, and appear at an earlier age, whereas the second would be expressed at a more mature age and be related to cognitive functions. The study of the hidden face of development that emphasizes transitory adaptations and the discontinuity in means of adaptation is useful in clarifying this distinction. In this view, deficits preventing primitive actualization of the communicative function may account for "a dysfunctional cortex," as in the case of early deprivation of experience (Fein, Humes, Kaplan, Lucci, & Waterhouse, 1984; Rutter, 1979). We can then propose the existence of two sets of social skills. The first, based on "here and now" mediators, would involve stimulus-bound responses and carry emotional contents. The second, appearing at about 12 months of age, involves what Zelazo and Leonard (1983) call "active thought" (p. 37) and is supported by a qualitative change in central processing capacities.

Other than Zelazo and Leonard's set of concomitant structural changes (vocalizing and pointing to social stimuli, functional and symbolic use of objects, obvious fear of strangers, and separation protest), the appearance of active joint attention (Bakeman & Adamson, 1984), active joint topics (Eckerman & Stein, 1982), indicating skills (Bates, Benigni, Bretherton, Camaioni, & Volterra, 1979; Rutter, 1979), and long interactions as opposed to one-turn interactions (Jacobson, 1981; Mueller & Brenner, 1977), accounts for this developmental change, which, to put it differently, can be explained by the emergence of a "theory of mind" (Leslie, 1987). This distinction can be usefully applied to imitation.

Immediate imitation -- which appears early in the child's development, and which is probably an innate mechanism, relatively independent of cognitive development, since even severely retarded children display it (see Gibson, 1978) -- would belong in the group of primary social factors as a primitive means of interacting and learning. Delayed imitation, viewed by Piaget and Inhelder (1945) as a marker of nascent representational capacity appearing around the 1st year of life and linked with symbolic play and language (Ungerer & Sigman, 1981), would be part of the qualitative change in social and cognitive development (Meltzoff, 1985).

Within this framework, two assumptions were made. First, we hypothesized that autistic children behave at best like three-year-old toddlers, without the capacity to predict their partners' social behaviors. In other words, they act without "a theory of mind" (Baron-Cohen, Leslie, & Frith, 1985). To test this hypothesis, we studied nonspeaking autistic children meeting speaking nonautistic familiar children, using the 3rd-year repertoire of exchange with a peer-partner as a comparative criterion. The nonautistic speaking children were considered naive interaction partners insofar as they used action patterns that were not specifically adjusted to their autistic partners. This allowed us to analyze both the speaking nonautistic children's reactions to the autistic behaviors (i.e., Which behaviors were addressed to the autistic children? Did they elicit responses? What kind of responses?) and the autistic children's reactions, if any, to their partners' initiations.

The second assumption concerned the repertoire of social exchanges. Based on our previous findings with normal toddlers, we hypothesized that synchronized verbal and gestural imitation is a necessary step in the development of primitive sustained communication. To address this issue, we focused on the functional role of immediate echolalia and immediate noninduced imitation of gestures in communicative sequences. It is important to note that most of the previous research on imitation in autism studied deferred imitations of gestures or induced immediate imitation of gestures (Curcio, 1978; Hammes & Langdell, 1981; Sigman & Ungerer, 1984) and that the few studies dealing with spontaneous immediate imitation used expert-novice dyads (Dawson & Adams, 1984). The functional role of immediate echolalia was documented by Prizant (1983), and colleagues (McCaleb & Prizant, 1985; Prizant & Duchan, 1981; Schuler & Prizant, 1987), and by Howlin (1982), but without taking the partners' utterances into account. Furthermore, the partner was not naive and was usually a parent or medical expert.

Sixteen dyads of hospitalized children, composed of a nonspeaking autistic child (i.e., one without generative language) and a nonautistic child were videotaped in the same experimental setting with double objects, using the methodology previously described. The experiment took place in a familiar room in their hospital. A familiar adult was present when necessary. The adult was trained to follow a neutral behavioral protocol as often as possible and was not engaged in educational, care-giving, or therapeutic relationships with the children. Autistic youngsters were diagnosed according to DSM-III-R (American Psychiatric Association, 1987; Cohen, Paul, & Volkmar, 1987) and the Mises Scale (Mises, Fortineau, Jeammet, Lang, Mazet, Plantade & Quemada). Eight of these autistic children were echolalic and gestural-imitative, and 8 were mute and non-gestural-imitative.

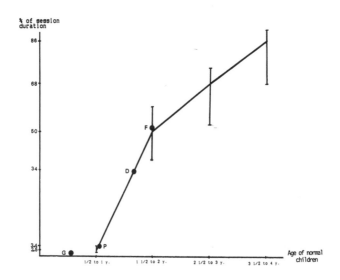

Figure 7.4

Density of socially-oriented behavior of 4 autistic children compared to prelinguistic children in dyadic peer conditions.

G = 10-year-old autistic child P = 14-year-old autistic child
D = 8-year-old autistic child   F = 10-year-old autistic child

The social performance of 4 echolalic and imitative autistic children was analyzed second by second. Their performance was compared with the social performance of 6-month-olds, and 2-, 3-, and 4-year-olds observed in the same experimental setting, with the exception of the infants, who were observed in infant-peer dyadic conditions in situ (Eckerman & Stein, 1982; Vandell, Wilson, & Buchanan, 1980). None of the 4 echolalic and gestural-imitative autistic children attained the 3-year-old level of social performance, but they were all essentially capable of sustaining a short social exchange (see Figure 7.4). Two of them were able to spontaneously produce a few verbal utterances, while the other two could only produce echolalic utterances (see Figure 7.5).

Social interactions were mainly based on spontaneous imitations of the partner's gestures or verbal utterances and were regarded as social behaviors by the partner, since they elicited the partner's social interest. These are reported in Figure 7.6. However, nonimitative autistic children were not able to show any social involvement.

140

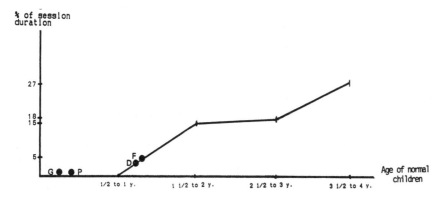

Figure 7.5

Density of verbal utterances (creative or echolalic) of 4 autistic children compared to prelinguistic children in dyadic peer conditions.

G = 10-year-old autistic child   P = 14-year-old autistic child
D = 8-year-old autistic child   F = 10-year-old autistic child

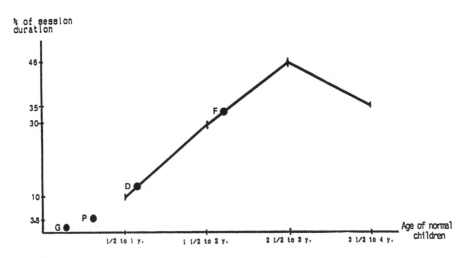

Figure 7.6

Density of spontaneous imitation of 4 autistic children compared to prelinguistic children in dyadic peer conditions

G = 10-year-old autistic child   P = 14-year-old autistic child
D = 8-year-old autistic child   F = 10-year-old autistic child

141

This research is still in progress; therefore, any generalizations would be premature. However, the first results suggest that our basic interest in transitory means of adaptation can not only improve our understanding of the early growth of social competence but may also be a means to understand dysfunction.

Conclusion

Having first illustrated the role of immediate imitation in the emergence of a transitory communication system among prelinguistic children, we have demonstrated this system's dependence on the immediate environment and its disappearance at age 4, when it is displaced by the language system. Autistic children, of any age, were described as highly dependent on the immediate context. Therefore, the first aspect of our approach has been to compare the communicative behaviors of autistic children paired with nonautistic partners, with those of prelinguistic dyadic systems, in terms of their shared characteristics of the unpredictability of the partner. Secondly, we are making comparisons between the social performances of autistic children and those of prelinguistic toddlers observed in the same experimental settings. We are thus seeking to test the hypothesis that the prelinguistic imitative system is a crucial milestone on the road to extended intensive interaction between partners. The first findings do indicate a strong connection between the ability to understand the partner's imitation as a meaningful social contact, the capacity to produce imitative responses as a means of social contact, and the level of communication achieved by the child. As we continue this research, we hope to shed light on the functional importance of imitation in the development of communicative competencies. We postulate that its role is transitory but crucial.

References

American Psychiatric Association (1987). *Diagnostic and Statistical Manual of Mental Disorders (DSM III)*, (3rd ed.).Washington, D.C.

Bakeman, R., & Adamson, L. (1984). Coordinating attention to people and objects in mother-infant and peer-infant interaction. *Child Development, 55*, 1278-1289.

Baron-Cohen, S., Leslie, A., & Frith, U. (1985). Does the autistic child have a theory of mind? *Cognition, 21*, 37-46.

Bartak, L., & Rutter, M. (1976). Differences between mentally retarded and normally intelligent autistic children. *Journal of Autism and Childhood Schizophrenia, 6*, 109-120.

Bartak, L., Rutter, M., & Cox, A. (1975). A comparative study of infantile autism and specific developmental receptive language disorder: 1. The children. *British Journal of Psychiatry, 126*, 127-145.

Bates, E., Benigni, L., Bretherton, Y., Camaioni, L., & Volterra, V. (1979). *The emergence of symbols*. New York: Academic Press.

Baudonnière, P-M. (1986). Effect of number of partners on modes of social exchanges among 2 1/2 - 3 year old peers. *Genetic, Social and General Psychology Monographs, 112*, 419-433.

Brazelton, T., Koslowski, B., & Main, M. (1974). The origins of reciprocity: Early mother-infant interaction. In M. Lewis & L. O. Rosenblum (Eds.), *The effect of the infant on its caregiver* (Vol. 1, pp. 49-77). New York: Wiley.

Cohen, D., Paul, R., & Volkmar, R. (1987). Issues in the classification of pervasive developmental disorders and associated disorders. In D. Cohen & A. Donnellan (Eds.), *Handbook of autism and pervasive developmental disorders* (pp. 151-172). New York: Wiley.

Curcio, F. (1978). Sensorimotor functioning and communication in mute autistic children. *Journal of Autism and Childhood Schizophrenia, 8*, 218-292.

Dawson, G., & Adams, A. (1984). Imitation and social responsiveness in autistic children. *Journal of Abnormal Child Psychology, 12*, 209-226.

De Myer, M. K., Alpern, G. D., Barton, S., De Myer, W., Churchill, Hintgen, J. N., Bryson, C., Pontius, W., & Kimberlin, C. (1972). Imitation in autistic, early schizophrenic and non-psychotic subnormal children. *Journal of Autism and Childhood Schizophrenia, 2*, 264-287.

De Myer, M. K., Hintgen, J. N., & Jackson, R. K. (1981). Infantile autism reviewed: A decade of research. *Schizophrenia Bulletin, 7,* 388-449.

Eckerman, C. O., Davis, C., & Didow, S. (in press). Toddlers' emerging ways of achieving social coordinations with a peer. *Child Development.*

Eckerman, C. O., & Stein, M. R. (1982). The toddler's emerging interactive skills. In K. H. Rubin & H. S. Ross (Eds.), *Peer relationships and social skills in childhood* (pp. 47-71). New York: Springer-Verlag.

Fein, D., Humes, M., Kaplan, E., Lucci, D., & Waterhouse, L. (1984). The question of left hemisphere dysfunction in infantile autism. *Psychological Bulletin, 95,* 258-281.

Fein, D., Pennington, B., Markowitz, P., Braverman, M., & Waterhouse, L. (1986). Toward a neuropsychological model of infantile autism: Are social deficits primary? *Journal of the American Academy of Child Psychiatry, 25,* 198-212.

Gibson, D. (1978). *Down's syndrome: The psychology of mongolism.* Cambridge, UK: Cambridge University Press.

Grusec, J., & Abramovitch, R. (1982). Imitation of peers and adults in a natural setting: A functional analysis. *Child Development, 53,* 636-642.

Hammes, J. G., & Langdell, T. (1981). Precursors of symbol formation in childhood autism. *Journal of Autism and Developmental Disorders, 11,* 331-344.

Hobson, R. P. (1986). The autistic child's appraisal of expressions of emotion: A further study. *Journal of Child Psychology and Psychiatry, 27,* 671-680.

Howlin, P. (1982). Echolalic and spontaneous phrase speech in autistic children. *Journal of Child Psychology and Psychiatry, 23,* 281-293.

Jacobson, J. L. (1981). The role of inanimate objects in early peer interaction. *Child Development, 52,* 618-626.

Kanner, L. (1943). Autistic disturbances of affective contact. *Nervous Child, 2,* 217-250.

Leslie, A. M. (1987). Pretense and representation: The origins of "theory of mind." *Psychological Review, 94, 4,* 412-426.

Maratos, O. (1973, April). *The origin and development of imitation in the first six months of life.* Paper presented at the annual meeting of the British Psychological Society, Liverpool.

McCaleb, P., & Prizant, B. M. (1985). Encoding new versus old information by autistic children. *Journal of Speech and Hearing Disorders, 50,* 230-240.

Meltzoff, A. (1985). Immediate and deferred imitation in fourteen and twenty-four month old infants. *Child Development, 56,* 62-72.

Mertan, B. (1988, July). *The effect of adult presence on peer-toddler communication.* Paper presented at the NATO Institute for Advanced Studies, Les Arcs, France.

Mises, R., Fortineau, J., Jeammet, P., Lang, J. L., Mazet, P., Plantade, A., & Quemada, N. (1988). Classification française des troubles mentaux de l'enfant et de l'adolescent [French classification system of child and adolescent mental disorders]. *Psychiatrie de l'enfant, 31,* 67-134.

Moss, E., & Strayer, F. (1988). Imitation and communication between young children, by J. Nadel. *Contemporary Psychology, 33,* 970.

Mueller, E., & Brenner, J. (1977). The origins of social skills and interaction among playgroup toddlers. *Child Development, 48,* 854-861.

Mueller, E., Lucas, T. (1975). A developmental analysis of peer interactions among toddlers. In M. Lewis & L. Rosenblum (Eds.), *Friendship and peer relations* (pp. 223-258). New York: Wiley.

Nadel, B. J. (1980). The functional role of imitation in personality development: Wallon's contribution. *French Language Psychology, 1,* 169-177.

Nadel, J. (1986a). *Imitation et communication entre jeunes enfants* [Imitation and communication among young children]. Paris: PUF.

Nadel, J. (1986b). Matching activities and the regulation of peer-toddler sustained activities. In J. LeCamus & J.Cosnier (Eds.), *Ethology and psychology* (pp. 57-65). Toulouse. France: Privat.

Nadel, J. (1987). Le développement de la communication selon Wallon: Un modèle méconnu [The development of communication according to Wallon: A misunderstood model]. *Studi di Psicologia dell' Educazione, 3,* 105-117.

Nadel, J., & Baudonnière, P-M. (1980). L'imitation comme mode prépondérant d'échange entre pairs au cours de la troisième année [Imitation as a predominant mode of exchange among three-year-old peers]. *Enfance, 1-2,* 77-90.

Nadel, J., & Baudonnière, P-M. (1982). The social function of reciprocal imitation in 2-year-old peers. *International Journal of Behavioral Development, 5,* 95-109.

Nadel, J., & Baudonnière, P-M., & Fontaine. A. M. (1983). Les comportements sociaux imitatifs [Imitative social behaviors]. *Recherches de Psychologie Sociale, 5,* 15-29.

Ornitz, E., Guthrie, D., & Farley, A. J. (1978). The early symptoms of childhood autism. In G. Sherban (Ed.), *Cognitive defects in the development of mental illness* (pp.207-229). New York: Brunner/Mazel. Pawlby, S. J. (1977). Imitative interactions. In H. R.Schaffer (Ed.), *Studies in mother-infant interactions* (pp.203-223). New York: Academic Press.

Piaget, J. (1945). *La formation du symbole chez l'enfant* [The formation of symbols in childhood]. Neuchatel/Paris: Delachaux & Niestle.

Prior, M. R. (1979). Cognitive abilities and disabilities in infantile autism: A review. *Journal of Abnormal Child Psychology, 7*, 357-380.

Prizant, B. M. (1983). Language acquisition and communicative behavior in autism: Toward an understanding of the "whole" of it. *Journal of Speech and Hearing Disorders, 48*, 296-307.

Prizant, B. M. & Duchan, J. F. (1981). The functions of immediate echolalia in autistic children. *Journal of Speech and Hearing Disorders, 46*, 241-249.

Rutter, M. (1978). Language disorder and infantile autism. In M. Rutter & E. Schopler (Eds.), *Autism: A reappraisal of concepts and treatment* (pp. 1-25). New York: Plenum Press.

Rutter, M. (1979). Maternal deprivation, 1972-1978: New findings, new concepts, new approaches. *Child Development, 50*, 283-305.

Rutter, M. (1983). Cognitive deficits in the pathogenesis of autism. *Journal of Child Psychology and Psychiatry, 24*, 513-531.

Rutter, M., & Garmezy, N. (1983). Developmental Psychopathology. In E. M. Hetherington (Ed.), *Handbook of child psychology* (Vol. 4, pp. 775-835). New York: Wiley.

Schuler, A. (1979). Echolalia: Issues and clinical applications. *Journal of Speech and Hearing Disorders, 44*, 411-434.

Schuler, A., & Prizant, B. M. (1987). Facilitating communication: Prelanguage approaches. In D. Cohen & A. Donnellan (Eds.), *Handbook of autism and pervasive developmental disorders* (pp. 301-315). New York: Wiley.

Sigman, M., & Ungerer, J. A. (1984). Cognitive and language skills in autistic, mentally retarded, and normal children. *Developmental Psychology, 20*, 293-302.

Trevarthen, C., & Hubley, P. (1978). Secondary intersubjectivity: Confiding and acts of meaning in the first year. In A. Lock (Ed.), *Action, gesture and symbol* (pp. 183-227). London: Academic Press.

Ungerer, J., & Sigman, M. (1981). Symbolic play and language comprehension in autistic children. *Journal of the American Academy of Child Psychiatry, 20*, 318-337.

Uzgiris, I. (1981). Two functions of imitation during infancy. *International Journal of Behavioral Development, 4*, 1-12.

Uzgiris, I. C., & Kruper, J. C. (in press). The links between imitation and social referencing. In S. Feinman (Ed.), *Social referencing and the social construction of reality in infancy*. New York: Plenum.

Vandell, D., Wilson, K., & Buchanan, N. (1980). Peer interaction in the first year of life. *Child Development, 51*, 481-488.

Veuriot, F., & Nadel, J. (1988). *Le rôle de l'imitation dans la communication prélangagière: Analyse micro-événementielle et développementale* [The role of imitation in prelinguistic communication: A developmental micro-event analysis]. Unpublished dissertation, Universite Paris-V.

Wallon, H. (1934). *Les origines du caractère chez l'enfant* [The origins of character in the child] (3rd ed., 1973). Paris: PUF.

Wing, L. (1976). *Diagnosis, clinical description and prognosis*. In L. Wing (Ed.), *Early childhood autism* (2nd ed., pp. 15-64). New York: Pergamon Press.

Wing, L. (1982). Language and social impairment in autism and severe mental retardation. In S. M. Chess & A. Thomas (Eds.), *Annual progress in child psychiatry and child development* (pp. 290-315). New York: Brunner/Mazel.

Wing, L., & Gould, J. (1979). Severe impairments of social interactions and associated abnormalities in children: Epidemiology and classification. *Journal of Autism and Developmental Disorders, 9*, 11-30.

Yando, R., Seitz, V., & Zigler, E. (Eds.). (1978). *Imitation: A developmental perspective*. Hillsdale, NJ: Erlbaum. Zelazo, P. R., & Leonard, E. I. (1983). The dawn of active thought. In K. W. Fischer (Ed.), *Levels and transitions in children's development*, (Vol. 21, pp. 37-49). San Francisco: Jossey-Bass.

144

8

Co-adaptation Within the Early Peer Group: A Psychobiological Study of Social Competence

F. F. Strayer

Laboratoire d'Ethologie Humaine
Département de Psychologie
Université du Québec à Montréal

Biosocial models of human development posit two different but complementary processes that regulate the impact of early experience on the growth of individual competence. *Experience-dependent adaptation* entails forms of developmental change induced by specific but relatively unpredictable information present in the organism's immediate environment. Such developmental change is contrasted with *experience-expectant adaptation*, which involves adjustments to patterns of information that characterize natural developmental settings for a given species. This second form of adaptation can be influenced more directly by genetic information that either predisposes individual sensitivity and responsiveness to particular patterns of early stimulation, or provides motivational dispositions that lead the young organism to actively seek or construct characteristic forms of early experience (Greenough, Black, & Wallace, 1987).

Although hominid evolution undoubtedly depended upon both of these forms of ontogenetic adaptation, the developmental study of early competence has often presumed that growth of social skills results primarily from experience-dependent adaptation. For example, psychologists have usually assumed that the development of children's early competence depends most directly upon access to adequate socialization experiences. From this perspective, individual differences in social competence reflect variations in the quality or quantity of external support from the social environment. Such emphasis upon environmental determinants of individual competence accords well with commonsense notions that during the course of human evolution, the emergence of more sophisticated learning capacities was associated with increasing developmental plasticity and, consequently, progressively greater freedom from biological, or genetic, constraint. However, within the framework of experience-expectant adaptation, demonstration of differential impact of time-based, or maturationally "expected," forms of stimulation on the growing organism would indicate a continuing influence of biological factors in the development of individual social competence. At a theoretical level, the nature of such biological constraints must in part be induced from comparative studies that attempt to reconstruct the probable evolutionary history of our species. However, at an empirical level, the study of the biological foundations of early competence must be anchored in demonstrations of age-graded

B. H. Schneider et al. (eds.), Social Competence in Developmental Perspective, 145–174.
© 1989 by Kluwer Academic Publishers.

regularities, or species-specific constancies, in the natural setting where early adaptation and development take place.

Among nonhuman primates, biological constraints on behavioral development generally involve differential sensitivity to particular forms of information in the immediate social environment. For example, research on primate social adaptation has demonstrated innate capacities for the recognition of species-typical communication signals (Sackett, 1966), species-characteristic forms of social relationships at different moments in the life cycle (Harlow & Harlow, 1965), and species-specific dispositions that lead to predictable social structures in groups of animals observed in their natural settings (Kummer, 1968). Comparative analyses of different species sharing similar habitats leave no doubt that experience-dependent adaptation by itself cannot account for the great diversity in social functioning that characterizes monkeys and apes. Experience-expectant adaptation must be invoked to explain why two distinct species persist in maintaining radically different modes of social adaptation even when they co-exist within the same ecological habitat (Kummer, 1971).

For developmental psychobiologists, at least some of the observed differences in human social adaptation may reflect genetically regulated sensitivity to "anticipated" information in the natural environment of the developing child. For the moment, the best-documented illustration of biologically constrained social adaptation concerns species-specific learning processes that underlie children's acquisition of formal language during the first 2 or 3 years of life. Communicative competence is undoubtedly influenced by patterns of early language stimulation, but it is also canalized by the organism's genetic disposition to differentially perceive, process and respond to linguistic stimuli (Lenneberg, 1967). Recent theories in developmental psychobiology have proposed similar interactionist models emphasizing both biological constraint and diversity of early experience to account for developmental change in an increasing variety of psychological characteristics (Lerner, 1984). For example, researchers examining the biological bases of learning processes have elaborated a biosocial model to explain the evolutionary origins of human intelligence. Humphrey (1976) argues that mutual adaptation within stable social contexts favors progressive transformations in species-specific representational capacities. Increasing abilities to store and process relevant information about social relationships within particular group settings contributes directly to personal survival within the collective social unit. In this model, strategic coordination with other group members is viewed as a fundamental aspect of individual adaptation. The biological function of early socialization becomes the acquisition of minimal levels of social competence necessary for optimal co-adjustments with familiar partners. Processes of co-adaptation maximize the likelihood of individual survival and indirectly increase reproductive fitness. The greater reproductive fitness of more socially competent individuals leads to an increased probability that offspring in subsequent generations will also develop the particular representational abilities that were associated with more optimal social functioning. According to this model, the driving force behind the emergence of advanced cognitive abilities among the primates has been the more fundamental need to process relevant information essential for the production of situationally adjusted and socially appropriate behavior.

The extension of this comparative argument to human development leads to the provocative hypothesis that the ontogeny of both cognitive and affective functions depends upon the active role of the organism in assuring optimal interactive experience with familiar social partners. Such social experience provides contexts where information is repeatedly exchanged in order to coordinate ongoing mutual activity. Synchrony in social participation involves processes of co-adaptation that ultimately lead to increased similarity in both thoughts and feeling between familiar social partners. A psychobiological model of social competence proposes that developmental differences in such co-adaptive processes result both from variations in social support provided by partners during interaction and from variations in the child's capacity to perceive, assimilate and adequately react to information within the prevailing social context. Instead of focusing upon differences in inherent abilities as basic parameters in the development of early competence, a psychobiological model examines co-adaptive processes within the natural social setting that lead to variation in children's access to socially pertinent information as well as diversity in their optimal use of existing behavioral resources.

Traditional psychological models of individual competence have often emphasized information-processing skills that develop during interactions with inanimate objects. In contrast, a psychobiological model proposes that information gleaned from the social environment orients early growth and generates phenotypic variability in the emerging regulation of socioaffective and cognitive activity. Accepting social relations as the prime mover of both cognitive and affective development has direct implications for how we understand the psychological impact of experience with objects and the development of social and representational activity during early childhood (Charlesworth, 1976). In natural settings, physical objects generally serve as instruments that facilitate social interaction (Musatti, 1986). Both adults and children use objects to focus dyadic participation and to modulate their mutual exchange of information (Nadel, 1986). The strategic shifting of attention between a social partner and a physical object probably requires an important increase in the complexity of representational activity during the course of social interaction. However, coordinating social interaction with multiple social partners places even more demands on a child's information-processing skills. Competent social communication requires representing information about the cognitive and affective state of the social partner, abstracting information about the meaning of particular messages, as well as projecting goals for the regulation of the ongoing episode. As the number of active partners engaged in a social sequence increases, there is a corresponding increase in the complexity of information-processing demands placed upon the young child. The capacity to assimilate and strategically adjust to such demands in different social contexts provides the most appropriate index of developmental change in children's level of social competence.

Past research has already demonstrated a number of direct links between children's information processing-skills and the quality of early social relations. Growth in representational ability has been associated with the formation of a stable primary attachment bond (Main, Kaplan, & Cassidy, 1985; Pipp & Harmon, 1987) as well as with the diversity of stable social relationships outside the family setting (Strayer, Moss & Blicharski, 1988). Studies examining the influence of attachment on cognition in the first 3 years report that security of attachment is associated with more active exploration and more advanced representational abilities, greater skill in dealing with the physical environment, greater task-persistence, and greater interest in exploratory play (Frodi, Bridges, & Grolnick, 1985; Harmon, Suwalsky, & Klein, 1979; Hazen & Durrett, 1982). In contrast, insecure attachment has been linked to immaturity in play with people and objects. Insecure-resistant toddlers appear to show the least object engagement and to require the most parental support (Main et al., 1985). Such preliminary description of how primary social bonds shape patterns of information processing are consistent with a co-adaptation model of early social competence. Affective and attentional mechanisms activated during the course of social interaction structure children's emerging representational activity in qualitatively different ways.

However, an exclusive focus on the primary attachment figure as the principal agent of cognitive and affective socialization minimizes the potential contribution of other individuals to the development of early social competence. For psychobiologists, the central role of maternal responsiveness as a determinant of early adjustment must be attenuated by a more complete consideration of the diversity of social resources available during early childhood (Hinde, 1983; Trivers, 1972). For example, parental investment theory predicts that from early infancy, the primary attachment bond is synergistically associated with other relational systems, leading to the establishment of multiple socioaffective relationships within a broader social ecology (Strayer, 1984). Such views draw attention to the diversity of individuals (grandparents, fathers, siblings, playmates, and peers) who are part of the stable social world of the young child. These individuals also serve as important agents of early socialization. All such social partners help shape the child's emerging capacity to function within a particular socio cultural context.

Interest in the collective context of early development raises questions about diversity and regularity in the kinds of social information obtained in the interpersonal settings where early socialization takes place. The style of interpersonal communication between socializing agents, as well as the different roles that they assume while jointly interacting with the child, provide concrete experiences that directly shape the child's emerging perception and representation of the social world. A psychobiological analysis of adaptive processes underlying the acquisition of these early cognitive, affective, and behavioral skills requires a more complete descriptive analysis of the stable characteristics of interpersonal relationships common in early childhood. During interaction with familiar social partners, young children repeatedly encounter and engage in patterns of social exchange that canalize both their representational and their social abilities. If such early social relationships have invariant aspects common across settings and cultures, then it is quite likely that the development of early social competence involves both experience-dependent and experience-expectant adaptation.

An Ethological Study of Social Competence With Peers

Questions about the nature and function of early peer relations have preoccupied researchers on the development of social competence for at least 50 years. Parten (1932) proposed a classic approach to the description of developmental change in social play. Her research focused upon physical proximity between peers, direction of visual attention, and degree of mutual involvement. The empirical analysis of these aspects of children's social behavior led to the conclusion that during the preschool period, children become progressively more sophisticated in coordinating cooperative activity with age-mates. A quite different approach to the study of peer relations dealt more directly with the social impact of observed behaviors. Influenced by theories of social learning, this approach to naturally occurring social behavior focused on its presumed value as a positive or negative reinforcer for the social partner (Hartup, Glazer, & Charlesworth, 1967). At a descriptive level, this functionalist approach redirected attention to the distinction between aggressive and cooperative social involvement, as well as to potential age changes in prosocial and antisocial peer activity. Although such a dichotomous classification was more general than Parten's earlier description of age-graded forms of peer play, the newer functional analysis did not address questions about the development of specific patterns of social behavior during early childhood.

McGrew's (1972) critique of such learning oriented studies in child psychology stressed their apparent lack of concern for the description of basic action units and their often arbitrary assignment of different behaviors to single global categories. In part as a reaction to this critique, research in child ethology attempted to provide more explicit empirical criteria for higher-order classifications of morphologically described action patterns. For example, Blurton-Jones (1972) used factor analysis of temporal association and frequency of 22 behavioral items observed during free play to reveal three independent classes of social involvement. The first consisted of both "rough and tumble play" and "cooperative task activities"; the second included different patterns of aggressive activity; whereas the third reflected more affiliative forms of social involvement. In spite of their apparent methodological divergence, these three approaches to early social behavior share the common focus of tracing develc ental change in individual adaptation. Their preoccupation with differences in raics of social activity often led to the presumption of more or less stable behavioral styles. Such views neglect tactical adjustments that children make as participants in a co-adaptive process where individual actions are shaped by the ongoing activity of social partners.

Contemporary research in social ethology examines individual social activity within the dynamic context of group social organization. The notion that individual growth and development take place within a dynamic social system was originally introduced by Crook (1970). In his comparative analyses of primate social organization, Crook stressed that individual modes of social adaptation are constrained by the set of established relationships that constitute the social ecology of any stable group. From this perspective, the use of social participation as an index of individual competence neglects the importance of transitory adjustment by the individual as he or she moves from one interpersonal setting to another. Social behavior is not evenly distributed among all possible partners; instead, particular actions are directed toward specific group members, who, in turn, usually respond in a predictable manner. In natural groups, both the quality and the quantity of social activity tend to remain similar within particular dyadic contexts over time. The observation of regularities in dyadic patterns of social exchange was the basic empirical information that sustained many of the initial discussions concerning how primate social relationships and social roles within the primate group determine individual behavioral development.

The introduction of an integrated analytic framework specifying distinct levels of social analysis helped to clarify much of the conceptual confusion that hindered previous descriptive research on processes of individual adaptation and social coordination (Hinde & Stevenson-Hinde, 1976). The application of this framework to the study of preschool (range in age from 1 to 6 years) social behavior led to the development of empirically based definitions of social adaptation in terms of individual actions, social exchange, dyadic relationships, and roles within the structured peer group (Strayer, 1980b). The resulting multidimensional analyses of peer group social ecology show that the availability of preferred social partners serves as a fundamental constraint on the manifestation of acquired social skills. These findings have two major implications for research on the development of early social competence. At a theoretical level, models purporting to explain the acquisition of social abilities within the peer setting must begin to distinguish between competence and performance in much the same way as more traditional models for the development of language or thought. On a more practical plane, these initial results indicated the need to elaborate more refined age-graded procedures that would allow the description of peer relationships throughout the course of early childhood.

The convergent allocation of particular social activities toward specific social partners has been used as a means of identifying social relations among non human primates (Strayer & Harris, 1979). Rather than focusing upon differences in the absolute rate of an individual's production of various forms of behavior, dyadic analysis examines covariation in the allocation of social acts among members of a stable group. Activities directed by the same individual toward different social partners are treated as analytically distinct entities. In an extension of this analytic approach to groups of young children, Strayer (1980b) suggested that the social ecology of the preschool group could be discussed in terms of two major classes of peer activity. Drawing from the work of Kummer (1971) and McGrew (1972), he labeled these classes in terms of their cohesive and dispersive functions. Basic categories of social activity promoting group cohesion included affiliative behaviors such as *orientation*, *approach*, and *contact* and object activity such as *offer*, *give*, *take*, and *share*. In contrast, agonistic activity such as *attack*, *threat*, and *competition* lead to the disruption of communication among members of the peer group. Summarizing evidence from a series of independent studies, Strayer (1980a) illustrated how these two functional classes of social behavior could be employed to assess qualitatively different dimensions of peer relationships as well as different social structures within the early peer group.

The Ethological Study of Co-adaptation within the Peer Group

The systematic application of methods from primate social ethology to the study of children's adaptation within stable peer groups has paralleled trends in the behavioral biology literature. During the 1970s, a number of independent researchers reported empirical data stressing the importance of social dominance hierarchies as an organizational feature of preschool groups (Abramovitch, 1976; Hold, 1977; Missakian, 1976; Sluckin & Smith, 1977; Strayer, Chapeskie, & Strayer, 1978; Strayer & Strayer, 1976; Vaughn & Waters, 1978). More recently, La Frenière & Charlesworth (1983) have addressed the underlying assumption that the establishment of a group dominance hierarchy contributes to the reduction of intra group aggression. Their findings suggest that the organization of peer conflict in terms of stable dominance relations leads to a reduction in overt aggression during sequential periods of the school year. However, since their study focused only upon a single age level, they do not provide direct information on age-related changes in the nature of peer group social organization. Ethological studies with school-age (range in age from 6 to 12 years) children indicate that social dominance persists as a unifying aspect of peer group social organization throughout the grade school and adolescent periods (Savin-Williams, 1976; Weisfeld, 1980; Weisfeld, Omark, & Cronin, 1980).

Following efforts to document the nature of social dominance, a number of researchers began to explore how cohesive forms of social activity are related to group dominance structure. Initial findings indicated that social dominance was directly related to patterns of peer friendship and popularity (Strayer, 1980a, 1980b), social attention (Abramovitch & Strayer, 1978), and imitation and leadership (Savin-Williams, 1980; Strayer, 1980b, 1981). However, other studies questioned the central role of dominance as an organizing principle for the early peer group (Vaughn & Waters, 1981). How diverse social activities are organized and coordinated within the early peer groups remains an important question in descriptive research on the diversity of social activity among young children. There was also some suggestion in the child ethology literature that the coordination of social activities may vary as a function of the average age of the peer group. For example, Missakian (1980) reported variations in both patterns and rates of conflict between different-age children in a mixed-age peer group. Similarly, our research has suggested that although social dominance hierarchies are quite similar among 4- and 5-year-old children, prosocial activities relate to dominance status in a slightly different manner at the two age levels (Strayer, 1980b, 1981). Surprisingly, there is still relatively little empirical evidence about when dyadic dominance relations and group social structures emerge as stable characteristics

150

of the peer group. More detailed information about the developmental processes underlying the early socialization of agonistic and affiliative behavior is a prerequisite for formulating and testing hypotheses about the adaptive significance of preschool social behavior. The extension of the social ethology framework in the descriptive study of groups of younger children can provide necessary normative data for the study of developmental changes in the organization of cohesive and agonistic activities in the early peer group.

Research Methods

The participants in this first study were 134 French-speaking children who attended a community day-care center in Montreal. The children, who ranged in age from 1 to 6 years, were members of the initial two cohorts in a 4-year longitudinal study of preschool social adaptation. The children were organized into five age-stratified groups that were constituted in September of each year. (See Table 8.1 for the children included in the first series of analyses.) The center provided services for a large variety of families, including trades people, professionals, students, and welfare recipients. About one third of the children came from single-parent homes. Daily activities for each of the groups were divided into periods of structured activity, free play, meal time, and nap time. Most children attended the center for a full day (9:30 a.m. to 5:00 p.m.). Each class had a permanent male and female teacher, who were occasionally replaced by part-time staff of either sex.

Table 8.1

Summary of Participants

	Cohort 1			Cohort 2		
Group	$\underline{N}$	Age (mo.)	SD	$\underline{N}$	Age (mo.)	SD
1 year	9	18	6.22	10	15	4.60
2 years	11	28	6.10	9	25	1.04
3 years	14	37	4.35	12	35	4.20
4 years	18	49	8.50	18	47	4.30
5 years	16	66	5.45	17	68	9.90

Records of social behavior were obtained for all 10 groups using direct observation procedures during periods of free play and structured activities. Data-collection procedures involved 24 5-minute focal samples for each child. In addition, supplementary observations of dyadic conflict were collected for all groups using matrix completion procedures (Altmann, 1974). These later observations were included to facilitate analyses of social dominance relations. For each observational record, the initiator of an act, the action, the target, and the target's response were noted. If any of the required elements in this minimal syntax was not available, the social exchange was not included for data analysis. A change of social partners and/or a period of 10 seconds between the end of one action and the onset of another was used to separate social-interaction sequences.

The description of peer-directed behavior required noting specific elements selected from a Social Action Inventory (Strayer, 1980a). A résumé of the coding categories included in the current analyses is provided in Table 8.2. All data were collected by full-

The description of peer-directed behavior required noting specific elements selected from a Social Action Inventory (Strayer, 1980a). A résumé of the coding categories included in the current analyses is provided in Table 8.2. All data were collected by full-time research staff with extensive training in the direct observation of preschool social behavior. Prior to the beginning of each phase of observation, inter observer reliabilities with respect to the use of coding categories were assessed using both correlational and agreement procedures.

Table 8.2

Principal Categories and Patterns of Social Behavior

I. Directed social actions

A. **Affiliation**
   1. Orientation   glance, look at, watch, turn toward
   2. Signal   beckon, point, show, wave, smile, play face
   3. Approach   step, walk, and run toward; follow
   4. Contact   touch, pat, hold hands, embrace, kiss, shoulder hug
B. **Agonism**
   1. Attack   bite, hit, grab, kick, pull, push, throw at, assault
   2. Threat   fragment hit, fragment kick, throw, chase, facial display, body display
   3. Competition   object struggle, steal, supplant

II. Terminators of social exchange

A. **Affiliation**
   1. Reorient   look away, look at other, turn away, turn to other
   2. Withdraw   step, walk, and run away
B. **Agonism**
   1. Submission   gaze avert, crouch, cringe, flinch, cry
   2. Retreat   step back, flee
C. **No Response**   ignore, miss social overture

Reliability indices were consistently above 85% for the complete coding system and slightly higher than 90% for the coding of selected forms of social conflict from video records of agonistic interaction. Percentage agreement coefficients were also calculated at the midpoint of each observational phase. The values of these reliability indices ranged form 83% to 98% (mean = 90.2%, SD = 5.08).

Social Activity as a Function of Age

Analyses of age differences in the hourly rate of social activity indicated a striking increase in the frequency of affiliative activities. The frequency of orientation and approach more than doubled from 1- to 5-year-olds; contact also increased but at a somewhat slower rate, reaching an apparent plateau in the 4-year-old groups. In contrast, agonistic activity was much less frequent at all age levels. The rate of attack and competition remained nearly constant until age 3 and decreased steadily thereafter. Interestingly, the use of threat, the least frequent form of aggressive behavior, increased between 1 and 3 years of age and then decreased in conjunction with other forms of agonistic activity. Although the preliminary analyses of initiated activity showed changes in behavioral rates as a function of age, they revealed little about how the allocation of different actions toward particular social partners may change during the course of the preschool period. In order to address the question of regularities in interpersonal exchange, the next set of analyses examined the covariation of selected social activities across the possible dyadic contexts within each of the 10 peer groups.

Table 8.3

Principal Components of Dyadic Activity

	1 year		3 years		5 years	
Factors	Aff.	Ago.	Aff.	Ago.	Aff.	Ago.
Attention	.30	.13	.73*	.20	.81*	.12
Approach	.82*	.36*	.97*	.19	.75*	.15
Contact	.27	.03	.45*	.29	.66*	.21
Competition	.40*	.63*	.35*	.59*	.31*	.34*
Threat	.12	.68*	.19	.56*	.17	.64*
Attack	.27	.97*	.13	.83*	.08	.71*
Eigen Value	1.09	2.83	2.98	1.12	2.63	1.24
Variance	18.10	47.10	49.60	18.60	43.90	20.70

Principal Components of Dyadic Activity

Initiated categories of social activity were compiled in separate dyadic matrices for each social group. These matrices summarized the dyadic distribution of observed behaviors among group members for each observational session. Another child's response to an initiated act was also tabulated in these matrices if it entailed an action pattern in one of the selected behaviorial categories. The majority of previous studies of social behavior in the early peer group have used marginal totals of such dyadic matrices as primary indices of social involvement. However, in the study of dyadic relationships, the unit of analysis is the directional dyad. For the description of interpersonal relationships, the set of cells within the dyadic matrix are of primary interest. Actions directed by each member of a given dyad (A <--> B) to the other represent different analytic cases (A -->B and B --> A); thus, if there are N children in a social group, there are N squared minus N directional dyads that may serve as cases in the dyadic analysis. Each of the six behavioral matrices was restructured as a single vector representing the frequency of initiation of each activity for the set of dyadic cases in each peer group. To examine natural covariation among different forms of social behavior, correlational and principal component analyses were conducted to determine the convergence of behavioral categories as underlying dimensions of interpersonal relations within each of the 10 groups. Factors were extracted with a standard eigen threshold of 1.00 and were rotated using the Varimax option. Table 8.3 provides a summary of representative results obtained for groups of 1-, 3-, and 5-year-old children.

The principal component analyses of dyadic activity identified two orthogonal factors. In the youngest group, attack, threat, and competition had the highest loadings on the first factor. The grouping of these behaviors on the same factor readily identifies it as an agonistic dimension of social participation. The second factor was defined primarily by the category approach although it also had a secondary association with competition. Because of variability in their dyadic distribution, orientation and contact were not strongly related to either of the two principal factors for the youngest groups. Affiliation in this first analysis was interpreted as an emergent dimension of social participation. In contrast, for

153

the two older groups, the affiliative factor emerges as the most important dimension of dyadic involvement, whereas the agonistic factor accounted for a smaller but still significant part of the residual variance. Indeed, for all of the older groups, the variables associated with the first factor were orientation, approach, and contact, whereas attack, threat, and competition were clustered on the second factor. Finally, although, with age, there was an increasing trend for independence between agonistic and affiliative indices, competition was significantly correlated with both social factors in all 10 groups.

It is interesting to note that both the cohesive and the dispersive dimensions of social activity discussed in the primate and child ethology literature are evident at all age levels in this analysis. These cross-sectional contrasts also demonstrate that in spite of its relatively lower frequency, agonistic activity emerges as a main source of variation in the dyadic allocation of social behaviors. In contrast, affiliative activities become the primary source of behavioral convergence for the identification of social relations among groups of older children. The dyadic analysis of naturally occurring peer interaction indicates potentially important developmental changes in early peer relations between 1 and 3 years of age. Newly established patterns of social participation appear to become consolidated in the 3-year-old peer group and remain stable for the rest of the preschool period.

Developmental Changes in Social Participation

To determine the degree of regularity in age-graded features of peer participation, separate principal component analyses were compared across cohorts at each age level. In general, the obtained number of factors, eigen values, and explained variance were very similar from one year to the next and from one age level to another. Comparison of results obtained for the 1-year-olds indicated some group differences in the covariation of orientation, contact, and threat as well as in the stability of the respective associations of these variables with the two principal factors. However, in both cases, agonistic activities were more directly associated with the first factor and affiliative activities more strongly associated with the second. Thus, although the overall analyses for these two groups did not indicate a unique pattern of association between all six behavioral indices and the underlying social factors, they confirmed that the major source of variability in social participation at this age was due to differential allocation of agonistic activity and that affiliative activities among the 1-year-olds represented a less coherent mode of dyadic involvement.

Comparison of the 2-year-old groups indicated more variable ordering of the primary social factors. In Cohort 1, findings were very similar to those shown for the youngest group in Table 8.3. In contrast, the 2-year-old analyses in Cohort 2 showed a first factor defined primarily by contact and associated with approach, orientation, and attack, whereas the second factor reflected primarily competition and threat. Thus, for the second group of 2-year-olds, the order of the principal factors was inverted; affiliation accounted for more of the total variance than agonistic activity. In spite of these between-group differences, a complete dissociation between affiliative and agonistic components of dyadic activity was consistently lacking in the four youngest groups. The variability in the dyadic patterning of social participation among the 2-year-olds suggested that children at this age may be in a transitional phase. The behavioral ecology of their peer group may be evolving away from the agonistic mode that characterized the 1-year-old children and toward an organization in which more prosocial forms of participation account for a greater proportion of variability in the dyadic allocation of individual acts.

With the 3-year-olds, the principal component analyses provided a more clear-cut picture of social participation. The usual categories defining peer affiliation were tightly clustered on the first factor and those pertaining to agonistic activity on the second factor. With the sole exception of competition, all categories had exclusive loadings on a single factor. Moreover, the value of these loadings was generally much higher than those obtained with the two younger age levels. The robustness of the replication of results presented in Table 8.3 suggests that the prevalence of affiliation over agonism is well established in the 3-year-old peer group. A very similar organization of social participation was also obtained for the 4- and 5-year-old groups. In each of these analyses of dyadic participation, affiliative activity emerged as the first dimension and agonism as the second dimension of dyadic social activity. At each age level, Cohort 1 findings were well replicated by the factor structures obtained with groups from Cohort 2. The relatively high loadings of each category on a single social factor suggest that the independence of these principal components of social participation among 3-year-olds is maintained throughout the rest of the preschool period. Once again, the only exception to this clear separation of agonistic and affiliative activity involved competition. This category of activity remained significantly correlated with both dimensions of social participation throughout the latter 3 years of the preschool period.

Peer Conflict and Dominance Relations

Social dominance relations were evaluated using three primary categories of initiated conflict: attack, threat, and competition. In all cases, the critical behavior for identifying a dominance exchange entailed noting submission or retreat by the recipient of these behaviors. Although the frequency of dominance exchanges varied across groups, there was no evidence of a systematic linear trend in the absolute number of observed encounters as a function of age. In general, conflict was more frequent among children at the three younger ages (mean episodes per group was 321, SD = 66), whereas 4- and 5-year-olds were involved in substantially fewer dominance bouts (mean episodes per group = 163, SD = 39).

In all 10 groups, clear status hierarchies were evident. Figure 8.1 illustrates the nature of the obtained hierarchical networks. In each case, individuals are ordered on the diagonal according to their serial position in the group dominance hierarchy. The arrows in these social networks indicate that a dyadic relationship was established according to observed conflict outcomes. An intersecting line above the diagonal indicates either that there was no observed dominance relation for the dyad in question or that the child with a lower group status dominated in that particular dyadic context. The latter case represents a nonlinear relation and is portrayed in the diagram by an arrow beneath the diagonal. The frequency of such nonlinear relationships was extremely low. In each of the 10 groups, fewer than 10% of the observed relations violated predictions from the linear transitive model of social dominance.

Visual inspection of these three hierarchies in Figure 8.1 reveals the first of two important age changes in the nature of the group status structures. For the youngest group, nearly three quarters of the possible dyadic dominance relations were established by observed aggressive exchanges. For the 3-year-olds, this proportion decreased slightly, whereas for the 5-year-old groups, there was a substantial reduction in the percentage of observed dominance relations. This latter difference is especially noteworthy, because considerably more time was devoted to matrix completion sampling with the older children. Thus, in spite of this additional sampling, the relative number of established dyadic dominance relations for the older groups remained considerably lower than the values obtained at the younger age levels. Such findings suggest either that older children have a greater capacity to sustain social relationships without the overt expression of social dominance or that with age, children begin to employ other, more symbolic means of asserting their social dominance with peers.

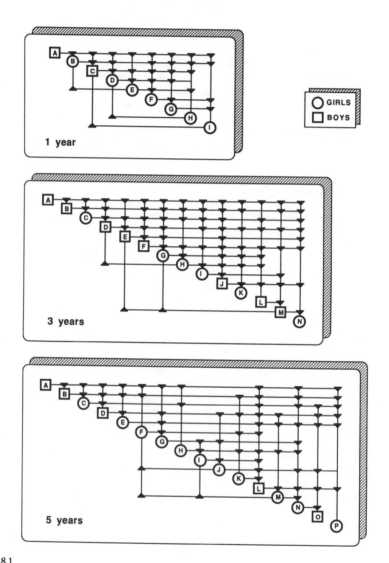

Figure 8.1

Hierarchical networks representing social dominance structures for three preschool groups.

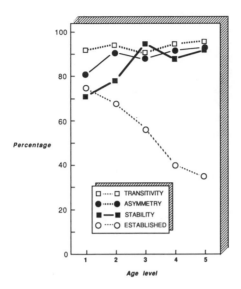

Figure 8.2

Descriptive parameters of preschool status hierarchies as a function of age.

A second age-related change in the nature of peer dominance involved the temporal stability of the obtained group status structures. Our assessment of temporal stability was performed by dividing the agonistic data into early and late observational periods. Each subset of data was analyzed independently to produce early and late dominance matrices for each group. The columns and rows of the resulting matrices were then reordered to maximize fit to the linear dominance model. Finally, Spearman correlation coefficients were calculated between the resulting rank orders for each of the 10 groups. All of these correlation coefficients were positive, ranging from .48 to 1.00. Figure 8.2 provides a summary of four descriptive parameters of social dominance as a function of age. Although both dyadic asymmetry and linear transitivity of dominance relations increased slightly as a function of age, these first two descriptive indices of social dominance were remarkably stable throughout the period under study. In contrast, both the percentage of established dominance relations and the stability of the obtained rank orders showed substantial and systematic change as a function of age. These final results indicate that changes in the nature of peer group dominance during the first 5 years of life are most evident in terms of reductions in the overt expression of agonistic status differentials as well as in the progressive emergence of temporally stable group status hierarchies.

Peer Affiliation and Interpersonal Attraction

In each of the 10 groups, the relative rate of affiliative activity far exceeded the rate of agonistic activity. Generally, over 80% of the total recorded behavior involved some form of positive social initiation. However, the ratio of initiated agonistic activity to initiated

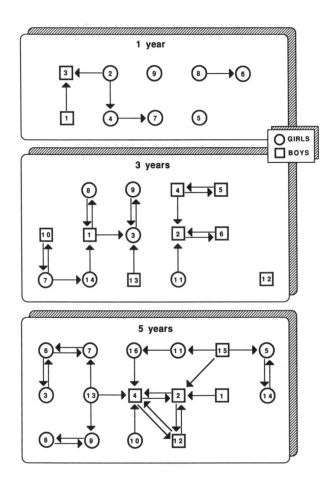

Figure 8.3

Reciprocal networks showing affiliative bonds in three preschool groups.

affiliation varied systematically as a function of age. A substantially higher proportion (over 90%) of cohesive behaviors was evident among the oldest children, whereas proportionately fewer affiliative activities (barely more than 60%) were evident among the 1-year-olds. Separate analyses of the receipt of total affiliative acts showed that in each of the 10 groups, certain children obtained significantly more than their expected share of the group's total cohesive activity (chi-square > 6.61, $p < .01$) (for the details of this analysis, see Soczka, 1973, and Strayer, 1980b). Certain children in each group were more often chosen as preferred social partners by many other group members and could therefore be identified as the more popular members of the group. Similar analyses examining individual allocation of affiliative behavior also revealed significant individual preferences within each of the 10 groups. Thus, affiliative acts were generally allocated by individuals to peer group members in a nonrandom fashion. However, social preferences were not necessarily evident for all group members. Figure 8.3 shows a graphic representation of individual social choices at three age levels. These illustrations represent behavioral sociograms of the affiliative structure of each group. Popular children appeared to be more central in these group networks, whereas other peer group members assume peripheral or even isolated roles (see also Strayer, 1980b).

The Coordination of Affiliative and Agonistic Activity

Our subsequent analyses of the coordination of affiliative activity with social dominance in the peer group focused on the overall allocation of cohesive behaviors as a function of children's position within the group dominance hierarchy as well as the correspondence between dominance rank and the frequency of being chosen as a preferred social partner by other group members. The first set of analyses focused upon the question that has guided most of the prior research on the distribution of social attention according to dominance status. The analysis requires tabulating the total received activity for each individual and correlating this measure with the status rank in the dominance hierarchy. Four of the 10 correlations were significant. In Cohort 1, three groups showed a trend toward a positive association between the receipt of affiliative behavior and social dominance status. However, in Cohort 2, only the oldest group showed a similar correlation. Thus, in general, there was a consistent trend for more affiliative activity to be allocated to higher-status individuals only among the 5-year-olds.

Table 8.4

Asymmetrical Choices Toward High- and Low-Status Peers

Age level	High-ranking	Low-ranking	p Level
1 year	3	9	.93
2 years	5	4	.50
3 years	10	6	.23
4 years	17	8	.05
5 years	15	2	.00

Note: Binomial one-way test for attraction to high rank.

A major problem with the preceeding analysis is that it fails to control for individual differences in activity levels between particular members in each peer group. For example, the positive correlations between received affiliation and dominance status may merely reflect a tendency for more dominant children to interact more frequently together and thus to increase their joint receipt of all forms of social activity. An analysis at the level of dyadic relations avoids this problem because the identification of preferred social partners is calculated from each child's total affiliative production rather than from the total activity of the entire peer group. In the youngest groups there was a slight but not significant tendency for dominant children to choose lower-ranking group members as preferred social partners. For the 2-year-olds, affiliative choices were uncoordinated with status differentials. However, among the three older groups, there was an increasing trend for affiliative choices to be directed to higher-ranking group members. This trend attained statistical significance in the two 5-year-old groups. The emerging trend for older children to choose higher-ranking group members as significant affiliative targets was to some extent obscured by a parallel tendency for increasing reciprocity in the choice of preferred playmates. In a final analysis, we separated mutual affiliative preferences from significant but asymmetrical dyadic choices. Table 8.4 shows the distribution of asymmetrical social choices toward higher- and lower-ranking peers as a function of age. The removal of reciprocal choices in the analysis of preferred social partners provides a much more vivid demonstration of how affiliative activity becomes coordinated with dominance status during the later preschool years. At the two older age levels, a disproportionate number of nonreciprocated social choices is clearly directed toward higher-ranking group members.

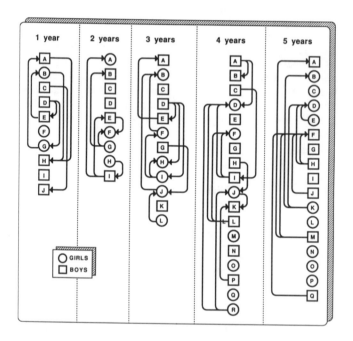

Figure 8.4

Coordination of asymmetrical affiliative choices and dominance status differentials for children in the first cohort.

The developmental shift in the coordination of asymmetrical choices with dominance status is illustrated in Figure 8.4. For the two 1-year-old groups, the general trend is for higher-status children to selectively choose subordinate group members as preferred affiliative partners. In fact, the initiation of three quarters of the observed asymmetrical choices was attributable to the four highest-ranking group members. In contrast, among the 3-year-olds, nearly half of the significant choices were directed by lower-status group members. However, with only a single exception all of these choices were directed to higher-ranking peers. Finally, in the 5-year-old groups, nearly all of the nonreciprocated preferences were directed by group members in the lower half of the dominance hierarchy to higher-ranking peers. In all but two cases, asymmetrical affiliative preferences were for peers of higher social status.

Social Ecology and Constraints on Co-adaptation

This descriptive study of the social ecology of the early peer group was undertaken to clarify how group processes might constrain individual behavior and thus represent a necessary framework for the more meaningful interpretation of naturally occurring social activities as indices of early social competence. The present analysis of social constraints in the peer group focused on the differential allocation of behavioral activity as a function of the social partner and on the coordination of social acts between pairs of preschool children. An examination of differences between age groups in activity level indicated that the younger children were substantially less active than the three older groups. In addition, older children showed greater differences in the relative use of affiliative and agonistic activity. However, at all ages, affiliation was by far the children's most important form of social involvement. The principal component analysis of our six primary categories of dyadic activity revealed two qualitatively different forms of social participation. Although these dimensions of dyadic involvement were evident at each age level, our cross-sectional comparisons indicated a developmental shift in their relative importance as a function of age. For the groups of 1- and 2-year-olds, the three categories of agonistic activity were the primary source of convergence of dyadic activity, indicating that agonism is a well-established form of social participation among even the youngest preschool children. However, the lack of a complete association among all prosocial forms of activity with the second factor suggested that affiliation would be better viewed as an emergent dimension of social life in these younger groups. The most important developmental change occurred among the 3-year-olds; for these children, there was a clearer convergence of affiliative activities, and the affiliative dimension of dyadic involvement was established as a predominent mode of dyadic interaction. In the groups of 4- and 5-year-olds, subsequent changes consisted essentially in the consolidation of the two dimensions of social participation already evident at 3 years.

In general, findings concerning dyadic participation provide empirical support for the functional distinction between cohesive and dispersive activity employed in earlier studies of social relations among 4- and 5-year-olds (Strayer, 1980a). The classes of affiliative and agonistic activity defined by our factor analyses resemble the more intuitive categories of activity discussed in both the psychological and ethological literatures. Nevertheless, a possible limitation in the present dyadic analyses involves the restricted number of behavioral categories employed to describe dyadic involvement. Given the cross-sectional focus of these analyses, and especially the relatively large age span under study, a restriction in behavioral categories was necessary in order to avoid exaggerating the effect of anticipated differences in the more sophisticated social repertoires of the older groups of preschool children. Clearly, the present rudimentary indices of social involvement cannot be expected to reflect the full complexity of social communication commonly observed among 4- and 5-year-olds. These concerns raise legitimate questions about potential limits on the utility of the present findings with regard to assessments of social competence in the older groups of children from our sample. More sophisticated forms of social communication might alter in important ways the two-dimensional representation of early interpersonal relations with peers offered by the present analyses.

In a study focusing on social relations among 4- and 5-year-olds, Strayer, Tessier, and Gariépy (1985) adopted a similar analytic strategy using a more elaborated list of social action patterns. Their observational procedures included recording a variety of verbal and gestural communication as well as forms of object exchange. In spite of differences in behavioral categories, dyadic analyses revealed principal social factors that closely resemble those in Table 8.3. In addition, their findings indicated a strong and consistent relation between distal communication and the affiliative component of dyadic participation. In conjunction with the present findings, these analyses support a basic distinction between agonistic and affiliative dimensions as consistent aspects of interpersonal relationships throughout the preschool period. These ethological studies of peer relations provide initial evidence of potential regularities in early social experience that may have important ramifications for our understanding of the processes of adaptation underlying the development of preschool social competence. Such regularities in peer relationships may serve either as environmental constraints during experience-dependent adaptation or as species-characteristic contexts that call upon processes of experience-expectant adaptation.

If integration into a stable social unit offers important occasions for developing social skills, group membership also places important limitations upon individual activities. In past developmental research, it has often been unclear how to analyze the emerging patterns of social exchange that characterize early social relationships and social roles within a stable group. This research suggests that throughout the preschool period, the stability and organization of the early peer group depend upon a delicate balance struck between social activities promoting group cohesion and those leading to social dispersion (Kummer, 1971; McGrew, 1972). In this view, the group dominance hierarchy formalizes dyadic roles during periods of social conflict and thus serves as a regulatory system that minimizes dispersive aggressive exchanges between group members. In contrast, activities that directly promote group cohesion, attracting individuals to one another and maintaining them in a coordinated social unit, must be conceptualized as an orthogonal dimension of the group's social ecology.

A child who is more skillful in coordinating both agonistic and affiliative interaction with peers may establish more stable dyadic relationships and benefit from the resulting ability to recruit allies during social conflict with others. When successful, such recruitment would have a positive feedback effect on subsequent social exchange and ultimately enhance both affiliative and dominance status in the peer group. Recent analyses of triadic conflict among 5-year-old children indicate that strategic intervention in the conflict of other group members is influenced by affiliative bonds between the various participants (Strayer & Noël, 1986). Such preliminary findings suggest that Chase's (1979, 1985) model of tripartite interaction for the emergence of linear dominance hierarchies during group formation might also be extended to account for the developing coordination of affiliative choices and social dominance toward the end of the preschool period. Perhaps among the more sophisticated 5-year-old, dominance status no longer reflects individual differences in the ability to successfully impose a preferred solution to a common interpersonal problem but rather individual differences in the ability to identify and profit from social resources in the peer setting.

Such speculation suggests that the social organization of the early peer group contributes to the emergence of individual differences in social adjustment and that the resulting individual differences bear directly upon children's capacity to influence their social partners and upon their ability to obtain social resources. The social ecology of the early peer group provides a variety of differentiated settings for early social learning. Such learning may facilitate or inhibit the acquisition of fundamental behavioral, representational, and planning skills that are universal prerequisites for subsequent integration into the larger adult society. The attractiveness of dominant peers at the end of the preschool period may reflect a growing tendency for higher-status children to manifest more sophisticated social skills and thus to become more attractive as potential affiliative partners. However, the opposite could also hold. Perhaps popular children rise in dominance status because of their greater ability to establish "social contracts" of mutual aid with their peers. Cross-sectional analyses of co-adaptation among peers provide a necessary basis for formulating questions about patterns and processes of early social adaptation. However, questions about the development of early social competence require longitudinal assessments of diversity and stability in individual styles of social adaptation during successive encounters with different peer groups.

Individual Styles of Social Adaptation

The longitudinal analysis of styles of peer adaptation involves characterizing individual differences in modes of social functioning within different stable peer groups. In the following analyses, we again decided to focus upon spring evaluations in order to minimize the potential effects of group-formation processes on assessments of differences in social adaptation styles. To increase the number of children in our evaluation of stability in observed social styles, we included all children from the longitudinal project in this second set of analyses.

Research Methods

The total sample from the four cohorts included 20 peer groups with a total of 226 children. The number of children at each age level remained relatively constant from one cohort to the next: 34 children at 1 year, 33 children at 2 years, 44 children at 3, 60 children at 4, and 55 children at 5. The 67 children who had been observed in two consecutive spring sessions were selected as the sample of individual for the longitudinal comparisons. Observational procedures for the second two cohorts were identical to those in the first study. Basic parameters of the peer group social ecology for the latter 10 groups were quite similar to those already reported for the first two cohorts in the preceeding section.

Behavioral Indices of Social Style

The descriptive analysis of the social organization of the early peer group provides a number of quite different behavioral indices that could potentially be used to classify individual differences in early social adaptation. For example, we might classify children at each age level according to their rate of initiated social acts or their relative use of agonistic and affiliative gestures. At a relational level, another classification might be based upon the relative success of initiated agonistic or affiliative actions or upon the number and quality of dominance and affiliative relationships. Finally, at the level of group structure, we might wish to distinguish children according to their relative position within the group dominance hierarchy or with respect to their centrality within the affiliative network of their peer group. Each of these possible classifications would accentuate a particular facet of social functioning within the early peer group. A more elegant solution to the problem of differentiating styles of social adaptation involves the use of multivariate classification procedures. These analytic techniques simultaneously classify individuals in terms of similarity across a series of distinct descriptors. Each behavioral measure can be conceptualized as an element in a finite set of elements that constitute a general profile of individual social adaptation.

The application of multivariate classification procedures to identify modal styles of social adaptation requires a clear response to three important analytic questions. First, what behavioral indices are the most appropriate elements to include as parameters of individual social profiles? Second, what is the most appropriate way to measure the degree of similarity in obtained individual scores? Third, should the final classification procedure cluster individuals according to the degree of similarity or according to the extent of observed differences in the obtained social profiles? In the present context, the latter question has the simplest answer. Given the objective of identifying differences in modes of social adaptation, classification should proceed by establishing major differences in social functioning and progressively placing individuals in one or the other of these extreme categories. This classification procedure puts primary emphasis on discontinuities in observed social styles. The second question of how to calculate the index of similarity is more complex and considerably more technical. Often, in multivariate classification of individual profiles, the degree of similarity between individuals is reflected in the extent to which the obtained profiles are correlated. Individuals with identical profiles (correlation coefficient of +1.00) would be classified in the same category, whereas those with diametrically opposed scores (correlation coefficient of -1.00) would be placed in the opposite extreme groups. In fact, such a correlational approach is often recommended when the primary elements that compose the individual profile have similar statistical distributions. However, if the distributions of the classification criteria are potentially dissimilar, a general similarity index based upon calculation of Euclidean distances in a multidimensional space is usually preferred. Ultimately, these technical considerations lead us to the initial question of which indices to include in the description of individual social adaptation styles. In the present analysis, a series of nine indices were selected that reflect both quantitative and qualitative aspects of social participation as well as organizational aspects of interpersonal relationships between peers. The complete set of classification variables is listed in Table 8.5.

Table 8.5

Behavioral Indices of Peer Adaptation

1.	Group participation	Percentage of total group activity
2.	Initial conflict	Initiated agonistic acts per hour
3.	Received conflict	Received agonistic acts per hour
4.	Agonistic asymmetry	Ratio of initiated agonism to total agonistic involvement
5.	Dominance status	Rank in group dominance structure
6.	Initiated affiliation	Initiated affiliative acts per hour
7.	Received affiliation	Received affiliative acts per hour
8.	Affiliative investment	Ratio of initiated affiliation to total affiliative involvement
9.	Peer popularity	Number of significant preferences and mutual affiliative relations

The *social participation* score reflected the relative involvement in social activity observed for the entire peer group. This index combined both the child's own social initiations and initiatives by other group members to the child in a percentage measure corrected for total group activity. Thus, children who were socially active, either as the instigator or as the preferred partner, scored higher on the participation index. The next four measures dealt with the agonistic repertoire. Hourly rate of *initiated aggression* provided an index of aggressive tendencies, whereas rate of *received aggression* reflected the likelihood of a child's eliciting aggressive behavior from peers. The ratio of agonistic initiations to total involvement in conflict was used as an index of the *asymmetry of conflict* for each child. This index provided an unbiased measure of the tendency to balance initiation and receipt of conflict regardless of total involvement. The final agonistic index, *dominance status*, was measured in terms of the child's relative position within the top, middle, or bottom third of the group status hierarchy. A second series of four adaptation indices reflected the child's affiliative involvement in the peer group. Hourly rate of *initiated affiliation* and *received affiliation* indexed absolute rates of prosocial involvement; the *affiliative investment* score reflected asymmetries in the relative initiation and receipt of affiliative behavior; whereas the *popularity* score measured the total number of significant affiliative choices and mutual affiliative bonds. Because these measures of social functioning do not have comparable distributions, a Euclidean distance measure of similarity was used for multivariate classification of individuals at each age level.

Modal Patterns of Social Adjustment

Multivariate classifications of social adjustment styles were calculated separately for all children observed at each age level. In the first analysis, the 33 1-year-olds were treated as basic cases in a hierarchical cluster analysis with unique scores on each of the nine classification criteria. Figure 8.5 illustrates the results obtained using the Ward hierarchical clustering method with complete linkage. Three distinct clusters of children were clearly evident. To facilitate discussion the clusters in this dendogram were labeled with the letters *A*, *B*, and *C*. Subsequent analyses at each of the remaining age levels also revealed three primary clusters. However, for the three youngest groups, the relative number of children included in each cluster varied from one age level to another. For the 1-year olds, nearly 40% of the children were grouped in Cluster A, whereas 30% were placed in Cluster B and 30% Cluster C. Of the 33 2-year-olds, only 27% of the children were classified in Cluster A, whereas 48% were placed in Cluster B, and 24% in Cluster C. Finally, among the 44 3-year-olds, 47% of the children were grouped in Cluster A, 14% in Cluster B, and 39% in Cluster C. In contrast, at 4 and 5 years, the relative number of children per cluster seemed to stabilize: 40% were placed in Cluster A and 40% in Cluster B, whereas the remaining 20% were in Cluster C. The identification of three primary styles at each age suggested strong consistencies in social adjustment to the early peer group.

However, since these classification analyses were conducted separately for each age group, it was not clear that the obtained clusters of children necessarily shared common social characteristics at all age levels. To better document differences and similarities in social styles as a function of age, clusters were treated as homogeneous subgroups and compared on each of the nine classification indices for the five age levels. The first contrast focused upon levels of social participation and indicated that children in Cluster A were significantly less involved in peer exchange throughout the entire preschool period. Members of Clusters B and C had quite comparable levels of social involvement at each age level. Subsequent comparisons of agonistic and affiliative activity clarified these preliminary differences. Figure 8.6 presents the mean rate of agonistic and affiliative initiations for each of the three clusters at each age level. Both behavioral measures

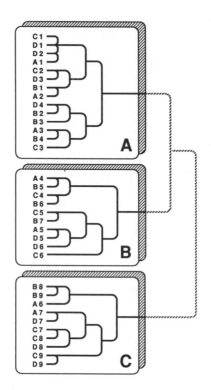

Figure 8.5

Classification of social styles for four groups of 1-year-olds.

showed developmental changes in peer-directed behavior. Individual rates of affiliative activity increased as a function of age for children in all three clusters. However, a comparison of mean rates at each age level indicated that Cluster A children were characteristically less likely to initiate affiliative episodes and that the other two clusters were quite similar. In contrast, age trends for the initiation of social agonism differed for each of the three subgroups. Members of Cluster A had the lowest rate of initiated agonism at each age level. In contrast, Cluster C children were consistently the most aggressive subgroup, although, with age, their rate of conflict progressively approached that of other members of their peer group. Children in Cluster B showed a moderate but progressively increasing rate of conflict for the first 3 years and subsequently appeared to maintain an intermediate level with respect to the other two groups of children. The comparison of rates of aggressive activity among the three social classes provided an unexpected insight concerning the often reported reduction of aggressive activity during the course of the preschool period. The present findings indicate that such a decline in social conflict is primarily due to changes in the behavioral activity of a particular subgroup of children who in the present analysis have been classified in Cluster C.

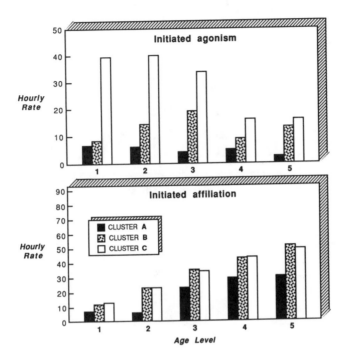

Figure 8.6

Mean rates of received social activity for each style of social functioning.

Similar analyses of the rate of received social activity are presented in Figure 8.7. Once again, both affiliative and agonistic measures showed important age-graded changes. The receipt of affiliative activities again reflected different developmental functions for the three classes of children. A gradual but consistent increase in received affiliation was evident for children classified in Cluster A. Children from Cluster B showed the strongest and most consistent growth in the rate of received affiliative acts throughout the entire preschool period. Especially at 5 years, Cluster B children obtained a surprisingly disproportionate share of the total affiliative activity in the peer group. Members of Cluster C increased their rate of received affiliation progressively during the first 4 years and subsequently declined at 5 years. Throughout the preschool period, these children were least often the target of social aggression from peers. In contrast, at each age level, Cluster B children were most frequently targeted for peer aggression. Finally, the lower rate of affiliative and agonistic initiations by Cluster A children was associated with a lower but relatively variable mean rate of receipt of both aggressive and affiliative acts from peers.

The between-cluster comparisons in rates of initiated and received social activity provided an initial portrait of both continuity and change in the three styles of social adaptation. Analyses of the five remaining social descriptors provided additional insights into the developmental changes that characterized children in each of our three clusters. Analyses of relational asymmetry in both affiliative exchanges showed no consistent

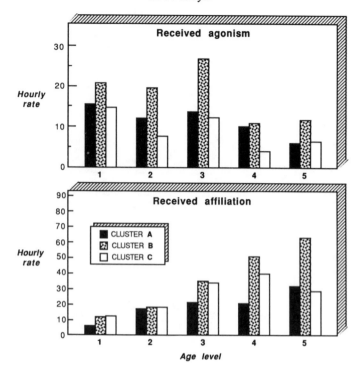

Figure 8.7

Mean rates of received social activity for each style of social functioning.

differences as a function of age or cluster membership. Apparently, initiation and receipt of affiliative activity was equally balanced at all age levels and differed little from one social style to the other. The corresponding analysis of asymmetry in agonistic exchange showed strong style differences between Cluster A and Cluster C children. Both subgroups maintained a high level of differentiation in

interactive roles during peer conflict. Regardless of age, members of Cluster C initiated nearly 75% of their episodes of interpersonal conflict, whereas Cluster A children initiated only about 25%. Children in Cluster B progressively increased their relative initiation of conflict with age (from 38% at 1 year to 60% at 5). In conjunction with findings on social activity, these differences in coordination of dyadic exchange indicated that the classification of social adjustment styles might be associated with social roles within the peer group. Figure 8.8 compares the three clusters in terms of dominance status and peer popularity as a function of age. Cluster C children showed a consistent trend to occupy high status positions in the dominance hierarchy, whereas Cluster A children were consistently in the lower third of the group structure. Once again, Cluster B children were consistently between these two extremes and appeared to be most differentiated from the other two groups at 5 years. Finally, the popularity index indicated that Cluster B children emerged as the most attractive members of their peer group at the end of the preschool period.

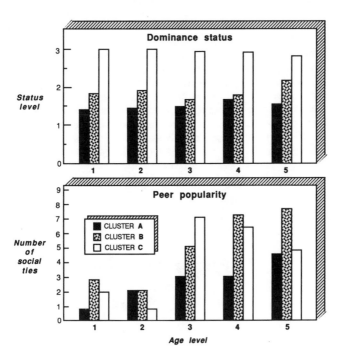

Figure 8.8

Mean social status indices for each style of social functioning.

From these comparative analyses of rates of behavioral activity, patterns of dyadic relations, and social roles within the peer group, it becomes possible to provide a tentative age-graded characterization of the three primary styles of social adaptation. Members of Cluster A appear to be withdrawn, relatively inactive, and subordinate members of the peer group. Children in Cluster B are socially active and perhaps more secure in their balanced use of both the agonistic and the affiliative parts of their social repertoire. With age, these children appear to be increasingly more attractive social partners for other children in their peer group and emerge at 5 years as the most popular members of the peer group. Finally, members of Cluster C are also active participants in the peer setting but are more assertive in their agonistic relations with other group members. Their greater aggressivity becomes increasingly associated with an attenuation of their own prosocial initiatives and with a decrease in their general attractiveness as social partners for peers.

Temporal Stability of Social Styles

These comparative analyses of social adjustment styles suggest that the three primary modes of adaptation to social pressures within the early peer group may reflect different ontogenetic pathways for individual social development. Although some of the characteristics associated with each social style change systematically as a function of age, many of the behavioral indices show surprising stability from one age level to the next. At a theoretical level, it is tempting to consider these early peer experiences as important social events that canalize the subsequent development of individual competence. However, the demonstration of consistency in particular modes of social adaptation from one age level to the next does not necessarily imply corresponding differentiated pathways for individual development. For the psychobiologist, it is essential to determine whether these empirically derived styles of social adaptation result from intrinsic differences in early social dispositions or instead reflect phenotypic variation in the expression of the child's potential for short-term adjustment to predictable forces within the early social peer environment. In order to respond to this question, modes of adaptation must be compared for the same child over time. In the present context, it is essential to assess the degree of stability in the style of social adaptation from one social setting to the next.

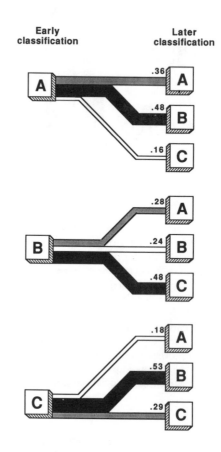

Figure 8.9

Temporal changes in the classification of social adjustment styles.

Our final set of analyses explored the question of the temporal stability of social styles from the end of one school year to the next. These analyses focused upon a subset of 67 children who were members of the observed peer groups during two consecutive spring sessions. A simple cross-tabulation of cluster membership from one year to the other showed that nearly two thirds of the children changed their mode of social adaptation. Such findings do not support a strong deterministic model of early social development. Instead, they suggest that early experience with peers primarily influences short-term adaptation within a particular group setting. A closer consideration of the direction of the observed changes suggests a somewhat novel view of the development of early peer competence (see Figure 8.9). The modal tendency for each of the social styles was to change. Nearly half of the Cluster A children were in Cluster B the following year. Slightly more than a third remained in Cluster A, and about one in six became members of Cluster C. Similarly, nearly half of the Cluster B children were classified in Cluster C the following year, whereas a quarter remained in Cluster B and the rest were placed in Cluster A. Over half of the Cluster C children were reclassified as Cluster B, less than a third maintained their previous mode of social functioning, and one in six changed to Cluster A. The relative instability of classification in styles of social adaptation has direct ramifications for models of individual social development and peer group social ecology.

Discussion and Conclusions

At a developmental level, variability in primary modes of adaptation indicates that in spite of the possible short-term stability of interactive roles, dyadic relationships, and social status within the early peer group, children maintain a substantial degree of plasticity in their primary social repertoires. The development of particular routines that do not necessarily optimize the child's functioning within a specific social setting does not disrupt the acquisition of basic social skills that will be applied in other interpersonal contexts. More important, early contact with peers probably provides concrete representational and affective experience that contributes to the child's emerging competence, even though the overt expression of these new abilities is inhibited by prevailing social facts of the immediate peer group. With respect to the social ecology of the early peer group, the nature of change from one social style to another indicates that the Cluster A style of social adjustment becomes increasingly infrequent with age. The reduction in the number of *withdrawn-inactive* children during the course of the preschool years represents a potentially important benefit of early socialization in a setting co-constructed with same-age peers.

The second developmental finding indicates that the majority of children in the preschool peer group alternate between *involved-attractive* and *aggressive-dominant* modes of social functioning. Such a result suggests an underlying dialectic in modes of social adaptation throughout the preschool years. The establishment and maintenance of early peer relations involves keeping an optimal balance between cohesive and dispersive forces that arise during dyadic and polyadic interaction in the preschool setting. Early experience of both assertive and supportive modes of social adaptation assures a more diversified repertoire of social action, permitting increasingly strategic adjustments to social pressures in the particular interpersonal contexts. A greater diversity of available social tactics provides the potential means for assuming a more active role during social communication and balancing individual contributions in the co-construction of interpersonal relationships. Optimal choices of appropriate tactics in a given social setting may be the defining characteristic of mature or competent social participation.

Rather than defining social competence in terms of successful integration within a stable peer group, the present psychobiological perspective draws attention to developmental functions of early social experience with peers. Socialization within the preschool peer group serves as an early example of developing capacities to co-construct effective strategies for regulating interpersonal communication. Early differences in the ability to generate, assimilate and recall information about interaction with peers lead to qualitative differences in children's social knowledge base. Even when social information has no immediate advantage for enhancing group adjustment, nor any discernable effect on ongoing social activity, growing knowledge about social dynamics in the peer group has developmental value because it facilitates, and ultimately constrains, the elaboration of future interpersonal relationships.

References

Abramovitch, R. (1976). The relation of attention and proximity rank in the preschool children. In M. Chance & R. Larsen (Eds.), *The social structure of attention.* London: Wiley.

Abramovitch, R., & Strayer, F.F. (1978). Preschool social organization: Agonistic spacing and attentional behaviors. In P. Pliner, T. Kramer, & T. Alloway (Eds.), *Recent advances in the study of communication and affect* (Vol. 6, pp. 197-217). New York: Plenum

Altmann, J. (1974). Observational study of behavior: Sampling methods. *Behavior, 49,* 227-267.

Blurton-Jones, N. (1972). Categories of child-child interactions. In N. Blurton-Jones (Ed.), *Ethological studies of child behavior* (pp. 97-127). Cambridge: Cambridge University Press.

Charlesworth, W.R. (1976). Human intelligence as adaptation: An ethological approach. In L. Resnick (Ed.), *The nature of intelligence* (pp. 213-234). Hillsdale, NJ: Erlbaum.

Chase, I.D. (1979). Models of hierarchy formation in animal societies. *Behavioral Science, 19*(6), 374-382.

Chase, I.D. (1985). The sequential analysis of aggressive acts during hierarchy formation: An application of the "jig-saw puzzle" approach. *Animal Behaviour, 33,* 86-100.

Crook, J.H. (1970). Social organization and the environment: Aspects of contemporary social ethology. *Animal Behaviour, 19,* 197-209.

Frodi, A., Bridges, L., & Grolnick, W. (1985). Correlates of mastery-related behavior: A short-term longitudinal study of infants in their second year. *Child Development, 56,* 1291-1299.

Greenough, W.T., Black, J.E., & Wallace, C.S. (1987). Experience and brain development. *Child Development, 58,* 539-559.

Harlow, H.F., & Harlow, M.K. (1965). The affectional systems. In A. Schrier, H. Harlow, & F. Stollnitz (Eds.), *Behaviour of nonhuman primates* (pp.). New York: Academic Press.

Harmon, R., Suwalsky, J., & Klein, R. (1979). Infants' preferential response for mother versus an unfamiliar adult. *Journal of the American Academy of Child Psychiatry, 18,* 437-449.

Hartup, W.W., Glazer, J.A., & Charlesworth, R. (1967). Peer reinforcement and sociometric status. *Child Development, 38,* 1017-1024.

Hazen, N., & Durrett, M. (1982). Relationship of security of attachment to exploration and cognitive mapping ability in two-year-olds. *Developmental Psychology, 18,* 751-759.

Hinde, R.R. & Stevenson-Hinde, J. (1976). Towards understanding relationships: Dynamic stability. In P. Bateson, & R. Hinde (Eds.), *Growing points in ethology* (pp. 451-479). Cambridge: Cambridge University Press.

Hinde, R.R. (Ed.). (1983). *Primate social relationships: An integrated approach.* Oxford: Blackwell Scientific Publications.

Hold, B. (1977). Rank and behavior: An ethological study of preschool children. *Homo, 28,* 158-188.

Humphrey, N.K. (1976). The social function of intellect. In P. Bateson, & R. Hinde (Eds.), *Growing points in ethology* (pp. 303-317). Cambridge: Cambridge University Press.

Kummer, H. (1968). *Social organization of hamadryas baboons.* Chicago: University of Chicago Press.

Kummer, H. (1971). *Primate societies; Group techniques in ecological adaptation.* Chicago: University of Chicago press.

La Frenière, P.J., & Charlesworth, W.R. (1983). Dominance, attention, and affiliation in a preschool group: A nine-month longitudinal study. *Ethology and Sociobiology, 4*(2), 55-67.

Lenneberg, E. (1967). *The biological foundations of language.* New York: Wiley.

Lerner, R.M. (1984). *On the nature of human plasticity.* Cambridge: Cambridge University Press.

Main, M., Kaplan, N., & Cassidy, J. (1985). Security in infancy, childhood and adulthood: A move to the level of representation. In I. Bretherton, & E. Waters (Eds.), *Growing points of attachment theory and research.*

Monograph of the Society for Research in Child Development, 50, 41-65.

McGrew, W.C. (1972). *An ethological study of children's behavior.* New York: Academic Press.

Missakian, E.A. (1976, June). *Aggression and dominance relations in peer groups of children six to forty-five months of age.* Paper presented at the Annual Conference of the Animal Behavior Society, Colorado.

Missakian, E.A. (1980). Gender differences in agonistic behavior and dominance relations of synanon communally reared children. In D.R. Omark, F.F. Strayer, & D.G. Freedman (Eds.), *Dominance relations: An ethological view of human conflict and social interaction* (pp.397- 414). New York: Garland STPM Press.

Musatti, T. (1986). Early peer relations: The perspectives of Piaget and Vygotsky. In E. Mueller, & C. Cooper (Eds.), *Process and outcome in peer relationships* (pp. 25-53). New York: Academic Press.

Nadel, J. (1986). *Imitation et communication entre jeunes enfants* [Imitation and communication among young children]. Paris: Presses Universitaires de France.

Parten, M.B. (1932). Social participation among pre-school children. *Journal of Abnormal Psychology, 24,* 243-269.

Pipp, S., & Harmon, R. (1987). Attachment as regulation: A commentary. *Child Development, 58,* 633-647.

Sackett, G.P. (1966). Monkeys reared in visual isolation with pictures as visual input: Evidence for an innate releasing mechanism. *Science, 154,* 1468-1472.

Savin-Williams, R.C. (1976). An ethological study of dominance formation and maintenance in a group of human adolescents. *Child Development, 47,* 972-979.

Savin-Williams, R.C. (1980). Dominance and submission among adolescent boys. In D.R. Omark, F.F. Strayer, & D.G. Freedman (Eds.), *Dominance relations: An ethological view of human conflict and social interaction* (pp. 217-230). New York: Garland STPM Press.

Sluckin, A., & Smith, P. (1977). Two approaches to the concept of dominance in preschool children. *Child Development, 48,* 917-923.

Soczka, L. (1973). Ethologie sociale et sociométrie: Analyse de la structure d'un groupe de singes crabiers (*Macaca fascicularis irus*) en captivité [Social ethology and sociometry: An analysis of group structure in crab-eating macaques]. *Behaviour, 50,* 254-269.

Strayer, F.F. (1980a). Child ethology and the study of preschool social relations. In H.C. Foot, A.J. Chapman, & J.R. Smith (Eds.), *Friendship and social relations in children* (pp. 235-265). New York: Wiley.

Strayer, F.F. (1980b). Social ecology of the preschool peer group. In W.A. Collins (Ed.), *The Minnesota symposium on child psychology* (Vol. 13, pp. 165-196). Hillsdale, NJ: Erlbaum.

Strayer, F.F. (1981). The organization and coordination of asymmetrical relations among young children: A biological view of social power. In M.D. Watts (Ed.), *New directions for methodology of social and behavioral science* (Vol. 7, pp. 33-49). San Francisco: Jossey-Bass.

Strayer, F.F. (1984). Biological approaches to the study of the family. In R.D. Parke, R.N. Emde, H.P. McAdoo, & G.P. Sackett (Eds.), *The family: Review of child development research* (Vol. 7, pp. 1-19). Hillsdale, NJ: Erlbaum.

Strayer, F.F., Chapeskie, T.R., & Strayer, J. (1978). The perception of preschool social dominance relations. *Aggressive Behavior, 4,* 183-192.

Strayer, F.F., & Harris, P.J. (1979). Social cohesion among captive squirrel monkeys *(Saimiri sciureus).* *Behavioral Ecology and Sociobiology, 5,* 93-110.

Strayer, F.F., & Moss, E., & Blicharski, T. (1988). Bio-social bases of representational activity during early childhood. In T. Winegar (Ed.), *Social interaction and the development of children's understanding* (pp. 21-44). Norwood, NJ: Ablex.

Strayer, F.F., & Noël, J.M. (1986). The prosocial and antisocial functions of preschool aggression: An ethological study of triadic conflict among young children. In C. Zahn-Waxler (Ed.), *Altruism and aggression: Biological and social origins* (pp. 107-131). New York: Cambridge University Press.

Strayer, F.F., & Strayer, J. (1976). An ethological analysis of social agonism and dominance relations among preschool children. *Child Development, 47,* 980-988.

Strayer, F.F., & Tessier, O., & Gariépy, J.L. (1985). L'activité affiliative et le réseau cohésif chez les enfants d'âge préscolaire. In R. Tremblay, M. Provost, & F.F. Strayer (Eds.), *Ethologie et développement de l'enfant* [Ethology and child development] (pp. 291-308). Paris: Stock/Laurence Pernoud.

Trivers, R. (1972). Parental investment and sexual selection. In B. Campbell (Ed.), *Sexual selection and the descent of man, 1871-1971* (pp. 136-179). Chicago: Aldine.

Vaughn, B., & Waters, E. (1978). Social organization among preschooler peers: Dominance, attention and sociometric correlates. In D.R. Omark, F.F. Strayer, & D. Freedman (Eds.), *Dominance relations: An ethological view of human conflict and social interaction* (pp. 359-380). New York: Garland STPM Press.

Vaughn, B., & Waters, E. (1981). Attention structure, sociometric status and dominance: Interrelations, behavioral correlates and relationships to social competence. *Developmental Psychology, 17,* 275-288.

Weisfeld, G.E. (1980). Social dominance and human motivation. In D.R. Omark, F.F. Strayer, & D.G. Freedman (Eds.), *Dominance relations: An ethological view of human conflict and social interaction* (pp. 273-

286). New York: Garland STPM Press.

Weisfeld, G.E., Omark, D.R., & Cronin, C.L. (1980). A longitudinal and cross-sectional study of dominance in boys. In D.R. Omark, F.F. Strayer, & D.G. Freedman (Eds.), *Dominance relations: An ethological view of human conflict and social interaction* (pp. 205-216) New York: Garland STPM Press.

9

Development of Communicative Competencies in Early Childhood: A Model and Results

Pierre-Marie Baudonnière, Marie-José Garcia-Werebe,
Juliette Michel, and Jacqueline Liégeois

Laboratoire de Psycho-biologie de l'Enfant,
CNRS, Paris, France

> Science is meaningless without facts,
> but
> facts are meaningless if we don't
> know how they are obtained.

During the past 5 years, investigations of social development at the Laboratoire de Psycho-biologie de l'Enfant in Paris have centered on the ontogeny of communicative competence during early childhood. This general theme has been subdivided into a number of more specific topics that have become the particular interest of different research groups at the laboratory. Children's capacities to initiate socially directed behaviors, to respond to actions that have been directed to themselves, to synchronize these social exchanges, and to successfully transmit messages to social partners emerge progressively from birth during the course of social interaction with familiar others.

In general, our knowledge about the development of such communicative skills has been based upon detailed analyses of dyadic interaction in the adult-child context. However, with regard to our own research activities, such a context imposes very specific limitations because of the inherent asymmetry of adult-child social relationships. Often, the superior competence of the adult partner compensates for the rudimentary skills of the younger partner. As a result, we are unable to determine the actual communicative capacity of the very young child. To circumvent this problem, we have developed a research method that focuses upon child-child social communication using a particular paradigm which permits systematic manipulation of a number of associated variables such as physical setting, number and familiarity of partners, and age effects.

The developmental model of competence in peer communication can be summarized as follows:

B. H. Schneider et al. (eds.), Social Competence in Developmental Perspective, 175–193.

Months	Typical Communicative Behavior
6 - 9	Interest in animate partner.
9 - 16	Social behavior directed toward partner.
16 - 18	Observation of partner's manipulation of objects.
18 - 24	Delayed imitation of partner's manipulation using same object.
24 - 27	Attempts at simultaneous manipulation using same object.
27 - 36	Immediate reciprocal imitation using identical objects and vocal/verbal behavior.
36 - 48	Transition from role identification to role differentiation.
48 - 60	Transition from role differentiation to complementarity in pretend play.

The current problem is to define an appropriate methodology to test this model.

Methodologically speaking, early communicative performance, but not necessarily communicative competence, can be assessed in studies of mother-toddler interactions. Similar limitations are evident in assessments of communicative skills in a particular nursery school group. In order to establish the limits of communicative competence, children's communication must also be explored in the more controlled setting of interpersonal dyadic exchange. However, the study of adult-child interaction remains the central focus of most recent research with children under 3 years of age, while the analysis of social interactions within infant day-care groups is fast becoming a second major area of interest. From our perspective, it is quite surprising that so few researchers have been concerned with children's more private interpersonal interactions.

The principal rationale used to explain this apparent lack of interest in the development of interpersonal exchange involves the conditions under which young children can be readily observed. According to many ethologists, it is necessary to record behavioral data in settings where the behavior generally occurs. This is often referred to as the "natural setting." Thus, "naturalistic observation" is thought to assure meaningful and ecologically valid data, which ultimately guards against misunderstanding the observed phenomena.

The first problem that we must discuss is the notion of "natural setting" for the human species. A school or nursery school is just an "habitual setting" for some members of the species. The habitual setting is, in fact, more accurately designated as the by-product of an institutional organization that presents rules, constraints, and habits that are often more directly linked to socioeconomic imperatives than to children's developmental or social needs. The human milieu cannot be understood as other than a social by-product. Metaphors that assimilate children's environments into ecological models do not necessarily offer apt renderings of the social skills underlying particular cultural features of the human milieu.

Scientifically speaking, we must ask what advantages and/or guarantees are afforded by studying communicative competencies in their habitual setting. Are there not more drawbacks than advantages in choosing to observe behaviors in an habitual setting rather than in an experimental or quasi-experimental one? Obviously, it is not because a setting is habitual that it is worth being studied from a scientific point of view. Furthermore, behaviors demonstrated in the habitual setting do not necessarily represent the child's current behavioral capacities. Behaviors must always be viewed as by-products of the system of constraints — both social, biological, and environmental — in which the organism is observed. Such constraints are all the more important when we consider that observational settings are not freely chosen by the subjects, which is almost always the case for toddlers in preschool play groups. Thus, to better understand the development of communicative competencies, exogeneous constraints must be taken into account and their effects evaluated, even when the behaviors under observation are produced in an habitual setting.

The immediate problem is how to analyze the particular system of constraints within which the child is functioning. In an habitual setting, the number and diversity of variables to be taken into account are very important. Currently, however, differences in setting are extreme from one study to another. Settings may differ in group composition, use of space, pedagogical method, teacher-child ratio, and sex and age ratios, to name but a few conditions. How to synthesize coherent findings rather than anecdotal reports from such a diversity of settings remains a serious challenge. To attribute purported effects to a specific antecedent variable and to interpret higher-order statistical interactions among such variables is even more difficult. We chose to study toddlers' and preschoolers' interpersonal communication using experimental procedures.

Experimental Settings

Dyads of volunteer children played together in a room familiar to them in their day-care center or kindergarten. However, each space was rearranged in order to standardize settings across locations. This 15-square-meter setting contained 10 categories of objects in duplicate.

The duplicates were arranged by category to avoid any situational ambiguity. When given a choice among 10 different categories of objects, the children had to be in a position to know immediately whether they were taking an object as a function of the object that the partner was holding. This means that the subjects had to be clearly aware of the number of matching objects and that the situation had to facilitate this awareness. If the duplicates had been placed randomly in the setting, the researcher would have had no means of interpreting whether a child's behavior indicated unawareness of duplicates or a deliberate choice of an activity different from that of the partner.

The 10 categories of objects were arranged in standard fashion either on the floor, on small tables, or suspended from the ceiling (see Nadel & Baudonnière, 1980, 1982). The objects were chosen for the variety of activities for which children use them. There were two cowboy hats, two umbrellas, two pairs of sunglasses, two soccer balls, two inflated balloons, two towels, two dolls, two chairs, two stuffed dogs, and two musical mobiles hanging from the ceiling.

One door was always accessible during the sessions and subjects could leave whenever they wanted to. Analysis of modes of interaction in young children does not lend itself easily to enclosed spaces because enclosed spaces give children a vague sensation of being locked up. Therefore, session length was not set in advance but rather depended on the subjects themselves, who, by leaving the room, indicated the end of a session. There were numerous reasons for leaving, and no one global interpretation fit them all. Each session was videotaped in its entirety without the children's knowledge by a hidden mobile video camera equipped with a zoom lens.

Dependent Measures

The dependent measures, chosen for their relevancy and sensitivity as well as their reliability, were relatively straightforward with respect to categorization and coding. Four measures were used: object holds, physical proximity, partner-directed glances, and vocal or verbal utterances.

The motivation for choosing these dependent measures over more standard behavioral categories used in the current literature requires further justification. Behavioral categories present notorious definition problems. First, it would be necessary to agree on the notion of "behavioral unit." Second, in the majority of cases, researchers have used predefined categories which often constitute subjective filters, especially when they are associated with time sampling. In addition, even though the behavioral categories are generally taken from Parten (1932), lists and/or category definitions tend to vary from one author to another, making it difficult — at times, impossible — to compare findings.

The behavioral categories chosen are generally heterogeneous in terms of the type and duration of the behavioral units that they are designed to group together or set apart (e.g., glances at partner, takes, gives, cries, imitates) and form behavioral units which are heterogeneous in nature and duration. Therefore, we prefer to use variables correlated with behavior which do not require a priori interpretations.

Object Holds as a Measure of Frequency of Imitative Behavior

The value of centering analysis on the seemingly indirect measure of object holds to evaluate frequency of imitative behavior has been dealt with elsewhere (Baudonnière, 1985, 1986, 1987a; Nadel & Baudonnière, 1980, 1982; Nadel, Baudonnière & Fontaine, 1983). Other authors (Abramovitch & Grusec, 1978; Lubin & Field, 1981) have employed a priori definitions of imitative behavior to distinguish these from fortuitous occurrences of similar forms of behavior. Therefore, the only behaviors that were scored were reproductions of unusual actions produced within 10 seconds after the model behavior. For any trained observer of 2- to 3-year-olds, it is clear that this selection criterion is meaningless. No one can expect children to be systematically original in all of their activities, and there is a priori no reason to suspect that original actions are imitated more frequently than other actions, at least not in this age range. In addition, the originality of a behavior is not necessarily perceived in the same manner by 2-, 3- and 4-year-olds as it is by the experimenter. The lag between production and reproduction is not ironclad proof of a connection between these two behaviors. Children's activities during production of the model behavior may temporarily make it impossible for them to imitate the model and this sometimes generates a delay of over 10 seconds between model and imitation. For example, this occurs frequently for the use of the sunglasses or cowboy hats, which are difficult for 2-year-olds to manipulate.

To bypass these numerous obstacles, it was necessary to devise other more reliable solutions than this definition of imitation. Starting from the principle that the object is a mediator for all activities as of the 2nd year of life (Eckerman & Whatley, 1977; Eckerman, Whatley & Kutz, 1975; Mueller & Brenner, 1977; Mueller and Lucas, 1975; Nadel, 1986; Nadel and Baudonnière, 1982, 1985), the dependent measure of imitation chosen here was based on the ways in which the subjects used the duplicates of objects available to them.

The line of reasoning is that if two children whose prevalent mode of exchange is immediate imitation are brought together, and if objects are important bases or mediators for social and/or cognitive activities, then a situation in which all the objects are in duplicate should prompt children to interact by using holds of matching objects rather than solitary holds. Holds and discards of objects thus become evidence for the density of imitative behavior between partners.

This approach makes it possible to disconfirm the hypothesis of the prevalence of imitation because, in this "open" situation, the subjects are perfectly free to prefer solitary activities and to disregard their partner's ongoing behavior or to seek out other forms of exchange if they so desire. The choice of object holds also provides a reliable behavioral measure because each hold and each discard constitute events that are easy for the experimenter to code and can furnish unambiguous data on the imitative or nonimitative form of activity exhibited by each partner.

This is feasible because the subjects are given a choice of 10 categories of objects in duplicate. The children's choices at any point in time during the session are thus never constrained because they can either appropriate both matching objects in a given category, choose objects other than the one(s) that the partner is holding, or choose objects identical to the partner's.

A composite measure designed to evaluate object holds in dyads has been described elsewhere (Baudonnière, 1986, 1987a, 1988). This composite measure expresses, for any point in time during the session, a subject's behaviors in terms of the number of objects that the subject is holding that match or differ from those of the partner, thereby indicating whether the subject indeed favors matching holds. This measure is a ratio, calculated second by second, of the number of objects held in common to the total number of objects held at that time.

Ratio values range from 0 to 1 (where 0/0 indicates that the child is holding no objects). It can be seen that any value greater than 0.50 indicates a tendency toward matching choices of objects with the partner's choices. On the contrary, any value equal to or less than 0.50 indicates that the child, at this point in the session, prefers holding of objects different from those that the partner is currently holding. This composite measure has the additional advantage of distinguishing between partners because, for a given second in the session, the ratio can be 1.0 for one member of the dyad (1/1) and 0.25 for the other (1/4).

Physical Proximity

Physical proximity is commonly used as a measure in this type of study (Connolly & Smith, 1972; Eckerman et al., 1975; Mueller, 1972; Mueller, Bleier, Krakow, Hedegus & Cournoyer, 1977). Certain authors assign physical proximity a crucial role in early toddler contact (Eckerman & Stein, 1982). Before true mastery of language, communication at a distance is problematic, and physical proximity of the partners therefore constitutes a good measure of their social contact.

Coding (second by second) includes indications of whether or not children were located at less than 1 meter from each other (intersecting routes when crossing the room were not included). This criterion is a standard measure in studies of this age range and was selected because it corresponds to the distance from which two children can touch each other with their outstretched arms.

Orientation of Glance

Glances toward the partner are frequently employed as a measure in this type of study (Abramovitch & Grusec, 1978; Doyle, Connolly & Rivest, 1980; Eckerman and Stein, 1982; Eckerman et al., 1975; Lougee, Grueneich & Hartup, 1977). It was used by certain authors as the criterion for socially directed behavior (Becker, 1977; Bronson, 1981; Mueller & Brenner, 1977). However, orientation of glance is not defined in an identical fashion in all these works, nor is it measured with the same degree of precision. Glance can have multiple functions and accomplish various goals. A glance at a partner can indicate interest in that partner, observation, gleaning information on the partner's activities, and so forth. Therefore, no one communicative function can be attributed to it. In addition, it is not always necessary to look directly at the partner to see what the partner is doing. Peripheral vision may be operating, and at times, auditory information is amply sufficient. In this case, what value is there in using such a polyvalent behavioral measure?

If a small number of glances in the partner's direction suggests disregard and sustained interest is measured by frequent glances, then the duration of glances toward the partner should be highly indicative of the amount of attention one partner pays to the other. Glances for each child were analyzed second by second and classified into three categories: looks toward the partner, absence of glances toward the partner, and noncodable (impossible-to-determine) visual orientation.

Vocal and Verbal Utterances

Analyzing vocal and verbal utterances at this age is often tricky. Few studies have dealt directly with spontaneous utterances of 2- to 4-year-olds in peer interaction situations in the absence of adults. Only Mueller (1972) investigated verbal utterances of 3 1/2- to 5-year-olds in a situation highly comparable to the present one, without an adult present. All the other studies, including Mueller's subsequent work (Mueller et al., 1977), took place in the presence of an adult. However, it is common knowledge that the presence of adult partners affects the frequency of recourse to verbal utterances, even in younger children. Therefore, we have little basis for comparison. In addition, pronunciation at this age range is not always accurate, and although speech may sometimes be incomprehensible to adults, they can still make hypotheses about what is being said.

These two obstacles were decisive in our choice to employ, at least initially, a nonlinguistic analysis. Coding was restricted to frequency and duration (sampling unit = 1 second) of vocal and/or verbal utterances per child. These were classified into four categories as a function of (a) vocal content (shouts, song, exclamations, etc.), (b) verbal content (words, identifiable sentences, etc.), (c) whether these utterances were clearly solitary (without glances at the partner, with the back turned, unrelated to the partner's current activity, etc.), and (d) whether these utterances were addressed to the partner (encouragement, vocal or verbal imitation, questions accompanied by visual contact, etc.).

Scoring

Each child was recorded continuously during the entire session with a 1-second sampling unit. Most of the scoring was performed by two judges either simultaneously or separately. The few disagreements that occurred concerned the exact time of the start or end of an event. Disagreement was rare with regard to type of event or category classification. This was due to the nature of the measures selected, which left little room for differences in interpretation.

The Composite Variable

As stated earlier, no single dependent measure can account for a subject's privileged activity or mode of exchange. Rather, by combining dependent variables, hypotheses can be better assessed.

The basic issue is the way heterogeneous measures are combined. One solution is to analyze the relative duration of each dependent measure: simultaneous holds of matching objects, number of partner-directed verbal utterances, degree of physical proximity, partner-directed glances, and so on. This procedure, however, would only be valid in those rare cases where a single mode of social exchange is prevalent. In all other cases where behavior and mode of exchange vary over the session, which one could more reasonably expect, the relative duration of each dependent measure would be no more than weakly informative as to the modes of communication utilized by the subjects.

An alternative consists of comparing the four dependent measures second by second and analyzing their covariance. For example, do the children look more at their partners when they are closer to them? Are object holds accompanied by physical proximity? Have verbalizations acquired the status of communication at a distance? The method of data collection used in this study allows for this type of comparison, yielding I+ or I-, V+ or V-, P+ or P-, R+ or R-. The value of such an analysis, however, is questionable.

Analyzing the covariance of the dependent measures disregards the specific function of each observed behavior. Nothing can be gained by analyzing the relative duration of the comparative durations of the four dependent measures or their presence in the same second because this does not take into account the different and possibly antithetical or complementary functions of the dependent measures in characterizing the role that these behaviors play in social exchange. Verbalization can be encouragement, a glance of confirmation, physical proximity, holding matching objects, or other behaviors. This explains the fact that there is little value in scoring the occurrence of different behavioral measures in the same time unit.

The problem comes down to a sequential relationship across behaviors. Can the temporal boundaries for the consequences of a glance, verbalization, or imitation be set *a priori*? What are the relevant temporal spans: 1, 3, 5 or 10 second(s)? The obvious answer is that there is no one yardstick and that the problem must be expressed in different terms to arrive at a workable solution.

The method chosen provides a means of combining the behavioral measures, scored separately, without *a priori* hypotheses as to their sequential dependency. Each session was divided *a posteriori* into 10-second frames. The 10-second frame is short enough to reveal changes over a session and long enough to allow the function of the behaviors coded by dependent measures to emerge.

The remaining problem concerns quantitative assessment of variation for the four behavioral measures in the 10-second time frame. Current knowledge of these measures only allows for empirical assessment. After data analysis, a different threshold was set for each measure: over 50% of the frame for I+, using the ratio number for matching holds/total number of objects, and for P+, indicating physical proximity. The threshold for glance toward the partner was set at 3 seconds. For verbal utterances, the discriminant cutoff point was at least one directed utterance per frame over the course of 10 seconds for the three age groups.

Each measure can thus range from 0% to 100% for each 10-second frame over the entire session. The four measures therefore code each frame continuously for the session. If a subject favors immediate imitation during the entire session, for example, I+ will appear for each frame; if exchanges are predominantly verbal, then V+ will be close to 100%.

Using this methodology, a variety of different research projects were conducted. The following are three examples of more recent results. The first study examines the evolution of communicative abilities from the ages of 1 to 4. The second explores the influence of peer friendship on the emergence of dyad-specific language among 3- to 5-year-olds. The third examines behavioral flexibility in mixed-age dyadic situations during this same period (see Baudonnière, 1988, p. 70).

The Beginning of Social Interaction between Peers during the 2nd Year of Life: Effect of Familiarity

A large number of recent studies has shown that children become increasingly social with each other during the 2nd year of life (Becker 1977; Bronwell, 1982; Eckerman et al., 1975; Lewis & Rosenblum, 1975; Mueller & Brenner, 1977). In fact, the 2nd year seems to be principally marked by an emerging competence with respect to sustained interactions as well as increases in the frequency of social contact and in the complexity of interaction sequences. Although nonreciprocal contact may be typical of the 1st year, such a characterization of peer communication is less valid for the 2nd year. During this period, the probability of responses from the dyadic partner does not change dramatically. However, the amount of socially directed behavior is clearly augmented, and as a result, we note an important increase in the hourly rate of reciprocal exchange between peers. Many authors (see Hartup, 1983) report that socially coordinated activity such as imitation occurs during the 2nd year; however, it is only in the 3rd year that reciprocal imitation emerges as a predominant mode of social communication.

How do children pass from a period during which they display low levels of social interaction to one in which they are capable of sustaining imitative interactions? Several hypotheses can be proposed: Even though, during the 2nd year, the presence of a peer affects the partner's behavior, during this same period, interest in objects seems clearly more important in terms of both duration and frequency (Baudonnière & Michel, 1988). What are the reasons for this asymmetry of interest? Are objects more interesting because they serve as props which lend themselves to varied manipulation and novel exploration? Are the familiar partners relatively less attractive because they are familiar or because they are difficult to engage? Few studies have addressed these questions. Jacobson (1981) proposed that due to familiarity, the partner is relatively uninteresting. If this hypothesis were correct, we should expect the density of social interaction between unfamiliar children to be higher than that between familiar peers. Even if Jacobson's argument seems nonintuitive and unpersuasive, his hypothesis is sufficiently important to warrant systematic experimental evaluation.

Little attention has actually been paid to the role of familiarity between children and its effect on quality and quantity of early peer social interaction. A few studies, however, have experimentally manipulated peer familiarity. Schwartz (1972) found that 4-year-old children showed more positive affect, motility, and verbalization with a friend than either with a stranger or alone. Lewis and Rosenblum (1975), like Becker (1977), reported more extensive social interaction among familiar as opposed to unfamiliar peers. Rubenstein and Howes (1976) showed that the presence versus absence of a familiar peer raised the complexity of toddlers' object play. Bronson (1974) predicted lower levels of social interaction among familiar as opposed to unfamiliar peers on the grounds that the feedback from unfamiliar peers is too delayed and variable. Finally, Doyle, et al. (1980) found that with a familiar peer, social play was more frequent and that when children were interacting socially, the cognitive level of play was also higher.

To examine the effects of familiarity between toddlers on the density of social interaction, and to analyze the growth and form of interaction in order to assess changes over the period of 10 to 30 months, we selected a sample consisting of 96 children from six Parisian kindergartens, half of whom were familiar and half of whom were unfamiliar with their experimental partners. They were equally divided over four age groups: 10 to 14 months, 16 to 20 months, 22 to 26 months, and 28 to 32 months. In dyads, the age difference between the 2 children was less than 1 month.

It was predicted, contrary to Jacobson's (1981) hypothesis, that an unfamiliar partner would not be more attractive and would not incite higher levels of social interaction than a familiar one. Specifically, it was hypothesized that a familiar peer would increase the frequency of social interaction in all four age groups under consideration.

We examined both familiar and unfamiliar dyads in the same setting using the same behavioral measures. Moreover, we studied a long age period, starting at the beginning of the 2nd year and extending up to the middle of the 3rd year. This allowed us to address the following questions: Does familiarity between partners affect social interaction as early as 1 year of age? With reference to our model, could we find evidence for the evolution of interest from the object per se to delayed imitation, and then for immediate and reciprocal imitation between partners?

Results

Most of the sessions lasted 18 minutes. The differences observed in the duration of the sessions are attributable to familiarity. Two sessions in the unfamiliar condition lasted less than 6 minutes, and three less than 12 minutes. In the familiar condition, only two sessions lasted less than 12 minutes. These groups were not excluded from the analysis.

Matching Holds. Figure 9.1 shows that matching holds are more frequent in familiar dyads than in unfamiliar dyads. The figure also indicates that this type of behavior increases with age. We can see, too, that familiarity has a different influence at different ages. The effect of an unknown partner is very important for all ages except 2 years of age, where the differences are insignificant. On the other hand, the effect of age differs according to the degree of familiarity. In the familiar condition, we can see a progressive increase in matching holds, whereas, in the unfamiliar condition, the increase is more abrupt (from 16 to 20 months and from 22 to 26 months) and remains stable for older children.

These results demonstrate the importance of matching holds in 2 1/2-year-old children. The findings clearly indicate that the importance of imitative behavior, understood as the emphasis on holding the same object as the partner, reaches a peak at 2 1/2 years of age. This provides confirmation that the predominance of immediate imitation in social exchange among familiar peers can emerge even in the presence of an adult.

Physical Proximity between Children. Proximity seeking is greater for familiar peers. In this condition, the frequency of close proximity increases with age up to 2 years of age and remains stable for older children. In contrast, in unfamiliar dyads, periods of proximity between children decrease during the 2nd year but increase in the 3rd (see Figure 9.2).

Physical proximity to the Adult. Proximity to the adult is analyzed in order to verify that the peer is the privileged partner in this situation where there is a possibility of interaction with two different partners. Figure 9.3 summarizes this data. It seems that the frequency of close adult-child proximity is low for all ages and under both conditions of familiarity. Nevertheless, even if these behaviors are infrequent, it is necessary to compare this data with data on close peer proximity. This comparison shows that only unfamiliar 2-year-olds are more frequently close to adults than to peers.

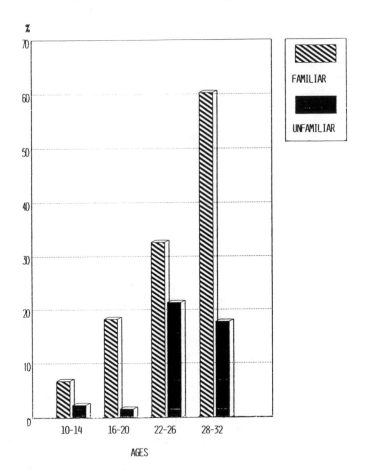

Figure 9.1

Matching Holds

Interest in Objects. When the two children are interested in the same category of object, we can determine whether this interest is directed at the same exemplar as the partner's or at the other exemplar of the same category. Furthermore, we can determine whether the interest in this same category of object is still evident after the partner stops using the object or only while the object is being carried so that synchronized manipulation of the object can occur.

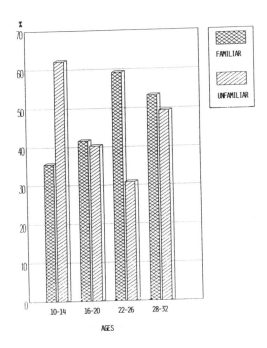

Figure 9.2

Proximity between children

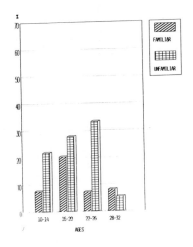

Figure 9.3

Proximity to Adult

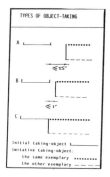

Figure 9.4

Types of object grasp

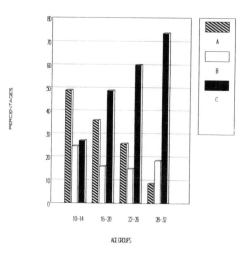

Figure 9.5

Percentage distribution of types of object grasp

Conclusion

The results of the present study show peer familiarity to be a salient variable in children's interaction. A familiar peer increases the frequency of social exchange and close proximity. The study also demonstrates that between 10 and 30 months of age, children pass from a state in which they display limited social exchanges with the individual to a state in which they display sustained interactions with reciprocal imitation.

Friendship among Preschool Children

Interest in the study of friendship among children stems from the fact that friends have a particular status among peers and these relationships play an important role in children's social development. The procedures commonly employed to study friendship (sociometrics or interviews) have been judged inappropriate by a number of authors. Foot, Chapman, and Smith (1980) argue that "the evidence concerning whether sociometric choices of children generally do correspond to preferences manifested in actual play associations is sufficiently confusing to give serious cause for concern about what measure is most valid".

Attempts to question children about their friends have not always been fruitful. Hinde, Titmus, Easton, & Tamplin (1985) feel that asking children to assess their friendships is "liable to indicate whom they would like to be friends with, rather than actual friendships, and is of variable reliability for preschoolers" (p. 234). Another approach which has gained wider acceptance is based on observation of friends' interactions at home, in laboratories, in day-care institutions, or in nursery schools. The research conducted within this framework opens up an efficient way to study friendship in children (Corsaro, 1979; Doyle, 1982; Howes, 1983; Vandell & Mueller, 1980).

In the present study, we adopted the latter approach, using an experimental setting. The study was restricted to children aged 3 to 5 years, because friendships are thought to become more stable at this age. The first question we raised concerns the specificity of interactions between friends: Are these interactions different from those between peer acquaintances of the same age?

A number of authors have reported striking differences in interactions, which are thought to be related to the degree of familiarity of partners. Their studies have revealed the privileged character of interactions between preschool dyads composed of familiar and/or unknown partners. A summary of their findings shows that friendship dyads engage in more positive exchanges, mutuality, and sharing (Furman & Masters, 1980). Furthermore, joint activities of friends are characterized by more generosity, cooperation, integration, and sharing (Galejs, 1974). Also, friends exchange mutual glances, smile, and laugh at each other more frequently (Baudonnière, 1987b) and are more mobile and talkative (Baudonnière, 1987b; Schwartz, 1972). Finally, friends are more likely to imitate each other (Baudonnière, 1987b; Lewis & Rosenblum, 1975), and are more likely to engage in proximal activities by standing or sitting closer to each other (Aiello & Jones, 1971; see Baudonnière, 1987b).

All the studies mentioned above provide evidence for the existence of a privileged character of interactions between friends. But in all these studies, the dyads of friends and nonfriends were observed either in isolation or within a larger group, and were then treated separately. One of the major differences between the present research and previous works is that we tested the privileged character of interactions between friends in a specific social situation where friends were not alone or in contact with other familiar partners in a group but rather in a *triadic situation*, in the presence of a third familiar partner who was nevertheless not a friend. This situation was designed to shed light on the eventual solidity of friendship. In other words, it allowed us to test whether or not the presence of a third familiar child would impinge upon the privileged character of interactions between friends. Our main hypothesis was that this privileged character of interactions between friends would be strong enough to maintain itself in a triadic situation with a third familiar partner present.

A new experimental paradigm was chosen. The dyads of friends with a third child were placed in a situation with limited resources (matching objects) in order to test whether (a) the two friends would hoard these objects and use them for their own benefit and/or (b) they would also share them with the third child.

We hypothesized that the two friends would appropriate the matching objects during the greater part of the session, to the detriment of the third child. We also predicted that this third partner would attempt to gain possession of the matching objects when they were held by the friends (i.e., when these objects had attracted the friends' attention). It was predicted that the constraints imposed by the paradigm (two sets of objects for three children) would arouse interest in the identical objects when both of these objects were held by two of the three participants.

The children were observed in the absence of adults. This feature is important because, with the exception of our previous study (Baudonnière, 1987b), the investigations of children's friendships mentioned earlier have always been made in the presence of an adult. This is a critical consideration because the presence of an adult cannot be regarded as neutral even if the adult does not interfere. It is very difficult to control for this effect. In the situation used in our study, the absence of adults was essential so that the children could freely select a partner and objects. Since the purpose of the present study was to examine the privileged character of interactions between friends in order to identify the possible specificity of these interactions, our major focus was not to define children's friendships. This task has been the objective of other authors (e.g., Furman & Beirman, 1983; Hartup, 1975, 1983; Hinde et al., 1985; Howes, 1983). The definition of friendship presented below served as a basis for selecting the dyads of friends. It is comparable to the principal criteria used by the previously mentioned authors. Friendship is defined as a stable and close relationship (minimum duration: 2 months), expressed by a mutual and preferential search for each other (the two friends spend most of their time together in class and at play), and founded upon voluntary choice (i.e., not imposed by the family or by the teacher).

The sample was composed of 108 children (54 boys and 54 girls) aged 3 to 5 years, grouped into 36 same-sex triads (18 male and 18 female). Each triad was composed of a dyad of friends plus a familiar partner who was not a friend. All 3 were classmates. The age differences between friends varied from 0 to 7 months. Subjects were recruited from five Parisian kindergartens, and the majority of the children came from middle-class backgrounds. Only same-sex friendships were studied to avoid problems in choosing an appropriate third child and to avoid introducing another variable, since mixed-sex friendships are rare from childhood to adolescence (Hartup, 1983).

The children were brought together to the experimental room by the experimenter who had conducted the preliminary observations and was familiar with them. Before closing the door, the experimenter always stated: "You can take anything you want. I'll stay outside, and I'll wait for you outside." The observations were made from March to May (the school year begins in September), when children's relationships could be assumed to be more defined and stable.

Results

The data analysis is based on the first 18 minutes of each group session. In the majority of the groups, children spent little time (in terms of relative duration) without holding objects. Generally, it was the third partner who remained longer without holding any object and in solitary holds.

To evaluate the importance of simultaneous holds of matching objects, we calculated the percentage of time corresponding to the higher values of the ratio (> 0.50). This percentage was calculated separately for each of the dyad-partner combinations: F1-F2, F1-T3, F2-F1, F2-T3, T3-F1, T3-F2 (see Baudonnière, 1986).

The matching holds were differentiated according to the type of dyad. The differences between the friends and the third child were significant, but no significant differences in this ratio were observed for gender or age. The privileged character of interactions between friends was confirmed by their reciprocal offers of objects. There is a marked difference between the offers made by friends to each other as compared to offers made to the third partner (77.0% vs. 7.8% in male groups and 64.0% vs. 14.5% in female groups).

As predicted, the constraint imposed by the double set of identical objects, and the mode used by children to appropriate the objects, revealed their interest in objects that were held by the other children (generally, the two friends). Appropriation took place, according to the group, with or without competition and conflict. The third partner was more often the target of competition (friends against the third child) or the instigator (the third child against the two friends), especially in male groups.

The groups structured themselves according to the amount of physical proximity among partners required by the games. Consequently, the search for closeness varied according to the groups, the point in the session, and of course, the dyads. Friends more frequently sought to be close to each other than to the third child in all groups. The amount of verbal exchange varied according to the group as a function of its activities. Gender differences were significant, with girls producing more utterances than boys. Friends tended to communicate with each other rather than with the third partner. This preference was present in all groups and was true for both of the friends.

The results can be summarized as shown in Figure 9.6.

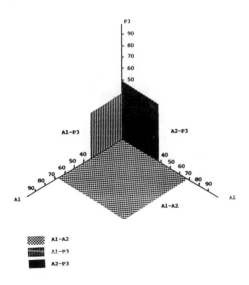

Figure 9.6

Simultaneous holds of identical objects and/or verbalizations

Interactions between Preschool Children in Mixed-Age Dyads: Effect of Age and Age Spacing

The purpose of this study was to analyze the effect of mixed-age situations between preschool children on the density of interaction and to examine the children's accommodation according to the partner's competencies.

We hypothesized that an important difference in communicative competencies among partners would preclude sustained exchanges. On the other hand, as soon as preschool children master language, the density of interactions would increase.

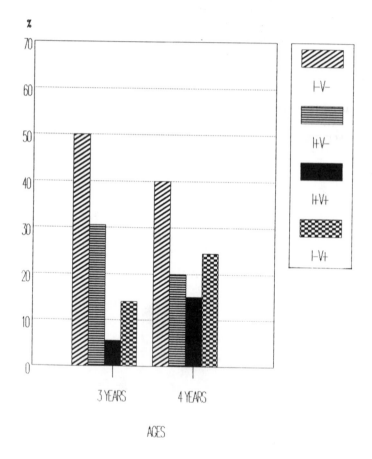

Figure 9.7

Breakdown in percentage of time sample units according to the privilege for imitation or directed verbalization

Thirty-six dyads from kindergartens were selected. These were broken down into 12 dyads of 3- and 5-year-olds (mean age difference: 2.1 years) and 12 dyads of 4- and 5-

year-olds (mean age difference: 1.1). For each condition, 6 same-sex and 6 mixed-sex dyads were formed. In all dyads, children were unfamiliar but from the same school.

The experimental procedure was a classical one. Children were filmed without their knowledge in a familiar room of their school, without the presence of an adult. We provided two identical sets of the 10 categories of objects.

The findings show that age differences of 1 or 2 years between children do not change the frequency or the relative duration of interactions, unless the age difference is associated with an important difference in communicative competencies (3 - 4 years and 3 - 5 years) but not when a co-mastering of language is present (4 - 5 years). During one-third of the time, preschool children did not interact in the 3 - 4 and 3 - 5 conditions as compared to 9% in the 4 - 5 condition, where sustained interactions were more frequent (65% of the session).

A low level of verbal and imitative interactions was found across the 3 - 4 and 3 - 5 dyads, for the younger as for the older children. Furthermore, directed verbalizations could be noticed between 4 and 5 years old. Therefore, older children do not seem to accommodate their social behavior to less competent younger children. Furthermore, younger children do not appear "stimulated" by more competent children, at least not until preschool children have achieved mastery of language.

Conclusion

Two points bear reiteration — one methodological, the other relative to the substantive findings obtained.

With regard to the methodology, this chapter should make clear the heuristic value of experimental paradigms in the study of multifaceted phenomena such as the emergence of the young child's communication abilities. We hope that by virtue of having used sound experimental techniques, our results will ultimately prove reliable and replicable. We have emphasized throughout the difficulties inherent in directly analyzing the behaviors in question, given the lack of consensus with regard to the concepts of "behavior" and "behavioral unit" in this area of inquiry. For this reason, the researcher must embark on paths that are somewhat more circuitous. We have tried to define and describe these less direct routes by including variables that correlate with the behaviors observed; these variables are much more readily quantifiable. This helps avoid, as far as possible, the tricky problem of how to quantify the content of interaction between children. Thus, our steps were taken deliberately, guided by the conceptual ambiguities in the field.

Second, several aspects of the model that we propose for the development of communication abilities have by now been subjected to empirical validation (Baudonnière, 1988; Nadel, 1986). Some may consider these validation studies too specific, or overly connected to our own experimental setup. We strongly disagree. The paradigm used is very suitable for testing this model. It has proved sensitive to the experimental manipulations undertaken, the subjects' ages, the age differences between partners, the degree of familiarity, and so forth. The research situation can be considered very revealing of communicative competencies. It yields results that are stable and, by virtue of the dependent measures involved, replicable variables.

References

Abramovitch, R. & Grusec, J. (1978). Peer imitation in a natural setting. *Child Development, 49,* 60-65.
Aiello, J. R. & Jones, S. E. (1971). Field study of the proxemic behavior of young school children in three subcultural groups. *Journal of Personality and Social Psychology,* 351-356.

Baudonnière, P.-M. (1985). Effet du mode de scolarisation (crèche ou maternelle) sur les échanges entre pairs de 2,6-3,0 [The influence of school attendance (in nursery school or kindergarten) on peer relations from 2.6 to 3 years]. *Enfance, 1-2*, 293-307.

Baudonnière, P.-M. (1986). Effect of number of partners on modes of social exchange among 2 1/2 - 3.0-year-old peers. *Genetic, Social and General Psychology Monographs, 112*(4), 419-433.

Baudonnière, P.-M. (1987a). *De l'émission à la communication :l'évolution des compétences à communiquer chez l'enfant de 2 à 4 ans* [From emission to communication: communication skills development among 2- to 4-year-old children]. Thèse, Université Paris V.

Baudonnière, P.-M. (1987b). Interactions dyadiques entre enfants de 4 ans : inconnus, familiers et amis. Le rôle du degré de familiarité [Dyadic interaction between 4-year-old children: strangers, acquaintances and friends. The influence of familiarity]. *International Journal of Psychology, 22*, 347-362.

Baudonnière, P.-M. (1988). *L'évolution des compétences à communiquer chez l'enfant de 2 à 4 ans* [Communication skills development among 2- to 4-year-old children]. Paris : PUF.

Baudonnière, P.-M. & Michel, J. (1988). L'imitation entre enfants au cours de la 2ème année : changement de cible et/ou changement de fonction? In J. Nadel (Ed.), *Psychologie française, 33*, pp. 29-36.

Becker, J. (1977). A learning analysis of the development of peer-oriented behavior in nine-month-old infants. *Developmental Psychology, 13*, 481-491.

Bronson, W. C. (1981). *Toddlers' behaviors with agemates*. Norwood, NJ: Ablex.

Bronwell, C. A. (1982). *Effect of age and age-mix on toddler peer interaction*. Paper presented at the International Conference on Infant Studies, Austin, TX.

Connolly, K. J. & Smith, P. K. (1972). Reactions of preschool children to a strange observer. In N. G. Blurton Jones (Ed.), *Ethological studies of child behavior*. London: Cambridge University Press.

Corsaro, W. A. (1979). "We're friends, right?": Children's use of access rituals in nursery school. *Language in society*, Vol. 8, Cambridge: Cambridge University Press, pp. 315-337.

Doyle, A. B. (1982). Friends, acquaintances and strangers: The influence of the familiarity and ethnolinguistic background on social interaction. In K. H. Rubin & H. S. Ross (Eds.), *Peer relationships and social skills in childhood*. New York: Springer-Verlag.

Doyle, A. B., Connolly, J. & Rivest, L. P. (1980). The effect of playmate familiarity on the social interactions of young children. *Child Development, 51*, 217-223.

Eckerman, C. O. & Stein, M. R. (1982). The toddler's emerging interactive skills. In K. H. Rubin & H. S. Ross (Eds.), *Peer relationships and social skills in childhood*. New York: Springer-Verlag.

Eckerman, C. O. & Whatley, J. L. (1977). Toys and social interaction between infant peers. *Child Development, 48*, 1645-1656.

Eckerman, C. O. Whatley, J. L. & Kutz, S. L. (1975). Growth of social play with peers during the 2nd year of life. *Developmental Psychology, 11*, 1, 42-49.

Foot, H. C., Chapman, A. J. & Smith, J. R. (1980). Patterns of interaction in children's friendship. In H. C. Foot, A. J. Chapman & J. R. Smith (Eds.), *Friendship and social relations in children*. New York: Wiley.

Furman, W. & Beirman, K. L. (1983). Developmental changes in young children's conceptions of friendship. *Child Development, 54*, 549-556.

Furman, W. & Masters, J. C. (1980). Peer interaction, sociometric status and resistance to deviation in young children. *Developmental Psychology, 16*, 229-336.

Galejs, W. (1974). Social interaction of preschool children. *Home Economics Research Journal, 2*, 153-159.

Hartup, W. W. (1975). The origins of friendships. In M. Lewis & L. A. Rosenblum (Eds.), *Friendship and peer relations*. New York: Wiley.

Hartup, W. W. (1983). Peer relations. In P. H. Mussen (Ed.), *Handbook of child psychology* (103-196). New York: Wiley.

Hinde, R. A., Titmus, G., Easton, D. & Tamplin, A. (1985). Incidence of "friendship" and behavior toward strong associates versus nonassociates in preschoolers. *Child Development, 56*, 234-245.

Howes, C. (1983). Patterns of friendship. *Child Development, 54*, 1041-1053.

Jacobson, J. L. (1981). The role of inanimate objects in early peer interaction. *Child Development, 52*, 618-626.

Lewis, M. & Rosenblum, L. A. (1975). *Friendship and peer relations*. New York: Wiley.

Lougee, M., Grueneich, R. & Hartup, W. W. (1977). Social interaction in same and mixed-age dyads of preschool children. *Child Development, 48*, 1353-1361.

Lubin, L. & Field, T. (1981). Imitation during preschool peer interaction. *International Journal of Behavioral Development, 4*, 443-453.

Mueller, E. (1972). The maintenance of verbal exchanges between young children. *Child Development, 43*, 930-938.

Mueller, E., Bleier, M., Krakow, J., Hedegus, K. & Cournoyer, P. (1977). The development of peer verbal interaction among two-year-old boys. *Child Development, 48*, 284-287.

Mueller, E. & Brenner, J. (1977). The origins of social skills and interaction among play group toddlers. *Child Development, 48,* 854-862.

Mueller, E. & Lucas, T. (1975). A developmental analysis of peer interaction among toddlers. In E. D. Lewis & L. A. Rosenblum (Eds.), *Friendships and peer relations,* New York: Wiley.

Nadel, J. (1986). *Imitation et communication entre jeunes enfants* [Imitation and communication among young children]. Paris: PUF.

Nadel, J. & Baudonnière, P.-M. (1980). L'imitation, comme mode d'échange prépondérant entre pairs au cours de la troisième année [Imitation as a main exchange medium between children in their third year of life]. *Enfance, 1-2,* 77-90.

Nadel, J. & Baudonnière, P.-M. (1982). The social function of reciprocal imitation in 2-year-old peers. *International Journal of Behavioral Development, 5,* (1), 95-109.

Nadel, J. & Baudonnière, P.-M. (1985). L'objet: moyen d'étude des compétences à communiquer [Studying communication skills through the use of objects]. In P.-M. Baudonnière (Ed.) *Etudier l'enfant de la naissance à 3 ans, comportements.* Paris : CNRS.

Nadel, J., Baudonnière, P.-M. & Fontaine, A.-M. (1983). La fonction sociale de l'imitation réciproque [The social role of reciprocal imitation]. *Recherches en Psychologie Sociale, 5,* 15-29.

Parten, M. B. (1932). Social participation among preschool children. *Journal of Abnormal and Social Psychology, 27,* 243-269.

Rubenstein, J. & Howes, C. (1976). The effect of peers on toddler interaction with mother and toys. *Child Development, 47,* 597-605.

Schwartz, J. C. (1972). Effects of peer familiarity on the behavior of preschoolers in a novel situation. *Journal of Personality and Social Psychology, 24,* 276-284.

Vandell, D. L. & Mueller, E. (1980). Peer play and friendships during the first two years. In H. C. Foot, A. J. Chapman and J. R. Smith (Eds.), *Friendships and social relations in children.* New York: Wiley.

Section III

Ongoing Social Development in Middle Childhood and Adolescence

Introduction to Section III

Barry H. Schneider

Profound changes in the child's physical and interpersonal surroundings accompany the start of structured schooling; these have marked impact on peer relations and their measurement. The child begins to spend extended periods of time in structured school lessons, during which peer interaction is limited and subtle (Loranger, 1984). This restricts, but does not eliminate, the utility of direct observation as a research tool. At the same time, adult monitoring of children's social interaction declines. Though teachers spend increasing amounts of time with children, academics become more prominent in teacher-pupil exchanges. Independence from parents increases as direct parental supervision declines. While researchers can still gain some useful information about children's peer relations from both parents and teachers, researchers can maintain only limited confidence in these data, which are important in their own right because they portray the adults' impressions of the children's social development, whether or not these impressions correspond with those of the children (Byrne & Schneider, 1986; Schneider & Byrne, in press).

The child's emerging cognitive capacities permit conceptualization and description of friendships, likes and dislikes within the peer group, and feelings of social success or failure. Researchers can capitalize on these abilities by using children's self-ratings and ratings by peers. While providing information on one's own behavior may compromise objectivity somewhat, this must be balanced against the unique advantage of self-report instruments in permitting access to private experiences that may mediate social interaction. However, most theorists and researchers place a premium on information obtained from a child's peers, who experience the individual's social behavior more directly and are the best interpreters of the peer group's standards and norms.

When using either self-report or peer informant measures in studying children during middle childhood, it is easy to lose sight of the fact that the responder is not equipped with an adult's full cognitive apparatus. It has been found, for instance, that children in the first few years of structured schooling may not possess a clear cognitive schema for social withdrawal (Younger & Boyko, 1987). This, of course, may limit the validity of self-reports and peer ratings of this construct.

Each of the research tools mentioned so far (observation, parent and teacher ratings, self-report, sociometrics) has its advantages and drawbacks. As one might imagine, they often yield markedly disparate pictures of a child's social competence (see Gresham, 1981). It is important that the reasons for this poor congruence among measures be explored rather than dismissed atheoretically as "measurement error." Section Three opens with a brief summary of a conversation hour led by Sharon Foster at the NATO Advanced Study Institute on Social Competence in Developmental Perspective in which she addressed the links between observable social behavior and peer assessments of social status.

The dialectic between children's social behavior and the evaluation of this behavior by peers receives in-depth scrutiny in Chapter 11 by Toon Cillessen and Tamara J. Ferguson. They consider the proposition that children are data-based in their evaluations of each other -- that is, that they base their opinions on the social behaviors that they experience.

197

B. H. Schneider et al. (eds.), Social Competence in Developmental Perspective, 197–198.
© 1989 by Kluwer Academic Publishers.

Unfortunately, impressions are slow to change, leading Cillessen and Ferguson to hypothesize that children's peer relationships are self-perpetuating in nature. In testing this hypothesis, they make use of LISREL statistical treatment techniques, a recent innovation that enables the researcher to use correlational data under certain very specific circumstances to estimate the likelihood of a theoretical model that contains causal inferences. Their model includes the two most frequent dimensions of childhood social behavior that have emerged from factor analyses of adults' descriptions of troublesome child behaviors (see Reference 4).

Chapters 12 and 13 are devoted to the consequences of aggression on children's social development. A host of previous studies have demonstrated that aggressive behavior in childhood is a stable predictor of adjustment problems in later life (see Asher & Parker, this volume). In Chapter 12, John D. Coie, Christina Christopoulos, Robert Terry, Kenneth A. Dodge, and John E. Lochman explore the links between aggressive behavior, active rejection by the peer group, and psychological disorder. Their large sample, follow-up into adolescence, and differentiation among types of aggression as well as types of aggressive relationships contribute to this study's value in confirming the findings of previous research.

In Chapter 13, Peter K. Smith makes explicit the differences between real and feigned aggression (rough-and-tumble play). He outlines the possible positive contributions of rough-and-tumble play to prosocial development and psychological adjustment. Smith makes use of ethological theories of social dominance (see Strayer, this volume) in exploring the functions of this type of play. Hopefully, these views will help adults who are unsure about the desirability of such playful "roughhousing" and how to respond to it.

The perceptive reader will detect throughout Section Three the feeling of the research community that aggression places a child far more at risk than withdrawal. However, recent research is increasingly devoted not to comparing these dimensions in terms of long-term risk but to clearly delineating the specific rules that govern the risk associated with both social aggression and withdrawal. This finer-grained investigation has resulted in a search for subtypes of both aggression and withdrawal (see also Rubin & Mills, 1988), as well as enhanced attention to age, sex, and situational differences.

References

Byrne, B. M. & Schneider, B. H. (1986). Student-teacher concordance on dimensions of student social competence: A multitrait-multimethod analysis. *Journal of Psychopathology and Behavioral Assessment, 8,* 263-279.

Gresham, F. (1981). Assessment of children's social skills. *Journal of School Psychology, 19,* 120-133.

Loranger, M. (1984, June). *Social skills in the secondary school.* Paper presented to the Conference on Research Strategies in Children's Social Skills Training, Ottawa, Ontario, Canada.

Rubin, K. H., & Mills, S. L. (1988). The many faces of social isolation in childhood. *Journal of Consulting and Clinical Psychology, 56,* 916-924.

Schneider, B. H. & Byrne, B. M. (in press). Parents rating children's social behavior: How focused the lens? *Journal of Clinical Child Psychology.*

Younger, A. J. & Boyko, K. A. (1987). Aggression and withdrawal as social schemas underlying children's peer perceptions. *Child Development, 58,* 1094-1100.

Examining the Impact of
Social Behavior on Peer Status

Sharon L. Foster

West Virginia University

Scholars and practitioners have devoted considerable attention during the last decade to the creation of and evaluating programs for enhancing children's peer relations. These efforts are based on the assumption that peer acceptance and rejection are the direct results of how children interact with their peers. Assuming this hypothesis to be true, creating an effective social skills training program requires specifying those behaviors functionally related to peer status. In other words, investigators must isolate pivotal social behaviors which children of different ages need to acquire to function effectively with peers in situations they routinely encounter. This requires in turn that they develop methods for deciding which of the myriad of interpersonal behaviors cause fluctuations in peer acceptance.

In examining the functional effects of behavior on peer acceptance, several factors must be considered (Foster, 1983), each of which has been shown to relate to children's evaluations of and responses to social behavior. The first, of course, is the nature of the behavior itself. In addition, the situational context of the behavior must be examined, together with child characteristics (e.g., age, sex, race) that may influence the results of the behavior on others. The nature of the outcome produced by the behavior defines its function, and can be explored in terms of who the behavior effects, who judges its effects, and whether short or long-term impact is emphasized. Further, it is important to isolate behaviors that are causally (not merely correlationally) related to peer acceptance and rejection.

Various research methods have examined which behaviors exert greatest influence on peer status. Perhaps the earliest and most popular method involves correlational studies, in which numbers of positive and negative peer nominations received by children are correlated with rates of behavior (e.g., Vaughn & Waters, 1981). With a similar strategy, the known-group comparison, investigators compare the behavior of groups of accepted, rejected, average, and (sometimes) neglected and controversial children in naturalistic settings (e.g., Dodge, Coie, & Brakke, 1982). The best of these studies compare behavior in different situations (e.g., Dodge et al., 1982), sometimes finding only minimal correlations in behavior across situations (Foster & Ritchey, 1985). Most of these studies have been limited, however, by their relatively molar categorizations of behaviors and situations, although a few recent studies have examined child behavior in more specific situations (e.g., a peer group entry task; Putallaz & Gottman, 1981). Perhaps the most important limitation of correlational and known-group studies is that behaviors associated with peer status are only correlates: although behavior is a plausible cause of status, it is also possible that the experience of rejection or acceptance produced the child's behavior.

Deriving more precise information requires more specific examination of behaviors and situations using designs that permit stronger causal inferences. Short-term longitudinal play

B. H. Schneider et al. (eds.), Social Competence in Developmental Perspective, 199–201.
© *1989 by Kluwer Academic Publishers.*

group studies, pioneered by Coie and Kupersmidt (1983) and Dodge (1983), examine behavior in a single situation: peer play. In Coie and Kupersmidt's study, boys interacted during a series of hour-long play sessions after school. Trained observers coded videotapes of boys' play session behavior. Research assistants drove each child home after each session and casually asked who the boy liked and did not like, thus gathering sociometric data. By observing the evolution of peer status among previously unacquainted children, stronger cause-effect statements about the relationship between behavior and peer status could be made than with known-groups comparisons. Indeed, even when placed in groups of unacquainted peers, boys who were rejected by classroom peers re-established their rejected status after about two group sessions. Concommitent with this,rejected boys displayed more aversive physical and verbal behavior than did boys who were popular with peers. Similarly, Dodge (1983) found that boys who became rejected displayed higher rates (relative to boys who attained average status) of inappropriate play, hostile verbalizations, hitting peers, and excluding others, while having lower rates of social conversation.

Despite the advances made possible by this methodology, the behavior of participants was still evaluated in the context of other behaviors. In the Dodge study, for example, rejected boys' high rates of aggression occurred in the context of lower social conversation, and it is unclear how these individual behaviors-- alone and in combination--influenced peer judgments. Furthermore, friendship and liking judgments in settings like schools are preceded by a history of interactions comprised of diverse positive and negative behaviors, again highlighting the potential importance of the social-behavioral context in evaluating the impact of a given response.

Experimental studies document that the behavioral context can influence the social impact of behavior. In some investigations of this kind (e.g., DiLorenzo & Foster, 1984), two children are videotaped following scripts that manipulate behavior (e.g., refusal of requests vs. compliance vs. neutral behavior) and contextual variables (e.g., provocative vs. cooperative initiation by a peer). Other children unfamiliar with the child actors view the videotapes and provide sociometric ratings of the actors. This method enables the investigator to control both behavior and situation, and to isolate causal relations between behavior and sociometric ratings. The results of these studies demonstrate the importance of the behavioral context: compliance with another's request, for example, leads to higher peer ratings than noncompliance, unless it is accompanied by critical remarks. In the behavioral context of criticism, compliance has no influence on peer ratings (Ritchey, 1981).

Experimental studies sacrifice external validity for experimental control, and thus the generalizability of these studies is questionable. A final method used to explore behaviors that influence liking borrows a strategy called the "critical incidents technique" from industrial-organizational psychology. With this strategy, interviewers ask children to describe recent incidents where a peer behaved in a way that made the subject like the peer more (or less) (see Foster, DeLawyer, & Guevremont, 1986). Content analyses of children's responses permit the investigator to examine responses that are salient and/or frequent for children. If situational descriptions are obtained, profiles of liked and disliked behaviors within particular situations can be derived (see Zarbatany, Rankin, & Hartmann, this volume). Despite high face validity of responses, however, the method leads to questions about whether children are able to verbalize those factors that actually cause shifts in liking and whether their reports are accurate. Furthermore, the fact that most children cite events (both positive and negative) involving friends leads to questions about whether the behaviors subjects describe would have the same effects if performed by disliked peers.

Despite different methodologies, none of which is flawless, the results of various studies show considerable convergence regarding the behaviors associated with peer rejection.

Results of correlational, known-groups, experimental, and critical incidents studies all indicate that negative peer judgments are consistently related to verbal and physical aggression and to off-task, disruptive behavior. Results are less consistent with regard to positive behaviors, perhaps because observational studies have often used molar categories whereas experimental and interview studies have employed more molecular foci. Nonetheless, taken as a group, studies generally indicate the importance of friendly-sociable initiations, cooperative shared activities, and considerate behavior such as unsolicited helping and favors.

The results summarized above are based on numerous studies using diverse methodologies. Together they support the hypothesis that children's behavior has a major impact on how peers judge their likeability. They also support, however, the importance of examining the social impact of behavior in its behavioral and situational contexts, with the ultimate goal of understanding what constitutes effective and ineffective performance in important social situations for children of differing ages, genders, and socio-cultural backgrounds. Finally, this research highlights the importance of studying the processes by which children form important social judgments about peers.

References

Coie, J.D., & Kupersmidt, J.B. (1983). A behavioral analysis of emerging social status in boys' groups. *Child Development, 54,* 1400-1416.

DiLorenzo, T.M., & Foster, S.L. (1984). A functional assessment of children's ratings of interaction patterns. *Behavioral Assessment, 6,* 291-302.

Dodge, K.A. (1983). Behavioral antecedents of peer social status. *Child Development, 54,* 1389-1399.

Dodge, K.A., Coie, J.D. & Brakke, N.P. (1982). Behavior patterns of socially rejected and neglected preadolescents: The roles of social approach and aggression. *Journal of Abnormal Child Psychology, 10,* 389-410.

Foster, S.L. (1983). Critical elements in the development of children's social skills. In R. Ellis and D. Whitington (Eds), *New directions in social skills training* (pp. 229-265). Beckenham, UK: Croon-Helm.

Foster, S.L., DeLawyer, D.D., & Guevremont, D.C. (1986). A critical incidents analysis of liked and disliked behaviors and their situational parameters in childhood and adolescence. *Behavioral Assessment, 8,* 115-133.

Foster, S.L., & Ritchey, W.L. (1985). Behavioral correlates of sociometric status of fourth, fifth, and sixth-grade children in two classroom situations. *Behavioral Assessment, 7,* 625-638.

Putallaz, M., & Gottman, J.M. (1981). An interactional model of children's entry into groups. *Child Development, 52,* 986-994.

Ritchey, W.L. (1981). *The effects of children's approval and compliance on peer and teacher ratings.* Doctoral dissertation, West Virginia University.

Vaughn, B.E., & Waters, E. (1981). Attention structure, sociometric status, and dominance: Interrelations. behavioral correlates, and relationships to social competence. *Developmental Psychology, 17,* 275-288.

Zarbatany, L. Rankin, D.P., & Hartmann, D.P. (1988, July). The preadolescent peer context: Important activities and behavioural prescriptions. Paper presented at NATO Advanced Study Institute, Les Arcs (Bourg-St-Maurice), France.

10

Self-Perpetuation Processes in Children's Peer Relationships

Toon Cillessen

Catholic University of Nijmegen

and

Tamara J. Ferguson

Utah State University
and
Catholic University of Nijmegen

At least two related indicators of social competence can be identified in the literature (Asher & Coie, in press). The first is the quality of a child's actual social behavior in a given context--most notably, in the peer group. The second is the social status or position that a child acquires in that group. The relationship between social behavior and social status has been demonstrated very clearly in several studies (Coie, Dodge, & Kupersmidt, in press). The goal of this chapter is to specify some of the processes that may account for the emergence and maintenance of status in the peer group, social behavior in the peer group and the social status-social behavior link.

Possible Determinants of Social Status

Research has attempted to identify which factors determine and maintain a child's status in the peer group. The bulk of earlier research treated social status as due to characteristics of the target child (e.g., the rejected child). One research tradition focused on what may be labeled *extra-peer group correlates* of social status, which refer to characteristics that the child brings with him or her to the peer group (e.g., physical attractiveness and the presence of mental or physical handicaps). The second research tradition focused on the extent to which the child's own social behavior in the peer group and knowledge about peer group interactions determines social status--that is, on what may be labeled *intra-peer group correlates* of social status. Evidence is accumulating that extra-peer group factors contribute to the status that a child obtains in the peer group. In particular, it has been shown that social status is related to physical attractiveness, body build, birth order, and the presence of mental or physical handicaps (see Hartup, 1983;

B. H. Schneider et al. (eds.), Social Competence in Developmental Perspective, 203–221.
© *1989 by Kluwer Academic Publishers.*

Vaughn & Langlois, 1983). The child's social competence is also influenced by parent-child relations (Lieberman, 1977; Pastor, 1981; Waters, Wippman, & Sroufe, 1979) and parent-parent relations (Hetherington, 1979). These variables can also be classified as extra-peer group correlates, but their effects are indirect through their influence on the child's social skills.

Children's behaviors in an established peer group are also predictive of their status in that peer group and in unestablished peer groups (e.g., Coie & Kupersmidt, 1983; Dodge, 1983). Coie, Dodge, and Kupersmidt (in press) review the behavioral differences found between sociometric status types within different age groups in research that has used peer-based or adult-based measures of social interactive behavior and objective codings of interactions between children (e.g., Coie, Dodge, & Coppotelli, 1982; Dodge, Schlundt, Schocken, & Delugach, 1983). Although some inconsistencies exist (see Coie & Dodge, 1988), it has been concluded that social acceptance is related to helpfulness, being considerate of others, following the rules for peer interaction and active engagement in positive peer interaction, whereas social rejection is related to aggression, rule violations, hyperactivity, and disruptiveness.

Finally, social-cognitive variables are related to social status. These variables include the child's knowledge of social skills, the way a child processes social information, and the child's level of social-cognitive reasoning about peer relations. The child's knowledge of social skills has frequently been measured using hypothetical stories, in which the child has to come up with many different possible solutions for the main story character's behavioral strategy. Although a child may know how to behave competently in peer situations (competence) but may fail to behave according to this knowledge (performance), Spivack, Platt, & Shure (1976) hypothesize that the most effective solutions to hypothetical situations will actually appear in the child's behavior. Knowledge of social skills has, in fact, been shown to be related to young children's actual social behavior (Richard & Dodge, 1982). In addition, Renshaw and Asher (1983) suggested that children's goals in social situations might be the cause of dysfunctional behavior or the use of antisocial strategies in hypothetical *or* actual situations.

The child's level of social-information processing has been elaborated in a recent model by Dodge (1986). According to Dodge's model, a competent social response depends on the processing of social cues in five consecutive steps (encoding social cues, representation and interpretation of cues, response search, response decision, response enactment). Results show that socially incompetent children might be deficient in one or more steps of this model. For example, Dodge (1980) found that compared to nonaggressive boys, aggressive boys attributed malevolent intent more frequently in ambiguous situations. In addition, Dodge and Newman (1981) showed that aggressive boys were less inclined to search for more information after provocation than nonaggressive boys. Finally, research by Perry, Perry, and Rasmussen (1986) demonstrated that aggressive and nonaggressive children differed in their evaluation of the effectiveness of aggressive responses.

The Self-Perpetuating Nature of Children's Peer Relationships

While these links are clearly present, the research nevertheless operates under assumptions that may lead to nonoptimal decision making regarding what types of intervention programs should be developed (Trouwer, 1981; van der Ploeg, 1975, 1981; van der Ploeg & Defares, 1971). Social status is treated as a property of the target child--that is, as a weighted function of a set of more or less stable characteristics of the child (including extra- and intra-peer group factors). Moreover, although status is the result of peer judgments in a peer context, situational and judgmental processes are seldom taken into account. One notable premise in this literature, therefore, is that children are consistently and primarily "data-based" in their perceptions of, and behavior toward, one another (e.g., Coie, in press). The guiding assumption, moreover, is that characteristics of the target child that are potentially modifiable (e.g., knowledge and/or utilization of socially skilled behavior) will lead to changes in others' perceptions of, and behavior toward, the child. A concrete example will serve to illustrate this point. Imagine that a child is persistently rejected by the peer group and that the child subsequently receives training designed to improve his or her social skills. According to a data-based conception of the status-behavior link, an improvement in the child's social skills should lead to more adaptive social behaviors when the child returns to the already established peer group and, therefore, to a more popular status.

Research with adults indicates, however, that this assumption may be a tenuous one. This research shows that university students and other individuals (such as teachers) form stable expectations about others' behaviors and personalities. Such expectations may be based, for example, on perceivers' actual behavioral encounters with the target other, on what perceivers have simply heard about the target other, and/or on the stereotypes that perceivers have about certain characteristics of the target other (e.g., that physically unattractive people are aggressive). Once formed, such expectations are resistant to change, as attested to by research using different paradigms (see, e.g., Jones, Farina, Hastorf, Markus, Miller & Scott, 1984; Snyder, 1981; Snyder & Gangestad, 1981; Snyder, Tanke, & Berscheid, 1977; Swann & Ely, 1984; Yarkin, Harvey, & Bloxom, 1981; see also Babad, Inbar, & Rosenthal, 1982, for a discussion of invalid critiques of this type of research).

Resistance to changing an expectation manifests itself in a variety of ways. In particular, research indicates that *cognitive bolstering* is involved. Specifically, individuals usually show better memory for expectation-consistent than -inconsistent behavior, they are more likely to give expectation-consistent than -inconsistent interpretations of even expectation-inconsistent behavior, and they make more confident predictions or more stable attributions about expectation -consistent than -inconsistent behavior.

Adults also manifest resistance to changing their expectations at the behavioral level by engaging in what is known as *behavioral confirmation* (see, e.g., Hamilton, 1981). Given a particular person-based expectation or a group-based expectation (such as a stereotype) of a target person, adults behave toward the target in ways that actually reconfirm their prior expectations of the target by eliciting expectation-consistent behaviors from the target (e.g., Greenwald, 1982; Mischel, Ebbessen, & Zeiss, 1976; Snyder, 1981; Snyder & Swann, 1978; Snyder & Uranowitz, 1978). If the target person's resultant behavior is consistent with his or her self-expectation, then the behaviors emerging from interactions are likely to reaffirm the target's self-expectation as well (e.g., Swann & Ely, 1984).

This research therefore shows that cognitive bolstering and behavioral confirmation work as a "self-fulfilling prophecy" (Merton, 1957) or in a "self-perpetuating" way (Snyder, 1981). A detailed description of these processes has been given by Darley and Fazio (1980), and their description reveals how self-perpetuating mechanisms can explain the stability in social behavior, social status, and their link across time. Figure 10.1 describes the six steps in Darley and Fazio's model. When a perceiver meets a target in an interactive situation, a set of expectations about the target will be triggered in the perceiver (1). The perceiver will then behave toward the target according to this set of expectations (2). The target interprets (3) and responds (4) to the perceiver's behavior. Finally the target's response is interpreted by both parties (5, 6). The perceiver's interpretations of the target's behavior are then reflected in the perceiver's disliking judgments, which will then partly determine the target's status in interactions with another child in the same or another peer group and thereby also explains the transference of the target's status to new peer groups.

The considerations outlined above pertain to situations in which it is the *perceivers* who treat the target in a manner consistent with their expectations. However, as implied in the preceding section, we submit that cognitive bolstering and behavioral confirmation may also occur in the target individual (cf. Swann, 1983; Trouwer, 1981). The pertinence of these processes to the target individual can be illustrated by

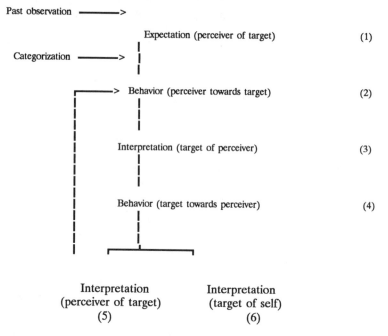

Figure 10.1

Schematic representation of Darley and Fazio's model.
Note: Expectancy confirmation processed arising in the social interaction sequence. *American Psychologist*, 1980, 35, 867-881.

considering how a child could obtain a particular social status in new peer groups, such as when the child first begins attending school or when the child transfers from one school to another. Consider, once again, the concrete example of a child who has been rejected by an established peer group. Research shows that children who are rejected by an established peer group also manifest maladaptive social behaviors in new peer groups. Since peers in a new group are unfamiliar with the child, it does not seem plausible that the child's reputation could explain his or her maladaptive behavior in the new peer group. We would argue, however, that the child's reputation does serve as a likely indirect explanation if one considers the repercussions of his or her reputation for (a) the child's own self-expectations, (b) the child's expectations of how others will behave toward him or her, and (c) the child's resultant behavior.

While there is little research with children regarding the relations among self-expectations, projected self-expectations and awareness of others' expectations of self (cf. Harter, 1983; Rosenberg, 1979; Shrauger & Schoeneman, 1979), this research does suggest that the child's previous experience in the peer group affects the child's expectations of himself or herself and the expectations that the child has regarding others' (including peers') behaviors toward him or her. The child brings these expectations with him or her even to newly established peer groups. These previously formed expectations may guide the formation of scenariolike anticipations of what events will occur as interactions in the new peer group unfold--for example, the new peers may be imagined to behave in accordance with the child's experience in other peer groups and in the family. These scenarios may actively guide the child's interactional strategy in the new peer group, resulting in interactions similar to past interactions and thereby ultimately leading to a social status in the new peer group compatible with the child's status in previous peer groups. The target child may thereby inadvertently initiate his or her own cognitive bolstering and behavioral confirmation processes, as research with university and high school students seems to bear out (Trouwer, 1981; see also La Gaipa & Wood, 1981).

Our argument up to this point has been that cognitive bolstering and behavioral confirmation are two major contributors to the maintenance of the child's status and behavior in established peer groups as well as to the emergence and subsequent maintenance of social status and behavior in new peer groups. We are thus essentially arguing that little change takes place in the viability of such processes within the age range (4 to 12 years) that has been the focus of much research on children's peer relations. While this claim has never been directly examined, it is indirectly borne out by research from various domains. For example, research shows that children as young as 4 years (and perhaps even younger) selectively remember and interpret boys' or girls' behaviors to make them consistent with these children's gender stereotypes (see Harter, 1983; Huston, 1983). Similar findings have been reported in research assessing how a target child's physical attractiveness affects children's interpretations of aggressive behavior (see Rule & Ferguson, 1983, 1984). Research in our own and others' laboratories bears out these findings with respect to reputational factors and expectations formed on the basis of observations of an individual target child's behavior (e.g., Dodge, 1980; Dodge & Frame, 1982; Ferguson, Olthof, Luiten, & Rule, 1984; Ferguson, van Roozendaal, & Rule, 1986; Hymel, 1985; Rule & Ferguson, 1983, 1984). Hence, the research indicates that even kindergarten-age children (ages 5-6 years) form stable self- and other-expectations and that such expectations guide the use of subsequent expectation- (in)consistent information in making various judgments. These findings would lead one to expect little difference across the 4-to-12-year age range in terms of the operation of either cognitive bolstering or behavioral confirmation.

At this point, it should be noted that the self-perpetuation hypothesis taken to its extreme actually leads one to expect perfect stability in social status (and by implication, in social behavior and the social status-social behavior link across time). This expectation is not borne out by the extant literature, which we will illustrate by giving a few examples regarding the stability of social status only. For example, Roff, Sells & Golden (1972) report stability coefficients of .53, .48, and .45, respectively, for combined social status-related scores for each of the three one-year intervals between the third grade (8-9 years) and sixth grade (11-12 years) of elementary school (6-12 years). Similarly, Rubin and Daniels-Bierness (1983) report only a moderate correlation (.48) between status measured in kindergarten and in first grade. In addition, Coie and Dodge (1983) report decreasing stability for social status-related scores with increasing measurement intervals (e.g., .65 vs. .36 for a 1- vs. a 4-year interval starting in the third grade of elementary school).

A variety of methodological factors can obviously account for these results (including differences in sample composition, Cairns, 1983; and temporal erosion, Campbell, 1971). Methodological considerations aside, these differences are actually consistent with what one would expect based on research guided by various models of the development of interpersonal understanding (see Berndt, 1983; Bigelow, 1977; Damon, 1977; La Gaipa & Wood, 1981; Selman, 1980; Youniss, 1980). This research shows that children's reasons for (dis)liking one another change across the 4-to-12-year age range. To give but a few examples, research shows that young children (ca. 4 to 6 years) form expectations based primarily on concrete/externally observable characteristics (such as physical appearance, cf. research on stereotypes reported earlier), older children (ca. 7 to 8 years) form expectations based on these characteristics but also on relational characteristics (such as shared interests), and even older children (ca. 11 to 12 years) form expectations based primarily on more abstract/less easily observable characteristics such as shared values or attitudes (cf. Damon & Hart, 1982; Harter, 1983; Livesley & Bromley, 1973; Oppenheimer & de Groot, 1981; Oppenheimer & Thijssen, 1983; Shantz, 1983; van Hekken & van Bekkum, 1976). Further research (cf. Shantz, 1983) shows that children form expectations based on negative behaviors and personality characteristics at a young age (ca. 4 to 6 years). However, it is only at a later age that children heavily weigh information about positive behaviors or personality characteristics to form expectations (ca. 7 to 8 years) and that children begin to consistently integrate positive and negative information to form less univalent expectations (ca. 11 to 12 years).

We believe that these findings are crucial to understanding the results on the stability of social status. That is, the extent to which one finds stability in social status and social behavior and the extent to which earlier status predicts later social behavior may depend on (a) whether changes have taken place in the social behaviors and interaction types that actually contribute to the formation of expectations by children-as- perceivers and (b) whether these changes, in relation to characteristics of the target child, could lead to a different social status. A concrete, although rather simplified, example will serve to illustrate this point. Imagine two target children. Assume that Child A is characterizable in terms of uniformly positive lower-level and higher-level characteristics (e.g., physically attractive and cooperative), whereas Child B is characterizable in terms of negative lower-level attributes (e.g., physically unattractive) but positive higher-level attributes (e.g., cooperative). The increase with age in the use of higher-level attributes to form expectations of a person's (dis)likability should lead to no change in Child A's status and peers' behaviors toward Child A, but it could lead to a change in Child B's status and peers' behaviors toward Child B, thereby resulting in imperfect stability in social status and social behavior for Children A and B as a group. Of course, any research concerned with accounting for the temporal (in)stability in children's social status and social behavior should investigate whether the obtained (in)stability reflects these kinds of developmental changes.

To summarize, perceivers confirm their expectations cognitively and treat targets in ways that cause them to confirm the perceivers' expectancies behaviorally. This set of relationships applies not only to the perceivers' expectations about the targets, but also to the targets' own self-expectations (Darley & Fazio, 1980; Miller & Turnbull, 1986; Snyder, 1981). A target child's new behavior may be internalized in the child's self-conception, thereby channeling the child's own future expectations and behavior which results in a confirmation of the initial expectancies in new interaction contexts. We will argue that these processes play a role in explaining the stability of a child's position in the peer group and his or her related pattern of socially (in)competent behavior in such a group.

Test of the Model

One purpose of our research is to explain the stability of children's social status and behavior in terms of these self-perpetuation processes. Before specifying the model that we actually tested, it is important to give you an idea of the methods and procedures that we employed in the research designed to shed light on these issues.

The data that we summarize here are part of a much larger longitudinal research project involving 231 four-to-eight-year -old boys. The boys were selected for participation because of their popular, rejected, or neglected status in the eyes of their classmates at the beginning of 1986; their social status according to classmates was once again determined at the beginning of 1987. In addition, in both 1986 and 1987, each of these boys participated in a series of four one-hour sessions with two other boys of his age. The three boys in each group were either of the same social status (the group consisted of either three popular boys or three rejected boys) or of different social status (the group consisted of one popular, one rejected, and one neglected boy). In half of these groups, the three boys were classmates and therefore already knew each other. In the remaining half, the boys were age-mates from different schools and therefore were initially unacquainted with each other. Each of the four one-hour sessions was separated by a one-week interval, and each session consisted of three or four phases.

During the preplay interview, each of the three boys was questioned about his expectations of his own and his interaction partners' behaviors. During the play phase, the three boys engaged in cooperative games, competitive games, and a free-play subphase. In two of the four sessions, a "division of rewards" task was also included. And finally, after the play phase, each boy was asked questions designed to estimate social status in these small groups as well as to measure his interpretation of his own and his interaction partners' behaviors during the play phase. The measures that we derived from these play sessions are the ones most crucial to our currently available tests of cognitive bolstering and behavioral confirmation. In addition, other measures were used to shed more light on the hypothesized relationships. These include teacher judgments of behavioral and personality dimensions; a teacher checklist for social-emotional, physical, and academic problems; a test for knowledge of social skills; and measures of physical attractiveness, body build, family constellation, and socioeconomic status.

The model shown in Figure 10.2 consists of the several constructs that were each measured at two different times. The left part of the model contains the constructs measured in the first session in which the boys participated. The right part of the model contains the same constructs measured once again in the third session. In each session, measures were taken of target children's own self-expectations, interpretations of their own behavior, their actual behavior and their social status. Measures were also taken of perceivers' expectations of the target children's behaviors as well as of the perceivers' interpretations of the target children's behavior. In this way, we could determine the so-called short-term stability of each of the constructs (for example, did children's social behavior remain stable between the first and third sessions?). More important, we could also assess the short-term links among expectations, behavior interpretations, and social status--both contemporaneously and across time--at least at the microlevel represented by Sessions 1 and 3. Once all of the behavioral data have been scored, we will also be able to test these relations at a more macrolevel--namely, across the four sessions of each wave and across both waves.

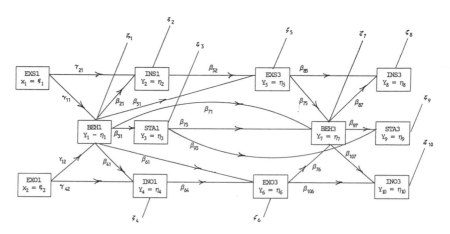

Figure 10.2

LISREL VI model of relations between expectations (EX), interpretations (IN), status (STA) and behavior (BEH) for the self (S) and other (O) in Sessions 1 and 3.

Descriptive Results

Stability of social status. In 1986 (Wave 1), social-status data were collected in 54 first-grade classes (393 boys, mean age = 5.2 years, range = 4.3-7.0 years; 427 girls, mean age = 5.3 years, range = 4.0-6.9 years) and in 43 third-grade classes (336 boys, mean age = 7.2 years, range = 5.4-9.3 years; 368 girls, mean age = 7.1 years, range = 5.4-9.6 years). Status was measured using Asher, Singleton, Tinsley, and Hymel's (1979) rating method.

In Wave 1, social status was determined using Newcomb and Bukowski's (1983) probability procedure for 435 first-grade boys (mean age = 5.2 years, range = 4.0-7.0 years) and for 349 third-grade boys (mean age = 7.1 years, range = 5.4-9.3 years). The distribution of status types found in 1986 was: popular 22.7%; rejected, 19.0%; neglected, 1.8%; controversial, 1.4%; and average, 55.1%.

Stability coefficients were then determined for the 231 boys who had been selected for participation. Table 10.1 presents the percentage of boys whose status remained stable for the total group, organized according to the boys' age and 1986 status classification. The first entry in each cell represents status stability using a strict criterion (*alpha* = .05). Stability coefficients using a much more lenient criterion (*alpha* = .20) are presented in parentheses.

Table 10.1

One-Year Stability of Social Status

Group	Both age groups (*n*=231)	First grade (*n*=114)	Third grade (*n*=117)
All status groups	.43 (.56)	.33 (.47)	.53 (.66)
Popular group	.51 (.70)	.40 (.60)	.62 (.79)
Neglected group	.00 (.04)	.00 (.00)	.00 (.08)
Rejected group	.47 (.58)	.34 (.45)	.60 (.71)

These data show moderate to good status stability for first and third graders over a one-year interval. Three trends in the data are important and should be noted. First, status is more stable for third graders as compared to first graders, which is consistent with the idea that older children make more reliable judgments than younger ones. Second, the neglected group is extremely unstable, to say the least. These results are consistent with past results and it seems pointless to attach any meaning to the other data that we have on these children, although we will report the results. Finally, the popular group is slightly more stable than the rejected group, which is consistent with the recent idea that the rejected category is a more heterogeneous one.

Social status and social behavior. Session-independent behavioral and personality differences among the social-status groups were analyzed using Q-sort judgments that had been made by the boys' teachers (Block & Block, 1980). For this purpose, six behavioral dimensions and two personality dimensions were used. The six dimensions of social behavior are cooperation, competition, disruption, shyness, help seeking, and leadership (see Table 10.2). The two personality dimensions are ego resiliency and ego control. We have Q-sort results for *both* waves for only 113 out of a total of 231 boys. This group consists of 45 popular boys, 13 neglected boys, and 55 rejected boys. In order to be able to analyze across the one-year interval, the data for these 113 boys are used here.

Scores for ego resiliency and ego control were computed by correlating the scores on the total set of 100 items with expert profiles for resiliency and control. For each of the six behavioral dimensions, a scale of five Q-sort items was constructed. These scales were constructed by first selecting a set of about 10 items for each scale based on item content and then selecting the 5 best items for each scale after performing a factor analysis. The items comprising each scale are listed in Table 10.2.

The scale homogeneity coefficients (Cronbach's *alpha*) for each of the six behavioral subscales in Wave 1 and Wave 2 are reported in Table 10.3. The one-year stability (Pearson correlation coefficients) of each of the six behavioral dimensions and the two personality dimensions are also reported in Table 10.3. The help-seeking dimension appears unreliable, but all dimensions appear moderately to extremely stable across the one-year interval.

Separate 3 (Status) x 2 (Age) x 2 (Time) analyses of variance were performed for the six behavioral dimensions and the two personality dimensions, treating time as a within-subjects factor. The univariate analysis of variance on the *shyness* dimension yielded no significant effects. As you will see, teachers' perceptions on the other dimensions reaffirm earlier results attesting to the behavioral competence of popular children relative to their rejected counterparts. The analysis of variance for the *cooperation* dimension yielded a

Table 10.2

Social Behavior Dimension Item Composition

Cooperation
  Is considerate to other
  children
  Is helpful and cooperative
  Has stable friendships
  Is honest and shares
  Has empathy with other
  children

Fighting
  Blames other children
  Is dishonest and unfair
  Is restless and agitated
  Teases other children
  Is verbally and physically
  aggressive

Shyness
  Is anxious and frightened
  Tries to avoid tension and
  retreats from stressful
  situations
  Is anxious in ambiguous
  situations
  Has low self-esteem and a sense of inferiority
  Is shy and withdrawn and does not make contacts very easily

Leadership
  Is open and direct when disagreeing
  with something or someone
  Demonstrates verbal fluency
  Has self-confidence
  Is assertive
  Is bossy

Disruption
  "Is trying" to others without being
  punished
  Wants to be the focus of attention
  Is disobedient
  Cannot delay gratification
  Is obstinate and stubborn

Help seeking
  Wants to be liked by others
  Is unsatisfied with own achievements
  Tries to please others
  Seeks affirmation
  Lacks independence

Table 10.3

Reliability and Stability Data for the Six Behavioral Dimensions and Two Personality Dimensions

Dimension	Item *alpha* Wave 1 ($n=167$)	Item *alpha* Wave 2 ($n=130$)	Stability/ Pearson *r*'s ($n=113$)
Cooperation	.84	.82	.49 (p=.000)
Competition	.83	.82	.60 (p=.000)
Disruption	.75	.71	.59 (p=.000)
Shyness	.80	.78	.59 (p=.000)
Help seeking	.46	.45	.42 (p=.000)
Leadership	.75	.60	.54 (p=.000)
Ego resiliency	--	--	.70 (p=.000)
Ego control	--	--	.57 (p=.000)

significant main effect for status--$F(2,107) = 8.74$, $p = .001$. The popular group ($M = 32.02$) scored significantly higher on cooperation than the rejected group ($M = 26.51$), while the neglected group ($M = 29.43$) had an intermediate position and did not differ significantly from the other two status groups.

A Status x Time interaction was also found for cooperation--$F(2,107) = 5.82$, $p = .004$. The means for this interaction are presented in Table 10.4. As can be seen in Table 10.4, the popular group's level of cooperation was constant across the two waves, and it scored higher on cooperation than the rejected group. The rejected group scored below the popular group in Wave 1, improved significantly over the year, but still scored below the popular group in Wave 2. The so-called neglected group scored as well as the popular group in 1986 but then declined significantly over the year to a level intermediate between (and not different from) the rejected group's Wave 1 and Wave 2 scores.

Table 10.4

Mean Cooperation Scores for Popular, Rejected, and Neglected Boys in Wave 1 (1986) and Wave 2 (1987)

	Wave 1	Wave 2
Popular (*n*=45)	32.00$_a$	32.04$_a$
Neglected (*n*=13)	32.54$_a$	26.31$_{bc}$
Rejected (*n*=55)	25.31$_c$	27.71$_b$

Note: Cells not sharing a common subscript differ significantly at $p \leq .05$.

The analysis of variance on the *fighting* dimension yielded a significant main effect for status--$F(2,107) = 11.50$, $p = .000$. Planned comparisons showed that the rejected group ($M = 22.57$) and the neglected group ($M = 20.70$) both scored significantly higher than the popular group ($M = 15.38$) on the fighting dimension, with no other significant between-group comparisons.

For *disruption*, a main effect was found for status--$F(2,107) = 7.47$, $p = .001$. The rejected group ($M = 22.70$) and the neglected group ($M = 22.97$) both scored higher on disruptiveness than the popular group ($M = 17.26$) but did not differ significantly from each other. A main effect for time was found $F(1,107) = 4.21$, $p = .043$--showing significantly more disruption in Wave 2 ($M = 20.96$) as compared to Wave 1 ($M = 20.16$) for all three groups. A significant Status x Time interaction (see Table 10.5)--$F(2,107) = 3.57, p = .032$--shows that the disruptiveness scores for the popular group and the rejected group do not change over time. The popular group scored lower on disruptiveness than the rejected group at both measurement times. The neglected group did not differ from the rejected group in Wave 1 or Wave 2 but increased significantly from slightly below the rejected group at Wave 1 to slightly above the rejected group at Wave 2. In combination with the results for cooperation, the neglected group was the group that changed the most as reflected in teachers' judgments of social behavior. This result is very much in line with the fact that the neglected group was shown to be a very unstable sociometric group.

For *help seeking*, only an effect for status was found--$F(2,107) = 4.14$, $p = .019$. Planned comparisons demonstrated that the popular group scored significantly lower ($M = 21.32$) on help-seeking behavior than both the neglected ($M = 24.62$) and the rejected ($M = 23.71$) groups, which did not differ significantly from each other.

For *leadership*, a significant Age x Time interaction was found--$F(1,107) = 13.67$, $p = .000$--as presented in Table 10.6. Planned comparisons show that the first graders remain constant over the year. Third graders scored significantly lower than the first graders in Wave 1, but increased significantly in their leadership behavior over the year. These data have a very interesting interpretation if we take into account the ages of both age groups at both measurement times. The development of leadership behavior demonstrates an inverted U-shaped function, with its lowest point around 7.5 years. Of course, this is a very tentative conclusion from our data.

Table 10.5

Disruption Means for Popular, Rejected, and Neglected Boys in Wave 1 (1986) and Wave 2 (1987)

	Wave 1	Wave 2
Popular ($n=45$)	16.27_d	18.24_{cd}
Neglected ($n=13$)	20.62_{bc}	25.31_a
Rejected ($n=55$)	23.24_{ab}	22.16_{ab}

Note: Cells not sharing a common subscript differ significantly at $p \le .05$.

Table 10.6

Leadership Means for First-Grade and Third-Grade Boys in Wave 1 (1986) and Wave 2 (1987)

	Wave 1	Wave 2
First-Grade ($n=64$)	30.84_a	29.13_{ab}
Third-Grade ($n=45$)	28.20_b	30.92_a

Note: Cells not sharing a common subscript differ significantly at $p \le .05$.

Finally, the univariate analyses for *ego resiliency* and *ego control* each yielded an effect for status--$Fs(2,107) = 10.86$, $p = .000$ and 5.19, $p = .007$, respectively. Planned comparisons demonstrated that the popular group ($M = .49$) scored significantly higher on ego resiliency than both the neglected ($M = .26$) and the rejected ($M = .22$) groups, which did not differ significantly from each other. In addition, the popular group ($M = -.07$) scored significantly lower on ego undercontrol than both the neglected ($M = .07$) and the rejected ($M = .07$) groups, which did not differ from each other.

Social cognition and social status. An adapted version of Shure and Spivack's (1974) Preschool Interpersonal Problem Solving test was used. In this test, children were asked to generate as many different solutions as they could for a series of hypothetical social conflict situations. In our test, four types of social situations were used: (a) competition between two children over an attractive toy, (b) a child's destroying the favorite toy of another child, (c) a group-entry situation with unfamiliar peers, and (d) conflicting social goals between two children who are playing together.

Each boy's total number of answers on the test was computed in each wave relative to the number of stories used, and the answers were scored by two females using a 29-category coding system. Reliability was determined on 29% of the data of Wave 2 and yielded an overall reliability of .88 (Cohen's *kappa*). One category was extremely infrequent, with a *kappa* of .00, and was excluded from further analyses.

The remaining 28 categories formed four clusters: prosocial solutions, antisocial solutions, solutions that implied withdrawal from the conflict situation, and socially irrelevant answers (i.e., answers in which the child did not deal with the presented social conflict). The number of answers in each cluster was computed by summing the frequencies of the individual categories within each cluster. Proportion scores resulted from dividing cluster frequencies by the total number of answers given. For analyses purposes, five scores resulted for each wave: the total number of solutions given and the proportions of prosocial, antisocial, withdrawn, and irrelevant solutions. Table 10.7 presents the intercorrelations between these five scores in Wave 1 (above the diagonal) and Wave 2 (below the diagonal) and their stability from Wave 1 to Wave 2 (on the diagonal).

Table 10.7

Social Skills Dimensions: Intercorrelations and One-Year Stability

	Prosocial	Antisocial	Withdrawn	Irrelevant	Total
Prosocial	.23**	-.48**	-.30**	-.26**	-.02
Antisocial	-.71**	.41**	-.59**	-.28**	-.01
Withdrawn	-.20**	-.45**	.06	.08	.04
Irrelevant	-.27**	-.07	-.11	.08	.00
Total	-.23**	.05	.16*	.15*	.29**

Note: **$p<.010$; *$p<.050$. Scores above (below) the diagonal are for the Wave 1 (Wave 2) assessment.

Most important, for the present purposes, is the stability for the social-skills clusters. Across the one-year interval, prosocial, antisocial, and total responses are fairly stable, while the withdrawn and irrelevant clusters do not demonstrate stability.

A 3 (Status) x 2 (Age) x 2 (Time) analysis of variance was performed for each of the clusters (total, prosocial, antisocial, withdrawn, and irrelevant). As you will see, the most striking result of these analyses is the almost complete absence of differences among the three status groups. The analysis of variance on the *total answers* yielded a main effect for age--$F(1,204) = 13.01, p = .000$. Third graders generally generated more answers per story than first graders ($Ms = 3.50$ vs. 3.11). A main effect for time was also found--$F(1,204) = 83.18, p = .000$, indicating that children gave more answers in Wave 2 than in Wave 1 ($Ms = 3.65$ vs. 2.95).

There was also a significant interaction between age and status for total answers-- $F(2,204) = 3.75, p = .025$. Table 10.8 presents the means for this interaction. It is clear from this table that the neglected group gave significantly fewer answers than the popular and rejected group in Wave 1.

Table 10.8

Status x Time Interaction for Total Answers

	Wave 1	Wave 2
Popular ($n=87$)	2.90$_b$	3.55$_a$
Neglected ($n=24$)	2.51$_c$	3.77$_a$
Rejected ($n=99$)	3.10$_b$	3.70$_a$

Note: Cells not sharing a common subscript differ significantly at $p \le .05$.

For *prosocial* responses, significant main effects were found for age--$F(1,204) = 7.79$, $p = .006$ and time--$F(1,204) = 8.56, p = .004$. Third graders scored proportionally more prosocial responses than first graders ($Ms = .48$ vs. $.44$), and more prosocial answers were found in Wave 2 than Wave 1 ($Ms = .48$ vs. $.44$).

For *antisocial* responses, a significant Status x Age interaction was found--$F(2,204) = 3.21, p = .042$. The relevant means are presented in Table 10.9. Since this interaction effect is not highly significant, planned comparisons failed to reveal significant differences between cell means. Inspection of the means in Table 10.9 demonstrates that the interaction is probably caused by the fact that the neglected group had a somewhat higher proportion of antisocial responses compared to the popular and rejected group in Wave 1, but a slightly lower proportion in Wave 2. The neglected group's decline from 40% antisocial answers in 1986 to 27% in 1987 just failed to pass the criterion for significance.

A main effect for time was found for the *withdrawal* responses--$F(1,204) = 17.55, p = .000$. Fewer withdrawal responses were scored in Wave 2 than in Wave 1 ($Ms = .13$ vs. $.19$). Finally, no significant effects were found for *irrelevant* responses, which averaged 5% for all status and age groups across the one-year interval.

Table 10.9

Status x Age Interaction for Antisocial Responses

	First Grade	Third Grade
Popular	.31 ($n=45$)	.33 ($n=42$)
Neglected	.40 ($n=12$)	.27 ($n=12$)
Rejected	.33 ($n=51$)	.33 ($n=48$)

LISREL Analysis

The currently available sample size of 108 boys for this analysis was not large enough to test the model shown in Figure 10.2 as a latent variable model with six indicators per variable. Therefore, the model was tested using LISREL VI for each of the six behavioral categories separately. These categories were derived from the videotape recordings of the boys' social behavior during the tower game. The following six behaviors were observed: cooperation, fighting, disruption, shyness, help seeking and leadership. To give a few examples, the *cooperation* category included the behaviors helping, making a proposal, positive reinforcement, and positive reactive behavior; the *fighting* category included the behaviors negative verbalization, protest/argue, threat, strong attack, negative reactive behavior, fighting, and object/position struggle; and the *disruption* category included the behaviors disturbing behavior, ignoring behavior, and inappropriately leaving the field.

To determine reliability, one-sixth of the videotaped material was scored twice. Except for cooperation in Session 1, all categories were scored reliably. Reliability coefficients varied from .79 to .99 for all other categories in Session 1 and from .87 to .99 for all categories in Session 3.

With the exception of the *leadership* category, Table 10.10 indicates that the model generally accounts for a relatively high proportion of the variance with comparatively small amounts of residual variance to be explained. Due to lack of fit for leadership, this variable was not further analyzed.

Based on maximum-likelihood estimates, standardized parameter estimates were also computed. As an example, the standardized solution for fighting is presented in Table 10.11. The same pattern of estimates was found for cooperation, disruption, shyness and help seeking. Children's social status and behavior were both stable, as indicated by the high values of parameters ß93 and ß71. The parameters estimating the status-behavior link did not, however, always show consistent results.

A very consistent pattern was found for the coefficients estimating the effects between expectations, behavior, and interpretations for both target and perceiver measures in Sessions 1 and 3. Stated briefly: The effect of expectations on interpretations (e.g., *gamma*

216

Table 10.10

Goodness-of-Fit Indices for the Model in Figure 10.2

Index	Cooperation	Fighting	Disruption	Shyness	Help seeking	Leadership
Coefficient of determination	.09	.22	.33	.24	.49	.26
X^2 (df)	202.76 (44)	244.47 (44)	196.99 (44)	229.21 (44)	123.95 (44)	--
Goodness-of-fit index	.77	.77	.80	.80	.85	.47
Adjusted goodness-of-fit index	.60	.60	.64	.63	.74	.06
Root mean square residual	.17	.19	.16	.13	.11	--

42) was higher than both the effect of expectations on behavior (*gamma* 12) and the effect of behavior on interpretations (*beta* 41). In addition, the effect of interpretations on new expectations (*beta* 64) was higher than the effect of behavior on new expectations (*beta* 61), with only a few exceptions.

Table 10.11

Standardized Effect Estimates for Fighting

Coeff.	Effect	Coeff.	Effect	Coeff.	Effect
B11	.08	B51	-.14	B75	-.08
B21	.24	B61	-.27	B85	.34
B12	.07	B71	.30	B76	.11
B42	.38	B52	.03	B106	.49
B21	.10	B73	.26	B87	-.06
B31	.10	B93	.69	B97	-.17
B41	.30	B64	.45	B107	.05

Conclusions

Our preliminary test of the self-perpetuation explanation of the stability of social status and behavior in groups of boys indicates that there is promise to this approach. Although the coefficients of determination were not very high, the fit measures of around .80 give indications of the existence of cognitive bolstering and behavioral confirmation effects at a microlevel. This is in line with Dodge, Pettit, McClaskey, and Brown's (1986) publication on the relationship between social-information-processing patterns and social behavior.

The effect estimates showed stronger cognitive-bolstering than behavioral-confirmation effects. This difference may very well reflect the low relationship that is frequently found between actual behavior and people's attitudes or beliefs about behavior. These analyses are nevertheless currently incomplete, and several technical questions can only be resolved when the complete data set becomes available. In addition, the mechanism of behavioral confirmation can be more completely specified in the model. Extra arrows are needed between perceivers' expectations, perceivers' behaviors toward the targets, and the targets' own behaviors. For this purpose, we are busy observing children's social behavior treating the dyad as the unit of analysis. Finally, we are in the process of scoring the data in a sequential way that gets at cognitive bolstering and behavioral confirmation more directly than was possible using the LISREL technique.

In closing, one important feature of the research project is that it bridges the gap in the social-developmental literature between children's *ideas* about one another and children's actual *behavior* toward one another. Clearly, there are age-related differences in which aspects of behavior and in which types of interactions contribute to children's expectations of themselves and others as individuals *and* as friends. We believe that these age-related differences are crucial to accounting for any observed temporal instability in children's social status and social behavior. In addition, as noted earlier, most basic and applied research has focused on social status as a property of the target child only. We, however, have our doubts about the completeness of this point of view. A second important feature of our project is, in fact, that it allows us to assess how the target child's *peers* and the composition of the peer group may actually be contributing to his or her social status and behavior in the peer group. Knowing how and the extent to which peers make a contribution clearly has implications for the types of interventions that should be developed to ameliorate poor-quality peer relations. We are obviously quite curious and excited about the results that will be found once all the data are available.

References

Asher, S. R., & Coie, J. D. (in press). *Peer rejection in childhood.* New York: Cambridge University Press.

Asher, S. T., Singleton, L., Tinsley, B., & Hymel, S. (1979). A reliable sociometric measure of preschool children. *Developmental Psychology, 15,* 443-444.

Babad, E., Inbar, J., & Rosenthal, R. (1982). Pygmalion, Galatea, and the Golem: Investigations of biased and unbiased teachers. *Journal of Educational Psychology, 74,* 459-474.

Berndt, T. J. (1983). Social cognition, social behavior, and children's friendships. In E. T. Higgins, D. N. Ruble, & W. W. Hartup (Eds.), *Social cognition and social development: A sociocultural perspective.* Cambridge, United Kingdom: Cambridge University Press.

Bigelow, B. J. (1977). Children's friendship expectations: A cognitive-developmental study. *Child Development, 48,* 246-253.

Block, J. H., & Block, J. (1980). The role of ego-control and ego-resiliency in the organization of behavior. In W. A. Collins (Ed.), *The Minnesota Symposium on Child Psychology: Development of cognition, affect, and social relations* (Vol. 13, pp. 39-101). Hillsdale, NJ: Erlbaum.

Cairns, R. B. (1983). Sociometry, psychometry, and social structure: A commentary on six recent studies of popular, rejected, and neglected children. *Merrill-Palmer Quarterly, 29,* 429-438.

Campbell, D. T. (1971). Temporal changes in treatment-effect correlations: Aquasi-experimental model for institutional records and longitudinal studies. In G. V. Glass (Ed.), *The promise and perils of educational informational systems.* Princeton, NJ: Educational Testing Service.

Coie, J. D. (in press). Towards a theory of peer rejection. In S. R. Asher & J. D. Coie (Eds.), *Peer rejection in childhood.* New York: Cambridge University Press.

Coie, J. D., & Dodge, K. A. (1983). Continuities and changes in children's social status: A five-year longitudinal study. *Merrill-Palmer Quarterly, 29,* 261-282.

Coie, J. D., & Dodge, K. A. (1988). Multiple sources of data on social behavior and social status in the school: A cross-age comparison. *Child Development, 59,* 815-829.

Coie, J. D., Dodge, K. A., & Coppotelli, H. (1982). Dimensions and the types of social status: A cross-age perspective. *Developmental Psychology, 18,* 557-570.

Coie, J. D., Dodge, K. A., & Kupersmidt, J. B. (in press). Peer group behavior and social status. In S. R. Asher & J. D. Coie (Eds.), *Peer rejection in childhood.* New York: Cambridge University Press.

Coie, J. D., & Kupersmidt, J. B. (1983). A behavioral analysis of emerging social status in boys groups. *Child Development, 54,* 1400-1416.

Damon, W. (1977). *The social world of the child.* San Francisco: Jossey-Bass.

Damon, W., & Hart, D. (1982). The development of self-understanding from infancy through adolescence. *Child Development, 53*, 841-864.

Darley, J. M., & Fazio, R. H. (1980). Expectancy confirmation processes arising in the social interaction sequence. *American Psychologist, 35*, 867-881.

Dodge, K. A. (1980). Social cognition and children's aggressive behavior. *Child Development, 51*, 162-170.

Dodge, K. A. (1983). Behavioral antecedents of peer social status. *Child Development, 54*, 1386-1399.

Dodge, K. A. (1986). A social information processing model of social competence in children. In M. Perlmutter (Ed.), *Minnesota Symposium on Child Psychology* (Vol. 18, pp. 77-125). Hillsdale, NJ: Erlbaum.

Dodge, K. A., & Frame, C. M. (1982). Social cognitive biases and deficits in aggressive boys. *Child Development, 53*, 620-635.

Dodge, K. A., & Newman, J. P. (1981). Biased decision making processes in aggressive boys. *Journal of Abnormal Psychology, 90*, 375-379.

Dodge, K. A., Pettit, G. S., McClaskey, C. L., Brown, M. M. (1986). Social competence in children. *Monographs of the Society for Research in Child Development, 51*(2), 1-80.

Dodge, K. A., Schlundt, D. C., Schocken, I., & Delugach, J. D. (1983). Social competence and children's social status: The role of peer group entry strategies. *Merrill Palmer Quarterly, 29*, 309-336.

Ferguson, T. J., Olthof, T., Luiten, A., & Rule, B. G. (1984). Children's use of observed behavioral frequency vs. behavioral covariation in ascribing dispositions to others. *Child Development, 55*, 2094-2105.

Ferguson, T. J., van Roozendaal, J., & Rule, B. G. (1986). The informational basis for children's impressions of others. *Developmental Psychology, 22*, 335-341.

Greenwald, A. G. (1982). Ego task analysis: An integration of research on ego-involvement and self-awareness. In A. Hasdorf & A. Isen (Eds.), *Cognitive Social Psychology* (pp. 109-148). New York: Elsevier North Holland.

Hamilton, D. L. (1981). Stereotyping and intergroup behavior: Some thoughts on the cognitive approach. In D. L. Hamilton (Ed.), *Cognitive processes in stereotyping and intergroup behavior* (pp. 333-354). Hillsdale, NJ: Erlbaum.

Harter, S. (1983). Developmental perspectives on the self-system. In P. H. Mussen (Ed.), *Handbook of child psychology* (Vol. 4, pp. 275-386). New York: Wiley.

Hartup, W. W. (1983). Peer relations. In P. H. Mussen (Ed.), *Handbook of child psychology* (Vol. 4, pp. 103-196). New York: Wiley.

Hetherington, M. E. (1979). Divorce: A child's perspective. *American Psychologist, 34*, 851-858.

Huston, A. C. (1983). Sex-typing. In P. H. Mussen (Ed.), *Handbook of child psychology* (Vol. 4, pp. 387-468). New York: Wiley.

Hymel, S., & Rubin, K.H. (1985). Children with peer relationships and social skills problems: Conceptual, methodological, and developmental isues. In G. J. Whitehurst (Ed.), *Annals of child development* (Vol. 2). Greenwich, CT: JAI Press.

Jones, E. E., Farina, A., Hastorf, A. H., Markus, H., Miller, D. T., & Scott, R. A. (1984). *Social stigma: The psychology of marked relationships.* New York: Freeman.

La Gaipa, J. J., & Wood, H. D. (1981). Friendship in disturbed adolescents. In S. Duck & R. Gilmour (Eds.), *Personal relationships: Vol. 3: Personal relationships in disorder.* London: Academic Press.

Lieberman, A. F. (1977). Preschoolers' competence with a peer: Relations with attachment and peer experience. *Child Development, 48*, 1277-1287.

Livesley, W. J., & Bromley, D. B. (1973). *Person perception in childhood and adolescence.* London: Wiley.

Merton, R. K. (1957). *Social theory and social structure.* Glencoe, IL: Free Press.

Miller, D. T., & Turnbull, W. (1986). Expectancies and interpersonal processes. *Annual Review of Psychology, 37*, 233-256.

Mischel, W., Ebbessen, E. B., & Zeiss, A. R. (1976). Determinants of selective memory about the self. *Journal of Consulting and Clinical Psychology, 44*, 92-103.

Newcomb, A. F., & Bukowski, W. M. (1983). Social impact and social preference as determinants of children's peer group status. *Developmental Psychology, 19*, 856-867.

Oppenheimer, L., & de Groot, W. (1981). Development of concepts about people in interpersonal situations. *European Journal of Social Psychology, 11*, 209-225.

Oppenheimer, L., & Thijssen, F. (1983). Children's thinking about friendships and its relation to popularity. *The Journal of Psychology, 114*, 69-78.

Pastor, D. L. (1981). The quality of mother-infant attachment and its relationship to toddlers' initial sociability with peers. *Developmental Psychology, 17*, 326-335.

Perry, D. G., Perry, L. C., & Rasmussen, P. (1986). Cognitive social learning mediators of aggression. *Child Development, 57,* 700-711.

Renshaw, P. D., & Asher, S. R. (1983). Children's goals and strategies for social interaction. *Merrill-Palmer Quarterly, 29,* 353-374.

Richard, B. A., & Dodge, K. A. (1982). Social maladjustment and problem solving in school-aged children. *Journal of Consulting and Clinical Psychology, 50,* 226-233.

Roff, M., Sells, B. B., & Golden, M. M. (1972). *Social adjustment and personality development.* Minneapolis: University of Minnesota Press.

Rosenberg, M. (1979). *Conceiving the self.* New York: Basic Books.

Rubin, K. H., & Daniels-Beirness, T. (1983). Concurrent and predictive correlates of social status in kindergarten and grade 1 children. *Merrill Palmer Quarterly, 29,* 337-351.

Rule, B. G., & Ferguson, T. J. (1983). Developmental issues in attribution, moral judgment and aggression. In R. M. Kaplan & V. Konecni (Eds.), *Aggression in children and youth* (pp. 138-161). Den Haag: Martinus Nijhoff.

Rule, B. G., & Ferguson, T. J. (1984). An overview of the relations among attribution, moral evaluation, anger and aggression. In A. Mummendey (Ed.), *Social psychology of aggression: From individual behavior towards social interaction* (pp. 143-156). Berlin: Springer-Verlag.

Selman, R. L. (1980). *The growth of interpersonal understanding.* New York: Academic Press.

Shantz, C. U. (1983). Social cognition. In P. H. Mussen (Ed.), *Handbook of Child Psychology* (Vol. 3, pp.495-555). New York: Wiley.

Shrauger, J. S., & Schoeneman, T. J. (1979). Symbolic interactionist view of self-concept: Through the looking glass darkly. *Psychological Bulletin, 86,* 549-595.

Shure, M., & Spivack, G. (1974). The preschool interpersonal problem solving tests (PIPS). Unpublished manual, Hahnemann Community Mental Hospital, Philadelphia, PA.

Snyder, M. (1981). On the self-perpetuating nature of social stereotypes. In D. L. Hamilton (Ed.), *Cognitive processes in stereotyping and intergroup behavior* (pp. 183-212). Hillsdale, NJ: Erlbaum.

Snyder, M., & Gangestad, S. (1981). Hypothesis-testing processes. In J. H. Harvey, W. Ickes, & R. F. Kidd (Eds.), *New directions in attribution research* (Vol. 3). Hillsdale, NJ: Erlbaum.

Snyder, M., & Swann, W. B. (1978). Hypothesis-testing processes in social interaction. *Journal of Personality and Social Psychology, 36,* 941-950.

Snyder, M., Tanke, E. D., & Berscheid, E. (1977). Social perception and interpersonal behavior: On the self-fulfilling nature of social stereotypes. *Journal of Personality ;and Social Psychology, 35,* 656-666.

Snyder, M., & Uranowitz, S. W. (1978). Reconstructing the past: Some cognitive consequences of person perception. *Journal of Personality and Social Psychology, 36,* 941-950.

Spivack, G., Platt, J. J., & Shure, H. B. (1976). *The problem-solving approach to adjustment: A guide to research and intervention.* San Francisco: Jossey-Bass.

Swann, W. B. (1983). Self-verification: Bringing social reality into harmony with the self. In J. Suls & A. G. Greenwald (Eds.), *Psychological perspectives on the self* (Vol. 2). Hillsdale, NJ: Erlbaum.

Swann, W. B., & Ely, R. J. (1984). A battle of wills: Self-verification versus behavioral confirmation. *Journal of Personality and Social Psychology, 46,* 1287-1302.

Trouwer, P. (1981). Social skill disorder. In S. Duck & R. Gilmour (Eds.), *Personal relationships: Vol. 3: Personal relationships in disorder.* London: Academic Press.

van der Ploeg, J. D. (1975). *Isolement, angst en agressie: Een sociaal psychologisch onderzoek naar de randfiguur in de inrichtingsgroep* (Isolation, anxiety, and aggression: A social psychological investigation of outsiders in an institution). Alphen a/d Rijn, Netherlands: Samson.

van der Ploeg, J. D. (1981). Interactie en rejectie in de groep (Interaction and rejection in the group). In J. de Wit, H. Bolle, & J. M. van Meel (Eds.), *Psychologen over het kind (Psychologyists Over the Child)* Groningen, Netherlands: Wolters-Noordhoff.

van der Ploeg, J. D., & Defares, P. B. (1971). *Randfiguren in duplo: Een sociaal psychologisch onderzoek naar de isolitari in de inrichtingsgroep* (Double outsiders: A social psychological investigation of isolated people in institutions). Assen, Netherlands: Van Gorcum.

van Hekken, S. M. J., & van Bekkum, J. J. (1976). Ontwikkelingen in 'waarnemen van de ander' en de relatie van deze ontwikkelingen met sociaal gedrag in de kinderjaren (The development of person perception and its relationship to social behavioral development during childhood). In J. de Wit, H. Bolle, & J. M. van Meel (Ed.), *Psychologen over het kind.* Groningen, Netherlands: Tjeenk Willink.

Vaughn, B. E., & Langlois, J. H. (1983). Physical attractiveness as a correlate of peer status and social competence in preschool children. *Developmental Psychology, 19,* 561-567.

Waters, E., Wippman, J., & Sroufe, L. A. (1979). Attachment, positive affect, and competence in the peer group: Two studies in construct validation. *Child Development, 50,* 821-829.

Yarkin, K. L., Harvey, J. H., & Bloxom, B. M. (1981). Cognitive sets, attribution, and social interaction. *Journal of Personality and Social Psychology, 41,* 243-252.

Youniss, J. (1980). *Parents and peers in social development: A Sullivan-Piaget perspective.* Chicago: University of Chicago Press.

11

Types of Aggressive Relationships, Peer Rejection, and Developmental Consequences

John D. Coie, Christina Christopoulos, and Robert Terry

Duke University

Kenneth A. Dodge

Vanderbilt University

John E. Lochman

Duke Medical Center

The phrase *social competence* has been used in the literature to refer to two separate lines of research. The first line has focused on the development and maintenance of close friendships (Berndt, 1986; Furman, 1982, 1985; Gottman, 1983; Gottman & Parker, 1986; Selman, 1981; Youniss, 1980) and the second on the ability to interact effectively in a more general social environment, like the peer group (Asher & Coie, in press; Asher & Hymel, 1981; Coie, Dodge, & Coppotelli, 1982; Hartup, Glazer, & Charlesworth, 1967; Putallaz & Gottman, 1981). Such differentiation reflects researchers' acknowledgment that both areas are important components of social competence. At the same time, it indicates their awareness that close friendships and peer relations may be quite distinct in nature and function. Furman (1985), for example, proposed that intimacy, affection, loyalty, and availability are primarily obtained in the context of close friendships, whereas a sense of inclusion is more likely to develop within the context of peer relations. In the present chapter, we will focus on the peer relations side of social competence, and we will discuss some of the aspects of poor peer relations that appear particularly problematic or are predictive of adjustment problems in later life.

Early peer relationship difficulties repeatedly have been identified as predictors of later psychological and social maladjustment (Conger & Miller, 1966; Janes, Hesselbrock, Myers, & Penniman, 1979; Roff, 1975; Roff & Wirt, 1984). On the other hand, aggressive behavior in childhood has also been associated with adolescent delinquency and adult crime (Feldhusen, Thurston, & Benning, 1973; Kupersmidt, 1983; Magnussen, Stattin, & Duner, 1983). However, very little is actually known about the behavioral correlates and the predictive value of poor peer relations and aggression jointly. Our aim is to examine briefly the connection between poor peer relations (as reflected in rejected peer status) and aggression in early childhood and personal adjustment in adolescence. More specifically, we will present some of our own data on the prediction of adolescent adjustment based on third-grade (i.e., eight-year-old children) social status and aggressiveness. Then, we will describe the behavior of rejected-aggressive boys in play groups to illustrate cross-sectional differences and similarities in the nature of aggression

B. H. Schneider et al. (eds.), Social Competence in Developmental Perspective, 223–237.
© *1989 by Kluwer Academic Publishers.*

in six-year-old (first grade) and eight-year-old (third grade) group contexts. The longitudinal data demonstrate the importance of peer rejection and aggression as predictors of disorder in later life. The cross-sectional data, involving some of the same third-grade boys who were part of the longitudinal study, illustrate some of the ways in which rejected-aggressive children may fail to keep up with early changes in the norms for social interaction in the peer group.

The Association Between Rejection and Aggression

Rejected peer status has been viewed as a general index of problematic peer relations. However, the construct of peer rejection does not appear to be homogenous in nature. Preliminary cluster analyses in our lab suggest that teachers may be able to differentiate among four subgroups of rejected children. The first subgroup appears to consist of the rejected-aggressive children; the second cluster contains the rejected children who are physically unattractive; the third cluster includes the rejected children who exhibit a number of strange behaviors (e.g., strange noises; odd comments; acting silly and immature; strange, inappropriate, and irritating behaviors); and finally, the fourth cluster consists of those rejected children who may be average on all of the above characteristics. Validation of these preliminary results would then suggest that we should turn the focus of our research and intervention efforts toward specific subgroups of rejected children.

It is true that when peers and trained unfamiliar observers provide information about rejected children's behavior, the most compelling reason for peer rejection appears to be aggressive behavior (Coie, Dodge, & Kupersmidt, in press). Approximately 30% to 40% of rejected children are viewed as aggressive (Coie & Koeppl, in press). Moreover, not only is aggressive behavior a correlate of peer rejection but it may be an antecedent of rejected status (Coie & Kupersmidt, 1983; Dodge, 1983). Despite the significant associations between rejection and aggression, however, it is important to keep in mind that not all rejected children are aggressive, just as not all aggressive children become rejected by their peers. Lesser (1959), for example, found that standing up for oneself was not related to peer rejection.

The magnitude of the relation between aggression and peer status depends on a number of research factors. The subjects' age is one such factor. Among children above the ages of seven or eight, the evidence for a relation between aggression and rejection is more compelling than among younger children (Coie, Belding, & Underwood, 1988). The reason for this age difference appears to be the differential prevalence rates for aggression in these two age groups. During the preschool years, aggression is more prevalent, and as a result, it is not perceived as deviant, whereas aggressive behavior during elementary school is considered out of the norm and may lead to rejection.

The subjects' sex is the second important variable in the relation between rejection and aggression. This relation appears to be stronger for boys than for girls, possibly because girls exhibit less aggression.

A third factor in the relation between rejection and aggression is the method by which aggression is measured. The most frequently used measures of aggression are: peer nominations, teacher ratings, and behavioral observations by trained observers. Each technique has its own advantages and disadvantages. Given the amount of time children spend together at school, one would expect peers to be the most accurate reporters of low-frequency aggressive behavior. However, their level of cognitive development may not allow them to distinguish between the children whom they dislike and those who are aggressive. Moreover, their judgments may be influenced by their past interactions with the child being assessed. Teachers, on the other hand, are more mature observers and may be able to make more objective judgments, but they may not witness those aggressive episodes that take place on the playground or in the lavatories. Also, teachers may not be able to differentiate between aggression and other forms of problem classroom behavior, such as disruptiveness. Finally, trained observers offer the least-biased judgments of children's behavior in the school environment. However, the intrusiveness of their presence may affect the rate of aggressive behavior exhibited by the children and thus may lead to an underestimation of the prevalence of aggressive behavior.

Coie and Dodge (1988) examined the relation among peer-, teacher-, and observer-reported aggressive behavior in first- and third-grade boys. Peers and teachers, who interact on a day-to-day basis with the child being assessed, agreed significantly on their reports of aggressiveness ($r = 0.59$), but neither one agreed with observer-reported aggression. Despite the inconsistent relations among the three sources, however, all three of them present rejected children as more aggressive than the average status group.

Finally, the sociometric method employed to determine peer status also affects the rejection-aggression association. Three types of sociometric measures have been used to assess social status. Children have been asked to nominate the classmates they like most (positive nominations). They have been asked to rate each of their classmates on a likability scale (peer ratings). And finally, children have been asked to nominate peers they like most and peers they like least. Usually, these liking and disliking nominations are combined to divide children into social-status groups (Coie et al., 1982; Newcomb & Bukowski, 1983).

Depending on the sociometric measure employed, the relation between rejection and aggression has varied substantially. Positive nominations by themselves do not appear to relate to aggressiveness (Hartup, Glazer, & Charlesworth, 1967; Olweus, 1977), whereas when status is measured with both positive and negative nominations, a stronger association with aggressiveness appears (Cantrell & Prinz, 1984; Carlson, Lahey, & Neeper, 1984; Coie et al., 1982; Coie, Finn, & Krehbiel, 1984; Coie & Whidby, 1986; Dodge, Coie, & Brakke, 1982; French & Waas, 1985). Peer ratings are moderately associated with aggressive behavior (Hymel & Rubin, 1985; LaGreca, 1981).

The Relation of Rejection and Aggression to Concurrent Behavior and Delinquency in Adolescence

So far, we have discussed the factors that may affect the association between aggression and rejection. Next, we would like to discuss the few studies that have examined the relation of rejection and aggression to concurrent behavior and delinquency in adolescence. Kupersmidt, Patterson, and Griesler (1987) studied the agreement between subjective and objective assessment of social competence for rejected, aggressive, rejected-aggressive, and nonrejected-nonaggressive children. The subjective measure of social competence was children's self-report on Harter's social competence subscale, whereas the objective measure of social competence was the mean of same-sex peer ratings of likability received. Rejected and rejected-aggressive children presented themselves as significantly more socially competent than their peers reported them to be. The results for the aggressive group were in the same direction but did not reach statistical significance. These results seem to suggest that rejected, rejected-aggressive, and possibly aggressive children do not acknowledge their interpersonal difficulties and present themselves as very competent in the social domain.

Coie and Dodge (1988) went one step further and differentiated between rejected children who use aggression as a means of getting their way and dominating others (proactive aggression) and those who, when provoked, get angry and strike back (reactive aggression). Proactively aggressive, rejected boys were nominated by their peers as disruptive but with leadership qualities and a sense of humor. Reactively aggressive boys, however, were not viewed as leaders nor as having a sense of humor. This study, then, demonstrates the need for further differentiation even within the rejected-aggressive group.

The importance of poor peer relations and aggressive behavior in childhood as separate predictors of later adjustment has been addressed in a series of studies (see Parker & Asher, 1987, for a comprehensive review). Parker and Asher concluded that rejection had the strongest predictive relation to dropping out of school, whereas aggression was most closely linked to delinquency. There have been few studies in which the joint role of peer rejection and aggression has been examined. In one small sample study in which both variables were jointly considered (Kupersmidt & Coie, 1988), slightly different results emerge when the total mixed-race sample was considered and when only the white, majority subsample was analyzed.

Study 1: Rejection and Aggression as Predictors of Adolescent Outcome

One implication of this review of the prediction literature is that childhood aggression and peer rejection might be more effective predictors of adolescent and adult disorder if they were considered jointly rather than singly. Actually, some of our data seem to support this conclusion. These data come from a sample of early adolescents who had just completed their first year of middle school. Middle school consists of grades six through eight and is attended by children in the age range of 12 to 15 years. These subjects had been followed longitudinally from the third grade and assessed on peer social status and aggression each year. Many of these subjects were only 12 years old at this first point of outcome assessment, and so the question could be raised as to whether this is an appropriate point in development to begin assessing outcomes on the sample.

There are two reasons for thinking that outcome analyses on a sample of 12- and 13-year-olds may be instructive for the study of developmental patterns of maladjustment. One very poignant reason is suggested by the fact that several female members of this sample gave birth before the completion of the school year. Thus, some members of this sample were facing adult responsibilities despite a decided lack of preparedness. Although most of the sample were not facing this extreme kind of life transition, the first year of middle school appears to be an important developmental period, and it may be worthwhile to consider childhood predictors of success and failure during this period. A number of developmentalists (e.g., Berndt, 1987; Eccles, Midgley, & Adler, 1984) suggest that the transition from elementary school to middle school is difficult for children. This may be particularly so for minority children (Felner, Primavera, & Cauce, 1981) such as the predominantly black, low-income sample being studied here.

This study began with a screening of 571 children during the middle of their third-grade school year. The screening included sociometric testing and peer assessments of social behavior, including aggressiveness ("starts fights"). These same measures were administered each year until the sample entered sixth grade, the first year of middle school. Outcome data were collected from three independent sources. At the end of the sixth-grade year, teachers rated the 361 adolescents who had continued in this school system. They rated both their academic adjustment and their general adjustment to middle school as satisfactory or unsatisfactory. A representative subsample of 177 of these subjects were interviewed using Hodges' (1986) Child Assessment Schedule and the National Youth Survey (Elliott & Huizinga, 1983) on conduct disorder. The mothers of each of these 177 subjects completed the Child Behavior Checklist (Achenbach & Edelbrock, 1981).

In all of the analyses that follow, we faced the problem of the positive correlation between two of our independent variables, rejection and aggression. Because of the lack of independence between these variables, it was necessary to implement the analytic strategies of hierarchical modeling. Essentially, one begins with the most complex model (for example, a model with both main effects of rejection and aggression plus their interaction). One then proceeds by testing the more complex models against a series of simpler alternative models, until the simplest model that is statistically significant is obtained. This "simplest" model contains the effects necessary to "explain" the data.

In third grade, teachers' reports of general adjustment to middle school were predicted by both aggression and rejection. The prediction ratio of maladjustment was almost three times as high for rejected or aggressive children compared to nonaggressive-nonrejected children. Similarly, both aggression and rejection in fourth grade (nine-year-olds) were predictive of poor middle school adjustment. Table 11.1 provides the breakdown for this aggression by rejection comparison.

Table 11.1

Proportion of Children Making a Poor Adjustment to Middle School Based on Predictions From Third- and Fourth-Grade Peer Status and Aggressiveness

| | Third-grade data | | Fourth-grade data | |
	Aggressive	Nonaggressive	Aggressive	Nonaggressive
Rejected	0.50 (*n* = 8)	0.24 (*n* = 21)	0.40 (*n* = 15)	0.29 (*n* = 35)
Nonrejected	0.25 (*n* = 28)	0.11 (*n* = 304)	0.30 (*n* = 27)	0.11 (*n* = 324)

Mothers' reports of early adolescent adjustment were significantly predicted by peer rejection in both the third and the fourth grade, but not by aggressiveness in either grade. This was true for both internalizing and externalizing problems. Table 11.2 illustrates the extent of these rejected versus nonrejected comparisons.

Table 11.2

Mean Internalizing and Externalizing Scores on the Child Behavior Checklist in Terms of Peer Status and Aggressiveness in Third and Fourth Grade as Reported by Mothers

| | Third-grade data | | Fourth-grade data | |
	Internal	External	Internal	External
Rejected (*n* = 44)	17.71	19.46	Rejected (*n* = 54) 17.50	19.45
Nonrejected (*n* = 88)	12.04	12.73	Nonrejected (*n* = 81) 11.76	12.30

The prediction of adolescent adjustment as reported by the subjects themselves is more complicated and involves differences for males and females as well as for type of disorder. When predictions from the third-grade data were evaluated, only aggression predicted disorder, and it did so only for males. Males who had been aggressive in third grade reported more conduct disorder in early adolescence. Grade-four data proved to be predictive of disorder among male and female adolescents. In this case, rejection was the more consistent predictor. As Tables 11.3 and 11.4 indicate, rejection predicted self-reported internalized psychological problems in males as well as more total disorder. However, rejection and aggression both predicted more conduct disorder among females as well as more total disorder.

Table 11.3

Proportion of Middle School Boys Who Experience Early Adolescent Disorders, in Terms of Peer Status and Aggressiveness in Fourth Grade

	Males Internalized Psychological Problems	Conduct Disorder
Rejected-aggressive ($n = 15$)	0.13	0.53
Rejected-nonaggressive ($n = 18$)	0.28	0.44
Aggressive-nonrejected ($n = 9$)	0.00	0.50
Nonaggressive-Nonrejected ($n = 39$)	0.13	0.33

Table 11.4

Proportion of Middle School Girls Who Experience Early Adolescent Disorders, in Terms of Peer Status and Aggressiveness in Fourth Grade

	Females Internalized Psychological Problems	Conduct Disorder
Rejected-aggressive ($n = 1$)	0.00	1.00
Rejected-nonaggressive ($n = 20$)	0.05	0.45
Aggressive-nonrejected ($n = 4$)	0.25	0.50
Nonaggressive-Nonrejected ($n = 34$)	0.09	0.15

Some of the complexity and inconsistency of these prediction results may be due to the relatively small sample followed. It is possible to draw some general conclusions, however. Rejection in childhood is a consistent predictor of multiple forms of disorder according to parent and teacher reports. Aggression is often a contributing predictor variable, and it makes sense to think that the combination of the two variables is most likely to identify children at risk for disorder in adolescence.

Study 2: The Relation of Rejection and Aggression to Concurrent Behavior in Newly Formed Play Groups

Although the preceding data are just the first slice of longitudinal assessment of the predictive linkages between childhood social relations and adjustment in later life, they do support the hypothesis that peer rejection and aggressiveness are each significant predictors of multiple indices of disorder. One way to address the question of why this might be true is to take a closer look at the social behavior and peer relationships of these children at earlier points in development. This was possible with two cohorts of males who were invited to become members of newly acquainted play groups that met each day for one week during the summer after the sociometric screening and the peer behavioral assessment. The group sessions were videotaped, and the interactions of group members were coded by trained observers, blind to the boys' social status and aggression ratings.

The first cohort was composed of a subsample of the 9-year-old males from the prediction cohort; the second one was composed of 7-year-old boys. There were 29 groups in all, each made up of 6 boys of rejected, popular, neglected, and average status, as determined by the earlier sociometric screening. Each of these group members had no prior acquaintance with the others. Data describing the results of each individual act by social status have been described in detail elsewhere (Dodge, Coie, Pettit, & Price, 1987). We will not review these findings except to note that rejected boys initiated more aggressive acts of all kinds. There was one interesting interaction effect involving age and status, and this effect will be mirrored in many of the results we will report here. At the 7-year-old level, both popular and rejected boys displayed more proactive aggressive acts than average boys (proactive aggression included acts such as bullying or instrumentally oriented aggression [Dodge & Coie, 1987]).

In the remainder of this chapter, we wish to examine various aspects of the aggressive interactions that took place in these groups. We will consider these interactions in two ways. First, we will describe quantitative and qualitative aspects of the aggression episodes that took place in these groups. Aggression does not just consist of individual acts but usually involves a series of interactions between two or more persons. Thus, we examined the series of aggressive interactions that began with an act of aggression by one boy and continued until acts of aggression between the initiator and the target had ceased or were interrupted by extended interactions with other group members. Interactions between the aggressor and the target child just prior to the initial aggressive act were coded for the degree to which this aggressive act was justified. Participants' roles in the aggressive interchange that followed were coded, as well as the means by which the episode was resolved. Moreover, the seriousness of the episode was rated in terms of the severity of violence involved. These data would then allow us to answer the question of whether aggressive-rejected boys differ from aggressive-nonrejected boys just in terms of the quantity of aggression they initiate or whether there are important qualitative differences.

The second approach to understanding aggressive interactions was to look at the kinds of relationships that aggressive- rejected boys develop in new peer groups. The fact that 50% of all the aggressive interactions in these groups took place between only 20% of all the dyads led us to focus on dyadic relationships, which we further differentiated into high-conflict and asymmetrically aggressive dyads. This approach would then allow us to determine whether aggressive-rejected boys are more often found in one of these two types of dyads.

Quantitative and Qualitative Aspects of Aggressive Behavior

In the analyses that follow, we compared four types of boys at each age level: rejected-aggressive boys, rejected-nonaggressive boys, nonrejected-aggressive boys, and nonrejected-nonaggressive boys. Rejected status was decided by using the system developed by Coie et al. (1982); a boy was considered aggressive if he received a z-score of higher than 1 on the peer behavioral nomination of "starts fights." The analysis of quantitative aspects of aggressive behavior was conducted with both frequencies and proportions, and it will be presented in that order.

Total frequency of aggression was primarily predicted by rejection. The hierarchical modeling analysis showed that although both aggression and rejection were significant predictors by themselves, aggression did not add to prediction above the effects of rejection. Rejection, on the other hand, did add to predictability above and beyond aggression. Thus, it appears that in these groups, rejection, not aggression, was more useful in explaining total frequency of aggression. The effect of rejection was further qualified by an interaction with age. Nine-year-old rejected boys started more aggressive episodes than their nonrejected counterparts, whereas there was little difference between rejected and nonrejected 7-year-olds.

There were also differences with respect to the frequency of types of aggression. For reactive aggression, there was only an age difference, with 9-year-olds *(M* = 0.82 per session) involved in less reactive aggression than 7-year-olds *(M* = 1.17 per session). The results for proactive aggression mirrored that for total aggression. Rejection, not aggression, was the most useful predictor but was qualified by an interaction with age level. Again, 9-year-old rejected children initiated more proactive aggressive episodes than nonrejected children, but this comparison did not hold for the 7-year-olds.

If one considers the proportion of reactive versus proactive aggression initiated, however, the results were somewhat different. Rejection was no longer significantly associated with proportional types of aggression, whereas an aggression-by-age interaction was obtained. Seven-year-old aggressive subjects tended to have proportionally more reactive aggression (30%) and less proactive aggression than nonaggressive 7-year-olds (20%), whereas 9-year-old aggressive children had less reactive aggression (16%) and more proactive aggression than nonaggressive 9-year-olds (27%).

These results, then, suggest an interesting relationship between rejection, aggression, and age. Frequency of aggression appears to be primarily responsible for peer perceptions of social rejection, particularly for older children, whereas it is the proportion of type of aggression that appears to influence peer judgments of aggressiveness. As we noted earlier, proactive aggression among early school-age children did not seem to be related to either peer rejection or having a reputation for starting fights. Thus, the quantitative analysis of aggressive behavior presented a fairly clear picture. The qualitative aspects of aggression, however, were more complex.

While 9-year-old rejected boys were more likely to be involved in serious episodes *(M* = 1.28 per session) than nonrejected 9-year-olds *(M* = 0.45 per session), there was no difference in serious aggression for rejected and nonrejected 7-year-olds *(M's* = 0.89 and 0.84, respectively). Aggressiveness was not related in any way to initiating serious aggression. Analyses of the proportion of episodes that were serious were not significant, indicating that involvement in serious aggression is probably a consequence of frequent involvement in all kinds of aggression.

One important question for us was whether rejected- aggressive children initiated more unprovoked aggressive episodes than other boys. This proved to be true among the older age group but not among the younger group, where it was the nonrejected-aggressive children who initiated twice as much unprovoked aggression as all the other children of their age.

Another important qualitative dimension of aggression is the extent to which children escalate an episode in which they are involved. What is the contingent probability that if one is the aggressor and the target responds, the aggressor will escalate? Does this contingent probability change as a function of rejection, aggression, and age? The frequency analyses showed that rejected boys were more likely to escalate episodes *(M* =

0.5 per session) than were nonrejected children for both age groups ($M = 0.33$ per session). On the other hand, when the proportional episodes in which subjects escalated the level of aggression were analyzed, there were no differences among the older boys. As above, however, it was the nonrejected-aggressive, younger children who escalated episodes more (0.22) than any of the other groups (0.04).

The resolution of aggression episodes is another important issue. For all boys, the largest proportion of episodes were ended as a result of one or both boys, being distracted by something happening in the group, and the conflict ended without any clear resolution. This was also true when rejected boys initiated the aggression, possibly because they were involved in more fights overall. Unlike other boys, however, only rejected older boys tended to force the other child to submit before they stopped their aggression. Furthermore, we found that rejected- aggressive boys rarely submitted. In general, the younger children were proportionately more distracted from continuing fights, while the older boys tended to resolve fights more often with someone's submitting.

One result of coding aggressive episodes is that it became clear just how many isolated acts of aggression occurred in these groups--acts to which the target of aggression made no apparent response. Our analyses of the frequency of these unreciprocated acts of aggression yielded two significant two-way interaction effects, both involving rejected status. One was an interaction of rejection with aggression, and as Table 11.5 illustrates, it is the rejected-aggressive boys who most often initiated these single acts of aggression. The other interaction effect (cf. Table 11.6) indicates that only in the third grade do rejected

Table 11.5

Frequency of Single, Unreciprocated Aggressive Acts Initiated per Session, by Rejection and Aggressiveness

	Aggressive	Not Aggressive
Rejected	6.98 ($n = 21$)	4.39 ($n = 12$)
Nonrejected	2.77 ($n = 23$)	3.38 ($n = 100$)

Table 11.6

Frequency of Single, Unreciprocated Aggressive Acts Initiated per Session, by Rejection and Grade Level

	First grade	Third grade
Rejected	5.03 ($n = 23$)	6.12 ($n = 21$)
Nonrejected	4.15 ($n = 57$)	2.58 ($n = 55$)

boys commit more of these acts than nonrejected boys. Taken together, these findings suggest that by the third grade, peers have begun to respond in markedly different fashion to the aggressive behavior of rejected-aggressive boys. It is as though they have learned to disregard many acts of aggression by these boys because of the noxious consequences of responding in self-defense. As the preceding data show, rejected boys tend to escalate the level of aggression once the target resists them. They continue to fight until the other boy submits, and because they are most often involved in serious aggression, peers may come to view them as being dangerous.

Types of Aggressive Relationships

Our interest in getting a more thorough understanding of aggressive behavior led us to study the types of aggressive relationships children become involved in. One such type, high-conflict dyads, is characterized by high rates of aggression of each member toward the other. These boys say they dislike each other, but they continue to interact with each other at a high rate. A second type of dyad, asymmetrically aggressive dyads, is marked by one member's regularly aggressing against the other, but this aggression is not reciprocated. The "bully" in this dyad makes frequent demands on the "victim," who responds with submission. It should be noted that the number of dyads is fairly small because of the strictness of the requirement we imposed regarding the consistency with which these relationships hold true across time.

The analysis of the data showed that both rejection and aggressiveness were singularly predictive of membership in a high, mutually aggressive dyad, by ratios of close to 2 to 1. However, neither variable was significantly associated with this circumstance once the other variable was statistically adjusted for. This finding, then, indicated that, for all practical purposes, one variable was equivalent to the other in predicting participation in mutually aggressive relationships.

The other interesting type of aggressive relationship is the asymmetric dyad, or the bully-victim pair. Neither rejection nor aggression was significantly predictive of being the bully in this relationship, although a trend indicates that rejected- aggressive children were more prone to be bullies. More interesting is the analysis of those children who bully more than one child. It was the older rejected-aggressive children (44%) who tended to have multiple victims more than any of the other boys. Most telling was the fact that all of the older rejected- aggressive children who were bullies had multiple victims (100%), whereas only 31% of the other bullies had more than one victim. Furthermore, in these asymmetric dyads, it is primarily the low-aggressive children (25% vs. 10%) who are the victims.

Implications of the Findings

There is an interesting developmental narrative embedded in the data we have just described. This narrative reflects a changing relation between aggression and peer social adjustment over the early period of school years when children learn to become members of a stable social group outside the family. Although individual differences in aggressiveness exist and were the major focus of our research program, there were compelling age-group differences that suggest a shift in the social functions and consequences of aggression during these early school years. Aggression was much more frequent among the groups of 7-year-olds than among the 9-year-olds. This fact was mirrored in observations of these same age groups in their school settings several months prior to the conduct of these experimental groups (Coie & Dodge, 1988). These differences in sheer frequency of aggression may help explain why aggressiveness (and particularly proactive aggressiveness) in the new groups was related to peer rejection among the 9-year-olds but not among the 7-year-olds. Wright, Giammarino, and Parad (1986) have demonstrated the way peer evaluation shifts according to the behavioral norms of the peer group. They found aggression to have very little relation to peer status in highly aggressive groups but to be significantly related to status in groups where aggression was generally less frequent.

One reason aggression may be a more common occurrence among the younger boys is that it is a primary mechanism for establishing social dominance hierarchies in the peer group (Strayer, 1980). If this is true, then it is understandable that a high frequency of proactive aggression is characteristic of both rejected and nonrejected first-grade boys. High-status first-grade boys will act aggressively in new peer group situations as a way of establishing their positions in these groups. Strayer (1980) observed that submissive responses to attacks and threats characterize dominance relations of both primates and children. We found that nonrejected-aggressive 7-year-old boys (boys who were, in fact, popular) made more unprovoked attacks than other boys, whereas this was primarily true of rejected-aggressive boys in the 9-year-old groups. Likewise, rejected 9-year-olds insist on submission of the other as a condition for stopping aggressive episodes, while there were no differences in this regard for rejected and nonrejected first graders.

It is clear that different norms for aggression are developed during the first few years of school, at least for boys. Perhaps, by the time boys are as old as 9, they develop other ways of establishing dominance structures in place of assertive aggression. Alternatively, these structures may become established more quickly among the 9-year-olds, and so high-status boys do not have to persist in their use of physical force, whereas the process takes much longer among 7-year-olds.

The above discussion suggests that while the same general relation holds between global peer assessments of aggression and peer rejection for 7- and 9-year-old boys, there are important transitions in the qualitative aspects of aggression and peer status. One interesting question is whether boys who are aggressive but not rejected in first grade change their behavior by third grade or acquire more negative peer status. Our review of longitudinal data on this first-grade sample indicates that both things happen but that aggressive-nonrejected boys are almost three times as likely to be rejected in third grade as nonaggressive-nonrejected boys.

As we have already observed, during the period of 7 to 9 years of age, important changes are taking place regarding the role of aggression in handling social problems. There is decreasing use of aggression to solve conflicts and manage power issues. The qualitative data provide several possible reasons for this change. Among older boys, aggression is more likely to involve seriously hurtful acts. Fights have less of the playful quality of preschool rough-and-tumble activity. Second, fights among the older boys more often become resolved with a clear winner and loser. Thus, there is more at stake for older boys, from a psychological standpoint. When someone is likely to get hurt and when there is the risk of being clearly identified as losing, boys may become less inclined to take steps that will result in a fight. Therefore, as boys grow older, they begin to recognize when it makes sense to let some negative exchanges pass without comment or overt reaction. Rejected boys do not seem to keep pace with these changing norms for aggressive behavior. They continue to use direct aggression as a way of getting what they want or to express frustration and resentment. While, on the surface of things, they may seem to be getting away with this inappropriate behavior, to the extent that other boys fail to reciprocate, they also pay a serious price for this social deviance. Other boys dislike them and increasingly avoid interacting with them.

The frequency with which rejected-aggressive boys become members of high, mutually aggressive dyads illustrates some of the social consequences of deviant aggressive behavior. One consequence is that these boys' most important peer relationships, those with peers with whom they most often play, may be marked by frequent conflict and antipathy. Because of this, they are deprived of some of the rewarding features of relationships that are experienced by most other boys. Another negative consequence is that they become limited in their choice of relationships to boys who are much like themselves. Patterson (in press) describes this sequence of deviant peer group formation as one that ultimately contributes to heightened delinquency. These two possibilities may help explain why it was the rejected-aggressive third graders who had the poorest levels of adjustment when the early adolescent screening was conducted.

Conclusions

In their comprehensive review of the prediction literature, Parker and Asher (1987) concluded that a solid case could be made for considering both peer rejection and aggression to be significant predictors of disorder in later life. They suggested that aggression was a better predictor of delinquency and that peer rejection was a better predictor of school adjustment problems. They also argued that these differential patterns of prediction might be a consequence of the way prediction studies were planned, since most investigators of antisocial behavior included aggression in their predictor variables sets but rarely included peer rejection measures, whereas peer rejection was more often employed as a predictor variable in school adjustment studies. The data we have just presented suggest that the combination of the two variables is predictive of multiple forms of poor adjustment in early adolescence, even when the interdependent nature of the two variables is controlled.

These prediction results, however, must not be regarded as making precise statements about developmental links between types of childhood social processes and adolescent adjustment. Although the sample was not small by the standards of most other prediction studies, the number of adolescents who fit the disorder criteria was relatively small, which, in turn, can make a difference in the relative predictive power of the two variables. More definitive results will come with future replication samples.

A second point of qualification should also be considered. Adjustment was assessed at a fairly early point in adolescence, and because this was a major life transition for these adolescents, one must expect to see some instability in their adjustment at that time. Thus, it will be important to see how many of these subjects continue to have problems or get into trouble in later adolescence.

Nonetheless, the results of this study are consistent with earlier research and furthermore make sense from a logical standpoint. There is a clear connection between childhood aggression and conduct disorder among adolescent boys, particularly by their own admission. This finding is congruent with the Parker and Asher (1987) conclusion. Logically, this represents a continuity of behavior from childhood to adolescence, since much of the admitted conduct disorder consists of violence toward other persons, particularly peers.

Interestingly, it is the nonaggressive-rejected boys who reported more internalized problems, although mothers reported internalized problems for rejected children. There is some evidence that nonaggressive-rejected children are more distressed by their rejected status, or more aware of it, than aggressive- rejected children (Parkhurst & Asher, 1987; Williams & Asher, 1987). It is possible that these earlier negative feelings may eventually be transformed into more recognizable forms of psychological distress in adolescence. Although such a statement is admittedly speculative, the fact that aggressive-rejected children may not be as sensitive to their peer status as other rejected children is consistent with the behavioral data on aggression in first and third grade. These data suggest that aggressive-rejected boys are not keeping up with age-related changes in the norms for aggressive behavior in the peer group.

The longitudinal data presented here provide support for the contention that rejected children are an appropriate target for preventive intervention programs. Rejection eventually leads to some form of social distancing or isolation (Coie & Kupersmidt, 1983; Dodge, 1983). Those rejected children who are not aggressive may experience this distancing by peers more directly than aggressive-rejected children, and thus, they may feel the pain of social rejection more intensely. Peers may be reluctant to express their dislike for aggressive children directly, because they recognize that this may result in more aggressive retaliations. Nonetheless, aggressive children may have less rewarding and intimate peer relationships than other children (Parker & Asher, 1988). When children are faced with the multiple stresses and transitions of adolescence, Sullivan (1953) has argued that the peer network and close friendships are important. Rejected-aggressive children are apt to be deprived of this social support. They are not only deprived of reassurance and encouragement by peers, but they may have less opportunity to learn how other peers handle similar stresses. Thus, not surprisingly, they have greater difficulty in making the life adjustment of this period.

References

Achenbach, T. M., & Edelbrock, C. S. (1981). Behavioral problems and competencies reported by parents of normal and disturbed children aged four through sixteen. *Monographs of the Society for Research in Child Development, 46* (1, Serial No. 188).

Asher, S. R., & Coie, J. D. (in press). *Peer rejection in childhood: Origins, consequences and intervention.* New York: Cambridge University Press.

Asher, S. R., & Hymel, S. (1981). Children's social competence in peer relations: Sociometric and behavioral assessment. In J. D. Wine & M. D. Smye (Eds.), *Social competence* (pp. 125-157). New York: Guilford Press.

Berndt, T. (1986). Sharing between friends: Contexts and consequences. In E. C. Mueller & C. R. Cooper (Eds.), *Process and outcome in peer relationships* (pp. 105-127). New York: Academic Press.

Berndt, T. J. (1987). *Changes in friendship and school adjustment after the transition to junior high school.* Paper presented at the biennial meeting of the Society for Research in Child Development, Baltimore.

Cantrell, V. L., & Prinz, R. J. (1984). *Multiple perspectives of rejected, neglected, and accepted children: Relationship between sociometric status and behavioral characteristics.* Paper presented at the annual meeting of the Association for the Advancement of Behavioral Therapy, Philadelphia.

Carlson, C. L., Lahey, B. B., & Neeper, R. (1984). Peer assessment of the social behavior of accepted, rejected, and neglected children. *Journal of Abnormal Child Psychology, 12,* 189-198.

Coie, J. D., Belding, M., & Underwood, M. (1988). Aggression and peer rejection in childhood. In B. B. Lahey & A. Kazdin (Eds.), *Advances in clinical child psychology* (Vol. 11, pp. 125-158). New York: Plenum.

Coie, J. D., & Dodge, K. A. (1988). Multiple sources of data on social behavior and social status. *Child Development, 59,* 815-829.

Coie, J. D., Dodge, K. A., & Coppotelli, H. A. (1982). Dimensions and types of social status: A cross-age perspective. *Developmental Psychology, 18,* 557-569.

Coie, J. D., Dodge, K. A., & Kupersmidt, J. (in press). Peer group behavior and social status. In S. R. Asher & J. D. Coie (Eds.), *The rejected child.* New York: Cambridge University Press.

Coie, J. D., Finn, M., & Krehbiel, G. (1984). *Controversial children: Peer assessment evidence for status category distinctiveness.* Paper presented at the annual meeting of the American Psychological Association, Toronto.

Coie, J. D., & Koeppl, G. K. (in press). Expanding the framework of intervention with rejected children. In S. R. Asher & J. D. Coie (Eds.), *The rejected child.* New York: Cambridge University Press.

Coie, J. D., & Kupersmidt, J. B. (1983). A behavioral analysis of emerging social status in boys' groups. *Child Development, 54,* 1400-1416.

Coie, J. D., & Whidby, J. B. (1986, April). *Gender differences in the basis for social rejection in childhood.* Paper presented at the annual meeting of the American Educational Research Association, San Francisco.

Conger, J. J., & Miller, W. C. (1966). *Personality, social class, and delinquency.* New York: Wiley.

Dodge, K. A. (1983). Behavioral antecedents of peer social status. *Child Development, 54,* 1386-1399.

Dodge, K. A., & Coie, J. D. (1987). Social-information processing factors in reactive and proactive aggression in children's peer groups. *Journal of Personality and Social Psychology, 53,* 1146-1158.

Dodge, K. A., Coie, J. D., & Brakke, N. P. (1982). Behavior patterns of socially rejected and neglected preadolescents: The roles of social approach and aggression. *Journal of Abnormal Child Psychology, 10,* 389-410.

Dodge, K. A., Coie, J. D., Pettit, G. S., & Price, J. M. (1987, April). *Peer status and aggression: Developmental and contextual analyses.* Paper presented at the biennial meeting of the Society for Research in Child Development, Baltimore.

Eccles, J. E., Midgley, C. M., & Adler, T. F. (1984). Age-related changes in the school environment: Effects on achievement motivation. In J. H. Nichols (Ed.), *The development of achievement motivation.* Greenwich, CT: JAI Press.

Elliott, D. S., & Huizinga, D. (1983). Social class and delinquent behavior in a national youth panel. *Criminology: An Interdisciplinary Journal, 21,* 149-177.

Feldhusen, J. F., Thurston, J. R., & Benning, J. J. (1973). A longitudinal study of delinquency and other aspects of children's behavior. *Journal of Criminology and Penology, 1,* 341-351.

Felner, R. D., Primavera, J., & Cauce, A. M. (1981). The impact of school transitions: A focus for preventive efforts. *American Journal of Community Psychology, 9,* 449-459.

French, D. C., & Waas, G. A. (1985). Behavior problems of peer-neglected and peer-rejected elementary-age children: Parent and teacher perspectives. *Child Development, 56,* 246-252.

Furman, W. (1982). Children's friendships. In T. Field, G. Finley, A. Huston, H. Quay, & L. Troll (Eds.), *Review of human development* (pp. 327-342). New York: Wiley.

Furman, W. (1985). What's the point? Issues in the selection of treatment objectives. In B. H. Schneider, K. H. Rubin, & J. E. Ledingham (Eds.), *Children's peer relations: Issues in assessment and intervention* (pp. 41-54). New York: Springer-Verlag.

Gottman, J. M. (1983). How children become friends. *Monographs of the Society for Research in Child Development, 48* (3, Serial No. 201).

Gottman, J. M., & Parker, J. G. (1986). *Conversation of friends: Speculation on affective development.* New York: Cambridge University Press.

Hartup, W. W., Glazer, J., & Charlesworth, R. (1967). Peer reinforcement and sociometric status. *Child Development, 38,* 1017-1024.

Hodges, K. (1986). *Manual for the child assessment schedule.* Unpublished, Duke University Medical School, Durham, NC.

Hymel, S., & Rubin, K. H. (1985). Children with peer relationships and social skills problems: Conceptual, methodological, and developmental issues. In G. J. Whitehurst (Ed.), *Annals of child development* (Vol. 2, pp. 251-297). Greenwich, CT: JAI Press.

Janes, C. L., Hesselbrock, V. M., Myers, D. G., & Penniman, J. H. (1979). Problem boys in young adulthood: Teachers' ratings and twelve-year follow-up. *Journal of Youth and Adolescence, 8,* 453-472.

Kupersmidt, J. B. (1983, April). *Predicting delinquency and academic problems from childhood peer status.* Paper presented at the biennial meeting of the Society for Research in Child Development, Detroit.

Kupersmidt, J. B., & Coie, J. D. (1988). *The prediction of delinquency and school-related problems from childhood peer status.* Unpublished manuscript.

Kupersmidt, J. B., Patterson, C. J., & Griesler, P. C. (1987, November). *Self-report and objective assessments of adjustment among rejected, aggressive, and rejected-aggressive children.* Paper presented at the Association for the Advancement of Behavior Therapy, Boston.

LaGreca, A. M. (1981). Peer acceptance: The correspondence between children's sociometric scores and teachers' ratings of peer interactions. *Journal of Abnormal Child Psychology, 9,* 167-178.

Lesser, G. S. (1959). The relationship between various forms of aggression and popularity among lower-class children. *Journal of Educational Psychology, 50,* 20-25.

Magnussen, D., Stattin, H., & Duner, A. (1983). Aggression and criminality in a longitudinal perspective. In K. T. Van Dusen & S. R. Mednick (Eds.), *Prospective studies of crime and delinquency* (pp. 277-301). Hingham, MA: Kluwer-Nijhoff.

Newcomb, A. F., & Bukowski, W. M. (1983). Social impact and social preference as determinants of children's peer group status. *Developmental Psychology, 19,* 856-867.

Olweus, D. (1977). Aggression and peer acceptance in adolescent boys: Two short-term longitudinal studies of ratings. *Child Development, 48,* 1301-1313.

Parker, J. G., & Asher, S. R. (1987). Peer relations and later personal adjustment: Are low-accepted children "at risk"? *Psychological Bulletin, 102,* 357-389.

Parker, J. G., & Asher, S. R. (1988, July). *Peer group acceptance and the quality of children's best friendships.* Paper presented at NATO Advanced Study Institute, Savoy, France.

Parkhurst, J. T., & Asher, S. R. (1987). *Two social concerns of aggressive-rejected children.* Paper presented at the biennial meeting of the Society for Research in Child Development, Baltimore.

Patterson, G. (in press). Factors relating to stability and changes in children's aggressive behavior over time. In D. J. Pepler & K. H. Rubin (Eds.), *The development and treatment of childhood aggression.* Toronto: Erlbaum.

Putallaz, M., & Gottman, J. M. (1981). Social skills and group acceptance. In S. R. Asher & J. M. Gottman (Eds.), *The development of children's friendships* (pp. 116-149). New York: Cambridge University Press.

Roff, J. D., & Wirt, R. D. (1984). Childhood aggression and social adjustment as antecedents of delinquency. *Journal of Abnormal Child Psychology, 12*, 111-126.

Roff, M. (1975). Juvenile delinquency in girls: A study of a recent sample. In M. Roff & D. F. Ricks (Eds.), *Life history research in psychopathology* (Vol. 4, pp. 135-151). Minneapolis: University of Minnesota Press.

Selman, R. L. (1981). The child as a friendship philosopher. In S. R. Asher & J. M. Gottman (Eds.), *The development of children's friendships* (pp. 242-272). New York: Cambridge University Press.

Strayer, F. F. (1980). Child ethology and the study of preschool social relations. In H. C. Foot, A. J. Chapman, & J. R. Smith (Eds.), *Friendship and social relations in children* (pp. 235-266). New York: Wiley.

Sullivan, H. S. (1953). *The interpersonal theory of psychiatry.* New York: Norton.

Williams, G. A., & Asher, S. R. (1987). *New approaches to identifying rejected children at school.* Paper presented at the annual meeting of the American Educational Research Association, Washington, DC.

Wright, J. C., Giammarino, M., & Parad, H. W. (1986). Social status in small groups: Individual-group similarity and the social "misfit." *Journal of Personality and Social Psychology, 50*, 523-536.

Youniss, J. C. (1980). *Parents and peers in social development: A Sullivan-Piaget perspective.* Chicago: University of Chicago Press.

12

The Role of Rough-and-Tumble Play in the Development of Social Competence: Theoretical Perspectives and Empirical Evidence

Peter K. Smith

University of Sheffield, United Kingdom

Play has often been held to be an important aspect of children's development. Indeed, the last 50 years have seen the rise of a "play ethos", at least in Western societies, which has held play to be an essential element of cognitive and social development; only recently has this play ethos come under critical scrutiny (Smith, 1988). In their research on children's play, however, psychologists have most commonly focused on play with objects and on fantasy and sociodramatic play based on objects. Whether it is the descriptions of Piaget (1951), the classification scheme of Smilansky (1968), or the play tests used by clinicians (e.g., Lowe & Costello, 1976), the child's play with objects has been the most easily observed, the most often described, and apparently the most appreciated as distinctively human in its nature and development.

Thus, one of the most social forms of play has also been one of the most neglected-- rough-and-tumble play (R&T). This is play that may superficially appear aggressive because it involves wrestling, grappling, hitting, kicking, restraining, chasing, and fleeing--but in a playful mode. Although such play warranted a chapter in Groos' (1901) book "The Play of Man", it received little attention through the succeeding decades, apart from some passing mention by anthropologists watching children in non-Western societies. Perhaps its affinities to animal play and the fact that it apparently has less educational value led to its being preferentially ignored or undervalued by social scientists in the behaviorist era, with its reaction against social Darwinism and any hints of links to our animal past (Humphreys & Smith, 1984). It may be no accident that interest in rough-and-tumble play (R&T) appeared in the late 1960s and early 1970s in the work of the human ethologists. Nicolas Blurton-Jones (1967), following the observations of Harlow and Harlow (1965) on rhesus monkeys, gave the first modern description of R&T in human children, and this influenced others such as Bill McGrew, Sean Neill, and myself. Owen Aldis' (1975) book *Play fighting*, a largely descriptive study, put the topic more firmly on the behavioral map. Ken Rubin

B. H. Schneider et al. (eds.), Social Competence in Developmental Perspective, 239–255.
© *1989 by Kluwer Academic Publishers.*

(1982) added R&T as a distinct category to augment the influential Smilansky classification scheme. Besides further work in Sheffield, by Annie Humphreys (Humphreys & Smith, 1984, 1987) and Michael Boulton (Boulton & Smith, in press), recent contributions to the topic have come from Tony Pellegrini (1987, in press), Douglas Fry (1987) and others. All this renewal of attention has coincided with a resurgence of interest in nonhuman play, much of which involves playfighting (e.g., Fagen, 1981; Pellis, 1988; Symons, 1978).

R&T should be of particular interest to those of us concerned with social competence in childhood. It is viewed favorably by some parents and teachers, less favorably by others. It is linked closely to the topics of friendship, cooperation, dominance, and aggression. It has been hypothesized to be influential in the development of various aspects of social competence. It may also be a sensitive indicator of a child's social skills, or lack of them--a key issue to which I will give more attention later.

Recent studies of R&T have used a variety of methods: ethological and observational; ethnographic; sociometric; interview and questionnaire. In this chapter, I aim to first review what we know about R&T, then consider theoretical perspectives on this form of behavior in animals and humans, and finally look at the empirical evidence on how R&T relates to social competence, focusing particularly on R&T in children as an indicator of social-skills adjustment.

R&T: An Overview

Several authors have examined physical play between parents and their children. In very young children, social play, like social communication and interaction generally, will show its most advanced forms when assisted or "scaffolded" by older children or adults. These early kinds of physical play may well be the developmental precursors of R&T between peers in the later preschool (ages 3-4) and school years.

Power and Parke (1981) have described physical play patterns in a study of mothers and fathers with infants of about 8 months of age. For example,

> Father picks up 7 month old Nathan, tosses him into the air, and then throws his head back so that he and Nathan are face to face. As Nathan giggles and chortles, father lowers him, shakes him, and tosses him up in the air again (p. 147).

MacDonald and Parke (1986) have systematically studied the types of such physical play and how they vary with age and sex of child and parent. Generally, they found that physical play between parent and child increased in frequency up to around 2 or 3 years, then declined. The most common forms of such play were tickle, chase, play with ball, bounce on knee, roll on soft surface, pattycake, wrestle, swing, horsey, piggyback, and tumble. Some of these, at least, would clearly count as R&T forms.

In this study, as in several others in the United States (see the review in MacDonald & Parke, 1986) and the United Kingdom (Smith & Daglish, 1977), boys were found to engage in more physical play than girls, and fathers to engage in more physical play than mothers. For wrestling in particular, fathers do more than mothers, and boys receive more than girls. Parent-child wrestling peaks at 3 to 4 years, and, like all the physical play categories, shows a modest tendency to decrease with the age of the parent.

From 3 to 4 years, R&T has been observed between peers in nursery schools and playgrounds--for example, as wrestling, tumbling, grappling, and chasing. Again, in many though not all studies, it is reported that there is a higher frequency in boys than in girls. It appears to be common through the school years at least up to adolescence. In our observations in school playgrounds during recess we have found that it takes up some 10% of time throughout the middle school period (ages 8-11). This figure naturally varies considerably; R&T is much more common on soft grassy surfaces than on harder concrete or tarmac surfaces. Factors such as the number and composition of the children on the playground, the equipment available, and the attitude of adult supervisors are also important (e.g., Smith & Connolly, 1980).

R&T between children is probably a cultural universal. Besides the United Kingdom and the United States, it has been described in many European countries and, albeit briefly, in many studies of non-Western cultures such as the six cultures study of Whiting & Whiting (1975). More substantial descriptions have come from Mel Konner (1972) in observations of the Kalahari San and particularly from Douglas Fry (1987) in observations of the Mexican Zapotec people.

R&T can resemble real fighting. Sometimes, playground supervisors and dinner ladies (part-time staff who supervise lunchtime play in British schools) have difficulty distinguishing the two: "Well, if you do see them, and think they're fighting you go and say, 'no fighting'; and they say, 'it's all right, we're only playing', and I let them get on with it" (middle school dinner lady, cited in Sluckin, 1981, p. 41). Sometimes, psychologists have failed to distinguish between R&T and actual fighting. For example, Ladd (1983) defined rough-and-tumble as "unorganised agonistic activity with others (e.g., fights or mock-fights, wrestling, pushing/shoving)" (p. 291).

Nevertheless, studies in the United Kingdom and the United States, and Fry's work among the Zapotec, concur in showing that at least in the majority of cases, and at least in early and middle childhood, R&T and real fighting can be clearly distinguished. They are, of course, by definition different in intent, but how is this difference inferred by nonparticipants? Ethological and observational studies suggest that a number of criteria, summarized in Table 12.1, discriminate between the two forms of behavior (Blurton-Jones, 1967; Fry, 1987; Smith & Boulton, in press; Smith & Lewis, 1985).

These criteria have been inferred by adult researchers. However, children themselves are obviously aware of the differences and can report on them. We have been using two approaches to examine these differences.

In one, we show a videotape containing what we judge to be episodes of both playful fighting and aggressive fighting, and ask children whether they think each episode is playful or real fighting and why. Some children as young as 4 years can make judgments that agree significantly with those of other children and adults (Smith & Lewis, 1985), and when they can give a reason the most common is based on the restraint criterion--for example, "He was only doing it gently" or "He thumped him". By 8 to 11 years of age, there is a high level of consensus on episodes, and common criteria are restraint, outcome ("At the end they separated"), and actions of onlookers ("Everyone was encouraging them"). Even at this age, though, about a quarter of the children only give an unelaborated judgment of intent (albeit usually accurate), such as "He's only playing" or, "He was really hurting him."

The other technique we have used is to interview children directly. In a study of 8- and 10-year-olds, we found that the great majority claimed they could distinguish play-fighting from serious fighting. When we asked them how they could tell, common criteria were: facial/vocal expression, restraint, outcome, and actions of onlookers. The presence or absence of particular actions was often a determining factor, too -- for instance, "He wasn't punching him", or "He was kicking him." In this study, the greater salience of facial/vocal expression as a criterion probably results from the limitations of videotape in preferentially capturing these aspects of the action.

Table 12.1

Criteria Discriminating between R&T and Real Fighting in Children

Criterion	R & T	Real fighting
1. Circumstances leading to an encounter.	There is no conflict over resources.	There is frequently conflict over resources such as space or equipment.
2. The way an encounter is initiated by one child and responded to by another.	One child invites another, who is free to refuse.	One child frequently challenges another, who cannot fail to respond without losing face.
3. Facial and vocal expression of participants during an encounter.	Play, face, laugh, or smile; or neutral expression.	Staring, frowning, red face, puckering up and crying.
4. Number of participants involved.	Often there are two, but more participants may be involved in a connected short episode.	There are seldom more than two children involved.
5. Reaction of onlookers.	The encounter attracts little if any interest from nonparticipants.	The encounter attracts attention from nonparticipants; sometimes a crowd of onlookers will gather around.
6. Self-handicapping.	A stronger or older child will often self-handicap, not using maximum strength.	Self-handicapping is normally absent.
7. Restraint	A participant will often show restraint in the force of a blow.	Restraint occurs to a lesser extent or is absent.
8. Reversals	Participants may take it in turns to be on top or underneath in a wrestle, or to chase or be chased in a chase/flee game.	Turn taking is not usually observed.
9. Relationship between participants immediately after an encounter has ended.	Participants often stay together in another activity.	Participants often separate.

These studies all suggest that R&T and real fighting are clearly separate. However, observational studies have shown that some episodes may have mixed motivation. For example, Smith and Lewis (1985) found that some 2% to 3% of incidents had conflicting criteria, such as one child might be smiling or laughing but the episode might end with the other child's running away angry. Such episodes have appeared infrequently in our observations of preschool children and of 8- to 11-year-olds (Humphreys & Smith, 1987). They were also rare in Fry's (1987) observations of 3- to 8-year-old Zapotec children. But when we interviewed 8- to 10-year-olds, 78% thought that a play fight could lead to a serious fight as a result of accidental injury, or misperception of accidental injury, and especially if the play partner was not a close friend. These results suggest that R&T would only become hostile accidentally. However, Neill (1976), in an observational study of 12-

to 13-year-old boys in a London school, reported an actual mix of playful and hostile episodes to be not uncommon. For example, he stated that "the attacker might start vigorously, causing distress, and then become more playful, often after pinning the other boy down" (p. 217). One crucial factor in the difference between Neill's results and those of other investigators may be the age of the children, which will be discussed in more detail later.

Theoretical Perspectives on R&T

Social play can be observed in a large number of mammalian species, as well as some birds (Fagen, 1981). The behaviors used in social play obviously vary with the species, but many of the behaviors -- such as lunging, pouncing, grabbing, inhibited biting, wrestling, butting, balking, parrying and chasing -- are to some degree similar to behaviors shown in actual fighting or, in some cases, predatory behaviors. The playful intent of such play-fighting episodes is often signaled by some metacommunicative gesture such as a play bow or gambol (e.g., in canids) or an open-mouthed play face (e.g., in primates).

There are now a large number of high-quality ethological studies of play-fighting in a variety of mammalian species, including rodents, ungulates, ursids, canids, felids, and primates. Robert Fagen (1981) provided a superb overview of this work as of the beginning of the 1980s.

Up to that time, a very large number of functions had been ascribed to mammalian play. As Fagen (1981) commented, the numerous beneficial effects hypothesized for play give this behavior the status of a wonder-working elixir. Apparently, play can do almost anything! Play is cited as the source of virtually any skill or information that can result from experience with conspecifics or with the physical environment during development (p. 279).

So far as social play and in particular play-fighting were concerned, some of the main functional hypotheses advanced were:

learning fighting skills
learning predatory or predator-avoidance skills
learning social rank
enhancing social rank
promoting social cohesion
promoting social cooperation
learning social signals
learning complex, varied patterns of social interaction
developing behavioral flexibility

Evidence can be brought to bear on these hypotheses from experimental studies involving deprivation or supplementation of play; from correlations with naturally occurring variations in play between individuals, sexes, and related species; from the variation of play through the life cycle; from correlations with contextual factors such as time of day, season, and choice of play partners; and from close examination of the "design features" of play -- namely, the detailed nature and form of play behaviors.

The evidence for some of the hypothesized functions of mammalian play-fighting is stronger than for others. In a review paper (Smith, 1982), I suggested that play-fighting functioned primarily as practice for competitive social skills (fighting, predatory, and predator-avoidance skills). It might be difficult for juveniles to safely get adequate practice in such competitive social skills. Play-fighting, with its similarity in form to actual fighting, or in some cases to predatory or predator-avoidance behavior, might have evolved as a risk-free way of getting such practice. I also suggested that in the higher primates, notably the chimpanzee, social play might have been additionally selected as a means of providing practice in complex social skills such as tripartite interactions.

Although the hypothesis that play-fighting serves as practice for adult fighting skills has probably been the front-runner (e.g., Jamieson & Armitage, 1987; Smith, 1982; Symons, 1978), it has come under criticism. It almost certainly oversimplifies the diversity of functions for which social play may have come to be selected through the range of mammalian species. For example, in a review of play in ungulates, Byers (1984) hypothesized that although social play first evolved in these species because of selection for fighting skills, its function can be modified in particular species. The forms of play seen among the collared peccary, for instance, involving adults as well as juveniles in coordinated herd activity, suggested to him that in this species, social play functioned to promote and maintain social cooperation and group cohesion.

Developing this line of argument, Pellis (1988) has distinguished between forms of play-fighting according to whether the goal or target of a play-fight is or is not similar to the goal of actual fighting, as well as whether the tactics of attack and defense are similar in the two cases. He argues that in several rodent species, the goal in a play-fight (often, attempting to bite the nape of the neck) is different from the goal in a real fight (often, attempting to bite the rump); also, the detailed behavioral tactics are frequently different. These differences in design features clearly weaken the argument that such play is practice for fighting skills.

Martin and Caro (1985) have raised more fundamental issues related to the search for the functions of play, including social play. First, they argue that the costs of play are probably small; therefore, the benefits need not be very large in order for play to have been selected. Indeed, they suggest that the ease with which play can be suppressed by other motivations such as fear, hunger, or fatigue indicates that it is a low-priority activity. Any benefits of play might thus be difficult to detect. In addition, such benefits might be obtainable by other means (the problem of equifinality), might only be gained above a certain threshold, and might have short- or long-term effects. They conclude that "there is no direct evidence that play has any important benefits" in nonhuman species but that it is "a facilitative developmental determinant of minor importance" (p. 97). This view remains controversial, and it is arguable that Martin and Caro have underestimated the actual costs of play; nevertheless, this review clearly points to the lack of firm evidence on the topic and the difficulty in obtaining such evidence.

Another interesting development in theories of mammalian play has been the consideration of "cheating" in play, discussed by Fagen (1981). The "cheating" hypothesis is that

> animals may exploit opportunities to change play into agonistic fighting. An animal would begin play, then make an escalated attack on its playmate. By doing so it would damage or intimidate its opponent, thus gaining access to a current or a future resource. An initial play attempt could also serve to deceive watching adults, who might then disregard the pair long enough for the cheater to harm its partner (p. 337).

Although an animal might gain a short-term advantage over another by cheating in a play-fight in this way, a consequence might be that it would come to be avoided as a play partner. This would be one example of the "tit-for-tat" strategy that Axelrod and Hamilton (1981) have shown can punish selfish cheating and instead provide an evolutionary basis for cooperation. Individuals could be selected for their ability to abide by the play convention, so that they could continue to get the benefits of play bouts in the future.

However, there remain circumstances in which cheating might be expected. These include (a) play bouts with strangers, who will probably not be encountered again, and (b) play bouts with individuals who are rapidly changing in dominance position. There is some evidence from the literature on play in primates that such cheating bouts can occur, though they seem to be infrequent. For example, Kurland (1977) described some cases in which Japanese macaque play-fights escalated into violent attacks between unrelated and relatively unfamiliar participants. In all such cases, it is important but sometimes difficult to distinguish what Fagen calls "honest mistakes", (p. 338) -- that is momentary transgressions due to an individual's not realizing its own strength or failing to recognize a play signal -- and "cheating" in a more intentional sense.

That many primates are capable of using behaviors intentionally to deceive others is becoming apparent from a growing body of evidence, much of it anecdotal but impressive in its scope and variety (Byrne & Whiten, 1988). Many of these anecdotes concern giving alarm signals when no predator is present or failing to go to a food source when in view of a more dominant animal. However, there are some relevant observations of play behavior. Both Breuggeman (1978), in observations of rhesus monkeys, and Lawick-Goodall (1968), in observations of chimpanzees, have described how a mother may initiate play with an infant in order to distract the infant from suckling; or an older sibling may play with a younger sibling briefly to distract it from the mother, so that the older sibling can then get the mother's attention. These are examples of manipulation rather than cheating. They do little harm and are not likely to be retaliated against. They are, nevertheless, examples of the social manipulation of the play convention. Deception, cheating, and manipulation are also, of course, features of human behavior. They can appear in childhood from the 2nd year onward -- for example, in sibling relationships (Dunn & Kendrick, 1982) and we could in theory expect them to be found in social play situations. If we suppose that R&T does have some benefits for the participants, then R&T bouts can be viewed as a resource. Charlesworth (1988) has argued that there may be five major classes of resource-directed actions -- namely, cooperation, manipulation, deception, intimidation, and aggression. He and his colleagues have found evidence for such strategies in group problem-solving situations in preschool children. If we attempt to apply these to the case of R&T, a cooperative strategy would be one that respected the play convention. However, a manipulative strategy might use play for other ends (e.g., distracting from another resource); a deceptive strategy might involve starting a bout playfully but escalating it to aggression; an intimidating strategy might start with aggression and modulate into play. Such forms of manipulation and cheating in R&T could be expected to be within the social-cognitive competence of children and to be predicted on theoretical grounds, at least in certain circumstances.

Empirical Evidence on the Developmental Significance of Children's R&T

If it is difficult to pin down the functions of play-fighting in mammals, it is even more difficult to do so for R&T in humans. There may well be cultural values put on play, and benefits accruing from play, that do not necessarily coincide with any biological function or benefit (Humphreys & Smith, 1984). We can look at the possible developmental benefits that R&T may have, bearing in mind that such benefits may or may not be essential, may be very specific or quite general, may be immediate or delayed, and may or may not be functions in any evolutionary sense of the term.

R&T might, in earliest times, have provided practice for fighting and hunting skills, and this is supported by some anthropological observations. Konner (1972) remarked that "it is very striking that most of the component behaviors in rough-and-tumble play ... can be seen in Zhun/twa (San) children annoying large animals ... or trying to kill small ones" (p. 299). Wrestling R&T in children is fairly similar to actual fighting, with the goal of wrestling often being to obtain a superior position (Aldis, 1975). The goals and tactics of play-fighting do not differ greatly from real fighting, as they do in many rodents (Pellis, 1988), though there are some differences (Fry, 1987). This functional hypothesis could explain the sex difference usually found in R&T, since males generally engage in more physical fighting and hunting. Such outcomes of R&T would not necessarily be so beneficial in modern urban societies, albeit fighting skills may still carry some benefits in terms of children's position in the peer group.

If children were practicing fighting skills in R&T, then we would expect them to choose partners of similar strength so as to get optimal practice. Comparisons we have made of R&T partner choice and sociometric rankings for strength suggest that R&T partners are often more closely matched for strength than chance would predict (Boulton and Smith, in press; Humphreys and Smith, 1987). While this supports the practice-fighting hypothesis, we also found that partners in non-R&T activities are similarly more closely matched for strength. This matching may therefore be a general feature of friendship choice and not a specific feature of R&T partner choice.

R&T might also be related to social dominance (Meany, Stewart, & Beatty, 1985). One variant of this hypothesis is that individuals learn the strength of others in a noninjurious way and, hence, determine their ranking in the group. Leaving aside the fact that there are other ways of discovering this, the restraint and self-handicapping that characterize R&T would seem to make it an ineffective way of learning strength and rank position. When we interviewed 8- and 10-year-olds, about half of them said that you could *not* tell who was stronger in a play-fight, mainly for these reasons.

Another variant of this hypothesis is that an individual could maintain or improve dominance position by asserting this in a nonaggressive way in R&T. Again, the existence of restraint and self-handicapping argue against this. To maintain or improve dominance in R&T, one might need to "cheat" a little and actually demonstrate at some point that one could pin down or hurt another child. Interestingly, the 8- and 10-year-olds whom we interviewed who said that you *could* tell who was stronger in a play-fight, most commonly cited reasons such as being able to get another person down or infliction of pain or injury. Neill (1976) explicitly supported this hypothesis in 12- to 13-year-old boys when he claimed that a mixture of hostility and R&T might be

> a means of asserting or maintaining dominance; once the weaker boy has registered distress the bond can be maintained by the fight taking a more playful form, but if he does not do so at the start of the fight, the stronger boy may increase the intensity of the fight until he does (p. 219).

This suggests that R&T may at times be brought into use for dominance assertion rather than that this is a primary function or benefit of R&T. There would be little incentive for partners to regularly accept R&T initiations if it only resulted in dominance being imposed on them. Examination of the sociometric status of play partners at 7 to 11 years shows that there is not usually a predominance of stronger initiator choosing weaker partners, as such a hypothesis would predict; Humphreys and Smith (1987) did find such a pattern in one class of 11-year-olds but this finding has not been replicated (Smith & Boulton, in press).

R&T might also have more socially cooperative benefits. It might help to form or maintain friendships between those children who play together in R&T bouts, for example.

There is no *direct* evidence for this, but it is now well established that from 3 and 4 years up to 11 years, children tend to choose as R&T partners other children whom they like, at above chance levels. When we interviewed 8- and 10-year-olds we found that some 50% of best friends were nominated as children with whom they liked to play-fight or play-chase. There are, of course, plenty of other ways for children to make friends, and some children engage in very little R&T, so this is unlikely to be an essential benefit of R&T. The finding that children choose friends for R&T is compatible with other theories, such as practice fighting, since the chances of R&T staying in a "cooperative" rather than a "cheating" mode would be expected to be greater if the partner were a friend. When we interviewed 8- and 10-year-olds, we found that the reported likelihood of a child's retaliating if accidentally hit in a play-fight was much higher if the partner was not a friend.

However, the most popular recent hypothesis among psychologists studying R&T in childhood is that it facilitates social skills. This is true of both parent-child physical play and peer-peer R&T. On the basis of their descriptions of parent-child physical play, Power and Parke (1981) argue that

> the descriptive analysis of the physical bouts ... showed that these bouts often serve as contexts for a wide range of communicative and affectively charged social interactions between parents and their infants. Therefore, through such interactions fathers may play an important role in facilitating the development of communicative skills and the formation of social relationships ... We might expect that early physical play may be important both as an antecedent of later peer-peer play and in the regulation of agonistic and aggressive interactions (p. 160).

In a subsequent study, MacDonald and Parke (1984) observed mothers and fathers interacting in the home with their 3- or 4-year-old child. In line with their general hypothesis, they found that children whose parents (and especially fathers) engaged in more physical play with them tended to be more popular at nursery school and to be rated more positively by teachers (for example, as being more involved, less apprehensive). They concluded that

> through physically playful interaction with their parents, especially fathers, children may be learning the social communicative value of their own affective display, as well as how to use these signals to regulate the social behavior of others. In turn, they may learn to accurately decode the social and affective signals of other social partners (p. 1273).

Such arguments are based on the observations that physical play can involve highly intense stimulation, which is generally seen as pleasurable to the child but which must be carefully modulated by the parent and to some extent by the child to avoid overstimulation, withdrawal, and other negative consequences.

Parke, MacDonald, Beitel, and Bhavnagri (1987) replicated the correlation between physical play with fathers and popularity with peers, though at borderline significance levels. Correlations of physical play with emotional decoding ability (identifying facial expressions) were however only significant for girls and with fathers, not for boys or with mothers. In addition, MacDonald (1987) has looked at the amount of parent-child physical play in the homes of 3- to 5-year-olds who were *popular, rejected* or *neglected* at nursery school, using the sociometric status types of Coie, Dodge, and Coppotelli (1982). In line with the hypothesis, it was found that neglected children received much less physical play from parents. Rejected children did not, however (although a small effect was found in the second part of the observational session when it was suggested to parents that they might engage in physical play). MacDonald states that the parental physical play with rejected children was more characterized by overstimulation and avoidance of stimulation than was the case for the popular children. He also points out that no cause-effect relations can be deduced; for example, both quantity of play and peer popularity might derive from temperamental differences among the children.

So far as peer-peer R&T is concerned, Pellegrini (1987) has hypothesized that it has functional significance for social-cognitive skills. In part, this is based on argument from design. Children need specific social skills to recognize R&T as opposed to aggression. R&T exercises reciprocal turn-taking skills such as chasing, then fleeing. Pellegrini also reviews some of the correlational evidence relating R&T to social skills. The few available earlier studies do not seem to support the hypothesis. Ladd's (1983) study of middle school children found more R&T in rejected children, and a significant correlation with *unoccupied*, but the meaning of this is obscured by his confounding of R&T and actual fighting, as mentioned earlier. Rubin and Daniels-Beirness (1983) found near-zero and one negative correlation of R&T with sociometric popularity in 5- and 6-year-olds, and Rubin, Daniels-Beirness, and Hayvren (1982) found similar near-zero or negative relations between R&T to popularity in 4- and 5-year-olds. Their definition of R&T was not given. Dodge (1983), in a study of 7- and 8-year-old boys, found the highest level of "aggressive play (often called rough-and-tumble play)" (p. 1388) in *controversial* children, with *average* children showing the least. Controversial and popular children received the most positive responses to their "aggressive play" interactions. However, these results must be treated with caution, since there were only 3 controversial children in the sample. Also, it is not clear from the definition how well "aggressive play" matches with R&T. Dodge's comment that "aggressive, rough-and-tumble play ... has been shown to have high probabilities of receiving negative peer responses" (p. 1397) suggests that it differs from R&T, which usually gets a positive or neutral response (Humphreys & Smith, 1987).

Finally, Coie and Kupersmidt (1983) reported observations on groups of 4 boys, aged 9 to 11 years, who were either familiar or unfamiliar with each other. Rough-and-tumble play, defined as a physical prosocial category, did not differ by sociometric status type for unfamiliar children, but for familiar children was most frequent in average and rejected children, least frequent in neglected children, with popular children in between.

However, in observations of 5- to 9-year-olds, Pellegrini (in press) found that different patterns of results were obtained for popular and rejected children. In the case of popular children, R&T led to games with rules and very seldom resulted in aggression; in the case of rejected children, R&T led to aggression some 28% of the time. Also, for popular children, R&T correlated significantly with a measure of social skills (Interpersonal Cognitive Problem Solving), whereas for rejected children this correlation tended to be negative, and R&T correlated with teachers' ratings of antisocial behavior. In further work, Pellegrini (1988) has reported results using our videotape interview method which suggest that popular children give a much wider range of responses than rejected children; that is, they give a much greater spread of responses across the various categories, even though the rank ordering of the categories is similar for the two kinds of children.

The correlational findings of MacDonald and Parke (1984) on parent-child physical play, and Pellegrini (in press) on peer-peer R&T, give some support to the hypothesis that such forms of play can enhance children's popularity in the peer group, perhaps through fostering social skills such as encoding and interpreting social cues or selecting behavior that will regulate affect within optimal levels or help to maintain the interaction. The available evidence is not entirely consistent, and its being correlational is open to various interpretations. Nevertheless, such a hypothesis would fit well with the social-skills model of competence proposed by Dodge, Pettit, McClaskey, and Brown (1986). These latter authors hypothesize an information-processing model of social skills, involving sequentially the encoding and interpreting of social cues and the generation, selection, and enactment of appropriate behavioral responses. Rejected and neglected children are thought to be deficient in some aspects of this process, such that, for example, they are less competent at entering a game with peers or at dealing with provocations. The skills that children need in initiating and regulating R&T and in distinguishing R&T from real fighting would seem to be very similar to the skills that they need for entering a game or for dealing with provocations. Thus, on the Dodge et al. (1986) model, frequency of and competence in R&T could be expected to be linked to social skills and to popularity. The evidence from MacDonald and Parke (1984) and from Pellegrini (in press) supports both this expectation and the hypothesis that rejected children, rather than showing less R&T, show less cooperative R&T -- specifically R&T that is less well regulated for affect (MacDonald, 1987) and that more often leads to aggression (Pellegrini, in press). (Neglected children, however, may simply show less R&T, as Coie & Kupersmidt, 1983, found.) These hypotheses are illustrated in Figure 12.1, with arrows going each way to indicate that all the directional links are plausible; it is not crucial to this model which way the cause-effect predictions go, and anyway, all three factors might be mutually reinforcing popularity (might allow more practice of social skills, etc.).

What exactly is the non-cooperative R&T that is linked to peer rejection? The presupposition of the theory behind this model would seem to be that such non-cooperative R&T is due to "honest mistakes" (p. 338) in Fagen's (1981) terminology. That is, it results from less adept interpretation of the meaning of R&T invitations or less adept regulation of the affect in the encounter through restraint, self-handicapping, or turn taking. If this is so, then help for rejected children in the form of social-skills training might include some specific training in R&T skills as well as other skills, as already implemented in a number of studies (e.g., Bierman, Miller & Stabb, 1987).

Such an interpretation is supported by some observations. For example Sluckin (1981), in his ethnographic study of playground behavior, commented that

> there are undoubtedly a certain number of children who fail to distinguish and react appropriately to rough and tumble (pretend) and real aggression. In First School I saw two non-English speaking children for whom this was a problem. Both these boys lashed out at others who continually taunted them, misinterpreting these actions as aggressive rather than a friendly invitation to a chasing game. Happily, a sensitive teacher stepped in and successfully urged the others to "be gentle" with the individuals concerned (p. 40).

However, there is another perspective to be reintroduced at this point. Some non-cooperative R&T might be the result, not of lacking social skills, resulting in misinterpreting signals or choosing inappropriate responses, but rather of having quite *sophisticated* social skills directed toward non-cooperative ends. That is, some non-cooperative R&T might result from intentional deception, intimidation, or manipulation on the part of one of the participants. This possibility is also discussed in Fagen's (1981) theoretical analysis. There is evidence for both deceitful and manipulative R&T in primates, and there is evidence for deceit, intimidation, and manipulation in other aspects of children's behavior (e.g., Charlesworth, 1988).

The observational work on children that has been carried out in the tradition of psychology and ethology (i.e., recording the occurrence and sequence of particular behavior categories) has not often found evidence for deceptive, intimidating, or manipulative R&T. The main exception is Neill's (1976) observations of 12- and 13-year-old boys, referred to earlier, according to which some boys deliberately use R&T conventions to continue an interaction whose overriding intent is to assert dominance. We have seen rather few clear

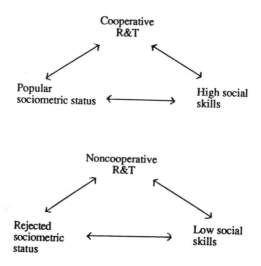

Figure 12.1

Hypothesized relation of R&T to peer popularity and rejection.

instances ourselves, though the ones we have observed are more common in older children (M.J. Boulton, personal communication, July 1988). Fry (1987) has also commented that

> the clear distinction between play and aggression apparent among 3 to 8 year old Zapotec children may blur somewhat for Zapotec 12-16 year olds. At times, horseplay among teenagers appeared on the basis of facial expression to become somewhat serious, but then shifted back to obvious play once again (p. 298).

Interestingly, rather more evidence for non-cooperative R&T seems to come from ethnographic studies of playground behavior, rather than from psychological/ethological studies. Sluckin's (1981) study of 5- to 9-year-olds falls more into the ethnographic category, since he tried to record the main features of behavior sequences in context, rather than the occurrence of specific categories, and also interviewed the children extensively. Besides the "honest mistakes" in R&T that he observed, described above, it is clear from his account that some children used, or tried to use, R&T play conventions in deceitful, intimidating or manipulative ways. For example,

> *Ivan* grabs Ashok (9:6) round the neck and says: we're only playing, aren't we Ashok? *Ashok* refuses to accept this verbal definition of the situation and defensively shouts: "No. *Ivan* goes off" (p. 40).

Sluckin argued that many 7-, 8- and 9-year-olds seemed adept at moving between R&T and actual aggression as a way of trying to control others -- for instance, by redefining a situation to their advantage as Tim does in the following extract:

Nick (9:9) tells Tim who is holding Bob: You'd better leave him alone. *Nick* grabs Tim who lets Bob go. *Tim*: as soon as you've let go of me, I'll hurt him some more. *Nick* grabs Tim again. *Tim*: It's only a game, it's only a game (p. 36).

An ethnographic study of 6- and 10-year-olds in a school in West Berlin, by Oswald, Krappmann, Chowduri, and von Salisch (1987), refers to "fooling around" or "horseplay" (p. 212) in the children. They commented that for 6-year-olds

there were instances when fooling around degenerated into annoyance or a quarrel, and others where actions designed to indicate fooling around were met with irritation on the part of the intended recipient. In most cases, however, the fooling was clearly high-spirited, and, unlike such play among older children, was devoid of elements that could be perceived as encroachment. In contrast, the fooling around we observed in 10-year-olds often incorporated elements that could be regarded as disturbing, annoying, or even trespassing beyond limits. The children were able to present their behavior in a manner that clearly indicated that they were fooling around, and not serious or hurtful in their intentions. Nonetheless, over a protracted period of fooling around this scheme could go awry; suddenly a thump was painful, or it was no longer sufficiently clear whether or not a gesture was intended to be disparaging. In such cases the nature of the interaction was reversed and the situation ended in verbal abuse or a scuffle. With some social skill, however, it was often possible to restore the interaction to the level of fooling around. In some sequences we gained the impression that children deliberately held the interaction at the boundary between playfulness and seriousness, between fooling around and annoyance (p. 213).

In another ethnographic study of a racially mixed U.S. school, Hanna (1982) describes even more sinister results in what she calls "meddlin" in 7- to 11-year-olds. Misunderstandings could arouse racial sensitivity and lead to fights -- for example, when a black fourth grader grabbed a white boy in a stranglehold and demanded: "Boy, you be my slave!" Hanna comments that

what is overlooked as trivial play or "horsing around" in the classroom or informal areas of the school covers a great deal of children's social life ordinarily hidden from adult's eyes. Children receive experiential lessons from each other -- the "meddlin" curricula may subvert formal education (p. 341).

There seems to be some consensus among the small number of relevant studies that deceptive, intimidative, and manipulative forms of R&T become more frequent with age. Nevertheless, psychological/ethological studies tend to suggest that such forms of non-cooperative R&T are infrequent up to 10 or 11 years of age, whereas the ethnographic studies tend to suggest that they are more frequent in the middle school period (not all ethnographic studies do so; for example Finnan, 1982, and Thorne, 1986 do not comment on deception, intimidation, or manipulation in chasing games).

Besides the age of the children, it may well be that other factors such as social and ethnic background, and composition of the group, are important factors here. So, also, are sociometric status types. Following the lead of MacDonald and Parke (1984), Pellegrini (in press) and others, it will clearly be useful for future researchers to bear these issues in mind. If some frequency of deceptive, intimidative, or manipulative R&T *is* established, this may offer some challenge to the social-skills model presented in Figure 12.1, since the children engaging in these behaviors may well have quite sophisticated social skills rather than lacking them. It is entirely possible that the hypothesis that popular children have good social skills and children of other sociometric status have less good social skills is oversimplified. The evidence is certainly mixed, and at times, results are interpreted more favorably for the hypothesis than might seem reasonable. For example, Feldman and Dodge (1987) concluded that "deviant children (rejected and neglected) were found to respond deficiently compared to average and popular children" in teasing situations (p. 211), but in fact, one main result on which this conclusion is based is that rejected and neglected children showed a higher endorsement of aggressive responses in such a situation. This is interpreted as *deficient*. Yet this same study found a significant increase with age in endorsement of aggressive responses in this situation. This is interpreted as "changing subculture norms" (p. 225). However, it could just be that some rejected children have different subculture norms, too, or different goals for their interactions, without lacking social skills per se. This argument might be even more plausibly applied to controversial status children. There are very little data on R&T in controversial children, but their status and their likely similarity to some children who are playground "bosses" in ethnographic studies (Hargreaves, 1967; Sluckin, 1981), liked by some but disliked by others, suggests that even if some rejected children are lacking in social skills (and perhaps make honest mistakes in R&T), controversial children might have different goals in their interactions and, in some senses, may not be unsuccessful in their objectives. This possibility is shown in Figure 12.2. Value judgments about what is "successful" and what is "deficient" become salient at this point, and rightly so. When does social-skills training become moral judgment training?

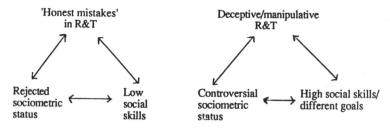

Figure 12.2

Hypothesized further breakdown of the relationship shown in Figure 12.1 between non-cooperative R&T and sociometric status.

In further research, it will also be useful to try to blend some features of both the ethological and ethnographic traditions. For example, Pellegrini's (in press) results would be even more interesting if we knew more about *how* R&T turned into aggression in rejected children; were these episodes honest mistakes or intentional? Generally, the meaning of a behavior in context may sometimes get insufficient attention in observational studies, including some that I have done. Equally, ethnographic reports would be enhanced by some more precise definition of terms such as *fooling around*, *horseplay*, and *meddlin*;

by a more quantified approach to the frequency of certain types of activity; and by paying more attention to the psychological characteristics of the individual children.   A combination of both clear, accurate and quantifiable observations, together with attention to the meaning of encounters in context and perhaps also interviewing children themselves, will be necessary for further progress to be made in this area.

References

Aldis, O. (1975). *Play fighting.* New York: Academic Press.

Axelrod, R. & Hamilton, W.D. (1981). The evolution of cooperation. *Science, 211,* 1390-1396.

Bierman, K.L., Miller, C.L. & Stabb, S.D. (1987). Improving the social behavior and peer acceptance of rejected boys: Effects of social skill training with instructions and prohibitions. *Journal of Consulting and Clinical Psychology, 55,* 194-200.

Blurton-Jones, N. (1967). An ethological study of some aspects of social behavior of children in nursery school. In D. Morris (Ed.), *Primate ethology* (pp. 347-368). London: Weidenfeld & Nicholson.

Boulton, M.J., & Smith, P.K. (in press). Issues in the study of rough and tumble play. In M. Bloch and A. Pellegrini (Eds.), *The ecological context of children's play.* Norwood, N.J.: Ablex.

Breuggeman, J.A. (1978). The function of adult play in free-ranging Macaca mulatta. In E.O. Smith (Ed.), *Social play in primates* (pp. 169-191). New York: Academic Press.

Byers, J.A. (1984). Play in ungulates. In P.K. Smith (Ed.), *Play in animals and humans* (pp. 43-65). Oxford, England: Basil Blackwell.

Byrne, R., & Whiten, A. (1988). *Machiavellian intelligence; Social expertise and the evolution of intellect in monkeys, apes and humans.* Oxford, England: Oxford University Press.

Charlesworth, W.R. (1988). Resources and resource acquisition during ontogeny. In K.B. MacDonald (Ed.), *Sociobiological perspectives on human development* (pp. 24-77). New York: Springer-Verlag.

Coie, J.D., Dodge, K.A., & Coppotelli, H. (1982). Dimensions and types of social status: A cross-age perspective. *Developmental Psychology, 18,* 557-570.

Coie, J.D., and Kupersmidt, J.B. (1983). A behavioral analysis of emerging social status in boys' groups. *Child Development, 54,* 1400-1416.

Dodge, K.A. (1983). Behavioral antecedents of peer social status. *Child Development, 54,* 1383-1399.

Dodge, K.A., Pettit, G.S., McClaskey, C.L., & Brown, M.M. (1986). Social competence in children. *Monographs of the Society for Research in Child Development, 51*(2), 1-85.

Dunn, J. & Kendrick, C. (1982). *Siblings: Love, envy and understanding.* London: Grant McIntrye.

Fagen, R.M. (1981). *Animal play behavior.* New York: Oxford University Press.

Feldman, E. & Dodge, K.A. (1987). Social information processing and sociometric status: Sex, age, and situational effects. *Journal of Abnormal Child Psychology, 15,* 211-227.

Finnan, C.R. (1982). The ethnography of children's spontaneous play. In G. Spindler (Ed.), *Doing the ethnography of schooling* (pp. 358-380). New York: Holt, Rinehart and Winston.

Fry, D.P. (1987). Differences between playfighting and serious fights among Zapotec children. *Ethology and Sociobiology, 8,* 285-306.

Groos, K. (1901). *The play of man.* London: William Heinemann.

Hanna, J.L. (1982). Public social policy and the children's world: Implications of ethnographic research for desegregated schooling. In G. Spindler (Ed.), *Doing the ethnography of schooling* (pp. 316-355). New York: Holt, Rinehart & Winston.

Hargreaves, D.H. (1967). *Social relations in a secondary school.* London: Routledge & Kegan Paul.

Harlow, H.K., & Harlow, M.K. (1965). The affectional systems. In A.M. Schrier, H.F. Harlow & F. Stollnitz (Eds.), *Behaviour of non-human primates,* Vol. II. London, England: Academic Press.

Humphreys, A.P. & Smith, P.K. (1984). Rough and tumble in preschool and playground. In P.K. Smith (Ed.), *Play in animals and humans* (pp. 241-266). Oxford: Basil Blackwell.

Humphreys, A.P. & Smith, P.K. (1987). Rough and tumble, friendship, and dominance in schoolchildren: Evidence for continuity and change with age. *Child Development, 58,* 201-212.

Jamieson, S.H. and Armitage, K.B. (1987). Sex differences in the play behavior of yearling yellow-bellied marmots. *Ethology, 74,* 237-253.

Konner, M.S. (1972). Aspects of the developmental ethology of a foraging people. In N. Blurton-Jones (Ed.), *Ethological studies of child behaviour* (pp. 285-304). Cambridge, England: Cambridge, University Press.

Kurland, J.A. (1977). *Kin selection in the Japanese monkey*. Basel, Switzerland: Karger.

Ladd, G. (1983). Social networks of popular, average, and rejected children in a school setting. *Merrill-Palmer Quarterly, 29*, 283-307.

Lawick-Goodall, J. van (1968). The behaviour of free-living chimpanzees in the Gombe Stream Reserve. *Animal Behaviour Monographs, 1*, 161-311.

Lowe, M. & Costello, A.J. (1976). *Manual for the symbolic play test*. Windsor, England: National Foundation for Educational Research.

MacDonald, K. (1987). Parent-child physical play with rejected, neglected and popular boys. *Developmental Psychology, 23*, 705-711.

MacDonald, K. and Parke, R.D. (1984). Bridging the gap: Parent-child play interactions and peer interactive competence. *Child Development, 55*, 1265-1277.

MacDonald, K. and Parke, R.D. (1986). Parent-child physical play: the effects of sex and age of children and parents. *Sex Roles, 15*, 367-378.

Martin, P. & Caro, T.M. (1985). On the functions of play and its role in behavioral development. In J.S. Rosenblatt, C. Beer, M.C. Busnel, & P.J.B. Slater (Eds.), *Advances in the study of behavior* (Vol. *15*, pp. 59-103). Orlando FL: Academic Press.

Meany, M.J., Stewart, J., & Beatty, W.W. (1985). Sex differences in social play: The socialisation of sex roles. In J.S. Rosenblatt, C. Beer, M.C. Busnel, P.J.B. Slater (Eds.). *Advances in the study of behavior* (Vol. *15*, pp. 3-58). Orlando FL: Academic Press.

Neill, S.R.StJ. (1976). Aggressive and non-aggressive fighting in 12 to 13 year-old preadolescent boys. *Journal of Child Psychology and Psychiatry, 17*, 213-220.

Oswald, H., Krappmann, L., Chowduri, F. & von Salisch, M. (1987). Gaps and bridges: Interactions between girls and boys in elementary school. *Sociological Studies of Child Development, 2*, 205-223.

Parke, R.D., MacDonald, K.B., Beitel, A. & Bhavnagri, N. (1987). The role of the family in the development of peer relationships. In R. Peters (Ed.), *Social learning and systems approaches to marriage and the family* (pp. 17-44). New York: Bruner/Mazel.

Pellegrini, A. (1987). Rough-and-tumble play: Developmental and educational significance. *Educational Psychologist, 22*, 23-43.

Pellegrini, A.D. (1988). What is a category? The case of rough-and-tumble play. Unpublished manuscript.

Pellegrini, A. (in press). Elementary school children's rough-and-tumble play and social competence. *Developmental Psychology*.

Pellis, S.M. (1988). Agonistic versus amicable targets of attack and defense: Consequences for the origin, function, and descriptive classification of play-fighting. *Aggressive Behavior, 14*, 85-104.

Piaget, J. (1951). *Play, dreams and imitation in childhood*. London: Routledge & Kegan Paul.

Power, T.G. and Parke, R.D. (1981). Play as a context for early learning. In L.M. Laosa & I.E. Sigel (Eds.)., *Families as learning environments for children* (pp. 147-178). New York: Plenum.

Rubin, K.H. (1982). Non-social play in preschoolers: Necessarily evil? *Child Development, 53*, 651-657.

Rubin, K.H. and Daniels-Beirness, T. (1983). Concurrent and predictive correlates of sociometric status in kindergarten and grade one children. *Merrill-Palmer Quarterly, 29*, 337-351.

Rubin, K.H. and Daniels-Beirness, T. & Hayvren, M. (1982). Social and social-cognitive correlates of sociometric status in preschool and kindergarten children. *Canadian Journal of Behavioral Science, 14*, 338-347.

Sluckin, A.M. (1981). *Growing up in the playground: The social development of children*. London: Routledge & Kegan Paul.

Smilansky, S. (1968). *The effects of sociodramatic play on disadvantaged preschool children*. New York: Wiley.

Smith, P.K. (1982). Does play matter? Functional and evolutionary aspects of animal and human play. *The Behavioral and Brain Sciences, 5*, 139-184.

Smith, P.K. (1988). Children's play and its role in early development: A re-evaluation of the "play ethos". In A.D. Pellegrini (Ed.), *Psychological bases for early education* (pp. 207-226). Chichester, England: Wiley.

Smith, P.K. & Boulton, M. (in press). Rough-and-tumble play, aggression and dominance: Perception and behavior in children's encounters. *Human Development*.

Smith, P.K. & Connolly, K.J. (1980). *The ecology of preschool behaviour*. Cambridge, England: Cambridge University Press.

Smith, P.K. & Daglish, L. (1977). Sex differences in parent and infant behaviour in the home. *Child Development, 48*, 1250-1254.

Smith, P.K. & Lewis, K. (1985). Rough-and-tumble play, fighting and chasing in nursery school children. *Ethology and Sociobiology, 6*, 175-181.

Symons, D. (1978). *Play and aggression: A study of rhesus monkeys.* New York: Columbia University Press.

Thorne, B. (1986). Girls and boys together but mostly apart: Gender arrangements in elementary schools. In W.W. Hartup & Z. Rubin (Eds.), *Relationships and development* (pp. 167-184). Hillsdale, NJ.: Erlbaum.

Whiting, B.B. & Whiting, J.W.M. (1975). *Children of six cultures: A psycho-cultural analysis.* Cambridge, MA: Harvard University Press.

Section IV

Setting Factors in Children's Social Development: The Influences of Families and Schools

Introduction to Section IV

Grazia Attili

Until recently, social cognition has been the primary focus of study in the social-development field. In the last decade, peer relationships have received increased attention as researchers have become sensitized to the impact of early peer interactions on the development of social-cognitive skills and, conversely, to the effects of social-cognitive competencies on children's ability to enter and sustain peer interactions.

The link between general, basic competencies such as social competence (see Section One, this volume) and the capacity for successful peer relationships has been stressed both by psychologists--whether their intent is to describe these processes, as Piagetians do, or to develop applied interventions (see Section Five, this volume)--and by ethologists. Piagetian-inspired researchers have devoted primary attention to children's basic social-cognitive abilities, whereas ethologists have focused on their capacities for different modalities of interaction. However, these researchers have largely overlooked the extent to which emotional factors might affect the development of children's interaction skills as well as the mutual influences between children's behavior on the one hand and family, school, and environmental factors on the other hand. Indeed, the dialectic between these systems and its effect on the display of social skills within peer groups appears to be one of the most urgent and promising topics of research in the area of interventions to improve children's maladjusted behavior.

The neglect of these fundamental processes can be understood as a manifestation of the revolution against the psychoanalytic model and of the overzealous application of Piagetian theory. Until the early 1970s, the influences of psychoanalysis (which emphasizes relationships with adults) and of the Piagetian model (which emphasizes the egocentric nature of the young child's thinking) may have discouraged the study of interpersonal relationships other than those between mothers and their children. However, this state of affairs has largely been reversed in recent years.

The social significance to the young child of play and exploration that involve social objects other than the mother has increasingly been traced. Nevertheless, scholars have usually considered the adult-child and child-child systems as functionally independent. This ignores the fact that children need to engage in accurate social reality testing with regard to their peer relations and that their social interaction with peers may be somewhat dependent on the security acquired from adult contacts. Individual differences in social behavior directed at peers and at unfamiliar adults may be affected to a certain extent by the child's previous relationships at home and by the environmental conditions and opportunities provided by his or her school.

The emphasis in this section is on the setting factors that affect children's social competence. Drawing upon Bronfenbrenner's (1979) ecological model of human development, the contributors to this section outline their position that children's social behavior must be considered within the context in which development occurs. Chapters 14, 15, 16, and 17 explore the diversity of such influences on the social interaction of both preschoolers and school-age children. These include the spatial arrangements of the child's school; features of the family, school, and neighborhood environments; the quality of the

259

B. H. Schneider et al. (eds.), Social Competence in Developmental Perspective, 259–262.
© 1989 by Kluwer Academic Publishers.

child's relationships with the mother and father; and the mother's beliefs concerning socially competent and incompetent behaviors.

Alain Legendre (Chapter 14) pursues the theme that environmental and developmental foci need to be integrated. In his work, environmental psychology goes beyond simply identifying the aspects of the physical environment that might possibly affect children's behavior to considering the individual characteristics likely to enable a child to adapt to that physical environment. Factors that permit field independence are studied in two groups of children 2 to 3 years old, an age at which the verbal communication system is not yet fully mastered. Adaptation to spatial constraints is explained as a function of children's competence at initiating and maintaining interaction with peers. Children who are better able to form preferred relationships with their peers are better able to sustain close proximity among themselves within small play areas when separated from adult caregivers by visual obstacles. Before mastery of the verbal communication system, children seem to find it difficult to feel safe interacting with an unfamiliar peer out of an adult's sight. With the formation of preferred relationships, children begin to share the meaning of their common activities with their playmates. Hence, the close proximity of a friend in areas far from an adult becomes less threatening than the presence of an unfamiliar peer and enables the child to overcome the feeling of insecurity associated with being away from the an adult's comforting presence.

Legendre does not analyze the social skills and interaction style that influence children's success at forming long-lasting relationships. These abilities and children's accuracy in perceiving peers' aggressive and prosocial behaviors are of central importance in Gary W. Ladd's work (Chapter 15). He examines the consequences in terms of peer rejection and subsequent school maladjustment of individual child characteristics such as prosocial versus aggressive interaction style. Nevertheless, Ladd's results indicate that children's experiences in the family, neighborhood, and school can also contribute to their adjustment. Parents' management of children's peer relations during preschool years, for example, can greatly influence their social success when they enter new kindergartens and foster academic and social success when they enter grade school. This is particularly true when parents are able to supervise peer contacts in noninterfering ways. Having been enrolled in preschool also predicts grade school adjustment insofar as it prepares children to face both positive and stressful experiences such as separating from parents and becoming comfortable with new peers and adults. Children's involvement in relationships with neighborhood friends and the types of children they choose as friends also affect school adjustment. While having neighborhood friends was generally associated with positive school adjustment, this did not apply to children who tended to relate with younger companions outside of school; they may find it difficult to relate to age-mates in the school setting. Of course, the causality may be in the opposite direction: Children who have difficulty relating to age-mates in school may find it easier to associate with their juniors in the neighborhood. The negative consequences of these asymmetrical relationships can probably be attributed to their long duration and high frequency. From a totally different framework, certain benefits may accrue from interacting with a younger partner and confronting the mismatch between one's own level of cognitive complexity and the playmate's. In fact, Doise and Mugny (1984) found that children improve their intellectual abilities by interacting with younger playmates. In facing the cognitive difficulties of another child, they reflect upon problem-solving tasks in a productive way. Reviewing the findings gathered by himself and his colleagues, Ladd suggests several strategies useful in preventing both overall school adjustment problems and difficult school transitions. These strategies include helping children learn prosocial behaviors and encouraging parents to constructively direct their children's peer experiences both in and out of school.

The link between family and school settings is also the topic of Chapter 16 by Grazia Attili, though she explores the impact of different aspects of family life on children's social competence. Whereas Ladd focused on parental socialization processes, Attili has studied how parental styles affect children's emotional security and their capacity to interact successfully with peers in preschool settings. She has traced connections between children's relationships with their mothers and fathers and their relations with peers in preschool, as well as the covariance of these factors with children's temperamental characteristics and the mothers' mood.

Joint activities with the mother and father are found to relate to social success in the preschool setting. Conversely, being disconfirmed (i.e., ignored or responded to irrelevantly) and being overcontrolled by parents relate to social failure in preschool. Parental overcontrol is associated mainly with children's social isolation and uneasiness, whereas children who are highly disconfirmed by parents tend to be involved in hostile, negative interactions and are very often targets of aggression. Disconfirmation by mothers is associated with maternal depression and with nonadaptive, difficult behavior on the children's part. Overcontrol by mothers is related to their inward irritability and to high levels of distractibility in their children. These findings are similar in direction to the results of research on the link between the different types of attachment bonds and behavior problems in school. Nevertheless, they underscore the need to go beyond the study of mother-child attachment and explore many other important aspects of family relationships as well the contributions of the child's individual characteristics and the mother's affective state as interactive influences on children's social success with peers.

The impact of mothers' expectations and beliefs on the development of their children's social competence is considered by Kenneth H. Rubin, Rosemary S. L. Mills, and Linda Rose-Krasnor (Chapter 17). These scholars investigated the extent to which these belief systems are likely to guide the socialization behaviors that mothers expect to display toward their children. Among many results, they found that the mothers' beliefs concerning the importance, timing, and causes of social-skills development relate to children's classroom behaviors. Mothers who believe that social skills are important have children who are more likely to have prosocial goals, who use indirect requests to achieve their goals, and who experience social success. Children who mainly achieve their goals by crying have mothers who feel that social skills are not important. Children with social difficulties tend to have mothers who believe that it would be difficult to change their children's poor social performance and who believe that factors internal to the children, such as personality, cause the development of their social skills. With regard to the mothers' suggested interaction strategies, Rubin and colleagues report that moderate-power assertion was the preferred response to children's aggression. In contrast, the preferred response to withdrawal was low-power assertion.

The research reported in these four chapters is not based on the same theoretical framework, nor did the authors use the same methodology--though direct observation was the most frequently employed technique. Legendre's ecological approach called for observation in semistructured situations in experimental settings. Working within an evolutionary perspective, Attili used ethological observation in natural settings to assess the quality of children's relationships, plus questionnaires and rating scales to measure children's and mothers' characteristics. Rubin and colleagues used observation plus interviews to study parents' socialization strategies and ideas about development. Ladd's research tools were sociometrics as well as peer and teacher nominations.

Common to these four chapters, however, is their basic focus on the same problem: the interdependence between family, school, and peer systems in development. When various research teams approach a single question from different standpoints and investigate that question using different techniques, as is the case in Section IV, science can only be strengthened and our understanding enriched.

References

Bronfenbrenner, U. (1979). *The ecology of human development.* Cambridge, MA: Harvard University Press.
Doise, W., & Mugny, G. (1984). *The social development of intellect.* Oxford, United Kingdom: Pergamon.

13

Young Children's Social Competence and Their Use of Space in Day-Care Centers

Alain Legendre

Laboratoire de Psycho-biologie de l'Enfant,
CNRS, Paris, France

Environmental psychology theorists have called for the development of "transactional" models that emphasize the bidirectional relationship between environment and behavior (Barker, 1976; Bronfenbrenner & Crouter, 1983; Stokols, 1978; Wohlwill, 1970). However, the influence of environmental features on children's behavior has often been studied without considering the behavioral characteristics that could enable a child to better adapt to environmental constraints.

The environmental psychology of young children is a relatively recent area of research. In this early phase, studies in the field mainly seek to identify the principal components of the physical environment that can affect children's behavior (Barker, 1968; Gump, 1978). The influence of diverse aspects and features of play materials has already been tested systematically: amount of play equipment (Johnson, 1935; Rohe & Patterson, 1974; Smith & Connolly, 1980); size and type of materials (DeStephano & Mueller, 1982; McLoyd, 1983; Rubin, Fein & Vandenberg, 1983); and position of play equipment -- that is, located centrally versus peripherally (Witt & Gramza, 1970). Many other studies have focused on the effects of play-space density: social density, groups of differing size in the same-size space (Hutt & Vaizey, 1966; Loo, 1972; McGrew, 1970), and spatial density, manipulation of play-space size with same-size group (McGrew, 1972; Smith & Connolly, 1980). However, the influence of spatial arrangements is less well documented (Ledingham & Chappus, 1986; Legendre, 1983, 1985; Moore, 1983a; Neill, 1982a, 1982b).

Nevertheless, most of these studies deal essentially with the general effects of the environmental variable on *populations* of children. Those populations are roughly segregated by age group according to school grade levels (e.g. day-care centers, preschool), and the studies are often not clearly related to developmental issues. Moreover, except for gender, individual characteristics likely to influence the transactional relationships between the child and the physical environment have seldom been examined. A few studies have sought to explain the inter individual differences in adaptation to environmental constraints as a function of the development of specific cognitive (Goldbeck, 1985) or social competences (Vandenberg, 1981). However, such studies of children's adaptation to the environment represent, perhaps, as Wohlwill (1980) pointed out, "the clearest challenge for a true integration between the environmental and the developmental foci" (p. 357).

B. H. Schneider et al. (eds.), Social Competence in Developmental Perspective, 263–276.
© 1989 by Kluwer Academic Publishers.

Children's development permits progressive field independence with respect to the physical, social, and even emotional context. However, before the verbal communication system becomes predominant, peer exchanges are highly context-dependent (see the chapter by Nadel & Fontaine presented elsewhere in this book). Difficulties in referring to absent features restrict children's interactions to the actual features provided by the physical environment. Nevertheless, developmental studies of children's social competences have revealed a notable increase in peer interactions during the 3rd year (Finkelstein, Dent, Gallagher, & Ramey, 1978; Holmberg, 1980). This supports the claim that transitory communication systems already assume an important *adaptive function* in children's integration into settings such as day-care centers.

The important role of reciprocal imitation in peer exchanges between the ages of 21 and 30 months has been demonstrated by Nadel & Baudonnière (1982) (see the chapters by Baudonnière, Garcia-Werebe, Michel, & Liégeois; and Nadel & Fontaine presented elsewhere in this book). Studies have also shown that during the 3rd year, children's complex interactions rely on the shared meaning of preverbal routines (Brenner & Mueller, 1982; Deleau, 1987; Howes & Hunger, 1986). Such routines — different from stereotyped activities — are extremely dependent both on the physical supports and on the few partners with whom the child shares specific games and situations defining their common interactive context.

This suggests that during the 3rd year, establishing privileged relationships with a few partners should be critical for the development of sustained interaction within peer groups. Studies in social ethology support this idea; analyses of the social organization within such groups do confirm the presence of an emerging social network (see the chapter by Strayer presented elsewhere in this book). However, this network does not yet structure the group as a whole; it is more of a weak association of several subgroups of two, three, four or, more exceptionally, five children (Smith & Connolly, 1980; Strayer, 1980; Strayer, Tessier, & Gariepy, 1985).

Thus, before the verbal communication system is mastered, it is worthwhile to examine whether those children who show higher competence in initiating and maintaining interactions with peers adapt to environmental constraints better than their age-mates. I postulated that the children's skill at interacting with peers and, specifically, their competence in establishing stable relationships with privileged partners should, at this age, not only enhance integration into the social context but also support a better exploitation of the physical environment, especially its spatial resources.

In order to test this hypothesis, I examined the relationships between 2- to 3-year-old children's social competence and their adaptation to "closed spatial arrangements" in day-care centers. Previous studies in environmental psychology have demonstrated that such closed spatial arrangements, which present important environmental constraints, restrict young children's use of space (Legendre, 1987; Moore, 1983b; Neill, 1985).

The first objective of this research was to investigate the interdependencies between the children's use of available space and their skill at interacting with peers. In this first part of the study, interest was centered on the individuals and their competence in communicating under specific environmental conditions. The analyzed systems correspond to the microsystems as defined by Bronfenbrenner (1977).

The second objective was to study the influence of peer relationships on children's social use of different areas of the playroom. Primary emphasis was placed on the strength of the social relationship rather than on individual competences. Consequently, the integrated systems under investigation were *dyads* of children and their spatial environment.

264

Thus, this second part of the study dealt more directly with the social ecology of young children's groups.

These two different approaches are part of a wider area of research on the transactional relationships between the environment and the developing person. They are attempts to clarify certain aspects of the complex network of interconnections that links young children's behavior to the social and physical components of the environment.

Method

Participants

Observations were made in two different day-care centers:

- *Group A*: 16 children (7 girls and 9 boys); mean age: 29 months (age range: 24 to 35 months).
- *Group B*: 16 children (7 girls and 9 boys); mean age: 32 months (age range: 26 to 37 months).

Data Collection

Data were collected during morning free-play periods. Two adult caregivers were seated in their usual location in the room. They responded to children's requests but did not initiate activities with them.

Three video cameras filmed the children without their knowledge. This video system enabled us to simultaneously observe each child in the group for a given length of time. For each group, six 15-minute sessions were videotaped over a one-month period.

Coding

The videotapes permitted us to code timed sequences of events, with a coding interval of 3 seconds. Every 3 seconds, we noted:

- Whether the child was engaged in interaction
- The partner(s) with whom the child was interacting
- The precise location of the child on a grid (see figure 13.1)

Interaction was defined as a sequence of mutual exchanges of socially directed behaviors (SDB) (Mueller & Lucas, 1975). The sequence started when the target of an SDB returned an SDB to the initiator; it ended with the last SDB occurring within 6 seconds of the partner's last SDB. This means that an interactive sequence could go on as long as there was no interruption of the SDB interchange lasting longer than 6 seconds.[1]

---

[1]A more detailed coding of the children's behavior was done. At every successive interval, the momentary state of the child/environment microsystem was taken into consideration: self-centered activity (absence of motor and verbal behavior or self-solace behavior), activity directed toward features of the physical environment, social attention (onlooker), socially directed behavior, and social interactions (dyadic interactions were distinguished from polyadic ones). The character (affiliative, agonistic, ambiguous, heterogeneous) of the overtures and interactions was also noted. A detailed French paper on the data collection, coding system, and database can be supplied upon request (Legendre, Fontaine, & Barthes, 1988).

The mean observation time per child in terms of location was 82 minutes, ranging from 48 to 90 minutes (some children were absent from some of the six sessions, came late, or were momentarily outside the playroom). The mean observation time per child in terms of behavior was 67 minutes, ranging from 40 to 84 minutes. (Sometimes, the children's positions with respect to the cameras did not permit analysis of their behavior even though their location within the room could be coded precisely; this explains the discrepancy between location and behavior observation times.)

Results

Interactive Skills and Use of Space

Closed spatial arrangement. Both day-care settings had a closed spatial arrangement in which the layout of the furniture created obstacles that formed major visual and physical boundaries. These boundaries combined with the caretakers' location to form three types of social space:

- *S1 — adult-proximal space:* 2 meters around where the caregivers usually stood. In this area, a child was in the immediate proximity of an adult.
- *S2 — eye-contact space:* More distant part of the room where a child could rapidly establish eye contact with an adult without moving.
- *S3 — beyond-eye-contact space:* An area where a major visual boundary separated the child from adults, so that the child had to move in order to initiate eye contact (see Figure 13. 1).

Results of a previous study (Legendre, 1987) demonstrated that in closed spatial arrangements, as compared with arrangements that lack major visual boundaries, children spent more time in the adult-proximal space than in other parts of the playroom.

In the two day-care centers, the children's spatial distribution was consistent with previous results. The children's positions are represented by black dots on the floor plans of the playrooms shown in Figure 13.1. Each dot in a square on the grid corresponds to 1 percent of the total number of positions recorded for all children in a group; that percentage was computed in such a manner that every child in the group loaded the same in the final results.

For both day-care centers, the adult-proximal space was the most densely occupied area of the room (see Figure 13.2). The density there was considerably higher than in either eye-contact space or beyond-eye-contact space. (Density of occupation was calculated as the percentage of child positions recorded within an area divided by the surface of that area, measured in square meters.)

These results confirm that in closed spatial arrangements, visual boundaries restrict children's use of space. Such closed spatial arrangements constitute an appropriate context in which to test whether peer-interactive competence, or the ability to develop stable relations, permits a child to better use the space provided.

Spatial autonomy and interactions with peers. *Spatial autonomy* is an index of the percentage of time spent outside the adult-proximal space, which is weighted to take into account the distance from caregivers. It is computed by summing the percentage of time spent within eye-contact space and twice the percentage of time spent outside eye-contact space.

266

Figure 13.1

Maps of the two day-care centers: Children's spatial occupancy

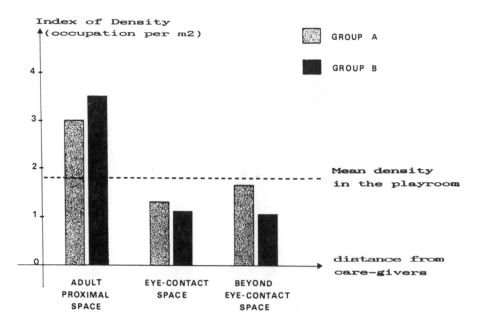

Figure 13.2

Density of occupation inside the three social spaces

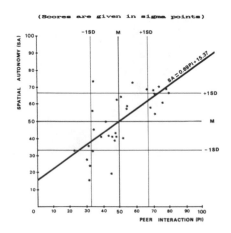

Figure 13.3

Regression line of spatial autonomy on the time spent in peer interactions.

For the 32 children of the two day-care centers, the correlation computed between spatial autonomy scores and percentage of time spent interacting with peers was high and positive (Bravais Pearson $r = +0.69$, $p > 0.01$). The same correlation computed independently for each day-care center was similar (Group A: $r = +0.78$; Group B: $r = +0.63$). The regression line (see Figure 13.3) illustrates that a high score in interaction with peers is predictive of a higher degree of spatial autonomy in closed arrangements.

Use of the social areas and peer-interactive competences. To get a more detailed view of the children's occupation of different social spaces as a function of their interactive skills, three subsets of children were distinguished on the basis of the percentage of time that they spent interacting with peers:

- low-scoring children (scores below the group mean minus one standard deviation);
- medium-scoring children (scores around the mean plus or minus one standard deviation);
- high-scoring children (scores above the mean plus one standard deviation).

Figure 13.4 clearly shows the strong relationship between use of the three different social spaces and competence at initiating and maintaining interactions with peers. High-scoring children were observed in the beyond-eye-contact space more often than either low- or medium-scoring children. In contrast, low-scoring children spent a larger proportion of their time in the adult-proximal area than either high- or medium-scoring children. For both groups, the distribution of time spent in the three social spaces by the high-scoring children was significantly different than the distribution for children whose scores were low (Kolmogorov-Smirnov two-sample test — Group A: $K = 15.8$, $p < 0.001$; Group B: $K = 14.74$, $p < 0.001$).

It is important to note that for the 32 children, the correlation computed between spatial autonomy and the percentage of time spent in interaction with adults was low and negative (Bravais Pearson $r = -0.16$). The same correlation computed independently for each day-care center was low for both, but negative for only one of them (Group A: $r = -0.39$; Group B: $r = +0.06$).

These results indicate that for 2- to 3-year-old children, interacting with adults is independent of the children's use of spatial resources. In contrast, greater competence at interacting with peers allows children to use all the areas of a playroom more freely. Children who spend an important proportion of their time in interactions with peers evidence greater spatial autonomy from adults than their age-mates. This suggests that the prominent role played by caregivers as mediators of child interactions within social and physical environments during the first 2 years becomes less important as children's interactive competence with peers develops.

Peer Relations and Social Use of Space

One of the more important contributions of the ecological approach to psychology is that it encourages us to examine the position of the system under study with respect to inclusive, enclosed, and connected environmental systems. The inclusive relationships between systems refer to Bronfenbrenner's model (1977), in which "the ecological environment is conceived topologically as a nested arrangement of structures, each contained within the next" (p. 514). However, inclusive relationships are not the only possible ones: Two

269

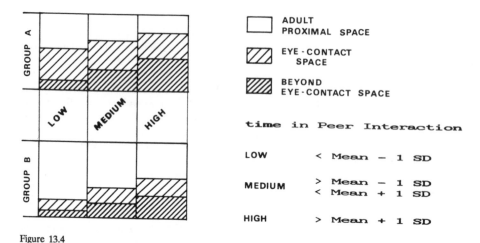

Figure 13.4

Use of the three social spaces as a function of the competence at interacting with peers.

systems can be connected by an interdependence relationship. With respect to a day-care-center group, investigating the interdependence between the microsystems defined by the different children within this setting may help us clarify the complex network of relationships that link their behavior to the immediate environment. Therefore, such an ecological perspective could prompt us to reconsider the examined system and its basic units of analysis.

The results presented in the first section of this chapter were based on an analysis of the microsystem defined by the child in a specific physical and social setting. The main focus of interest was the individual, and the results were concerned with the relations between the child's interactive skills and his or her *personal* use of space.

But if the focus of interest switches from the child's individual competence to peer relations, it seems more appropriate to change the basic unit of analysis from individuals to dyads. This change allows us to analyze the interdependence between the strength of the dyadic bond linking two children and that particular dyad's *social* use of space.

Types of Peer Dyads. By examining the proportion of time that children spent interacting together within every dyad of each group ($n = 232$), it was possible to distinguish four types of dyads (see Figure 13.5):

270

- *NP — nonpartners*: dyads made up of children who had no interaction together during the observation time. They represent 25 percent of all possible dyads.[2]
- *OP — occasional partners*: dyads made up of children who interacted together less than 3% of the observation time. They represent 50 percent of all possible dyads.
- *UP — usual partners*: dyads made up of children who interacted together more than 3% and less than 10% of the observation time. They represent 15 percent of all possible dyads.
- *PP — privileged partners*: dyads made up of children who interacted together more than 10% of the observation time. They represent 10 percent of all possible dyads.

Such a distribution shows that only a few dyads shared more than 10% of their time in interaction together, and that such privileged partners interacted up to an impressive score of 40% of the observation time. It is interesting to note that interactions between these privileged partners represent 45% of the total time that children spent interacting with peers. Furthermore, the number of privileged partners per child was restricted to 1 (mean = 1, mode = 1; only 1 child shared interaction time with 3 privileged partners); notice that the mean number of privileged partners plus usual partners was restricted to 3. These results indicate that in such 2- to 3-year-old peer groups, nearly half of a child's peer interactions occur with only 1 of the 15 possible partners. This is consistent with the claim that during the 3rd year, sustained exchanges are based on preverbal routines that can be elaborated with only a few peers through repeated interactions.

Dyadic proximity as a function of peer relations and types of social spaces. Dyadic proximity corresponds to the percentage of the observation time during which two children of a particular dyad were located within 2 meters of each other.

The respective influence of the three types of social space (*T3*) and the four types of dyads (*G4*) was examined by analysis of variance (*S <G4>* x *T3* program VAR3; see Rouanet & Lépine, 1977).

Social space was the main factor affecting dyadic proximity. Time spent in dyadic proximity decreased dramatically with distance from an adult. This effect was particularly obvious in Group B ($F = 140$, df 2, 216, $p < 0.001$) and also significant in Group A ($F = 51.6$, df 2, 232, $p < 0.001$).

The second factor was the type of dyad; dyadic proximity increased with the amount of time that children spent interacting together (Group A: $F = 25.6$, df 3, 116, $p < 0.001$; Group B: $F = 10.4$, df 3, 108, $p < 0.001$).

A more interesting finding involves the interaction between these two factors. Figure 13.6 shows how the main factor, social space, is mediated by the type of dyadic relationship. For non- or occasional partners in both groups, the percentage of time spent in proximity to one another decreased dramatically once the children were outside the adult-proximal space. In Day-Care Center B, the effect of social space had less influence on privileged and usual partners. However, the interaction between the two factors was not important enough to be significant. In contrast, this interaction was very important in Day-Care Center A ($F = 8.9$, df 6, 232, $p < 0.001$). Figure 13.6 shows that social space had no effect on usual partners and that there was an inverse relation with respect to privileged

---

[2] These percentages are computed on the basis of the observation time during which the two children of a given dyad were actually both present in the room. We eliminated the dyads whose observation time was less than 25 minutes.

partners, who spent more time in proximity when they were outside the adult-proximal space, either in eye-contact space or in beyond-eye-contact space!

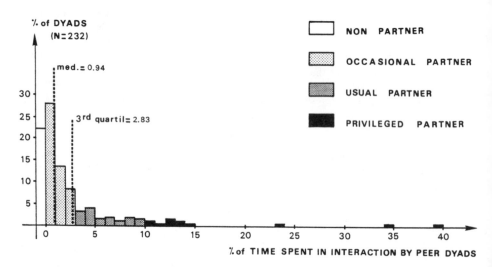

Figure 13.5

The four types of partners: distribution of time spent in interaction by peer dyads.

Derived from ethological analyses of social bonding in animals, proximity has often been used as an index for relationships among young children (Attili, 1986; Burgess & McMurphy, 1982; Strayer, 1980). The preceding results indicate that in adult-proximal space, dyadic proximity is independent of peer acquaintance. It is obvious that in this area, children mainly seek the adult's attention and that conversely, the closest adult is a prime potential competitor for young children's attention (Hartup, 1983). Therefore, in order to use proximity as an efficient and reliable index of peer relationships in field settings, the index must be more precisely defined. I propose *dyadic proximity outside the adult-proximal space*, defined as the percentage of the observation time during which two children of a particular dyad satisfy the following three conditions:

1. They are located within 2 meters of each other
2. They are outside the adult-proximal space
3. They are not separated from each other by a physical or visual boundary.

In Day-Care Center A, the correlation between time spent in dyadic proximity outside the adult-proximal space and time spent interacting together was very high and positive

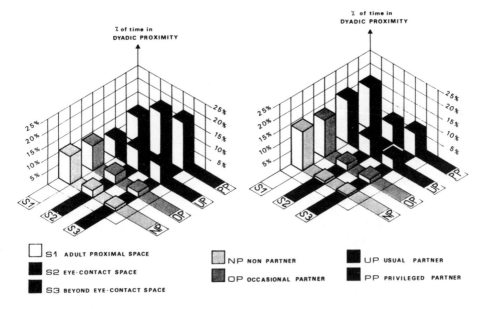

Figure 13.6

Dyadic proximity as a function of peer relations and types of social spaces.

(Bravais Pearson $r = +0.89$). In Day-Care Center B, this correlation was more moderate but still high and positive (Bravais Pearson $r = +0.68$).

Considering the "type of dyad" factor, objections might be raised that the effects of this factor on the social use of space may be attributed not only to the strength of the children's social bond but also to the individual characteristics of the children constituting the different types of dyads, such as age, sex, interactive competence, and personal use of space. To accurately analyze the effects of the kind of social relationship established between the children, one must control for the individual characteristics of the children constituting the different types of dyads.

For this purpose, we matched the children in privileged partner dyads with different partners in such a manner that the resulting pairs were dyads of non- or occasional partners (see Table 13.1). Therefore, as the children are the same in the two sets of dyads, individual factors cannot be incriminated when comparing these paired dyads. Furthermore, the gender variable was strictly preserved (the same number of girls, boys or mixed dyads).

In both day-care centers, the distribution of dyadic proximity in different social spaces was significantly different for the two types of dyads (Kolmogorov-Smirnov two-sample test − Group A: $K = 6.79, p < 0.01$; Group B: $K = 6, p < 0.01$). The percentage of time that privileged partner dyads spent in dyadic proximity in the beyond-eye-contact area was significantly greater than the percentages for non- or occasional partners (Mann & Whitney − Group A, two samples: $N = 6, U = 0, p < 0.01$; Group B two samples: $N = 10, U = 12, p < 0.01$).

Such results confirm the importance of considering peer relationships to understand children's social use of different areas of playrooms.

273

Table 13.1

Paired Dyads of Privileged and Non- or Occasional Partners in Group A

Privileged Partners		Non- or Occasional Partners	
B6 - G9	39.7%	B6 - B16	0.0%
G2 - G3	34.3%	G2 - G14	0.2%
B15 - B16	14.9%	B15 - G3	0.0%
B11 - G14	14.7%	B11 - G9	0.0%
B5 - G9	12.6%	G9 - G14	1.1%
B7 - G14	10.9%	B7 - G5	1.0%

G = girl; B = boy. % = percentage of time that the children of a dyad spent interacting together.

Conclusion

Within stable groups of 2- to 3-year-olds, children's use of space is closely related to their competence at initiating and maintaining interaction with peers.   In closed spatial arrangements, children whose interactive competences with peers are low exhibit restricted use of space: These children are more dependent on the location of the caregivers within the room. In contrast, children who spend a larger portion of their time interacting with age-mates show better adaptation to spatial constraints.

Results demonstrate that strong relationships between peers facilitate the social use of areas separated from adults by major visual boundaries. Privileged partners can stay side by side in beyond-eye-contact spaces, whereas non- or occasional partners do not remain together outside the adult-proximal space.   Such results suggest that before the verbal communication system is mastered, difficulties in communicating between peers render children's close proximity in areas far from adults uncomfortable, if not insecure.   In order to stay with a peer in areas away from adults, 2- to 3-year-old children must share a common context of exchange built on repeated interactions.   Sharing the meaning of specific games and activities certainly facilitates children's anticipation of their partner's behavior, which makes proximity at a distance from adults a situation that is no longer uncomfortable. Furthermore, results show that this can be an attractive situation for privileged partners. The reassuring function fulfilled almost exclusively by adults up to the second birthday seems to be partially replaced by the establishment of stable and privileged social relationships within the peer group. This finding leads to the conclusion that the relative autonomy from spatial constraints shown by the most socially competent children is still highly dependent on social context, and particularly on peer relationships, during the 3rd year.

Acknowledgments: I would like to thank Anne-Marie Fontaine for her help in data collection and coding, and Benedicte Mouëza for her help in the production of figures.

References

Attili, G. (1986). The development of preferred relationships in preschool children: Child-child and child-adult relationships. In R. Gilmour & S. Duck (Eds.), The emerging field of personal relationships (pp. 173-187). Hillsdale, NJ: Erlbaum.
Barker, R. G. (1968). *Ecological psychology.* Palo Alto, CA: Stanford University Press.

Barker, R. G. (1976). On the nature of environment. In H. Proshansky, W. Ittelson, & L. Rivlin (Eds.), *Environmental psychology: People and their physical setting* (2nd ed., pp. 12-26). New York: Holt, Rinehart and Winston.

Brenner, J. and Mueller, E. (1982). Shared meaning in boy toddlers' peer relations. *Child Development, 53,* 380-391.

Bronfenbrenner, U. (1977). Toward an experimental ecology of human development. *American Psychologist, 32(7),* 113-129.

Bronfenbrenner, U. and Crouter, A. C. (1983). The evolution of environmental models in developmental research. In P. H. Munsen (Ed.), *Handbook of child psychology: Vol. 1* History, Theory and Methods. W. Kessen, Vol. Ed.; 4th ed., pp. 357-414). New York: Wiley.

Burgess, J. W. & McMurphy, D. (1982). The development of proxemic spacing behavior: Children's distance to surrounding playmates and adults changes between 6 months and 5 years of age. *Developmental Psychobiology, 15(6),* 557-567.

Deleau, M. (1987). *Communication et développement des conduites sémiotiques chez le jeune enfant* [Communication and semiotic behavior development in the young child]. Unpublished doctoral dissertation, Université de Paris VIII, Saint-Denis.

DeStephano, C. T. & Mueller, E. (1982). Environmental determinants of peer social activity in 18-month-old males. *Infant Behavior and Development, 5,* 175-183.

Finkelstein, N. W., Dent, C., Gallagher, K. & Ramey, C. T. (1978). Social behavior of infants and toddlers in a day-care environment. *Developmental Psychology, 14(3),* 257-262.

Goldbeck, S. L. (1985). Spatial cognition as a function of environmental characteristics. In R. Cohen (Ed.), *The development of spatial cognition* (pp. 225-254). Hillsdale, NJ: Erlbaum.

Gump, P. V. (1978). School environment. In I. Altman & J. Wohlwill (Eds.), *Human behavior and environment: Advances in theory and research: Vol. 3. Children and the environment* (pp. 132-176). New York: Plenum.

Hartup, W. W. (1983). Peer relations. In P. H. Munsen (Ed.), *Handbook of Child Psychology: Vol. 4. Socialization, Personality and Social Development* (E. M. Hetherington, Vol. Ed.); (pp. 693-774). New York: Wiley.

Holmberg, M. C. (1980). The development of social interchange patterns from 12 to 42 months. *Child Development, 51,* 448-456.

Howes, C. & Hunger, O. (1986). Play with peers in a child care setting. In M. Bloch & A. Pellegrini (Eds.), *The ecological context of children's play.* Norwood, NJ: Ablex.

Hutt, C. T. & Vaizey, M. J. (1966). Differential effects of group density on social behaviour. *Nature, 209,* 1371-1372.

Johnson, M. V. (1935). The effect on behavior of variation in the amount of play equipment. *Child Development, 6,* 56-58.

Ledingham, J. E. & Chappus, F. T. (1986). Behavioral mappings of children's social interactions: The impact of play environment. *Canadian Journal of Research in Early Childhood Education, 1,* 137-148.

Legendre, A. (1983). Appropriation par les enfants de l'environnement architectural [Children's appropriation of their structural environment]. *Enfance, 4,* 389-395.

Legendre, A. (1985). L'expérimentation écologique dans l'approche des comportements sociaux des jeunes enfants en groupe [Environmental experimentation in relation to social group behavior of young children]. In P.-M. Baudonnière (Ed.), *Etudier l'enfant de la naissance à trois ans* (pp. 165-181). Paris: Collection Comportement CNRS.

Legendre, A. (1987). Transformation de l'espace d'activités et échanges sociaux de jeunes enfants en crèche [Transformation of play areas and social exchanges among young nursery school children]. *Psychologie française, 32* (1-2), 31-43.

Legendre, A., Fontaine, A.-M., and Barthes, D. (1988). *L'écologie expérimentale: collecte, codage et gestion des données* [Experimental ecology: data collection, processing and management]. Unpublished manuscript, Laboratoire de Psycho-biologie de l'Enfant, CNRS, 41 rue Gay-Lussac, 75005 Paris.

Loo, C. M. (1972). The effects of spatial density on the social behavior of children. *Journal of Applied Social Psychology, 2,* 372-381.

McGrew, P. L. (1970). Social and spatial density effects on spacing behaviour in preschool children. *Journal of Child Psychology and Psychiatry, 11,* 197-205.

McGrew, W. C. (1972). *An ethological study of children's behaviour.* New York: Academic Press.

McLoyd, V. C. (1983). The effects of the structure of play objects on the pretend play of low-income preschool children. *Child Development, 54,* 807-814.

Moore, G. T. (1983a, August). *Effects of the definition of behavior setting on children's behavior.* Paper presented to the American Psychologists Association, Population and Environmental Psychology. Anaheim, CA.

Moore, G. T. (1983b, April). *Some effects of the organization of socio-physical environment on the cognitive behavior in a child care setting.* Paper presented to the Society for Research in Child Development, Detroit.

Mueller, E. & Lucas, T. (1975). A developmental analysis of peer interaction among playgroup toddlers. In M. Lewis & L. A. Rosenblum (Eds.), *Friendships and peer relations*. New York: Wiley.

Nadel, J. & Baudonnière, P.-M. (1982). The social function of reciprocal imitation in 2-year-old peers. *International Journal of Behavioral Development, 5(1)*, 95-109.

Neill, R. S. St. J. (1982a). Experimental alterations in playroom layout and their effect on staff and child behaviour. *Educational Psychology, 2*, 103-119.

Neill, R. S. St. J. (1982b). Preschool design and child behaviour. *Journal of Child Psychology and Psychiatry, 23(3)*, 309-318.

Neill, R. S. St. J. (1985). *The behavioral effects of weekly alterations in room environment of a preschool playgroup*. Department of Education, University of Warwick, United Kingdom.

Rohe, W. & Patterson, A. H. (1974). The effects of varied levels of resources and density on behavior in day care centers. In D. Carson (Ed.), *Man-environment interactions*. Milwaukee: EDRA.

Rouanet, H. & Lépine, D. (1977). Comparisons between treatments in repeated measurement design: ANOVA and multivariate methods. *British Journal* of Mathematical and Statistical Psychology, *23*, 147-163.

Rubin, H. R., Fein, G. G., and Vandenberg, B. (1983). Play. In P. H. Munsen (Ed.), *Handbook of child psychology: Vol. 4* Socialization, Personality and Social Development. (E.M. Hetherington, Vol. Ed.; pp. 693-774). New York: Wiley.

Smith, P. K., & Connolly, K.J. (1980). *The ecology of preschool behaviour*. Cambridge: Cambridge University Press.

Stokols, D. (1978). Environmental psychology. *Annual Review of Psychology, 29*, 253-295.

Strayer, F. F. (1980). Child ethology and the study of preschool social relations. In H. Foot, A. Chapman & J. Smith (Eds.). *Friendship and social relations in children* (pp. 235-266). New York: Wiley.

Strayer, F. F., Tessier, O., & Gariepy, L. (1985). L'activité affiliative et le réseau cohésif chez les jeunes enfants [Affiliation and cohesif networks among young children]. In R. E. Tremblay, Provost, M. A. & Strayer, F. F. (Eds.), *Ethologie et développement de l'enfant* (pp. 291-308). Paris: Stock.

Vandenberg, B. (1981). Environmental and cognitive factors in social play. *Journal of Experimental Child Psychology, 31*, 169-175.

Witt, P. A. & Gramza, A. E. (1970). Position effects in play equipment preferences of nursery school children. *Perceptual and Motor Skills, 31*, 431-434.

Wohlwill, J. F. (1970). The emerging discipline of environmental psychology. *American Psychologist, 25*, 303-312.

Wohlwill, J. F. (1980). The confluence of environmental and developmental psychology: Signpost to an ecology of development? *Human Development, 23*, 354-358.

276

14

Children's Social Competence and Social Supports: Precursors of Early School Adjustment?

Gary W. Ladd

Purdue University

Schools are among the most pervasive socialization contexts in our culture, and among the most influential for shaping the course of human development over the life span. Yet, as much as 20% to 30% of the school-age population (Achenbach & Edelbrock, 1981; Glidewell & Swallow, 1969; Rubin & Balow, 1978) experience substantial adjustment problems in the classroom and, thus, are at risk for a variety of interpersonal, emotional, and career difficulties in later life (see Cowen, Pederson, Babigian, Izzo, & Trost, 1973; Kohlberg, LaCrosse, & Ricks, 1972; Ladd & Asher, 1985; Parker & Asher, 1987). Many school adjustment problems appear to have lasting or cumulative effects; problems that arise early in children's school careers are often perpetuated by social-psychological factors (e.g., reputational bias, self-fulfilling prophecies), or are exacerbated when nascent difficulties undermine later progress (see Butler, Marsh, Sheppard, & Sheppard, 1985; Coie & Dodge, 1983; Horn & Packard, 1985; Perry, Guidubaldi, & Kehle, 1971). Given the pervasiveness of this problem, and the potential costs to both the individual and society, research on early school adjustment is needed. In particular, there is a need to identify the factors that forecast children's school adjustment as they enter grade school (approximately age 5 or 6) and progress through the primary grades (ages 6-12). Findings from this research will expand the empirical, "generative base" (cf. Cowen, 1980) that is needed to devise and extend prevention programs for young children.

Unfortunately, research on school adjustment has proceeded in the absence of clearly articulated theories. Due to this void, there are few guiding frameworks to assist researchers in defining the concept of school adjustment, debating its meanings, and arriving at operational definitions of its attributes and features. Moreover, in the absence of explicit models, there are no carefully articulated meaning contexts that will allow researchers to systematically deduce and explore potential "causes" (typically antecedents or precursors) of school adjustment, or generate "useful" interpretations for the fact patterns they obtain in empirical investigations.

As a consequence, the term *school adjustment* is used loosely in the literature, and may refer to a variety of aspects of children's social and academic functioning. Frequently, rather narrow domains of school functioning (achievement, peer relations, problematic classroom behavior) are targeted for investigation, and relations among measures that represent different domains receive little attention. In other words, because researchers lack an overarching framework, they have tended to investigate aspects of children's school

B. H. Schneider et al. (eds.), Social Competence in Developmental Perspective, 277–291.
© *1989 by Kluwer Academic Publishers.*

experience (e.g., their achievement or classroom peer relations) as separate phenomena, and have neglected the relations between them.

A related concern is that the concept of school adjustment, as it is currently used in the literature, is seldom defined in a way that ties it clearly to the school context. Consequently, confusions may arise over its meanings. In particular, it may be difficult for researchers to discriminate "school" adjustment from other forms of adjustment measured during childhood. Part of this problem may be resolved by defining school adjustment in terms of the child's success at coping with the task/demands of the school environment. Moreover, researchers could begin to incorporate the changing demands of school environments (e.g., those posed by entrance into vs. continuation in, grade school) into the concept of school adjustment. As the capacities of the child and the demands of schooling change, so may the criteria that define adjustment and the adaptive value of particular child attributes and environmental resources.

Finally, the absence of explicit models of school adjustment may have restricted researchers' efforts to identify the antecedents and precursors of school adaptation, and study them in a systematic fashion. Although many potential antecedents of school adjustment have been investigated (e.g., child competencies, classroom atmospheres, family stress), they have often been studied independently rather than jointly, and in the context of cross-sectional rather than longitudinal research designs. Undoubtedly, the process by which children adapt to school is complex, and influenced by many factors. Insight into how these factors combine, converge, and interact to produce higher or lower levels of school adaptation will likely not be achieved by studying these elements individually. Moreover, the process by which these potential precursors impact upon children is undoubtedly not a static one, thereby restricting what researchers can learn from correlations obtained in cross-sectional studies. Rather, the events that shape school adjustment, and the processes of coping and adaptation, are dynamic in nature, and also call for carefully planned longitudinal investigations.

In sum, there is a need to construct more comprehensive models of school adjustment. In particular, models are needed that define adjustment in terms of the outcomes children experience as they cope with the demands of schooling. It may also be important to develop models that define adjustment in relation to important shifts and changes in the school environment and in the child--that is, models that have a developmental orientation. In terms of the antecedents and precursors of school adjustment, models are needed that focus on linkages between precursors/processes (i.e., the means by which children are prepared for school, and adapt to differing school environments) and adjustment outcomes (i.e., the criteria by which children are judged to be adjusted or maladjusted). Beyond this, it will be important to develop research strategies and designs that are suited to understanding the *process* of school adjustment.

The purpose of this chapter is to propose a new model of early school adjustment, and to review relevant empirical findings gathered by my colleagues and me. The assumptions and concepts that comprise this model have been drawn from many sources; its present form owes a heavy debt to recent person-by-environment theories of adaptation (cf. Garmezy, Masten, & Tellegen, 1984; Heller & Swindle, 1983; Ladd & Price, 1987). Within this perspective, school adjustment is viewed as an outcome of children's attempts to adapt to the demands of the school environment. The types of adjustment outcomes children experience are hypothesized to be a function of both their personal-social characteristics, including organismic factors (e.g., sex, intelligence) and behavioral competence (e.g., skills vs. deficits at coping with demands), and features of their interpersonal environments (e.g., formative experiences, relationships that prepare and support vs. preclude and discourage adaptive responses). A schematic representation of the model can be found in Figure 14.1.

Briefly, this model is based on the assumption that the origins of early school adjustment lie both in the child (i.e., the degree to which the child possesses particular abilities, skills, or adaptive attributes), and in her interpersonal environment (i.e., the degree to which the child participates in relationships and experiences that prepare her for, and support her in, dealing with the demands of school). As such, this model provides a framework for testing alternative hypotheses concerning the unique and/or joint contributions of child attributes and environmental supports/stressors to early school adjustment. Its usefulness will be most apparent to those researchers who wish to determine whether specific child characteristics (e.g., gender, intelligence, social skills) combine with differing environmental supports/stressors (e.g., the child's prior experience in school-related settings, high versus low levels of parental school involvement, perceived teacher support) to forecast various indices of school adjustment.

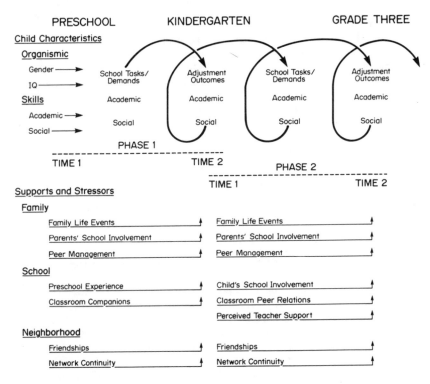

Figure 14.1

A model of early school adjustment depicting the interface between child characteristics, task/demands of the school environment, and interpersonal supports and stressors in the family, school, and neighborhood.

Various hypotheses about the unique and/or joint contributions of individual child characteristics and differing interpersonal supports and stressors can be generated from the model and empirically tested. For example, hypotheses similar to the additive

279

(compensatory) and interactive (protective) relations proposed by Garmezy et al. (1984) can be organized within the model and empirically compared. The following illustration may be instructive. An additive model implies that, in addition to any predictability offered by a particular child characteristic, environmental supports or stressors may contribute uniquely to school adjustment. In other words, an attribute that places children at risk for early school maladjustment (e.g., an aggressive behavioral style) may be: (a) partially offset (compensated for) by supportive features of the school environment or (b) exacerbated by environmental stressors. Similarly, attributes that increase the likelihood of school adjustment may be mitigated or enhanced by stressful or supportive features of the environment, respectively. For example, although children who display nonsocial behavioral styles in preschool might be anticipated to be at greater risk for school avoidance in kindergarten (approximately age 5, when children enter grade school), the magnitude of this risk might vary with the child's access to interpersonal supports or his exposure to stressors. The difficulties that withdrawn children face in coping with the social demands of school may be offset by a supportive relationship with the teacher or, conversely, exacerbated by stressful events occuring within the family.

In contrast, researchers with an interactive perspective might argue that the adaptive functions of child characteristics (e.g., intelligence) and interpersonal supports/stressors do not combine in an additive way (i.e., one adding to or subtracting from the other's contributions). Rather, the adaptive function of one variable may differ depending on the child's position or level on other variables. For example, it might be the case that stressful home or school environments take a greater toll on the achievement of high- as opposed to low-ability children (see Garmezy et al., 1984).

As can be seen in this illustration, the proposed model will allow investigators to consider multiple antecedents and concomitants of early school adjustment. Research based on this model may offer a more complete understanding of the contributions of child characteristics and interpersonal supports/stressors to the process of school adaptation. The usefulness of this model, however, also rests upon the specific constructs that are identified for investigation, and their hypothesized relationship to the task/demands of schooling. Thus, a further elaboration of the concept of school adjustment and its relationship to the constructs proposed in this model is warranted.

School Adjustment: Outcomes of Children's Adaptation to Changing Demands

In the present model, the concept of school adjustment is based on several fundamental premises about the task/demands of early grade-school environments (see Ladd & Price, 1987). It is hypothesized that school environments, due to their nature and design, confront all children with relatively uniform cognitive and interpersonal demands. The nature of these demands changes, however, as children progress from grade to grade and, thus, poses different types of adjustment opportunities and risks. For example, the demands children face as they enter school may differ from those encountered as they move from grade to grade in the same school. Within a particular time span (e.g., grade level), the outcomes of children's attempts to adapt to relevant demands can be viewed as indicators of their school adjustment.

Thus, the definition of *school adjustment* is partly dependent on the researcher's ability to specify the potential task/demands (and associated adjustment outcomes) inherent within the school environment at particular times during grade school. But what types of demands do children face as they enter school and progress through the primary grades, and what types of adjustment outcomes might evolve from their efforts to cope with these demands?

Previous theory and research suggest a number of important school demands and adjustment outcomes that may be relevant as children enter grade school and progress through the primary grades.

Entrance Into Grade School

As children enter kindergarten, they must gain acceptance into a new peer group (Holland, Kaplan & Davis, 1974), become comfortable with the new school environment (Ladd & Price, 1987), meet new school and teacher expectations (Bensen, Haycraft, Steyaert & Weigel, 1979), and develop the preacademic skills needed to succeed at scholastic tasks (Bogat, Jones & Jason, 1980; Holland et al., 1974). For each of these demands or "tasks", various outcomes may occur, depending on the types of adaptive factors and processes (considered below) that are present or operative in the child's environment. For example, children may become accepted or rejected by peers, embrace or withdraw from the school environment, develop a supportive or stressful relationship with the teacher, and succeed or fail to master various preacademic skills.

The Primary Years

Grade school is often the first time children are exposed to explicit performance standards, and receive direct feedback about the quality of their work. Children's capacity to cope with these demands may steer them toward a number of academic adjustment outcomes. Recent research (Berndt and Miller, in press; Eccles, 1983) suggests that in addition to actual achievement, academic school adjustment can be conceptualized in terms of three independent dimensions: achievement motivation (the students' degree of involvement and value that they attach to school learning), perceived competence (students' perceptions of scholastic competence), and classroom conduct (compliance/disruptiveness).

Within the interpersonal domain, children face tasks such as maintaining existing peer and teacher relationships, and forming new ones as they change grades. Children's social reputations and peers' expectations may follow them from grade to grade, perpetuating in-group/out-group distinctions, conformity pressures, and the type of social information that children receive about themselves (see Hymel, Wagner, & Butler, in press). Resolution of these demands may be associated with adjustment outcomes such as children's interpersonal motivations (peer involvement/avoidance), perceptions of interpersonal competence (perceived social competence and self-efficacy), and emotional well-being and self-worth. For example, children who are consistently rejected by peers tend to withdraw from peer activities (Coie & Kupersmidt, 1983; Dodge, 1983), develop lower levels of perceived social competence (Bukowski & Hoza, in press), and feel lonely and depressed (Asher & Wheeler, 1985; Vosk, Forehand, Parker, & Rickard, 1982). Children who fail to maintain or lack friendships tend to develop lower levels of self-esteem (Bukowski & Hoza, in press).

Adapting to School Demands: Factors That Mediate Adjustment Outcomes

Although there may be considerable uniformity in the demands posed by early grade school environments, children's characteristics (attributes that children "bring" to school), and features of their interpersonal environments (supportive vs. stressful milieus) may influence their ability to adapt to the challenges of school and, thus, contribute to school adjustment outcomes. Although many child characteristics and environmental features may have a

281

bearing on school adjustment, it may be useful to identify several key factors that appear to warrant further research attention. These factors are also depicted in Figure 14.1.

Child Characteristics

Certain child attributes (e.g., gender, IQ) and competencies (e.g., social and academic skills) appear to be important predictors of school progress. Girls, for example, are more likely to develop lower or inaccurate (underestimated) perceptions of their competence (Block, 1983; Dweck, 1986; Dweck & Elliott, 1983; Ladd & Price, 1986), and boys are at greater risk for conduct problems in the classroom (Garmezy et al., 1984; Ladd & Price, 1987). Children's IQ and basic academic skills predict achievement in the early primary grades (Stevenson, Parker, Wilkinson, Hegion & Fish, 1976), and their interpersonal styles (e.g., prosocial vs. aggressive) forecast later peer rejection, classroom disruption, and school avoidance (Ladd & Price, 1987; Parker & Asher, 1987). Less is known, however, about the contributions of specific child characteristics to different forms of school adjustment (e.g., academic versus social), and the importance of these attributes relative to environmental supports and stressors.

Environmental Supports and Stressors

Past research suggests that children's experiences and relationships in the family, the school, and the neighborhood may contribute to school adjustment outcomes. Most children live in families, and their experiences in this context may play an important role in early school adjustment. Exposure to stressful life events in the family may place children at risk for school maladjustment (see Cowen, Lotyczewski & Weissberg, 1984; Garmezy et al., 1984; Sandler & Ramsay, 1980), and the form of family stress may affect the type of adjustment problems children display in the classroom. Felner, Stolberg and Cowen (1975), for example, found that children who had recently suffered the death of a parent tended to be withdrawn at school, whereas those who had lost a parent through divorce were more likely to be disruptive and disorderly in the classroom. Prior theory and research (Bronfenbrenner, 1979) also suggest that cooperative linkages between the home and school environment (e.g., exchanging information about the child, fostering schoolwork at home) can facilitate children's progress in school. Beyond this, various socialization practices in the family, such as parents' management of children's peer relations, may have a bearing on children's school adjustment. Parents who arrange opportunities for their children to meet and play with agemates during the preschool years (approximately ages 2-5) may help their children to develop the interpersonal skills needed to establish relationships with unfamiliar peers as they enter grade school and move from grade to grade (see Ladd & Golter, 1988).

Experience with schooling and features of the school environment may also affect the degree to which children adapt to educational demands. Prior school experience may facilitate school adjustment, especially as children enter grade school. For example, as Ladd and Price (1987) have argued, children with considerable preschool experience may well have mastered tasks such as separating from parents, accepting the teacher's authority, meeting new peers, and negotiating large group settings. The result may be that these children face fewer adjustment demands as they enter school or, perhaps, the demands they do face are perceived as less discrepant with past experience and, therefore, less stressful to accomodate.

Once children are in grade school, features of the school environment may have an important bearing on adjustment processes and outcomes. Within this context, it is hypothesized that children's interpersonal relationships with peers and teachers play an important role in their school adjustment by serving as sources of support or stress. The importance of supportive peer relationships is underscored by evidence indicating that the quality of children's classroom peer relations forecasts school avoidance, disruption, and failure (Coie & Krehbiel, 1984; Kupersmidt, 1983; Parker & Asher, 1987). Moreover, children's self-esteem and achievement appear to suffer in the absence of supportive school friendships (Bukowski & Hoza, in press; Krappman, 1985). Perceived teacher support is associated with enhanced motivation to achieve (Nicholls & Thorkildsen, 1988).

School adjustment may also be influenced by children's friendships in the neighborhood or nonschool settings (see Cowen et al., 1984; Ladd & Price, 1987). It is hypothesized that the features of the friendships children form outside the school context may vary in ways that facilitate or impede school adjustment. One potentially important feature is the type of companionship children pursue in the neighborhood. For example, children who choose to relate with younger companions in the neighborhood may find grade school classrooms, which tend to be comprised of agemates, a less familiar or more stressful environment. It is also possible that children may compensate for failures to develop supportive peer relationships at school by doing so in the neighborhood.

Another relevant feature may be the stability of children's friendships in the neighborhood. It is apparent from research with adults that the continuity of an individual's close personal relationships is related to her success in coping with life's demands. It may also be the case that children benefit from developing stable friendships in the neighborhood, especially during periods of transition at school (the transition to grade school, moving from grade to grade).

Preliminary Investigations and Findings

We have investigated several aspects of the model of school adjustment depicted in Figure 14.1, and will use the following pages to describe some of our studies and findings. To date, our research program has been focused primarily on factors that forecast children's adjustment to "new" school environments (e.g., the transition into preschool, and from preschool to kindergarten). Toward this end, we have attempted to identify both child characteristics and features of children's interpersonal environments (i.e., family, school, and neighborhood) that may have an important bearing on school adjustment.

Child Characteristics

Children's social skills, particularly their interaction style with peers, and organismic attributes, such as gender and mental age, have occupied a position of central importance in our work. Currently, there is growing evidence to suggest that children's social skills influence the degree to which they succeed at developing supportive peer relationships in the classroom (e.g., see Ladd & Price, 1987; Ladd, Price & Hart, 1988). Moreover, it also appears that even young children develop accurate and stable perceptions of peers' aggressive and prosocial behaviors, and that these perceptions are related to their liking preferences and friendship choices in the classroom (e.g., see Ladd & Mars, 1986; Masters & Furman, 1981).

Ladd, Price and Hart (1988, in press) conducted a short-term longitudinal study of children's entrance into preschool classrooms, and examined the relation between children's behavioral styles at the outset of the school year (i.e., prosocial vs. antisocial) and their peer acceptance at the middle and end of the school year. The types of social skills children displayed on the playground among peers during the early weeks of school were predictive of their eventual status among classmates. Whereas children with prosocial styles (e.g., cooperative play) tended to become better liked and less rejected by classmates, those with antisocial styles (e.g., arguing, physical aggression) were more likely to become disliked and rejected. Moreover, children who became rejected by peers had more difficulty finding consistent play companions than did accepted children, and were also seen by their teachers as less well adjusted in school. These findings suggest that, in new school environments, children's success in establishing supportive peer relationships is partly determined by the types of social skills they display in early social encounters with peers. However, it was unclear from these findings whether the interaction styles documented by Ladd, Price and Hart (1988, in press) were stable characteristics that children possessed prior to school entry, or transient responses to the new school situation.

Further evidence pertaining to this question was gathered by Ladd and Price (1987) in a longitudinal study of the transition from preschool to kindergarten (the first year of grade school). Two aspects of children's behavioral styles were assessed in preschool, including the frequency of their prosocial and antisocial behaviors toward peers, and the number of different peers with whom they tended to conduct prosocial versus antisocial interactions (i.e., the range of positive vs. negative peer contacts). These measures, which reflected children's interactive styles in preschool, were used to predict their emerging peer relations in new schools with unfamiliar kindergarten classmates. Organismic characteristics, such as children's mental age and gender, were also taken into account in analyses designed to evaluate the predictive efficacy of their preexisting social skills.

Results indicated that children's styles of interacting with peers in preschool did, in fact, forecast their peer acceptance and rejection in kindergarten. Children who displayed a broader range of positive peer contacts in preschool (i.e., they used prosocial behaviors with many as opposed to only a few peers) achieved more supportive peer relations in kindergarten. Conversely, greater use of antisocial behaviors, and a broader range of negative peer contacts in preschool, predicted peer rejection in kindergarten. Important sex differences in the predictive power of children's social skills were also found. Cooperative play (prosocial) and arguing (antisocial) behaviors in preschool emerged as better predictors of kindergarten peer acceptance and rejection, respectively, for girls than for boys. The stability coefficients obtained for these behavioral measures from preschool to kindergarten were also higher for girls than for boys. In contrast, measures of physical aggression and the range of negative peer contacts observed in preschool were stronger predictors of kindergarten peer rejection for boys than for girls. Moreover, the corresponding stability coefficients were higher for boys than for girls. No relationships were found between children's mental age and their acceptance or rejection in kindergarten.

Another important finding to emerge from the Ladd and Price (1987) study was that children's behavioral styles in preschool also predicted teachers' perceptions of classroom maladjustment in kindergarten. More specifically, children who were aggressive toward peers in preschool tended to be seen by kindergarten teachers as disruptive and hostile in the classroom. The same results were found for boys whose preschool peer interactions had been characterized by a broad range of negative contacts. An additional finding, however, was that boys with more negative contacts in preschool were also seen by kindergarten teachers as hyperactive and distractible. Taken together, these findings suggest that children's social skills, particularly their styles of relating to peers, are not merely a unique response to a particular setting but rather a social disposition that is maintained across school contexts and predictive of current and later school adjustment. Moreover, there appear to be important gender differences in the types of social skills that place children at risk for adjustment problems in new school environments.

The Interpersonal Environment: Family, School, and Neighborhood

We have also investigated several of the environmental supports/stressors depicted in the proposed model of school adjustment (see Figure 14.1). One aspect of the *family* environment that has been investigated is parents' management of children's peer relations in nonschool settings (e.g., the home and neighborhood). Ladd and Golter (1988) were interested in determining whether parents' management practices, particularly their efforts to initiate and monitor children's nonschool peer contacts during preschool, would predict children's school adjustment in grade school. Parents were asked to complete logs of their management activities, and scores were derived to index the proportion of children's neighborhood peer contacts that parents had initiated (i.e., arranged for the child), and monitored in a direct manner (e.g., watching children closely, guiding their play) versus an indirect manner (e.g., periodically observing children's activities). Results indicated that parental initiation was related to children's peer status in kindergarten, but only for boys. Boys whose parents tended to initiate peer contacts during preschool became better liked and less rejected by peers in kindergarten. Parents' styles of monitoring were related to later school maladjustment for both boys and girls. Children whose parents tended to use direct as opposed to indirect forms of monitoring during preschool tended to become less accepted and more rejected by peers in kindergarten. Furthermore, direct as opposed to indirect monitoring styles were predictive of later classroom behavior problems, such as disruptiveness and aggression. One implication of these findings is that the types of peer experiences that parents arrange and how they supervise these contacts during preschool may affect children's later school adjustment, especially their ability to establish supportive social ties with classmates. For example, it may be the case that direct monitoring represents a type of parental control that prevents children from independently mastering and generalizing peer-related social skills. Another possibility is that children who tend to be directly supervised by parents at home may not be as well prepared for settings that afford less adult guidance and attention (e.g., classrooms) and, thus, respond to what is perceived as a lack of structure by becoming more disruptive or unruly.

In addition to managing children's peer relations in the home and neighborhood, parents may help children adjust to school by providing them with opportunities to relate with peers in a variety of community settings (e.g., playground, library, pool, church, school). By exposing children to different settings, peers, and rules for behavior, parents may help children become more autonomous and comfortable in new environments and more skillful at establishing new relationships. To explore this hypothesis, Ladd and Price (1987) employed parents' reports of the diversity of community settings in which children had regular peer contact during preschool to forecast children's school adjustment following their entrance into kindergarten. They found that children who had participated in multiple peer contexts during early childhood were more comfortable in the new school environment, and displayed lower levels of school avoidance. Specifically, the measure of preschool peer contexts predicted lower levels of classroom anxiety and requests to see the school nurse at the beginning of kindergarten, and fewer absences from school at both the beginning and the end of kindergarten.

We have also investigated several aspects of the *school* environment that are hypothesized to be antecedents and concomitants of children's school adjustment (see

Figure 14.1). As part of a larger investigation of the transition from preschool to kindergarten, Ladd and Price (1987) obtained measures of the duration of children's experience in preschool classrooms, and the percentage of time that children spent playing with younger, same-age, and older peers in these settings. These measures were deemed to be important antecedents of kindergarten adjustment for the following reasons. First, kindergarten tasks--such as separating from parents, accepting the teacher's authority, and establishing new peer relationships--may be more familiar to children with considerable preschool experience and, therefore, easier to accomodate. Second, because most grade-school classrooms require that children relate with agemates, children who have demonstrated a preference for younger companions in preschool may be at a disadvantage. Moreover, overinvolvement in this type of relationship may be associated with lower maturity demands and, ultimately, failure to develop age-appropriate social skills and relationships (see Ladd, 1983, 1984).

In addition to these potential antecedents, Ladd and Price (1987) hypothesized that features of the new school environment, such as the peer composition of kindergarten classrooms, might influence children's subsequent school adjustment. Based on past research indicating that friends and familiar peers can be an important source of emotional support in novel situations (e.g., Ispa, 1981; Schwarz, 1972), it was anticipated that the proportion of familiar peers in children's kindergarten classrooms would be positively related to their school adjustment.

In fact, Ladd and Price (1987) found that all three factors were related to children's posttransition school adjustment. Children with greater preschool experience displayed fewer anxious behaviors during the early weeks of kindergarten, and those who preferred to relate with younger classmates in preschool developed negative attitudes toward school that endured throughout the school year. Children who began kindergarten in classrooms with familiar peers were less anxious at the outset of the school year, and made fewer requests to visit the school nurse. These children were also more likely to develop stable, positive attitudes toward the new school environment.

As hypothesized in the proposed model of school adjustment, children's peer relations in *nonschool setting* (e.g., the neighborhood) may also have an important bearing on their school adjustment. Recent investigations by Ladd (1983, 1988) and Ladd, Hart, Wadsworth, and Golter (1988) are among the first to describe the features of children's nonschool peer relations during the preschool and early elementary years. These studies reveal that children as young as 3 tend to have frequent play companions in the neighborhood, and that the number of neighborhood companions increases steadily for both boys and girls throughout both preschool and grade school.

The potential benefits of nonschool peer relationships for children's school adjustment have been explored in studies by Ladd et al. (1988) and Ladd and Price (1987). In a study of the transition from home to preschool, Ladd et al. (1988) found that children who played primarily among agemates in the neighborhood (as opposed playing among younger or older peers) received higher school adjustment ratings from teachers following their entrance into preschool. A related finding was obtained by Ladd and Price (1987) in their study of the transition from preschool to kindergarten. Specifically, preschoolers who tended to associate with younger peers in the neighborhood were more likely to develop negative attitudes toward kindergarten.

In addition to the form of companionship children pursue, the stability of their peer relationships in nonschool settings may facilitate adjustment to new school environments. Support for this premise was obtained by Ladd and Price (1987). They found that children who retained a larger proportion of their nonschool peer relationships, as they moved from preschool to kindergarten, tended to develop more favorable attitudes toward the new school environment.

Implications and Future Directions

Our data suggest that early school adaptation may be a complex process that is affected by many factors. Consistent with our model, both characteristics of the child and the child's interpersonal environments (i.e., social supports or stressors) were found to be important predictors of adjustment outcomes in new school settings.

Of the characteristics that children "bring" to the school setting, attributes such as their social skills and interaction patterns with peers appear to be important precursors of school adaptation. Our findings suggest that, as children enter new classrooms, those who interact cooperatively with peers *and* pursue an extensive pattern of peer contacts (i.e., they "sample" many play partners from the pool of available classmates) tend to become better accepted by their classmates. These children also tend to be more successful at finding and maintaining specific play partners (i.e., consistent companions or "friends"). Not surprisingly, teachers perceive these children to have higher levels of classroom social adjustment. In contrast, children who begin the school year by aggressing against peers, and engaging in negative interactions with a broad range of classmates, tend to become disliked by their new classmates and are viewed as poorly adjusted by their teachers. The negative peer reputations that these children develop early in the school year often persist, and appear to limit their choice of play partners and activities as the school year progresses.

The fact that these patterns of behavior were found to differ by gender, and remained relatively stable across school settings is also worthy of comment. Of the two behavioral "styles" described above, the antisocial style that forecasted school maladjustment was more common and stable among boys than among girls. This finding may mean that more boys than girls are at risk for early school maladjustment. On the other hand, it may also mean that we have not yet discovered some of the avenues by which girls develop social adjustment problems in school. The stability of this behavioral style across school settings suggests that, for males in particular, the tendency to engage in antisocial interactions with many peers may be the result of child disposition rather than an idiosyncratic response to a particular setting. As discussed below, this finding may have important implications for prevention and intervention.

In addition to the characteristics children bring to school, our findings also suggest that features of children's interpersonal environments and relationships have an important bearing on school adjustment. Moreover, these data suggest that when studying adaptation to new school environments, it may be important to consider qualities of children's family, school, and neighborhood relationships. Within this purview, both children's previous interpersonal relationships, and those that accompany their current school experience may be important.

Within the family, socialization activities sponsored by parents may play an important role in preparing children for school. Our data suggest that parents' management of children's peer relations at home and in the community may be related to children's later school adjustment. Specifically, children whose parents tended to foster contact with peers at home and in the community (e.g., at the community pool or library) during preschool, tended to have higher levels of social adjustment when they entered new kindergarten classrooms. Moreover, higher levels of adjustment were found for children whose parents supervised their peer contacts in indirect, noninterfering ways.

Findings pertinent to the school context highlight the importance of both prior experience in this setting, and the nature of children's relationships with classmates. Experiential antecedents, such as children's school and peer experiences during the preschool years, may enhance or inhibit their adaptation to new grade-school classrooms. We found that children who associated primarily with younger companions during preschool tended to develop less favorable school attitudes, and displayed higher levels of school avoidance once they entered grade school. It would appear that, although companionship with younger children may be common and appropriate during preschool (e.g., many preschool classrooms are mixed-age), overinvolvement in this type of relationship may not prepare children for the social demands of age-segregated grade-school classrooms.

The duration of children's prior school attendance also emerged as a significant predictor of early grade-school adjustment. The negative relation found between the length of children's preschool attendance and their anxious behaviors in kindergarten is consistent with the hypothesis that prior school experience prepares children for such tasks as separating from parents, spending time away from home, and becoming comfortable with new peers and teachers.

Once children enter school, features of the existing classroom environment may also influence school adjustment. Our data suggest that early school adjustment, following the transition from preschool to grade school (kindergarten), is enhanced when children are placed in classrooms with familiar peers. Perhaps the presence of familiar peers reduces the strangeness of new classrooms, and makes attendance less stressful.

A third context that may be important to children's school adjustment is the neighborhood. We found that children's peer relationships in the neighborhood, specifically the stability of their ties with neighborhood friends, forecasted school adjustment during the transition to kindergarten. The continuity of these relationships may have provided children with an enduring source of support, and a greater sense of predictability in an otherwise-changing social environment.

The findings reviewed in this chapter also suggest potentially useful strategies for researchers and educators interested in preventing children's school adjustment problems. In particular, our research on adjustment to new classrooms has led us to think that preventive programming could be most effective if it were designed to assist children both before and during key school transitions. Because much of our past work has been focused on the transition from preschool to kindergarten, we shall use this period as the basis for examples and illustrations.

It may be useful to intervene prior to a transition (e.g., during preschool) to modify behavioral dispositions that appear to be both stable and predictive of later adjustment difficulties. For example, helping children learn how to refrain from aggressive acts and pursue more extensive positive contacts in preschool might prepare them to make new friends and establish more favorable social reputations when they enter grade-school classrooms. Preemptive interventions might also focus on supportive "formative" experiences in family and school settings. Toward this end, parents might arrange for children to attend preschool, and develop neighborhood friendships with agemates prior to the time they enter grade school. Extensive social experiences, such as developing ties with peers in a variety of community settings, may also be helpful.

As children undertake the transition from one school environment to another (e.g., from preschool into kindergarten), it may be helpful for parents to engineer as much continuity as possible in children's neighborhood peer relationships. Helping children maintain ties among friends in the neighborhood may foster a sense of stability as their social ties in the school environment change. Also, it may behoove school administrators to plan the peer composition of new classrooms so that children find the new environment less strange or unfamiliar. Use of a "buddy system" or pairing children with friends or familiar peers as they enter school may be an effective as well as an economical way to promote early school adjustment.

To conclude, although not all the proposed linkages between school adjustment and features of children's family, school, and neighborhood environments have been examined, those that have been explored show considerable promise and warrant further investigation. It will also be important for researchers to identify other child characteristics and interpersonal supports that may be related to early school adjustment outcomes. There is also a need for further investigation of the unique and combined effects of various child characteristics and interpersonal relationships. For example, our work suggests that supportive features of new school environments (i.e., beginning school with familiar vs. unfamiliar classmates) partially compensates for the risks posed by maladaptive child characteritics (e.g., an antisocial behavioral style). However, many other combinations of child characteristics and environmental supports/stressors may operate to influence early school adjustment, and remain to be investigated.

There is also a need for studies of school adjustment within different and varied time frames. For example, most of the studies reviewed here provide data on children's adjustment to new school environments, and are relevant to key transition periods, such as grade school entrance. However, additional studies are needed to replicate and extend this work, and to explore the antecedents and concomitants of school adjustment during the preschool, elementary school, middle school (approximately ages 13-15), and high-school (approximately ages 16-18) years.

References

Achenbach, T. M., & Edelbrock, C. S. (1981). Behavioral problems and competencies reported by parents of normal and disturbed children aged four through sixteen. *Monographs of the Society for Research in Child Development, 46,* (Serial No. 188).

Asher, S. R., & Wheeler, V. A. (1985). Children's loneliness: A comparison of rejected and neglected peer status. *Journal of Consulting and Clinical Psychology, 53,* 500-505.

Bensen, G. P., Haycraft, J. R., Steyaert, J. P., & Weigel, D. J. (1979). Mobility in sixth graders as related to achievement, adjustment, and socioeconomic status. *Psychology in the Schools, 16,* 444-447.

Berndt, T. J., & Miller, K. (in press). Motivational and behavioral correlates of academic achievement. *Journal of Educational Psychology.*

Block, J. (1983). Differential premises arising from differential socialization of the sexes. *Child Development, 54,* 1335-1354.

Bogat, G. A., Jones, J. W., & Jason, L. A. (1980). School transitions: Preventive intervention following an elementary school closing. *Journal of Community Psychology, 8,* 343-352.

Bronfenbrenner, U. (1979). *The ecology of human development.* Cambridge, MA: Harvard University Press.

Bukowski, W., & Hoza, B. (in press). Popularity and friendship: Issues in theory, measurement, and outcome. In T. J. Berndt & G. W. Ladd (Eds.), *Peer relationships in child development.* New York: Wiley.

Butler, S. R., Marsh, H. W., Sheppard, M. J., & Sheppard, J. L. (1985). Seven-year longitudinal study of the early prediction of reading achievement. *Journal of Educational Psychology, 77,* 349-361.

Coie, J. D., & Dodge, K. A. (1983). Continuities and changes in children's social status: A five-year longitudinal study. *Merrill-Palmer Quarterly, 29,* 261-282.

Coie, J. D., & Krehbiel, G. (1984). Effects of academic tutoring on the social status of low-achieving, socially rejected children. *Child Development, 55,* 1465-1478.

Coie, J. D., & Kupersmidt, J. B. (1983). A behavioral analysis of emerging social status in boys' groups. *Child Development, 54,* 1400-1416.

Cowen, E. L. (1980). The wooing of primary prevention. *American Journal of Community Psychology, 8,* 258-284.

Cowen, E. L., Lotyczewski, B. S., & Weissberg, R. P. (1984). Risk and resource indicators and their relationship to young children's school adjustment. *American Journal of Community Psychology, 12,* 353-367.

Cowen, E. L., Pedersen, A., Bagigian, H., Izzo, L. D., & Trost, M. A. (1973). Long-term follow-up of early detected vulnerable children. *Journal of Consulting and Clinical Psychology, 41*, 438-446.

Dodge, K. A. (1983). Behavioral antecedents of peer social status. *Child Development, 54*, 1386-1399.

Dweck, C. S. (1986). Motivational processes affecting learning. *American Psychologist, 41*, 1040-1048.

Dweck, C. S., & Elliott, E. S. (1983). Achievement motivation. In E. M. Hetherington (Ed.), *Handbook of child psychology*, (Vol. 4, pp. 643- 691). New York: Wiley.

Eccles, J. (1983). Expectancies, values and academic behaviors. In J. T. Spence (Ed.), *Achievement and achievement motivation.* (pp. 75-146). New York: Wiley.

Felner, R. D., Stolberg, A., & Cowen E. L. (1975). Crisis events and school mental health referral patterns of young children. *Journal of Consulting and Clinical Psychology, 43*, 305-310.

Garmezy, N., Masten, A., & Tellegen, A. (1984). The study of stress and competence in children: A building block for developmental psychopathology. *Child Development, 55*, 97-111.

Glidewell, J. C., & Swallow, C. S. (1969). *The prevalence of maladjustment in elementary schools.* Report prepared for the Joint Commission on Mental Illness and Health of Children. Chicago: University of Chicago Press.

Heller, K., & Swindle, R. W. (1983). Social networks, perceived social support, and coping with stress. In R. D. Felner, L. A. Jason, J. N. Moritsugu, & S. S. Farber (Eds.), *Preventive psychology: Theory, research, and practice* (pp. 87-103). New York: Pergamon Press.

Holland, J. V., Kaplan, D. M., & Davis, S. D. (1974). Interschool transfers: A mental health challenge. *Journal of School Health, 64*, 74-79.

Horn, W. F., & Packard, T. (1985). Early identification of learning problems: A meta-analysis. *Journal of Educational Psychology, 77*, 597-607.

Hymel, S., Wagner, E., & Butler, L. J. (in press). Reputational bias: View from the peer group. In S. R. Asher & J. D. Coie (Eds.), *Peer rejection in childhood.* New York: Cambridge University Press.

Ispa, J. (1981). Peer support among Soviet daycare toddlers. *International Journal of Behavioral Development, 4*, 255-269.

Kohlberg, L., LaCrosse, J., & Ricks, D. (1972). The predictability of adult mental health from childhood. In B. Wolman (Ed.), *Manual of child psychopathology.* New York: McGraw-Hill.

Krappman, L. (1985). The structure of peer relationships and possible effects on school achievement. In R. A. Hinde, A. N. Perret-Clermont, & J. Stevenson-Hinde (Eds.), *Social relationships and cognitive development.* (pp. 149-166). Oxford, England: Clarendon Press.

Kupersmidt, J. B. (1983, April). *Predicting delinquency and academic problems from childhood peer status.* Paper presented at the biennial meeting of the Society for Research in Child Development, Detroit.

Ladd, G. W. (1983). Social networks of popular, average, and rejected children in school settings. *Merrill-Palmer Quarterly, 29*, 283-307.

Ladd, G. W. (1984). Expanding our view of the social world: New territories, new maps, same directions? *Merrill-Palmer Quarterly, 30*, 317-320.

Ladd, G. W. (1988). Friendship patterns and peer status during early and middle childhood. *Journal of Developmental and Behavioral Pediatrics, 9*, 229-238.

Ladd, G. W., & Asher, S. R. (1985). Social skill training and children's peer relations. In L. L'Abate & M. Milan (Eds.), *Handbook of social skills training and research* (pp. 219-244). New York: Wiley.

Ladd, G. W., & Golter, B. S. (1988). Parents' initiation and monitoring of children's peer contacts: Predictive of children's peer relations in nonschool and school settings? *Developmental Psychology, 24*, 109-117.

Ladd, G. W., Hart, C. H., Wadsworth, E. M., & Golter, B. (1988). Preschooler's peer networks in nonschool settings: Relationships to family characteristics and school adjustment. In J. Antrobus, M. Hammer, & S. Salzinger (Eds.), *Social networks of children, adolescents, and college students* (pp. 61-92). New York: Lawrence Erlbaum & Associates.

Ladd, G. W., & Mars, K. T. (1986). Reliability and validity of preschoolers' perceptions of peer behavior. *Journal of Clinical Child Psychology, 15*, 16-25.

Ladd, G. W., & Price, J. M. (1986). Promoting children's cognitive and social competence: The relation between parents' perceptions of task difficulty and children's perceived and actual competence. *Child Development, 57*, 446-460.

Ladd, G. W., & Price, J. M. (1987). Predicting children's social and school adjustment following the transition from preschool to kindergarten. *Child Development, 58*, 1168-1189.

Ladd, G. W., Price, J. M., & Hart, C. H. (1988). Predicting preschoolers' peer status from their playground behaviors. *Child Development, 59*, 986-992.

Ladd, G. W., Price, J. M., & Hart, C. H. (in press). Preschoolers' behavioral orientations and patterns of peer contact: Predictive of peer status? In S. R. Asher & J. D. Coie (Eds.), *Peer rejection in childhood.* New York: Cambridge University Press.

Masters, J. C., & Furman, W. (1981). Popularity, individual friendship selection, and specific peer interaction among children. *Developmental Psychology, 17*, 344-350.

Nicholls, J., & Thorkildsen, T. (1988). *Achievement goals and beliefs: Individual and classroom differences.* Manuscript submitted for publication.

Parker, J. G., & Asher, S. R. (1987). Peer acceptance and later interpersonal adjustment: Are low-accepted children at risk? *Psychological Bulletin, 102*, 357-389.

Perry, J. D., Guidubaldi, J., & Kehle, T. J. (1971). Kindergarten competencies as predictors of third-grade classroom behavior and achievement. *Journal of Educational Psychology, 4*, 443-450.

Rubin, R. A., & Balow, B. (1978). Prevalence of teacher-identified behavior problems. *Exceptional Children, 45*, 102-111.

Sandler, I. N., & Ramsay, T. B. (1980). Dimensional analysis of children's stressful life events. *American Journal of Community Psychology, 8*, 285-302.

Schwarz, J. C. (1972). Effects of peer familiarity on the behavior of preschoolers in a novel situation. *Journal of Personality and Social Psychology, 24*, 276-284.

Stevenson, H. W., Parker, T., Wilkinson, A., Hegion, A., & Fish, E. (1976). Longitudinal study of individual differences in cognitive development and scholastic development. *Journal of Educational Psychology, 68*, 377-400.

Vosk, B., Forehand, R., Parker, J.B., & Rickard, K. (1982). A multimethod comparison of popular and unpopular children. *Developmental Psychology, 18*, 571-575.

15

Social Competence Versus Emotional Security: The Link between Home Relationships and Behavior Problems in Preschool

Grazia Attili, Istituto di Psicologia del CNR, Rome, Italy

Social competence is an important area of research in the field of human development. In theory, it should be possible to use a comparative analysis of both cross-sectional and longitudinal studies to increase our understanding in this area. However, the term *social competence* has been applied to such a wide range of behaviors that it might be more useful to consider the various definitions as separate constructs, more or less related to each other, than as a single homogeneous theoretical concept (Dodge, Pettit, McClaskey, & Brown, 1986). Furthermore, the particular skills that have been studied, and the research that has been conducted on them, have been influenced by the highly diverse perspectives of the social and developmental theorists.

When measuring behavioral adjustment, competence is indicated by an individual's ability to respond to specific problematic situations and tasks (Goldfried & d'Zurilla, 1969; Schwartz & Gottman, 1976). In research on children's social competence, the most commonly studied skills include skills useful in peer group entry attempts and those useful in dealing with provocation by a peer (Dodge, 1980; Dodge et al., 1986; Dodge, Schlundt, Schoken, & Delugach, 1983; Putallaz & Gottman, 1981). These skills have often been investigated in conjunction with children's social-cognitive abilities (Shantz, 1983), social-information processing patterns, and overall social competence (Dodge et al., 1986; Rubin & Krasnor, 1986).

One major limitation of these studies is that the measures have been obtained through peer and/or teacher ratings, rather than in natural settings. This minimizes the usefulness of the findings because of the raters' inevitable bias and expectations regarding the children's behavior. Social-information processing patterns have been assessed by analysing children's judgments about videotaped responses to specific situations. The quality of these situations is highly accurate (Rubin & Krasnor, 1986) and their repertoire is large (Spivack, Platt, & Shure, 1976). Nevertheless, the situations used to generate the responses are still formulated by adults rather than by children. Social competence can also be assessed in a structured laboratory setting, such as by placing two peers in a playroom and asking a third child to initiate play with the first two. While this approach is an efficient means of measuring the specific variables under investigation, it again lacks the complexity of a real-life setting.

B. H. Schneider et al. (eds.), Social Competence in Developmental Perspective, 293–311.
© *1989 by Kluwer Academic Publishers.*

Research dealing with children at risk for psychopathology (Garmezy, Masten, & Tellegen, 1984) has stressed the role of social competence in the appearance of later disturbance. Due to the assumption that rejected, withdrawn, and/or isolated children are an at-risk population, attempts have been made to identify these children in order to prevent the development of psychopathology through appropriate intervention. These studies have applied sociometric techniques to assess children's social competence. To be popular and likeable and to be socially competent are considered synonymous constructs (Coie, 1985). Receiving positive nominations from peers (being popular) is considered an indication of social skills, whereas receiving neither positive nor negative nominations (being neglected) or receiving only negative nominations (being rejected) is considered an indication of a lack of social skills. However, when data from studies of this sort are compared with information obtained by direct observation, the correlations are only moderate to low (Rubin, LeMare & Lollis, 1988).

Aggression has also played a large role in social skills research because aggressive behavior patterns that are stable over time may ultimately lead to rejection by peers (Coie & Kupersmidt, 1983; LaFreniere & Sroufe, 1985). A lack of cognitive capacities, such as the ability to view a situation from another's perspective, has been investigated to determine the role of cognitive capacities in aggression. It has been suggested that aggressive children have a limited behavioral repertoire for dealing with social problems (Feshbach, 1984; Rubin & Krasnor, 1986). However, the findings of studies linking aggressive behavior to low peer status have been inconsistent. Nevertheless, when aggression is broadly defined to encompass a wide range of behaviors and then compared with measures of peer disliking as opposed to peer liking, findings are consistent. Hartup (1983) has proposed that the apparent inconsistency of findings may stem from variations in the definitions and measures used to study aggression and peer status rather than indicating an actual lack of correlation between the two.

In summary, when one traces research on social competence and related skills, one discovers that this construct has been defined so inconsistently that it would be very difficult to compare the studies. However, limiting research inquiries to the question "How are aspects of social functioning related?" (i.e., "How do cognitive skills relate to effective behavior?") rather than asking "What is social competence?," as Dodge et al. (1986) have suggested, is misleading, insofar as it obscures our understanding of ongoing individual adaptation within an ontogenetic process.

Social Competence as an Integrated Construct

Social skills depend on the specific situation and the age of the individual. However, the assessment of social competence or incompetence should transcend the limitations of situations, tasks, and age in order to advance a developmental perspective. That is, an integrated definition of competence must be maintained in developmental research to permit the study of continuity in the discontinuous process of human development. Achieving that objective requires a definition of social competence that is valid across age spans, different social interactions, and varied situations (Waters & Sroufe, 1983). Not only are there differences in the specific skills available to children, adolescents, and adults, but skills that are successful in interactions with some partners may not be successful in interactions with others.

An evolutionary approach might yield an integrated definition of competence (Attili, in press b). Ethologists assume that social and cognitive skills must have evolved together to facilitate the management of interpersonal relationships. The main biological function of intellect is therefore to support social life rather than to contribute to practical problem solving. A higher primate must be skilled at exploiting others' behavior and at adjusting its own behavior to that of others in a continuous effort to balance costs and benefits. Survival and biological fitness are thus dependent on social success (Humphrey, 1976).

Social competence can be viewed as the result of natural selection when it brings individuals short- and long-term benefits (i.e., survival, reproduction, and inclusive fitness). Based on these ideas, we might define social competence as "the ability to manage those particular relationships that are important at a specific stage of development, in a certain environment, to maximize the individual's short- and long-term benefits." This definition is not so different from the one proposed by Waters and Sroufe (1983), although their definition focuses mainly on the short-term function of competence. They wrote: "The competent individual is one who is able to make use of environmental and personal resources to achieve a good developmental outcome" (p. 81). The construct proposed in this chapter is similarly valid from a developmental perspective. However, it is not useful to insist that developmental gain be present in order to regard an adaptive behavior as socially competent. This point can be illustrated with an example used by Waters and Sroufe (1983). Infants who learn to withdraw from human contact in response to rejection or abuse by their mothers (Egeland & Sroufe, 1981; George & Main, 1979) are exhibiting an adaptive response in terms of survival. According to the definition I have proposed, they are very competent individuals. Yet, in Waters and Sroufe's definition, those infants would not be considered competent because their withdrawal will prevent contact with other adults and peers. I believe that competence, as defined by the evolutionary construct outlined previously, is the correct use of situation-specific responses. It may be that what constitutes competent behavior with a particular partner in a particular situation at a particular age may in fact be considered incompetent behavior with a different partner in a different situation at a different age and at a different stage of development. The distinction between what is considered socially competent or incompetent does not depend merely on identifying the appropriate response for a given situation. Factors that lead individuals to be inflexible in their interactions across a changing environment must be studied, although the immediate objective here is to develop a satisfactory definition of the construct.

Competence and Development

Mother-Child Bond. The relationships that are most crucial to an individual in terms of ensuring optimal social development and biological fitness vary with age. Individuals are adapted by natural selection to be socially competent. For instance, an infant in distress who cries, clings, and then smiles at the mother for making a contact is a very competent individual.

The mother's sensitivity and responsiveness to an infant's signals may be considered indices of the infant's success. Social success, so defined, would thus be understood as an interaction between several variables, such as the interaction between the unique combination of affect, cognition, and behavior that characterizes Individual A (the child, for example) and the unique combination of factors that characterizes Individual B (the mother). In other words, a mother's sensitivity to her infant's signals would depend on her own characteristics and expectations, such as mood or past experiences, as well as on the child's characteristics and behaviors, such as intensity and frequency of crying. The use of competent behaviors enables the infant to survive and hence maximizes the mother's reproductive success. Each interactant brings to a social exchange a history of both previous and/or concurrent experiences involving his or her relationship with that partner as well as with other partners. The association between emotional, cognitive, and social factors characterizes the individual's social life at a very early age.

Peer Relationships. Peer relationships are the most important social interactions in early and late childhood. The development of social-cognitive abilities is fostered when these relationships occur with age-mates. In addition, the reciprocal nature of peer interactions facilitates children's understanding of the rules that regulate social exchanges (Attili, 1985; Attili & Felaco, 1986). Furthermore, in many respects, peer relationships can be considered a training ground for the development of skills that will be crucial in adulthood. For example, the ability to accurately interpret a partner's behavior and to adapt one's own behavior based on that of the partner are skills that when adequately learned in childhood, will lead to successful functioning both in adult sexual relationships and as parents.

The idea of assessing different behaviors for different age groups does not mean that we must dismiss social competence as an integrated and homogeneous construct. According to the perspective proposed in this chapter, for example, the skills that preschool children (ages 3 - 5) require for effective peer interaction tend to involve managing dyadic or triadic relationships in face-to-face interactions rather than improving group-entry skills. In order to define the construct of social competence, we must have an initial understanding of the central issues that should be considered social competencies. It is only through such a comprehensive understanding of social competence that we will be able to identify the particular aspects of children's social lives toward which intervention programs should be directed (Attili, in press b) in order to prevent the development of psychopathology.

Social Competence Versus Emotional Security

The ways in which children manage their peer relationships are more strongly influenced by their past and/or concurrent life experiences than is the case with other relationships. In view of this, it is surprising that research in this area has very rarely attempted to understand the interplay of emotional, social, and cognitive factors that characterizes peer interactions by examining the impact and interactive effects of school and home relationships. This is even more surprising because the main objective of research focusing on the establishment of satisfactory peer relations is to identify predictors of later adjustment or maladjustment.

Negative and unsuccessful behavior in peer interaction situations cannot simply be attributed to the cognitive capacities, self-concept, and personality traits of the individuals involved. Rather, we must consider the role of social competence, an organizational construct that may be defined as the ability to coordinate resources in order to reach adaptive goals. To define social competence merely as one of several personal resources, such as self-efficacy or locus of control (see the classic work of White, 1959), limits or reduces the utility of this construct. Waters and Sroufe (1983) have stressed that "competence may prove to be a more valuable construct when assessed in terms of qualitative individual differences in the coordination of resources.... Personal resources [instead] are conceptualized in terms of quantitative individual differences" (p. 83). For example, a child will assimilate the mother's and father's behaviors and moods, peer responses, and past and present experiences to ensure successful outcomes in interactions with peers.

The Link Between Home and School Relationships: The "Attachment" Approach

The link between home and extrafamilial relationships has been investigated primarily by attachment theorists. With respect to competence, their aim has been to prove that the construct can be validated by establishing a network of relationships within and across ages (Waters & Sroufe, 1983).

Ainsworth, Blehar, Waters and Wall (1978) found that secure attachment at the age of 1 year (Group B babies) is related to play, to exploring novel aspects of the environment, and to exploratory behavior at home. Children who were securely attached at 12 months were similarly attached at 18 months and at 6 years of age (Main, Kaplan & Cassidy, 1985; Waters, 1978). The attachment pattern was found to be stable, as well, for the group of children who were classified as ambivalent and unable to be comforted after the stress of separation from the mother (Group C babies) and for children who avoided contact with the mother upon reunion (Group A babies). The children in both of these latter groups were unable to explore the environment even while the mother was present.

These results seem to indicate that effective attachment relationships foster experiences, such as play and exploration, that will lead to positive adaptation in the next developmental stage. The securely attached infants (Group B) have been found to be more autonomous and more sociable as toddlers (Pastor, 1981), to have better self-control (Egeland, 1983), to be involved in more positive interactions, to use more positive affect in their social exchanges, and to be more affectively expressive as preschoolers (Sroufe, Schork, Motti, Lawroski, & LaFreniere, 1984) than infants in the other groups.

Conversely, it has been shown that children who experienced hostile feelings toward their mother (Group A and C babies) demonstrated hostile and aggressive patterns of behavior toward playmates in preschool. Furthermore, the behavior in preschool of children who exhibited an anxious/avoidant pattern of attachment in infancy differed from the behavior of children who exhibited an anxious/resistant pattern or were ambivalently attached as infants. The anxious/avoidant group were described by teachers as hostile, socially isolated and disconnected while the latter group were characterized as impulsive, tense, and/or helpless and fearful. Both of these behavior patterns are hypothesized to result from the type of mothering to which the children were exposed in their early years. Mothers of anxious/avoidant children are described as rejecting and emotionally unavailable, while mothers of anxious/resistant or ambivalent children are seen as inconsistent and over involved in caring for their children. The difficulties that these children have in peer relationships are hypothesized to arise from their inability to express anger directly in their relationship with the mother (Erickson, Sroufe, & Egeland, 1985). These findings demonstrate that the combination of affect, cognition and behavior necessary for successful adaptation depends to a large extent on the effectiveness of attachment in the mother-child relationship.

Although I agree in principle, it is misleading and confusing to define "social competence" as the capacity to explore the environment at 12 months, compliant behavior toward the mother, autonomy as a toddler, and positive behaviors toward peers in preschool (Waters & Sroufe, 1983). According to the theoretical construct presented in this chapter, social competence is merely a response by an individual that leads to success in a specific relationship, in a given situation. For example, in a stressful environment, attachment behavior directed toward mother represents socially competent behavior because the mother is the most protective figure in that situation. Specific behavior directed toward peers in preschool can be considered socially competent insofar as it enhances development of the cognitive and social skills that the child must have in order to become a socially competent adult. The behavior of the anxious/avoidant and anxious/ambivalent children -- Groups A and B, respectively -- can also be considered socially competent within the particular situation studied. The lack of play and exploration found in the behavior patterns of these children demonstrates their social competence in a potentially stressful situation. Through the use of avoidant or ambivalent behaviors these children are able to maintain some proximity to an attachment figure who, despite being highly anxiety-provoking for them, is nonetheless their attachment figure. The lack of exploratory behavior is appropriate for these children due to the nature of their relationship with the mother. Consequently, exploratory behavior cannot be taken *per se* as an index of social competence.

Attachment theorists have hypothesized that emotional factors related to previous and/or concomitant aspects of the relationships that children form with the attachment figure are directly related to the children's social competence in preschool (Erickson et al., 1985; Sroufe et al., 1984). The construct validity of social competence is increased by relying on data from several sources, as evidenced by the effect of consistent rejecting and inconsistent mothering of Group A and Group C children by their attachment figure. A construct based on emotional correlates due to external factors, such as aspects of mother-child attachments, is more reliable than one based on absolute scores on single measures.

Behavior in Preschool and Relationships Other Than Attachment Bonds: Ecologically Based Observations

Attachment is only one aspect of children's familial relationships. Furthermore, attachment behavior is displayed when the attachment system is activated, such as under conditions of stress. However, these situations do not occur as frequently as attachment theorists imply. Mother-child relationships are characterized by several types of interactions in everyday life. Also, fathers are playing increasingly important roles in children's lives. Unfortunately, we are still unsure of what role certain aspects of children's home relationships with mothers and fathers play in the real-life occurrence of incompetent behaviors in preschool.

Research projects involving ecologically based observations are difficult to design, inconvenient to arrange, and very time-consuming. Direct observation leads to problems, too, in defining and scoring due to the wide range of behaviors that can be displayed. Nevertheless, naturalistic settings offer many advantages when it comes to studying a construct such as social competence, especially when the skills are analyzed according to the definition proposed in this chapter.

One of the advantages is that the scored behavior is similar to the real-life conditions to which the findings will be generalized. Second, within these settings, we can identify individual styles of responding by considering which selection the subject makes with respect to all the available response options. Furthermore, behavioral observation permits assessment of the *content* of children's behavior as well as the *process* of parent-child and peer interactions. Also, we are able to assess the *reciprocal* and/or *complementary* nature of interactions rather than depending on others' (peers' or adults') *perceptions* of children as passive subjects whose behavior is considered in isolation -- that is, apart from any influence by interactants. Through the use of direct observational techniques, researchers can focus their studies on the interactants' responsivity, affect, social communication, and patterns of control (Attili, in press b).

The findings discussed in this chapter represent a portion of the results from an extensive project aimed at discovering how children's individual characteristics, in terms of their temperamental variables, and mothers' moods are related, as well as the nature of the relationships that children form with different partners in different contexts. For example,

298

we are studying children's interactions with fathers, mothers, and other children at home as well as with peers and teachers at preschool (Attili, 1987; Attili, 1989; Attili, in press a; Attili, in press b; Attili, Alcini & Felaco, 1988; Attili, Felaco, & Alcini, 1988; Attili, Felaco, Alcini, & Travaglia, 1988).

Method: Subjects

Thirty-four two-parent families were studied. We used a small sample size because the aim of our research was to consider as many variables as possible in order to provide an accurate, though not completely exhaustive, account of children's real lives. Psychological research that uses few subjects yet measures many variables should be considered a valuable means of generating and formulating plausible hypotheses as well as a preliminary step toward future studies that will be able to analyze only a few significant variables while using many subjects. The need for extensive observation of the subjects' complete behavior patterns in more than one situation constrained the study's size. Not only is recording and coding sequences of behavior time-consuming, but in addition, we could not increase the number of observers involved without jeopardizing the reliability of their observations.

The families' socioeconomic status ranged from unskilled to professional, although the majority fell into the semiskilled socioeconomic category. All of the children (16 female, 18 male) were around 4 years old and were firstborn and most of them had one sibling. The children were enrolled in different classes in three separate preschools and each had been attending preschool for at least 6 months.

Procedure

Assessments of Mother-Father-Child Interaction. Interactions between mother-father-sibling (when a sibling was present) and the subject child were observed at the home and recorded on audiotape. There were two 40-minute visits, scheduled one week apart, with each family. The experimenters supplied a collection of toys on both days and asked the parents to do whatever they liked, to do what they were accustomed to doing with the child, or to introduce the child to the toys as they normally would. The interactions were then coded using Hinde's (1983) modified version of Lytton's (1980) coding scheme.

For each focal child, coded behaviors were divided into the following categories:

1. *Degree of involvement.* These codes assessed the extent of the mother's and/or father's involvement in the child's activity without reference to the type of activity in which the child was engaged. This involved the assessment of: (a) the time that the mother and child, father and child, and mother and father and child spent at the same activity (joint activities); (b) the time that the mother and/or father were busy doing something apart from the focal child (parents busy); and (c) the time that the mother and/or father were available to the child although not necessarily interacting with him or her (parents available).

2. *Participation.* Codes in this category assessed the closeness of the focal child's physical contact with the mother and/or father.

3. *Neighbors.* This coding specified which parent was in closer proximity to the child. (These first three codes were measured in terms of duration.)

4. *Interactions.* The codes in this last category are based on an interaction grammar - - that is, they define the moves used by the child to communicate with others and used by others to communicate with the child. By identifying the subjects, verbs, objects, and qualifiers, we can get an understanding of what the child says and does to others; what others say and do to the child; the quality of the interaction, in terms of how it relates to

the previous interaction; and its descriptive quality. Both the event and its duration and the event were coded and recorded in terms of frequency during the particular interval being observed.

The interaction grammar consisted of approximately 80 verbs and 16 qualifiers. The frequency of interactions that had the focal child as subject and object was recorded. These interactions were: friendly behavior, in terms of touching and hugging; exchanging objects; neutral conversation; teaching in terms of reading to and giving information; hostility expressed in several ways, including specific aggression (a type of aggression whose aim is to take an object or a place away from another individual), teasing aggression (harassment of others, hurting another physically or verbally without a specific reason), game aggression (hurting that arises in the course of a game), and defensive aggression (hurting another physically or verbally as a defensive reaction to aggressive acts); threatening, criticizing and interfering behavior; control patterns, such as inhibiting, commanding or suggesting; assertive behaviors; and prosocial behaviors. Qualifiers assessed the quality of the interactions and whether the social behavior was an initiation, an answer, a disconfirmation (a statement in which the subject ignores a previous comment, answers irrelevantly, or treats the previous speaker as though he or she did not exist), or a compliance (in which the listener acquiesces to a control statement).

Preschool Assessments. The same children were observed during free-time periods in their classroom for two 40-minute intervals spaced one week apart. The children's interactions with their teachers and peers were recorded using the same procedure as for the assessment of family interactions. Two codes, social participation and activity, were added for the school observations. The first measured the degree of each child's involvement with others and how one child influences another in terms of playing alone, group-parallel play, and interactive play. The latter code included such categories as sensorimotor play, intellectual play without physical movement, and role-play (Attili, in press b).

Assessment of the Child's Temperament. At the conclusion of the second home visit, each parent was asked to rate the child's temperamental characteristics using the McDevitt and Carey (1978) 3- to 7-year-old temperament scale, which is based on the conceptualization of Thomas and Chess (1977). This scale assesses temperament according to nine categories developed by the New York Longitudinal project. These categories are: activity level, rhythmicity in physiological reactions such as eating and sleeping time, approach to/withdrawal from new physical environments, adaptability to changes in situations, intensity of affective reactions, mood (positive vs. negative), persistence in attempts to perform a task, distractibility, and sensory threshold. Using this scale, it is also possible to calculate an overall temperament rating of difficult or easy, based on the ratings obtained in the categories of rhythmicity, approach/withdrawal, adaptability, intensity, and mood.

Assessment of the Mother's Mood

The children's mothers completed an 18-item self-report scale (IDA scale). The mother replies to items such as "I can laugh and feel amused" based on a 5-point Likert scale ranging from "never" to "always". This scale provided a rating of their depression, anxiety, and outward and inward irritability (Snaith, Costantopoulos, Jardin, & McGuffin, 1978).

Results

We analyzed matrices of correlations concerning all the variables related to preschool behaviors, children's temperament, and mothers' mood as well as the following home categories: (a) teaching and giving instructions and information; (b) control of the child by inhibiting, commanding, or suggesting; (c) disconfirming the child, by ignoring the child, answering the child irrelevantly, and/or treating the child as though he or she did not exist; and (d) joint activities with the child. The home categories were assessed using the mother, the father, or both as the subject(s). Only significant correlations and correlations at the limit of significance have been reported. There were few significant or interesting correlations between the parents' teaching and giving instructions and all the other categories. Conversely, the correlations between the other home variables and the children's behavior at school, along with the mothers' mood and children's temperament, were very interesting.

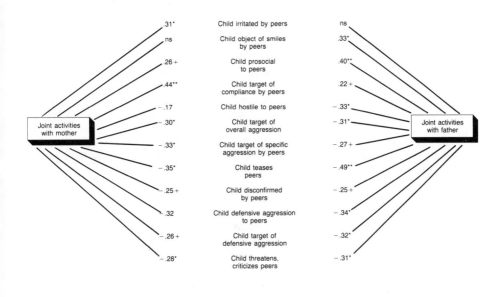

Note: Figures are given if the coefficient for one parent was significant or approached significance.
+ < .10; *p < .05; **p < .01; ***p < .001 (two-tailed)

Figure 15.1

Joint Activities with Parents and Behavior in Preschool: Spearman Correlation Coefficients

Mother-Child/Father-Child Joint Activities and Behavior in Peer Groups: Correlates

Children who were involved in joint activities with their mothers were similarly involved with their fathers ($r = .76$, $p<.001$). Children who were involved at home with mothers and fathers (considered separately) in doing things together were more likely to have age-mates comply with their requests and were less likely to be ignored and disconfirmed by peers at preschool (see Figure 15.1). Furthermore, these children were less likely to be targets for hostility by peers, especially with respect to specific aggression. (As noted earlier, this is a type of aggression that children use in order to take toys or space away from others.) These children were less hostile, too, (the correlation coefficient was significant only for the father-child activities) and did not tease age-mates as frequently, nor did they exhibit or receive defensive aggression, since they were less often attacking or being attacked. The peaceful quality of the interactions in which these children were involved was demonstrated by a lack of threats, criticisms, or interference with respect to their age-mates' activities. These children were also more prosocial than children who spent less time in joint activities with their parents and were more likely to be imitated by their peers (the correlation was significant only for mother-child joint activities) and to be the object of smiles (the correlation was significant only for father-child joint activities). The correlation coefficients between these home items and the mother's mood and children's temperament were not significant.

These findings suggest that children's positive relationships with both parents form a positive environmental resource on which their social competence and effectiveness in preschool are based. A child's social success can be clearly measured in terms of whether or not that child is the target of specific behaviors on the part of his or her peers. Children who experienced a high level of joint activity with their parents were mostly the target of compliance by peers and were unlikely to be the target of aggression. It should be stressed that these children teased and harassed their age-mates less than children who were not as involved in joint activities with their parents, and that teasing and harassing are a type of aggression that has been found to be more disliked than other types of hostility within peer relationships (Shantz, 1986).

Also, children who received compliance from peers frequently exchanged objects and toys with their age-mates, started conversations with them, were physically friendly, and exchanged smiles with peers. Any involvement in negative interactions was reciprocal in nature. This type of behavior included being hostile to peers who were criticizing and threatening, or controlling peers in response to submissive acts (Attili, in press).

Being Hostile and Being the Target of Aggression in Preschool: School and Home Correlates -- the Child's Temperament and the Mother's Mood

Lack of social success in preschool can be measured in terms of age-mates non-compliance with the child's requests and with the child's being a target of hostility by peers. Children who were targets of aggression were usually hostile as well. Both the children who were targets of aggression and those who were hostile to peers were almost exclusively involved in negative interactions (see Table 15.1). Furthermore, they were shifting from activity to activity without becoming involved, were less involved in interactive play and educational activities such as painting, and they spent less time playing alone.

15. Social Competence vs. Emotional Security

Table 15.1

Aggressive children and children targets of aggression; behavioral correlates in preschool and aspects of home relationships. Spearman Rank-order correlation

	Child target of aggression in preschool	Child hostile to peers
Mother disconfirms child	.29*	ns
Mother controls child without giving reason	.32*	.32*
Father controls child without giving reason	ns	.26+
Joint activities with Mother	-.30*	-.17
Joint activities with Father	-.32*	-.33*
Child hostile to peers	.73***	---
Child addresses specific aggression	.60***	.88***
Child target of specific aggression	.75***	.56***
Child addresses teasing aggression	.22+	.42**
Child target of teasing aggression	.59***	.43**
Child addresses games aggression	.48**	.59***
Child defensive aggression	.77***	.83***
Child target of defensive aggression	.57**	.55**
Child threatens peers	.61***	.57***
Child threatened by peers	.37**	.57***
Child submits	.58***	.52**
Child receives submission	.34**	.41**
Child controls	.27*	.45*
Child target of controls	.33*	.39**
Child initiates interaction	.40*	.35*
Child non-complying	.47**	.53**
Child transitional	-.49**	-.32*
Child disconfirms peers	.27*	.30*
Child disconfirmed by peers	.29*	.29*
Child plays arts	-.26+	-.30*
Child role plays	ns	-.39**
Child interactive play	-.37**	-.48**
Child plays alone	-.28*	-.31*
Child automanipulates, cries	.38*	ns
Child active	-.39*	ns
Child non-adaptable	-.33*	ns
Child intense	-.32*	-.31*
Child non-persistent	-.26+	ns
Child withdrawal	-.24+	ns
Child low sensory threshold	-.34*	ns
Child difficult	-.26+	ns
Mother inward irritable	.34+	ns

+p<.10; *p<.05; **p<.01; ***p<.001 (two tailed). Figures are given for both columns if either coefficient was significant or approached significance.

The more hostile the child was, the less involved he or she was in role-play. Children who were targets of aggression were rated by their mothers as less active, more adaptable,less intense, more persistent, less withdrawn, and having a higher sensory threshold. The children's temperamental characteristics were rated by the mothers at home and then compared to the children's school behavior. However, we need to understand the relationship between the children's characteristics and the mothers; behavior and mood, and how these two variables affect the children's emotional security and behavior in preschool. It was found that children who were largely ignored (disconfirmed) and controlled at home by their mothers, and who were less involved with both parents in joint activities, were often the target of aggression by peers in preschool. Furthermore, their mothers exhibited inward irritability, which was not the case with aggressive children.

Disconfirmation by the Mother and/or Father and Behavioral Correlates in Preschool

Children who were ignored and treated by their mothers as though they did not exist were treated similarly by their fathers ($r = .40$, $p < .01$). The children's behavior was linked more strongly to the mothers' disconfirmation than to the fathers'. Considering disconfirmation by father and mother separately, the more the children were disconfirmed at home, the more they acted out in preschool in ways that led to their receiving threats and criticisms from peers and to their being targets of hostility, especially targets of specific aggression. In addition, these children displayed specific aggression toward their peers but little teasing aggression. The conflicts were terminated through submission of the disconfirmed children. Furthermore, these children were found to be controlling with respect to their peers (correlations concerning the last five categories were significant only for disconfirmation by the mother), were less involved by peers in rough play, and exchanged less prosocial behavior with age-mates (correlations were significant only for disconfirmation by the father) (see Figure 15.2). Although these children did receive initiations from peers, these were mostly negative in nature, and the children (only those children disconfirmed by the father) tended to receive fewer replies to their openings (see Figure 15.3). In addition, these children (those disconfirmed by the father) did not comply with age-mates' requests, nor did the peers comply with the children's (both those disconfirmed by the father and the mother) requests.

Their emotional insecurity led these children to imitate their companions (correlations were significant only for disconfirmation by the father) and to be physically friendly with them (correlations were significant for disconfirmation by the mother). Evidence of their uneasiness in preschool was indicated by their high levels of automanipulation, such as crying, playing noisily, and creating disorder in the environment. They (only those children disconfirmed by the mother) also played alone for the most part which is further evidence of their uneasiness. Being disconfirmed by both parents (which refers to summing up of disconfirmation by both the mother and the father) was correlated with being the target of aggression by peers ($r = .31$, $p < .05$), with being the target of specific (instrumental) aggression by playmates ($r = .36$, $p < .02$), and with receiving mild control from peers ($r = .33$, $p < .05$). Correlation coefficients for children's being parentally disconfirmed and their receiving interaction initiations and answers from peers were not significant. The other correlations followed patterns similar to those found when mothers and fathers were considered separately.

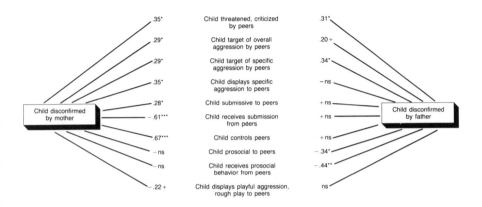

Note: Figures are given if the coefficient for one parent was significant or approached significance.
+ < .10; *p < .05; **p < .01; ***p < .001 (two-tailed)

Figure 15.2

Disconfirmations by parents and behavior in preschool. Spearman Correlation Coefficients.

Disconfirmation by Parents, Aspects of Home Relationships and the Child's Temperament

We assessed the associations between mother disconfirmation, father disconfirmation, and the parents' and child's behaviors within the home relationships. It was found that the more the parents ignored the child, the less likely that the child would comply with their requests. Interestingly, disconfirmations by the mother were associated with her assertion of control without giving reasons. Disconfirmations by the father were also correlated with assertion of control by the father as well as with the child's receiving many instructions and much information from him (see Figure 15.4). Mothers who disconfirmed their children tended to be depressed and rated their children as being nonadaptable and difficult.

The overall picture of these children and their interactions with their mothers is similar to that of children who were hypothesized to be anxiously attached (specifically, those who exhibited anxious/avoidant patterns of attachment in infancy) in a study by Erickson et al. (1985). Those children were characterized by their teachers as hostile, socially isolated, and disconnected in the preschool setting. Their behavior in preschool was described as acting out and was explained as being a defensive reaction on the part of children who had "an attachment figure who was rejecting, emotionally unavailable and perhaps depressed" (Erickson et al., 1985, p. 149).

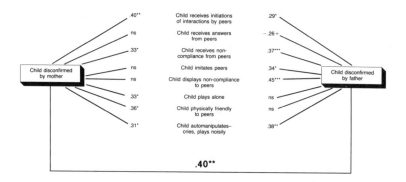

Figure 15.3

Being disconfirmed by mother and/or by father and behavior in preschool. Rank-Order Spearman.

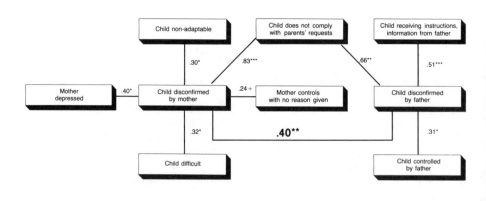

Figure 15.4

Disconfirmations by mother and by father, aspects of children's behavior and parents' behavior within home relationships, mothers' mood and children's temperamental characteristics. Correlation Coefficients.

15. Social Competence vs. Emotional Security

Controls by the Mother and the Father. Aspects of Home Relationships, Behavior in Preschool, and the Child's Temperament. The correlations for children who were controlled by their parents were different from those discussed above. Mothers' control patterns were correlated with the children's behavior in preschool to a greater extent than fathers' control patterns. These children tended to be isolated in preschool and onlookers (shifting from activity to activity without becoming involved). This category should not be confused with playing alone or with displaying less social behavior, although the latter may be true for these children. Youngsters who were overly controlled by their parents tended not to respond to interaction initiations from peers and were less physically friendly and assertive. Although they did attempt to control their peers, these children were in fact controlled by them but noncompliant to peer requests (all the above correlations were significant only for controls by the mother). Furthermore, they were unlikely to seek help, were less prosocial, and were rarely targets of prosocial activities by peers. In addition, they (only those who were overcontrolled by the father) tended to disconfirm their peers and were reciprocally disconfirmed by them. They were also less involved in intellectual activities and conversations with peers and displayed distress through behaviors such as crying frequently and playing noisily (see Figure 15.5).

Parents who controlled their children did so without giving reasons (the authoritarian parenting style described by Baumrind, 1971) and also gave instructions and information to them. The mothers scored high on inward irritability (as did fathers) and rated their children as highly distractible.

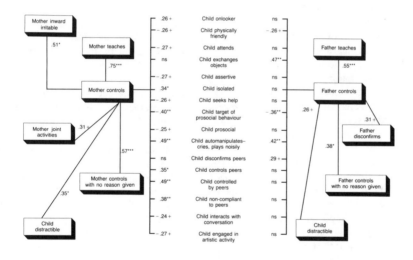

Note: Figures are given if the coefficient for one parent was significant or approached significance.
+ < .10; *p < .05; **p < .01; ***p < .001 (two-tailed)

Figure 15.5

Controls by parents: correlates.

The withdrawn children analyzed by Erickson et al. (1985) were described by teachers as passive, showing little interest in their surroundings, and not engaging in play. These children, who had been anxious/resistant in their attachment patterns in infancy, were also described as tense, helpless and fearful, all of which are patterns hypothesized to result from ambivalent/inconsistent or overinvolved caregiving.

Conclusion

In this chapter, I have urged the use of an integrated definition of the construct of social competence in order to facilitate the study of continuity in the discontinuous process of human development. Within an evolutionary perspective, we have considered social competence as the ability to best manage those specific relationships that are most important at a specific stage of development in a specific environment. In contrast to attachment theorists, I have restricted the domain of competence to behavior that is directly effective within the social environment. I believe that the construct of competence gains validity when it is based on the entire network of a child's relationships. In other words, social competence should be based on the interplay of social, cognitive, and emotional factors.

The coordination of affect, cognition, and behavior that children need to successfully manage peer relationships is to a great extent fostered by the quality of their home relationships with their mothers and fathers. Cross-situation relationships (as well as cross-age bonds) provide the resources that children need in order to achieve their adaptive goals. This definition of social competence is an organizational construct rather than a personal one (Waters & Sroufe, 1983).

The nature of the construct of social competence as a qualitative rather than a quantitative concept suggests that we must focus on how to assess it at different developmental stages, in different situations, and with different partners rather than trying to define fixed indices that will be valid across both situations and partners. Ethological observations in natural settings have been a powerful tool in the study of social competence from a developmental perspective. This approach allows researchers to assess the *content* of children's behavior as well as the *process* of their interactions. Even more important, ethological observation can be used to assess the quality of children's relationships in both the home and school settings.

The few researchers who have analyzed social competence as an organizational construct, based on resources from cross-situation and cross-age relationships, are attachment theorists. However, children's home relationships cannot be reduced simply to attachment interactions. The attachment pattern is merely one aspect of children's home relationships that is aroused under certain conditions of stress. Furthermore, mothers are not the only important figures in children's everyday life. Fathers have been shown to be important caregivers as well. Failure to consider the extent to which aspects of home relationships beyond attachment bonds contribute to the development of children's social competence and effectiveness in preschool would, in turn, restrict consideration of those factors that may lead to emotional disturbances manifested as behavior problems at preschool. For example, the quality of children's everyday home relationships with mothers and fathers might have greater value for predicting later disturbances than behaviors of the parents whose children display insecure attachment patterns. Whether or not the interaction styles identified were linked to anxious attachment patterns is still an open issue.

It was found that joint activities with the parents at home correlated with social success in preschool. Conversely, being disconfirmed (i.e., ignored and treated as though one did not exist) and being overcontrolled without being given reasons resulted in children's being socially unsuccessful in the preschool setting. Children who were highly disconfirmed by their parents tended to be involved in hostile and negative interactions and were often targets of aggression. Overcontrol by parents, in contrast, was associated mainly with isolation and uneasiness on the children's part in preschool.

Disconfirmation by the mothers was associated with maternal depression, indicated by low ratings on items such as "I have kept up my old interests" and "I can laugh and feel amused," as well as with nonadaptable and difficult behavior on the children's part. Overcontrol by mothers correlated positively with their inward irritability -- which was identified by high ratings on items such as "I feel like harming myself," "I get angry with myself or call myself names," and "The thought of hurting myself occurs to me" -- and with high distractibility on their children's part.

The behavior of the children who were disconfirmed by their parents was similar to the behavior problems common to children who exhibited anxious/avoidant patterns of attachment in infancy. Children who were overcontrolled by their mothers displayed behavior in preschool that is similar to the behavior of children who exhibited anxious/resistant attachments at an early age (Erickson et al., 1985). Research on the associations between attachment patterns and parents' styles of interaction with their children in the home is unfortunately still lacking.

The data presented here may be explained as reflecting a circular pattern, in which children who are perceived by their mothers as nonadaptable and difficult may contribute to the mothers' feelings of depression and to their disconfirming the children at home. This reaction on the part of the mothers may lead to the children's non-compliance to the mothers' requests, which, in turn, may increase the degree of disconfirmation by the parents. As the children become more difficult and less adaptable, the mothers become increasingly depressed. This circular model could be intensified if the mothers become aware (perhaps through preschool teachers) that their children are aggressive and destructive in the school setting, further convincing them that the children are difficult and thereby escalating the mothers' depression.

A similar circular pattern can be seen in the case of isolated children and their overcontrolling parents. Distractible children may be overcontrolled by their mothers if the mothers are irritable, which, in turn, may be due to their inability to modify their children's behavior. If the mothers become aware that their children are isolated in preschool, they might attribute it to the children's high distractibility. As a result, the mothers would become even more controlling and the children even more anxious.

The findings discussed in this chapter have demonstrated that environmental resources that lead to the coordination of affect, cognition, and behavior are important in every aspect of children's relationships. Furthermore, correlations between home and school variables cannot be explained merely in terms of parents' modeling effects (as in Putallaz, 1987). Certain interaction styles used by parents with their children in everyday home life can have a devastating effect on the children's social success in preschool. This is because those styles affect the children's emotional security. However, it may also be that parenting styles are affected by the children's behavior in preschool. The link between preschool behavior and aspects of everyday home relationships should be taken into consideration when deciding how, and where, to intervene.

Acknowledgments: I am very grateful to the children and parents who participated in this study as well as to Paola Alcini, Lello Felaco, Lia Formisano, Guido Travaglia, and Patrizia Vermigli, who helped with the data collection, observation coding, questionnaire scoring and statistical analysis.

References

Ainsworth, M., Blehar, M., Waters, E., & Wall, S. (1978). *Patterns of attachment*. Hillsdale, NJ: Erlbaum.

Attili, G. (1985). The extent to which children's early relationships are adapted to promote their social and cognitive development. In R. A. Hinde, A. N. Perret-Clermont, & J. Stevenson-Hinde (Eds.), *Social relationships and cognitive development* (pp. 50-65). Oxford, England: Oxford University Press.

Attili, G. (1987). Father as preferred parent and peer-peer interaction in preschool. *Proceedings of the China Satellite ISSBD Conference* (Vol. 2, pp. 32-47).Beijing.

Attili, G. (in press a). Emotional factors affecting social skills within peer relationships. *Rassegna di psicologia*.

Attili, G. (in press b). Successful and disconfirmed children in peer groups: Indices of social competence within an evolutionary perspective. *Human Development*.

Attili, G., Alcini, P., & Felaco, L. (1988). Differenze madre-padre nella valutazione di caratteristiche temperamentali di bambini. [Mother-father differences in rating temperamental characteristics of 4-year olds]. *Il Giornale Italiano di Psicologia, 15*, 269-285.

Attili, G., & Felaco, L. (1986). Natura e sviluppo delle relazioni tra coetanei: L'influenza del grado di familiarita e dell'amicizia sul comportamento sociale infantile. [Nature and development of peer relations: The influence of degree of familiarity and friendship on children's social behavior]. *Il Giornale Italiano di Psicologia, 13*, 275-295.

Attili, G., Felaco, R., & Alcini, P. (1989). Temperamento e relazioni interpersonali. [Temperament and interpersonal relationships]. *Eta Evolutiva, 11*, 58-69.

Attili, G., Felaco, L., Alcini, P., & Travaglia, G. (1988). La dialettica tra alcuni aspetti della relazione padre-bambino/madre-bambino e il comportamento non verbale all'interno della scuola materna. [On the dialecticamong several aspects of father-child/mother-child relations and non-verbal behavior in nursery school]. *Atti del XXI Congresso degli Psicologi Italiani, 1*, 113-120. Milan, Edizioni Guerini.

Baumrind, D. (1971). Current patterns of parental authority. *Developmental Monographs, 4*(1, Pt. 2), 1-103.

Coie, J. D. (1985). Fitting social skills intervention to the target group. In B. Schneider, K. H. Rubin, & J. Ledingham (Eds.), *Peer relations in childhood: Issues in assessment and training* (pp. 141-156). Springer-Verlag: New York.

Coie, J. D., & Kupersmidt, J. (1983). A behavioural analysis of emerging social status in boys' groups. *Child Development, 54*, 1400-1416.

Dodge, K. A. (1980). Social cognition and children's aggressive behavior. *Child Development, 51*, 162-170.

Dodge, K. A., Pettit, G. S., McClaskey, C. L., & Brown, M. M. (1986). Social competence in children. *Monographs of the Society for Research in Child Development, 51* (2, Serial No. 213).

Dodge, K. A., Schlundt, D. E., Schocken, I., & Delugach, J. D. (1983). Social competence and children's sociometric status: The role of peer group entry strategies. *Merrill-Palmer Quarterly, 29*, 309-336.

Egeland, B. (1983). Comments on Kopp, Krakow, and Vaughn's chapter. In M. Perlmutter (Ed.), *Minnesota Symposium in Child Psychology* (Vol. 16, pp. 129-135). Hillsdale, NJ: Erlbaum.

Egeland, B., & Sroufe, L. A. (1981). Attachment and early maltreatment. *Child Development, 52*, 44-52.

Erickson, M. F., Sroufe, L. A., & Egeland, B. (1985). The relationship between quality of attachment and behaviour problems in preschool in a high-risk sample. In I. Bretherton & E. Waters (Eds.), *Growing points of attachment theory and research: Monographs of the Society for Research in Child Development, 50* (1-2, Serial No. 209), 147-166.

Feshbach, N. (1984). Empathy, empathy training and the regulation of aggression in elementary school children. In R. M. Kaplan, V. J. Konecni, & R. W. Novaco (Eds.), *Aggression in children and youth* (pp. 177-192). NATO ASI Series D, *Social and behavioral sciences*. The Hague: Martinus Nijhoff.

Garmezy, N., Masten, A. S., & Tellegen, A. (1984). The study of stress and competence in a building block for developmental psychopathology. *Child Development, 55*, 97-111.

George, C., & Main, M. (1979). Social interactions of young abused children: Approach, avoidance and aggression. *Child Development, 50*, 306-318.

Goldfried, M. R., & d'Zurilla, T. J. (1969). A behavioural-analytic model for assessing competence. In C. D. Spielberger (Ed.), *Current topics in clinical and community psychology* (Vol. 1, pp. 151-196). New York: Academic Press.

Hartup, W. W. (1983). Peer relations. In E. M. Hetherington (Ed.) & P. H. Mussen (Series Ed.), *Handbook of child psychology*: Vol. 4. Socialization, personality, and social development (pp. 103-196). New York: Wiley.

Hinde, R. A. (1983). Unpublished coding manual.

Humphrey, N. K. (1976). The social function of intellect. In P. P. G. Bateson & R. A. Hinde (Eds.), *Growing points in ethology* (pp. 303-317). Cambridge, England: Cambridge University Press.

LaFreniere, P. J., & Sroufe, A. (1985). Profiles of peer competence in the preschool: Interrelations among measures, influence of social ecology, and relation to attachment history. *Developmental Psychology, 21*, 56-69.

Lytton, H. (1980). *Parent-child interaction: The socialization process observed in twin and singleton families.* New York: Plenum Press.

Main, M., Kaplan, N., & Cassidy, J. (1985). Security in infancy, childhood and adulthood: A move to the level of representation. In I. Bretherton & E. Waters (Eds.), *Growing points of attachment theory and research: Monographs of the Society for Research in Child Development, 50* (1-2, Serial No. 209), 66-104.

McDevitt, S., & Carey, W. (1978). The measurement of temperament in 3-7 year old children. *Journal of Child Psychology and Psychiatry*, Allied: Discipl., *19*, 245-253.

Pastor, D. L. (1981). The quality of mother-infant attachment and its relationship to toddlers' initial sociability with peers. *Developmental Psychology, 17*, 323-335.

Putallaz, M. (1987). Maternal behavior and children's sociometric status. *Child Development, 58*, 324-340.

Putallaz, M., & Gottman, J. M. (1981). An interactional model of children's entry into peer groups. *Child Development, 52*, 986-994.

Rubin, K. H., & Krasnor, L. R. (1986). Social cognitive and social behavioral perspectives on problem solving. In M. Perlmutter (Ed.), *Minnesota Symposium on Child Psychology*. (Vol. 18, pp. 1-68). Hillsdale, NJ: Erlbaum.

Rubin, K. H., LeMare, L. J., & Lollis, S. (1988). Social withdrawal in childhood: Developmental pathways to peer rejection. In J. R. Asher & J. D. Coie (Eds.), *Children's status in the peer group*. New York: Cambridge University Press.

Schwartz, R., & Gottman, J. M. (1976). Toward a task analysis of assertive behavior. *Journal of Consulting and Clinical Psychology, 44*, 910-920.

Shantz, D. (1986). Conflict, aggression and peer status: An observational study. *Child Development, 57*, 1322-1332.

Shantz, L. V. (1983). Social cognition. In J. H. Flavell & E. M. Markman (Eds.), P. H. Mussen (Series Ed.), *Handbook of child psychology*: Vol. 3. Cognitive development (pp. 495-555). New York: Wiley.

Snaith, R. P., Costantopoulos, A. A., Jardin, M. Y. & McGuffin, P. (1978). A clinical scale for the self-assessment of irritability. *British Journal of Psychiatry*, 1-32, 164-171.

Spivack, G., Platt, J. J., & Shure, M. B. (1976). *The problem-solving approach to adjustment*. San Francisco: Jossey-Bass.

Sroufe, L. A., Schork, E., Motti, E., Lawroski, N., & LaFreniere, P. (1984). The role of affect in emerging social competence. In C. Izard, J. Kagan, & R. Zajonc (Eds.), *Emotion, cognition and behavior* (pp. 289-319). New York: Cambridge University Press.

Thomas, A., & Chess, S. (1977). *Temperament and development*. New York: Brunner/Mazel.

Waters, E. (1978). The reliability and stability of individual differences in infant-mother attachment. *Child Development, 49*, 483-494.

Waters, E., & Sroufe, L. A. (1983). Social competence as a developmental construct. *Developmental Review, 3*, 79-97.

White, R. (1959). Motivation reconsidered: The concept of competence. *Psychological Review, 66*, 297-333.

16

Maternal Beliefs and Children's Competence

Kenneth H. Rubin and Rosemary S.L. Mills

University of Waterloo

and

Linda Rose-Krasnor

Brock University

Maternal Beliefs and Children's Social Competence

How children acquire the capacity to interact competently with others and how they develop forms of less competent social behavior are critical questions in the study of child development. Because social relationships are of such central importance in everyday life, there may well be no skills more important than those required to sustain relationships. Thus, the achievement of social competence can be considered one end point of successful development. Aside from its intrinsic value, social competence may also be a marker of adaptive socio-emotional development. Children who lack social competence usually evidence a variety of other difficulties and are considered to be at risk for maladjustment later in life. For example, aggression and social withdrawal are two forms of problematic social behaviors in childhood that not only tend to persist but also tend to forecast poor personal and social adjustment in later years (e.g., Moskowitz, Schwartzman, & Ledingham, 1985; Parker & Asher, 1987; Rubin & Mills, 1988a).

Given the significance of social competence, it is important to explore its origins and consequences. A child's social skills are likely a function of various factors *internal* to the child such as cognitive ability (e.g., Green, Forehand, Beck, & Vosk, 1980) and physical appearance (Langlois & Downs, 1979), as well as of factors *external* to the child such as the reinforcement of specific behaviors by peers (Patterson, Littman, & Bricker, 1967). It is likely also that *parents* play a significant role in the development of their children's social competencies. This latter notion is clearly consistent with several major theories of child development.

From a *behavioral* perspective, parents shape specific social behaviors through conditioning and modeling processes. Children's tendencies to directly imitate adult communicative, prosocial and aggressive behaviors have been reported consistently in the literature; in addition, critical social behaviors have been described as responsive to reinforcement principles (Radke-Yarrow & Zahn-Waxler, 1986). A strong link between parental socialization techniques and the quality of children's peer relationships has been

313

B. H. Schneider et al. (eds.), Social Competence in Developmental Perspective, 313–331.
© *1989 by Kluwer Academic Publishers.*

central to proponents of social learning theory (Bandura, 1977; Sears, 1961). It has long been suggested that behaviors learned in the family are generalized to extra-familial peer settings. Although this premise has been supported in a number of studies (e.g., Patterson, 1979), in actuality, there have been surprisingly few studies of this association.

Psychoanalytic theorists have posited that the child's early relationship with the mother establishes an internalized model for future relationships with peers as well as with other adults. The quality of this early primary relationship is thought to depend primarily on the *mother's* behaviors. Similarly, parental behaviors are thought to determine the degree to which young children identify with their parents and internalize their moral standards and constraints (Maccoby & Martin, 1983). Accordingly, the development of the superego is thought to provide children with the ability to control aggression and with the motivation to perform prosocial acts. These two attributes are essential contributors to the child's status in the peer group and are criterial to the definition of social incompetence (Dodge, 1983).

Ethological adaptations of psychoanalytic models also provide the rationale for a strong association between "parenting" and the development of children's social skills (Ainsworth, 1973). Traditionally, the quality of the infant's attachment with his or her primary caregiver is thought to have its roots in maternal competence, responsiveness, and acceptance of the child. Thus, the links between security of attachment in infancy and the quality of peer relationships in childhood are attributed, at least partially, to maternal sources.

In our earlier writings, we have described two developmental models in which the infant's dispositional characteristics, together with the parents' ability to respond to those characteristics with sensitivity and nurturance, determine the quality of the infant/toddler-parent relationship and in turn the development of the child's social competence (see Rubin, LeMare, & Lollis, in press; Rubin & Lollis, 1988, for descriptions of these models). For example, in the first model, we link rather disparate areas of research and suggest that babies who are easily aroused by and overly sensitive to novel or unfamiliar stimuli, and whose parents are unresponsive, insensitive, and neglectful are more likely to develop an anxious-resistant attachment by infancy and to become anxious and socially withdrawn by early childhood, than are babies who are not so easily aroused and whose parents are able to respond nurturantly. Furthermore, we have postulated that some consequences of anxious withdrawal from the peer milieu may be the development of social relational difficulties, negative self-perceptions, and (ultimately) internalizing difficulties. Indeed, in data from the Waterloo Longitudinal Project, we have found some evidence that anxious withdrawal in early childhood is predictive of self-reported feelings of loneliness and depression in early adolescence (Rubin, Hymel, & Mills, in press; Rubin & Mills, 1988a).

A second developmental pathway that we have described (Rubin, LeMare, & Lollis, in press) begins with a temperamentally difficult baby who is neglected or responded to with insensitivity and inconsistency by his or her parents. Given such conditions, an insecure attachment relationship of an avoidant/hostile nature may result. Subsequently, when the child enters the peer milieu, he or she may evidence aggressive behavior directed proactively toward peers. One consequence of such negative behavior will likely be rejection by peers. Ultimately, the lack of interventive or ameliorative conditions may result in the development of externalizing disorders by late childhood or early adolescence. Once again, data from the Waterloo Longitudinal Project reveals a predictive connection between early aggression and peer rejection and subsequent assessments of hostile, aggressive, conduct-disordered behavior in early adolescence (Hymel, Rubin, Rowden, & LeMare, in press).

From our reading of the literature, it appears as if almost all major psychological theories that deal with the development of social competence place a primary responsibility on parental attributes and behaviors. These theories have provided historically the basis for a large number of empirical studies assessing the relations between parental characteristics and children's social skills. This body of research can be divided into three general streams.

The first research stream, and perhaps the oldest, centers on parental socialization strategies. In the earliest studies, parenting strategies were assessed by interview or questionnaire methodologies (Maccoby & Martin, 1983). The data indicated generally that rejecting, restrictive, and authoritarian parenting styles were negatively related with children's social competence, whereas warmth, responsivity, and authoritative techniques were associated positively with social skills (Baldwin, 1955; Baumrind, 1967).

More recently, observational measures of parenting have been used and researchers have reported that children's social skills can be predicted from parental behaviors. Mothers of popular children, for example, have been found to be less demanding, less disagreeable, more feeling-oriented and more likely to use positive verbalization than mothers of less popular children (Putallaz, 1987). Peer popularity has also been associated with observed parental use of reasoning behaviors (Roopnarine, 1987) and explanations (Roopnarine & Adams, 1987). In addition to these social status variables, differences in children's social behaviors have been associated with parental behaviors. Stevenson-Hinde, Hinde and Simpson (1986), for example, found that the amount of mother's positive interactions with her child at home inversely predicted the child's negative peer behaviors at preschool.

A second research stream has focused on the effects of early security of attachment. The research has generally demonstrated a reliable association between the quality of the parent-infant relationship and later social skills in the peer group (e.g., Sroufe & Fleeson, 1986). Although promising, longitudinal data supportive of this link are only slowly beginning to accumulate.

The third major research stream linking parental and child domains consists of studies concerning parents' cognitions or ideas about development; their attributions, expectations, and appraisals of children's behavior; and their expressed goals and the socialization strategies they believe to be most appropriate for promoting child development. Although this research stream has its origins in the early interview and questionnaire studies concerning socialization (e.g., Emmerich, 1969), it is actually the most "contemporary" stream given that it has been affected substantively by the cognitive and social-cognitive "revolution" that swept child social development research in the 1970s and early 1980s. Recent studies in this stream has demonstrated, for example, that parental attributions about children's behaviors influence their strategic and affective responses to those behaviors (Bugental & Shennum, 1984; Dix, Ruble, Grusec, & Nixon, 1986; Sameroff & Feil, 1985). Parental attributions, however, have not yet been directly and reliably linked to children's social skills. The association between parental cognitions and child behavior is thus an intriguing, underresearched, and most likely a highly complex one.

Recent reviews of parental beliefs and ideas (e.g., Goodnow, 1988; Miller, 1988; Sigel, 1982, 1985) have highlighted the significance of this domain for understanding the socialization process; these authors have emphasized collectively the need for additional data clarifying the relation between parental belief structures, parenting behaviors, and child "outcomes." A variety of theoretical models suggest the importance of parent-child interactions for the development of children's social skills, and these empirical data have yielded promising but incomplete support. Little is known about those factors that serve to influence variations in the quality of these interactions. It is this lack of knowledge that has inspired the latest series of studies in our research programme.

The Significance of Setting Conditions

As we see it, there may be certain conditions that set the stage for the development of parent-child relationships and that enhance or inhibit the development of social competence throughout childhood. We suggest that parent-child relationships and peer relationships, as well as the social skills that are enhanced or debilitated by these relationships, develop under an "umbrella" that we refer to as "setting conditions." These setting conditions, which are described below, include the socioecological, personal-social, and parental beliefs contexts within which development occurs.

Socioecological Setting Conditions. Despite Bronfenbrenner's seminal work concerning the significance of socioecological factors in human development (Bronfenbrenner, 1979; Bronfenbrenner & Crouter, 1983) and the work of other theorists who have considered such factors to play an important determining role in child development (Antonucci, 1976; Belsky, 1984; Belsky, Robins, & Gamble, 1984; Cochran & Brassard, 1979; Maccoby & Martin, 1983), there has been little research concerning the impact of the socioecological milieu, that is, environmental conditions existing external to the individual--on the parent-child relationship and the development of the child. Nevertheless, there is growing evidence that socioecological factors may set the stage for positive and negative developmental "outcomes" by influencing parental values, attitudes, and expectations concerning children as well as the quality of parent-child interaction. Thus, being economically disadvantaged, unemployed, or poorly housed may produce sufficient stress in the family so as to interfere with the ability of a parent to be sensitive and responsive to the needs of a child (e.g. Belsky, 1984; Belsky, Robins, & Gamble, 1984). For example, economic poverty and the stress that often accompanies it have been found to be associated with parental conflict (Elder, Caspi, & Burton, 1987) and parental anger, inconsistency, and punitiveness in child-rearing (Conger, McCarty, Yang, Lahey, & Kropp, 1984; Radke-Yarrow, Richters, & Wilson, 1988).

Personal-Social Setting Conditions. A second setting condition is comprised of those variables which stem from inter- and intra-individual sources rather than from external sources. This personal-social setting condition (Rubin, LeMare, & Lollis, in press) includes such variables as the psychological maturity and well-being of the parents, disruptions in the family system, and the availability of social support. Thus, the development of children's social competence may be influenced by factors such as maternal age and psychological functioning, marital conflict or breakdown, and the lack of a supportive social network. We know, for example, that older mothers interact more sensitively with their infants than younger mothers (Ragozin, Basham, Crnic, Greenberg, & Robinson, 1982); that infants' attachment relationships with the mother may prove to be insecure when she is or has been depressed (Radke-Yarrow, Cummings, Kuczynski, & Chapman, 1985; Spieker & Booth, 1988) and that mothers with more committed occupational identities and less role conflict report more confidence as parents and evidence more positive perceptions of their children (Alvarez, 1985; Frank, Hole, Jacobson, Justkowski, & Huyck, 1986). We know also that mothers who experience affectionate and relatively conflict-free marital relationships feel competent in their parenting roles and are observed to be sensitive, affectionate parents (Engfer, 1988). Finally, the availability of social support from relatives, friends, and spouse is negatively related to maternal restrictiveness and punitiveness (Colletta, 1979; Desfossés & Bouchard, 1987).

Needless to say, personal-social and socioecological setting conditions can interact with one another in both positive and negative ways. High-risk mothers who are single and poor and who lack social support are more likely to have insecure relationships with their infants than those who have the support of a partner as well as extra-familial social support (Spieker & Booth, 1988). Similarly, mothers who are poor feel less stress and are less authoritarian in their relationships with their preschoolers when they receive socio-emotional support from their mates and relatives (Zur-Szprio & Longfellow, 1981).

Parental Beliefs. The third setting condition that likely affects the development of social competence is comprised of the beliefs that parents have concerning developmental timetables, causes of development, the importance that parents attach to certain aspects of development, and parental cognitions about how children should best be socialized. Researchers have examined such issues as when it is that parents believe particular milestones should be reached (timetables) (Goodnow, Knight, & Cashmore, 1986), what characteristics parents consider most important for their children to develop (values) (Emmerich, 1969; Kohn, 1977; Stolz, 1967), why it is that these characteristics do or do not develop on time (causal attributions) (Dix & Grusec, 1985), and how it is that parents believe they can foster these characteristics (socialization strategies) (Emmerich, 1969). While much of this research is concerned with the development of physical-motor and cognitive skills, and there is a notable lack of relevant data concerning social development (see Goodnow, 1988; Miller, 1988 for recent reviews), there seems little doubt that parental belief systems are significant for the development of social competence. Surely, if parents have inaccurate perceptions concerning when it is possible for children to begin forming friendships, or if they believe that the causes of maladaptive social behaviors derive from biological or dispositional factors, or if they believe in folkloristic notions such as "spare the rod, spoil the child," then such beliefs should have some influence on the ways in which they respond to their children's behaviors and, in turn, the quality of the relationship that develops between them. These effects should, in turn, have some impact on children's social development.

It is important to note that parental belief systems most likely interact with the other setting conditions to facilitate or inhibit the quality of parent-child interaction. For example, with regard to socioecological setting factors, it has been found that parents of higher socioeconomic status are more likely than their counterparts of lower status to believe that children learn best by being active processors rather than passive recipients of direct instruction (McGillicuddy-DeLisi, 1982). In addition, there have been ample numbers of studies in which low performance by children on a variety of cognitive measures has been associated with parental teaching styles involving direct instruction; more perspectivistic or "distancing" teaching styles, on the other hand, are associated with competent performance (e.g., Hess & Shipman, 1965; Sigel, 1982). Given that beliefs may mediate behaviors and may themselves be influenced by sociocultural factors, the interrelations between parental beliefs and other setting conditions appear to be a significant, but as yet, understudied area vis-à-vis the development of social competence.

Our recent efforts to understand why parent-child relationships vary in quality have focused on the setting condition of parental beliefs. Of the three setting conditions, parental beliefs directly concern the child and hence are most closely related to the actual enactment of child-rearing strategies. As such, we consider the link between beliefs and strategies to be basic to an information processing model of parenting behavior. The processing model we offer herein is similar to that which we have described in our earlier writings concerning the development of social information-processing skills in children (Rubin & Krasnor, 1986).

An Information-Processing Model of Parenting Behavior. Briefly, the model specifies cognitive and affective processes that guide both parents' *proactive* behavior (the strategies they use to promote skilled or competent social behavior in their children) and their *reactive* behavior (the strategies they use to modify or eliminate the unskilled or unacceptable behaviors their children display). In the present report, we begin by considering proactive parental behavior. Such behavior is likely guided, at least in part, by the *goals* parents have concerning their children's social development. What are the social skills that parents aspire to promote in their children? For example, do parents want their children to be proficient at making friends? Do they want their children to learn how to share with others or be able to communicate effectively and persuasively with peers? If parents have such aspirations for their children, when is it that they believe particular social skills should be learned? Second, what socialization *strategies* do parents believe are most effective in implementing these goals? Third, what *intervening factors* occur in the flow from parental goals to the choice of socialization strategies? For example, it may be that parents' cognitions and perceptions concerning their own children's developmental and personality characteristics have an influence on their choice of socialization strategies.

We then consider information processes that likely guide the reactive strategies that parents use when their proactive goals are not met. When the desired skills are not evidenced "on time" and/or when maladaptive social behaviors are displayed, how do parents react *affectively*? To what causes do they *attribute* these problematic behaviors, and what *strategies* do they think they would use to modify them? Finally, we address the question of *why* it is that parents differ from one another in their affective reactions to and causal attributions about problematic social behaviors. Specifically, we examine the association between socioecological and personal-social setting factors and parental beliefs concerning the development of socially inept behaviors, and present data suggesting that parents' reactive socialization strategies may be a product of both setting factors and parental beliefs.

Maternal Beliefs Concerning the Development of Social Competence

In the first study, we examined parents' proactive beliefs, that is, when it is they expect children to learn specific social skills, how it is that they believe these skills are developed, and what they believe should be done to aid in the development of these skills. We also examined the relations between these parental beliefs and their children's social competence in preschool (see also Rose-Krasnor, 1988a, 1988b).

Fifty-eight mother-preschool child pairs participated in this initial study. The children (31 boys, 27 girls) attended one of nine preschools or day-care centers and were approximately 4-years of age (M=50.1 mo., S.D.=7.8 mo.).

Maternal Beliefs. The mothers were interviewed and asked a series of questions concerning their beliefs about the development of three social skills: (a) making friends; (b) sharing possessions; and (c) leading or influencing others. Mothers were first asked to rate, on a five-point scale, the importance of attaining each of the three skills.

Next, each mother was asked the reasons why she thought children might succeed or why they might fail in attaining these social goals. For each failure attribution, the mother was asked to indicate how difficult it would be for parents to change that reason. Attributions were classified into one of three general categories: (a) *child-centered* (e.g., "just born that way," "too insecure," "poor language skills"); (b) *external-direct* (e.g., "was never taught how," "wasn't punished for hitting others"); (c) *external-indirect* (e.g., "never had a chance to play with others," "was allowed to make decisions on her own").

318

Mothers were also asked to describe what parents should or should not do to help their child learn the three social skills. These socialization strategies were coded as being either high, moderate, or low in power assertion or as involving information seeking or planning. Strategies involving strong force or coercion--such as punishment, strong commands, and threats--were labeled *high* in power assertion. Strategies such as reasoning, modeling, and gentle directions were designated *moderate* in degree of power assertion. Parents also responded quite nondirectively at times (e.g., by redirecting the child's behavior); these responses were considered *low* power. Other responses were considered to be quite indirect because they did not involve direct interaction with the child; these included *information-seeking* (e.g., consulting the teacher) and *planful* strategies (e.g., arranging opportunities for peer play). Finally, there was a category for those responses that indicated that the parent would do *nothing*. Due to the low frequency of the low-power and information seeking strategies, these codes were combined with the moderate-power category.

Children's Social Competence. In order to assess the children's social competence, each child was observed during free play in his or her preschool classroom for 10 3-minute periods over 3 separate days. Observers used a micro-computer to record the child's social problem-solving goal, strategies, targets, and outcomes. *Goal* categories included (a) seeking assistance, (b) initiating or directing joint peer play, (c) initiating or directing solitary play, (d) stopping other's actions, and (e) seeking attention. *Strategy* categories were (a) verbal or nonverbal prosocial action, (b) verbal or nonverbal aggression, (c) direct commands, (d) indirect commands, and (e) questions. *Outcomes* were coded as failures, successes, requests for clarification, and partial successes.

In addition to the observational codings of social competence, each child's preschool teacher was requested to provide ratings on the Behar and Stringfield (1974) Preschool Behavior Questionnaire. This measure yields three reliable factors for Aggressive-Disruptive, Fearful-Anxious, and Hyperactive-Distractible behaviors (Rubin & Clark, 1983).

Results

A brief description of our major findings is presented below. A more detailed description of the study may be found in Rose-Krasnor (1988b).

Maternal beliefs. Mothers indicated that they expected children to master the three social skills *prior* to entering preschool. Thus, mothers expected that children should be able to make friends (M=1.92 yr.) significantly earlier than either sharing (M=2.61 yr.) or successfully leading or influencing others (M=2.78 yr.). Mothers also rated making friends and sharing as more important skills to master than being able to influence others.

Insofar as the attributional data were concerned, we discovered that mothers most frequently suggested that social skills developed as a result of child-centered causes. Least common were external-direct causes. This pattern differed across the social skills, however. For example, external-direct causes were more commonly given for the development of sharing skill than for friendship or leadership; child-centered attributions, however, were more frequently suggested for friendship and leadership abilities than for sharing. Thus, the mothers appeared to feel that friendship and leadership skills developed more "naturally" than sharing, and thus required less external direction.

The data also allowed examination of the relations between the parental *goals* of socializing each of three social skills and the *strategies* they suggested as most appropriate to help children learn these skills. Mothers more often suggested moderate-power, planful, and no response strategies than high-power socialization techniques across all three social skills domains. It is important to note, however, that some strategies were advocated more often than others for the socialization of the three particular social skills. For example, the development of sharing was seen to require the employment of *more* high- and moderate-power strategies than was the case for the other two skills. On the other hand, the development of friendship initiation and leadership skills was thought to require more planful and no response strategies than was the case for the development of sharing. Thus, the development of sharing was viewed by mothers as requiring greater and more direct parental involvement than the development of the abilities involved in making friends and influencing others. These results nicely complement the causal attribution data reported above, in which mothers indicated that the development of sharing stemmed from external-direct causes and that making friends and influencing others were more child-centered abilities.

Relating maternal beliefs and children's social skills. Over the 30 minutes of observation, an average of 37.4 (S.D.=15.8) social problem-solving attempts was recorded per child. Data concerning the frequencies of goals, strategies, and outcomes are reported in Rose-Krasnor (1988b). In this chapter, we describe the relations between the maternal beliefs data and the relative distribution of children's social goals, strategies, and outcomes. It should be noted that age was partialled form each of the computed correlations.

We begin first by noting the relations between maternal beliefs about the importance of the three social skills (a total score across all three skills) and their children's classroom behaviors. The data indicated that mothers who believed strongly that social skills are important had children who were more likely to have prosocial goals, who employed a relatively high frequency of indirect requests to achieve their goals, and who experienced a high degree of strategic success. Mothers who felt that the attainment of these skills was not so important had children who were more likely to have many stop action goals, to cry in order to achieve their goals, and to be rated by teachers as hyperactive-distractible. In short, we discovered that mothers who viewed the attainment of social skills as highly significant tended to have children who were socially competent.

Second, mothers who believed that it would be difficult to change their children's poor social performance had youngsters who demonstrated a number of difficulties. The children were more likely to attempt to stop the behaviors of others, they were less likely to use indirect requests to meet their social goals, and they were relatively unsuccessful in reaching their social goals.

Third, insofar as attributions are concerned, mothers who suggested more *external-direct* causes for the development or non-development of social skills, tended to have children who showed a relatively high overall frequency of directive attempts. In particular, the number of external-direct attributions offered by mothers was positively associated with their children's goals to begin social action and negatively associated with their children's attention-seeking goals. Children of these mothers also showed higher success levels and were rated by their teachers as less hyperactive than their peers.

When correlations for positive and negative characteristics were examined separately, positive child behaviors (i.e., relatively high levels of begin action, success and relatively low levels of attention-seeking and hyperactivity) were primarily associated only with external-direct attributions for positive outcomes, while only one negative behavior (hyperactive) was associated with external-direct attributions for unskilled outcomes.

On a hypothetical internal-external continuum of control and causality, external-direct and child-centered attributions are at opposite ends. Maternal child-centered attributions, across tasks and outcomes, were negatively correlated with children's direct and indirect commands. These children also had higher social failure and lower success percentages than their peers, and were rated by their teachers as more fearful and hyperactive. In contrast to the analyses for external-direct causes, child-centered attributions for positive and negative outcomes showed almost identical correlational patterns.

External-indirect attributions reflect causal beliefs that fall somewhere between child-centered and external-direct causes on the internal-external continuum. These attributions are primarily external in content but carry an implicit assumption of active child participation. For example, several mothers suggested that the most important reason why a child would be skilled at making friends was that the child's parents have brought their own friends home. The child, therefore, could watch how friends interact. In this example, the child needs to actively process the external input in order to become skilled (e..g., needs to abstract relevant information from models or practice observed skills in a social environment). External-indirect causal attributions made by the mothers were positively correlated with the child's direct and indirect commands and with social success. They were inversely related to social failure and teacher ratings of fearful behavior. When examined separately, the correlations for causal attributions regarding positive and negative outcomes showed patterns that were similar in direction, but weaker for positive than for negative outcomes.

Finally, insofar as parental beliefs concerning socialization strategies were concerned, we found that children whose mothers suggested the use of *high power* to socialize social skills were more likely to have assistance seeking goals, to approach teachers as social targets, and to use indirect and questioning social strategies. These children were less likely to try to stop others' actions and less likely to use aggressive social strategies to meet their goals. Their teachers rated them as fearful and anxious.

The suggestion of *moderate power* strategies was associated positively with a relatively dependent, adult-oriented interaction style. That is, children whose mothers advocated the use of moderate power produced a high relative frequency of attention seeking goals and a low relative frequency of begin action goals. These children made few directive attempts, and they had a high frequency of attempts in which they approached teachers as social targets.

Suggestions of *planful* strategies by the mothers were associated with a more assertive and independent style. Children whose mothers made frequent suggestions of planful strategies were less likely to seek attention, and were more likely to use aggressive, prosocial, and direct command strategies to meet their social goals. They were also less likely to have teachers as social targets and were less likely to persist after failure. Maternal choice of *no response* strategies showed no relation to observed social behavior.

Summary and Discussion

In summary, the data described in our first study make it quite clear how complex the parent-child interactive system must be as it relates to the development of children's social competence. Given the correlational, non-longitudinal nature of the study, the conclusions offered below must be considered speculative. However, they may provide some guidance for others who are sufficiently interested in following up on our conjectures.

First, we found that some mothers were more strongly committed than others to aid in the development of their children's social skills. Indeed, children of mothers who placed a high priority on the *goal* of social skill attainment, demonstrated well-developed social competencies. Thus, it may be that maternal socialization efforts are mediated by strong beliefs in the importance of social skill attainment and that such efforts are positively reinforced by their children's acquisition of social skills. Interestingly, we also found that mothers whose children were relatively socially competent believed that social skills, and the lack thereof, were caused by both direct and both indirect factors *external* to the child, such as parental teaching and the provision of opportunities for peer play. The implication of these data is that when a socially competent child demonstrates poor social performance, the mother's belief in the external role of causation, in conjunction with a relatively high value placed on social skills will probably increase the likelihood of effective parental action.

For children who did not evidence social competence, however, the picture painted was not so bright. The data revealed that mothers whose children had relatively poor social skills believed that once attained, poor social skills would be difficult to change. Furthermore, mothers of children with relatively poor social skills placed less importance on the development of social skills and were more likely to believe that the development of social competence was caused by factors *internal* to the child, such as personality or biogenetic factors. These beliefs have rather significant implications because they may serve to *decrease* efforts to aid in the socialization of social skills when social incompetence is manifested. The outcome of these beliefs may be to increase the probability of social maladjustment in the child.

Finally, the analyses of preferred strategies for teaching social skills indicated that mothers seemed to choose strategies that matched their children's interaction style. Mothers of children who were relatively adult-oriented and non-assertive tended to suggest strategies in which parents take primary control (direct teaching as well as punishment). In contrast, mothers of relatively assertive and independent children suggested the use of more indirect strategies to teach social skills. In their view, parents should become involved in arranging the environment to facilitate their children's social development, but should not specifically direct their children's social activities.

As with the attributional data, the direction of causality for these relations is impossible to determine. We simply cannot tell whether mothers adapted their preferred teaching styles to match their children's behavior or whether the children's behaviors developed as a result of the mothers' preferred styles. It is most probable that both processes led to the evolution of a complementary fit between mother and child. One implication of this "fit" between maternal cognitions and child behavior may be that it makes the pattern of parent-child interaction more consistent over time. Relatively high rates of *directive* adult involvement are likely to increase adult-oriented, non-assertive child behaviors. The planful management style offered by other mothers is likely to enhance assertive, independent behaviors in their offspring because initiatives are left to the child. Well-matched parent-child systems such as these, if they remain stable, will probably be more difficult to change as the child grows older.

The most important conclusion to be drawn from these findings is that meaningful relations do exist between maternal beliefs concerning the development of children's social skills and children's behaviors as observed in the classroom. We now turn to a study of maternal beliefs concerning children's *problematic* social behaviors. In this study, we ask what mothers feel, think, and do about these behaviors, and whether relations exist between these reactions and the setting conditions of socioecological context and personal-social resources.

Maternal Beliefs Concerning Problematic Social Behaviors

In the previous study, we described the beliefs that mothers have concerning their roles in the development of social competence. As such, these beliefs can be construed as

concerning the *proactive* socialization of desired skills. Parents, however, must not only be concerned with the proactive socialization of social skills, but they must also consider how to *react* to their children's display of problematic social behaviors. In this section, we describe the cognitive and affective reactions that mothers typically have to their children's display of two forms of problematic social behavior--aggression and withdrawal. The data consists of mothers' emotional appraisals, causal attributions, and anticipated socialization strategies vis-à-vis these behaviors. We consider also some of the socioecological and personal-social setting conditions that may influence variations in maternal reactions to their children's manifestation of aggression and withdrawal. Finally, we examine how mothers' affective reactions and attributional interpretations of their children's aggression and withdrawal may be related to their expected strategies.

Cognitive theories (e.g., Lazarus & Folkman, 1984; Weiner & Graham, 1984) suggest that *emotional reactions* to events depend on how the events are appraised. As indicated in the previous section, mothers expect their children to have developed some social skills by very early in childhood. We know also that by middle childhood, if not sooner, they perceive both aggression and withdrawal as problematic behaviors (Bacon & Ashmore, 1985). It is quite likely, then, that when problems of aggression and withdrawal occur, even in early childhood, mothers have some negative emotional reactions. But precisely what these reactions are and how strong they are we do not know. Evidence indicating that antisocial acts such as aggression make mothers feel more angry than other types of transgression (Grusec, Dix, & Mills, 1982) prompted us to speculate that anger might be a predominant reaction to aggression, and a stronger reaction to aggression than to social withdrawal. However, if anger is not the predominant response to withdrawal, then what is? Moreover, because emotional reactions are rarely unmixed (Diener & Iran-Nejad, 1988), it is also relevant to ask what other emotional reactions mothers have to aggression and withdrawal, and whether they differ for these two types of behavior.

Mothers not only react emotionally to their children's behaviors; they also attempt to interpret them. Thus, we assume that the ways in which mothers attempt to modify problematic social behaviors are mediated by their *causal beliefs* about these behaviors. Of special relevance is whether particular problematic social behaviors are attributed to external factors such as the situation the child is in, or to internal factors such as the child's personality. Because the behaviors of growing children are continually changing, it is unlikely that, in general, mothers would attribute very many behaviors to traits or enduring dispositions, particularly in early childhood. Moreover, we know that mothers' interpretations of their young children's behaviors are positively biased (Dix et al., 1986; Goodnow, 1984; Gretarsson & Gelfand, 1988). In early childhood, then, it seems unlikely that mothers would attribute either aggression or withdrawal to traits or permanent dispositions in the child. But it is not clear to what causes mothers do attribute these behaviors, and whether there are any differences between aggression and withdrawal in the types of causes that predominate in their thinking.

Finally, it is probably the case that the socialization strategies that mothers choose in reaction to their children's maladaptive behaviors depend on the particular behaviors displayed (Grusec & Kuczynski, 1980). Yet, there has been a paucity of research on the techniques parents think that they would use to modify or eliminate problematic social behaviors. Most of the available evidence concerns reactions to aggression. For example, in one study, mothers were asked what they would do if their elementary school-age child committed certain transgressions (Grusec et al., 1982). Mothers' responses indicated that they would use more force and less empathy training with antisocial acts such as aggression than they would with other types of transgressions--namely, those involving a failure to act prosocially (e.g., not sharing). Extrapolating from this evidence, it seems likely that mothers would respond more forcefully to aggression than to social withdrawal. More difficult to predict is what they think they would do about social withdrawal. For example, do they think it calls for explicit training and, if so, what techniques do they think they would use?

In the study that follows, we describe mothers' affective, attributional, and socialization reactions to their preschool children's aggressive and withdrawn behaviors and the relations between them.

The sample consisted of 132 mothers and their 4-year-old children (56 girls, 76 boys). The children attended one of 18 preschools or day-care centers. Mothers ranged widely in age (21 to 55), educational level (from not having completed high school to having advanced degrees), and occupational background.

Parental Beliefs. Mothers' causal attributions, emotional appraisals, and anticipated socialization strategies in response to aggression and social withdrawal were assessed by presenting them with descriptions of hypothetical incidents of peer-directed aggression and withdrawal, through either home interviews or mailed questionnaires. There were four stories, two describing aggressive acts with peers occurring either in an activity group or at home, and two describing social isolation at preschool or at a birthday party. Following each story, mothers were first asked how they would feel seeing their own child act this way several times in a row. Answers were rated on a 3-point scale for each of nine *emotions*: angry, embarrassed, amused, disappointed, concerned, pleased, surprised, puzzled, and guilty. Next, mothers answered two open-ended questions: "Why do you think your child has been acting this way?" and "What, if anything, would you do about your child's behavior?"

Causal beliefs were coded in terms of both locus and type of attribution. Distinctions were drawn between attributions made to internal stable factors, internal unstable factors, and external factors. Internal stable factors included such characteristics as *traits* or dispositions having the quality of consistency across situations and over time. Internal unstable factors involved *age or age-related* factors (e.g., a passing stage or a skill not yet learned), *transient states* (e.g., mood, fatigue), and *acquired habits*. External factors referred to *situational factors* that may have influenced the child's behavior.

Anticipated socialization strategies were coded as in the first study. As such the categories included the suggestions of using either high-, moderate-, or low-power assertion or information -seeking, planning, or no response.

Measures of socioecological and personal-social setting conditions. Mothers provided information concerning their age, education, and occupation, among other variables. In addition, each parent completed a life-events questionnaire consisting of a list of 30 life events considered by mental health professionals and teachers to require a certain amount of social readjustment on the part of the preschool child (Coddington, 1972). Finally, parents completed a questionnaire that assessed the availability of personal resources and social support (Personal Resources Questionnaire, Brandt & Weinert, 1981).

Results

A brief description of major findings is presented herein. More detailed descriptions of the study, including all archival statistical data may be found in Mills and Rubin (1988) and Rubin and Mills (1988b).

Parental Beliefs. When asked how they would feel if they observed their children behaving in a consistently aggressive manner, mothers reported that their predominant reaction would be one of *concern*, with anger and disappointment comprising secondary affective reactions. In response to the consistent observation of social withdrawal, once again the predominant affective reaction was concern followed closely by puzzlement and surprise. With respect to how mothers differentiated emotionally between aggression and withdrawal, we found that mothers felt more angry, disappointed and embarrassed about aggression than withdrawal, and they felt more puzzled about withdrawal than about aggression. Interestingly, mothers' affective reactions to their daughters' and sons' display of aggression and withdrawal did not differ.

With regard to causal attributions, we found that mothers did not view aggression and withdrawal as stable characteristics in early childhood. They attributed both behaviors primarily to *temporary* internal states such as age or mood. Relative to withdrawal, aggression was much more likely to be attributed to factors relating to the child's age. No other attributional differences between aggression and withdrawal were found. Again, mothers did not differentiate between daughters and sons.

The analysis of mothers' suggested socialization strategies revealed that *moderate*-power assertion was the preferred strategic response to aggression, whereas *low* power was the preferred response to withdrawal. It is important to note that both high- and moderate-power assertive techniques were chosen more often in response to aggression than withdrawal; low-power, information-seeking, and planful strategies were suggested more often in response to withdrawal. Again, mothers made no distinctions between how they would react strategically to this behavior in their sons versus their daughters.

Relations between setting conditions and parental beliefs. Are socioecological and personal-social stressors associated with maternal belief systems? Our first set of analyses concerned the relations between these setting condition factors and maternal affective reactions to their children's display of aggressive and withdrawn behaviors. We expected that mothers who reacted most negatively to their children's agonistic and solitary behaviors would be those who were experiencing the most environmental and personal-social stress. Our speculations were partially supported by the relations found between maternal occupational status and educational level (both socioecological setting conditions), the availability of social support (a personal-social setting condition), and the affective reactions of anger and disappointment in response to aggression and withdrawal. Thus, mothers of low occupational status often showed *disappointment* at their children's withdrawn behaviors. Low educational level and the lack of social support were associated with maternal *anger* in response to aggression. Interestingly, mothers of low occupational status and educational level were likely to report feelings of guilt in response to aggression; furthermore, low occupational status was related to guilt in response to withdrawal.

We also expected that mothers under a good deal of stress would be more likely to blame their children for their problematic social behaviors--that is, a positive association was predicted between the experience of stress and the suggestion that problematic behaviors resulted from factors internal to their children. In support of these speculations, we found that mothers with low levels of social support were more likely to attribute their children's aggressive behaviors to dispositional factors. Furthermore, mothers of low educational level were more likely to attribute their children's withdrawal to a trait.

Finally, we expected that the experience of stress would be associated with maternal choices of socialization strategies in response to their children's aggression and withdrawal. Furthermore, we expected that maternal attributions about and feelings toward children's maladaptive behaviors might contribute either independently or interactively (with the other setting condition variables) to predict the choice of socialization strategies. To examine these hypothesized relations, a series of hierarchical multiple regression analyses was computed, entering first into the equation maternal causal attributions (traits) and negative feelings (anger and disappointment) about children's problematic behaviors, followed in a separate step by the setting condition variables of the mother's occupational and educational status (socioecological conditions), and social support and the experience of negative life events (personal-social conditions). The dependent variables were the choice of high-, moderate-, and low-power assertive techniques and no response to their children's display of aggressive and withdrawn behavior.

We found that the choice of *high*-power assertive strategies in reaction to children's display of *aggression* was predicted not only by the maternal affective response of anger and disappointment, but also by maternal lack of social support. An interaction effect revealed that among mothers who reported anger in response to their children's agonistic behavior, the more social support available to them, the less they chose to use high-power assertive strategies. In short, the availability of social support tempered the relation between maternal anger in response to their children's aggression and the mother's own reactive choice of high-power strategies.

The choice of *high*-power strategies in response to *withdrawal* was predicted significantly by the experience of many negative life events in the previous year and by the lack of available social support. Given that the preferred strategic reaction of choice to withdrawal was the use of low-power techniques, these data are rather compelling. It is not unreasonable to suggest that the use of coercive strategies to deal with social withdrawal is an inappropriate overreaction. Thus, the fact that stress predicted such a maternal choice is rather telling.

A second significant result was evidenced for the choice of *low*-power strategies in response to withdrawal. The choice of this modal response to withdrawal was significantly predicted by the lack of a negative affective response to such behavior. Finally, the choice of *not responding* was significantly predicted by maternal beliefs that the primary cause of socially withdrawn behavior emanated from dispositional, trait-like factors.

Summary and Discussion

The second study concerned maternal beliefs about their children's aggressive and withdrawn behaviors and whether such beliefs are associated with socio-ecological and personal-social setting condition factors. As one might expect, mothers reported more intense negative reactions to their children's aggressive behaviors than to their withdrawn behaviors. Although the predominant affective response to both behaviors was that of concern, aggression elicited significantly more reported anger and disappointment, whereas withdrawal elicited more puzzlement and surprise. These data suggested that the construct of withdrawal may be somewhat of a mystery for mothers of 4-year-olds. Indeed, until fairly recently, withdrawal has remained an enigma for psychologists! We know now that, in general, social solitude in the preschool years is *not* a non-normative form of behavior, and that it is not associated concurrently with indices of maladaptation (Rubin, 1982). In actuality, quiet, sedentary, constructive solitary activity is viewed by teachers as rather benign. Yet, we also know that from early in childhood, the phenomenon is fairly stable (Rubin, Hymel, & Mills, in press), that sedentary, quiescent solitude prior to the elementary school years is predictive of internalizing difficulties five years hence (Rubin, Hymel, & Mills, in press); and that by the early elementary school years, it is associated concurrently with numerous indices of maladaptation such as anxiety and poor self-image (Rubin, 1985). Finally, we know that social withdrawal becomes increasingly salient to parents, teachers and peers with the increasing age of the child (Bacon & Ashmore, 1985; Younger, Schwartzman & Ledingham, 1986). Certainly, by the mid-to-late years of childhood, social withdrawal is a highly salient behavior. Given the complexity of the phenomenon, it is therefore not surprising that mothers would not know what to make of their preschool-aged child's display of social withdrawal.

The attributional data indicated that mothers viewed both aggression and withdrawal as caused by temporary or transient states such as mood or fatigue. Aggression was more often assumed than withdrawal to be caused by age-related phenomena ("She's only 4; she'll grow out of it."). Finally, mothers indicated that aggressive behavior most often should be dealt with by moderate power assertive responses, low-power was the preferred response to withdrawal. Furthermore, the forceful strategies of high- and moderate-power were advocated more often for children's aggression whereas low-power, information seeking, and planful socialization strategies were associated more often with withdrawal. Thus, as with the affective data, mothers appeared to have a clearer, personal, idea of the meaning of aggression than of withdrawal. Aggression more often elicited anger and thus could be viewed as an unwanted, negative form of behavior; as a consequence, aggression was dealt with more harshly than withdrawal. Withdrawal, on the other hand, elicited surprise, and as such, low-power assertive techniques or the seeking of information about the behavior were the socialization reactions of choice.

It is important to add, at this point, that these data probably reflect the amount of information available to parents from media sources about aggressive and withdrawn behaviors in childhood. Moreover, as children are being "prepared" for elementary school, teachers and parents are likely to focus their educational and disciplinary efforts on the inhibition of aggression and on the reinforcement of quiet, constructive play. Consequently, it is no wonder that solitary play is reacted to with puzzlement and a search for more information.

Despite the more negative view of aggression, it is nevertheless the case that reactions to both behaviors shared several similarities. For example, both behaviors elicited a high degree of concern. The suggestion of coercive, high power assertive responses would have to be considered as non-preferred *overreactions* to both behaviors. Moreover, both behaviors were far less likely to be attributed to the child's personality or to biological/genetic factors than to transient states. It is interesting, therefore, that when high-power assertive strategies and dispositional causal attributions were chosen, the mothers were more likely to be experiencing a good deal of stress or a lack of social support.

The clearest example of the relation between parental beliefs and the other setting conditions concerns what we would consider a most inappropriate parental response to withdrawal; that is, the use of coercive, high-power assertive strategies. We found that the choice of such techniques was predicted by the experience of many negative and critical life events in the previous 12 months. Not reacting with high power, however, was predicted by the availability of social support. In many ways these data are reminiscent of Garmezy's (1983) discussions of "stress-resistant" children--children who experience a good deal of stress and yet appear to be invulnerable to these stressors. The children who are most stress-resistant are likely to have parents who themselves have access to familial and extra-familial support. Garmezy's description of stress resistance reminds us further of an insightful statement by Patterson (1983) who indicated that it is not children who are directly at risk because of stress, it is the family system."

In our study, we focussed on the *mother* and we found that the availability of social support moderates the influence of negative life circumstances and predicts the low use of coercive socialization reactions to withdrawal. Furthermore, in another set of analyses, we discovered that maternal anger, which predicts the use of high-power in response to aggression, is moderated by the availability of social support. In short, when mothers are stressed by environmental circumstances or by momentary affective reactions to aversive behavior, the existence of a supportive environment serves to moderate their choice of socialization behaviors. These data are rather significant given that we know, from our first study that mothers who chose to use forceful, coercive strategies were those whose children were the least socially competent.

Although we have suggested some interpretations of our findings, we offer them tentatively and with full acknowledgement that several significant factors are missing from both studies. For one, we simply asked mothers to *say* how they would respond to the exhibition of aggression and withdrawal; consequently, we cannot be certain how the mothers would actually respond to such behaviors in their children. For another, we investigated only one-half of the typical child's parenting unit; we have not examined *paternal* belief systems or how fathers would interact with their children. And finally, we studied mothers of normal *preschool-age* children; we have examined neither the *developmental* relations between setting conditions and child behavior nor the behaviors of extreme groups of aggressive and withdrawn boys and girls as they relate to parental beliefs and behaviors. In the current phase of our research, we are beginning to examine these factors.

Conclusion

In the present report, we set out to consider parental *beliefs* concerning socially competent and incompetent behaviors. First, we asked mothers questions concerning the importance, the time-tabling, and the causes of social skills development. In a second study, we asked mothers what they would think, feel, and do about displays of aggression and withdrawal by their children. We also examined the links between their beliefs and the setting factors of socioecological and personal-social contexts. Finally, in the first study, parental beliefs were linked to observations of children's behaviors. The data gleaned from these studies illustrate the importance of considering the potential role of setting conditions in general, and parental beliefs in particular, in the child's social development. Mothers' beliefs appear to play some role in guiding not only their proactive efforts to teach social skills but also the reactive strategies that they adopt when their children display problematic social behaviors. These beliefs, together with the environments of demands and resources within which mothers carry out their role, appear to be important in determining how they choose to teach their children social skills or to react to their children's social difficulties. Of particular significance are maternal tendencies to attribute social skills and difficulties to causes within the child rather than to external causes, because these tendencies appear to be associated with maternal stress and poor social adjustment.

In summary, our initial studies have yielded some meaningful concurrent relations between maternal beliefs, socioecological and personal-social setting conditions, and children's social competence. We believe that mothers' current belief systems have emerged out of their earlier relationships with their children, as well as out of their personal-social and socioecological histories. Moreover, these belief systems will likely guide their socialization behaviors in everyday interactions with their children, and in turn, will influence the quality of the parent-child relationship. It is the character of this relationship that provides the basis for the future development of social competence.

References

Ainsworth, M.D. (1973). The development of infant-mother attachment. In B. Caldwell & H. Ricciuti (Eds.), *Review of child development research. Vol. 3* (pp. 1-94). Chicago: University of Chicago Press.

Alvarez, W.F. (1985). The meaning of maternal employment for mothers and their perceptions of their three-year-old children. *Child Development, 56*, 350-360.

Antonucci, T.C. (1976). Attachment: A life-span concept. *Human Development, 19*, 135-142.

Bacon, M.K., & Ashmore, R.D. (1985). How mothers and fathers categorize descriptions of social behavior attributed to daughters and sons. *Social Cognition, 3*, 193-217.

Baldwin, J. (1955). *Behavior and development in childhood.* New York: Dreyden.

Bandura, A. (1977). *Social learning theory.* Englewood Cliff, NJ: Prentice-Hall.

Baumrind, D. (1967). The development of instrumental competence through socialization. In A. Pick (Ed.), *Minnesota symposia on child psychology, Vol. 7* (pp.3-46). Minneapolis: University Minnesota Press.

Behar, L., & Stringfield, S.A. (1974). A behaviour rating scale for the preschool child. *Developmental Psychology, 10*, 601-610.

Belsky, J. (1984). The determinants of parenting: A process model. *Child Development, 55*, 83-96.

Belsky, J., Robins, E., & Gamble, W. (1984). The determinants of parental competence: Toward a contextual theory. In M. Lewis (Ed.), *Beyond the dyad* (pp. 251-279). New York: Plenum.

Brandt, P.A., & Weinert, C. (1981). The PRQ - A social support measure. *Nursing Research, 30*, 277-280.

Bronfenbrenner, U. (1979). *The ecology of human development.* Cambridge, MA: Harvard University Press.

Bronfenbrenner, U., & Crouter, A.C. (1983). The evolution of environmental models in developmental research. In W. Kessen (Ed.), *Handbook of child psychology: Vol 1. History, theory, and methods* (pp. 357-414). New York: Wiley.

Bugental, D.B., & Shennum, W. (1984). "Difficult" children as elicitors and targets of adult communication patterns: An attributional transactional analysis. *Monographs of the Society for Research in Child Development, 49* (1, Serial No. 205).

Cochran, M., & Brassard, J. (1979). Child development and personal social networks. *Child Development, 50*, 601-616.

Coddington, R.D. (1972). The significance of life events as etiologic factors in the diseases of children. A survey of professionals. *Journal of Psychosomatic Research, 16*, 7-18.

Colletta, N. (1979). Support systems after divorce: Incidence and impact. *Journal of Marriage and the Family, 41*, 837-846.

Conger, R.D., McCarty, J.A., Yang, R.K., Lahey, B.B., & Kropp, J.P. (1984). Perception of child, child-rearing values, and emotional distress as mediating links between environmental stressors and observed maternal behavior. *Child Development, 55*, 2234-2247.

Desfossés, E., & Bouchard, C. (1987), April). *Using coercive behaviors with children: Stressors, conflictual relationships and lack of support in the life of mothers.* Paper presented at the Biennial Convention of the Society for Research in Child Development, Baltimore.

Diener, E., & Iran-Nejad, A. (1988). The relationship in experience between various types of affect. *Journal of Personality and Social Psychology, 50*, 1031--1038.

Dix, T.H., & Grusec, J.E. (1985). Parent attribution processes in the socialization of children. In I.E. Sigel (Ed.), *Parental belief systems: The psychological consequences for children* (pp. 201-233). Hillsdale, NJ: Lawrence Erlbaum.

Dix, T.H., Ruble, D.N., Grusec, J.E., & Nixon, S. (1986). Social cognition in parents: Inferential and affective reactions to children of three age levels. *Child Development, 57*, 879-894.

Dodge, K.A. (1983). Behavioral antecedents of peer social status. *Child Development, 54*, 1386-1389.

Elder, G.H., Caspi, A., & Burton, L.M. (1987). Adolescent transitions in developmental perspective: Historical and sociological insights. In M. Gunnar (Ed.), *Minnesota Symposia on Child Psychology* (Vol. 21). Hillsdale, NJ: Erlbaum.

Emmerich, W. (1969). The parental role: A functional cognitive approach. *Monograph of the Society for Research in Child Development, 34*, (8, Serial No. 132).

Engfer, A. (1988). The interrelatedness of marriage and the mother-child relationship. In R. Hinde & J. Stevenson-Hinde (Eds.), *Relations between relationships within families* (pp. 194-118). Oxford, U.K.: Oxford University Press.

Frank, S., Hole, C.B., Jacobson, S., Justkowski, R., & Huyck, M. (1986). Psychological predictors of parents' sense of confidence and control and self- versus child-focused gratifications. *Development Psychology, 22*, 348-355.

Garmezy, N. (1983). Stressors of childhood. In N. Garmezy & M. Rutter (Eds.), *Stress, coping and development in children* (pp. 43-84). New York: McGraw-Hill.

Goodnow, J.J. (1984). Parents' ideas about parenting and development: A review of issues and recent work. In M.E. Lamb, A.L. Brown, & B. Rogoff (Eds.), *Advances in developmental psychology* (Vol. 3, pp. 193-242). Hillsdale, NJ,: Erlbaum.

Goodnow, J.J. (1988). Parents' ideas, actions, and feelings: Models and methods from developmental and social psychology. *Child Development, 59,* 286-320.

Goodnow, J.J., Knight, R., & Cashmore, J. (1986). Adult social cognition: Implications of parents' ideas for approaches to development. In M. Perlmutter (Ed.), *Cognitive perspectives on children's social and behavioral development. Vol. 18. The Minnesota Symposia on Child Psychology* (pp. 287-329). Hillsdale, NJ: Erlbaum.

Green, K., Forehand, R., Beck, S., & Vosk, B. (1980). An assessment of the relationship among measures of children's social competence and children's academic achievement. *Child Development, 51,* 1149-1156.

Gretarsson, S.J., & Gelfand, D.M. (1988). Mothers' attributions regarding their children's social behavior and personality characteristics. *Developmental Psychology, 24,* 264-269.

Grusec, J.E., Dix, T., & Mills, R. (1982). The effects of type, severity, and victim of children's transgressions on maternal discipline. *Canadian Journal of Behavioural Science, 14,* 276-289.

Grusec, J.E., & Kuczynski, L.(1980). Direction of effect in socialization: A comparison of the parent vs. the child's behavior as determinants of disciplinary techniques. *Developmental Psychology, 16,* 1-9.

Hess, R.D., & Shipman, V.C. (1965). Early experience and socialization of cognitive modes in children. *Child Development, 36,* 869-886.

Hymel, S., Rubin, K.H., Rowden, L., & LeMare, L. (in press). A longitudinal study of sociometric status in middle and late childhood. *Child Development.*

Kohn, M.L. (1977). *Class and conformity: A study in values* (2nd edition). Chicago: University of Chicago Press.

Langlois, J., & Downs, C. (1979). Peer relations as a function of physical attractiveness: The eye of the beholder or behavioral reality? *Child Development, 50,* 409-418.

Lazarus, R.S., & Folkman, S. (1984). *Stress, appraisal, and coping.* New York: Springer.

Maccoby, E.E., & Martin, J.A. (1983). Socialization in the context of the family: Parent-child interaction. In P.H. Mussen (Series Ed.) and E.M. Hetherington, (Vol. Ed.) *Handbook of child psychology; Vol. 4. Socialization, personality, and social development* (pp. 1-101). New York: Wiley.

McGillicuddy-DeLisi, A. (1982). The relationship between parents' beliefs about development and family constellation, socio-economic status, and parents' teaching strategies. In L.M. Laosa & I.E. Sigel (Eds.), *Families as learning environments for children* (pp. 261-299). New York: Plenum.

Miller, S.A. (1988). Parents' beliefs about children's cognitive development. *Child Development, 59,* 259-285.

Mills, R.S.L., & Rubin, K.H. (1988, June). *Socialization factors associated with aggression and withdrawal in early childhood.* Paper presented at the Annual Convention of the Canadian Psychological Association, Montreal.

Moskowitz, D.S., Schwartzman, A.E., & Ledingham, J.E. (1985). Stability and change in aggression and withdrawal in middle childhood and early adolescence. *Journal of Abnormal Psychology, 94,* 30-41.

Parker, J.G., & Asher, S.R. (1987). Peer acceptance and later personal adjustment: Are low-accepted children "at risk"? *Psychological Bulletin, 102,* 357-389.

Patterson, G.R. (1979). A performance theory for coercive family interaction. In R. Cairns (Ed.), *The analyses of social interactions: Methods, issues and illustrations* (pp. 119-162). Hillsdale, NJ LEA.

Patterson, G.R. (1983). Stress: A change agent for family process. In N. Garmezy & M. Rutter (Eds.), *Stress, coping and development in children* (pp. 235-264). New York: McGraw-Hill.

Patterson, G.R., Littman, R., & Bricker, W. (1967). Assertive behavior in children: A step toward a theory of aggression. *Monographs of the Society for Research in Child Development, 32,* (Serial No. 113).

Putallaz, M. (1987). Maternal behavior and children's sociometric status. *Child Development, 58,* 324-340.

Radke-Yarrow, M., Cummings, E.M., Kuczynski, L., & Chapman, M. (1985). Patterns of attachment in two- and three-year-olds in normal families and families with parental depression. *Child Development, 50,* 884-893.

Radke-Yarrow, M., Richters, J., & Wilson, W.E. (1988). Child Development in a network of relationships. In R. Hinde & J. Stevenson-Hinde (Eds.), *Relations between relationships within families.* Oxford, U.K.: Oxford University Press.

Radke-Yarrow, M., & Zahn-Waxler, C. (1986). The role of familial factors in the development of prosocial behavior: Research findings and questions. In D. Olweus, J. Block & M. Radke-Yarrow (Eds.) *Development of antisocial and prosocial behavior* (pp. 207-234). Orlando: Academic Press.

Ragozin, A.S., Basham, R.B., Crnic, K.A., Greenberg, M.T., & Robinson, N.M. (1982). Effects of maternal age on parenting role. *Developmental Psychology, 18,* 627-634.

Roopnarine, J.L. (1987). Social interaction in the peer group: Relationship to perceptions of parenting and to children's interpersonal awareness and problem-solving ability. *Journal Applied Developmental Psychology, 8,* 351-362.

Roopnarine, J.L., & Adams, G.R. (1987). The interactional teaching patterns of mothers and fathers with their popular, moderately popular, or unpopular children. *Journal of Abnormal Child Psychology, 15*, 125-136.

Rose-Krasnor, L. (1988a, May). *Maternal beliefs and preschool social skill*. Paper presented at the Fifth Biennial University of Waterloo Conference on Child Development, Waterloo, Ontario.

Rose-Krasnor, L. (1988b). Parental socialization and peer skills. Unpublished grant report to the Social Sciences and Humanities Research Council of Canada.

Rubin, K.H. (1982). Non-social play in preschoolers. Necessarily evil? *Child Development, 53*, 651-657.

Rubin, K.H. (1985). Socially withdrawn children: An "at risk" population? In B. Schneider, K.H. Rubin, & J. Ledingham (Eds.), *Children's peer relations: Issues in assessment and intervention* (pp. 125-139). New York: springer-Verlag.

Rubin, K.H., & Clark, M.L. (1983). Preschool teachers' ratings of behavioral problems: Observational, sociometric, and social-cognitive correlates. *Journal of Abnormal Child Psychology, 11*, 273-285.

Rubin, K.H., Hymel, S. & Mills, R.S.L. (in press). Sociability and social withdrawal in childhood: Stability and outcomes. *Journal of Personality.*

Rubin, K.H., & Krasnor, L.R. (1986). Social-cognitive and social behavioral perspectives on problem solving. In M. Perlmutter (Ed.), *Cognitive perspectives on children's social and behavioral development. Vol. 18. The Minnesota Symposia on Child Psychology* (pp. 1-68). Hillsdale, NJ: Lawrence Erlbaum.

Rubin, K.H., LeMare, L., & Lollis, S. (in press). Social withdrawal in childhood: Developmental pathways to peer rejection. In S.R. Asher & J.D. Coie (Eds.), *Children's status in the peer group.* New York: Cambridge University Press.

Rubin, K.H., & Lollis, S. (1988). Beyond attachment. In J. Belsky & T. Nezworski (Eds.), *Clinical implications of attachment.* Hillsdale, NJ: Erlbaum.

Rubin, K.H., & Mills, R.S.L. (1988a). The many faces of social isolation in childhood. *Journal of Consulting and Clinical Psychology, 56*, 916-924.

Rubin, K.H., & Mills, R.S.L. (1988b). *Mothers' and fathers' emotional reactions and socialization responses to their children's aggression and withdrawal.* Paper presented at the Fifth Biennial University of Waterloo Conference on Child Development, Waterloo, Ontario.

Sameroff, A., & Feil, L.A. (1985). Parental concepts of development. In I. Sigel (Ed.), *Parental belief systems: The psychological consequences for children* (pp. 83-105). Hillsdale, NJ: LEA.

Sears, R.R. (1961). Relation of early socialization experiences to aggression in middle childhood. *Journal of Abnormal and Social Psychology, 63*, 466-492.

Sigel, I.E. (1982). The relationship between parents' distancing strategies and the child's cognitive behavior. In L.M. Laosa & I.E. Sigel (Eds.), *Families as learning environments for children* (pp. 47-86). New York: Plenum.

Sigel, I.E. (Ed.) (1985). *Parental belief systems.* Hillsdale, NJ: LEA.

Spieker, S., & Booth, C. (1988). Maternal antecedents of attachment quality. In J. Belsky & T. Nezworski (Eds.), *Clinical implications of attachment* (pp. 95-135). Hillsdale, NJ: Erlbaum.

Sroufe, L.A. & Fleeson, J. (1986). Attachment and the construction of relationships. In W. Hartup & Z. Rubin (Eds.), *The nature and development of relationships.* Hillsdale, N.J.: Erlbaum.

Stevenson-Hinde, J., Hinde, R., & Simpson, A. (1986). Behavior at home and friendly or hostile behavior in preschool. In D. Olwens, J. Block, & M. Radke-Yarrow (Eds.), *Development of antisocial and prosocial behavior* (pp. 127-145). Orlando, FL: Academic Press.

Stolz, L.M. (1967). *Influences on parent behavior.* Stanford, CA: Stanford University Press.

Weiner, B., & Graham, S. (1984). An attributional approach to emotional development. In C. Izard, J. Kagan, & R. Zajonc (Eds.), *Emotions, cognitions, and behavior* (pp. 167-191). New York: Cambridge University Press.

Younger, A.J., Schwartzman, A.E., & Ledingham, J. (1986). Age related differences in children's perceptions of social deviance: Changes in behavior or perspective? *Developmental Psychology, 22*, 531-542.

Zur-Szprio, S., & Longfellow, C. (1981, April). *Support from fathers; Implications for the well-being of mothers and their children.* Paper presented at the biennial Meeting of the Society for Research on Child Development, Boston.

Section V

Translating Theory Into Practice:
Social Competence Promotion Programs

Challenges Inherent in Translating Theory and Basic Research into Effective Social Competence Promotion Programs

Roger P. Weissberg

Yale University

The first four sections of this volume contribute substantially to the expanding theoretical and research literature on the emergence of social competence and its relation to mental health. For example, several chapters identify associations between social competence deficits and current and later interpersonal, academic, and psychological problems (e.g., Asher & Parker, Chapter 1; Coie, Christopoulos, Terry, Dodge, & Lochman, Chapter 11). Others suggest that social competence serves as a protective factor against psychopathology (e.g., Garmezy, Chapter 2; Ladd, Chapter 14). These chapters provide strong rationales for social competence promotion (SCP) programs both to treat and prevent social maladjustment in children and adolescents.

As investigators attempt to establish effective intervention and preventive SCP programs, one key issue is the extent to which basic research and theory can inform their successful design and implementation. The three chapters comprising Section Five highlight many of the concerns and complexities that confront SCP program developers (Caplan & Weissberg, Chapter 19; Furman, Giberson, White, Gavin, & Wehner, Chapter 18; Schneider, Chapter 17). They are consistent in their assessment that knowledge of social competence research and theory is a necessary, albeit insufficient factor for conducting successful interventions.

A variety of training approaches have been employed to promote social competence in children and adolescents (Ladd & Mize, 1983; Michelson, Sugai, Wood, & Kazdin, 1983). The common objective of these procedures is to train a combination of behavioral, cognitive, and/or affective skills that will enhance individuals' capacities to interact effectively with others and to handle social tasks adaptively. Social skills training interventions have been applied successfully to children and adolescents with such diverse target problems as aggressiveness and social isolation. Recent reviews also indicate that the promotion of social competence through educational interventions for all school children represents an important strategy for the primary prevention of a variety of negative psychosocial outcomes (Zins & Forman, 1988; Weissberg & Allen, 1986).

Despite of their optimism about the potential benefits of SCP training, the authors in Section Five also emphasize the difficulties in the design and implementation of SCP interventions. In developing a heuristic framework for establishing SCP programs,

335

B. H. Schneider et al. (eds.), Social Competence in Developmental Perspective, 335–338.
© 1989 by Kluwer Academic Publishers.

Weissberg, Caplan, and Sivo (1989) note that basic research and theory provide an instructive start to investigators as they develop initial plans about a program's goals, training methods, and content. Although the first sixteen chapters of this volume offer many constructive ideas and research findings to enrich the conceptual base for SCP program developers, several other considerations become critical as researchers attempt to translate theory and empirical findings into SCP programs that successfully promote adaptive social behavior and positive developmental outcomes. Successful SCP program development also requires attention to the tasks of program design, implementation, evaluation, and institutionalization (Weissberg et al., 1989).

Program *design* involves writing a developmentally and culturally sensitive curriculum and associated teaching materials with clearly specified, replicable guidelines for effective implementation. The creation of a detailed, informative training manual, however, does not automatically result in a properly implemented program. Program *implementation* involves the adaptation of a curriculum to suit the specific needs and characteristics of trainers and trainees as well as the ecological realities of the setting in which the program is conducted. Furthermore, steps must be taken (e.g., high quality supervision and on-site coaching of trainers) to ensure that the individuals who provide SCP training carry out the program with fidelity to the intervention model (Hall & Hord, 1987). Program *evaluation* concerns the use of valid and reliable assessment procedures to document: the extent and quality of program implementation; intervention impact on children's skills and behavior; and the combination of implementation, program, and ecological factors that contribute to the promotion of children's social competence. Finally, program *institutionalization* requires the clear delineation of critical program practices and the establishment of system-level supports and policies to facilitate the high-quality maintenance of service delivery during future years.

Each of the following chapters offers several important considerations for investigators who aspire to forge the difficult link between SCP theory and application. In Chapter 17, Schneider discusses the implications of a meta-analysis suggesting that social skills training (SST) is a moderately effective treatment approach for children with peer relationship and behavior problems. Despite the generally positive findings, this chapter identifies several "cleavages between theory and practice" that contribute to the variability of SST outcome findings. After examining the validity of various theoretical assumptions underlying SST and how they inform intervention practices, Schneider illustrates how variables that are seemingly unrelated to theoretically based SST models of behavior change may actually influence treatment outcomes.

Schneider's chapter highlights the importance of social skills trainers' behaviors--such as friendliness, spontaneity, and self-assurance--that may enhance positive outcomes. Although such factors are rarely included as explicit components of theoretical SST training models, they are especially important as they motivate children and adolescents to understand and apply the target skills. Even some ostensibly unimportant variables such as the age of a trainer may influence the effectiveness of treatment. For example, adolescents may be more responsive to modeling and feedback offered by a peer rather than an adult. Schneider also argues for the necessity of implementing social skills programs properly, and expresses concern that few researchers document the fidelity and quality of program implementation. Finally, the social environment is viewed as a powerful force that may enhance or inhibit the child's ability to enact the skills learned in the context of training. Thus, while certain treatments may succeed based on what occurs in the training setting, others may require modification or the involvement of significant others (e.g., family members, teachers) in a child's life in order to foster positive developmental outcomes.

Introduction to Section V

In Chapter 18, Furman, Giberson, White, Gavin & Wehner emphasize the importance of system-level influences when conducting school-based, primary prevention programs that train teachers to enhance their students' social competence. In discussing their own school-based SCP research, Furman et al. offer the bold hypothesis that systems processes may contribute more powerfully than program-specific processes in producing positive effects on students' behaviors. Although research has demonstrated that many SCP strategies (e.g., fostering cooperative interactions, changing students' motivational structures, teaching social or cognitive skills) have potential to improve children's peer relations, it appears likely that program effectiveness has less to do with specific training components or theoretical approaches and more to do with understanding how to collaborate with a system so that a program will be implemented effectively.

Furthermore, Furman et al. identify many systems variables that may influence whether or not a program succeeds. For example, the format and quality of teacher training--which involves the establishment of rapport between consultants and teachers, the presentation of SCP materials, consultant modeling of training methods, practice by teachers with feedback, and follow-up coaching in the classroom--relates to both implementation practices and program effects. The receptiveness and support of school principals and district administrators (the officials responsible for the administration of American schools) can also determine the extent to which a program is implemented, as well as whether a program will be continued from year to year. Furman et al.'s descriptions of their consultation experiences, especially one of their unsuccessful efforts, compellingly illustrate how knowledge of a setting and system-entry practices centrally influence if and how well SCP programs are conducted.

The authors point out that a major shortcoming in the intervention evaluation literature is the failure of most investigators to assess how well SCP programs are implemented. In many instances, programs fail to produce positive results because they are implemented idiosyncratically, poorly, or not at all. The authors emphasize the need for employing a systematic approach to evaluate change, to identify modal patterns of implementation, and to ascertain the relationships between program implementation and behavioral outcomes.

In Chapter 19, Caplan and Weissberg underscore the importance of developmental and ecological variables in designing and implementing school-based, primary prevention SCP programs for young adolescents. Three conditions critical for the development of socially competent behavior are emphasized in their programming efforts: (a) young adolescents must have the cognitive, affective, and behavioral skills to succeed in a social setting; (b) they must have multiple opportunities for meaningful positive involvements to apply these skills; and (c) those with whom they interact must consistently reinforce competent behavioral performance (Hawkins & Weis, 1985). Following this framework, they propose that SCP programs should employ a systematic combination of training approaches to: (a) improve the abilities of students to coordinate cognition, affect and behavior so that they may adaptively respond to meaningful social tasks and situations; and (b) create classroom settings and social supports to promote positive interpersonal functioning and developmental outcomes.

The authors review theory and empirical findings from basic research that have informed their program development efforts. For example, they identify physical, cognitive, psychosocial, emotional, and environmental variables that affect the behavior and development of young adolescents, and indicate how these factors influence their selection of target skills, training methods, as well as the social tasks on which they focus. They also highlight how Dodge's (1986) theoretical and empirical work regarding his social information processing model and the domain-specific nature of social competence have guided their design of two competence-building programs.

Caplan and Weissberg discuss several developmental and ecological variables that pose difficulties in the design and implementation of effective SCP programs. For example, the diversity among young adolescents in terms of physical maturity, cultural background, emotional development, academic performance, and psychosocial concerns complicate efforts to create programs and provide training. Furthermore, the departmentalized structure and academic emphasis of middle schools (schools for early adolescents) often present barriers to fitting much needed SCP training into the existing curriculum. As in the previous chapters, Caplan and Weissberg point out that training teachers to implement programs with fidelity and motivating students to learn and apply skills are challenges that require considerable expertise. In other words, the way in which programs are taught is equally important to the specific content conveyed.

In conclusion, although these three chapters recognize the important contribution that basic research offers to SCP program development efforts, they also point out that the nature of this contribution is somewhat limited. In reality, many factors influencing the outcome of SCP interventions can not be anticipated prior to program implementation. Such factors are often elucidated in the process of conducting action research. The authors also suggest that greater two-way communication between basic and applied social-competence researchers will be informative and advantageous to both groups. In some cases, intervention may contribute to the clarification of theory and basic research about social competence as much as theory and basic research inform practice.

References

Dodge, K. A. (1986). A social information processing model of social competence in children. In M. Perlmutter (Ed.), *Cognitive perspectives on children's social and behavioral development* (pp. 77-125). Hillsdale, NJ: Lawrence Erlbaum Associates.

Hall, G. E., & Hord, S. M. (1987). *Change in schools: Facilitating the process.* Albany, NY: State University of New York Press.

Hawkins, J. D., & Weis, J. G. (1985). The social development model: An integrated approach to delinquency prevention. *Journal of Primary Prevention, 6,* 73-97.

Ladd, G. W., & Mize, J. (1983). A cognitive-social learning model of social-skill training. *Psychological Review, 90,* 127-157.

Michelson, L., Sugai, D. P., Wood, R. P., & Kazdin, A. E. (1983). *Social skills assessment and training with children.* New York: Plenum Press.

Weissberg, R. P., & Allen, J. P. (1986). Promoting children's social skills and adaptive interpersonal behavior. In L. Michelson & B. Edelstein (Eds.), *Handbook of prevention* (pp. 153-175). New York: Plenum Press.

Weissberg, R. P., Caplan, M. Z., & Sivo, P. J. (1989). A new conceptual framework for establishing school-based social competence promotion programs. In L. A. Bond & B. E. Compas (Eds.), *Prevention in the schools.* Menlo Park: Sage.

Zins, J. E., & Forman, S. G. (Eds.). (1988). Primary prevention: From theory to practice [Special issue]. *School Psychology Review, 17(4).*

17

Between Developmental Wisdom and Children's Social-Skills Training

Barry H. Schneider

University of Ottawa

The purpose of this chapter is to explore some of the links--and many of the cleavages-- between theory and practice in the area of children's social development. The proposition considered herein is that current practice in children's social-skills training (SST) can be accurately regarded as the *in vivo* application of descriptive models and basic research in the field, as is often implied in the introductory statements of writings on children's SST. The scope of this chapter is broadened however, to mention the controversy about the value of intervention in the area of children's cognitive development, because that debate has directly involved the classic theorists in developmental psychology and, to a large extent, influenced more general attitudes towards applied intervention. Furthermore, many of the issues in that controversy are strikingly relevant to children's social development as well.

This chapter will begin by tracing several roots of this classic skepticism about intervention in general within developmental psychology and some possible rejoinders. It also examines some potential applications of developmental constructs that have often been overlooked in the clinical child psychology literature. Piaget is far from the sole source of inspiration for contemporary developmental psychology. The focus on Piaget in this chapter is due not only to the depth of his impact on the field, but also to the fact that the implications of his work for directive interventions with children are arguable and controversial. The outlook of other major theoricians in the field can rarely be seen as agnostic. Most psychoanalysts would probably regard SST as a totally superficial enterprise. Nevertheless, the sociometric movement of the early twentieth century flourished in blatant defiance of the widespread Freudian influence in Europe and America. Within the sociometric movement, peer assessments were used to determine an individual's role in the group--as they often are in contemporary social development research. Psychodrama and "spontaneity training" were used to empower the individual to experience the roles of others and thereby achieve enhanced social adjustment (Moreno, 1956). Social learning theory has also had a profound impact on the field of child development. Most of its adherents could be counted among the proponents, if not the initiators, of interventions of some form.

B. H. Schneider et al. (eds.), Social Competence in Developmental Perspective, 339–353.
© 1989 by Kluwer Academic Publishers.

Barry H. Schneider

Social Development: Is "Mother Nature" Best?

In the field of cognitive development, advocates of structured teaching are often pitted against "Piagetians" (see, e.g. Vuyk, 1981) because of the premium that Piaget placed on learning that occurs by independent discovery. Though Piagetians did indeed conduct training studies, their intent was to duplicate as far as possible the conditions under which children learn naturally and to demonstrate that training procedures which provide opportunities for spontaneous discovery engender cognitive growth, whereas the "tutorial approach" does not (Brainerd, 1978, Vuyk, 1981). Brainerd (1978) has summarized Piaget's objections to the training in general. Piaget felt, first of all, that any learning that accrues from artificial intervention would be short-lived. As well, it would in some ways be inferior in quality to "natural" learning. Most damning of all, Piaget implied that whatever might be learned through "tutorial" methods would soon be learned by the child anyway.

Piaget's skepticism about intervention evolved logically from the reverence for the natural processes of development that pervaded all his work. Though post-Piagetians dispute the specifics of the ages and stages proposed by Piaget, and though many theorists vehemently attack most basic assumptions of Genevan theory, this "Rousseauian" reverence for the natural processes of development has remained and pervaded the field of child development. Such reverence will surely be among Piaget's most enduring contributions. However, it is easily overdone. Swept by the optimism of this viewpoint, one can ascribe almost curative powers to the natural processes of development: If the best learning occurs spontaneously, it would not be illogical to wait for learning to occur spontaneously rather than to intervene systematically. Such thinking is not atypical of many parents' concept of the process of development, in which many difficulties experienced by children are considered manifestations of a passing phase. Furthermore, this stance is consistent with the inattention to individual differences in development that is characteristic of the Geneva school, which is often criticized by cognitively-oriented researchers interested in the problems of performance decalages within cognitive stages (e.g., Longeot, 1978) but can profitably be extended further. Piaget did not pretend any clinical mission; his work did not address the problems of children who display atypical patterns of development, whether manifested in cognitive problems with school learning or in peer relations.

Questions similar to those raised by opponents of cognitive training have been asked of social-skills trainers: Are the benefits of SST enduring? Are they as "good" as spontaneous acquisition of social competence? Would the children acquire the new skill without the training? How relevant is the debate about the value of cognitive training to the evaluation of SST? Before this question can be tackled, it is necessary to determine what type of learning social-skills trainers hope to engender; otherwise they could be condemned for failing to achieve something that they do not strive for in the first place. It could be argued that most advocates of SST at least implicitly operate from, and seek to impart in their clients, an understanding of human relationships characterized by mutual respect and reciprocity. However, this understanding is rarely presented completely or directly either to colleagues or to the children involved. Rather, the intervention focuses on some specific aspect of mutually respectful relating--be it making initial contact with the other, improving self-expression within the relationship, or resolving difficulties that may arise. In working with children, large-group relationships, such as those occurring between classmates and playground associates, have traditionally received more attention than more intimate, dyadic relationships, though this is changing somewhat (see Duck, this volume; Furman & Robins, 1985). At times, the perspective of mutuality becomes obscure as an intervention is implemented. This has led to corrective measures within the field, such as the criticisms directed at of some assertiveness trainers who place exclusive emphasis on "standing up for oneself" without accompanying this with enhancement of relationship-building skills (see Argyle, 1981; 1985). Similar objections might also be raised with regard to some "social-skills" programs intended for children, which focus primarily on compliance behaviors. These programs should be regarded as incomplete or mislabeled, but not as unhelpful. In any event, they are not typical of the SST field.

We are becoming increasingly aware of the fact that many of the rejected youngsters at whom SST is directed have an understanding of peer relationships that differs fundamentally from the outlook of children who enjoy successful peer relations. One such clue is provided by Dodge's work on cue detection (Dodge & Frame, 1982), which indicates that rejected, aggressive youngsters tend to perceive the intentions of others as hostile more readily than do their non rejected counterparts. Perhaps this work will inspire a more direct focus on children's understanding of relationships in the planning of interventions.

Brion-Meisels and Selman (1984) have categorized social- development interventions in terms of their structural or functional emphases. They describe structural interventions as "theory-driven" because of their explicit focus on the organization of new forms of interpersonal knowing. They contrast these with "problem-driven" functional interventions, which are directed at skills useful in situations of interpersonal conflict, most of the interventions discussed in this chapter would fall into this latter group. Brion-Meisels and Selman wisely describe the distinction between structural and functional interventions as one of emphasis, not one of kind.

In deciding how genuine or enduring the changes engendered by SST might be, it is imperative to consider the emphasis of the intervention. A "structural" intervention should engender changes in interpersonal understanding whether or not these translate into behavior change in conflict situations. A "functional" intervention should lead to meaningful changes in the specific conditions or behaviors targeted, whether or not there are more global spinoffs. With this in mind, let us return to the comparison of "artificially-induced" and "spontaneous" change in children's social behavior.

There are several bodies of knowledge relevant to this comparison, but in each case, gaps in the data base preclude a definitive answer. First of all, relatively little is known about how social competence is acquired naturally, though there has been considerable research on its long-term stability and amenity to short-term change. As documented in a review by Parker and Asher (1987; see also Asher & Parker, this volume), longitudinal studies have documented at least moderate long-term persistence of difficulties related to social competence deficits. Despite the shortcomings of these studies, it is reasonable to conclude that many deficits of social competence are unlikely to disappear spontaneously. This particularly applies to aggressive behavior; the long-term course of childhood withdrawal is less clear (Coie, 1985; Rubin, 1985; Strauss, 1988).

There are considerable and useful data on short-term changes in children's social development. Furman, Rahe and Hartup (1979) assigned socially withdrawn preschool children to two conditions that involved interaction in a small playroom with a partner of either the same age or younger. There was no direct teaching of social-skills, though toys that would facilitate social interaction were presented. In comparison with no-"treatment" controls, those who participated in the playroom sessions displayed improvement in social interaction. Unfortunately, it is difficult to decide whether these findings favor "natural" or "artificial" learning. The children's social behavior improved without didactic SST. However, the playroom set up was totally contrived by the experimenters, which could be seen as an intervention of sorts. Perhaps the evidence accrued from this study might be claimed by those "organic lamp" theorists (see Langer, 1969) who, while affirming the organism's self-generative role in development, emphasize the need for environments that provide needed nourishment and set the scene.

Beirman and Furman (1984) directly compared a didactic "coaching" program with play sessions that, again, provided enhanced involvement with peers but no didactic SST. The children in this study were preadolescents disliked by their classmates. Both conditions engendered benefits in comparison to untreated controls, albeit on different indices of social competence. A third condition, which included both systematic training and semi structured opportunities for interaction, was the most beneficial of all. Although these results (and those of related studies) do not provide unqualified support for "artificial" SST, neither are they consistent with the position that Mother Nature is the best teacher of social-skills.

As will be detailed below, there is considerable evidence for the short-term effectiveness of social-skills interventions with children, but few researchers have been as systematic as Beirman and Furman in comparing didactic and non-didactic approaches. Short-term benefits of these interventions have been found in both cognitive and motoric aspects of children's social development. However, long-term follow-up studies have been few.

Thus, in attempting to resolve the question of whether SST can meaningfully improve upon the spontaneous learning of social skills, we are confronted by missing data on both sides. Hopefully, research will better elucidate both the natural processes involved in becoming socially competent and the long-term impact of intervention.

Intervention as the Action Component of Theory

Though clearly influenced by both theory and descriptive research, practitioners have rarely made explicit the connection between intervention procedures and the theoretical models that underlie them. Here again, the field of cognitive development offers some insight as to how even a well-conceived intervention procedure can be ineffective. Given an intervention procedure based on a theoretical model, several conditions are necessary for the effectiveness of the intervention; these are enumerated by Brainerd (1978). Most fundamentally, the model itself must be valid. Second, the prescribed procedures must be representative of the model. Finally, the procedures must be properly implemented. Any unsuccessful intervention can be attributed to the failure to satisfy one or more of these conditions.

Are the Models Valid?

Let us consider each of these conditions in turn in an effort to establish what is reasonable to expect of SST. How valid are the theoretical models which underlie SST? The fact that these models are rarely well articulated in this highly empirical literature makes such an evaluation difficult . However, Ladd's (1985) review of the basic assumptions in children's SST probably best sketches the model most adherents would endorse. According to Ladd, children's SST is predicated on the basic assumptions that: (a) that children experiencing peer relations problems lack social skills; (b) they acquire these skills during SST; and (c) their peer relations improve as result.

With regard to the first assumption, Ladd categorizes the types of social-skills deficits identified in most SST as social-cognitive, behavioral or affective. Social-cognitive skills include, for example, the ability to generate a variety of solutions in problematic situations. Behavioral deficits include the inability to integrate oneself into an existing peer group. Affective deficits refer to social competence problems involving underlying anxiety, self-deprecation and other inhibitors.

342

It is the social-cognitive and behavioral deficits that have been most frequently targeted in the training literature. There is considerable evidence that such deficits are at least correlated with peer rejection, yet results are not entirely unanimous (see Asher, 1985; Coie & Kupersmidt, 1983; Ladd, 1985; Putallaz & Gottman, 1981; Rubin & Daniels-Beirness, 1983). While a fair number of children surely exist who are deficient in the social-cognitive and behavioral skills discussed, there is some question as to whether most peer relations problems are caused by not knowing the skills themselves or by not putting them into practice. By focusing on these social-cognitive and behavioral skills deficits, most social-skills trainers have been working on the judicial and legislative branches of interpersonal relating (to take liberties with a metaphor offered by Peters [1959]) at the expense of the executive component which would be responsible for coordinating the social-cognitive and behavioral skills with the situation at hand.

Specific executive skills must be associated with an effective executive branch of social behavior. Ladd is probably referring to some of these as affective deficits. Some contemporary British social-skills trainers are addressing the executive component in their call for a shift from models characterized by the "reductionistic" training of specific social skills with essentially passive trainees. They would rather appeal to the more global process by which individuals actively generate socially skilled behavior (called "social *skill* training"--as opposed to "social *skills* training"--by Trower [1984]), though training of specific social skills can be seen as a useful adjunct in this enterprise (Trower, 1984). These ideas, which recall Moreno's (1956) crucial construct of spontaneity, have had more impact on theory than on practice and been more extensively applied to adults than to children. In contrast, Gresham (1986), whose work is with children, appears to have excluded the executive component from the realm of social skills. He makes a distinction between social-skills deficits and social-performance deficits. In his model, skills deficits refer to the acquisition of specific abilities--the "legislative" component most likely. Gresham has implied that performance deficits rather than skills deficits tend to be more extensively implicated in the social rejection of children at risk.

Nonetheless, support for Ladd's first assumption--that rejected children lack social skills--is not lacking even for the traditional social-cognitive and behavioral targets of SST. Presumably, support is enhanced if we broaden the scope to include the affective dimension or executive component as discussed. We would be on far shakier ground if our models were to maintain that the skills deficit *caused* the children's maladjustment. To begin with, it is unclear and unlikely that social behavior difficulties have one single cause. In many cases, multiple factors are implicated, perhaps including social-skills deficits; deficient linguistic, academic and motor skills; and physical appearance, all of which are to some degree modifiable (Hops & Finch, 1985).

Interestingly, intervention may emerge as one of the best ways of clarifying the causal pathways involved. Let us consider some examples from the field of remedial education to illustrate this type of paradigm. Bryant and his colleagues (Bradley & Bryant, 1983; Bryant & Goswami, 1986), exploring remedial techniques with reading-disabled youngsters, faced the problem of multiple factors impinging on reading development in attempting to illustrate the importance of the concept of rhyme in learning to read. He conducted an intervention in which the concept of rhyme was incorporated into a longitudinal study of reading development. This design permits the training of one potential "causal" ability while holding the others constant. Rogosa (1988), in his scathing attack on the misuse of structural equation modeling by making causal inferences from correlational data in the absence of a theoretical framework, referred to a similar paradigm used by Powers and

Swindon (1984) in coaching students for university entrance exams as an example of the judicious use of an intervention to elucidate causal relationships.

Assuming that there is theoretical justification for the skills presented, what about the techniques? Our models would be highly tenuous if we felt the need to train social skills in the same ways that children learn them naturally. For each of the major training techniques--modeling, coaching, operant reinforcement, social-cognitive methods--there might still be purists who think that the training method approximates the child's spontaneous learning of social behavior. However, in each case, the empirical support available would be quite meager. Nevertheless, these "artificial" techniques do seem to be effective. For example, modeling by parents or peers would probably account for only a small part of the child's "natural" acquisition of social skills (see Maccoby & Martin, 1983; Youniss, 1980). Yet, modeling is a very effective way of training social skills "artificially"--probably more effective than any attempt to replicate in the laboratory the child's spontaneous "discovery" of social skills. Similar arguments could be offered for the other major training techniques.

Do the Prescribed Procedures Accurately Represent the Model?

Assuming that there is an adequate theoretical rationale for the skills taught, the next logical focus is the intervention itself. Are the skills taught the same as those which play a part in the underlying theoretical rationale? The problem here is that the skills presented in training must of necessity be reduced to presentable, teachable form. The natural drama of a social interchange must be presented without some of the full living color, background music, and expressive skill that naturally form part of the exchange. What is lost in the adaptation? If the traditional psychotherapist can be accused of extensive preoccupation with *how* clients do things rather than with *what* they do, the social-skills trainer can be accused of exactly the reverse.

Let us consider an example in the area of children's problem solving. It has been demonstrated in many (but not all) studies that unpopular children have difficulty with such social-cognitive skills as generating alternative solutions to a social problem: their solutions may be fewer in number or of inferior quality (Durlak, 1983; Higgins & Thies, 1981; Spivack, Platt & Shure, 1976). Thus, we can probably accept the rationale for teaching this skill. However, in training problem solving, we have in mind something further: the way in which the problem-solving skills will, hopefully, be used. We want the children to first think through their alternatives when faced with a problem situation, rationally decide between alternatives, then go out and behave in accordance with these decisions. Therefore, the problem-solving skills inherent in the intervention procedure imply a rational, purposive model of cognitive control not necessarily implicit in the related descriptive research or typical of *in vivo* behavioral control. The training may approximate a computer program whose output leads to more friendships--all the necessary commands are there. But the child involved will not process the commands as a computer does. The difference will be the enormous tension inherent in a human being's attempts to achieve cognitive control of behavior, perhaps reversing a lifetime of impulsive responding. This process of achieving control may be more important than the details of the "commands" and might merit greater consideration in the intervention. This is already evident in some recent intervention programs.

There may be other differences between the way social skills are taught and the way the same skills are conceptualized. In his very useful structured learning approach, Goldstein (1980) trains a series of discrete social skills, most of which could be supported by theory and research. These skills are divided into sequential component steps, which the trainees memorize and then practice. Unless corrected by a particularly skilled trainer, the trainees may mechanically display the series of skill steps, ignoring what may be the most important element in social skills training: learning to be friendly and spontaneous (M. Argyle, personal communication, 1984). Hopefully, such mechanical recitation of skill steps is just one stage in the learning process. Redoubled efforts to include the affective as well as the cognitive, to bring in the living color of a true social exchange, will surely bring added benefit to the field. This may involve going *beyond* the underlying theoretical models in developing the art and science of SST.

Are the Interventions Conducted Properly? Do Children Learn Social Skills in SST?

The conceptual soundness of an intervention does not ensure its effectiveness. It must be implemented in a way that maximizes its impact on children. When teaching *anything*, it is a fundamental error to assume that children will understand, much less use, whatever is *told* to them. Furthermore, even if the prescribed procedures are well conceptualized and meaningful to children, there has often been no verification that they have been implemented as prescribed. Improvements here are well underway; these should help preserve one of the most attractive features of SST--namely, its usefulness in professionally supervised programs conducted by students, teachers and paraprofessionals.

Much SST is conducted by beginners. Other forms of intervention--from psychoanalytic to behavioral, as well as more traditional aspects of the school curriculum have seen thousands of hours of supervision and reams of writing devoted to every crucial juncture in the therapy or teaching process. Few would want this for SST, which has always been seen as a primary or secondary prevention technique developed for application in schools and communities. Yet far too little attention is paid to SST technique even within this framework of prevention. Self-confidence must be an important component of the backdrop to a successful social exchange. We cannot be sure that the many inexperienced social-skills trainers ever model the necessary self-confidence, because most people are not confident while performing a task for the first time. Other personal qualities that may well be associated with success as a social-skills trainer are largely unknown at present.

Weissberg (1985) has emphasized the importance of proper trainer preparation even if the intended trainer is a teacher with many other classroom responsibilities. Problems have been reported where this has not been done. Teachers are accustomed to helping children find the "right answer" in many academic tasks. This same tendency to help children find the "right answer" may be transferred to such SST procedures as the generation of alternative solutions, where the intent is often to foster the processes of creative thinking, not tell children what to do (M. Shure, personal communication, 1982). Teachers are accustomed to using language as the major medium of presentation. However, visual aids and appropriate kinetic experiences may increase the impact of many lessons on the students who need them most; this may well apply to social skills curricula. Finally, there is a danger that an SST "package" may be relegated to an insulated compartment of the school day. If the underlying principles are not applied as appropriate to interpersonal exchanges, disciplinary encounters, and other opportunities for learning, it may be difficult for the children to understand how to generalize what they learn. These obstacles--and opportunities--illustrate the importance of an active, creative role for those who implement SST.

Even if we were invited to offer systematic preparation to prospective social skills trainers, we would have a very limited data base and an impoverished fund of case studies in the literature to use as a basis for such training. More careful consideration needs to be given to such issues as group formation, how the SST should be explained, when to terminate, and how to deal with obstacles to progress. Wolpin (1975) insightfully describes an experience with adult assertiveness training that was highly successful after only one session. The client, according to a follow-up report left the session totally absorbed with the need to use his newly-acquired skills. He spent 2 hours in mental rehearsal of his "homework assignment" before going out to deal with a minor financial problem. The client's success led to a tremendous change in his self-confidence and, apparently, in his future transactions. Wolpin emphasized not the content of the SST, but the way the client "got into it". Since we are concerned about fostering developmental growth in many settings (see Bronfenbrenner, 1979) and over extended periods of time, we may well need to find out exactly what we must do to help children in SST "get into it." If we did so, we would be, in a way, borrowing from the general philosophy and tone of classical Piagetian theory, which emphasizes the active, creative, and constructive role of the individual in learning.

As introduced above, it is my contention that the problem of generalization of SST may best be addressed by actively encouraging and motivating the trainees rather than viewing them as passive elements in the training process. Let us consider the somewhat analogous problem faced by Powers and Swindon (1984), whose goal it was to prepare high school students for the Scholastic Aptitude Test, a test of university ability. Of all the ways devised to get the students to actually use the study materials given them, sending them letters reminding them that the exam was forthcoming and that study will bring payoff, was the most effective. While it is not clear whether such a "gimmick" will enhance generalization of SST, the underlying message may well do so: that SST should be implemented as ongoing process with the attention to motivational factors.

It would be tempting to view SST as the "action arm" of the psychology of children's social development. This is only partially justified because, as we have seen, some important elements are lost in the translation from theory to practice. Perhaps the best estimate of the seriousness of that loss is the data on how much meaningful change is engendered by SST (cf. below). We must remember, however, that these data pertain to SST as it is commonly practiced, not the potential impact of SST after a number of refinements--including those implied in the previous discussion--many of which would not really be difficult to bring about.

The Social Context of Peer Relations: Implications for Intervention

The following discussion is devoted to the context in which children's social relationships occur. While Piaget did have much to say about social relations, his work was heavily criticized for its inattention to the larger context in which social relationships occur: family, school, community and society. Piaget had little patience for the "sterile disputes aimed at determining to what extent the action and thought of people are based on social factors and to what extent they are due to individual initiative" (Piaget, 1979, p. 6), though he had much to say about the latter and little about the former. Piaget's views in this regard are diametric to those of many American developmentalists, who have emphasized a systemic point of view (Bronfenbrenner, 1979; Oppenheimer, this volume; Sameroff, 1983).

Implementers of SST have also tended to pay insufficient attention to the larger context. This particularly applies to those who implement SST on a one-to-one basis, though SST packages distributed for community use have also disregarded circumstances particular to specific subcultures and socioeconomic conditions. This may not be entirely due to oversight. Many proponents have been attracted to SST as an alternative to previous approaches in behavior therapy which required control over the entire immediate environment. This position is best enunciated by E. Lakin Philips, who, in his enumeration of the theory underlying SST, noted that in a situation of person-environment conflict, it is easier to change the person than to change the environment (Philips, 1978). Furthermore, some may find working with an individual more manageable than confronting a maladaptive system. However, failure to consider the child's social environment can impair effectiveness. Conversely, careful scrutiny of the world in which the child lives can help SST professionals design a more effective intervention procedure. Let us turn to an example of environmental effects and their subtle impact on intervention effectiveness.

Our colleagues in the area of parent training are one step ahead of the social skills field in their "failure analysis"--the close inspection of the instances in which parent training has failed--in an effort to understand why. Wahler and Dumas (1987) report an interesting case in which traditional training of parenting skills was a complete failure. Careful probing of the client's life circumstances revealed that she, a single mother, was constantly embroiled in heart rending arguments with members of her extended family. So upset by these arguments that lacked the energy to implement the parenting skills she had learned in training. Wahler and Dumas were able to demonstrate that unpleasant exchanges with this mother's relatives coincided with coercive exchanges with her daughter. Simply making the mother aware of this connection was sufficient to prompt some use of the skills previously presented. Could a similar contingency--and a similar opportunity--not occur in SST, as in the case of a child who, because of many arguments at home, engages in self-defeating exchanges with classmates?

Let us design an SST program for such a child. Knowledge of the child's circumstances could have some bearing in the selection of target skills. Besides helping the child cope at home, we would want to facilitate the emergence of friendships that could provide support and comfort despite the hostility at home--to make the child more resilient and less vulnerable to the family stress (see Garmezy, this volume). Therefore, skills in approaching others, forming friendships, and disclosing oneself appropriately would be among the ideal target skills. We might choose not to provide training in role-taking or empathy, which, though it might bring some dividends in the area of peer relations, could unwittingly cause the child to be emotionally "dragged down" by the surrounding unhappiness at home. The uncritical use of a social skills "package", in ignorance of the context of this child's peer relations, could thus diminish the impact of training.

While many social skills trainers are guilty of ignoring these setting factors in the design of training programs, we may be relying too heavily on the setting to promote generalization and transfer of training. We have become acutely aware of the fact that there are many children who will learn social skills in the training or laboratory setting but not use them in their schools or homes. It is tempting to devise some way of getting the parents and teachers to promote the use of skills learned. This may be of considerable value, but we must also take into account the possibility that the teacher may place much more emphasis on such behavior as compliance with classroom rules than on relationships among the pupils (Walker & Rankin, 1983). Similarly, parents have been found to vary considerably in terms of how important they consider friendship building for their children (Rubin & Sloman, 1984). While we should of course continue such efforts to secure teacher and parent support for SST, this support may thus not be without its limits; hence, the accent in the previous section on mobilizing the child's own motivation.

Barry H. Schneider

Does Social-Skills Training Facilitate Social Development?

The controversy as to whether "artificial" learning is as "good" as spontaneous natural development is really an empirical one. If it can be demonstrated that training can facilitate meaningful change in the long run, we can consider the question answered. This applies equally to cognitive and social development.

What is the track record of children's SST? In an effort to address that question, I (Schneider, 1988) conducted a Rosenthal-type meta-analysis of 85 studies which involved random assignment of children to treatment and control groups, and reported data in a format suitable for meta-analysis. This meta-analysis was limited to published studies conducted with children up to age 18 in which there was a planned, systematic intervention intended to improve children's social behavior. Training approaches included videotaped and live modeling, directed problem-solving discussions and "coaching"--instructing children with regard to friendship-forming behavior. More than one of these techniques was used in most of the studies.

Schneider found that the overall effect size r (see Rosenthal, 1984) was 0.41, which is very significantly different from zero (p <.001). Rosenthal's binomial effect size display is probably the best way of understanding this statistic. Accordingly, we could estimate an improvement rate of 69.8% for experimental subjects, compared with 30.2% for controls. Even greater effectiveness is apparent when one eliminates peripheral variables, such as academic achievement, from the analysis, permitting a more direct focus on peer acceptance and observed social behavior. Importantly, the effects at follow-up (obviously calculated only for those studies which included follow-up components), though not as high as the effects at the conclusion of treatment, were still substantial: $r = 0.35$. Unfortunately, this follow-up statistic is based on the relatively small group of studies for which follow-up data were reported. Until more extensive and longer-term follow-up data appear, even the most die-hard advocate of SST will be ill-equipped to affirm conclusively that the benefits of SST are more than transitory. These effect sizes can be considered moderate, and essentially comparable to those derived in other meta-analysis conducted on other forms of intervention with children with atypical developmental patterns (see the meta-analytic review by Weisz, Weiss, Alicke & Klotz, 1987).

Missing Links: Some Potentially Useful Applications of Developmental Theory

Although child developmental journals have devoted considerable attention to SST, there has been surprisingly little study of the impact of developmental change on the design or outcome of these interventions.

Training Differentiated by Age of Trainee

Most developmentalists would be highly skeptical of any suggestion that either any specific social skills target or training technique--or the whole enterprise--is equally applicable to children of all ages. Figure 17.1 represents details of my (Schneider, 1988) meta-analysis, mentioned above. Here, the effect sizes are depicted as a function of trainee's age, and grouped by major training technique. As shown, the age effects may be different according to the techniques applied. Modeling procedures, which require less cognitive mediation than others, appear most effective with preschoolers (ages 3 and 4 years). The more complex training packages--which use a variety of techniques--seem more effective with older children.

348

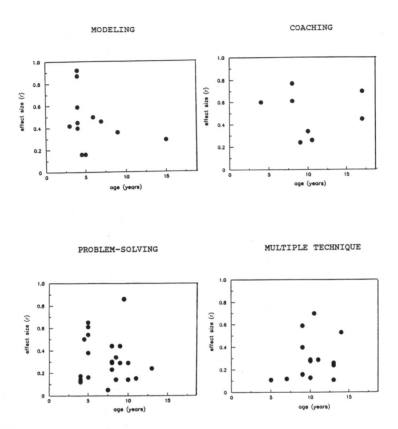

Figure 17.1

Effect sizes for modeling, coaching, problem-solving and multi-treatment interventions as a function of mean chronological age of child subjects.

Though relevant data are not as readily available, there may also be important developmental changes in *what* skills should be taught, not just *how* they should be taught. As noted by Gottman (1983), this aspect of intervention is too often overlooked. The more basic skills of joining a group may be more relevant at some ages than others. As children get older, it may be more crucial to assist them in forming fewer but more intensive friendships, and to resolve difficulties that arise within such friendships. The reader is referred to Sullivan's (1953) stage model as a source of ideas for such stage differences in the content of SST.

"Readiness" for SST

One component of many developmental models is the concept of readiness: can the child understand the material to be learned? Is the intervention relevant to the child's developmental level? This has received surprisingly little attention in SST. Some programs (e.g., Spivack & Shure, 1974) call for considerable amount of time to be spent on vocabulary thought to serve as a foundation for SST. This indicates an awareness of the possible limitations on children's understanding of what is presented, which has often been ignored. At the present time, no real cognitive or personality profile of the child who is ready for SST can be derived from research. Thus, many children may not be ready in some sense for the specific intervention. As well, there have been few attempts to exclude "prerequisite" training in cases where most of the children involved have already mastered the "prerequisites". This is imperative because of the very limited time usually available for the important undertaking of SST. Classic cognitive-developmental theory is again of some use in suggesting (in spirit if not in letter) the level at which SST might be pitched. In structural interventions designed to promote cognitive development, optimal efficacy can be achieved by *directed* (rather than passive) exposure to reasoning *one* stage above the child's current level (Kohlberg, 1971). If we extrapolate freely, we might hypothesize that, even in functional interventions, children are best presented material which clearly affords opportunities for growth, without being out of reach.

Though we seldom reflect on this, SST typically involves adults attempting to assist children with problems that belong to the children and not really to the adults. There may be important developmental differences in children's responsiveness to this approach. Most developmentalists have traditionally portrayed a decline in adult influence over the course of childhood and adolescence. This may have important implications for determining the age of intervention, and for involvement of peer trainers (see Strain & Fox, 1981). It should be noted, however, that some theorists have recently emphasized the continuity of adult influence throughout the course of development. Wintre, Hicks, McVey, and Fox (1988) investigated children's choices of consultants for various hypothetical problems presented on videotape. When confronted with interpersonal problems with peers, 8 year-old respondents most often indicated that they would seek help from a familiar adult. This shifted dramatically as the subjects entered adolescence, with 11-, 14-, and 17 year olds increasingly indicating preferences for familiar peers as consultants. Adult experts were rarely indicated as sources of help by children of any age. These findings may point to the diminishing impact of adults as consultants on older children's peer problems, as well as a need for role induction in situations where "experts" conduct SST.

On the Decision to Conduct an Intervention

As we have seen, children's SST is not without its conceptual problems and technical difficulties. Nevertheless, it does bring benefits to many children. Some may wish to relegate this "action arm" of children's social development to others until the knowledge base that serves as the foundation for intervention is augmented. Several factors are relevant to this decision.

Among these factors is the individual's sense of clinical mission. If no one develops applied interventions until we have securely put into place more pieces of the social development puzzle, we might leave many children with peer relations problems waiting for a long time. It would be irresponsible to attribute curative properties to the natural processes of development and assure children that these difficulties will probably disappear, because, as discussed above, they often will not.

Furthermore, it does not follow that problems must be permanent to be painful. With the important proviso that the intervention can be kept brief and enjoyable, it is entirely appropriate to see interventions as serving two purposes: one of prevention for those children whose social failure might not disappear with time, and one of support for those whose peer relations problems are hurtful though transitory.

Although we cannot guarantee success to all trainees, let us remember several critical properties of SST when properly conducted:

1. It is easily applicable to large-scale community-based primary prevention programs.
2. When used in secondary prevention or treatment, it is lower in time and cost than most other interventions available for children with atypical development patterns, such as psychodynamic psychotherapy.
3. It requires less restructuring of the child's total environment than such approaches as token economy or family therapy.
4. While its effectiveness can be seen as moderate, negative effects appear to be few.
5. Many adults may find SST more acceptable than the other approaches mentioned.

Therefore, although some might question the use of techniques that have limits and require further development, others might question their disuse or the use of more intrusive interventions if SST might have helped relieve the problem, or helped prevent it in the first place. The intent of the arguments raised above is to call for realism in our expectations regarding these procedures, and for the incessant redoubling of efforts to refine them. In the course of improving SST, we would benefit from frequent reference to the theoretical heritage in the psychology of human development--both for specific content and for its many more general guidelines useful in understanding children's social behavior and its modifiability.

Acknowledgments: Roger Weissberg's helpful comments on an earlier draft are gratefully acknowledged. This chapter was prepared while the author was an academic visitor at the Department of Experimental Psychology, University of Oxford. Appreciation is extended for their hospitality.

References

Argyle, M. (1981). The contribution of social interaction research to social skills training. In J. D. Wine and M. D. Smye (Eds.) *Social Competence* (pp. 261-286). New York: Guilford Press.

Argyle, M. (1985). Social behavior problems and social skills training in adolescents. In B. H. Schneider, K. Rubin and J. E. Ledingham (Eds.) *Children's peer relations: Issues in assessment and intervention* (pp. 207-224). New York: Springer-Verlag.

Asher, S. R. (1985). An evolving paradigm in social skills training research with children. In B. H. Schneider, K. Rubin and J. E. Ledingham (Eds.) *Children's peer relations: Issues in assessment and intervention* (pp. 157-174). New York: Springer-Verlag.

Beirman, K. L. & Furman, W. (1984). The effects of social skills training and peer involvement on the social adjustment of preadolescents. *Child Development, 55,* 151-162.

Bradley, L. & Bryant, P. E. (1983). Categorising sounds and learning to read: A causal connexion. *Nature, 301,* 419-421.

Brainerd, C. (1978). *Piaget's theory of intelligence.* Englewood Cliffs, NJ: Prentice-Hall.

Brion-Meisels, S. & Selman, R. L. (1984). Early adolescent development of new interpersonal strategies: Understanding and interventions. *School Psychology Review, 13,* 292-301.

Bronfenbrenner, U. (1979). *The ecology of human development.* Cambridge, Mass.: Harvard University Press.

Bryant, P. & Goswami, U. (1986). Strengths and weaknesses of the reading level design: A comment on Backman, Mamen and Ferguson. *Psychological Bulletin, 100,* 101-103.

Coie, J. (1985). Fitting social skills intervention to the target child. In B. H. Schneider, K. Rubin and J. E. Ledingham (Eds.) *Children's peer relations: Issues in assessment and intervention* (pp. 141-156). New York: Springer-Verlag.

Coie, J. D. & Kupersmidt, J. B. (1983). A behavioral analysis of emerging social status in boys groups. *Child Development, 54,* 1386-1399.

Dodge, K. A. & Frame, C. L. (1982). Social cognitive biases and deficits in aggressive boys. *Child Development, 53,* 620-635.

Durlak, J. (1983). Social problem solving as a primary prevention strategy. In R. Felner, L. Jason, J. Moritsugu, & S. Farber (Eds.). *Preventive psychology: Theory, research and practice* (pp. 31-48). New York: Pergamon.

Furman, W., Rahe, D. F., & Hartup, W. W. (1979). Rehabilitation of socially-withdrawn children through mixed-age and same-age socialization. *Child Development, 50*, 915-922.

Furman, W. & Robins, P. (1985). What's the point?--Issues in the selection of training objectives in B. H. Schneider, K. Rubin & J.E. Ledingham (Eds.) *Children's peer relations: Issues in assessment and intervention* (pp. 41-56). New York: Springer-Verlag.

Goldstein, A. P. (1980). *Skillstreaming the adolescent.* Champaign, IL: Research Press.

Gottman, J. G. (1983). How children become friends. *Monographs of the Society for Research in Child Development, 48*, 3.

Gresham, F. M. (1986). Conceptual issues in the assessment of social competence in children. In P.S. Strain, M.J. Guralnick and H.M. Walker (Eds.) *Children's social behavior: development, assessment and modification* (pp. 143-180). Orlando: Academic Press.

Higgins, J. & Thies, A. (1981). Problem solving and social position among emotionally disturbed boys. *American Journal of Orthopsychiatry, 51*, 356-358.

Hops, H. & Finch, M. (1985). Social competence and skill: A reassessment. In B. H. Schneider, K. Rubin and J. E. Ledingham (Eds.) *Children's peer relations: Issues in assessment and intervention* (pp. 125-140). New York: Springer-Verlag.

Kohlberg, L. (1971). Stages of moral development as a basis for moral education. In C.M. Beck, B.S. Crittenden & E.V. Sullivan (Eds.) *Moral Education: Interdisciplinary Approaches* (pp. 23-92). New York: Newman Press.

Ladd, G. W. (1985). Documenting the effects of social skill training with children: Process and outcome assessment. In B.H. Schneider, K. Rubin, and J. E. Ledingham (Eds.) *Children's peer relations: Issues in assessment and intervention* (pp. 243-269). New York: Springer-Verlag.

Langer, J. (1969). *Theories of development.* New York: Holt, Rinehart and Winston.

Longeot, F. (1978). Les stades opératoires de Piaget et les facteurs de l'intelligence. (Piaget's operative stages and factors of intelligence). Grenoble: Presses Universitaires de Grenoble.

Maccoby, E. E. & Martin, J. A. (1983). Socialization in the context of the family: Parent-child interaction. In P. H. Mussen (Ed.) *Handbook of Child Psychology* (4th Edition) (pp. 1-102). New York: Wiley.

Moreno, J. L. (1956). (Ed.) *Sociometry and the science of man.* New York: Beacon House.

Parker, J. G. & Asher, S. R. (1987). Peer relations and later personal adjustment: Are low-accepted children at risk? *Psychological Bulletin, 102*, 357-389.

Peters, R. S. (1959). Freud's theory of moral development in relation to that of Piaget. *British Journal of Educational Psychology, 29*, 250-258.

Philips, E. L. (1978). *The social skills basis of psychopathology.* New York: Grune & Stratton.

Piaget, J. (1979). *Behaviour and evolution* (D. N. Smith, Trans.) London: Routledge-Paul. (Original work published 1975).

Powers, D. E. & Swindon, S. S. (1984). Effects of self-study for coachable test item types. *Journal of Educational Psychology, 76*, 266-278.

Putallaz, M. & Gottman, J. M. (1981). Social skills and group acceptance. In S. R. Asher and J.M. Gottman, (Eds.) *The development of children's friendships* (pp. 116-149). Cambridge; Cambridge; University Press.

Rosenthal, R. (1984). *Meta-analytic procedures for social research.* Beverly Hills, CA: Sage.

Rogosa, D. (1988, April). Casual models do not support scientific conclusions. Paper presented at the annual meeting of the American Educational Research Association. New Orleans.

Rubin, K. H. (1985). Socially withdrawn children: An at-risk population? In B. H. Schneider, K. H. Rubin and J. E. Ledingham (Eds.) *Children's peer relations: Issues in assessment and intervention* (pp. 125-139). New York: Springer-Verlag.

Rubin, K. E. & Daniels-Beirness, T. (1983). Concurrent and predictive correlates of sociometric status in kindergarten and grade one children. *Merrill-Palmer Quarterly, 29*, 337-352.

Rubin, Z. & Sloman, J. (1984). How parents influence their children's friendships. In M. Lewis (Ed.) *Beyond the dyad.* (pp. 223-250). New York: Plenum.

Sameroff, A. J. (1983). Developmental systems: Contexts and evolution. In P. H. Mussen (Ed.) *Handbook of Child Psychology*, 4th Edition (pp. 237-294). New York: Wiley.

Schneider, B. (1988, April). Children's social skills training: What works best? Paper presented to the annual meeting of the American Educational Research Association, New Orleans.

Spivack, G. Platt, J. J. & Shure, M. B. (1976). *The problem-solving approach to adjustment.* San Francisco: Jossey-Bass.

Spivack, G. & Shure, M. B. (1974). *Social adjustment of young children.* San Francisco: Jossey-Bass.

Strain, P. S. & Fox, J. J. (1981). Peers as behavior change agents for withdrawn classmates. In B. B. Lahey and A. E. Kazdin (Eds.) *Advances in clinical child psychology* (Vol 4, pp. 167-198). New York: Plenum.

Strauss, C. C. (1988). Social deficits of children with internalizing disorders. In B. B. Lahey and A. E. Kazdin (Eds.) *Advances in clinical child psychology* (Vol. 11, pp. 159-192). New York: Plenum.

Sullivan, H. S. (1953). *The interpersonal theory of psychiatry.* New York: Norton.

Trower, P. (1984). A radical critique and reformulation: from organism to agent. In P. Trower (Ed.) *Radical approaches to social skills training* (pp. 48-88). London: Croom-Helm.

Vuyk, R. (1981). *Overview and critique of Piaget's genetic epistemology, 1965-1980.* New York: Academic Press.

Wahler, R. G. & Dumas, J. E. (1987). Family factors in childhood psycho-pathology: Toward a coercion-neglect model. In T. Jacob (Ed.) *Family interaction and psychopathology: Theories, methods and findings* (pp. 581-627). New York: Plenum.

Walker, H. M. & Rankin, R. (1983). Assessing the behavioral expectations and demands of less restrictive settings, *School Psychology Review, 12,* 274-284.

Weissberg, R. P. (1985). Designing effective social problem-solving programs for the classroom. In B. H. Schneider, K. H. Rubin, and J. E. Ledingham (Eds.) *Children's peer relations: Issues in assessment and intervention* (pp. 225-242). New York: Springer-Verlag.

Weisz, J. R., Weiss, B., Alicke, M. D. & Klotz, M. L. (1987). Effectiveness of psychotherapy with children and adolescents: A meta-analysis for clinicians. *Journal of Consulting and Clinical Psychology, 55,* 542-549.

Wintre, M. G., Hicks, R., McVey, G. & Fox, J. (1988). Age and sex differences in choice of consultant for various types of problems. *Child Development, 59,* 1046-1055.

Wolpin, M. (1975). On assertion training. *Counselling Psychologist, 5,* 42-44.

Youniss, J. (1980). *Parents and peers in social development.* Chicago: University of Chicago Press.

18

Enhancing Peer Relations in School Systems

Wyndol Furman, Ronita Giberson, Allison S. White, Leslie A. Gavin, and Elizabeth A. Wehner

University of Denver

In this chapter, we present a systems perspective for school intervention programs and describe our efforts to apply such a perspective in our consultation programs for teaching teachers ways to improve their students' peer relations. Our work is derived from the literature on peer intervention programs (see Furman, 1984; Hops, 1982). Several common themes have emerged in that literature. First, a number of promising approaches have been developed, including coaching or social skills training programs, social cognitive interventions, and cooperative group programs. Second, we don't have a good understanding of why the programs have at least short-term effects, particularly considering that the specific nature of changes or lack of changes varies from study to study. For example, social skills training programs have sometimes resulted in changes in both sociometric status and peer interactions; in other instances, changes have been observed in only one domain; and in a few instances, no changes at all have been observed (Furman, 1984). These results also underlie the third common theme heard in the literature: Serious concerns exist about the generalization and maintenance of treatment effects (Hops, 1982). Few have examined such effects, and fewer have found them.

Other psychotherapy literature indicates that generalization and maintenance of treatment effects do not occur by chance and must be programmed (Goldstein & Kanfer, 1979). Yet few efforts have been made to explicitly promote generalization. In fact, although one or two exceptions exist, social-skills-training programs have usually been conducted by a member of the research staff. The teachers have not been the change agents, nor have they received instructions in how to maintain the treatment effects after the program has ended. Can one realistically expect changes to generalize or persist under such conditions?

On the other hand, social cognitive and cooperative group programs are often classroom-based ones designed to be conducted by teachers. Even here, it is not clear what kind of teachers will choose to carry out the programs and what kind of training or institutional support is necessary to implement the programs successfully. Although the descriptions of the selection of teachers are frequently cursory, it appears that the teachers are usually a select group of motivated volunteers. Participating teachers are often paid for conducting the programs, or they receive special perquisites (e.g., aides to assist in the sessions, course credit). The training component of most social cognitive programs is also quite extensive. For example, Elardo and Caldwell (1979) conducted the "Aware" sessions

B. H. Schneider et al. (eds.), Social Competence in Developmental Perspective, 355–369.

themselves for the first month and then met weekly with the teachers for the next four months.

Similarly, Weissberg, Gesten, Carnrike, Toro, Rapkin, Davidson & Cowen (1981) conducted a 14 week program in which the consultants held weekly workshops for the teachers and their aides, made biweekly observations of classroom lessons, and regularly met with small groups of teachers. It seems unlikely that such training programs would be implemented in a typical school. The cooperative group training programs are more realistic (e.g., 1-day workshops), but the issues concerning the selection of teachers still apply.

Some investigators have been trying to solve these problems by having school districts adopt the programs systemwide. Regardless of whether a program is formally adopted or not, it is not clear what proportion of teachers implement the program effectively or, for that matter, whether they actually implement it at all. As a rule, educational researchers have serious problems in implementing educational innovations, particularly when role changes are involved as they are here (Berman & McLaughlin, 1976; Fullan & Pomfret, 1977; Sarason, 1982). It is quite common for 25% or more of the teachers to be nonusers of a *required* innovation even in the second or third year of implementation (Hord, Rutherford, Huling-Austin, & Hall, 1987). Among those who implement an innovative program, there is marked variation in how well they implement it. Specifically, the majority of teachers implement programs in a disjointed, mechanical manner during the initial years. Many teachers may pick and choose different lessons from a program and do not implement the entire program (Durlak & Jason, 1984). We are unfamiliar with any peer intervention program that presents any results concerning the proportion of teachers implementing the program or implementing it well.

The questions concerning implementation are particularly serious in light of the fact that a teacher's primary objective in the classroom is not to improve peer relations. The demands on both teacher's time and classroom time are extensive. Some teachers, parents, and administrators may seriously question whether affective education is the school's or the family's responsibility.

Where does this leave us? We believe that investigators have shown that the programs *can* work--at least when it comes to short-term effects. At the same time, we believe that there is little evidence that the typical teacher is either able or willing to conduct peer enhancement programs on a regular basis. Whereas implementation issues may be relatively new to many of us in this field, educational researchers, practitioners, and school consultants are quite familiar with them. In the next part of this chapter, we will offer a brief review of relevant literature. Certainly, we cannot provide a comprehensive guide to conducting school consultation to teachers. Fortunately several excellent texts already exist (see Conolly, 1981; Hall & Hord, 1987; Meyers, Parsons, & Martin, 1979). What we will do, however, is outline some of the complexities that need to be addressed by either researcher or practitioner--that is, the ulcers with which you need to live. Following this, we will describe some of our experiences--both successful and unsuccessful. Three major theses will be advanced. First, in order to successfully effect change in the school, a systems perspective must be taken. Second, we can use the same model of behavior change--that is, a skills training model--to change the system as to change individual children's peer relations. Third, the processes primarily responsible for change may be systems processes and not simply program-specific processes. In other words, perhaps the reasons some programs are successful and others are not has little to do with the specific training components or theoretical approaches but instead has to do with our success or failure in working with and integrating into the system.

Finally, our points are intended for both the researcher and the clinical practitioner. Their goals and tools are different. Researchers are more limited than practitioners in what they can and cannot do after an intervention has been started. Yet by knowing more about how the system works, researchers, as well as practitioners, can learn to implement programs appropriately in the superstructure of the system. Moreover, they can examine how the system affects the process and outcome of an intervention.

A Systems Perspective

As others have observed (Lieberman & Miller, 1984; Sarason, 1982; Schmuck & Schmuck, 1974), we believe that a systems perspective must be applied to our understanding of the use of innovative techniques within the schools. The context in which teachers adopt and utilize an innovation may be the essential determinant of the success or failure of that innovation. Schmuck and Schmuck (1974) describe four distinct levels within the school system: (a) the individuals involved--teachers, students, and administrators; (b) the learning groups--classrooms and committees; (c) the school organization--the working of the organization and the social interactions among the individuals and units; and (d) the external environment--school board, budget, and parents. Each of these levels is considered in the following subsections.

Level 1--The Individuals. Teachers, students, and administrators all play important roles in the system. Teachers will be considered first, as they are the ones who both implement change and are most directly affected by it. In this section, we will initially consider the typical characteristics of the school system that generally affect teachers' implementation of innovations and then consider how individual differences in teachers may affect implementation.

Usually, norms exist for teachers' not sharing, observing, or discussing classroom successes and problems with each other (Lieberman & Miller, 1984; Lortie, 1975). One effect of this autonomy or isolation is that teachers learn about teaching largely on their own through a trial-and-error process. Each teacher acquires a teaching style that takes into account the rhythms of the school day, week, and year and the unique characteristics of each classroom (Lieberman & Miller, 1984). The teacher has great faith in this style because it has yielded effective results in the classroom (Bolster, 1983).

According to Lieberman and Miller (1984), a teacher's knowledge base is thought to be relatively weak as a consequence of learning to teach in isolation. Moreover, the base is usually not growing at an optimal rate, as it might through working with peers. Teachers are left to struggle with their problems alone, which can result in feelings of uncertainty and self-doubt (Lortie, 1975).

The process through which teachers' values and beliefs are developed also makes them very resistant to change. Wouldn't any of us be reluctant to give up hard-earned skills for an untried program? Stated simply, teachers are pragmatists (Doyle & Ponder, 1977-1978). Accordingly, those innovations that are seen as practical are most likely to be used, whereas those perceived as impractical have little chance of being tried unless mandated. Once the mandate is removed, teachers are likely to discard the innovations they perceive as impractical (Doyle & Ponder, 1977-1978).

Teachers and social scientists use different criteria for evaluating the usefulness of a program. As social scientists, we have primarily been concerned with effectiveness. Effectiveness, however, is not the only criterion used by teachers to judge the potential value of a program (Witt, 1986). In fact, the actual effectiveness may not be as important to determining the use of a program as the teachers' perceptions of effectiveness. Their perceptions are particularly critical because teachers may not have access to empirical data, nor may they put much stock in empirical research that has not been tested in the "real world" (Witt, 1986).

In addition to effectiveness or perceived effectiveness, teachers use three criteria to judge the practicality of an intervention: instrumentality, congruence, and cost (Doyle & Ponder, 1977-1978; Fullan, 1982). *Instrumentality* refers to the degree to which innovation procedures are clearly and concretely stated or illustrated. *Congruence* refers to how well the new procedures fit with a teacher's existing style, self-image, and preferred mode of interacting with students. The *cost* of a program refers to the ratio of the amount of return to the amount of investment. Cost includes not only material resources and teacher time but also the degree to which an innovation requires changes in the existing structure. Finally, teachers are also responsive to social factors such as recognition and particularly student enthusiasm (Doyle & Ponder, 1977-1978; Lortie, 1975). In fact, most of the rewards that teachers receive are from their students. To complicate matters further, though, the program's effectiveness must be apparent early on in the intervention process, as teachers are likely to make their judgments about the program quickly.

Up to this point, we have emphasized the typical characteristics of teachers that have an impact on the implementation of an innovation, but there are also individual differences among teachers that affect whether and how a program is implemented. For example, research on teachers' self-concept or self-efficacy suggests that those teachers who feel best about themselves make the most improvement during training programs (Sparks, 1983), make more use of training opportunities, and seek to develop skills in new areas to a greater extent (McKibbin & Joyce, 1980) than teachers who feel less positively about themselves. Similarly, conceptual flexibility has been found to be related to the instructional styles that teachers initially develop (Hunt & Joyce, 1967), to the ease with which individuals master new teaching skills (Joyce, Weil & Wald, 1973), and to the transfer of new skills to an existing repertoire (Showers, Joyce, & Bennett, 1987; Sparks, 1983). This work notwithstanding, we know relatively little about the effects of individual differences on the implementation of programs. For example, we have been unable to locate work on the effects of grade level, years of experience, or intelligence.

A second set of individuals in the cast of characters of the school system are students. Significantly less is known about their impact on the effectiveness of intervention programs. Lieberman and Miller (1984) observed that students' perception of their roles can vary from that of interested and challenged partners in learning to bored and passive recipients of directives. Such role perceptions can be expected to set the tone of the learning environment and, by extension, affect the outcome of any intervention.

Other variables of interest include the individual student's level of motivation, economic background, and level of achievement. It is not clear how these student characteristics relate to the effectiveness of an innovative program. In fact, evaluations of classroom-based social cognitive or cooperative group programs have not even distinguished between the effects on children with peer relationship problems and the effects on those without such problems. Is a program that is appropriate for nonproblem children powerful enough to correct for adjustment difficulties in problem children? We simply don't know. Some of our work suggests that cooperative programs may need to be supplemented with skills programs to have a lasting impact on unaccepted children (Bierman & Furman, 1984). Finally, the nature of the overall student population should be considered. For example, are the students a heterogeneous or homogeneous group?

Another central character is the school administrator. The principal's method of school leadership can best be understood in the context of interrelationships among individuals and so will be considered in that sub-section of the chapter. However, individual characteristics of the principal should also be addressed. Principals' perceptions of their primary role can range from that of overseer, referee, and plant manager to disciplinarian, scapegoat, and moral authority (Lieberman & Miller, 1984). Schmuck and Schmuck (1974) suggest that there is an inherent tension between the bureaucratic and the interpersonal aspects of the role. As was the case for teachers and students, the principal's role perceptions, experience as a leader, and views on innovation will affect the outcome of any innovative program.

Level 2--The Learning Group. The second level of analysis refers to the natural autonomous subgroups, such as classrooms, team-teaching dyads or triads, and committees. These groups are important because they are most often the arenas in which change takes place. Although teachers usually work in isolation in the classroom, strong interpersonal relationships are typically formed at the learning group level. For an innovation to be successful, it may be essential that the innovative efforts receive support from these relationships. Of course, from a researcher's point of view, the interactions among teachers present problems of statistical dependency, as each teacher's behavior may influence that of the others (Cronbach, 1976). A group's climate can also vary as a function of the rules within particular classrooms, the expectations of individuals/students and teachers for each other, and the relationships among members of the group. Innovators would be wise to consider the tenor and constellation of such small groups.

Finally, it is important to recognize that the children, as well as the teachers, are in systems. The system includes both children's relationships with teachers and their relationships in the peer group. Like the teachers' groups, these groups are important elements in the school system.

Level 3--The School Organization. The third level is made up of the interrelations of the autonomous subgroups. Sarason (1982) is credited with ground-breaking work in his descriptions of the inner workings of the school culture. A central element of the culture is the decision making process. Teachers feel more powerful if they are apprised of and involved in changes to their environment. Although it makes the researchers' job more difficult, teacher involvement in the planning and decision-making process is often cited as a necessary and critical ingredient for the success of an innovation (Berman & McLaughlin, 1976; Fullan, 1982; Purkey & Smith, 1985; Sarason, 1982).

Not only is the school principal the key power figure, but he or she sets the tone for all interactions in the school (Chesler, Schmuck, & Lippitt, 1975; Lieberman & Miller, 1984). Active principal support for innovations has been shown to result in more teachers' participating in innovations (see Chesler et al., 1975). Berman and McLaughlin (1976) found that teachers were able to support each other more effectively in their attempts at innovation when they were supported by their principal. The principal can also indirectly affect innovations by the general climate he or she establishes. Satisfied teachers may work productively to reach a principal's goals; dissatisfied teachers may attempt to sabotage any directive from the principal (Schmuck & Schmuck, 1974).

The structure of the school day provides another set of indications about the potential responsiveness of a particular school to innovation. Do teachers have free time to meet about an innovation? Are they burdened with extracurricular and administrative demands? Course credit or released time to work on innovations may increase the interest in and effectiveness of the innovations. Interestingly, offering extra pay to teachers as an incentive has not been found to be related to adopting the new skills (Berman & McLaughlin, 1976).

Level 4--The External Environment. The fourth level refers to outside groups or factors--including the school board, school budget, district superintendent and parents--each of which exerts tremendous influence on the individual school. Innovations that come with long-term district support (monetary and otherwise) stand a better chance of long-term success than those that do not. Many school systems may be unwilling to make peer enhancement programs a part of their regular curriculum despite the positive features of these programs. In addition, district level demands and support for projects often change over time, and the individual schools may need to change accordingly to maintain positive ties with the district. For this reason, programs that have been adopted may also be dropped in subsequent years as programs arise that respond to new issues.

Innovations and the Process of Change

In the previous section, we have tried to identify some of the factors that influence the functioning of the school system. When trying to implement an innovation or change this system, a number of other considerations must be taken into account.

Consultant Characteristics. One major issue is whether the change agent/facilitator should be someone within the system or someone from outside. External consultants can provide an objective view of the system.

They can enter with prestige and status, perhaps offering specialized expertise not present in the system. From the point of view of the researcher, a trained outsider is more likely to maintain a systematic, controlled approach to the intervention. On the other hand, insiders are familiar with the internal workings of the system. They are known to the staff and probably would not be met with the same skepticism and suspicion with which outsiders are often greeted. Old-timers in the school frequently assume that both the new person and the new program are likely to be transient (Crandall, Eiseman, & Louis, 1986). A team approach in which internal and external agents work together seems promising (Crandall et al., 1986). Having invested staff remain in the setting after the outside consultant leaves may help to maintain and institutionalize the changes.

Regardless of whether the person is an insider or an outsider, the consultant should have interpersonal skills such as sensitivity and flexibility, which have been found to be typically associated with effective helping behavior. Although it is clearly important for the consultant to understand what the process of teaching is like, some researchers have found that previous teaching experience by the consultants is negatively related to consultee satisfaction (Conolly, 1981).

Teacher Training. Not surprisingly, most of the knowledge available on teacher training comes from the education literature. It primarily addresses ways of teaching teachers how to institute new teaching programs, but the same principles may apply to teaching teachers to implement social skills training programs. Of course, teachers may feel less obliged to implement affective education programs than traditional academic programs.

With some slight variations, most of the "how-to" literature on consultation presents similar models for fostering behavior change within a system. The typical steps include the establishment of rapport, the presentation of material, demonstration and observation by the participants, practice by the participants, feedback, and follow-up coaching. Note the striking parallels to the general social-skills-training model we use.

Perhaps the most important step is establishing trust and rapport with participants. Time spent drinking coffee and talking casually about seemingly unrelated topics is important to the consulation process. Not only does it aid in developing relationships, but it also provides one with increased knowledge of the participants' characteristics and concerns. Ironically, it is a stage of the intervention process that we social scientists don't discuss and simply take for granted.

The in-service workshop is the medium used most often to present and teach material to staff. It is cost effective and efficient, and the group format provides the teachers with a sense of community and social support. Teachers can share questions and ideas, which aids in the learning process (Sparks, 1983). In general, the workshop is a microcosm of the overall consultation effort, with the effective components being: (a) study of theory or rationale for the innovation, (b) demonstration by an expert, and (c) practice and feedback by participants (Joyce & Showers, 1982).

Single-session workshops, however, have been shown to be ineffective in producing lasting change (Lawrence, 1974). A more promising approach begins with a series of workshops. These should be spaced over time so that new skills can be introduced gradually and ongoing discussions of concerns and problems can naturally arise. Broyles and Tillman (1985) found that workshop time was not well spent in introducing participants, making general comments about the material to be presented, or detailing the theoretical underpinnings of the program. Instead, they suggest sending introductory materials to the teachers ahead of time and addressing theoretical concerns at a later point. The workshop time should focus on practical, concrete material, with examples and applications for the classroom.

Even a series of workshops is not enough to effect long-lasting change. Joyce and Showers (1980, 1983) found that teachers need to practice new skills at least 5 times in the two weeks that follow training, with up to 30 instances of observation, feedback, and coaching before they are able to comfortably assimilate the skills into their daily routine.

Although teachers can *master* skills in a relatively short time, the follow-through to using new skills in the classroom is generally very poor (Berman & McLaughlin, 1976). Joyce and Showers (1983) found that with a learning program made up of theory, demonstration, practice and feedback, 80% of teachers can acquire the skills, but only 2% to 5% will end up integrating the skills into their classroom routine. Again, the parallels within the field of behavior therapy are striking.

Many point to the importance of consultant follow-up after the initial presentation of new ideas and skills in the workshop setting. This may be provided by the consultant's offering ongoing consultation services or meeting with teachers individually or in small groups to answer questions or review the finer points of the program. The consultant may visit classrooms, observing and offering suggestions to teachers. Teachers also need to receive regular feedback on changes in student behavior (Guskey, 1985) and continual support during the initial implementation phase when they are not yet committed to the program (Crandall, 1983; Guskey, 1985). Consultants cannot expect the support to come from within the system, at least not initially.

Joyce and Showers (1982) suggest a follow-up program involving teachers' coaching and supporting one another. With this component in place, the maintenance of skills increases from 2% to 5% all the way up to 80% (Joyce & Showers, 1982). Similarly, Sparks (1983) compared the outcomes of three programs: workshops plus trainer-provided coaching, workshops plus peer observation, and workshops alone. Results indicated that workshops plus peer observation was the most effective approach in fostering lasting change.

Crandall (1983) examined 61 innovative programs and found that attempts to change teacher attitudes and foster commitment to the new practices prior to implementation were generally unsuccessful. Significant changes in teacher beliefs and attitudes may also depend on evidence of change in their students (Bolster, 1983; Crandall, 1983). Guskey (1985) found that changes in beliefs occurred only after student improvement and not just with training or even with training and implementation.

Miles, Fullan, and Taylor (1978) found that prepackaged, rigidly structured change programs were less effective than more flexible programs. Berman and McLaughlin (1976) and others have emphasized the concept of mutual adaptation, wherein an innovation must adapt to the particular setting and teachers, and the setting must adapt to the demands of any innovative project. One common way of adapting to the setting is to have teachers involved in the planning and design process. Often, however, the teachers' alterations to the programs were such that the innovations lost their effectiveness (Crandall, 1983). This idea of mutual adaptation can also pose problems for the researcher, who may need to maintain control over the program and keep the components in a package constant.

Table 18.1

Stages of Concern: Typical Expressions of Concern About an Innovation

	Stages of concern	Expressions of concern
I M P A C T	6 Refocusing	I have some ideas about something that would work even better.
	5 Collaboration	I am concerned about relating what I am doing with what other instructors are doing.
T A S K	4 Consequence	How is my use of it affecting kids?
	3 Management	I seem to be spending all my time getting material ready.
S E L F	2 Personal	How will using it affect me?
	1 Informational	I would like to know more about it.
	0 Awareness	I am not concerned about it (the innovation).

Note: Adapted from *Taking Charge of Change*. (p. 31) by S. M. Hord, W. L. Rutherford, L. Huling-Austin, and G. E. Hall, 1987, Austin, TX: Southwest Educational Development Laboratory. By permission.

Evaluating the Process of Change

The most systematic work on evaluating change derives from the Concerns-Based Adoption Model (CBAM). Three components of implementing change are examined: (a) innovation configurations, (b) stages of concern, and (c) levels of use (Hall & Hord, 1987; Hord et al., 1987). The concept of *innovation configuration* is that there are a number of components in any innovation. Each teacher may decide to implement some and not others. Thus, not all teachers will be implementing the program in the the same manner. Some components may be critical, whereas others may not. One would want to conduct an assessment of the configuration of components to determine what is, in fact, being implemented. *Stages of concern* refer to the teachers' concerns about a program, which typically progress developmentally. Early on, they tend to be self-concerns, then task concerns, and perhaps finally concerns about the impact of the program (see Table 18.1). Finally, *levels of use* refers to whether and how well the program is being implemented. As can be seen in Table 18.2, levels of use include somewhat sequential degrees of implementation: (0) nonuse, (1) orientation (seeking information), (2) preparation, (3) mechanical use, (4A) routine, (4B) refinement, (5) integration (combining efforts with colleagues), and (6) renewal (making major modifications in the innovation).

The information concerning levels of usage is invaluable for evaluation, particularly if it appears that a program is not effective. Perhaps it is not being implemented properly! By knowing the innovation configuration, the nature of the teachers' concerns, and the levels of usage, one can determine what issues need to be addressed further in the consultation package or in booster sessions that follow. Thus, detailed information can be obtained about program implementation, why a program may be working or not, and what can be done to improve it. Any one investigator may only work with a limited number of teachers, but perhaps if the field were to adopt a common means of evaluating implementation, such as CBAM, results could be pooled to determine the modal pattern of implementation and the factors that may improve implementation of programs.

Table 18.2

Levels of the Use of an Innovation

Level 0 -- nonuse:	The individual has little or no knowledge of the innovation, no involvement with it, and is doing nothing toward becoming involved.
Level 1 -- orientation:	The individual has acquired or is acquiring information about the innovation and/or has explored its value orientation and what it will require.
Level 2 -- preparation:	The user is preparing for first use of the innovation.
Level 3 -- mechanical use:	The user focuses most effort on the day-to-day use of the innovation. Changes in use are made more to meet user needs than needs of students. The user is primarily engaged in an attempt to master tasks required to use the innovation.
Level 4A -- routine:	Use of the innovation is stabilized. Few if any changes are made in ongoing use. Little preparation or thought is being given to improving innovation use or its consequences.
Level 4B -- refinement:	The user varies the use of the innovation to increase the impact on students. Variations in use are based on knowledge of both short- and long-term consequences for students.
Level 5 -- integration:	The user is combining own efforts to use the innovation with related activities of colleagues to achieve a collective impact on students.
Level 6 -- renewal:	The user reevaluates the quality of use of the innovation and seeks major modifications of, or alternatives to the innovation in order to present the innovation in a way that will achieve increased impact on students.

Note: Adapted from *Taking Charge of Change*. (p. 55) by S. M. Hord, W. L. Rutherford, L. Huling-Austin, and G. E. Hall, 1987, Austin, TX: Southwest Educational Development Laboratory. By permission.

A Seeming Success

During the last two years, we have been examining the efficacy of a consultation program designed to teach educators how to treat and prevent peer relationship problems in their classrooms. The program was tried in a school with both elementary school grades (grades 1 to 6 with students ranging in age from 6 to 12 years old) and middle school grades (grades 7 to 8 with students ranging in age from 12 to 15). Before describing the program, we should describe the process of entry. First, we invited the principal to have her school participate, and then we presented the program at a faculty meeting, and had the teachers vote to participate. We felt it was important to enter the system informally as well. The consultants (two advanced clinical students) attended school functions, met informally with teachers, and in general worked to make themselves familiar and accepted in the school.

The core components of the project were workshops and ongoing consultation. Two workshops, each 75 minutes long, were presented to the entire school staff. The workshops had two main purposes: first, to educate and provide information and, second, to arouse interest in the project. The following topics were covered: the importance of peer relationships, the nature of problems in peer relationships, the value of classroom-based methods, and descriptions of both the approaches that would be available, and the consultation process. Didactic presentations were coupled with experiential/"hands on" exercises to increase enthusiasm and provide teachers with a realistic impression of the feasibility of using the techniques in their own classroom.

Six different approaches were offered to the teachers because it seemed unlikely that any one peer relationship improvement program would be appropriate for all teachers or all age groups. They included: two social skills training approaches--"Getting Along With Others" (Jackson & Jackson, 1983) for the lower grades and "Skill Streaming the Elementary School Child" (McGinnis & Goldstein, 1984) for the upper grades; two social-cognitive approaches--"Think Aloud" (Bash & Camp, 1985) for the lower grades and "Aware" (Elardo & Cooper, 1977) for the upper; a cooperative group technique--"Student Team Learning" (Slavin, 1980); and a simple collection of fun activities designed to help children get to know one another better and create friendships--"Fun With Friends."

Interested teachers were asked to implement a technique in their classroom five times within approximately a one month period. After the 5th session, the teacher was offered another 5-session package. The program was broken into two 5-session segments because our past experience indicated that some teachers found an initial commitment of 10 sessions to be too much, and 5 sessions provided enough information for them to evaluate the practicality of the program.

To assist the teachers in implementing the programs, the consultant met with them five times during each segment. These 30-minute consultation meetings were scheduled flexibly during the teachers' own free time. A standard seven-step sequence was followed: (a) *Meeting 1*: This meeting served as an opportunity for the consultant to become more familiar with the teacher, the teacher's style, and the classroom problems she or he wished to work on. Together, they selected an approach. (b) *Meeting 2*: The consultant and teacher discussed the "nuts and bolts" of implementing the approach and planned the first lesson. (c) *Joint Lesson*: The two jointly conducted the first lesson. (d) *Feedback*: The two reviewed the first lesson and planned the next one. (e) *Second lesson*: The teacher conducted a second classroom lesson while the consultant observed. (f) *Meeting 4*: The two reviewed the previous lesson, "troubleshooting" as much as possible, and planned out the remaining three lessons. (g) *Meeting 5*: The two reviewed the entire program and discussed further implementation of it. All teachers who had participated in the program were interested in continuing. We believed that this package was both long enough to provide sufficient training to enable a teacher to implement a program, yet not so long that an ordinary school psychologist, social worker, curriculum adviser, or teacher would be unwilling to undergo the process. In other words, we thought that the program was realistic, unlike some of the other more concerted efforts used in previous research.

What effects did the program have? Five of the 13 elementary school teachers participated in the program. None of the 4 middle school teachers did. We also collected pre- and postevaluations of teacher attitudes. Specifically, teachers completed a 17-item questionnaire that examined their openness to change, their perceived competence in coping with peer problems, their perceptions regarding how changeable peer relation problems are, their attitudes about cooperative group programs, their attitudes concerning the importance of affective education, and their extracurricular commitments. Although the sample was too small to permit us to draw any firm conclusions, the data suggested some positive changes. After participating, the teachers showed increases in their openness to innovative techniques, felt more competent in coping with peer relationship problems, and had more positive attitudes concerning cooperative group programs. Additionally, at the time of preevaluation, the nonparticipants reported both feeling more competent in coping with peer problems and feeling more overwhelmed by other responsibilities, suggesting that the reasons for not participating are diverse.

We continued our involvement for the first part of the next year. The consultants reviewed the approaches and consultation process at a faculty meeting. Several teachers who had previously participated spontaneously offered testimony regarding the benefits of the program.

Two types of packages were offered this year. Teachers who had participated previously were encouraged to participate in a booster package designed to foster the reimplementation of the old approach with a new class. Specifically, the consultant and teacher reviewed last year's experience. Then the consultant observed the teacher conducting a lesson and provided feedback. Three to four weeks later, they met again to discuss how the approach was working and to plan further implementation.

All teachers were also provided with the option of participating in the consultation program offered during the first year. All teachers who participated in the first year continued with consultation in the second year. Two received the booster package for their original approaches, two chose to add breadth and opted for receiving the standard package to learn a new approach, and 1 motivated teacher chose both to receive booster sessions and to learn a new approach. In addition, 5 new teachers chose to participate. All 10 teachers taught first- through fifth-grade classes. (The students in these classes ranged in age from 6 to 11 years old). Interestingly, all the different approaches had been selected by at least 1 teacher, suggesting that a range of techniques may be more appealing than any single one.

Two months later, the level of usage interviews described previously were conducted. Three teachers were using the program mechanically (Level 3). Two were using the program routinely (Level 4-A). The remaining four had modified the program to fit their classroom (Level 4-B), and in a couple of cases rather substantially (i.e., perhaps Level 6). Thus, most, if not all, teachers had learned the program from the short consultation experience, but the frequency of implementation varied substantially. Three reported using the program twice a week or more; four were using it weekly; one was using it every other week; and the remaining two were not using it at all.

Although the teachers were inconsistent in following up the program after our completion, they did report positive changes in the children's social skills. At the beginning

and end of the school year, each teacher completed social questionnaires for four of their students whom they perceived as having problems in social skills and four other randomly selected children (total N = 153 children). The 22 item questionnaire assessed five components of social skills: (a) problem-solving skills,
(b) prosocial behavior, (c) coping with provocation, (d) positive behavior toward nonfriends, and (e) small-group behavior. Compared to children in the nonparticipating teachers' classrooms, those in participating teachers' classrooms showed increases in all five skill domains (see Table 18.3). The changes were comparable both for children identified by teachers as having problems in social skills and for those who were not so identified, suggesting that the program had both remedial and preventive effects.

Table 18.3

Pretreatment and Posttreatment Ratings of Children's Social Skills

| | Participants | | Nonparticipants | |
	Pre	Post	Pre	Post
Skills				
Problem-solving skills	3.64	3.88	3.71	3.75
Prosocial behavior	3.69	4.06	3.84	3.79
Coping with provocation	3.65	3.84	3.84	3.67
Behavior toward nonfriends	3.91	4.18	4.06	3.84
Small group behavior	3.71	4.11	4.02	3.85

Note: Scores (range 1-5) represent participating and nonparticipating teachers' ratings of the social skills of a sample of their students. Higher scores reflect more skillfulness. Significant group-by-time effects were found for all variables.

We believe that we were relatively successful in implementing this program. Of course, even the beginning psychology student will observe that we have not adequately demonstrated that. The changes could reflect preexisting differences between the teachers who participated and those who did not. An ideal control group would be a second, comparable school in which the program is not offered until a subsequent year. One could then compare the changes in classrooms in which a program had been implemented with those in which a program would be implemented in the future. We originally planned to include such a comparison. In fact, an experimental school was to be that control group, but our original experimental school was a disappointing, though enlightening, failure--the topic we turn to next.

An Enlightening Failure

Prior to conducting this project, we had contacted another elementary school. As in the other case, we contacted the principal, she presented the project to the faculty, and faculty agreement was obtained. The consultants appeared in the school about a month later, after the initial evaluation data had been collected. The consultants presented two workshops. The first was well received, but in the second workshop, many questions were raised by the teachers, and several teachers were openly critical. The following day a group of teachers met with the principal, angry about what they viewed as their forced participation in an "outsiders'" project. Moreover, they felt that what was then a 10-session commitment was excessive, given their already full schedules. We felt it best to end our involvement in the school at that point.

The Lesson

Why did the project fail? The teachers did not have a good understanding of the project as a whole. We suspect that the principal had undersold the amount of work that would be required on the teachers' part. The school had not been involved in a research project before, and the staff found the process of obtaining parental permission, and so on to be a major headache. We had spent little time informally entering the school and had not included the teachers in our planning process. As a result, we made uninformed decisions about the initial level of commitment that could be expected. Finally, the teachers felt that the project had been thrust on them by outsiders. If it had been thrust on them by the principal, they probably would have passively resisted it; in the present case, however, they could simply reject it.

What is important to note is that our failure had little to do with the actual peer relationship approaches being offered. Except for the change in the amount of commitment initially required of the teachers, this project was essentially identical to the one described earlier. Instead, the entry process, the nature of the school culture, and the implementation procedures were responsible for both our failure in one case and our success in the other.

The system issues not only influenced our outcome, but they may also influence others' outcomes. Perhaps this is why the social-skills literature is full of inconsistencies. System issues need to be addressed in order for a program to have a chance of succeeding. In fact, we believe that the degree of success in getting teachers to participate or change their behavior or feelings is strongly determined by the degree to which these issues are properly addressed.

If the teachers don't participate in programs or implement them properly, then it is unlikely that the children will change in the desired manner. What if the teachers do implement the programs properly? In that case, we usually think that the treatment approach (e.g., reinforcement, modeling) and the specific skills that are targeted are the important determinants of the degree of change in the children. The outcome, however, may also be influenced by a number of other factors that are not specific to any particular program or even to any general approach. As has been pointed out by psychotherapy researchers, the therapeutic relationship, a plan for change, the encouragement and reinforcement of change, and the fostering of esteem may all be centrally involved in the process of change (see Shapiro & Morris, 1978). In the research on improving children's peer relationships, these factors have not received much attention. Some investigators have tried to rule out such factors by including an attention control group, but such a group controls both for too much and too little simultaneously (O'Leary & Borkovec, 1978). We wonder whether some of the variability in treatment outcomes may be a function of the change agents' relationships with the children or their ability to engage the children in the process.

Finally, as was noted previously, the children, as well as the teachers, are in systems. The research on cooperative techniques has shown that changing peer group attitudes or behaviors may often prove to be an effective means of bringing about changes in individual children (Bierman & Furman, 1984; Furman, 1984; Johnson & Johnson, 1975). Regardless of the approach used, the system in which the children are functioning may have a critical effect on the outcome.

In conclusion, we believe our current theories of social skills may not be fully capturing the process of change. Fostering cooperative interactions, changing motivational structures, or teaching social or social-cognitive skills are all thought to be means of improving children's peer relations. Each of them may work often, but each of them can fail. Thus, we cannot explain the process of change simply in terms of these mechanisms. Instead, we need to understand systems and the process of implementation. Certainly, we need the tools that the programs give us, and some tools may prove to be better than others. Yet the structure of the system is the essential framework. We need to fit our tools to the system.

Acknowledgments: This research was supported by a W. T. Grant Faculty Scholar Award to the first author. The contributions of the third and fourth authors are comparable in scope. Appreciation is expressed to Jennifer Connolly for her thoughtful comments about this paper and to Larry Epstein for his prompt assistance in the analyses.

References

Bash, M. A., & Camp, B. W. (1985). *Think Aloud classroom program*. Champaign, IL: Research Press.

Berman, P., & McLaughlin, M. W. (1976). Implementation of educational innovation. *Educational Forum, 40*, 345-370.

Bierman, K. L., & Furman, W. (1984). The effects of social skills training and peer involvement on the social adjustment of preadolescents. *Child Development, 52*, 171-178.

Bolster, A. S. (1983). Toward a more effective model of research on teaching. *Harvard Educational Review, 53*, 294-308.

Broyles, I., & Tillman, M. (1985). Relationships of inservice training components and changes in teacher concerns regarding innovations. *Journal of Educational Research, 78*, 364-371.

Chesler, M., Schmuck, R. A., & Lippitt, R. (1975). The principal's role in facilitating innovation. In T. E. Deal & M. Z. Ancell (Eds.), *Managing change in educational organizations* (pp. 176-186). Berkeley, CA: McCutchan.

Conolly, J. C. (1981). *Consultation in schools: Theory, research, procedures*. New York: Academic Press.

Crandall, D. P. (1983). The teacher's role in school improvement. *Educational Leadership, 41*, 6-9.

Crandall, D. P., Eiseman, J. W., & Louis, K. S. (1986). Strategic planning issues that bear on the success of school improvement efforts. *Educational Administration Quarterly, 22*, 21-53.

Cronbach, L. J. (1976). *Research on classrooms and schools: Formulation of questions, design, and analysis*. Stanford, CA: Stanford Evaluation Consortium.

Doyle, W. & Ponder, G. A. (1977-1978). The practicality ethic in teacher decision-making. *Interchange, 8*, 1-12.

Durlak, J. A., & Jason, L. A. (1984). Preventative programs for school-aged children and adolescents. In M. C. Roberts & L. Peterson (Eds.), *Prevention of problems in childhood: Psychological research and applications*. New York: Wiley.

Elardo, P. T., & Cooper, B. M. (1977). *Aware: Activities for social development*. Menlo Park, CA: Addison-Wesley.

Elardo, P.T. & Caldwell, B.M. (1979). The effects of an experimental social development program on children in the middle childhood period. *Psychology in the School, 16*, 93-100.

Fullan, M. (1982). *The meaning of educational change*. New York: Teachers' College Press.

Fullan, M., & Pomfret, A. (1977). Research on curriculum and instruction implementation. *Review of Educational Research, 47*, 335-397.

Furman, W. (1984). Enhancing peer relations. In S. Duck (Ed.), *Personal relationships 5: Repairing personal relationships*. New York: Academic Press.

Goldstein, A. P., & Kanfer, F. H. (1979). *Maximizing treatment gains: Transfer enhancement in psychotherapy*. New York: Academic Press.

Guskey, T. R. (1985). Staff development and teacher change. *Educational Leadership, 43*, 57-60.

Hall, G. E., & Hord, S. M. (1987). *Change in school: Facilitating the process*. Albany, NY: State University of New York.

Hops, H. (1982). Social skills training for socially withdrawn/isolated children. In P. Karoly & J. Steffan (Eds.), *Advances in child behavior analysis & therapy: Vol. 2. Intellectual and social deficiencies.* New York: Gardner Press.

Hord, S. M., Rutherford, W. L., Huling-Austin, L., & Hall, G. E. (1987). *Taking charge of change.* Alexandria, VA: Association for Supervision and Curriculum Development.

Hunt, D., & Joyce, B. (1967). Teacher trainee personality and initial teaching style. *American Educational Research Journal, 4,* 253-259.

Jackson, N.F. & Jackson, D.A. (1983). *Getting along with others: teaching social effectiveness to children.* Champaign, IL: Research Press.

Johnson, D.W. & Johnson, R.T. (1975). *Learning together and alone.* Englewood Cliffs, NJ: Prentice Hall.

Joyce, B., & Showers, B. (1980). Improving inservice training: The message of research. *Educational Leadership, 37,* 379-385.

Joyce, B., & Showers, B. (1982). The coaching of teachers. *Educational Leadership, 40,* 4-10.

Joyce, B., & Showers, B. (1983). *Power in staff development through research on training.* Alexandria VA: Association for Supervision and Curriculum Development.

Joyce, B., Weil, M., & Wald, R. (1973). The teacher-innovator: Models of teaching as the core of teacher education. *Interchange, 4,* 47-60.

Lawrence, G. (1974). *Patterns of effective inservice education: A state of the art summary of research on materials and procedures for changing teacher behaviors in inservice education.* Tallahassee: Florida State Department of Education (ED 176 424).

Lieberman, A., & Miller, L. (1984). *Teachers, their world, and their work: Implications for school improvement.* Alexandria, VA: Association for Supervision and Curriculum Development.

Lortie, D. C. (1975). *School-teacher: A sociological study.* Chicago: University of Chicago Press.

McGinnis, E., & Goldstein, A.P. (1984). *Skill-streaming the elementary school child.* Champaign, IL: Research Press.

McKibbin, M., & Joyce, B. (1980). Psychological states and staff development. *Theory Into Practice, 19,* 248-255.

Meyers, J., Parsons, R. D., & Martin, R. (1979). *Mental health consultation in the schools.* San Francisco: Jossey-Bass.

Miles, M., Fullan, M., & Taylor, G. (1978). *Organizational development in schools: The state of the art: Vol. III. OD consultants/OD programs in school districts.* New York: Center for Policy Research.

O'Leary, K. D., & Borkovec, T.D. (1978). Conceptual, methodological and ethical problems of placebo groups in psychotherapy research. *American Psychologist, 33,* 821-830.

Purkey, S. C., & Smith, M. S. (1985). School reform: The district policy implications of effective school literature. *The Elementary School Journal, 85,* 353-389.

Sarason, S. B. (1982). *The culture of the school and the problem of change (2nd ed.).* Boston: Allyn & Bacon.

Schmuck, R., & Schmuck, P. (1974). *A humanistic psychology of education.* Palo Alto, CA: National Press.

Shapiro, A. K., & Morris, L. A. (1978). The placebo effect in medical and psychological therapies. In S. L. Garfield & A. E. Bergin (Eds.), *Handbook of psychotherapy and behavior change: An empirical analysis 2nd ed.,* pp. 369-410. New York: Wiley.

Showers, J., Joyce, B., & Bennett, B. (1987). Synthesis of research on staff development: A framework for future study and state-of-the-art analysis. *Educational Leadership, 45,* 77-87.

Slavin, R. E. (1980). *Using student team learning.* Baltimore, MD: Johns Hopkins Team Learning Project.

Sparks, G. M. (1983). Synthesis of research on staff development for effective teaching. *Educational Leadership, 41,* 65-72.

Weissberg, R. P., Gesten, E. L., Carnrike, C. L., Toro, P. A., Rapkin, B. D., Davidson, E., & Cowen, E. L. (1981). Social problem-solving skills training: A competence-building intervention with second- to fourth-grade children. *American Journal of Community Psychology, 9,* 411-423.

Witt, J. C. (1986). Teachers' resistance to the use of school-based interventions. *Journal of School Psychology, 24,* 37-44.

19

Promoting Social Competence in Early Adolescence: Developmental Considerations

Marlene Zelek Caplan and Roger P. Weissberg

Yale University

Social competence promotion (SCP) during childhood and adolescence has been identified as an important means of fostering adaptive behavior and preventing psychopathology (Kent & Rolf, 1979; Kornberg & Caplan, 1980; Long, 1986; Report of the Prevention Task Panel, 1978). As a result, a variety of school-based SCP programs have been developed (see reviews by Durlak & Jason, 1984; Pellegrini & Urbain, 1985; Spivack & Shure, 1982; Weissberg & Allen, 1986). Many of these programs are designed for preschool- and elementary school-age children (ages 4-10), based, in large part, on the assumption that the earlier the intervention, the greater the likelihood of promoting social competence and precluding more serious problems later in life (Durlak & Jason, 1984).

However, as many SCP researchers point out, short-term childhood interventions neither ensure competent behavior throughout life nor "inoculate" individuals against psychopathology (Bloom, 1985; Rutter, 1982; Zigler & Berman, 1983). During the course of development, a number of socioecological transitions occur that precipitate new challenges for adaptation and positive developmental outcome (Bronfenbrenner, 1979). Each transition involves an alteration in activities and tasks, a redefinition of social roles, changing motives and concerns, a reorganization of social networks, exposure to different socializing agents, opportunities for novel experiences, and a restructuring in the ways of both perceiving and interacting with the world (Felner, Farber, & Primavera, 1983; Higgins & Parsons, 1983).

The question then arises as to how to create SCP programs most beneficial to students at different points in the life span. Recognition of the developmental tasks, changes, concerns, and pressures motivating behavior is essential if we are to create effective SCP programs that facilitate current and future adaptive functioning (Garmezy & Masten, 1986; Jessor, 1984). According to Sroufe and Rutter (1984), it is necessary "to understand both individual patterns of adaptation with respect to salient issues of a given developmental period and the transaction between prior adaptation, maturational change, and subsequent environmental challenges" (p. 17).

Our most recent work on social competence promotion centers on the period of early adolescence. This chapter highlights a number of developmental considerations in the design and implementation of school-based SCP programs for this age group. We begin by identifying several developmental tasks and challenges of early adolescence that create a need for SCP intervention during this period. We then articulate the conceptualization

B. H. Schneider et al. (eds.), Social Competence in Developmental Perspective, 371–385.
© *1989 by Kluwer Academic Publishers.*

of social competence guiding our work and describe two SCP programs currently being implemented in our local school system (Caplan, Jacoby, Weissberg, & Grady, 1988; Weissberg, Caplan, & Bennetto, 1988). Finally, we offer several recommendations for future SCP research with young adolescents.

Focus on Early Adolescence

At no time in the life span are the changes in intrapersonal, interpersonal, and social environments greater than in early adolescence (Erikson, 1964; Hill, 1980; Kimmel & Weiner, 1985; Lipsitz, 1977). While the characterization of adolescence as a period of "storm and stress" (Hall, 1904) has not held up to empirical scrutiny, changes occurring in the physical, cognitive, psychosocial, emotional, and environmental domains render children particularly vulnerable to current problems and subsequent dysfunction (Jessor, 1984; Rutter, 1980). Lipsitz (1977) suggests that early adolescence is a "period of plasticity" (p. 10) and should be recognized as an opportune time for intervention to promote adaptive development. Similarly, Jessor (1984) maintains that this period represents a critical point in development in which health-enhancing or health-compromising learning occurs, setting the stage for later life. Hill (1980) provides a useful framework for understanding the major issues and challenges of the early adolescent period. He describes a set of primary changes--biological, cognitive, and social-- that engender secondary changes in attachment, autonomy, achievement, identity, intimacy, and sexuality. In terms of biology, young adolescents are adapting to rapid and multifaceted physical and physiological changes, which, in turn, bring about alterations in social expectations, intimacy, and sexuality. For example, students must come to terms with their own physical and emotional changes and learn how to integrate these changes into their self-concept and social behavior. With respect to cognition, young adolescents are undergoing cognitive advances that allow them to consider hypothetical possibilities, think ahead to the future, reflect on their own thoughts, examine others' motives and intentions, and consider new perspectives regarding problem situations, social relationships, and moral dilemmas (Keating, 1980; Piaget, 1970). These cognitive advances have major implications for achievement, autonomy, and intimacy, as young adolescents can now experiment with various strategies of social behavior, integrate past and future behaviors, and relate more intimately with others. Socially, adolescents are coping with an evolving role that involves alterations in both adult and peer expectations. Parents often increase their demands in terms of schoolwork and chores around the home and expect greater social responsibility in the use of leisure time and academic performance (Kimmel & Weiner, 1985). New, more complex relations with agemates become established as young adolescents form closer relationships with same-gender peers (Sullivan, 1953) and begin new modes of interaction with opposite-gender peers (Montemayor & VanKomen, 1985).

Early adolescence involves a transformation in the relative influence of the various agents of socialization, as experiences outside of the home begin to displace those that were previously under the control of parents (Adelson, 1980). This growing peer orientation results in more time being spent in unsupervised activities, creating a vulnerability to participation in risky or health-compromising behavior (Berndt, 1979; Costanzo & Shaw, 1966). The opportunity and peer support for engaging in such activities, not evident at younger ages, contributes to this heightened risk. Frequently, such activities are encouraged by new peer role models, not only to express independence but also to strengthen bonds between peer group members (Jessor, 1984). Thus, minor delinquency and substance use become fairly common during adolescence, when pressure to conform is particularly high

(Costanzo & Shaw, 1966; Jessor, 1984). It is clear that the values of the peer group play an important role in determining whether competent social skills are actually translated into competent behavior (Parkhurst & Asher, 1985). Peers can serve to increase, maintain, or decrease the tendency to engage in risky behavior through direct interaction and also by setting norms related to the propriety of certain actions.

The sheer pervasiveness of these changes may create a vulnerability to problem behaviors, as young adolescents cope with feelings of inadequacy, shifting social controls, and expanding peer relations. Exposure to new models, often at odds with those observed in the home, contribute to the exploration of a new self-definition and social identity occasioned by the social organization of adolescent life itself. Furthermore, this period constitutes a time of key transitions and opportunities for novel experiences, such as smoking, drinking, and engaging in sexual activity (Petersen, 1982).

Adapting to school-related changes also represents an important task for young adolescents. The new environmental setting of the middle school (typically grades 5-8 or 6-8, ages 10-14) places increased demands on students to adapt to a larger educational environment, departmentalized classrooms, and a more taxing academic work load (Lipsitz, 1977). Theoretical and empirical evidence suggests that individuals often have particular difficulty negotiating this transition (Felner, Primavera, & Cauce, 1981). The shift has been associated with a rise in absenteeism, an increase in negative attitudes toward school, more referrals for disciplinary problems, less participation in extracurricular activities, a decrease in academic achievement, and for girls, lowered self-esteem (Kaplan, Martin, & Robbins, 1984; Simmons & Blyth, 1987). In addition to the transition itself causing difficulty, anticipation of the move to a new school setting can also foster anxiety. Gilchrist, Schinke, Snow, Schilling, and Senechal (1988) found that sixth graders (i.e., 11- and 12-year olds) preparing for seventh grade reported a high degree of anxiousness about the impending transition. The most common concerns included: adjusting to new surroundings, worry about academic competence, concern over new social networks, and pressure to engage in risk-taking behavior.

The developmental issues outlined in this section indicate the need for intervention during early adolescence. Successful adaptation in the face of these challenges has positive implications for later life, while failure to adapt can result in a variety of problem behaviors, including school difficulties, social isolation, depression, delinquency, substance abuse, and other health-compromising behaviors (Bachman, O'Malley, & Johnston, 1979; Bloom, 1979; Felner et al., 1983; Jessor & Jessor, 1977). Considering the large number of children whose current and future psychosocial functioning is of concern, it seems both logical and critical to establish effective SCP programs in the schools (Weissberg, Caplan, & Sivo, in press). Lipsitz (1977) maintains that the schools should not be "responsible for" but "responsive to" (p. 84) children as they progress through this difficult period in the life span. Among other things, schools can teach social skills; provide for satisfying social contacts; engage students in activities to build cohesiveness in personal, academic, and community life; provide support resources; and structure an environment where health is the norm (Jessor, 1984; Lipsitz, 1984; Perry, 1982; Rutter, 1980).

Given these perspectives, our work has focused on young adolescents in their first and second years of middle school (i.e., grades 6 and 7). The new environment places demands on children to cope with various intrapersonal, interpersonal, and environmental challenges and to behave in ways that require increased responsibility and decision-making (Elias, Gara, & Ubriaco, 1985). While changes in social activities, roles, and concerns during this age period may create numerous risks for both short- and long-term social adjustment, they may also offer opportunities and challenges that, if negotiated successfully, will provide a stronger foundation for positive developmental outcomes (Erikson, 1964; Higgins & Parsons, 1983; Hill, 1980; Jessor, 1984; Rutter, 1980). The next section describes the conceptualization of social competence guiding our current work with young adolescents, followed by a description of the programs being implemented in our local school setting.

Conceptualization of Social Competence

Many different definitions of *social competency* have been proposed. In recent years, there seems to be an emerging consensus that social competence has less to do with any one set of behaviors, skills, or traits and more to do with the coordination of cognition, affect, and behavior to successfully handle developmentally relevant social tasks (Dodge, 1986; Ford, 1982; 1985; Waters & Sroufe, 1983). Ford (1982), for example, refers to social competence as the "attainment of relevant social goals in specified social contexts, using appropriate means and resulting in positive developmental outcomes" (p. 324). Waters and Sroufe (1983), similarly, define the competent individual as "one who is able to make use of environmental and personal resources to achieve a good developmental outcome" (p. 81). Dodge (1986) refers to social competence as the "degree to which significant others rate an individual as successful in solving and completing relevant social tasks" (p. 75).

We suggest that SCP programs should employ a systematic, integrated combination of intervention approaches to: (a) enhance the capacities of children and adolescents to coordinate cognition, affect, and behavior so that they may effectively handle relevant social tasks and (b) create environmental settings and resources that support the promotion of adaptive behavior and positive developmental outcomes (Weissberg et al., 1988). The flexible coordination of these personal and environmental resources contributes to the performance of socially competent behavior. The specific personal resources that are taught, the teaching techniques employed, and the situations to which they apply will vary considerably depending on the developmental level and sociodemographic characteristics of the target population (Furman, 1980; Laosa, 1984).

A number of practical concerns for SCP researchers stem from these formulations: (a) What set of *personal resources* should be taught to facilitate positive developmental outcomes? (b) Which *social tasks* and developmental challenges should be emphasized in SCP programming efforts? (c) What *environmental settings* are most conducive to promoting the acquisition, maintenance, and generalization of social competence?

Choice of Personal Resources

Theoretically, there exists a vast array of personal resources that could be enhanced through school-based SCP programs for young adolescents. Personal resources might include cognitive, affective, and behavioral skills; personal beliefs and social attitudes; acquired information about relevant social issues and situations; and self-perceptions of performance efficacy in specific social domains or tasks (Ford, 1982; Waters & Sroufe, 1983; Weissberg et al., 1988).

According to a number of theorists (Dodge, 1986; McFall, 1982; Rubin & Krasnor, 1986), an individual's behavior in a particular social situation occurs as a function of the way in which social cues are processed. Skillful processing aids in the production of competent behavior, while deficits in processing may result in deviant behavior. Dodge (1986) has outlined five sequential social information-processing skills necessary for competent responses to social tasks: (a) decoding the social cues in the environment; (b) interpreting these cues in a meaningful, integrated way; (c) accessing and generating potential behavioral responses to the interpreted cues; (d) evaluating the consequences of alternative responses and selecting an optimal choice; and (e) enacting the selected response with behavioral effectiveness and self-monitoring its effects. Since multiple components are involved in a behavioral response, training children to use a processing framework may have stronger effects than focusing on only one or two discrete component skills--especially since difficulties at one level of processing may negatively affect performance at a later level.

To this basic model, other investigators have added the role that individuals' beliefs play in competent responding to social tasks. Slaby and Guerra (1988) note that the content, as well as the process, of cognition may serve to mediate behavior. For example, they report that high- and low-aggressive adolescents differ not only in the way in which they process information but also in their general social beliefs regarding the legitimacy of aggression and the expected outcomes for both the aggressor and the victim. This suggests the importance of understanding the beliefs held by individuals concerning the consequences of certain behaviors. Thus, if one's primary training objective is to reduce aggression, focusing both on information processing skills *and* on beliefs about aggression may be more effective than teaching information processing strategies independent of students' beliefs.

Related to beliefs is the role of children's goals in social interactions. Research indicates that there are individual differences in social goals and that these differences correlate with behavior and social status (Parkhurst & Asher, 1985; Renshaw & Asher, 1983; Rubin & Krasnor, 1986). With development, the nature and complexity of social goals undergo change. For example, Renshaw and Asher (1983) found that sixth graders (ages 11-12) as compared to third graders (ages 7-8) were consistently more oriented toward enhancing and maintaining relationships. They were also more likely to coordinate two goals simultaneously (e.g., group entry and preservation of self-image), indicating an increasing complexity of social goals. Espousement of specific values in early adolescence, furthermore, may be an important consideration in conceptualizing social competence. There is some evidence to suggest that negative, antisocial, or health-compromising goals (e.g., joking around a lot in class, fighting, skipping school, drinking) may be valued behaviors in early adolescence (Allen, Weissberg, & Hawkins, in press).

Social competence involves affective factors as well. Fear and anxiety may inhibit competent responding on particular tasks, whereas feelings of self-efficacy may contribute to success (Ford, 1985). Many social situations are emotionally charged (e.g., being teased or pressured to engage in risk-taking behavior), which may result in an inaccurate interpretation of social cues and consequent generation of maladaptive choices for responding to a social task. Furthermore, low frustration tolerance, impulsivity, and general impatience may work against the successful processing and enactment of socially competent behavior (Meichenbaum, 1978). Affective factors also become relevant when specified goals in a situation cannot be reached and must be reformulated or abandoned. It is then necessary for the child to cope with the emotions that often accompany failure (Lazarus, 1980).

Carrying out chosen solutions with behavioral skill represents another essential aspect of social competence. In his social information-processing model, Dodge (1986) refers to this as "enactment." Social skills training interventions that focus exclusively on this aspect of information processing (by teaching children specific behavioral responses to an array of problematic tasks) have produced short-term behavioral adjustment gains (Michelson, Sugai, Wood, & Kazdin, 1983). Recently, Weissberg and Allen (1986) have argued that the combination of behavioral social skills training and social-cognitive information-processing training will have a greater likelihood of producing short- and long-term positive developmental outcomes than will the independent use of either approach. This may be particularly important during early adolescence, when subtleties of behavior--such as self-confidence, comfort in social situations, and interpersonal sensitivity--become more central to social competence (Coie, Dodge, & Coppotelli, 1982; Kurdek & Krile, 1982).

Choice of Social Tasks

Recent research indicates that socially competent behavior in handling one social task does not necessarily generalize to competent responding in another. Dodge, Pettit, McClaskey, and Brown (1986) examined the reactions of children to situations involving peer group entry and peer provocation. Children's group entry-processing abilities, but not their provocation-processing abilities, predicted their competence at actual group entry in a laboratory task and on the playground. Similarly, children's provocation-processing skills, but not their group entry-processing skills, related to their competence in actual provocation situations. Given these findings, one cannot assume that generic skills training will equip individuals with the skills necessary to competently respond to all social tasks that they face.

Intervention outcome findings lend support to this domain-specific conceptualization of social competence. In a review of the literature on SCP interventions, Durlak (1983) notes that task-specific programs (e.g., those geared toward specific domains of social competence) often result in more beneficial outcomes than general SCP interventions designed to promote skills that could be applied to many social tasks. For example, there is evidence to suggest that programs designed to promote students' competencies to resist peer pressure to experiment with substances or competencies to avoid teen pregnancy may be more effective than generic skill-building programs designed to prevent a variety of negative outcomes.

Recently, SCP researchers have become increasingly interested in selecting developmentally relevant social tasks for which social information processing can be learned and to which it can be applied. Based on the reports of teachers and clinicians, Dodge, McClasky, and Feldman (1985) developed a set of critical problematic social situations relevant for elementary school-age children. The Taxonomy of Problematic Social Situations for Children consists of six situations: (a) peer group entry, (b) responding to ambiguous provocation by a peer, (c) responding to failure, (d) responding to success, (e) responding to peer group norms and expectations, and (f) responding to teachers' expectations. Clearly, similar taxonomies need to be derived for different age and ethnic groups. Although the range of social tasks undoubtedly varies depending on the unique problems of the individual, enough similarities occur in the experiences of agemates to render certain social task issues relevant for the majority of students (Dodge & Murphy, 1984).

In designing SCP programs for young adolescents, it is clear that the developmental literature highlights a number of important social tasks: establishing relationships with same- and opposite-gender peers; managing a new school structure with varied responsibilities; mastering a new social role; gaining independence from parental authority; coping with peer and media pressure to take dangerous risks; integrating physical and emotional changes into a developing self-concept and social behavior; and establishing adaptive, realistic goals for health, education, and leisure activities. Specific steps need to be taken in SCP programs to address the relevant social tasks and challenges that this particular age group encounters.

Choice of Environmental Setting to Promote Social Competence

Hawkins and Weis (1985) maintain that children not only should possess the relevant cognitive, affective, and behavioral skills to succeed in a particular setting but must also: (a) have multiple opportunities to practice these skills and (b) receive consistent reinforcement from socializing agents when competent behavior is displayed. Their model suggests that SCP programming efforts must be directed both at developing personal resources *and* creating environmental settings conducive to the development of social competence. It is essential to provide resources that reinforce children's real-life application, generalization, and maintenance of the skills being taught (Elias, 1987; Hawkins & Weis, 1985; Levine & Perkins, 1980).

Implementing SCP programs in the classroom setting offers a promising means of promoting such maintenance and generalization (Weissberg, 1985). Students can practice newly acquired skills both within and outside of the structured SCP lessons. Teachers can facilitate students' use of these skills as situations arise throughout the school day. Furthermore, the classroom setting provides students with the opportunity to benefit from peer modeling and peer reinforcement of social skills (Rose, 1982). Social skills interventions for groups (as opposed to individuals) have demonstrated the beneficial effect of peer inclusion on both target children and peers (Bierman & Furman, 1984). Given the powerful influences of the peer group for establishing norms of behavior, classroom-based SCP can also be inherently advantageous for facilitating a prosocial, health-promoting climate (Perry, 1982).

Although classroom-based SCP programs have excellent potential to improve the behavioral adaptation of young adolescents, there are a variety of factors relevant to this age group that may render such programs difficult to design and implement effectively. For example, the extreme diversity among middle school students in terms of their physical maturation, cultural background, emotional development, academic performance, and social relationships poses a great challenge to program developers. It is difficult to gear interventions to meet the needs of all students in a group because growth in each of these domains is not continuous, uniform, or synchronized (Lipsitz, 1984). Thus, while instructors may teach general SCP concepts to all students, individual attention may be necessary to identify and remediate their information processing deficits or to help them resolve specific difficulties that they encounter.

In addition, early adolescence can be a period of extreme self-consciousness (Elkind, 1967) which may sometimes hamper students' initial participation in classroom discussions. As a result, students may feel uncomfortable sharing problems in front of the entire group, especially if opposite-gender peers are present. Sensitivity to this issue when facilitating classroom discussions is essential. Students may also have the mistaken idea that their feelings and needs are beyond the understanding of others, particularly adults (Elkind, 1967). Classroom discussion among students can improve the accuracy of normative expectations regarding difficult social tasks that they may face. Recent research also suggests that same-age or older students who serve as facilitators in SCP programs may be very instrumental in promoting social competence (Botvin, Baker, Renick, Filazzola, & Botvin, 1984). Because peers are often referred to as sources for standards and models of behavior during early adolescence, they can help to promote an understanding that problems encountered are typical for students their age. Designing interventions in which teachers or other adults collaborate with peer leaders appears to be a very promising approach (Perry & Jessor, 1985).

Adapting programs to the ecology of the school setting can also pose difficulties for SCP developers, especially at the middle school level. Most middle schools are departmentalized. Consequently, teachers may only meet with a group of students for five periods a week, fostering concerns about completing the necessary academic coursework concurrently with SCP lessons. It is also difficult to determine which department (e.g., social studies, science, health, or language arts) should provide SCP training, the appropriate number and length of SCP curriculum lessons, which teachers should be charged with the responsibility for implementing the program, and the best ways for other school personnel (e.g., nonprogram teachers, principals, guidance counsellors, school psychologists, lunchroom monitors, in-house suspension staff) to be involved in SCP-training efforts.

Thus, while classroom-based SCP programs have a number of inherent advantages, there are also potential problems that stem from the developmental features of early adolescence and the ecology of the middle school. Sensitivity to the developmental issues of this age period as well as to the priorities and ecological realities of the school setting can aid in the structuring of an SCP program and increase the likelihood that it will become an integral part of the system's curriculum (Weissberg et al., 1988).

In the next section, we briefly describe two SCP programs for young adolescents currently being implemented in our local school system and highlight how a developmental perspective has influenced the choice of personal resources, social tasks, and environmental settings included in these SCP programs.

Description of Two Social Competence Programs for Young Adolescents

In New Haven, Connecticut, we have developed two complementary school-based SCP programs for young adolescents. The first is a general competency-building program designed to impart skills in stress management and impulse control, problem solving, and behavioral social skills to help students respond competently to a variety of social tasks. The second program, which builds on these core skills, focuses specifically on the social task of coming to terms with peer and media influences to experiment with alcohol and drugs. Given empirical findings suggesting that pressure to engage in risky or health-compromising behavior constitutes a primary stressor at this age level (Gilchrist et al., 1988; Jessor, 1984), we considered this an important social task to which developing skills and resources could be applied. Furthermore, theoretical and empirical work indicates that task-specific SCP programs may be more beneficial to students than task-general programs (Dodge et al., 1986; Durlak, 1983).

Both SCP programs are classroom-based, allowing for the daily encouragement and reinforcement of newly acquired skills by both teachers and peers. In addition to the core lessons, teachers are trained in "dialoguing" techniques that enable them to communicate effectively with students about real-life concerns (Spivack & Shure, 1982). The curriculum also includes follow-up activities to ensure maintenance and generalization of program concepts throughout the school year. We provide training to other school staff (e.g., counsellors, mental health professionals, in-house suspension teachers, vice-principals, and principals), enabling them to reinforce and extend the SCP concepts introduced by the teacher.

The programs incorporate affective factors (emotional monitoring and stress management), cognitive factors (goal setting, alternative solution generation, consequential thinking), and behavioral factors (social skills training). Curriculum lessons emphasize both the integration of the social information-processing steps and the application of this process to developmentally appropriate, real-life social tasks identified by teachers and students.

378

Direct instruction, group discussions of real-life problems, role-plays, cooperative and competitive games, and work sheets are used as instructional tools. Videotapes also serve as teaching aids, creating a springboard for discussion and providing a model for the adaptive integration of cognition, affect, and behavior (Harwood & Weissberg, 1987).

The Yale-New Haven Social Problem-Solving (SPS) Program for Young Adolescents

The 17-lesson curriculum comprises three basic units: (a) stress management and impulse control, (b) a six-step sequential social information processing model, and (c) behavioral social skills training (Weissberg, Caplan, & Bennetto, 1988). The structure and content of the curriculum are guided by the theoretical and empirical work of several investigators (e.g., Dodge et al., 1986; Elias, 1987; Rubin & Krasnor, 1986; Spivack & Shure, 1982; Weissberg et al., in press).

The first unit is designed to facilitate competence in stress management and impulse control. Given the number and variety of psychosocial stressors that affect young adolescents (Hill, 1980; Lipsitz, 1977), students are taught to recognize situations in their own lives that cause stress and their physical and emotional reactions to them. Students are then instructed in adaptive means of coping with these stressful life events, with an emphasis on self-instructional training to foster competence in self-control (Kendall & Braswell, 1985). In the second unit, students learn the following six-step framework to help them cope with relevant social tasks: (a) stop, calm down, and think before you act; (b) say the problem and how you feel; (c) set a positive goal; (d) think of lots of solutions; (e) think ahead to the consequences; and (f) go ahead and try the best plan. Young adolescents are developing a variety of cognitive skills (e.g., the ability to generate multiple solutions to problems and think ahead to the consequences) and metacognitive skills (e.g., the ability to reflect on their own behavior), which can aid in successful social information processing. However, several developmental features of this age period have influenced the selection and specific wording of the steps.

Given that self-control is of critical importance during middle childhood and early adolescence (Meichenbaum, 1978), the model teaches students to stop and calm down before beginning the cognitive process of problem-solving. Second, since some young adolescents may have negative, antisocial goals (Allen et al., in press), the use of the adjective *positive* in conjunction with *goal* is intended to serve as a prompt for prosocial values. Third, based on our understanding of the important role that beliefs play in competent responding to social tasks (Slaby & Guerra, 1988), the teaching of consequential thinking emphasizes evaluation of one's own beliefs regarding the legitimacy of certain behaviors (e.g., aggression) and its effects on others. Finally, the model focuses on step-by-step planning, the anticipation of obstacles, and persistence, all of which serve to promote means-end thinking, an important component of social competence during adolescence (Spivack & Shure, 1982).

Students also receive instruction in self-monitoring behavioral performance. This includes the capacities to: abandon ineffective strategies for handling relevant social tasks; try backup strategies or reformulate goals when necessary; and when faced with failure, cope adaptively with the resultant affect. In addition, emphasis is placed on understanding and, in some cases, modifying one's own beliefs regarding (a) expectations about successful coping with difficult social tasks and (b) behavioral strategies that can both benefit oneself and not hurt the other person(s) involved in problem situations.

The final phase of the program emphasizes the behavioral skills needed to respond competently to social tasks, such as assertiveness and communication skills. In the curriculum, behavioral enactment of responses to social tasks is role-played extensively, as presentation style and subtleties of behavior become more central to social competence in early adolescence (Coie et al., 1982; Fine, 1981; Kurdek & Krile, 1982). Behavioral social skills training, therefore, is combined with social-cognitive information processing training to increase the likelihood of producing competent responding to relevant social tasks.

The social tasks selected for inclusion in the curriculum stem from a list of frequently experienced stressful problems and social tasks reported by a sample of inner-city young adolescents (Santello, 1986). These include situations such as: coping with physical and verbal aggression, being blamed for something one did not do, and meeting new peers. The developmental issues detailed earlier also prompted us to highlight important social competence domains for young adolescents such as: responding to provocation by peers, managing stress, establishing more intimate relationships with same- and opposite-gender peers, and responding to teacher expectancies. Program teachers and students prioritize the topics they wish to emphasize from these situations.

Program evaluation findings, based on a total of 421 middle school students, indicate that this SCP training program has a variety of beneficial effects (Weissberg & Caplan, 1989). Relative to controls, program participants improved in their social information-processing skills, social relations with peers, and teacher ratings of behavioral adjustment. With respect to information-processing abilities, trained students improved more than controls in terms of the quantity, effectiveness, and planfulness of their solutions to social tasks pertaining to provocation by peers. Involvement with positive peers, as measured by self-report and teacher ratings, increased as a function of the program. Teacher ratings of student adjustment also indicated improvements in impulse control, sociability with peers, and academic performance. Positive program effects were also noted in the frequency of self-reported misbehavior (e.g., starting physical fights, getting sent out of the classroom, being suspended from school, stealing from a locker or desk). This evaluation represents one component of a large-scale study investigating the short- and long-term effects of SCP training on students' social skills, attitudes, and behavioral adjustment.

Interestingly, the program had no effect on cigarette, alcohol, or drug use. Beer, wine, and alcohol consumption were found to increase, both for program and control groups, from pre-to post-assessment. Thus, while the SCP program had positive effects on targeted behaviors, these skills did not automatically generalize across domains.

The Positive Youth Development (PYD) Program: A Substance Abuse Prevention Program for Young Adolescents

The identification of peer pressure to use substances as an important social task for young adolescents (Jessor, 1984) and our more general program's lack of effects on these variables prompted us to develop a separate SCP program. The PYD program is specifically geared toward the teaching of skills, beliefs, and information that can enable students to resist peer and media influences to experiment with substances.

Strategies to resist peer influences can be considered a specific subset of social information-processing skills. In the PYD curriculum, these skills are taught in a broad-based framework and then applied to specific situations involving alcohol and drugs. The 20-session program (Caplan et al., 1988) focuses on the same three units as the Yale-New Haven Social Problem-Solving Program: (a) stress management and impulse control (b) a sequential social information-processing model for responding competently to social tasks and (c) behavioral social skills training. In contrast to the more generic program, the social information-processing steps discussed and role-played in the latter part of the curriculum pertain primarily to the social task of resisting peer and media influences to experiment with substances. For example, one curriculum lesson is devoted to discussing and role-playing students' application of the social information processing framework to a situation in which a group of older students pressure a younger student to drink alcohol. Given the emerging complexity of goals in such situations, classroom discussion focuses not on the simple goal of "saying no" but rather on the more developmentally appropriate goal of "saying no" *and* either "maintaining a relationship with the other person" or "creating a favorable impression among peers."

The program is implemented twice per week for 10 weeks by masters-level health educators in conjunction with classroom teachers. The inclusion of health educators as program implementers is based on the belief that some students may be more comfortable discussing issues related to alcohol and drugs with someone other than the regular classroom teacher. However, reinforcement of competencies throughout the school day by classroom teachers represents an important aspect of program implementation.

Program evaluation findings, based on a sample of 282 students, indicate that the training program has positive effects on young adolescents' application of social information processing skills to peer pressure situations (Caplan, Weissberg, Grober, Sivo, Grady & Jacoby, 1989). Relative to control students, program students increased the quantity and quality of their strategies for resisting peer pressure and coping with stress from pre- to post-assessment. Teacher ratings of behavioral adjustment corroborated these findings, indicating that the program students demonstrated improved abilities in social problem-solving and stress management in school. Negative attitudes toward substances also increased as a function of the program. Moreover, the program had preventive effects on alcohol misuse. Relative to program students, controls showed a significant increase in the number of occasions on which they consumed excessive amounts of alcohol.

These preliminary results support the importance of designing domain-specific, contextually sensitive SCP programs. It is likely that the application of social information processing skills to relevant social tasks faced by young adolescents will benefit from extensive practice within the specified context (e.g., peer pressure situations) for maximum mastery and usage. Further research is needed to clarify the relative benefits of broad-based and task-specific SCP programming efforts.

Summary and Future Directions

In this chapter, we suggest that greater sensitivity to the developmental issues, challenges, pressures, and social environments impacting on young adolescents can aid in the creation of more effective SCP programs for this age group. Awareness of these factors can inform the choice of social information processing strategies, behavioral social skills, relevant social tasks, and environmental settings selected for the intervention. The SCP programs currently being implemented in our local setting represent two approaches to the promotion of social competence. In describing these programs, we have attempted to highlight how developmental considerations are informing the design and implementation of our work.

Clearly, SCP programming efforts could benefit from several other considerations as well. Given that short-term SCP programs are unlikely to produce lasting behavioral change, it seems critical to develop multiyear training programs. Preliminary data analyses of our recent programming efforts indicate that two years of SCP training, conducted during sixth and seventh grade, resulted in more beneficial outcomes for young adolescents than did one year or no years of training. One promising SCP-training model during the middle school years might entail: (a) the building of basic personal and social competencies (e.g., social information processing, behavioral social skills, stress management) upon entry into the middle school and (b) follow-up modules focused on key social tasks relevant to the particular age group (e.g., resisting peer pressure and preventing substance abuse; making positive educational and career choices and preventing delinquency; developing appropriate, positive social relations and preventing teen pregnancy). The domain-specific nature of social competence that has been theoretically advanced and empirically supported (Dodge et al., 1986) would advocate for this combined, integrated strategy of general skill training followed by an emphasis on developmentally relevant, targeted social tasks.

In designing effective SCP programs, it is also important to consider the possibility of beginning training prior to entry into the middle school, since research suggests that students experience a number of concerns regarding this transition (Gilchrist et al., 1988). Some SCP proponents (e.g., Bloom, 1985; Felner et al., 1983) have advocated the establishment of competence-training efforts for individuals across the life span as they cope with stressful life events. To this end, the National Mental Health Association Commission on the Prevention of Mental-Emotional Disabilities has recently recommended the creation of a comprehensive, sequential preschool through high school (ages 3-18) SCP curriculum (Long, 1986).

The articulation of a developmentally appropriate sequence and scope of SCP across the school years represents an important task for future investigators. We need to consult theory, research findings, and available curricula as we attempt to specify the processing skills, beliefs, social tasks, domains of competence, and training methods that should be emphasized at each grade level. Furthermore, the creation of system structures and policies to support effective SCP programming is critical for the effective implementation and long-term maintenance of educational programs such as these (Weissberg et al., in press). Societal concern about problems such as substance abuse, teen pregnancy, school dropout, delinquency, suicide, and AIDS has created a greater receptivity on the part of the community to implementing school-based SCP programs. However, unless formal structures and policies are established, this goal will be difficult to achieve.

In this chapter, we have discussed the need for SCP programming during one period in the life span, early adolescence, and described two interventions designed to promote social competence during these years. Reflection on the developmental issues, challenges, motivations, and social world characteristic of early adolescence has informed our effort. As SCP program developers begin the process of establishing multiyear training efforts, developmental considerations will prove essential in identifying the personal resources, social tasks, and environmental settings most conducive to the promotion of social competence at the different age levels.

Acknowledgments: The authors gratefully acknowledge the support provided by the William T. Grant Foundation Faculty Scholars Program in Mental Health of Children, the John D. and Catherine T. MacArthur Foundation Health and Behavior Network, the Justice Planning Division of the Connecticut Office of Policy and Management, and the Connecticut Department of Children and Youth Services. We also appreciate the editorial assistance of Loisa Bennetto.

References

Adelson, J. (1980). *Handbook of adolescent psychology.* New York: Wiley.
Allen, J., Weissberg, R. P., & Hawkins, J. (in press). The relation between values and social competence in early adolescence. *Developmental Psychology.*

Bachman, J. G., O'Malley, P. M., & Johnston, J. (1979). *Adolescence to adulthood: Change and stability in the lives of young men.* Ann Arbor, MI: Institute for Social Research.

Berndt, T. J. (1979). Developmental changes in conformity to peers and parents. *Developmental Psychology, 15,* 608-616.

Bierman, K. L., & Furman, W. (1984). The effects of social skills training and peer involvement on the social adjustment of preadolescents. *Child Development, 55,* 151-162.

Bloom, B. L. (1979). Prevention of mental disorders: Recent advances in theory and practice. *Community Mental Health Journal, 15,* 179-191.

Bloom, B. L. (1985). New possibilities in prevention. In R. L. Hough, P. A. Gongla, V. B. Brown, & S. E. Goldston (Eds.), *Psychiatric epidemiology and prevention: The possibilities* (pp. 31-52). Los Angeles: NIMH.

Botvin, G. J., Baker, E., Renick, N. L., Filazzola, A. D., & Botvin, E. (1984). A cognitive-behavioral approach to substance abuse prevention. *Addictive Behaviors, 9,* 137-147.

Bronfenbrenner, U. (1979). *The ecology of human development: Experiments by nature and design.* Cambridge, MA: Harvard University Press.

Caplan, M. Z., Jacoby, C., Weissberg, R. P., & Grady, K. (1988). *The Positive Youth Development Program: A Substance Abuse Prevention Program for Young Adolescents.* New Haven, CT: Yale University.

Caplan, M. Z., Weissberg, R. P., Grober, J. H., Sivo, P. J., Grady, K., & Jacoby, C. (1989). *Social competence promotion as a strategy to prevent substance use: Outcome findings with inner-city and suburban young adolescents.* Manuscript submitted for publication.

Coie, J. D., Dodge, K. A., & Coppotelli, H. (1982). Dimensions and types of social status: A cross-age perspective. *Developmental Psychology, 18,* 557-570.

Costanzo, P. R., & Shaw, M. E. (1966). Conformity as a function of age level. *Child Development, 37,* 967-975.

Dodge, K. A. (1986). A social information processing model of social competence in children. In M. Perlmutter (Ed.), *Minnesota Symposium on Child Psychology* (Vol. 18, pp. 77-125). Hillsdale, NJ: Erlbaum.

Dodge, K. A., McClasky, C. L., & Feldman, E. (1985). A situation approach to the assessment of social competence in children. *Journal of Consulting and Clinical Psychology, 53,* 344-353.

Dodge, K. A., & Murphy, R. R. (1984). The assessment of social competence in adolescents. In P. Karoly & J. J. Steffen (Eds.), *Advances in child behavioral analysis and therapy: Adolescent behavior disorders* (Vol. 4, pp. 61-96). Lexington, MA: Heath.

Dodge, K. A., Pettit, G. S., McClaskey, C. L., & Brown, M. M. (1986). Social competence in children. *Monographs of the Society for Research in Child Development, 51.*

Durlak, J. A. (1983). Social problem-solving as a primary prevention strategy. In R. D. Felner, L. A. Jason, J. N. Moritsugu, & S. S. Farber (Eds.), *Preventive psychology: Theory, research, and practice* (pp. 31-48). New York: Pergamon Press.

Durlak, J. A., & Jason, L. A. (1984). Preventive programs for school-aged children and adolescents. In M. C. Roberts & L. Peterson (Eds.), *Prevention of problems in childhood: Psychological research and applications* (pp. 103-132). New York: Wiley-Interscience.

Elias, M. J. (1987). Establishing enduring prevention programs: Advancing the legacy of Swampscott. *American Journal of Community Psychology, 14,* 259-275.

Elias, M. J., Gara, M., & Ubriaco, M. (1985). Social-cognitive problem solving in children: Assessing the knowledge and application of skills. *Journal of Applied Developmental Psychology, 7,* 77-94.

Elkind, D. (1967). Egocentrism in adolescence. *Child Development, 38,* 1025-1034.

Erikson, E. H. (1964). *Childhood and society.* New York: Norton.

Felner, R. D., Farber, S. S., & Primavera, J. (1983). Transitions and stressful life events: A model for primary prevention. In R. D. Felner, L. A. Jason, J. N. Moritsugu, & S. S. Farber (Eds.), *Preventive psychology: Theory, research, and practice* (pp. 199-220). New York: Pergamon Press.

Felner, R. D., Primavera, J., & Cauce, A. M. (1981). The impact of school transitions: A focus for preventive efforts. *American Journal of Community Psychology, 9,* 449-459.

Fine, G. A. (1981). Friends, impression management, and preadolescent behavior. In S. R. Asher & J. M. Gottman (Eds.), *The development of children's friendships* (pp. 29-52). New York: Cambridge University Press.

Ford, M. E. (1982). Social cognition and social competence in adolescence. *Developmental Psychology, 18,* 323-340.

Ford, M. E. (1985). Primary prevention: Key issues and a competence perspective. *The Journal of Primary Prevention, 5,* 264-266.

Furman, W. (1980). Promoting social development: Developmental implications for treatment. In B. B. Lahey & A. E. Kazdin (Eds.), *Advances in clinical child psychology* (Vol. 3, pp. 1-40). New York: Plenum.

Garmezy, N., & Masten, A. S. (1986). Stress, competence, and resilience: Common frontiers for therapists and psychopathologists, *Behavior Therapy, 17,* 500-521.

Gilchrist, L. D., Schinke, S. P., Snow, W. H., Schilling, R. F., & Senechal, V. (1988). The transition of junior high school: Opportunities for primary prevention. *Journal of Primary Prevention, 8,* 99-108.

Hall, G. S. (1904). *Adolescence: Its psychology and its relations to physiology, anthropology, sociology, sex, crime, religion, and education* (Vols. 1 and 2). New York: D. Appelton.

Harwood, R., & Weissberg, R. P. (1987). The potential of video in the promotion of social competence in children and adolescents. *Journal of Early Adolescence, 7,* 345-363.

Hawkins, J. D., & Weis, J. G. (1985). The social development model: An integrated approach to delinquency prevention. *Journal of Primary Prevention, 6,* 73-97.

Higgins, E. T., & Parsons, J. E. (1983). Social cognition and the social life of the child: Stages as subcultures. In E. T. Higgins, D. N. Ruble, & W. W. Hartup (Eds.), *Social cognition and social development* (pp. 15-62). Cambridge, England: Cambridge University Press.

Hill, J. P. (1980). *Understanding early adolescence: A framework.* Carrboro, NC: The Center for Early Adolescence.

Jessor, R. (1984). Adolescent development and behavioral health. In J. D. Matarazzo, S. M. Weiss, J. A. Herd, N. E. Miller, & S. M. Weiss (Eds.), *Behavioral health: A handbook of health enhancement and disease prevention* (pp. 69-90). New York: Wiley.

Jessor, R., & Jessor, S. L. (1977). *Problem behavior and psychosocial development: A longitudinal study of youth.* New York: Academic Press. Kaplan, H. B., Martin, S. S., & Robbins, C . (1984). Pathways to adolescent drug use: Self-derogation, peer influence, weakening of social controls, and early substance use. *Journal of Health and Social Behavior, 25,* 270-289.

Keating, D. P. (1980). Thinking processes in adolescence. In J. Adelson (Ed.), *Handbook of adolescent psychology* (pp. 211-246). New York: Wiley.

Kendall, P. C., & Braswell, L. (1985). *Cognitive-behavioral therapy for impulsive children.* New York: Guilford Press.

Kent, M. W., & Rolf, J. E. (1979). *Social competence in children.* Hanover, NH: University Press of New Hampshire.

Kimmel, D. C., & Weiner, I. B. (1985). *Adolescence: A developmental transition.* Hillsdale, NJ: Erlbaum.

Kornberg, M. S., & Caplan, G. (1980). Risk factors and preventive intervention in child psychotherapy: A review. *The Journal of Primary Prevention, 1,* 71-133.

Kurdek, L. A., & Krile, D. (1982). A developmental analysis of the relation between peer acceptance and both interpersonal understanding and perceived social self-competence. *Child Development, 53,* 1485-1491.

Laosa, L. M. (1984). Social competence in childhood: Toward a developmental, socioculturally relativistic paradigm. In J. M. Joffe, G. W. Albee, & L. D. Kelly (Eds.), *Readings in primary prevention of psychopathology* (pp. 261-285). Hanover, NH: University Press of New England.

Lazarus, R. S. (1980). The stress and coping paradigm. In L. A. Bond & J. C. Rosen (Eds.), *Competence and coping during adulthood* (pp. 28-74). Hanover, NH: University Press of New England.

Levine, M., & Perkins, D. V. (1980). Social setting interventions and primary prevention: Comments on the Report of the Task Panel on Prevention to the President's Commission on Mental Health. *American Journal of Community Psychology, 8,* 147-157.

Lipsitz, J. (1977). *Growing up forgotten: A review of research and programs concerning early adolescence.* Lexington, MA: Lexington Books.

Lipsitz, J. (1984). *Successful schools for young adolescents.* New Brunswick, NJ: Transaction Books.

Long, B. B. (1986). The prevention of mental-emotional disabilities: A report from a National Mental Health Association Commission. *American Psychologist, 41,* 825-829.

Meichenbaum, D. (1978). Teaching children self-control. In B. Lahey & A. Kazdin (Eds.), *Advances in child clinical psychology* (Vol. 2, pp. 1-33) New York: Plenum.

McFall, R. M. (1982). A review and reformulation of the concept of social skills. *Behavioral Assessment, 4,* 1-33.

Michelson, L., Sugai, D. P., Wood, R. P., & Kazdin, A. E. (1983). *Social skills assessment and training with children.* New York: Plenum.

Montemayor, R., & VanKomen, R. (1985). The development of sex differences in friendship patterns and peer group structure during adolescence. *Journal of Early Adolescence, 5,* 285-294.

Parkhurst, J. T., & Asher, S. R. (1985). Goals and concerns: Implications for the study of children's social competence. In B. B. Lahey & A. E. Kazdin (Eds.), *Advances in child clinical psychology* (Vol. 8, pp. 199-228). New York: Guilford Press.

Pellegrini, D., & Urbain, E. S. (1985). An evaluation of interpersonal cognitive problem-solving training efforts with children. *Journal of Child Psychology and Psychiatry, 26,* 17-41.

Perry, C. (1982). Adolescent health: An educational-ecological perspective. In T. J. Coates, A. C. Petersen, & C. Perry (Eds.), *Promoting adolescent health : A dialogue on research and practice* (pp. 73-86). New York: Academic Press.

Perry, C. L., & Jessor, R. (1985). The concept of health promotion and the prevention of adolescent drug abuse. *Health Education Quarterly, 12,* 169-184.

Petersen, A. C. (1982). Developmental issues in adolescent health. In T. J. Coates, A. C. Petersen, & C. Perry (Eds.), *Promoting adolescent health: A dialogue on research and practice* (pp. 61-72). New York: Academic Press.

Piaget, J. (1970). Piaget's theory. In P. H. Mussen (Ed.), *Carmichael's manual of child psychology* (Vol. 1, pp. 703-732). New York: John Wiley & Sons.

Renshaw, P. D., & Asher, S. R. (1983). Children's goals and strategies for social interaction. *Merrill-Palmer Quarterly, 29,* 283-307.

Report of the Prevention Task Panel (1978). *Task panel reports submitted to the President's Commission on Mental Health* (Vol. 4, pp. 1822-1863). Washington, DC: U.S. Government Printing Office.

Rose, S. R. (1982). Promoting social competence in children: A classroom approach to social and cognitive skill training. *Child and Youth Services, 5,* 43-59.

Rubin, K. H., & Krasnor, L. R. (1986). Social-cognitive and social-behavioral perspectives on problem-solving. In M. Perlmutter (Ed.), *Cognitive perspectives on children's social and behavioral development* (pp. 1-68). Hillsdale, NJ: Erlbaum.

Rutter, M. (1980). *Changing youth in a changing society.* Cambridge, MA: Harvard University Press.

Rutter, M. (1982). Prevention of children's psychosocial disorders: Myth and substance. *Pediatrics, 70,* 883-894.

Santello, M. D. (1986). *A survey of frequency and upset levels for adolescent problem situations.* Unpublished manuscript, Yale University, New Haven, CT.

Simmons, R. G., & Blyth, D. A. (1987). *Moving into adolescence: The impact of pubertal change and school context.* New York: Aldine De Gruyter.

Slaby, R. G., & Guerra, N. B. (1988). Cognitive mediators of aggression in adolescent offenders: 1. Assessment. *Developmental Psychology, 24,* 580-588.

Spivack, G., & Shure, M. B. (1982). The cognition of social adjustment: Interpersonal cognitive problem-solving thinking. In B. B. Lahey & A. E. Kazdin (Eds.), *Advances in clinical child psychology* (Vol. 5, pp. 323-372). New York: Plenum.

Sroufe, L. A., & Rutter, M. (1984). The domain of developmental psycho-pathology. *Child Development, 55,* 17-29.

Sullivan, H. S. (1953). *The interpersonal theory of psychiatry.* New York: Norton.

Waters, E., & Sroufe, L. A. (1983). Social competence as a developmental construct. *Developmental Review, 3,* 79-97.

Weissberg, R. P. (1985). Designing effective social problem-solving programs for the classroom. In B. H. Schneider, K. H. Rubin, & J. E. Ledingham (Eds.), *Children's peer relations: Issues in assessment and intervention* (pp. 225-242). New York: Springer-Verlag.

Weissberg, R. P., & Allen, J. P. (1986). Promoting children's social skills and adaptive interpersonal behavior. In L. Michelson & B. Edelstein (Eds.), *Handbook of prevention* (pp. 153-175). New York: Plenum.

Weissberg, R. P., & Caplan, M. Z. (1989). *The evaluation of a social competence promotion program with urban middle-school students.* Manuscript submitted for publication.

Weissberg, R. P., Caplan, M. Z., & Bennetto, L. (1988). *The Yale-New Haven Social Problem-Solving Program for Young Adolescents.* New Haven, CT: Yale University.

Weissberg, R. P., Caplan, M. Z., & Sivo, P. J. (in press). A new conceptual framework for establishing school-based social competence promotion programs. In L. A. Bond, B. E. Compas, & C. Swift (Eds.), *Prevention in the schools.* Menlo Park, CA: Sage.

Zigler, E., & Berman, W. (1983). Discerning the future of early childhood intervention. *American Psychologist, 38,* 894-906.

Appendix

Research Abstracts

Communication and Cooperation Among Young Children

Monique Alles-Jardel and Evelyne Genest

Université de Provence (Aix-Marseille), France

This work is situated within the double perspective of social ethology and developmental studies in peer interaction, a common subject of investigation by researchers in Canada and the U.S.A. on social competence. We have noticed that capacities of cooperation develop as the child grows up. We can note a progression from elementary peer interaction forms to increasingly elaborate forms of communication and cooperation. This notion of cooperation gives way to contradictory developmental hypotheses. Some assert that cooperation is the result of individual developmental processes, whereas others think that it is the result of social interactive processes, which begin with mother-infant interactions. Actually, this notion of cooperation is quite complex. Cultural values, influences of the family background, learning and cognitive development are all part of it.

In a first instance, we want especially to study the influence of family background and child rearing on the evolution of children's communicative and cooperative behaviour; and investigate if there are differences in cooperation and development between girls and boys.

We have also developed a behaviour checklist for the observations of children, according to the social ethological method. This list consists of different categories: communication acts, opposition acts, isolation acts and cooperation acts. The observations were conducted in a nursery, on 25 children aged between 24-36 months (10 boys and 15 girls). The children were regularly observed for ten-minute intervals. The observation time totalled 35-45 minutes per child.

We have developed a questionnaire for the parental data. The questionnaire was constructed considering different attitudes towards childrearing: Control, indulgence and nuances in communication.

Results. From the 4 categories (communication, opposition, isolation and cooperation acts), we have defined 3 indicator scores for each of the children, as frequencies of behaviours: Cooperation coefficient, decentration coefficient and combativeness coefficient. Summing up, one can say that parents' attitudes have an obvious influence over children's communication and cooperation capacities. The more the attitude toward childrearing is nuanced (adaptative), the more the children show cooperation.

Age also plays an important part; the capacity of cooperation increases during development. Among older children, girls have superior capacities of communication and cooperation than boys, independent of education. However, we cannot assert that girls have a childrearing type that makes them more able to cooperate. Adaptive upbringing helps younger children to cooperate earlier with peers; they seem to be less aggressive and less isolated. This type of upbringing favours the child's decentration abilities. Both genders, facing an adaptative education show a pugnacity that one can characterize as "positive and necessary" (assertiveness).

However overcontrolled upbringing seems to limit the capacity of the child to cooperate with his peers. Controlled upbringing provokes different reactions among girls and boys. Boys show a more marked assertiveness, while girls show isolation and sometimes withdrawal.

Adaptative upbringing is important during development because it seems not to exagerate this pugnacity but, on the contrary, it seems to maintain it within acceptable limits, and furthermore, it is balanced by acts of communication and cooperation.

In conclusion, this work has elucidated some important trends. However, one of the main difficulties is the evaluation of parents' childrearing style based on a questionnaire. By this method we can estimate the representation of ideal upbringing, but perhaps not the training they give their children. Another difficulty is the observation of the children in a natural situation.

Perceived Social Competence, Global Self-Esteem, Social Interactions and Peer Dependence in Early Adolescence

Preliminary results from a cohort-sequential study.
Françoise D. Alsaker

University of Bergen, Norway

The importance of social interactions for a person's mental health is well documented (e.g., Cowen et al, 1973). As noted by Wheeler and Ladd (1982) research indicates that self-perception of social competence may influence interpersonal behaviour in ways that affect the quality of peer relations. The first aim of the paper was to explain the relationships between social interactions, perceived social competence and global self-esteem. Two models were proposed: 1) A "common sense" model, based on Shavelson's writings (see Shavelson, Hubner & Stanton, 1976) and which states that one's experiences (social interactions) affect one's perceived social competence which, in turn, affects one's global self-esteem.

2) A "global self-esteem" model which assumes that social interactions affect both global self-esteem and one's perceived social competence, and that self-esteem also affects one's perception of social competence.

The second aim of the paper was to explore the relationship between peer dependence and the three constructs described above.

This study is part of a large-scale project (Olweus, 1978, 1987) extending over a period of two and a half years. Data were collected in four large representative adjacent age cohorts, drawn from 42 schools in Bergen, Norway. The entire sample at the first time of data collection (May 1983) included 1143 girls and 1330 boys aged 11 through 14 (modal ages). The data used in the present paper were collected in May 1984 and May 1985.

Self-esteem was measured with the *GLOBAL NEGATIVE SELF-EVALUATION* scale: GSE (Alsaker & Olweus, 1986), in part based on Rosenberg's RSE (Rosenberg, 1979). The *PERCEIVED SOCIAL COMPETENCE / ACCEPTANCE* scale (PSCA) was designed to tap both a sense of social self-efficacy and feelings of acceptance by peers. The *PEER DEPENDENCE* scale was aimed at measuring the importance of peers' evaluations and to what extent these evaluations could influence the subjects' behaviour. Experiences of social interactions were measured with two scales: A *PEER RELATIONS* scale tapping how many good friends the subjects had at school, and a *Victimization* scale, tapping if they had been physically or mentally bullied at school.

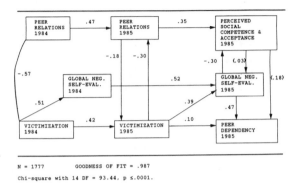

N = 1777   GOODNESS OF FIT = .987

Chi-square with 14 DF = 93.44, p ≤.0001.

Figure 20.1

Results from a LISREL analysis on the relation between peer relations, victimization, global negative self-evaluations, perceived social competence/acceptance and peer dependence over a two year period.

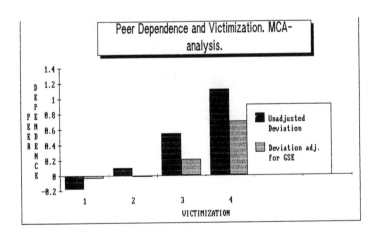

Figure 20.2

Results from a multiple classification analysis using victimization as the independent variable, peer dependence as the dependent variable and global negative self-evaluation as a covariate.

On the basis of our results, the common sense model was rejected. The global self-esteem model received some support, but had to be differentiated: Highly negative social

391

experiences, i.e., victimization in this context, seems to affect global self-esteem directly, but more common social experiences, such as having few or many friends, may play a greater role in the formation of perceived social competence.

The global self-esteem model was used as a basis for exploring the relationship between peer dependence and the other constructs mentioned above. A LISREL-analysis was conducted, the results of which are presented in Figure 20.1.

Negative global self-evaluations were found to affect peer dependence. Peer dependence was also weakly affected by victimization. Because of the skewed distribution of the victimization scale a multiple classification analysis was conducted.

Figure 20.2 shows that children having experienced many victimization episodes were significantly more dependent on their peers' evaluations than other children. It was concluded that the relationships between victimization, global self-esteem and peer dependence may develop into a vicious circle, which may remain stable over time.

References

Alsaker, F.D. & Olweus, D. (1986). Assessment of global negative self-evaluations and perceived stability of self in Norwegian preadolescents and adolescents. *Journal of Early Adolescence, 6*, 269-278.

Cowen, E.L., Pederson, A., Babigian, H., Izzo, L.D., & Trost, M.A. (1973). Long-term following of early detected vulnerable children. *Journal of Consulting and Clinical Psychology, 41*, 438-446.

Olweus, D. (1978). *Aggression in the schools: Bullies and whipping boys.* Washington, D.C.: Hemisphere.

Olweus, D. (1987). *Bully / victim problems among school children in Scandinavia.* Mimeo. Unpublished.

Rosenberg, M. (1979) *Conceiving the self.* New York: Basic Books, Inc., Publishers.

Shavelson, R.J., Hubner, J.J., & Stanton, G.C. (1976). Self-concept: Validation of construct interpretation. *Review of Educational Research, 46*, 407-441.

Wheeler, V.A. & Ladd, G.W. (1982). Assessment of children's self-efficacy for social interactions with peers. *Developmental Psychology, 18*, 795-805.

Peer Rejection and Self-Perception Among Early Elementary School Children: Aggressive-Rejectees vs Withdrawn-Rejectees

Michel Boivin, Line Thomassin and Michel Alain

Université Laval, Québec, Canada

Recent studies have shown that rejected children, a group thought to be at risk for maladjustment, are not a homogeneous population. For instance, both aggressive and withdrawn children may be rejected by their peers (Williams & Asher, 1987) and not all of these children display negative self-perceptions (Boivin & Bégin, in press; Hymel & Franke, 1985).

The purpose of this study was to compare the competencies and the self-perceptions of aggressive-rejected, withdrawn-rejected and average status third-grade children. The selection was based on Coie & Dodge's (1983) procedure and a combination of specific items on the aggression-disruption and sensitivity-isolation scales of the Revised Class Play (Masten, Morison, & Pellegrini, 1985). The aggressive-rejected subgroup was composed of 12 children (26% of the rejected sample: 3 girls and 9 boys) having a high score (Z score > 1) on aggression (Gets into a lot of fights; Too bossy; Interrupts when other children are speaking) and a low or normal score (Z score < 5) on withdrawal (Rather play alone than with others; Very shy). The withdrawn-rejected subgroup was formed of 15 children (32% of the rejected sample: 6 girls and 9 boys) high on withdrawal (Z score > 1) and low or normal aggression (Z score < 5). The children filled out the perceived Competence Scale (Harter, 1983) and Asher & Wheeler's (1985) Loneliness and Social Dissatisfaction Questionnaire. The teachers also completed the Teacher's Rating Scale of Child's Actual Competence (Harter, 1983) which parallels the 5 competence dimensions of the PCS.

The results revealed that when compared to the average group, a) Both subgroups were chosen more often by their peers as having their feelings hurt easily and being often left out and usually sad (withdrawn-rejected children were also chosen more often as being usually sad than aggressive-rejected children);
b) The teacher saw withdrawn-rejected as less competent on all five competence dimensions whereas the aggressive-rejected were seen as less competent only on the social acceptance, physical appearance and behavior/conduct dimensions; c) Withdrawn-rejected children perceived themselves as less accepted, less competent academically and behaviorally whereas aggressive-rejected children saw themselves to be less competent only on the behavior/conduct dimension; e) Finally, only the withdrawn-rejected children expressed more loneliness and social dissatisfaction.

This study indicates that the combination of rejection and withdrawal is associated with a general lack of competence and supports the view that withdrawn-rejected children are more at risk for internalizing problems. The difficulties of the aggressive-rejected children seem to be less general. Yet, the fact that these children do not see themselves as less accepted and do not express more loneliness and social dissatisfaction suggests that they may be less aware of their peer rejection (or less affected by it). These results support the view that they may have less motivation to change socially (Coie & Koeppl, in press). This preliminary study supports the relevance of distinguishing aggressive-rejected from withdrawn-rejected children and emphasizes the need to study prospectively the developmental trajectories of these children.[1]

References

Asher, S.R., & Wheeler, V.A. (1985). Children's loneliness: A comparison of rejected and neglected peer status. *Journal of Consulting and Clinical Psychology, 53,* 500-505.

Boivin, M., & Bégin, G. (in press). Peer status and self-perception among early elementary school children: the case of the rejected children. *Child Development.*

Coie, J.D., & Dodge, K.A. (1983). Continuities and changes in children's social status: A five-year longitudinal study. *Merrill-Palmer Quarterly, 29,* 261-282.

Coie, J.D., & Koeppl, G.K. (in press). Adapting intervention to the problems of aggressive and disruptive rejected children. In S.R. Asher & J.D. Coie (Eds.), Peer rejection in childhood. New York: Cambridge University Press.

Harter, S. (1983). Developmental perspectives on the self-system. In P.H. Mussen (Ed.), *Handbook of child psychology,* 4th Edition, vol. IV, New York: John Wiley and Sons Ltd.

---

[1]This study was supported by grants from The Social Sciences and Humanities Research Council of Canada and from the Québec FCAR research funds.

Hymel, S., & Franke, S. (1985). Children's peer relations: Assessing self-perceptions. In B. Schneider, K. Rubin, & J. Ledingham (Eds.), *Peer relationships and social skills in childhood: Issues in assessment and training.* New York: Springer-Verlag Inc.

Masten, A.S., Morison, P. et Pellegrini, D.S. (1985). A revised class play method of peer assessment. *Developmental Psychology, 21*, 523-533.

Williams, G.A., et Asher, S.R. (1987). *Peer and self perceptions of peer rejected children: Issues in classification and subgrouping.* Communication présentée au Biennal meeting of the Society for Research in Child Development, Baltimore, avril 1987.

Social Skills Training With Children as a Function of Group Setting

Paul E. Bourque and Denis Boucher

Université de Moncton, N.B., Canada

Social skills training is widely accepted as an effective intervention technique with children. However, few studies have determined the impact of the type of setting in which social skills training takes place. The purpose of the present study was to compare the effectiveness of a social skills training program using two different elementary school settings. In the first setting, social skills training was provided to target children within the classroom and to all the classmates, whereas in the second setting, the training was provided to a small group of target children only.

The sample consisted of 27 sixth grade elementary schoolchildren rated by their teachers as having social skills problems. Subjects were assigned either to the classroom group (CG), the small group (SG) or the waiting-list control (WLC). Each group included 7 boys and 2 girls with a mean age of 11. Sociometric data, behavioral observations and self-report measure of assertiveness were used as basic outcome measures.

Subjects in both training settings performed significantly better than the control group on the sociometric, behavioral and self-report measures. Overall, the social skills training program appears to have been effective and both training settings were equivalent for teaching social skills. It thus seems clear that, at least for schoolchildren, social skill training in small group setting is not more effective than in the classroom setting. Although the implications of the present results favor the provision of training to children with social skills problems in the least restrictive setting possible, i.e. the classroom, further replication studies are needed.

Interpersonal Skill Deficits of Adolescent Psychiatric In-Patients

Jennifer Connolly

York University, Downsview, Canada

Social impairment is symptomatic of many adolescent psychiatric disorders. Little is known, however, of the interpersonal skill deficits which may contribute to this impairment. In this study, the social problem-solving abilities of adolescent psychiatric in-patients are evaluated in relation to social status in the residential milieu.

In adolescence, critical problem-solving skills have been postulated to include sensitivity to social problems, consideration of alternate means to solve a problem, and consideration of consequences (Spivack, Platt & Shure, 1976). Research supporting the importance of these skills among psychiatrically disturbed adolescents is, however, meager and somewhat inconclusive. Deficits reported by some investigators (e.g., Platt, Spivack, Altman, Altman & Preizer, 1974) are not substantiated by others (e.g., Haley, Fine, Marriage, Moretti & Freeman, 1985). This inconsistency may be at least partially attributable to limitations of the Means-Ends Problem-Solving task (Spivack et al., 1976). This instrument, commonly used to measure adolescents' social problem-solving abilities, presents interpersonal dilemmas which are quite abstract in content and require good verbal comprehension. When testing adolescents with psychiatric disturbances, it may be necessary to use social tasks which present age-relevant problems in a concrete manner and to consider the content of the problem-solving efforts.

In the present study, a social problem-solving instrument was developed with these concerns in mind. Five sequences portraying everyday problematic situations are described both verbally and by means of illustrative photographs of high school student actors. Situations involving social initiation, assertiveness, peer provocation and help-seeking were selected on the basis of previous research identifying them as problematic for teenagers (Argyle, 1985). Problem-solving skill was examined in terms of: complexity of problem identification; solution quantity and solution quality; identification of the best solution; and consideration of probable consequences. Prior to conducting the study with the psychiatric patients, the responses of 61 high school students to the new instrument were evaluated. The results indicated that the test possessed interrater reliability; Kappa values averaged .81. Positive correlations between problem-solving ability and teacher ratings of social adjustment were also found.

Forty adolescent psychiatric in-patients who were admitted to a 15-bed adolescent treatment unit were administered the problem-solving test during the first week after admission. In addition, sociometric status, based on the average number of positive and negative nominations received during the first six weeks following admission, was calculated.

Among these adolescent in-patients, the interrater reliability was comparable to that found in the normal group. In addition, significant correlations were obtained between social problem-solving and peer rejection. Patients who were socially rejected were more inaccurate in their problem description, generated fewer solutions to the problems and were more likely to select aggressive solutions as the best course of action. No correlations with peer acceptance were found.

In summary, the results support the use of analyzing social problem-solving abilities using a procedure in which everyday situations are presented in a concrete manner. Using this measure, the findings confirm that social impairment among psychiatrically disturbed adolescents is related to deficits in their social problem-solving abilities.

References

Argyle, M. (1985). Social behavior problems and social skill training in adolescence. In B. Schneider, J. Ledingham & K. Rubin (Eds.), *Children's peer relations: Issues in assessment and intervention*. New York: Springer-Verlag. (pages 207-224.)

Haley, G.M.T., Fine, S., Marriage, K., Moretti, M.M., & Freeman, R.J. (1985). Cognitive bias and depression in psychiatrically disturbed children and adolescents. *Journal of Consulting and Clinical Psychology, 53*, (4), 535-537.

Platt, J., Spivack, G., Altman, N., Altman, D., & Preizer, S. (1974). Adolescent problem-solving thinking. *Journal of Consulting and Clinical Psychology, 42*, 787-793.

Spivack, G., Platt, J.J., & Shure, M.B. (1976). *The problem-solving approach to adjustment*. San Francisco: Jossey-Bass.

Children's Evaluations of Peer Entry and Conflict Situations: Social Strategies, Goals, and Outcome Expectations

Nicki R. Crick and Kenneth A. Dodge

Vanderbilt University

Children's social goals, their perceptions of the strategies they would use in peer social situations, and their expectations of the probable outcomes of social behaviors have been cited in several recent empirical and theoretical papers as important cognitive components that may underlie children's behavior in the peer group (see Ladd and Crick, in press, for a review). To date, studies of the relation between these cognitive components and behavior have focused largely on children with aggressive behavioral patterns (e.g., Perry, Perry, and Rasmussen, 1986). The goal of the present study was to examine this relation for children who exhibit withdrawn and prosocial behavioral patterns as well as for those who exhibit aggressive patterns.

Method

A total of 608 third- through sixth-grade children participated in two group assessment sessions. During the first session, children completed a peer assessment questionnaire in which they nominated peers for each of ten behavioral descriptors (e.g., those who start fights, those who are helpful and nice to other kids, those who hang back and don't play much with others) (Dodge and Coie, 1987; Williams and Asher, 1987). The total number of nominations children received for each of the behavioral descriptors was calculated and standardized within each classroom. These scores were then factor analyzed (varimax rotation) and a 3 factor solution (i.e., aggressive, withdrawn, and prosocial behavior) was obtained which accounted for 69.4% of the variation in the scores. Median splits of children's weighted factor scores were employed in order to create high and low groups for each of the three factors resulting in six groups: aggressive (n=319) versus nonaggressive (n=287), prosocial (n=332) versus nonprosocial (n=274) and withdrawn (n=318) versus nonwithdrawn (n=288).

During the second session, children completed a questionnaire designed to assess their outcome expectations (adapted from Crick and Ladd, 1987), strategy efficacy (adapted from Wheeler and Ladd, 1982), frequency of strategy usage, and social goals for peer group entry and peer conflict situations. Each of four hypothetical situations (two entry and two conflict) was presented to each subject. The subject was to consider each of four strategy types for each situation. For the conflict situations, the strategies were physical aggression, verbal commands (verbal aggression), avoidance of the conflict (withdrawn behavior), and compromise (prosocial behavior). For the entry situations, the strategies were physical aggression, verbal commands (verbal aggression), hovering (withdrawn behavior), and assertive entry bids (prosocial behavior). For each strategy, children were asked to rate how easy or hard it would be for them to use the strategy in the given situation (to assess strategy efficacy) and how often they would use the strategy if the situation happened to them a lot (to assess frequency of strategy use).

Children were also asked to evaluate each of three types of outcomes for each strategy included in the questionnaire. For the conflict situations, the outcome types were instrumental (i.e., the strategy would or would not accomplish an instrumental goal), relational (i.e., the peer would like or dislike me), and conflictual (i.e., the peer would or would not argue or fight with me). For the entry situation, the outcome types were instrumental, relational, and peer aversiveness (i.e., the peer would or would not be mean to me). Previous work suggests that these outcome types are salient for middle school-aged children (Crick & Ladd, 1987). For each situation, children were also asked to choose between an instrumental and a relational goal.

Results

Eight 2 (Aggressive vs. Nonaggressive) By 2 (Prosocial vs. Nonprosocial) By 2 (Withdrawn vs. Nonwithdrawn) multivariate analyses of variance were then performed, one for each of the four kinds of strategies within each of the two situation types. For each multivariate analysis, children's outcome expectation scores (three variables), strategy efficacy score, and strategy usage score served as the dependent variables. A similar, univariate ANOVA was also performed on children's social goal scores (for this analysis, scores were combined across the two situations). Follow-up univariate analyses were performed on significant effects where appropriate. Significant group differences are summarized below.

Compared with nonaggressive peers, those classified as aggressive reported: (1) more frequent use of compromise and physical aggression and less frequent use of avoidant behaviors in conflict situations, (2) more frequent use of verbal commands and physical aggression in group entry situations, (3) higher efficacy for verbal commands and physical aggresssion and lower efficacy for avoidant behaviors in conflict situations, (4) higher efficacy for entry bids, verbal commands, and physical aggression in group entry situations,

(5) higher expectations that compromise strategies used in conflict situations would result in retaliation by the peer (i.e., relatively negative conflictual outcome expectations), (6) more negative instrumental, relational, and peer aversive outcome expectations for entry bids used in group entry situations, and (7) more positive peer aversive outcome expectations for verbal command strategies and physical aggression used in entry situations. Relative to nonwithdrawn peers, those classified as withdrawn reported: (1) less frequent use of verbal commands and physical aggression in conflict situations, (2) less frequent use of physical aggression in group entry situations, (3) lower efficacy for verbal commands and physical aggression in conflict and group entry situations, (4) more negative instrumental outcome expectations for verbal commands and physical aggression used in conflict situations.

Compared with nonprosocial peers, those categorized as prosocial reported: (1) more positive instrumental outcomes for compromise strategies and verbal commands used in conflict situations, (2) more positive conflictual outcome expectations for avoidance in conflict situations, and (3) more positive instrumental outcome expectations for entry bid strategies used group entry situations. Also, analysis of children's goal scores showed that prosocial children chose relational goals rather than instrumental goals more frequently than their nonprosocial peers.

Only two of the 48 interaction terms were significant and these were not interpreted as robust.

Discussion

Similar to findings from previous studies (e.g., Perry, Perry, & Rasmussen, 1987), results suggest that aggressive children hold more positive evaluations of verbally and physically aggressive strategies relative to their nonaggressive peers (for both peer group entry and peer conflict situations). In contrast, aggressive children's evaluations of prosocial behaviors appear mixed. That is, relative to peers, they report more frequent use and higher efficacy for prosocial strategies but expect more negative outcomes to accrue. Also, aggressive children's perceptions of withdrawn behaviors appear to be more negative than those of peers. These findings are consistent with a social information processing theory that children who evaluate aggressive strategies and their associated outcomes favorably tend to behave aggressively (Dodge, 1986).

Findings for the withdrawn group indicate that these children hold more negative views of physically and verbally aggressive behaviors relative to their nonwithdrawn peers. Surprisingly, they do not appear to hold more positive perceptions of withdrawn behaviors than peers. These findings suggest that withdrawn children view aggressive behavior in highly negative ways and are likely to act in ways that will minimize the probability of an aggressive conflict.

The findings suggest that prosocial children expect more positive outcomes for prosocial behaviors and verbal commands used in conflict situations and for prosocial behaviors used in entry situations. Also, prosocial children seem to prefer being liked (a relational goal) more than achieving extrinsic outcomes (an instrumental goal).

In general, these findings support the hypothesis that children's goals, strategy evaluations, and outcome expectations contribute to their characteristic styles of social behavior.

Acknowledgments: This study was presented as a poster at the NATO Advanced Study Institute, *Social Competence in Developmental Perspective*, July, 1988, Les Arcs, France.

This work was partially supported by a Vanderbilt University Graduate Fellowship to the first author. We would like to express our appreciation to the elementary-school personnel and students who participated in this project. Special thanks to Zvi Strassberg, Tracy Arnold, Cynthia Ziegler, and Beth Harris for their assistance with data collection and data coding. Please send correspondence regarding this paper to Nicki R. Crick, Box 512, Department of Psychology and Human Development, Vanderbilt University, Nashville, TN, 37205.

References

Crick, N. R., & Ladd, G. W. (1987, April). Children's perceptions of the outcomes of social strategies: Do the ends justify being mean? In J.D. Coie (Chair), *Types of aggression and peer status: The social functions and consequences of children's aggression.* The Society for Research in Child Development, Baltimore, MD.

Dodge, K. A. (1986). A social information processing theory of social competence in children. In M. Perlmutter (Ed.), *Minnesota symposium on child psychology, 18,* 77-125. Hillsdale, NJ: Erlbaum.

Dodge, K. A., & Coie, J. D. (1987). Social information-processing factors in reactive and proactive aggression in children's playgroups. *Journal of Personality and Social Psychology, 53,* 1146-1158.

Ladd, G. W., & Crick, N. R. (in press). Probing the psychological environment: Children's cognitions, perceptions, and feelings in the peer culture. In C. Ames and M. Maehr (Eds.), *Advances in Motivation and Achievement,* Volume 6, JAI Press.

Perry, D. G., Perry, L. C., & Rasmussen, P. (1986). Cognitive social learning mediators of aggression. *Child Development, 57,* 700-711.

Wheeler, V., & Ladd, G. W. (1982). Assessment of children's self-efficacy for social interactions with peers. *Developmental Psychology, 18,* 795-805.

Williams, G. A., & Asher, S. R. (1987, April). Peer- and self- perceptions of peer rejected children: Issues in classification and subgrouping. Paper presented at the biennial meeting of the Society for Research in Child Development, Baltimore, MD, 1987.

Assessment of Reflection-Impulsivity Style in Preschoolers: Developmental Trends

Orlanda Cruz

University of Porto, Portugal

Reflection-impulsivity is a cognitive style which refers to the extent to which a subject delays a response when he/she is faced with a problem solving situation whose main feature is the response uncertainty. Children who respond fast and make many errors are called impulsive, whereas children who are slow to respond and make few errors are called reflective. These individual differences in performance are usually assessed through perceptual tasks that require the subject to make a choice among several alternative figures in order to match the standard one. The Kansas Reflection-Impulsivity Scale for Preschoolers (KRISP) is a test similar to the Matching Familiar Figures Test (MFFT) in what concerns the kind of tasks and instructions and was developed by Wright (1971, 1978) for a younger population (two and half to six and half years).

Given the problems raised by the operationalization of reflection-impulsivity in preschool aged children (Kogan, 1976) and the small number of empirical studies about the KRISP (Kogan, 1983), this research is intended to be a contribution to the assessment of this construct in this age range. In this sense the main purposes are:

- to conduct developmental analysis of the two response components--errors and latency--as well as their interrelations. Some conclusions concerning the psychological meaning of this construct are taken from this analysis.
- to raise some suggestions regarding future studies on the construct and/or the adaptation/standardization of the KRISP to the Portuguese population.

The KRISP was applied to a sample of 190 children equally distrubuted by sex and age level (three, four and five years old). From this initial sample 73 children were randomly picked (inside each age and sex subgroup) for a second administration in order to proceed the study of test-retest reliability.

Data analysis was subdivided into three parts:
1) Item analysis of the KRISP (hierarchic pattern of the items and factor analysis)
2) Reliability of the results of the KRISP (test-retest and internal consistency)
3) Developmental study of the results of the KRISP

Item analysis revealed that the obtained hierarchic pattern was not completely similar to the original sequence of the ten items, particularly in regard to the error component on one side, and the three age groups on the other. Two main factors were extracted from factor analysis: one regarding the latency component which explains the tendency to take long or short decision time and the other regarding the error component which translates the degree of difficulty/easiness in solving the items.

The internal consistency coefficients were higher than the stability coefficients in all age groups. These last ones are differentiated according to each of the components - the error stability coefficients are lower and equivalent for the several age groups.

The analysis of the results by age level shows: (1) a significant decrease on errors with an increase on age range, (2) an increase on latency between three and four years old and a decrease between four and five both not significant, (3) a low inverse correlation between the two components which did not increase with age (as one would expect) and (4) an absence of differences related to sex.

The differences found among the age levels lead us to conceptualize the error component in terms of performance accuracy which develops along with age and the latency component as the most important in the determination of stylistic tendencies since it differentiates the subjects apart from their inclusion in a certain age level. The absence of a moderate correlation between the two components doesn't seem a relevant basis for their exclusion as indexes of reflection-impulsivity. They seem to translate psychological dimensions (impulsivity/efficiency) that tend to be ignored due to many authors' tendencies to classify children on the basis of four traditional groups (Salkind & Wright, 1977).

References

Kogan, N. (1976). *Cognitive styles in infancy and early childhood*. Hillsdale, N.J.: Lawrence Associates Publishers.
Kogan, N. (1983) - Stylistic variation in childhood and adolescence. Creativity, metaphor and cognitive styles. In P.H. Mussen (Ed.), *Handbook of Child Psychology* (4th ed): Vol. III. New York: John Wiley & Sons.
Salkind, N. & Wright, J. (1977). The development of reflection-impulsivity and cognitive efficiency. *Human Development, 20,* 377-387.
Wright, J.C. (1971). *The Kansas Reflection-Impulsivity Scale for Preschoolers (KRISP)*. St. Louis: CEMREL, Inc.
Wright, J.C. (1978). *The KRISP: A normative evaluation*. Lawrence, Kansas: Center for Research in Early Childhood Education. Department of Human Development. University of Kansas.

Clinical Observations on the Development of Social Competence in a Group of Pre-Adolescent Boys

Phyllis Daen, PH.D. and James A. Fitzsimmons, M.S.W.

Washington, D.C., U.S.A.

Seven boys, ages ten to twelve, who were experiencing poor school performance and difficulties in peer relations and adult authority relationships were seen for group activity therapy over a period of four months. *House-(Tree)-Person* and *Kinetic Family Drawing* tests were administered at the initial session and again at the final group session. In addition, the boys created group drawings and murals, the former at the beginning and end of the therapy, the latter on a monthly basis. Improvements in peer social relations seemed to occur as the boys succeeded in altering their behavior, stepping back from their families, finding substitute linkages with the therapist (a member of the parent generation) and in developing a group sense. This introjection of new object ties, hypothesized as partially replacing the former ones, seemed to enable developing greater social competence.

Changes in the "Person" drawings were evident. A more mature sense of self was generally observed although one child experienced greater regression. Kinetic Family drawings, in general, became more sketchy and seemed to be less emotionally invested. The focus of the drawings of the group changed from inanimate objects (video and computer games) to images of a close group with a tall over-idealized leader (the therapist). The final group mural was noteworthy in the use of cut-out pictures integrated with the figure drawings. At the final session the boys continually asked the leader for permission and assistance and seemed to be seeking approval. None of the boys invaded each other's territory, a tendency that had been prevalent in earlier murals.

These observations are consistent with Anna Freud's view that social development is an alteration of relations to objects. By discarding the people who were important as love objects in the past, an early adolescent can overthrow the beliefs he/she formerly shared with them. This struggle against parents can be carried out in a variety of ways and may also alternate with periods of greater helplessness and dependence.

Persisting and Desisting Conduct Problem Boys from Kindergarten to Age 9

Claude Gagnon, Richard E. Tremblay, Pierre Charlebois and Serge Larivée

Université de Montréal

While almost all cases of sociopathy in adult life have been preceded by antisocial disturbance in childhood, only a third of those who engage in antisocial behavior during childhood develop personality disorders in adult life (Rutter, 1988). Thus, an important issue in developmental psychopathology is the stable or transient nature of behavioral disorders one can observe in some children during the first years of contact with the school and peer environments.

Within the longitudinal study of a sample of conduct problem kindergarten boys, an attempt has been made, through three successive teacher assessments, to distinguish between different developmental trajectories for subjects who persist, desist, or move in and out of the risk group over a four year period. Sixty four boys who scored above the 70th percentile, within a normative sample, on a teacher rating scale of aggressive-hyperactive behavior during kindergarten were reassessed twice, two and three years later. Forty seven percent of this risk sample in kindergarten remained in the at risk category in the two follow-up assessments. We labeled them the persisters. Twenty percent moved out completely of the risk category (the desisters). Thirty three percent moved out and in the risk category either at the first follow-up or at the second (the ambiguous). Comparisons were made between the three groups on different measures of social and intellectual competence.

The behavioral problems of the desisters, on all accounts, appeared to have been of a transient nature. The persisters were rated as more aggressive by their peers and by their mothers. Although not less intelligent, they tended to perform less well at school. However, they did not perceive themselves as less competent than the others on any of the self perceived competence subcales. The developmental trajectories of the third group is really ambiguous, within the risk category at some point, on some measures, and out of it at another point, on other measures. It is concluded that any early detection of young children who may need intervention must rely on more than one source of information and preferably at different points in time as some children may move in and out of risk as developmental and contextual factors in their lives change. The next best solution seems to be consecutive teacher assessments.

Interactions of autistic children with each other and with toys in a play-group situation

Pierre Garrigues, Guilhem de Roquefeuil and Michel Djakovic

INSERM Unité 70 - Montpellier, France

Behavioral repertories and interactional systems were studied in children 3 to 7 years of age, diagnosed as early psychotic or autistic. The working hypothesis was that access to attractive objects and their use in a free play situation in a small group evoke behaviors of social interaction and allow a study of the process by which communication is regulated.

Method. The situation video-filmed and analyzed was a 30-minute play session of a group of 4 children with 4 large toys, taking place in a 40-square-meter play room in the presence of a familiar adult. Occasionally a fifth child entered in the middle of the session. In all cases, the children habitually spent the day together, either in a child psychiatry department or a nursery school. A total of 54 psychotic or autistic children were observed and studied over 6 consecutive years. The behavioral variables were classifications of posture, movements, contact, imitation, and distance.

Results. The main results show:
- analogies between the autistic children 3 to 5 years of age and children from the nursery school, with respect to group rhythmic organization and behaviors when choosing the attractive object;
- differences in the response to a disturbance of this organization;
- a gradual development of interactional systems in certain autistic children observed over 6 consecutive years, from the ages of 3 to 7 years; communication emerged when the agonistic and affiliative systems coexisted, differentiated, and alternated.

Mother-Infant Communication in a Blank-Face Situation at a Precocious Infant Age (8 weeks)

M.L. Genta and A. Costabile

Universita' della Calabria, Italy

A total of 10 infants and their mothers participated in this study. The infants were 5 males and 5 females (8 weeks), all healthy full term. The mothers all had uneventful pregnancies and were well adapted to their infants. All the Ss came from upper middle class backgrounds, living in the same residential quarter in the surroundings of the University of Calabria.

Our ten mother-infant dyads were videotaped at home, in a playroom and in a standard situation, when the infant was in a contented and alert state. The Blank Face situation consisted of three phases:

Phase I: spontaneous communication (45 seconds, 24 patterns by infants, Looking at, Speaking to, Smiling at by mothers).

Phase II: Blank Face (45 seconds, 24 patterns by infants, Looking at by mothers);

Phase III: resuming spontaneous communication (45 seconds, 24 patterns by infants, Looking at, Speaking to, Smiling at by mothers).

The results were analysed as percentage scores (B distributions test, Phillips, 1973), indicating the trend of two-pattern-sequences in Phase I and Phase III. Notwithstanding the perturbation effect of Blank Face, spontaneous mother-infant communication is totally resumed in Phase III. However we could find only in Phase III the behavioural patterns of emotional disturbance and displacement activities by the infants ("halo effect"). We could find significant differences (One Tailed Binomial Test) between Phase I and III in : Speaking to (M)/Smiling at (I) (B/B - p = .002). In Phase III there were also interindividual sequences with infant distressed behaviour. Smiling at (M)/Looking elsewhere (I) (B/B - p = .002); Speaking to (M)/Excited Body Movements (I) (E/B - p = .004); Speaking to (M)/Grimace (I) (E/B - p = .011). These data confirm a kind of "halo effect" of the perturbation phase on the infants patterns in the last phase.

The analysis of the infants' sequences (eleven sequences characteristic of primary communication exchange), comparing the intra-individual sequences between the three phases, showed significant differences in: Mouth movements/Smiling (E/B - p = .001 - I Phase vs. III Phase); Open mouth/Smiling (E/B - p = .004 - Phase vs. II Phase); Smiling/Vocalizing (B/B - p = .011 - II Phase vs III Phase).

The analysis of mother-infant sequences shows that eight week old infants are capable of perceiving the affective structure in their mother's communicative acts and coherently vary their patterns with changes in mother's behaviour. The analysis of intra-individual infant sequences shows significant differences in the comparison between the three phases. It has been pointed out (Hopkins, 1983) that the association of *Looking* towards mother with *Smiling* and *Vocalizing* is a developmental milestone to which mothers are particularly sensitive. In fact, for the mother, this form of intrapersonal synchrony will give her infant's behaviour a socially-directed character, perhaps suggesting to her the first glimmerings of the infant's motives and intentions to communicate.

The Structure of Communication: Space and Interaction in a Pre-School Group

Mara Manetti and Maria Campart

Universita' di Genova, Italy

The goal of the present research was to investigate communication and play among socially disadvantaged children attending infant school.

The research was carried out in a class of 18 children aged between 3 and 6 years belonging to working and lower working class families. Previous preliminary observations had shown a number of constants: a generalized difficulty in paying attention on the verbal level of communication, an inappropriate use of physical/kinetic non-verbal communication, an almost total absence of peaceful behavior and a poor ability to concentrate and achieve continuity in play activities.

In socially and culturally disadvantaged groups, it is often possible that precise codes of communication are laid down. This can limit the child's range of interactional possibilities as much in terms of relationships as in regard to the school curriculum, and subsequently in life choices. On the other hand, a cognitive type of disadvantage and the concommitant expressive quality of symbolic forms displayed during play activity is explained not so much by the lack of experience or environmental stimulation as by the inability of adults to give their children the support they need to integrate the abundance of stimuli available (Udwin & Smukler, 1981). This reasoning follows Bateson's (1972) theme of deuter learning. In this perspective, children's relational and cognitive difficulties are attributed to a problem of learning, more precisely to the second type of learning previously mentioned. Such problems should be considered as dependent on a type of difficulty in coordinating the various codes a child has to sustain in the family context and in the school environment.

We assumed that variation in the environmental and physical structure of the classroom, together with the introduction of supplementary play material, could facilitate the emergence of social relationships and foster new styles of communication.

Procedures. The room was divided into four areas, theoretically in the first experiment, and then practically, with barriers, in the second. The observer recorded on videotape the events that took place and the children's interactions in each area for 15 minutes. The total observation time within the classroom was 60 minutes for each observation. The observations were carried out twice a week, over a period of three months.

Results. The research brought to light links between the way the classroom was set up in the second experiment (with barriers) and:
- the amount of time the children spent in different areas;
- the different types of group structures;

- the number of social exchanges initiated and received by the children;
- the type of social relationships between the children;

The results of the research were more significant than expected.

References

Bateson, G. (1972) *Steps to an ecology of mind*. San Francisco: Chandler Publishing Company.
Udwin, O. & Shmukler, D. (1981) The influence of sociocultural, economic and home background factors of children's ability to engage in imaginative play. *Developmental Psychology, 17*, 66-72.

Effects of the Presence of an Adult on Communication Between Toddlers

Biran Mertan & Jacqueline Nadel

Laboratoire de Psycho-Biologie de l'Enfant, Paris

Much research, both experimental and naturalistic, concerning social communication between children involves contexts in which at least one adult is present, without taking into consideration the effect of that presence on the children's communication. Surprisingly little research has focused on the influence of the presence of an adult in such settings.

We postulated that an adult's presence modifies the development of social interaction between toddlers. Behaviors such as close proximity, directed verbalizations, laughing and imitation occur less frequently when an adult is present. In the present study, we examine these behaviors under two conditions:

- With Adult Condition
- Without Adult Condition

Twelve triads of 30-36 month-old (mean age 32 months) familiar peers were video-recorded in their day-care centers without their knowledge. Eleven different age-appropriate objects, each in triplicate, were placed in the 18 m^2 experimental setting, in a familiar room of the day-care centers. The experimental setting is the same customarily used by Dr. Nadel's team. In order to locate the toddlers in three different social spaces, nine equal areas (1.4X1.4m) were marked on the floor.

After introducing the toddlers to the experimental setting, the adult assumed a position at a table and began to read. The adult's protocol required a **"neutral"** behavior; she never initiated interactions with the toddlers, but she accepted their offerings and responded briefly with a smile. After 12 minutes, the adult left the setting, leaving the toddlers alone for the last 8 minutes. The 20 minutes sessions were video-recorded in their entirety by a hidden mobile camera.

The adult's presence affected the frequency and the quality of social contact between toddlers. Indeed, results showed that toddlers were sensitive to the adult presence and they sought physical contact with her. The mean rate of toddlers' utilization of the sector S1 (where the adult was situated) was significantly higher (at $p < .05$ level (M1=19.5 vs M2=6) when the adult was present. When the adult was absent, the mean percentage of time samples during which the toddlers were in close proximity was significantly higher (at $p < .02$ level ($M1 = 5.3$ vs $M2 = 14.8$). They showed social attention toward each other. The verbal responses between toddlers was higher (at $p < .01$ level ($M1 = 1.1$ vs $M2 = 2.5$) when the adult was absent. This increase of social attention between toddlers did not result from the stress occasioned by the absence of the adult given that our results showed an increase in responsive laughs between toddlers (at $p < .001$ level).

Contrary to our prediction, the presence of an adult showed no effects on the frequency and the duration of imitative behavior. This result suggests that this predominant transitory register which is characteristic of the 2.6-3.0 age period, is robust enough not to be affected even when the adult is present in the experimental setting.

The Construction of Roles in Early Peer Interaction

Zilma de Moraes Ramos de Oliveira and Maria Clotilde Rossetti Ferreira

University of Sao Paulo, Brazil

A socio-interactionist constructivist approach, derived from the ideas of Mead, Moreno, Wallon, Vygotsky and Piaget, was used for the construction of a theoretical-methodological perspective to investigate early peer interaction. It proposes a frame for the analysis of the interactional process, that allows capturing the flux of interactions in a defined moment and context, by identifying the **roles being played** by the participants. Since human development occurs in dialogical matrices, each subject acts in various situations by playing specific roles, such as a baby being nursed, a partner in an interactional game, the leader of the group. Through his actions and in interaction with others, specific meanings are continuously constructed and shared with his partner(s), in a way that is both cognitive and affective.

This perspective of analysis was used to study some episodes recorded in a short term longitudinal study of two groups of children from low income families attending a State daycare center of Sao Paulo City. Each group (A & B) was observed during 15 minutes free play sessions spread over 12 months, in a playroom of the creche. The first author recorded the ongoing interactions with a portable VC equipment. Seventeen sessions were obtained for group A (2 boys and 3 girls, 21 to 23 months old at the beginning of data collection) and 14 sessions for group B (6 boys and 2 girls starting at age 33 to 45 months). A microanalytical transcription was made of the continuous flow of behaviours of each participant with a detailed description of the situation and objects involved. An effort was made to record postures, gestures, body & facial expressions and vocalizations which could help to apprehend ongoing interactions. Each tape was independently analyzed by two trained observers and their transcriptions were checked together, the disagreements being discussed by reviewing the relevant scenes. The presentation of one episode might help to illustrate some of the points raised.

Happy birthday episode, two girls aged 21 and 23 months

[Comments: the happy birthday song is usually sang around a cake, being followed by an excited and ritualized dialogue stimulating the others to greet and wish the person who is having the birthday all good things (tudo). The part which we consider relevant to make the episode understandable is presented below:
- E para ele/ela, tudo? (And what do we wish him/her, everything?)
- Nada (Nothing)
- E entao, como 'e que e? (And then, what do we say?)
- EEE! (We say is)]

Vania and Telma are sat side by side. Vania attempted to take a small wooden block away from Telma. Now she joins her hands, rests them on her lap, looks at the floor, raises her head and claps hands, shouting excitedly **eee**, while she looks at Telma who manipulates her block. Vania jumps, raising only her upper body, claps hands and shouts **tuto! tuto!**, looking at Telma's block. She repeats **tuto! tuto!** clapping hands and looking at Telma, who turns towards her proffering the block. Vania takes it, lays it on the floor in front of her, attentively observed by Telma. Vania picks the block up, let it drop and screams **abidi**, clapping hands. She shouts **aidite**, clapping hands, smiling and looking at the block on the floor. Observed by Telma, she claps hands, exclaiming **tudo! tudo!**, looking at Telma, who shows her another block and let it drop on the floor. Vania catches it while Telma makes a pile with some other blocks. Vania gives her block to Telma, who puts it over the pile. Telma claps rhythmically her hand on the top of the pile, while looking around and singing **para...**, with an intonation of "parabens" (happy birthday). She interrupts the song to take another block from Vania's hand, that she places over the pile. she begins to clap hands looking at Vania and shouting something. Vania looks at her for a while and then begins to clap hands, smiling and looking at the researcher who is recording the scene. Vania claps hands saying **beeeem** (with a tone of "parabens"), **tudo**, looking forward. She looks seriously at Telma who is arranging the blocks on the floor in front of her. Telma raises her upper body and claps hands, turning to look at Vania who claps her hands once with a distant gaze. Telma continues to clap hands looking at Vania who, then, smiles and begins to clap hands together with Telma, still looking forward, away from her partner. Telma and Vania clap hands together. Vania looks and smiles at Telma, who then opens and closes her arms dramatically shouting **eeee!**, while looking back at Vania. Vania claps hands. Telma repeats the gesture of opening and closing her arms and sings **a-ben-a** (with the tone of "parabens"), still looking at Vania, who looks back at her. Both clap hands together and shout **eee!** Telma looks around and claps hands saying **tei**, watched by Vania who also claps her hand. Then, the two girls begin to play with a large cylinder, dropping blocks inside it and taking them out. [Episode Duration> 1'32"].

The sequence presented demonstrates how the game is jointly constructed through the girls actions and interactions, that is through the roles they assume when they attribute some meaning to the situation. The fragments of the game are weaved together by the participation of each child, who tries to involve the partner in her own game, negotiating a shared meaning for their play. The roles emerge in small fragments which contain parts of well known scripts that can be performed by the children in the situation. In the birthday game, each girl behaves as a model for the other, in imitative sequences in which they assume the same role, although there are already moments of role discrimination. In a period when the self/other differentiation process is in its beginnings, the role play occurs chiefly through imitation and, in the example, through previously experienced rites.

The transformations observed in the way that the children of both groups played certain roles while coordinating them with the roles played by the others provided some cues for the discussion of the integrated processes of self-other differentiation and the ontogenesis of representation.

The authors acknowledge the help of FAPESP, CAPES, CNPQ, VITAE

Developmental Peculiarities of Graphic Recall in a Asperger's Syndrome Subject With Good Visual Memory

Laurent Mottron, Clinique de la Chesnaie, Chailles, France;
Jacqueline Nadel, C.N.R.S., Paris

The subject, an Asperger syndrome, has an high ability to memorize perceived space, higher than the average of untrained subjects, and close to that of professional draughtsmen. He has developed a crude represented space which associates systematic transformations of represented configurations by symmetry to lexically-determined orientations.

Several factors in this observation militate for "episodic" type of memorisation of perceived space, in the form of images stable through time:

a) The presence in the second recall of features which are not present in the first recall.

b) The order of recall of the same image is totally different, mainly through variations of possible combinations by contiguity and similarity.

c) The retaining of proportions over a long period of time.

d) The exceptional stability of spatial relations between two recalls separated by a short period.

e) The difference in quality between the real transformations in perceived space, extremely accurately reproduced, and the represented transformations of perspective in represented space, obtained by symmetry.

These characters favor the hypothesis that "islets of Abilities" of autistic subjects do not constitute islets of normal development, but the achievement of normal results through means which remain developmentally dated, and go back to very early stages, in this case to the beginning of the pre-operative period, before represented space reorganizes perceived space. Such a compensation which gives excellent results for visual memory does not allow a normal social relation which would require:

-   A transformation of perspective according to the point of view of the other rather that according to duplication by Symmetry.

-   A long-term memorisation of a semantic type.

Information Cues Provided by the Adult and Peer Interaction Among Preschool Children

Giovanna Tomada and Ersilia Menesini

University of Florence, Italy

According to recent research, several internal and external factors seem to influence individuals' interactional patterns in different types of relationships. Among the external factors, our attention focuses on the information provided by the adult to the child. The present research is part of a broader project on the relationships between information cues provided by the adult (as a positive or negative judgment on the partner) and interaction among children at different age levels. It aims to detect if and to what extent the adult's information influences the social behavior of a five-year-old child in a condition of collaborative play with a peer. In particular, our hypothesis is that the subject, after receiving from the adult a negative judgment on the partner's abilities to perform the play, will modify his own behaviors at the following levels: quantity of assembling performed, of initiatives and responses toward the other and of interactional patterns.

Fifteen five-year-old children attending the same kindergarten were observed. The observational setting was a play situation in which the subjects took part twice within a ten-day interval. In both situations they assembled a construction composed of different materials which presented the same level of difficulty. The ability of each subject to perform the task had been previously verified by testing. In the first situation, the experimenter introduced the partner saying: "Now one of your classmates is going to play with you." In the second situation, before introducing the peer, the adult provided a negative judgment on the playmate: "Now one of your classmates is going to play with you. You remember you built a castle together last time. Now you are going to build a village; he's had a try at this play but he wasn't able to do it." In both situations, the subjects' interacted by same-sex pairs with the same partner. In relation to our hypothesis, and in order to codify the quantity of assembling performed, we counted the number of pieces assembled by the target subject comparing it with the other's score. To analyze the interactional patterns, the verbal and nonverbal behaviors were codified according to two dimensions: *role* played by the subject during the interaction (initiation and response) and *meaning* of the behavior (collaborating, regulating, non-collaborating, disconfirming).

Our data show that the negative judgment on the peers' ability produced by the adult doesn't influence the quantity of work performed by the subject. However, it affects significantly the number and the quality of interactional behaviors: initiatives and responses increase; as well, the interactional patterns vary significantly from the first to the second situation. In particular, non-collaborating and disconfirming behaviors (both initiating and responding) increase, while the collaborating behaviors decrease ($.05 < p < .005$ - Student's$_{-}$ for dependent samples). Such data seem to provide interesting stimuli for a new

410

perspective in the study of peer social relationships, as they stress the role of adults in peer interaction.

Social Competence and Locus of Control: A Relationship Reconsidered

Nel Warnars-Kleverlaan and Louis Oppenheimer

University of Amsterdam

> In the bar of the famous theatre-restaurant Sardi's (New York) next to the printing-offices of the New York Times, 'success' or 'making it' is a compulsory drinking-talk. "Do I know your face from a poster?" asked the bartender to a young woman who hoisted herself on a stool. "Not yet", she said quite soberly, "I am working on it. But I believe in myself" (A.v.Dis, Casablanca, 1986, p. 41).

Importance

How important is the belief in having at least an illusion of control over one's own destiny? A brief survey of the psychological abstracts from 1988 (4 volumes), shows that locus of control is an intriguing subject for social scientists. Result of this survey, show 88 studies in which more than 12.500 persons participated. Salient topics in these studies are the relations between perceptions of personal control and achievement, physical health and functioning, job satisfaction, abnormality, social (in) competence and intervention.

Introduction

In the early thinking about locus of control it was assumed that internality (i.e. attributing control to the self) would be associated with a set of positive social outcomes. Being someone who perceives her or himself as personally responsible, implied that a child would, among other things, be more adaptive, more patient, more popular (Dalquist & Ottinger, 1983), more social competent, more information-seeking, more open to health programs, have a better self-concept, and demonstrate better adjustment patterns. The external child, on the other hand, (i.e. a child who attributes control to the environment) would be less adaptive, less successful at school, more vulnerable for physical and psychological problems and more prone to maladjustment (Nowicky & Duke, 1983). However it can be assumed that the relationship between internality and social competence is not as linear as presumably was supposed (Sobol & Earn, 1985; see Figures 20.3, 20.4, and 20.5).

Interpersonal relationships

1. Internal versus External. Children with an internally oriented locus of control view their interpersonal success and failure in terms of their own social skills or efforts, whereas children who are externally oriented view their success or failure as being a result of fate or luck, or the circumstances.

411

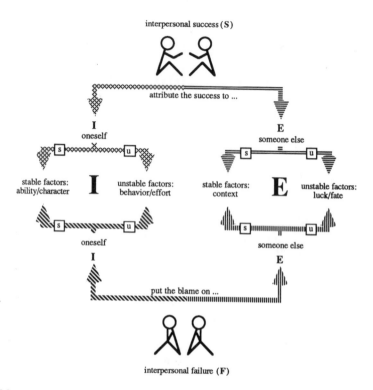

Figure 20.3

A schematic representation of the relationships among internal (I) and external (E) locus of control, interpersonal success (S) and failure (F) and stable (s) and unstable (u) factors.

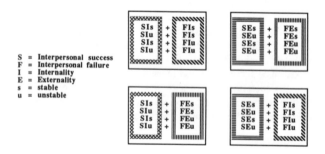

S = Interpersonal success
F = Interpersonal failure
I = Internality
E = Externality
s = stable
u = unstable

Figure 20.4

The hypothetical 16 combinations between the variables interpersonal success and failure, internal and external perceptions of control and stable and unstable factors.

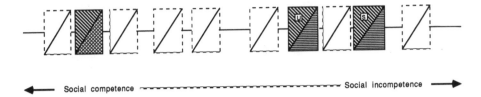

Social competence ⟵ ————————————————— Social incompetence ⟶

Figure 20.5

A schematic representation of the 16 hypothetical combinations on the continuum of social competence.

2. Success versus Failure. Some children may be noted for the manner in which they deny responsibility for failures, while they easily accept successes as self-relevant. Although the opposite situation, that is, the acceptance of responsibility for failure and the rejection of responsibility for success, may appear unlikely, it is related to 'difficult behavior' in school.

3. Stable versus Unstable. Emotional phenomena like depression and loneliness are less likely to occur when the child attributes responsibility for interpersonal failures to unstable personal factors, such as behavior or effort, rather than to stable person factors, such as character or ability.

Conclusion

It is neither internality nor externality per se that is related to social competent behavior. Instead it is the relationship between these two extreme forms of control orientation in regard to different kind of events that is important.

References

Dalquist, L.M. & Ottinger, D.R. (1983). Locus of control and peer status: A scale for children's perceptions of social interactions. *Journal of Personality Assessment, 47,* 278-287.

Nowicki, S. & Duke, M.P. (1983). *The Nowicki-Strickland life-span locus of control scales: Construct validation.* In H.M. Lefcourt (Ed.), *Research with the locus of control construct.* Vol.2. New York: Academic Pres.

Sobol, M.P. & Earn, B.M. (1985). What causes mean: an analysis of children's interpretations of the causes of social experience. *Journal of Social and Personal Relationships, 2,* 137-149.

Subject Index

Subject Index